THE ATTORNEY GENERAL,
POLITICS AND THE PUBLIC INTEREST

AUSTRALIA AND NEW ZEALAND
The Law Book Co. Ltd.
Sydney : Melbourne : Perth

CANADA AND U.S.A.
The Carswell Company Ltd.
Agincourt, Ontario

INDIA
N. M. Tripathi Private Ltd.
Bombay
and
Eastern Law House Private Ltd.
Calcutta and Delhi
M.P.P. House
Bangalore

ISRAEL
Steimatzky's Agency Ltd.
Jerusalem : Tel Aviv : Haifa

MALAYSIA : SINGAPORE : BRUNEI
Malayan Law Journal (Pte.) Ltd.
Singapore

PAKISTAN
Pakistan Law House
Karachi

4d

THE UNIVERSITY OF LIVERPOOL
LAW LIBRARY

CONDITIONS OF BORROWING

Members of Council, members and retired members of the University staff, and students registered with the University for higher degrees — 20 volumes for one month. All other readers entitled to borrow — 6 volumes for 14 days in term or for the vacation.

Books may be recalled after one week for the use of another reader.

THE ATTORNEY GENERAL, POLITICS AND THE PUBLIC INTEREST

by

JOHN Ll. J. EDWARDS, LL.D. (Cantab.)

of the Middle Temple, Barrister
Professor of Law and Founding Director,
Centre of Criminology, University of Toronto

LONDON
SWEET & MAXWELL
1984

Published in 1984 by
Sweet & Maxwell Limited of
11 New Fetter Lane, London.
Computerset by Promenade Graphics, Limited, Cheltenham.
Printed in Scotland.

British Library Cataloguing in Publication Data
Edwards, J. Ll. J.
    The Attorney General, politics and the public interest.
    1. Great Britain, *Attorney-General*
    I. Title
    354.41065   KD7107

    ISBN 0-421-30180-5

To
my grandchildren
Claire, Christopher and Erin

PREFACE

The 20 years that have elapsed since the publication of my earlier work *The Law Officers of the Crown* have witnessed a growing public awareness of the critical role assigned to the office of Attorney General under the British constitution. Parliamentarians, judges and lawyers, no less than ordinary citizens, have sometimes been bemused by the many disparate functions associated with this ancient office of State. Such controversial episodes of recent memory as the granting of immunity to Anthony Blunt, the efforts to ban the publication of the Crossman diaries and the thalidomide revelations, and the major confrontation that erupted between the Court of Appeal and Mr. Silkin in the famous case of *Gouriet* v. *Union of Post Office Workers*, have served to fuel renewed public questioning of the Attorney General's ability to demonstrate the independence and impartiality of his decisions whilst serving as a ministerial member of the Government. No wonder then that, from time to time, the cry is taken up that the only certain way to empty the Attorney Generalship of its political overtones is by removing its ministerial status and making the office a public service appointment.

As the State's chief public prosecutor, responsible for supervising the actions of the Director of Public Prosecutions, the latter model is often advanced as epitomising the qualities that should also be associated with the office of Attorney General. In examining the arguments for reform sight is not lost of the corresponding principle of accountability for decisions taken by the Attorney General, whether these involve proceedings in the civil courts or the criminal courts. The struggle for increased judicial participation in the Attorney General's public accountability has been actively pursued in the years covered by this study, alongside which there have been renewed efforts on the part of the House of Commons, through the medium of its Select Committee on Home Affairs, to render the actions of the Law Officers of the Crown subject to higher levels of public scrutiny. Stubborn resistance to both moves has been successful up to now but some changes may become inevitable in the years ahead.

The legal, constitutional and political aspects of all these developments, and the response of Attorneys General of different political allegiance, are addressed in the various chapters devoted to these questions. In doing so, the scope of the discussion has been broadened to take account of the experience of other countries, in the Commonwealth and in the United States, which long ago imported the office of Attorney General into their constitutional systems with individual adaptations. The occasion has also been taken to make good an omission from my earlier study by conducting a comparative review of the responsibilities of the Law Officers in Scotland and both parts of Ireland. This is particularly apt at this juncture since the responsibilities of Northern Ireland's former Law Officer are now shouldered by the Attorney General for England and Wales. As for Scotland, the merits of its system of procurators fiscal, in control of both the investigative and prosecution aspects of crime, has often been espoused as worthy of replication south of the border, a point of view that has recently been examined by the Royal Commission on Criminal Procedure. Its recommendations on a wide variety of topics pertinent to the role of the Attorney General and the powers of chief constables are critically assessed in a chapter devoted to police investigations and prosecutions. Whilst I was engaged in the final stages of proof reading this work the Government announced its intention to bring forward legislation that will establish a single national prosecution service for England and Wales. This objective, however, is not likely to be implemented in the immediate future. Meanwhile, it is to be hoped that the views I have expressed in this book will not only help to clarify the historical background to this age-old dispute but also to strengthen the position taken by the present Government.

In choosing the title for the present volume I have endeavoured to recognise the realities that surround the daily functioning of the office of Attorney General. This unique office stands astride the intersecting spheres of government and parliament, the courts and the executive, the independent Bar and the public prosecutors, the State and the citizenry at large. When speaking of politics as impinging on the diverse roles of the Attorney General this may involve the exercise of that official's statutory or prerogative powers, the action of the Director of Public Prosecutions or his superior in terminating an ongoing prosecution, as well as the Attorney General's difficult role as both the chief legal adviser to the Government and to the House of Commons. Experience during the period under review, 1964–84, demonstrates that the political ramifications of the Attorney General's actions may either be immediately apparent to everyone concerned or, a less likely situation, may surface as the public's reaction to the Attorney General's decisions becomes manifest. In each of these eventualities it is important to remember the various meanings attributable to the term politics.

At its worst, criticism may be directed towards what is perceived as the wrongful injection of partisan considerations into the course of action adopted by the Attorney General. This brand of political favouritism has no place in the trust imposed upon the office by constitutional convention. Any Attorney General who places the avoidance of embarrassment to his political party, his political colleagues or even his political opponents as the foremost consideration in fulfilling his official duties is in violation of that trust. At the same time it must be recognised that each incumbent, of whatever party affiliation, must face the difficult balancing exercise of weighing conflicting considerations as to the public interest that are the stuff of administering any department of State. The outcome of this kind of assessment of alternative choices of action involves a political judgment that may well go in opposite directions, according to the political and personal philosophy of the Attorney General in office. In examining the events of yesterday I have endeavoured to maintain the same balance, condemning any indications of a partisan approach and at the same time recognising the validity of political considerations of the kind distinguished above. The proverbial dispassionate observer who can identify unerringly where the public interest lies may be another of our legal fictions but it embodies the proper approach to the Attorney General's responsibilities to which all holders of that office must aspire.

My decision to write this book was facilitated by the understanding support of the publishers in encouraging me to write a companion volume rather than a new edition of *The Law Officers of the Crown*. Hopefully, the reader will be persuaded to refer to the earlier volume whenever the occasion demands recourse to the historical development of these servants of the Crown. The inclusion of a consolidated index that embraces both volumes is designed to make this kind of reference a less burdensome exercise.

I owe a particular debt of gratitude to the present Attorney General, Sir Michael Havers, and the staff of the Law Officers' Department who, in addition to affording me access to the department's State papers, responded patiently to my numerous queries. Although no longer a member of that Department, Mr. W. C. Beckett, now Legal Adviser to the Departments of Trade and Industry, generously undertook to read the entire manuscript and ensured that I had my attention drawn to errors of fact that might otherwise have distorted the portrayal of major events that occurred during his tenure as the Attorney General's senior professional adviser. The same kind of meticulous assistance was also extended to me by Mr. Jim Nursaw, Mr. Beckett's successor and now legal Adviser to the Home Office, and Mr. Henry Steel, the current Legal Secretary to the Law Officers' Department. Both officials helped to ensure that the text was brought up to date with respect to contemporary developments in the United Kingdom. Lord Elwyn-Jones and Mr. Sam Silkin, former occupants of the Attorney Generalship, likewise were kind enough to share with me their recollection of the controversial events that occurred during their regimes. Responsibility for the observations and conclusions with respect to those incidents is naturally mine alone. I also recall with pleasure my temporary attachment to the office of the Director of Public Prosecutions. During that all too short stay Sir Thomas Hetherington and his senior colleagues not only helpfully explained the organisation of the Department but also provided access to whatever papers that I requested for the purpose of better understanding the principles and practice governing the Director's discretionary powers.

Writing on the experience of the office of Attorney General in countries outside of England and Wales, without an intimate familiarity with the special conditions associated with such jurisdictions, is an exercise upon which I embarked with some trepidation. Apart from Canada, which has been my home and academic base for the past 25 years, I was fortunate, with the generous help of the Ford Foundation, to be welcomed as an interested visitor to each of the countries concerned and to be afforded

access to much research material that would not otherwise have crossed my
paths of inquiry. Acknowledgment of specific sources of information has
been made in the relevant footnotes. At this point I wish to pay especial
thanks to Mr. Norman J. Adamson, Legal Secretary to the Lord Advocate
and First Parliamentary Draftsman for Scotland, and Mr. W. G. Chalmers,
the Crown Agent for Scotland, both of whom generously read through the
chapter devoted to the Law Officers of Scotland and provided me with the
authoritative guidance that I needed in venturing to expound on Scottish
legal history and its distinctive system of criminal investigation and prosecutions. Any errors that have crept into my treatment of Scottish law and
history are entirely to be laid at my door.

The research entailed in a study of this kind could never have been discharged single handedly. I readily acknowledge the enthusiastic collaboration of a number of youthful colleagues and students who have lightened
my burdens. In this connection I recall with sincere appreciation the assistance of Philip Stenning, Ann Brumell, Mark Edwards, Shelley Roberts,
Audrey Korey and Eric Apps. The last mentioned of these undertook,
with rare insights, the preparation of the consolidated index. The same
appreciation is extended to the happy band of library staff in the University
of Toronto Law School and Centre of Criminology who constantly helped
in the task of tracking down references in the United Kingdom and further
afield. No less valuable has been the dedicated group of secretaries,
Kathryn O'Rourke, Patricia Kune, Geraldine Naunheimer and Joyce
Kawano, who uncomplainingly tackled the series of drafts from which the
book finally emerged.

Three foundations, the Ford Foundation, the Donner Canadian Foundation and the Law Foundation of Ontario, have been instrumental in facilitating the work that has produced this volume. I have especial cause to be
grateful for the financial assistance of the Donner Foundation whose support of my research efforts over many years and, in particular, of the
Centre of Criminology, University of Toronto, has been steadfast and
generous. To its President and Trustees I extend my enduring gratitude.

My final word of thanks, which can never be adequately expressed, is to
my wife Monica who has successfully combined being both my staunchest
source of encouragement and unrestrained critic throughout the preparation of this book.

January 1, 1984   J. Ll. J. E.

CONTENTS

TABLE OF CASES

TABLE OF STATUTES

1

The New Statutory Blueprints of 1978 and 1979

By the very nature of their decision-making process, in simultaneously having to weigh in the balance conflicting considerations derived from the law, the public interest and the realm of politics, the offices of Attorney General and Director of Public Prosecutions attract a degree of public attention that is inescapable. Events since the publication of *The Law Officers of the Crown*[1] in 1964 have only served to confirm the feeling that public concern is invariably directed towards the particular decisions made by the incumbents of the respective offices and much less towards gaining a proper understanding of their functions and responsibilities. Not that such attention is anything but healthy, involving as it does an assertion of the public accountability of the Attorney General and Director of Public Prosecutions of the day.

It would seem that things have not greatly changed since the enactment in 1879 of the Prosecution of Offences Act[2] setting up the first office of Director of Public Prosecutions.[3] Each occupant, in turn, has had to weather the storm of public criticism that sometimes has raged around his head, frequently involving allegations of partiality or capitulation to political pressures.[4] If the present tendency is to identify the existing office holder as the principal target of criticism on account of objectionable decisions that he may have taken, it was not always so. From the earliest part of the nineteenth century attention was repeatedly drawn to the anomalous situation exemplified in English law wherein there existed no responsible public prosecutor and the enforcement of the criminal law was left to the whim or strength of feelings of the injured party.[5] In their Eighth

---

[1] London, Sweet & Maxwell, 1964.

[2] 42 & 43 Vict., c.22.

[3] *Ibid.* s.2.

[4] For an account of the stream of complaints and strictures directed against Sir Augustus Stephenson's handling of the duties of D.P.P. between 1883 and 1894, including a description of the unseemly feud conducted publicly between Stephenson and Lord Chief Justice Coleridge, see Edwards, *Law Officers of the Crown*, pp. 376–386.

[5] *Op. cit.* pp. 337–338.

Report, published in 1845, the Commissioners on the Criminal Law[6] documented the defects of the existing system in which, they declared, "it happens but too often that prosecutions are conducted in a loose and unsatisfactory manner, from want of the means and labour essential to a just and satisfactory inquiry. Thus entrusting the conduct of the prosecution to a private individual opens a wide door to bribery, collusion and illegal compromises."[7] The Criminal Law Commissioners' recommendation that "the direct and obvious course for remedying such defects would consist in the appointment of public prosecutors" was to be echoed in the report and minutes of evidence of the Select Committee on Public Prosecutors appointed by the House of Commons in 1856.[8]

To many of the Committee's witnesses, drawn from the senior ranks of the judiciary, it was incomprehensible that English law had failed to adopt the system in vogue in Scotland for several centuries whereby the investigation of crimes and the enforcement of the criminal law was placed in the hands of state appointed procurators fiscal under the supervision of the Lord Advocate.[9] The same principle was seen to have been adopted in Ireland in the nineteenth century with its indigenous machinery of Crown Solicitors, Sessional Crown Solicitors and Crown Counsel responsible to the Attorney General of Ireland.[10] At one point, in 1854, the prospect of paralleling the Scottish and Irish systems was advanced through the initiative of a private member's Bill, but this was withdrawn upon the Attorney General's assurance that the government itself would take action.[11] After much procrastination by successive administrations, in withholding support from a series of further private members' Bills introduced in 1870 and 1871 which embraced the principle of public prosecutors, the Home Secretary eventually seized the initiative in 1873.[12]

Although none of these measures was to reach the statute book, within their provisions can be seen the embodiment of principles that continue to be debated up to the present time. For example, the Public Prosecutors Bill introduced in 1873 was formulated on the basic assumption that the ultimate source of ministerial responsibility for criminal prosecutions would rest in the Secretary of State for Home Affairs.[13] Specifically, provision was made for the appointment of a Solicitor to the Home Office who would superintend the local public prosecutors and take over the duties connected with government prosecutions then exercised by the Solicitor to the Treasury. In the proposed scheme the Solicitor to the Home Office would be subject to the overall supervision of the Home

---

[6] Parl. Papers, Vol. 14, No. 656.
[7] Edwards, *op. cit.* p. 340.
[8] Parl. Papers, Vol. 7, No. 206.
[9] Edwards, *op. cit.* pp. 344–345.
[10] *Ibid.*
[11] *Ibid.* pp. 349–352.
[12] *Ibid.* pp. 354–353.
[13] Bill No. 173 of 1873.

Secretary.[14] This assumption of the First Secretary of State as the ultimate source of accountability for the proposed new system of public prosecutors did not pass unchallenged and was rectified before the Prosecution of Offences Act 1879 was enacted,[15] marking the turning point in the long campaign waged throughout most of the nineteenth century to establish a more effective and responsible system of prosecutions in England and Wales.

Strangely, it might be thought, no public notice or celebration to mark the centenary of the creation of the office of Director of Public Prosecutions appears to have taken place in 1979. Such silence could hardly be taken as symptomatic of universal satisfaction with the record of that official's discharge of his public duties. On the contrary, recent years have witnessed a renewed clamour, by national organisations such as *Justice,* calling once again for the adoption in England and Wales of the Scottish system of state appointed prosecutors.[16] The persistence of this lobby, inside and outside Parliament, coupled with the expounding of similar objectives in the legal literature, did not pass unnoticed in circles where government policies are ventilated. The final impetus for a major review of police powers and practices, as well as the procedures followed in the office of the Director of Public Prosecutions, was provided by the criticisms contained in the 1977 Report by Sir Henry Fisher into what became known as the *Confait* case.[17] It was with no great surprise, therefore, that the terms of reference of the proposed Royal Commission on Criminal Procedure, announced by Prime Minister Callaghan in the House of Commons on June 24, 1977,[18] included a re-examination of the entire system of criminal prosecutions.

This aspect of the Commission's work was to form an essential part of the Government's remit, which envisaged a thorough review of the whole

---

[14] *Ibid.* cll. 3, 4 and 5, and see Edwards, *op. cit.* pp. 354–355.

[15] Edwards, *op. cit.* pp. 359–366. In the earlier versions of the Prosecution of Offences Bill the title used was "Solicitor of Public Prosecutions." During the passage of the measure through the House of Commons, the Home Secretary suggested as an alternative title "Crown Officer for Public Prosecutions," but this too was later withdrawn in favour of the title that has long since become the established but often misunderstood description of the present office of Director of Public Prosecutions.

[16] Justice, *The Prosecution Process in England and Wales,* 1970.

[17] H.C. Paper 90, discussed at pp. 410–411 *post.* Among the matters considered in the Fisher Report was the beneficial effects that might be expected to accrue if the Scottish system for the investigation and prosecution of serious crimes were to be adopted into English law. The D.P.P., at the time, Sir Norman Skelhorn, was opposed to the suggestion that his officers become responsible for supervising police investigations—*op. cit.* pp. 24–27. Sir Henry Fisher, however, was very careful to stress that "an inquiry such as mine into a particular case is not a sufficient foundation for fundamental changes in the law relating to police investigation and criminal prosecution (such, for instance, as the introduction of a system like that prevailing in Scotland). If such changes are to be contemplated, then something like a Royal Commission, which could go into all aspects of any proposed changes (including the cost) would be required." *Ibid.* pp. 6–7. For the initial responses of the Home Secretary, see H.C. Deb., Vol. 941, Written Answers, cols. 120–123, December 13, 1977 and by the Attorney General, see *ibid.* Vol. 945, cols. 26–27, February 27, 1978.

[18] H.C. Debates, Written Answers, cols. 604–605.

criminal process from the commencement of the police investigation up to the point of bringing a case to trial. Despite the somewhat feverish, occasionally tortuous, activities in the 1960s and 1970s of such bodies as the Law Commission, the Criminal Law Revision Committee, and several inter-departmental committees which had examined particular aspects of the substantive criminal law and criminal trial procedures, the Prime Minister was justified in describing these efforts as piecemeal and lacking in co-ordination. Hence the decision to address simultaneously the inter-related subjects of the investigation and prosecution of criminal offences. This, it was recognised, would inevitably lead the Commissioners to study the thorny question of how far should the police, who investigate the commission of an offence, be saddled with the further responsibilities of making the decision whether or not to prosecute and actually conducting the case for the prosecution at the trial itself. That other jurisdictions, especially Scotland, have long opted for a strict separation of functions was added reason for once again reviewing the role of the police in matters of prosecution.

Given the scope of the present work it follows that our major interest in the recommendations of the Royal Commission on Criminal Procedure will focus more particularly on those issues that surround the police—prosecutor relationship. It should be said at once that the Commission's examination of these issues is notably thorough and helpful in explaining the circumstances that contributed to the prevailing state of affairs, and why the *status quo* is defended so vigorously by the nation's chiefs of police. It also penetrates to the heart of such questions as to why the ranks of local prosecuting solicitors have been so forceful in their demands to gain a more independent status for themselves, and why they are so determined to change the solicitor-client relationship to the local chief of police that presently governs the vast preponderance of prosecution decisions in courts of summary jurisdiction. We will be examining each of these issues in due course.

For the moment, however, notice must be taken of the fact that shortly after the Royal Commission had embarked upon its task, and well before it had submitted its report in January 1981,[19] the Government proceeded to place on the statute book the Prosecution of Offences Act 1979,[20] thereby replacing the landmark enactment of the same title which in 1879 had brought into existence the office of Director of Public Prosecutions.[21] Furthermore, the same revisionary impetus was to be instrumental in revoking the no less important Prosecution of Offences Regulations 1946,[22] which in more detail had governed the scope of the Director of

---

[19] Cmnd. 8092. The chairman of the Royal Commission was Sir Cyril Phillips. For convenience sake, the Commission's Report will, from time to time, be referred to hereinafter as the Phillips Report.

[20] c.31.

[21] 42 & 43 Vict., c.22.

[22] S.R. & O. 1946 No. 1467.

Public Prosecutions' duties and his relationship to the police forces of
England and Wales, and seeing it replaced by the Prosecution of Offences
Regulations 1978.[23] In fairness to the Callaghan Government it must be
stated that public warning of its intentions had been made manifest by the
Prime Minister when the setting up of the Royal Commission on Criminal
Procedure was being made known to the House of Commons. It is
understood that an assurance had been sought from, and given by, Mr.
Callaghan to the Attorney General of the day, Mr. Sam Silkin, before the
Royal Commission announcement was made public,[24] which assurance was
designed to clear the tracks for the proposed tidying up measures that
primarily affected the working of the Department of Public Prosecutions.
"The Government" said the Prime Minister "do not . . . intend the
establishment of the Royal Commission, which will be concerned
essentially with matters of principle, to hold up the improvements we are
making within the existing structure. The Home Secretary and . . . the
Attorney-General will as a matter of urgent study be reviewing the
arrangements for prosecutions and inter-relationships between the Director of Public Prosecutions and other prosecutors. This review will include
the amendment of the Prosecution of Offences Regulations 1946, which
govern the offences that have to be referred by the police to the Director of
Public Prosecutions, and the implementation, within available resources,
of the recommendation of the 1962 Royal Commission on the Police that
every police force in England and Wales should have a prosecuting
solicitors' department."[25] It is with these new statutory blueprints, the
Regulations of 1978 and the Act of 1979 that our attention must first be
engaged.

FUNCTIONS AND POWERS OF THE DIRECTOR OF PUBLIC PROSECUTIONS:
    1879–1979

Whilst it is strictly true that the Prosecution of Offences Act 1879
marked the culmination of the long campaign to create "a responsible
public prosecutor" and represents, as it were, the centrepiece in the
semi-organised system of public prosecutions that to this day exists in
England and Wales, it should be noted that the 1879 statute has not
remained intact in all its provisions. Subsequent enactments in 1884[26] and
1908[27] represent rather more than tidying up measures, as shown in the
fuller analysis of these pieces of legislation which was undertaken in my
earlier work on *The Law Officers of the Crown*.[28] A brief summary of what

[23] S.I. 1978 No. 1357 (L.33). The new regulations came into operation on January 1, 1979.
[24] Personal communication to the author by Mr. Silkin on July 8, 1980.
[25] H.C. Deb., Written Answers, cols. 604–605, June 24, 1977.
[26] 47 & 48 Vict., c.58.
[27] 8 Edw. 7, c.3.
[28] *Op. cit.* pp. 375–376, 388–390, 397–401.

preceded the latest enactment may help to better understand the extent of the housekeeping changes effectuated in the Prosecution of Offences Act 1979.

First, let us examine the scope of the duties expressly imposed on the office of Director of Public Prosecutions. In the original statute of 1879 these duties were described in general terms that continue to bear a familiar ring at the present day. Thus, it was declared, it was the Director's duty "under the superintendence of the Attorney General, to institute, undertake, or carry on such criminal proceedings (whether in the Court for Crown Cases Reserved, before sessions of Oyer and Terminer or of the peace, before magistrates or otherwise). . . . "[29] The same section went on to develop the principle of an advisory role for the Director which time has shown to have been of the first importance. It required the Director "to give such advice and assistance to chief officers of police, clerks to justices and other persons, whether officers or not, concerned in any criminal proceeding respecting the conduct of that proceeding, or may be for the time being prescribed by regulations under this Act, or may be directed in a special case by the Attorney General."[30] As originally drafted the 1879 measure surprisingly gave no guidance as to the kinds of cases that should prompt the Director to take the initiative. This omission, however, was rectified before the measure was finally enacted, it being stated that action should be taken "in cases which appear to be of importance or difficulty, or in which special circumstances, or the refusal or failure of a person to proceed with a prosecution, appear to render the action of such Director necessary to secure the due prosecution of an offender."[31] Time and the hard school of experience have served to further illuminate this set of nebulous standards. There have also been some significant refinements in the statutory language used to describe the general ambit of the Director's responsibilities. Thus, the Prosecution of Offences Act 1908, s.2, declared that the Regulations, made under the parent statute, shall provide for the Director of Public Prosecutions taking action "in cases which appear to him to be of importance or difficulty, or which for any other reason require his intervention." The criterion for intervention, it will be noted, had become that of the Director's own judgment, not some external, objective assessment of the circumstances. And precisely the same formulation of the pertinent criteria is to be found in the latest enactment, the Prosecution of Offences Act 1979, s.2(2).

With respect to the formal institution or conduct of criminal proceedings the language of the 1979 enactment is consonant with the contemporary scene and reflects the changes in both the original and appellate courts of criminal jurisdiction that have taken place since the earlier provision was set down in the statute of 1879. Thus, section 2(1) of the Prosecution of

---

[29] 42 & 43 Vict., c.22, s.2.
[30] *Ibid.*
[31] *Ibid.*

Offences Act 1979 declares: "It shall be the duty of the Director, under the superintendence of the Attorney General—(a) to institute, undertake or carry on such criminal proceedings (whether in the criminal division of the Court of Appeal, or in the House of Lords on appeal under Part II of the Criminal Appeal Act, 1968, from the criminal division or from a divisional court of the Queen's Bench Division of the High Court, or in such a divisional court, or before the Crown Court, or before a magistrates' court, or otherwise). . . . " No expansion or retraction of the Director's original responsibilities can be discerned in the language quoted above. The same observation applies to the provision that immediately follows in the 1979 statute pertaining to the Director's advisory role which is "(b) to give such advice and assistance to chief officers of police, justices' clerks and other persons (whether officers or not) concerned in any criminal proceedings respecting the conduct of those proceedings." Furthermore, both categories of involvement by the Director are subject to an overriding power by the Attorney General "in a special case" to give directions to the Director of Public Prosecutions.[32]

Tampering with the Statutory Definition of the Director's Relationship to the Attorney General

This leads naturally into a consideration of the precise nature of the present relationship between the Attorney General and the office of Director of Public Prosecutions, as constituted by Parliament. And what residual powers, if any, in the field of public prosecutions continue to be reposed in the Home Secretary? In the run of the mill cases that daily occupy the attention of the Director and his staff these questions may never become a matter of high significance. Nevertheless, if constitutional impasses are to be avoided, with all the recriminations that usually accompany power struggles conducted in public, it is of vital importance that the respective lines of authority and responsibility be clearly defined in advance. That the theoretical possibility of confusion continues to exist is regrettably once more made manifest by the retention, under the Prosecution of Offences Act 1979, of the Home Secretary's statutory power of appointing each new incumbent to the office of Director of Public Prosecutions.[33] As an extension of the same power the Home Secretary may also appoint such number of Assistant Directors of Public Prosecutions as the Minister for the Civil Service shall sanction,[34] it being noteworthy that, as section 1(4) of the latest enactment provides, "An Assistant Director may do any act or thing which the Director is required or authorised to do by or in pursuance of any Act, or otherwise." This

[32] 1979, c.31, s.2(1).
[33] *Ibid.* s.1(1).
[34] *Ibid.* s.1(2).

repeats the similar provision contained in the Prosecution of Offences Act 1908, s.1(5).

The seeds of confusion are to be found in the debates marking the passage of the 1879 Bill which first conferred upon the Home Secretary, rather than the Attorney General, the final responsibility for making such appointments.[35] At that time, the forces opposing the decision to confer upon the Home Secretary the ultimate say in the choice of a new incumbent were trenchantly led by Lord Coleridge and Lord Selborne, both former Law Officers. The incongruity of making the discharge of the Director's statutory duties subject "to the superintendence of the Attorney General" whilst reposing in the Secretary of State for Home Affairs the power of appointment was vigorously pressed during the passage of the 1879 Bill.[36] It was to no avail. What was remarkable was the explanation advanced by Lord Cairns, the Lord Chancellor at the time, and the fallacies that it contained. In declining to make the change propounded by the former Attorneys General, the Lord Chancellor stated that "the positions of the Home Secretary and the Attorney General in the administration of the criminal law were essentially different. The Home Secretary was the head of a great Department, was responsible to Parliament for the general system of the administration of the criminal law of the country, and the Attorney General was not. The Attorney General was responsible for the way in which he discharged the duties of his own office. He had never heard of patronage of this description being placed in the hands of the Attorney General; and while the Secretary of State could be called to account in Parliament for the manner in which he had exercised it, it would not be so with the Attorney General."[37]

The same fallacious arguments, based on a non-existent distinction between the accountability to the House of Commons of the Attorney General and the Home Secretary, respectively, may no longer be subscribed to by those who saw fit to perpetuate in the 1979 statute the peculiar anomaly pointed out above. Moreover, in view of the considerable powers of patronage exercised by the Attorney General, from time immemorial up to the present day, in selecting and appointing Crown counsel to represent him as the State's chief Public Prosecutor, it makes no sense to claim that the patronage prerogative is the exclusive purview of the Secretary of State for Home Affairs. When writing in 1964, I expressed the view that the constitutional struggle for paramountcy of authority in relation to criminal law prosecutions, as between the Attorney General and the Home Secretary, had become a matter of historical record only and no longer contained the seeds of viable disputes of any practical importance.[38] A reading of the Report of the Royal Commission on

[35] See Edwards, *op. cit.* pp. 362–363.
[36] H.L. Deb., Vol. 247, ser.3, cols. 134–136.
[37] *Ibid.* col. 135.
[38] *Op. cit.* pp. 363, 389–390.

Criminal Procedure, and the ensuing recommendations of that Commission, prompt me to have second thoughts on the matter. This is, however, to anticipate a subject that must be for the moment deferred.

To place the historical record straight, it must be recalled that in the Prosecution of Offences Regulations of 1886, made pursuant to the Act of 1884 redesignating the office of Director of Public Prosecutions to be held jointly with that of the Treasury Solicitor, the Regulations made it mandatory for the Director to prosecute any case "where an order in that behalf is given to the Director by the Secretary of State or the Attorney General."[39] As late as 1924 there was ample evidence of the belief entertained by successive Home Secretaries that in matters of public security or of state interest it was the Secretary of State's prerogative to instruct both the Attorney General and the Director of Public Prosecutions to institute criminal proceedings in appropriate cases.[40] This position was subscribed to notwithstanding the explicit provision in the same Regulations of 1886 that "the action of the Director of Public Prosecutions shall in all matters, including the selection and instruction of counsel, be subject to the directions of the Attorney General."[41] The last vestiges of the Home Secretary's former involvement in matters of criminal prosecutions disappeared in 1946, the revised Regulations governing the prosecution of offences making no mention of the Home Secretary's power under the 1886 Regulations. Repeating the language of the earlier charter governing the office of Director of Public Prosecutions, regulation 5 of the 1946 Regulations declared that the Director's actions "shall in all matters . . . be subject to the directions of the Attorney General."

Such language permits of no equivocation. Why then, it may be asked, was this provision omitted altogether from the latest exposition of the Director's duties and responsibilities? I am referring here to the Prosecution of Offences Regulations 1978. According to regulation 2, the 1946 set of Regulations has been totally revoked. Read on their own it might be inferred that the latest statutory regulations have subtly and inconspicuously changed the vital relationship between the Director of Public Prosecutions and his constitutional superior, the Attorney General. This is, in fact, not so but such a conclusion does not appear on the face of the 1978 Regulations. Instead we must revert to the original statute, the Prosecution of Offences Act 1879, the basic provisions of which are still extant and which readily confirm the continued subservience of the Director of Public Prosecutions, in terms of legal authority, to the Attorney General for England and Wales. To clarify the relationship, it will be recalled that, under the terms of section 2 of the 1879 statute, which remains in effect, the Director in the discharge of his statutory powers acts "under the superintendence of the Attorney General." Moreover, the same enactment empowers the Attorney General, with the approval of the Lord

[39] Prosecution of Offences Act 1879 and 1884 (Regulations), reg. 1(c).
[40] Edwards, op. cit. pp. 197–198, 389.
[41] Ibid. reg. 10.

Chancellor and a Secretary of State, "to make, and when made, rescind, vary, add to, regulations for carrying into effect this Act," subject only to the final approval of Parliament.[42]

Given the central position accorded the Attorney General in determining the content of any revised set of regulations it must be assumed that the senior Law Officer of the Crown acquiesced, without demur, in the elimination of what was formerly regulation 5 in the Prosecution of Offences Regulations 1946. According to the inter-departmental working party which, under the chairmanship of the Deputy Director of Public Prosecutions, conducted a thorough review of the old 1946 Regulations,[43] "It was felt that the present regulation 5, placing the Director under the supervision of the Attorney General, was superfluous as it was already contained in section 2 of the 1879 Act."[44] The connotation of particular words in a statutory enactment, be it an Act or a Regulation made thereunder, can become an issue of fundamental importance if the perception of the parties immediately involved diverges according to their status and notions of what the proper relationship between them should be. The distinctions may be subtle and, to some minds, of no more than semantic importance. On the other hand, the change effectuated may contain the seeds of a delayed confrontation.

A hint of this potential for future trouble is contained in the working paper prepared within the office of the Director of Public Prosecutions for consideration by the inter-departmental working party, which consisted of representatives of the Home Office, the Director's office, the Association

---

[42] 42 & 43 Vict. c.22, s.8. The subsequent Regulations enacted in 1880 and 1886 bear the signatures of the Attorney General and, below that of the senior Law Officer, those of the Lord Chancellor and the Home Secretary of the day. The 1946 Regulations correctly follow the language of the parent statute of 1879 in that Lord Jowitt L.C., and J. Chuter Ede, the Home Secretary, are shown as "approving" the new regulations issued under the signature of Sir Hartley Shawcross as Attorney General. The "approval" of the Lord Chancellor as a prerequisite was removed by virtue of section 27 of the Administration of Justice Act 1965 (c.2), the "concurrence" of a Secretary of State being substituted for the former safeguards. Accordingly, the latest set of Regulations, promulgated before the Prosecution of Offences Act 1979 reached the statute book, bear the signature of the Attorney General, Mr. Silkin, to which the concurrence of the Home Secretary, Mr. Merlyn Rees, is duly affixed. The relevant change of authorisation, instituted by the Administration of Justice Act 1965, is repeated in the Prosecution of Offences Act 1979, s.9(1). One further amendment should be noted. According to the 1879 statute, quoted in the text above, an affirmative resolution by both Houses of Parliament is necessary to give validity to any such new set of prosecution regulations. In its place, section 27 of the Administration of Justice Act 1965 provides that the Attorney General's regulations shall be subject to annulment in pursuance of a negative resolution by either House of Parliament.

[43] The working party on prosecution arrangements was set up in 1977 in accordance with the Prime Minister's public announcement (see *ante*, fn. 25) that, prior to the establishment of the Royal Commission on Criminal Procedure, there would be studies within the existing framework of certain matters relating to prosecution authorities and procedures. In addition to conducting a review of the 1946 Regulations, the working party was asked to examine the inter-relationship between the D.P.P. and other prosecuting authorities, as well as the legal requirements for the consent of the Attorney General or the D.P.P. to the institution of proceedings for certain offences.

[44] Report of the Working Party, 1977, p.4.

of Chief Police Officers, the Prosecuting Solicitors' Society, the Commissioner of the Metropolitan London Police and a solitary representative from the Law Officers' Department. In arguing, as the working party did, for the deletion of the explicit statement contained in regulation 5 of the 1946 Regulations, on the grounds of its being superfluous, one may be forgiven for detecting a more threatening assault on the position and prerogatives of the Attorney General when the working paper proceeds to invite the working party to consider whether the Attorney General should continue to have the power to nominate counsel in prosecutions undertaken by the Director. Both in the 1886 and 1946 Regulations the principle is enshrined that "the action of the Director of Public Prosecutions shall in all matters, including the selection and instruction of counsel, be subject to the directions of the Attorney General." No reasons were advanced in support of the suggestion that the Attorney General's power of nominating counsel be truncated, such as the duplicity argument invoked to eliminate the more explicit language of regulation 5. The suspicion is left that at least the staff of the office of Director of Public Prosecutions would prefer a more independent status as prosecutors with less direction by their colleagues in the office of the Attorney General. Wherever the truth may lie, it is in my view unfortunate that the more ambiguous language of "superintendence by the Attorney General" is left to define the constitutional relationship between the Attorney and the Director. In situations of mutual respect, goodwill, and a shared understanding of the historical background to the evolution of the modern office of the Director of Public Prosecutions, disputes as to jurisdiction and ultimate control will probably never arise. These ideal conditions may one day evaporate and it is in those circumstances that resort may well be necessary to invoking the unequivocal language of the old 1946 charter as reasserting the unchallenged supremacy of the Attorney General as the final constitutional authority in matters of criminal prosecutions.

RELATIONSHIP OF THE DIRECTOR OF PUBLIC PROSECUTIONS TO OTHER PROSECUTING AUTHORITIES

In addition to elaborating on the statutory position of the Director of Public Prosecutions with respect to the Attorney General, the Prosecution of Offences Regulations also cover the inter-relationship of the Director with other prosecuting authorities.[45] These include government departments (e.g. the Departments of Health and Social Security and of the Environment), local authority councils (in relation to such areas as

---

[45] This relationship is basically advisory in character, entitling the D.P.P. to give advice, either orally or in writing, at his discretion whenever the circumstances appear to him to be of importance or difficulty or which for any other reason appears to him to require his intervention. The groups to whom such advice may be tendered include "Government Departments, clerks to justices, chief officers of police and such other persons as he may think right in any criminal matter . . . " Prosecution of Offences Regulations 1978 (S.I. 1978 No. 1357), reg. 4.

housing, building and planning, food and drugs, and environmental health), public utilities (*e.g.* gas, water and electricity boards), private agencies (*e.g.* National Society for the Prevention of Cruelty to Children), and private police forces that "police" airports, railways, harbours, docks and defence establishments.[46] All these authorities placed together pale in comparison with the role assigned to the regular police forces of this country as *the* prosecuting authorities. Whether the actual prosecutor at the trial is a senior police officer or a prosecuting solicitor employed in that capacity by the local authority, it is important to recognise that, to all intents and purposes so far as England and Wales are concerned, the prosecuting authority is vested in the chief officer of police.

Superimposed upon this authority, however, are certain statutory requirements and restrictions originally laid down by section 3 of the Prosecution of Offences Act 1884.[47] Until the recent amending statute and regulations governing the office of Director of Public Prosecutions were placed on the statute book, the local chief constable would have on his desk for constant guidance the Prosecution of Offences Regulations 1946. They served the machinery of prosecutions well for over 30 years but recent experience had pointed to several major deficiencies that called for attention. Principal among these weaknesses was the wording of the old regulations that, by their width of interpretation, impelled local chiefs of police to send complete reports of insignificant cases for the attention of the Director of Public Prosecutions and which, by modern standards, cast an unnecessary burden on the Director and his staff. Conversely, the feeling existed that several types of cases that ought to be referred to the Director were not sufficiently defined. In short, the criteria for determining what constitute cases "of importance or difficulty" or what special circumstances render the Director's intervention "necessary to secure the due prosecution of an offender," to use the well established indices set forth in the original Act of 1879, have changed as society's perception of certain crimes have become modified over a period of time. The law has not always kept in step with evolving community standards, and events that arouse public or political concern scarcely remain constant from one decade to another. It would be wrong, therefore, to suppose that the latest Regulations of 1979 are destined to achieve perpetuity in their present form.

---

[46] The Law Society, after 5 years of inactivity awaiting the recommendations of the Royal Commission on Legal Services, recently announced its intention to bring criminal proceedings under the Solicitors Act 1974 to protect the solicitors' monopoly on conveyancing—see *The Times,* February 17, 1983. For a full account of the various agencies, governmental and private, which regularly engage in "private" (*i.e.* non-police) prosecutions, see Research Study no. 10 (H.M.S.O. 1980), one of the ancillary projects initiated by the Royal Commission on Criminal Procedure. The study, entitled "Prosecutions by Private Individuals and Non-Police Agencies," was conducted by the staff of the Centre for Criminological Studies at Sheffield University and represents an invaluable source of otherwise uncollated information pertaining to a much neglected area of criminal prosecutions.

[47] 47 & 48 Vict., c.58.

The "Mandatory" List of Offences Reportable by the Police to the Director of Public Prosecutions

Whereas under the 1946 Regulations the approach had been that of casting a wide net to embrace every conceivable offence that might warrant the Director's intervention and assumption of control over the ensuing prosecution, the 1978 Regulations have developed a more refined instrument with a degree of flexibility that had been found lacking in the earlier charter. Henceforth, two categories are recognised. The first of these, the "mandatory" category, in which a report to the Director of Public Prosecutions must be made irrespective of the individual circumstances, includes those crimes that experience has shown are almost certain to be prosecuted by the Director.[48] They include offences punishable with death (*i.e.* treason but not murder); offences of homicide except cases of causing death by reckless driving; abortion; offences of treason, treason felony, misprision of treason, sedition, seditious libel or libel on holders of public offices; offences under particular sections of the Offences against the Person Act 1861,[49] and the Forgery Act 1913[50]; conspiracies, attempts or incitements to commit any of the above offences; and offences which may be the subject of an application under the Extradition Acts, 1870 to 1935 or the Fugitive Offenders Act 1967. Originally included within the above list were offences involving obscene exhibitions or publications.[51] These, however, were to remain there for a remarkably short time. Between September and December of 1978, no longer, a change of policy was given effect to in an amending regulation,[52] thereby relieving both chief constables and the Director of a flood of reports that, it was realised, requires a more refined set of criteria to determine exactly when the Director's intervention is called for. In all the offences listed within this "mandatory" category the chief officer of police must submit a report to the Director if there is a prima facie case for proceeding. Two additional classes of offences are also included within the "must" category. The most obvious of these are those crimes in which the prosecution has by statute to be undertaken by, or requires the consent of, the Attorney General, the Solicitor General or the Director of Public Prosecutions.[53] To round off this high profile category the chief officer of police is encouraged to report those cases where it appears that the advice or the assistance of the Director of Public Prosecutions is desirable.[54]

---

[48] The pertinent categories are listed in S.I. 1978 No. 1357, reg. 6(1).

[49] Sections 21, 23, 28, 29, 32 and 33.

[50] Sections 2(1), 3, 5 or uttering any such documents, seals or dies mentioned in those sections.

[51] 1978 Regulations, reg. 6(1)(*g*).

[52] S.I. 1978 No. 1846 (L.38), reg. 2. The change of policy appears to have resulted from the recommendations of the Committee on Obscenity and Film Censorship, [the *Williams Report*], Cmnd. 7772 of 1979—see especially pp. 128–129, and also *post*, fn. 92.

[53] S.I. 1978 No. 1357 (L.33) reg. 6(1)(*a*).

[54] *Ibid.* reg. 6(1)(*b*).

What is revealing is the list of offences that have been eliminated from the previous catalogue of mandatory reports laid down in the 1946 Regulations. There have been many efforts by criminological researchers to identify "serious" and "less serious" crimes according to an escalating barometer of public opinion. These lists have not always achieved wide acceptance. Now we have the verdict of Parliament based on the recommendations of the inter-departmental working party, to whose report reference was made earlier. Struck off the 1946 list of mandatory offences, and thus no longer requiring that a report in every such case be submitted for the attention of the Director of Public Prosecutions, are the following; the Punishment of Incest Act 1908 (now obsolete and governed by the Sexual Offences Act 1956,[55] ss.10 and 11); the Coinage Offences Act 1936[56]; conspiracies to pervert or defeat the course of justice; public mischief; fraudulent conversion by a public official, solicitor or trustee; offences of manslaughter, attempted murder, rape, abortion, carnal knowledge of mental defectives, defilement of girls under 13 years of age, indecent offences upon children or young persons, sexual offences against a child or young person involving the communication of a venereal disease, and cases in which there has been a previous conviction for the same or similar sexual offence and the offence charged is one that can be dealt with summarily.[57]

THE "FLEXIBLE" LIST OF OFFENCES REPORTABLE BY THE POLICE TO THE DIRECTOR OF PUBLIC PROSECUTIONS

Instead, the approach taken in the new 1978 Regulations is to provide for a second category that consists of a more flexible list of offences requiring reports to be submitted to the Director in accordance with criteria that may change from time to time and will not require the formal approval of Parliament before further possible changes are introduced. The statutory language used to achieve this objective is contained in regulation 6(2) which states: "The chief officer of every police area shall give to the Director of Public Prosecutions such information as he may require with respect to such other cases as the Director of Public Prosecutions may from time to time specify as appearing to him to be of importance or difficulty or for any other reason requiring his intervention." The thinking behind this approach is persuasive, arguing as it does that there is a wide band of offences which can be anything from trivial to very serious, depending on all the circumstances. The balance that has been struck in the initial schedule of offences within this second category is an attempt to identify those offences with which it is important that the Director of Public Prosecutions be concerned and at the same time avoid the possibility of his departmental officers becoming submerged with a

[55] 4 & 5 Eliz. 2, c.69.
[56] 26 Geo. 5 & 1 Edw. 8, c.16.
[57] See S.R. & O. 1946, No. 1467, reg. 6(2).

multitude of cases of minor importance. A further administrative device is intended to strengthen the maintenance of this balance. This is achieved by requiring the submission of only a shortened version of the normal report required with respect to the mandatory offences included within the first category. If, following the initial review, the Director elects to intervene, he can call for a full report of the circumstances, including copies of witnesses' statements, copies of material documents and any other relevant information.

So far as I am aware, the initial list of regulation 6(2) offences, the "flexible" list, corresponds exactly with that contained in the recommendations of the inter-departmental working party.[58] The flavour of contemporaneity is certainly captured in this schedule of offences, containing as it does the following crimes: conspiracy to manufacture controlled drugs; large scale conspiracy to supply controlled drugs in large amounts; large scale conspiracies to contravene immigration laws; causing death by reckless driving where the deceased is a close relative of the accused; rape where one woman is raped by more than one man on the same occasion or where one man rapes several women; kidnapping; robbery involving the use of firearms where injury is caused; large scale robbery involving property or money exceeding £250,000 in value; arson involving grave damage to public property; criminal libel; and coinage offences except those that are trivial. Closing up the list, as the most recent addition, are cases involving questions of EEC law. The exclusion of most sexual offences from this second category was dictated by the belief that it was best to leave it to the discretion of the police to decide which cases they might consider appropriate to report to the Director in the light of their local knowledge and experience. Offences of concealment of birth were omitted because they should be dealt with as quickly as possible. Another arguable exclusion is the offence of using a firearm with intent to endanger life, the reasons given being the width of possible circumstances surrounding such offences and the certainty that offences of attempted murder would have to be reported under the mandatory categories contained in regulation 6(1).

In considering the appropriateness of the allocation of offences to the first category of "must be reported" crimes, or to the second category of "in the Director's discretion" offences, it must be remembered that provision has also been made in the 1978 Regulations, repeating the policy contained in the old 1946 Regulations, whereby the police are given every encouragement to seek the advice or assistance of the Director of Public Prosecutions whenever such action is thought desirable by the chief of police.[59] What we now have, therefore, are clear guidelines based on many years of mutual experience on the part of both the police and the Director's

---

[58] This list is contained in Annex 2 to the Report of the inter-departmental working party, presented to the D.P.P. on February 22, 1978.
[59] 1978 Regulations, reg. 4.

office, with surrounding areas of elective action that permit speedy recourse to all the resources at the disposal of the Director of Public Prosecutions.

WITHDRAWALS AND REPORTS TO THE DIRECTOR OF PUBLIC PROSECUTIONS

Before leaving this inevitably detailed analysis of the regulations that govern the inter-relationship between the Director of Public Prosecutions and the country's police forces, a word must be said on the subject of withdrawals of criminal prosecutions. The sensitiveness of the issues surrounding this question was recognised in the Prosecution of Offences Act 1879 which required, under section 2, that the regulations under the Act provide for the Director of Public Prosecutions taking action, *inter alia,* "in cases . . . in which the refusal or failure of a person to proceed with a prosecution, appear to render the action of such Director necessary to secure the due prosecution of an offender." The same enactment provided, under section 5, that "It shall be the duty of every clerk to a justice or to a police court to transmit, in accordance with the regulations under this Act, to the Director of Public Prosecutions, a copy of the information and of all depositions and other documents relating to any case in which a prosecution for an offence instituted before such justice or court is withdrawn or is not proceeded with within a reasonable time." A requirement to report withdrawals, couched in language similar to that quoted above, has remained part of the duty of clerks to the justices up to the present time. The working party, in its report, referred to the burden upon the police to report withdrawals in every indictable case, cast by virtue of the 1946 Regulations. In serious cases, a police report would invariably constitute the major part of the information tendered to the Director's office by the justice's clerk and, in practice, the responsibility for submitting the relevant report has come to be assumed by the police, the clerk of the court discharging his statutory duty by satisfying himself that the particular chief constable had in fact reported. Insofar as the formal duty of the clerk of the court is concerned, the new Regulations have introduced a measure of alleviation in not requiring a report to be submitted to the Director of Public Prosecutions if there are grounds for believing that a satisfactory reason exists for the withdrawal or failure to proceed.[60]

Consideration was given, but rejected, to the necessity for expanding the duty imposed upon clerks to the justices to include cases of withdrawals or delays in the Crown Court. The reason advanced for this decision was that the same necessity that prevailed to counter abuses in the magistrates' court did not arise in a Crown Court because there the presiding judge has control of the proceedings and can reject any unsubstantiated motion to adjourn or withdraw the prosecution. Paradoxically, it is this very reason for not extending the statutory duty to report withdrawals in the Crown

---

[60] 1978 Regulations, reg. 19.

Court that demonstrates the ineffectual character of the original duty imposed on the lower courts under the 1879 statute. The object, presumably, of reporting circumstances of this nature is to ensure that any case which calls for the intervention of the Director is thereby taken over and prosecuted to its conclusion. Certainly, no statutory powers exist whereby the Director of Public Prosecutions can impose sanctions upon the original but inactive prosecutor to compel his proceeding with the case. Furthermore, the wording of the Prosecution of Offences Act 1879, and the ensuing Regulations made under its umbrella, only call for a report to be made to the Director of Public Prosecutions *after* the withdrawal has taken place.[61] By that time it is beyond the power of the Director, or any of his staff, to intervene and take remedial action to forestall the collapse of the case for the prosecution. The suggestion was floated before the working party that legislation be introduced that would enable the justices to refuse an application for withdrawal unless and until they were satisfied that such a course was not objected to by the Director of Public Prosecutions. The idea appears to have been still-born for the present, but if the nature and frequency of the problem ever comes to approximate the incidence of such withdrawals in some Commonwealth jurisdictions[62] a fresh look at the situation is likely to be called for and some curtailment of the withdrawal procedure may well be seriously considered.

CONSENT PROVISIONS—REFORM INITIATIVES WITHIN GOVERNMENT

When writing in 1964 I made a strong plea for a realistic appraisal of the much vaunted right of the private citizen to institute criminal proceedings.[63] At the same time it was pointed out how far the erosion of this fundamental tenet had proceeded under the growing weight of offences, the prosecution of which, by Parliamentary edict, is conditional upon the consent of the Attorney General, the Solicitor General, other ministers or the Director of Public Prosecutions being first obtained. The earliest example of such restrictions being imposed is to be found in the Roman Catholic Relief Act 1829.[64] Strong support for the principle of interposing the fiat of the Attorney General, to counter the perceived danger of bribery, corruption and improper compromises by private prosecutors, was forthcoming in the testimony given by Lord Chief Justice Campbell to the Select Committee on Public Prosecutors in 1856.[65] His views failed to gain the support of either the incumbent Attorney General, Sir Alexander Cockburn,[66] or the Select Committee itself.[67] Sporadically,

[61] 42 & 43 Vict., c.22, s.5.
[62] See, *e.g.* C. Sun, "The Discretionary Power to Stay Criminal Proceedings" (1973) 1 *Dalhousie Law Journal* 482 and S. A. Cohen, *Due Process of Law* (Toronto, Carswell, 1977), pp. 150–160.
[63] Edwards, *op. cit.* pp. 396–401.
[64] 10 Geo. 4, c.7, s.38.
[65] Parl. Papers (1854–1855), (481) Vol.xii, pp. 1 *et seq.*, especially at Qs. 674–677.
[66] *Ibid.* Qs. 2425–2428.
[67] Parl. Papers (1856) (206), Vol. vii, pp. 355–357.

however, during the rest of the nineteenth century examples can be found in the statute book in which the consent of either a Law Officer of the Crown[68] or, following the creation of the office, that of the Director of Public Prosecutions[69] was required for the institution or continuation of criminal proceedings. By far the biggest quota of illustrations of such a consent requirement is to be found in the social welfare legislation enacted during the post World War II period.[70] An examination of the statute book in the past two decades shows no significant reduction in the proliferation of consent provisions. At the last count in 1982, 42 Acts were listed as containing provisions—sometimes singly and frequently in a series of separate provisions within the same enactment—that require the consent of the Attorney General[71] to the institution or carrying on of criminal proceedings.[72] Occasionally, the consent of the Solicitor General is specified as an alternative control mechanism.[73] In many other instances the minister or other body responsible for administering the legislation is equated with the Law Officers of the Crown in having exclusive authority to launch a prosecution.[74] Further analysis of the statute book reveals a list of 64 statutes in which the consent of the Director of Public Prosecutions, either exclusively or in substitution for one of the Law Officers, is resorted to by Parliament as the device for controlling the enforcement of the relevant penal provisions.[75] A simple comparison between the number of enactments containing provisions vesting consent authority in the Attorney General and the Director of Public Prosecutions, respectively, confirms the belief that the latter's involvement as the dispenser of the fiat controlling

[68] *e.g.* the Newspaper, Printers and Reading Room Repeal Act 1869. For an interesting discussion of the enforcement practice with respect to this extant offence, and the role of the Attorney General, see (1982) 2 *Legal Studies* 180–189.

[69] One of the earliest examples was the Newspaper Libel and Registration Act 1881 (44 & 45 Vict. c.60), s.3 of which restricted the institution of criminal proceedings under the Act to cases in which the written fiat was obtained from "the D.P.P. in England or H.M.'s Attorney General in Ireland".

[70] See Edwards, *op. cit.* pp. 237–240.

[71] The full list of these statutory restrictions, involving preliminary recourse to the Attorney General's fiat, is to be found in Appendix 11 to the Written Evidence submitted by the D.P.P. to the Royal Commission on Criminal Procedure (1981). A comprehensive list, as of 1977, is also provided in H.C. Debates, Written Answers, cols. 37–39, March 14, 1977.

[72] In the explanatory memorandum that accompanied the Prosecution of Offences Bill 1979, attention is drawn to the fact that various expressions are used in the statute book to describe the commencement of criminal proceedings. Among these the term "initiation" of proceedings is frequently resorted to (*e.g.* s.12 of the Criminal Jurisdiction Act 1975) but never in relation to a consent provision. Special attention is drawn in the same memorandum to the use throughout the 1979 enactment of the preferred word the "institution" of criminal proceedings, as being the most common expression that encompasses all the various epithets used to describe the actual commencement of a prosecution.

[73] Examples are located in the Prevention of Corruption Act 1906 (6 Edw. 7, c.34), s.2.; Public Bodies Corrupt Practices Act 1889 (52 & 53 Vict. c.69), s.4(2).

[74] See, *e.g.* Clean Air Act 1956 (4 & 5 Eliz. 2, c.52), s.29(2); Mines and Quarries Act 1954 (2 & 3 Eliz. 2, c.70), s.164; Prevention of Oil Pollution Act 1971 (c.60), s.19(1); Water Act 1945 (8 & 9 Geo. 6, c.42), s.46.

[75] The latest summary of these provisions is contained in Appendix 12 of the D.P.P.'s written submission to the recent Royal Commission (*ante*, fn. 71). Excluded from this list are any Local Acts containing similar provisions.

the enforcement of statutory offences has now surpassed that of his ministerial superiors.

There is no need to look for any insidious motive behind this evolving parliamentary practice. In its wake we begin to see the formulation of a policy of restricting the Attorney General's involvement to those rare situations where, by the nature of the offence or the circumstances that are likely to surround its commission, it can be said that the widest interests of the State make it preferable that the senior Law Officer, as the responsible minister, exercise his best informed judgment before authorising proceedings to commence. To the extent that "new" consent provisions are piled upon earlier consent restrictions, with little apparent indication of a concerted attempt to develop policy guidelines,[76] it stands to reason that the recent tendency to designate the Director of Public Prosecutions as the authorising officer has left a large question mark beside many older provisions as to whether they should be allowed to continue in place. Recognition of this fact, and of the pressing need to tidy up the "consent" laws, is evident in the report of the working party set up in 1977 under the joint auspices of the Law Officers' Department and the Director of Public Prosecutions. Its efforts resulted in the introduction of the Consent to Prosecutions Bill in the House of Commons in February 1979.[77] Before the measure had proceeded very far through the legislative system a general election was called and Parliament was dissolved. We are left, therefore, with a forbidding morass of uncoordinated legislation, the scope and contents of which would normally defy the most enthusiastic analyst. Fortunately, this has been undertaken by the public officials in the two Departments directly connected with the problem. We shall gain a better appreciation of the incongruities of the existing consent offences if we follow the approach adopted by the crusading reformers inside government.

The first goal of the reformers was to draw up a select list of the most sensitive provisions that should continue to require the intercession of the Attorney General before criminal proceedings are brought. The seriousness of the offence, and the substantial public interest that will likely accompany the commission of the crime, were seen as the most pertinent

---

[76] Whether it is the Attorney General, the Solicitor General, or the D.P.P. whose consent is made necessary by statute, a facilitating provision in section 7 of the Prosecution of Offences Act 1979, has obviated the possibility of renewed challenges to the form in which the consent is expressed, as illustrated by *R.* v. *Cain and Schollick* [1975] 2 All E.R. 900. In noting the variation in the language used by Parliament in consent provisions, the Court of Appeal confirmed that, with respect to the offence before it, *i.e.* the Explosives Substances Act 1883, s.7(1), the statute contemplates the giving of consent by the Attorney General after proceedings have begun and not prior to the institution of proceedings before the examining justices. Referring to the fact that the form of consent used had been unchanged for 100 years or more the Criminal Division refused to sanction a change that would require greater particularity to be shown in the Attorney's grant of his consent. The 1979 statute confirms this approach, declaring any such document purporting to confer the necessary consent of a Law Officer or the Director as prima facie evidence of consent without further proof.

[77] Bill 88, introduced on February 15, 1979, in addition to transferring to the D.P.P. functions exercisable by the Law Officers relating to a variety of consent offences, also makes provision for such transfers in future.

criteria for retaining existing Attorney General's consent provisions within this list. Twelve Acts of Parliament containing such conditions were deemed to meet the more restrictive criteria in comparison with the existing 42 enactments that involve the issuance of the Attorney General's fiat. Some of the proposed retentions are probably well known, such as the broad range of offences in the Official Secrets Acts 1911 and 1920.[78] The exercise of the Attorney General's fiat in these kinds of cases will invariably occupy a high public profile. There is also an enormous list of revenue violations under the Customs and Excise Acts, and their updated EEC amendments, that may claim the attention of the Attorney General or the Solicitor General.[79] Normally, proceedings will be instituted by order of the Commissioners of Customs and Excise but it is open to a Law Officer to set a prosecution in motion in any case that he considers it proper to do so. Why this residual discretion should rest with the Law Officers is not readily apparent. If considered necessary, the Director could surely be assigned the responsibility.

The larger international implications that generally find the Attorney General being involved are represented in the consent provisions contained in the Genocide Act 1969,[80] the Hijacking Act 1971,[81] the Protection of Aircraft Act 1973[82] and the Prevention of Terrorism (Temporary Provisions) Act 1976.[83] The offences in these statutes carry very severe penalties, usually that of life imprisonment, and the same applies to the offences of developing, acquiring or retaining biological substances for hostile purposes or in armed conflict, under the Biological

---

[78] s.8 of the 1911 Act (1 & 2 Geo. 5, c.28) and s.8 of the 1920 Act (10 & 11 Geo. 5, c.75). For the factors that govern the exercise of the Att. Gen's consent powers in connection with prosecutions under the Official Secrets Acts, see the memorandum submitted by Sir Peter Rawlinson (as A.G.) to the Departmental Committee on s.2 of the Official Secrets Act 1911: the Franks Report, Cmnd. 5104 (1972), Vol. 2 (Written Evidence) pp. 4–8. Rawlinson's memorandum also states the arguments against transferring the consent discretion to the D.P.P. or a High Court judge. Among the more controversial cases in recent times involving the exercise of the Att. Gen.'s consent powers under s.1 of the 1911 statute see *Chandler* v. *D.P.P.* [1964] A.C. 763 (the anti-nuclear demonstration case), and under s.2 see *R.* v. *Aitken et al.* (*The Times*, January 13 to February 4, 1971, involving the *Sunday Telegraph* and its editor for printing disclosures relating to the Biafra civil war). For the relevance of "D" notices to any future prosecutions of the latter kind see the *Third Report of the Defence Committee, Session 1979–80* H.C. 773 and [1983] P.L. 37.

[79] 15 & 16 Geo. 6, c.44, ss.281(3) and 283(3).   [80] c.12, s.1(3).

[81] c.70, s.5(1).   [82] c.47, s.4(2).

[83] c.8, ss.1, 2, 9, 10 and 11. An exchange of letters (see *The Times,* August 2, 1980) between Sir Michael Havers and Sir Michael Swann, then chairman of the BBC, reveals the reasons why the Attorney General refrained from authorising a criminal prosecution under section 11 of the 1976 Act. The circumstances that gave rise to this incident were two television programmes, *Tonight* and *Panorama,* that, in the Attorney's words, "constituted little more than propaganda exercises by terrorist organisations to which [BBC] staff willingly gave their support . . . ." Only reluctantly and under pressure, according to Havers' letter, did the television crews cooperate with the security authorities in disclosing information that might have assisted in the apprehension and prosecution of the I.R.A. terrorists. In his reply, the BBC chairman referred to legal uncertainties surrounding the interpretation of the relevant statute and denied that there had been any intent to mislead. With the Attorney General's admonitions and warning, and the BBC's reiteration of the perils of imposing censorship of the media, the matter was allowed to rest.

Weapons Act 1974,[84] prosecutions for which are likewise subject to the consent of the Attorney General. Having regard to the range of serious offences that are made subject to the Director's consent, either originally or under the proposed transfer of responsibilities from the Attorney General, it may be wondered why offences under the Counter Inflation Act 1973[85] and the Housing Act 1957[86] (which concern proceedings against the local authority with respect to overcrowding in dwelling houses) should be retained in the proposed emasculated list of Attorney General's consent provisions. Much stronger arguments can be made in support of continuing the necessity for the Attorney's fiat in certain offences under the Public Order Act 1936.[87] The same arguments, for retaining control over what might otherwise be vexatious private prosecutions, apply to the requirement that the consent of the Attorney General is a precondition to any prosecution based on acts calculated to incite hatred against any racial group in Great Britain. Originally contained in the Race Relations Act 1965[88] and now incorporated into the Public Order Act 1936[89] under the terms of the Race Relations Act 1976,[90] this responsibility is considered an important part of the Attorney General's discretionary powers and there is no suggestion in the working party's report that it be transferred to the Director of Public Prosecutions.

In view of the strong and successful opposition led by the then Attorney General against the proposed consent clause in the Obscene Publications Bill in 1959,[91] it is noteworthy that no objection appears to have been mounted to divesting the Attorney General of consent responsibilities under the controversial Theatres Act 1968.[92] Several offences are created

---

[84] c.6, s.2(1).   [85] c.9, s.17(9).

[86] 6 Eliz. 2, c.56, s.85(1).

[87] 1 Edw. 8 & 1 Geo. 6, c.6, ss.1 and 2.

[88] c.73, s.6. For a useful review of the role of the Attorney General in connection with s.6 prosecutions, see A. Dickey, [1968] Crim. L.R. 489.

[89] 1 Edw. 8 & 1 Geo. 6, c.6, s.5A.   [90] c.74, s.70(5).

[91] Edwards, op. cit., pp. 240–243. Although the then Attorney General was successful in resisting pressures to impose consent powers upon his office with respect to prosecutions for obscene publications, the effect of amendments introduced by s.53 of the Criminal Law Act 1977 (c.45) is to require the D.P.P.'s consent to proceedings under either s.2 or 3 of the 1959 Act, where the obscene article in question is a moving picture film of not less than 16 millimetres and which was published, or kept to be published, for gain in the course of a cinematograph exhibition. Likewise, because of the provisions of s.25 of the Criminal Justice Act 1967 (c.80), which permits the issue of a search warrant only on an information laid by or on behalf of the D.P.P. or by a constable, the ordinary citizen is precluded from initiating forfeiture proceedings under s.3 of the 1959 Act. One further incongruity is to be found in the Children and Young Persons (Harmful Publications) Act 1955 (3 & 4 Eliz. 2, c.28), s.2(2) of which requires the consent of the Attorney General to prosecutions under its auspices. The reader, wishing to find his way successfully through this confusing patchwork of statutory provisions, should consult the Williams Report (see ante, fn. 52) (pp. 176–179) and the memorandum submitted to the Committee by the D.P.P. which contains the criteria used by his Department in classifying obscene material.

[92] c.54, s.8. The issues surrounding the enforcement of the relevant consent provisions in the Theatres Act 1968 and the Obscene Publications Acts 1959 and 1964 were examined anew by the Committee on Obscenity and Film Censorship in 1979 (Cmnd. 7772). The Committee, in its recommendations (ibid. pp. 159–166), favoured the restricting of criminal proceedings to cases brought by the police or by or with the consent of the D.P.P. In its Report the

by that statute including those of performing an obscene play (whether in public or private and whether for gain or not), incitement to racial hatred by means of a public performance of a play and likewise if the performance is likely to occasion a breach of the peace. Proceedings with respect to any of these offences, or the common law offence of publishing defamatory matter in the course of a play, may not be prosecuted except by or with the consent of the Attorney General.

THE CONSENT TO PROSECUTIONS BILL 1979

As already stated, the ambitious programme of transferring the consent powers of the Attorney General to the Director of Public Prosecutions met an unexpected roadblock in the House of Commons which declined to proceed further than the first reading of the Government's Consent to Prosecutions Bill in 1979.[93] Exactly why such opposition to the measure was encountered can only be conjectured and it may well have been the breadth of the assault upon provisions which, after all, had been originally inserted in the pertinent statutes by Parliament itself. In the first clause of the Bill all functions of a Law Officer contained in the enactments specified in the Schedule to the Act were to be transferred to the Director of Public Prosecutions or, if exercisable by a Law Officer concurrently with the Director, were to cease to be exercisable by the Law Officer. The list of enactments, 24 in all, that were embraced in the proposed mass transfer, extended from the Newspapers, Printers and Reading Room Act 1869[94] to the Solicitors Act 1974.[95] Among the more significant subject areas covered were the Explosives Substances Act 1883,[96] the Prevention of Corruption Act 1906,[97] the Coinage Offences Act 1936,[98] the Children and Young Persons (Harmful Publications) Act 1955,[99] and the Prevention of Oil Pollution Act 1971.[1]

The arguments advanced in favour of transferring these consent provisions from the Attorney General to the Director were more practical than theoretical. It was anticipated, for example, that professional time

---

Committee acknowledged that the provision which had aroused most antagonism among certain of its witnesses is that contained in the Theatres Act 1968, requiring the consent of the Attorney General to the bringing of a prosecution: "From the evidence . . . it seemed likely that had it not been for this restriction more prosecutions would have been brought under the Act not by the D.P.P. but by private prosecutors. As it is, the Act has only been used once. The Director told us that in the 10 years since the Act was passed only 28 cases of alleged offences under the Act have been referred to him; he thought this indicated that there was no great problem in this field." (*ibid.* p. 17).

[93] Bill no. 88.

[94] 32 & 33 Vict. c.24, Sched. 2, the entries relating to 2 & 3 Vict., c.12, s.4, and 9 & 10 Vict., c.33, s.1. The dearth of prosecutions under the 1869 Act is noted in Colin Manchester's call for the repeal *in toto* of the legislation, see (1982) 2 *Legal Studies* 180, at pp. 186–188.

[95] c.47, s.42(2).

[96] 46 & 47 Vict. c.3, s.7(1).

[97] 6 Edw. 7, c.34, s.2(1).

[98] 26 Geo. 5 & 1 Edw. 8, c.16, s.4(3).

[99] 4 & 5 Eliz. 2, c.28, s.2(2).

[1] c.60, s.19(1).

would be saved in the Law Officers' Department and the Law Officers themselves would cease to be burdened by run of the mill cases. It would also release professional time in the Department of Public Prosecutions by dispensing with the necessity of preparing, for the Attorney's benefit, a statement of the relevant facts in each case. The original intention of the working party, which initiated the suggested realignment of functions, was to render the offences subject to the Director's consent but with the proviso that he consult with the Attorney in serious cases. No such proviso found its way into the 1979 Bill.

Clause 2 of the Bill may also have touched the sensitivities of many members of Parliament. It was designed to facilitate future transfers of consent powers or other statutory functions, as between the respective Law Officers and the Director of Public Prosecutions, it being proposed that such transfers be effected by statutory instrument after an affirmative resolution had passed both Houses. Two other supplementary provisions in the Consent to Prosecutions Bill are worth noting. The first of these would enable the Attorney General to direct, either generally or specifically, that any consent discretion, conferred upon him by statute, be exercisable concurrently with the Solicitor General.[2] Some statutes already do this expressly (*e.g.* the Auctions (Bidding Agreements) Act 1927,[3] and the Cancer Act 1939[4]), without any indication as to why Parliament would wish to include the junior Law Officer in some enactments and not in others. And there is, of course, the existing provision in section 1 of the Law Officers Act 1944,[5] which enables the Solicitor General to discharge the functions of the Attorney General if the latter office is vacant, or its holder is unable to act owing to absence or illness, or the Attorney specifically authorises the Solicitor to act in any particular case. The other provision, contained in clause 4 of the 1979 Bill, reaffirms the important

[2] cl. 3(1). For this purpose "consent" is deemed to include "sanction, fiat, direction or order," see cl. 2(4). The breadth of this interpretation owes its origin to the meaning attributed to "consent" provisions in the Criminal Jurisdiction Act 1975 (c.59), s.12(3), and, prior to that enactment, to s.12 of the Criminal Justice Act 1925 (15 & 16 Geo. 5, c.86). It is repeated in the Prosecution of Offences Act 1979 (c.31), s.10. For what is believed to be the only reference to the "sanctioning" of a criminal prosecution see the Judicial Proceedings (Regulation of Reports) Act 1926 (16 & 17 Geo. 5, c.61), s.1(3). Resort to the language of "directing" the institution of criminal proceedings is exemplified by the Firearms Act 1976 (c.32), s.2(3).

[3] 17 & 18 Geo. 5, c.12, s.1(3).

[4] 2 & 3 Geo. 6, c.13, s.4(6).

[5] In my original study, *The Law Officers of the Crown,* when dealing with the subject of *nolle prosequi* (at p. 231), I mistakenly cited the Law Officers Act 1944, s.1(1) as authority for the Solicitor General's general power to act in place of the Attorney General in the exceptional circumstances envisaged by that Act. This is not so, since the terms of section 1(1) only deal with statutory consents and do not cover the common law powers of the Attorney in granting a *nolle prosequi* or in consenting to a relator action. For the same misapprehension contained in *Archbold,* see *post,* p. 447, fn. 18. Had the Consents to Prosecutions Bill (No. 88) been enacted without amendment, the same restrictions would have been applicable. No such obstacle exists with respect to the Solicitor General for Scotland deputising for the Lord Advocate (*post,* p. 286, fn. 2) or the Solicitor General of New Zealand deputising for that country's Attorney General (*post,* p. 447, fn. 19). It would seem advisable for the same policy to be adopted with respect to England and Wales.

constitutional principle that nothing in the proposed measure is to be taken as prejudicing section 2 of the Prosecution of Offences Act 1879 which, it will be recalled, states that it is the duty of the Director of Public Prosecutions to act under the superintendence of the Attorney General.

There is no need to dwell long in considering the next category of statutory offences with respect to which the Director of Public Prosecutions has expressed a willingness to dispense altogether with the consent requirements attached to his office. These conditions are to be found in statutes devoted to such disparate subjects as the Agricultural Land (Removal of Surface Soil) Act 1953,[6] the Betting, Gaming and Lotteries Act 1963,[7] the Fraudulent Mediums Act 1951,[8] the Pools Competitions Act 1971,[9] the National Health Service Act 1946,[10] and the Solicitors Act 1974.[11] The only surprise in this list is the apparent hesitation exhibited towards wielding the legislative scalpel. Taking all the proposed excisions together, they represent but a small inroad into the bulk of consent offences that will remain on the statute book.

This leaves us to consider the remaining category of offences the prosecution of which, from their inception, has been made subject to the consent of the Director of Public Prosecutions. It has been stated already that the quantum of these provisions has by now exceeded those which are subject to the consent of either the Attorney General and the Solicitor General. With the anticipated transfer at some future date of the additional consent offences we examined earlier, and presently exercisable by the Attorney General, it will be seen that the Director's office will further enlarge its discretionary jurisdiction. If the issue is confined to a choice between the Director's office and the office of the Attorney General as the most appropriate repository for this kind of responsibility, few would argue against confining the Attorney General's involvement to the most serious or the most publicly prominent cases. If the net effect of such a confining policy is to expand the participation of the Director of Public Prosecutions at the most sensitive stage in the criminal process, that of deciding whether or not to initiate a prosecution, this is already in line with the critical role assigned to the Director in his working relationship with the police.

In many other instances the Director acts as a kind of "long stop" where the offence is normally prosecutable with the concurrence of another body. That body may be the minister in charge of the government department which is responsible for administering the legislation, the inspectorate of weights and measures, an industrial assurance commissioner or a local authority. Illustrations of these statutory provisions are to be found in the

---

[6] 1 & 2 Eliz. 2, c.10, s.3.
[7] c.2, s.42(1).
[8] 14 & 15 Geo. 6, c.33, s.1(4).
[9] c.57, s.6(2).
[10] 9, 10 & 11 Geo. 6, c.81, s.35(11).
[11] c.47, s.44(1) & (4).

Coal Industry (Nationalisation) Act 1946,[12] the Electricity Act 1957,[13] the Gas Act 1972,[14] the Insurance Companies Act 1974,[15] the Nuclear Installations Act 1965[16] and the Radioactive Substances Act 1960.[17] There is another group of criminal offences that conforms to the central policy making role of the Director of Public Prosecutions in developing national standards for the institution of criminal proceedings. Examples of this kind of approach by Parliament are to be found in the Trading with the Enemy Act 1939,[18] the Sexual Offences Act 1956[19] (with respect to the crime of incest), the Sexual Offences Act 1967[20] (for crimes of buggery and gross indecency where either the accused or the victim is under the age of 21), the Suicide Act 1961[21] (pertaining to aiding and abetting or attempting to commit suicide), and the Criminal Act 1977[22] (relating to conspiracies to commit a summary offence). With respect to the former group of offences that are generally the primary concern of a government department or statutory body it is difficult to see any justification for conferring a "watchdog" role upon the Director. No information is readily available as to the incidence of cases in which the Director has been called upon to rectify the deficiencies of the discretionary authority. Intuition suggests that the relevant statistics would demonstrate a defunct jurisdiction that could be disposed of with no likelihood of weakening the fabric of law enforcement in those areas.

RATIONALITY OR EXPEDIENCY AS THE TRUE BASIS FOR RESTRICTING THE RIGHT
    OF PRIVATE PROSECUTION

Any attempt to derive a set of uniform principles that would provide a rational basis for the various categories of consent provisions is frankly an impossible task. Equally unrewarding, in general, is the attempt to locate the source of particular initiatives in inserting a consent provision into proposed new legislation. Where the measure originates in a single department of government and has a closely defined set of objectives, we can readily deduce whose hand lies behind the introduction of restraints with respect to the enforcement of its sanctioning provisions. And when objection is voiced on the part of the Law Officers to being saddled with another fiat responsibility it is obviously necessary to look elsewhere to discover the original impetus. Thus, in the recent Contempt of Court Act 1981, it was at the insistence of Parliament and over the strong objections

[12] 9, 10 & 11 Geo. 6, c.59, s.59(1).
[13] Electricity Act 1957, 5 & 6 Eliz. 2, c.48, s.30(8).
[14] c.60, s.43(1).
[15] c.49, s.18.
[16] c.57, s.25(3).
[17] 8 & 9 Eliz. 2, c.34, s.13.
[18] 2 & 3 Geo. 6, c.89, s.1(4).
[19] 4 & 5 Eliz. 2, c.69, Sched. 2, Pt. II, paras. 14, 15.
[20] c.60, s.8.
[21] 9 & 10 Eliz. 2, c.60, s.2(4).
[22] c.45, s.4(1).

of the Attorney General that future contempt proceedings are made subject to the fiat of the Attorney General first being obtained.[23] We need to go back to the Obscene Publications Bill in 1959 to locate a similar intensive debate on the principles that should govern the introduction of statutory limitations on the right to privately instituted criminal proceedings. The memorandum prepared by Sir Reginald Manningham Buller, the Attorney General at the time, and considered by the Select Committee reviewing the Bill,[24] is invariably cited by government departments, when submitting evidence to Royal Commissions or departmental committees, as the classic exposition of the relevant factors that should govern any resort to a consent formula in new statutory offences.[25]

The Attorney General's memorandum began with the ringing declaration that "the problem should be approached on the footing that it is a fundamental principle of English criminal law that proceedings may be instituted by private individuals, and, accordingly, the right to prosecute is unrestricted unless some very good reason to the contrary exists."[26] Formal adherence to this constitutional doctrine is contained in the Prosecution of Offences Act 1979, s.4 of which states that "Nothing in this Act shall preclude any person from instituting or carrying on any criminal

---

[23] Contempt of Court Act 1981 (c.49), see *post*, Chap. 6, pp. 171–176.

[24] See Report of the Select Committee on Obscene Publications, H.C. Paper 123 of 1958, Appendix 1 and Edwards, *op. cit.* pp. 140–143.

[25] pp. 140–143. A prominent example of dependence on the earlier exposition in 1958 is the Home Office submission to the Departmental [Franks] Committee on section 2 of the Official Secrets Act, 1911—see the written evidence to the Committee, *Report,* Vol. 2, pp. 124–127 and Appendix VII to Vol. 1, Cmnd. 5104 of 1972, pp. 138–139. Five kinds of overlapping reasons were identified in explaining the resort by Parliament to consent provisions, *viz.,*

    (a) to secure consistency of practice in bringing prosecutions, *e.g.* where it is not possible to define the offence very precisely, so that the law goes wider than the mischief aimed at or is open to a variety of interpretations;

    (b) to prevent abuse, or the bringing of the law into disrepute, *e.g.* with the kind of offence which might otherwise result in vexatious private prosecutions or the institution of proceedings in trivial cases;

    (c) to enable account to be taken of mitigating factors which may vary so widely from case to case that they are not susceptible of statutory definition;

    (d) to provide some central control over the use of the criminal law when it has to intrude into areas which are particularly sensitive or controversial, such as race relations or censorship;

    (e) to ensure that decisions on prosecution take account of important considerations of public policy or of a political or international character, such as may arise, for instance, in relation to official secrets or hijacking.

In a further attempt to provide some measure of clarification the Home Office paper concluded that "recent practice suggests that a control introduced on grounds (a), (b), or (c) would normally be thought appropriate to the Director of Public Prosecutions, a control on ground (e) would be thought appropriate to the Attorney General, and a control on ground (d) might be given to either, depending on the circumstances." This attempt at rationalisation of the statutory morass did not impress the recent Royal Commission on Criminal Procedure which stated that the Home Office's reasons, quoted above, "do not seem to be the basis of any coherent policy and an examination of the Acts concerned suggests that some of the restrictions have been arbitrarily imposed. . . . The only considerations that should apply, in our view, statutorily and absolutely to restrict prosecution relate to those very few cases where national interests may be thought to be particularly involved"—Cmnd. 8092, p. 162.

[26] Manningham Buller, *op. cit.* p. 23.

proceedings." So far so good, but there is no use denying the expanding inroads into this principle which are represented in the welter of statutory obstacles that must be surmounted by the private citizen who is of a mind to invoke the criminal law in pursuance of his constitutional rights. Furthermore, there is the overriding power, enshrined in the same section of the Prosecution of Offences Act 1979, quoted above, whereby the Director of Public Prosecutions "may undertake, at any stage, the conduct of those proceedings if he thinks fit." Originally enacted in section 2(3) of the Prosecution of Offences Act 1908, this power of the Director to assume control over the conduct of a privately instituted prosecution is all pervasive and effectually reduces the fundamental character claimed for the individual citizen's right of unrestricted access to the criminal courts in his or her own behalf.

What then are the important considerations in this debate? The first argument reviewed in the 1958 memorandum was that restriction was desirable to ensure uniformity in the administration of the criminal law by way of police prosecutions. It was pointed out that this purpose is largely accomplished under the Prosecution of Offences Regulations which, as we have seen under both the old and new codes, require chiefs of police to report to the Director of Public Prosecutions cases that fall within the ordained categories of offences calling for notification to the Director's office.[27] It is doubtful whether any offence, having the potential for public concern, has been omitted from these lists so that there already exists a review mechanism that falls short of actually curtailing the right to institute proceedings. Viewing the same argument that favours uniformity of practice in the broadest context, the Manningham Buller memorandum stated: "it is not proper . . . to impose any restriction on the right to prosecute for the purpose of obtaining uniformity in the administration of a law incapable of precise definition on the ground that . . . it is peculiarly liable to be regarded in a different light by different persons. Uniformity in the administration of the law is a matter for the courts themselves and should not . . . be achieved by interposing the decisions of the executive between them and the law which they administer."[28] This point of view is hardly consistent with the avowed purpose of making the Director of Public Prosecutions the supreme arbiter—subject only to the Attorney General—of instituting proceedings for a wide range of offences. Against this, it can be claimed, is the practical realisation that without the Director's benevolent or strict supervision the situation could quickly develop in which the policies of individual chief constables would readily produce a bewildering diversity of practice.

The reluctance of the judges to assume the role advocated in the 1958 memorandum and their preference for designating the Attorney General or the Director of Public Prosecutions as the state official clothed with that

---

[27] See *ante*, p. 13.
[28] Manningham Buller, *op. cit.* p. 24.

invidious responsibility is illustrated by the observations of Lord Goddard, C.J., in 1953 in relation to the privately instituted proceedings brought against the editor of *Lilliput* magazine for criminal contempt.[29] "In this class of case" the former Chief Justice declared, "I have always taken the view that it would be a good change if these actions were moved only by a Law Officer or on the instructions of the Attorney General because the object is to punish an editor who has committed contempt, not to assist the defence."[30] Other members of the Bench have not been averse either to making their views known publicly on the necessity for curtailing the right to institute a private prosecution. Whether in the individual circumstances the motives of a private prosecutor seem to be blatantly vexatious and oppressive may not be seriously questioned, but any move towards *statutorily* curtailing the citizen's basic rights should not rest on the lack of sympathy for the motives of those who elect to exercise their rights under the criminal law. Such was the situation in what became known as the *Bishop of Medway* case in 1979. That case, apart from its bizarre circumstances, was notable for the transformation in the views attributed to Lord Dilhorne. As the Attorney General responsible for the much cited memorandum submitted to the Select Committee on the Obscene Publications Bill in 1958, Sir Reginald Manningham Buller (as he then was) argued strenuously that on principle no case existed for departing from the basic constitutional rights of the private citizen. Twenty years later, in *Gleaves* v. *Deakin*[31] we find the former Attorney General taking sides with his judicial colleagues in the House of Lords in advocating, with respect to criminal libel, a further inroad into the fundamental principle that he had defended so successfully before the House of Commons. What is inevitable is that this particular debate, as to where the lines of prosecutorial responsibility should properly be drawn between the executive and judicial branches of government, will surface again and again in this book, and there it must rest for the moment.

Of the second ground advanced in the memorandum to the Select Committee in 1958 enough has probably been said already. Offences of obscenity (for which may be substituted any offence having undertones of subjective morality, religious or political opinion), it was said, are in their very nature liable to provoke vexatious legal proceedings in which the prosecution is initiated rather to gratify some whim of the prosecutor than to vindicate his rights or assist in the administration of criminal justice.[32] This argument reiterates the complaints uttered before the Select Committee on Public Prosecutors in 1856.[33] Where such an eventuality is patently obvious the case for imposing some *ad hoc* restrictions readily commands support. There exist other general powers of control such as the

---

[29] *The Times,* October 31, 1953.   [30] *Loc. cit.*
[31] [1979] 2 W.L.R. 665.   [32] *Op. cit.* p. 23.
[33] Edwards, *op. cit.* p. 343. *Cf.* the unsuccessful attempts, made during the passage of the Indecent Displays (Control) Act 1981 (c.42) through the Commons Standing Committee, to render private prosecutions subject to the prior consent of the D.P.P., *The Times*, March 12, 1981.

unrestricted right of the Director of Public Prosecutions to take over any criminal proceedings, summary or indictable, if he thinks fit. It is a moot question whether, in addition, each prosecution of particular offences requires the formal consent of the same Director or a Law Officer of the Crown.

One further consideration, that at first glance appears straightforward enough, in actuality contains the same seeds of dispute as to the proper ambit of the Attorney General's or the Director's functions in connection with prosecution decisions. When, owing to the difficulties of definition and drafting, the letter of the law becomes so wide that persons who have not offended against its spirit are caught then it is said to be appropriate that restriction be placed on the right to prosecute and that such restriction be subject to the fiat of the Attorney General or the Director of Public Prosecutions.[34] If such cases are triable by a jury, it can properly be argued that this restriction would to a very large degree require the Attorney General to perform the very functions which the law has assigned to the jury.[35] And, in any case, it once again poses the imponderable question as to where the dividing line is properly drawn between the judicial and executive branches of government. It will be necessary to return to this question later when the subjects of prosecutorial discretion, the relevant criteria,[36] and accountability to Parliament for the exercise of such discretionary powers, will be examined.

JUDICIAL REVIEW OF CONSENT DECISIONS

For the present we can confine our attention to the narrow issue of reviewability by the courts of the exercise of consent powers, whether these have been the subject of decisions by the Attorney General, the Solicitor General, a Minister of the Crown, the Director of Public Prosecutions or any other body designated as the statutory authority whose approval is necessary to the institution of a prosecution. Since the source of the discretionary power rests in statute law there are no inherent constitutional objections to the jurisdiction of the courts being invoked such as arise with respect to the prerogative powers of the Law Officers of the Crown.[37] Most of the celebrated cases which have been concerned with

[34] Manningham Buller, *op. cit.* p. 23, para. 2.

[35] *Ibid.* p. 24, para. 5.

[36] See the information provided by the D.P.P. to the Phillips Commission as to the number of "consent" cases referred in 1977 to the Attorney General and D.P.P., respectively, and the numbers where consent was withheld. It was found impossible to classify the grounds on which consent was withheld. The statistical tables are contained in Cmnd. 8092–1, Appendix 24, Tables 24.1 and 24.2.

[37] See, *e.g. Hanratty* v. *Lord Butler, The Times,* May 13, 1971, where the former Home Secretary was sued for negligence in not commuting the death sentence of a convicted murder. The Court of Appeal refused to allow the action to proceed on the ground that the prerogative of mercy is "one of the highest prerogatives of the Crown and the courts should refrain from enquiring into the manner of its exercise." This is in accord with the orthodox constitutional position. To like effect, the same court in *Blackburn* v. *Attorney General* [1971] 1 W.L.R. 1037 refused to entertain an application for a declaration relating to the signing of

the reviewability of the Attorney General's decisions fall within this latter category and deal with such questions as the entering of a *nolle prosequi* in indictable cases,[38] the institution of relator actions in matters affecting the general public,[39] and, until recently, the filing of *ex officio* informations.[40] These powers derive from the prerogative authority vested in the Attorney General and must be carefully distinguished from the discretionary powers that owe their origin to the actions of Parliament and which are to be found embedded in the long list of statutory provisions which have been reviewed in this chapter.

Where the necessary consent has been approved and criminal proceedings set in motion, the possibility of challenging the issuance of the statutory fiat will likely arise during the preliminary hearing or at the trial itself. The few reported cases on this question suggest that attention is generally directed towards satisfying the court that the procedural requirements surrounding the control mechanism have been properly met. These issues and more were considered in *R. v. Cain and Schollick*[41] where the accused appealed against their convictions on the ground that the document obtained from the Attorney General did not constitute a sufficient consent under section 7 of the Explosive Substances Act 1883. The Attorney's fiat purported to grant consent to the prosecution of the accused "for an offence or offences contrary to the provisions of the said Act." This formulation of the statutory consent was attacked on the ground that the wide and general terms in which it was couched meant in effect that the Attorney General, contrary to the requirements of Parliament, was delegating his duty to another. The Criminal Division of the Court of Appeal took the position that if the Attorney General considered that the prosecutor should be allowed to pursue any charge under the Act which was justified by the evidence, there was no objection to his giving his consent in the wide terms adopted in the instant case.

In elaborating the court's expectations of what the statute required Lord Widgery C.J., indirectly affirmed the existence of a judicial power of

the Treaty of Rome, the Master of the Rolls stating that Ministers of the Crown, when·they negotiate and sign a treaty, act on behalf of the country as a whole and exercise the royal prerogative. "Their action in doing so" declared Lord Denning "cannot be challenged or questioned in these courts"—*ibid.* p. 1040. In a note on "The Prerogative & Parliamentary Control" [1971] C.L.J. 178, D.G.T. Williams questioned whether the orthodox view is consistently adhered to by the judges and sought to explain the decisions restricting the scope of Crown privilege (see *post,* pp. 381–382) as an indication of judicial readiness to control the exercise, rather than define the ambit, of the prerogative. This interpretation is questionable and finds no support in the decisions pertaining to the prerogative powers associated with the Law Officers of the Crown, discussed in Chapter 6, *post.* For adherents to the view that no justification exists for continuing the distinction between judicial control of prerogative and statutory powers see Lord Denning M.R. in *Laker Airways Ltd.* v. *Dept. of Trade* [1977] 2 All E.R. 182 at pp. 192–193; *Re Toohey, ex p. Northern Land Council* (High Ct. of Aust.) (1981) 56 A.L.J.R. 164 *per* Mason J., at pp. 183–184; D.G.T. Williams, *loc. cit.* and A.W. Bradley, (Ed. of) Wade & Phillips, *Constitutional and Administrative Law* (4th ed.), p. 241.

[38] See *post,* pp. 444–447.
[39] See *post,* pp. 129–137, 140–145.
[40] See *post,* pp. 121–123, 438–442.
[41] [1975] 2 All E.R. 900.

review in such cases. According to Lord Chief Justice " . . . the purpose of requiring the Attorney General's consent to prosecutions under the 1883 Act is to protect potential defendants from oppressive prosecutions under an Act whose language is necessarily vague and general. Hence it is not necessary that the Attorney General should have considered and approved every detail of the charge as it ultimately appears in the indictment. His duty is to consider the general circumstances of the case, and decide whether any, and, if he thinks fit, which, of the provisions of the Act can properly be proved against the defendant. . . . If the Attorney General considers that the prosecutor should be at liberty to prove any charge under the Act which is justified by the evidence, there is no constitutional objection to his giving consent in the wide terms adopted in the present case. Furthermore, when consent is given in any terms it should be presumed that the Attorney General has made the necessary and proper enquiries before giving that consent."[42]

There is no suggestion, it will be noted, that the court should substitute its own judgment for that of the Attorney General in determining whether the particular circumstances warrant the decision to grant consent to the prosecution being brought. That decision rests exclusively, in cases falling within the Explosive Substances Act 1883, in the hands of the senior Law Officer of the Crown. As we have seen earlier, other statutes confer the discretionary authority on a variety of bodies ranging from the appropriate minister to the Director of Public Prosecutions. The principles adumbrated by the Court of Appeal in *R.* v. *Cain and Schollick* apply equally to such other designated bodies. As the Criminal Division further explained: "No doubt in every case of this kind it is open to the defendant to challenge the existence or otherwise of the Attorney General's consent. It will be sufficient response to such a challenge that the Attorney has applied his mind to the facts giving rise to the charge presently before the court . . . and gave his consent at whatever stage in those proceedings the relevant statute may require."[43]

This does not mean that the action of the Attorney General or other consenting power is beyond review by the courts. If, for example, the defendant could show that the Attorney General or the Director of Public Prosecutions had neglected to make "the necessary and proper enquiries" or had failed to "apply [his] mind to the facts giving rise to the charge" or in any other way could demonstrate that irrelevant considerations had dictated the exercise of the statutory discretion, there is the highest authority to justify expectations that the court would compel a review of the earlier decision and, in the meantime, vitiate the pending proceedings. As Lord Devlin stated in *Chandler* v. *D.P.P.*,[44] "The courts will not review the proper exercise of discretionary power but they will intervene to correct excess or abuse. This is a familiar doctrine in connection with

[42] *Ibid.* at p. 904.
[43] *Ibid.*
[44] [1964] A.C. 763 at p. 810.

statutory powers." Notwithstanding the absence in the law reports of any recorded instances in which the exercise of a consent power by the Attorney General, the Solicitor General or the Director of Public Prosecutions has been successfully challenged there is no reason to doubt that the fundamental principle, adverted to by Lord Devlin, embraces the whole range of statutory provisions reviewed in this chapter.

The grounds on which an excess of statutory authority can be established have been the subject of analysis by the House of Lords in a number of recent leading cases, foremost amongst which are *Padfield* v. *Minister of Agriculture*[45] and *Secretary of State for Education and Science* v. *Tameside Metropolitan Borough Council.*[46] In their exposition of the basic principles of law that govern judicial control of ministerial discretion there was agreement that the basic question for the court to determine is whether the minister or other body concerned was lawfully exercising its powers under the pertinent legislation. Moreover, the "unlawfulness" or "excess" by the responsible statutory authority can be established (a) by an outright refusal to consider the relevant matter, (b) by misdirecting itself in point of law, (c) by taking into account some wholly irrelevant extraneous considera- tion, or (d) by wholly omitting to take into account a relevant consideration.[47] Expressed with greater brevity, it was said that "The authority must not . . . allow itself to be influenced by something extraneous and extra judicial which ought not to have affected his decision."[48]

How far can these grounds be said to be appropriate when calling into question decisions pertaining to the institution of criminal proceedings by way of statutory consent? As we shall see later,[49] total objectivity in assessing the broad range of discretionary factors that relate to prosecuto- rial decisions is an unattainable goal. Added to which is a general adherence to the principle that the judiciary should not become embroiled in reviewing the decision to prosecute, lest the impartiality of the adjudicative process be seen to be diminished. Accordingly, it seems likely that the courts will exhibit considerable reluctance before passing judgment upon the relevancy of the various considerations that must be taken into account by the Law Officers or the Director of Public Prosecutions when deciding whether to issue a statutory fiat. This reluctance may diminish with the increasing public availability of the guidelines used in making decisions within the prosecution process. If this is so, and the circumstances warrant the court's scrutinising the decision of the Attorney General or the Director of Public Prosecutions, the outcome will surely be determined in accordance with the *Padfield* principles as stated above.

---

[45] [1968] A.C. 997.
[46] [1977] A.C. 1014.
[47] [1968] A.C. 997 at pp. 1041, 1058, 1061.
[48] *Ibid.* at p. 1046.
[49] See *post*, Chapter 14.

Only one limitation seems likely and that refers to the situation where the decision is not to grant consent and where no explanation is forthcoming—a normal practice at the present time. According to Lord Reid and Lord Pearce, speaking in the *Padfield* case,[50] a Minister's failure or refusal to give any reasons is no bar to the exercise of the court's surveillance. "If all the prima facie reasons" Lord Pearce maintained "seem to point in favour of his taking a certain course to carry out the intentions of Parliament in respect of a power which it has given him in that regard, and he gives no reason whatever for taking a contrary course, the court may infer that he has no good reason and that he is not using the power given by Parliament to carry out its intentions."[51] I find it difficult to imagine that such a presumption has a proper place in the special context of denying an application for consent to the institution of criminal proceedings. The rationale for exercising restraint with reference to negative decisions by the Attorney General and the Director of Public Prosecutions will be developed fully later.[52]

"Abuse" of statutory power may sometimes be indistinguishable from what has been described as a decision based on irrelevant or extraneous considerations. Included with the notion of abuse is conduct that manifests bad faith or *mala fides* on the part of the decision maker. The difficulties of adducing evidence that will satisfy the court of actual abuse of a consent power hardly needs emphasis, especially having regard to the very few occasions in which an explanation of any kind is made public by the Attorney General or the Director of Public Prosecutions within their appropriate fields of authority. In *Turner* v. *D.P.P.*,[53] a case which we shall have occasion to examine in more depth later,[54] the Director's decision to take over a private prosecution and terminate the proceedings was challenged, *inter alia*, on the ground that the Director of Public Prosecutions' purported exercise of his statutory powers under section 2(3) of the Prosecution of Offences Act 1908 was void on the ground of *mala fides*. No evidence was produced in support of this claim and the aggrieved plaintiff was left to question the unlawfulness of the Director's decision on the ground that the reasons behind the take-over of the private prosecution were not within the contemplated purposes of Parliament when it conferred the discretionary authority upon the Director of Public Prosecutions. The circumstances in *Turner* v. *D.P.P.* were unprecedented, Turner having launched a private prosecution against his accomplice who had given evidence for the Crown following a promise of immunity by the Director of Public Prosecutions. In rejecting the plaintiff's claim for a declaration that the Director's intervention was unlawful and *ultra vires,* the trial judge declared: "There is no doubt about the existence or the

---

[50] [1968] A.C. 997 at pp. 1032–1033 *per* Lord Reid.
[51] *Ibid.* pp. 1053–1054.
[52] See *post*, pp. 429–431.
[53] (1978) 68 Cr.App.R. 70.
[54] See *post*, pp. 460–461.

unfettered nature of the Director of Public Prosecutions' powers in this respect. As it is not suggested that he acted in bad faith and he clearly acted in the public interest . . . there is no case for the trial of a preliminary issue here."[55] In describing the Director's statutory power as "unfettered" it is doubtful whether Mars Jones, J., intended that it be given a literal interpretation. No evidence having been introduced to substantiate an abuse of power claim, the decision in *Turner* v. *D.P.P.* provides no more than indirect support for the application of the principles set down in the *Padfield* and *Tameside* judgments by the House of Lords.

The unusual circumstances of the *Turner* case were to be repeated a few years later in *Raymond* v. *Attorney General*,[56] and with the same result. Proceedings to obtain an order of *mandamus,* requiring the Director to pursue the charges laid by Raymond against his former confederate, were dismissed by the Divisional Court and the Court of Appeal, the latter doing so originally on jurisdictional grounds.[57] Undeterred, Raymond sought instead an injunction and a declaration designed to prevent the Director of Public Prosecutions from interfering in the plaintiff's privately launched prosecution. When these proceedings resurfaced in the Court of Appeal it was agreed that the major question concerned the limits of the Director's discretion to "undertake the conduct of a prosecution commenced privately." Speaking for the entire court, Sir Sebag Shaw stated[58]: " . . . there may be what appears to the Director substantial reasons in the public interest for not pursuing a prosecution privately commenced. What may emerge from those proceedings might have an adverse effect upon a pending prosecution involving far more serious issues. The Director, in such a case, is called upon to make a value judgment. Unless his decision is manifestly such that it could not be honestly and reasonably arrived at it cannot, in our opinion, be impugned. The safeguard against an unnecessary or gratuitous exercise of this power is that [under] section 2(7) of the Act of 1979 the Director's duties are exercised 'under the superintendence of the Attorney General.' That officer of the Crown is, in his turn, answerable to Parliament if it should appear that his or the Director's powers under the statute have in any case been abused." The Court of Appeal had no hesitation in dismissing the plaintiff's "fruitless pursuit of those engaged in the important and sensitive duties attaching to prosecutions."[59]

The important theoretical possibilities having thus been reasserted by the Court of Appeal, it only remains to observe that the citizen's recourse

[55] (1978) 68 Cr.App.R. 70 at p. 77.
[56] [1982] 2 W.L.R. 849.
[57] (1979) 70 Cr.App.R. 233. On that occasion the Master of the Rolls observed: "Mr. Raymond did put before us a suggestion that he might bring civil proceedings in order to obtain a declaration as to the powers or duty of the Director of Public Prosecutions. I would simply say that this is not the sort of case in which the court in its discretion would grant a declaration"—*ibid.* p. 235.
[58] [1982] 2 W.L.R. 849 at pp. 854–855.
[59] *Ibid.*

to the prerogative remedies of mandamus and certiorari, if they should arise again in future, are likely to be few and far between,[60] the principal obstacle being the applicability in statutory consent cases of the very standards that govern the issuance of the prerogative remedies. The doors to judicial review of the decisions made in these situations by the Law Officers of the Crown and the Director of Public Prosecutions are by no means closed but potential supplicants may find equal grounds for frustration when assessing the effectiveness of parliamentary accountability, as presently practised.[61]

[60] For an early example of an unsuccessful attempt to obtain an order of mandamus against the D.P.P. with respect to his refusal to grant consent under the Newspaper Libel Act 1881, s.3, see the judgments of the Divisional Court (*coram* Pollock B., and Manisty J.,) in *Ex parte Hurter* (1883) 47 J.P.R. 724. *Cf.* the refusal of the Irish Supreme Court to grant even a conditional order of mandamus against the Att. Gen. who had entered a *nolle prosequi* in circumstances similar to those portrayed in *Turner* and *Raymond* (*ante*). See *State (Killiam)* v. *A.G.* (1958) 92 I.L.T.R. 182 and criticisms noted *post* p. 264, fn. 25. See, too, the exploration of these issues by Bernard M. Dickens in "The Attorney General's Consent to Prosecutions" (1972) 35 M.L.R. 347.

[61] Another question that may surface more frequently than in the past is the extent of liability by the Attorney General or his agent, the D.P.P., for malicious prosecution. This issue has been the subject of a series of recent decisions by the Ontario High Court in which the trial judge in each case has pronounced in favour of immunity from such proceedings with respect to the Attorney General and his agents, the Crown Attorneys, when performing their duties as public prosecutors. See *Richman* v. *A.G. of Ontario* (1983) 41 O.R.(2d) 559 (Galligan, J.), *Owsley* v. *The Queen*, No. 7649/83 (Dupont, J.) and *Nelles* v. *A.G. of Ontario*, *The Globe and Mail*, August 20, 1983 (No. 12976/82) (Fitzpatrick J.). The basis for these decisions rests, in part, on the Proceedings against the Crown Act, R.S.O. 1980, c.382, s.5 of which excludes proceedings against the Crown for anything done by a person "while discharging responsibilities of a judicial nature vested in him," it being maintained that the duties of a Crown Attorney are quasi-judicial in nature and, therefore, protected by statute and common law from any possible civil liability. "The rule as to immunity" it was stated "is obviously designed not for the protection of the Crown officials but for that of the general public. Any injustices which may result to a litigant from improper actions on the part of such Crown officials must be deemed secondary to the primary general interest of society as a whole."

In support of this position the Ontario High Court justices relied upon the decision of the United States Supreme Court in *Imbler* v. *Pachtman* (1975) 424 U.S. 409, and the Scottish law as expressed in *Hester* v. *MacDonald* 1961 S.C. 370, where the Lord President (at p. 377) affirmed that: "Never in our history has a Lord Advocate been sued for damages in connection with [criminal] proceedings. On the contrary, our Courts have consistently affirmed the existence of such immunity on his part." A closer reading of the Lord President's judgment, however, suggests that the immunity of the Lord Advocate, and his agents, in proceedings by way of indictment derives from what Baron Hume described as follows: " . . . a constitutional trust is reposed in that high officer . . . and it will not be supposed of him that he can be actuated by unworthy motives in commencing a prosecution, or fall into such irregularities or blunders in conducting his process, as ought properly to make him liable in . . . amends." (*Crimes*, Vol. ii, p. 135). This rationale is far removed from that invoked by the justices of the Ontario High Court. The question of immunity was not raised before the English Court of Appeal in *Riches* v. *D.P.P.* [1973] 2 All E.R. 935. There, the Director opposed an action for malicious prosecution on the grounds that it disclosed no reasonable cause of action, and that the proceedings were vexatious and an abuse of the process of the court. In the course of his judgment, however, Stephenson, L.J. declared: "I do not wish to be taken as saying that there may never be a case where a prosecution has been initiated and pursued by the Director of Public Prosecutions in which it would be impossible for an acquitted defendant to succeed in an action for malicious prosecution, or as saying that the existence of the Attorney-General's fiat where required conclusively negates the existence of malice and conclusively proves that there was reasonable and probable cause for the prosecution. There may be cases where there has been, by even a responsible authority, the suppression of evidence which has led to a false view being taken by those who carried on a prosecution and by those who ultimately convicted. But that case is, as it seems to me, many miles from this one." *Ibid.* p. 941. If any credence is to be attached to the argument that the common law confers absolute immunity upon the Attorney General and his agents, including the D.P.P., it is noteworthy that no English precedents can be cited affirming the existence of such protection from civil suits, particularly proceedings for malicious prosecution. Stephenson L.J.'s dicta, as quoted above, are simply a modern and realistic appraisal of the circumstances that led Baron Hume to deny as being even conceivable. There is also considerable weakness in the "quasi-judicial" argument, since the same analogy has frequently been used to describe the police decision to initiate criminal proceedings by laying an information—see the authorities referred to *post*, Chapter 2, fns. 2 and 4. No similar immunity from malicious prosecutions suits, however, is seen to apply to police actions in setting the criminal law in motion.

2

Modern Interpretations of the Director of Public Prosecutions' Constitutional Status

Interpretation of the constitutional position which the Director of Public Prosecutions occupies in the administration of criminal law in England and Wales continues to be the subject, at times, of intense public debate. This debate generally surfaces in the wake of notable or controversial cases that engender a high public profile. At issue in such debates are two inter-related questions: first, what is the precise nature of the Director's relationship to the Attorney General and, secondly, what limits, if any, exist in manifesting the accountability of the Law Officers of the Crown to Parliament for the actions of the Director? In the previous chapter we examined the statutory provisions that govern the relationships between the State's principal officers in the area of criminal prosecutions. That analysis concentrated on the most recent evolution of the constitutional connection as contained in the specifics of the Acts and Regulations that cover a whole century of legislative history. What must concern us to no less degree are the views expressed, and the positions actually taken, by successive incumbents of the two offices. This body of evidence will further illuminate the constitutional position presently occupied by the Director of Public Prosecutions in England and Wales.

We are not here concerned directly with the comparative experience of other Commonwealth countries which, in their independence constitutions, have seen fit to incorporate varying versions of the English office of Director of Public Prosecutions.[1] Yet, as we shall see, these constitutions often reflect the areas of contention that have surrounded the original British model. Never far from the surface in all these discussions is the ideal goal of shielding the decision making process, whether or not to invoke the machinery of the criminal law, from political pressures and other considerations of an unacceptable nature. On the one hand, it is

---

[1] For a fuller treatment of these comparative constitutional provisions see Edwards, "Emerging Problems in Defining the Modern Role of the Office of Attorney-General in Commonwealth Countries," *1977 Meeting of Commonwealth Law Ministers, Minutes of Meeting and Memoranda*, (London, Commonwealth Secretariat), pp. 195–204.

argued that by rendering the office of Director of Public Prosecutions totally independent of any Minister of the Crown, including the Attorney General, the goal of impartiality can be safeguarded. Against this tenet is the paramount importance attached to the principle of ministerial accountability to Parliament for every action of the Director of Public Prosecutions. This responsibility, under English constitutional law, rests on the shoulders of the Attorney General.

To effectively discharge the Attorney General's constitutional duties in this regard there can be no question of completely insulating the Director's office in such a manner that renders the actions he takes immune from ministerial supervision. The words "control," "direction," "superintendence," and "supervision" permit of a wide disparity in meaning and are capable of arousing strong emotions when defining the power relationship between any two individuals, whatever the organisation.[2] In the adjacent field of policing, for example, it is only necessary to harken to the passions aroused in the breasts of chiefs of police when questions are raised as to the extent to which they are subject to the control and supervision of the local municipal authority or the Home Secretary, as the case may be.[3] Much has been written on the subject of the constitutional status of the police but it is doubtful even now whether there exists a consensus as to the true extent of

[2] The importance of defining the ambit of these terms, in the context of Canadian legislation pertaining to the relationship between the Minister (and Deputy Minister) responsible for the Royal Canadian Mounted Police and its Security Service, is elaborated upon by the *McDonald Commission of Inquiry into certain Activities of the R.C.M.P. 1981, Second Report*, Vol. 2, pp. 856–869, 1005–1014. In its discussion of the doctrine of accountability, the Royal Commission on Criminal Procedure adopted the terminology suggested by Geoffrey Marshall in his essay "Police Accountability Revisited" in Butler and Halsey (Eds.) *Policy and Politics*, (London, MacMillan, 1978), pp. 55–65. For the ensuing analysis of prosecutorial accountability, its scope and limitations, by the Phillips Commission, see its *Report*, Cmnd. 8092, pp. 139–142. Another helpful distinction to bear in mind is that adverted to by the late Professor E.C.S. Wade in a consultative memorandum prepared for the Royal Commission on the Police in 1962. In reply to the Commission's question: "What degree of independence does a chief constable have in enforcing the law?," Wade sought to distinguish between the "judicial" function of the police which demanded freedom from outside interference, and the "executive" function of maintaining law and order, under which rubric a chief constable should be open to direction on a limited range of "executive" matters—see Appendix II to the *Minutes of Evidence*, pp. 28–35.

[3] For a recent illustration of the intense passions generated by the debate surrounding this topic see the acerbic exchanges between Mr. James Anderton, Chief Constable of Greater Manchester (the largest police force outside London), and the chairman and deputy chairman of the Labour controlled county police committee. The controversy was generated by the police authority's censure of the chief constable for his handling of a local labour dispute with allegations of partiality towards management. Mr. Anderton replied with a public call for the abolition of elected police committees, appointed by the local authority concerned, and the substitution of non-political police boards. The former, according to Manchester's chief constable, represent "an enemy more dangerous, insidious and ruthless than any faced since the Second World War" and "the first conscious step . . . towards the political control of the police, without which the dream of a totalitarian one-party state in their country cannot be realised." The contrary philosophy, expressed in less strident terms, and aimed towards making the police more democratically accountable, is championed by Mr. John Alderson, formerly the Chief Constable of Devon and Cornwall. With regard to the Metropolitan London Police, whose Commissioner is directly responsible to the Home Secretary, the Labour Party is committed to ending that traditional relationship and replacing it with an

the independence claimed by chief constables in the discharge of their duties to enforce the criminal law.[4] Our present concern, however, is with the ambit of ministerial control over the office of the Director of Public Prosecutions, of which there is only one of its kind in English law. Parallels with the status claimed by chief constables must not divert us from the special constitutional relationship between the Attorney General and the Director of Public Prosecutions as it has been developed since the Prosecution of Offences Act 1879 first created the Director's office.

The Statute Law and Theobald Mathew's Views

As a reminder then let it be recalled that, in creating the office of Director of Public Prosecutions, the Prosecution of Offences Act 1879, s.2, declared that the Director was to act "under the superintendence of the Attorney General" who might also direct him "in a special case." That particular provision remains on the statute book at the present time. The consolidation of the Prosecution of Offences Regulations which took place in 1886 and was repeated in 1946 contained the more explicit language that "The Director of Public Prosecutions shall in all matters, including the nomination of counsel, be subject to the directions of the Attorney General." Reference has already been made in the preceding chapter to the elimination of regulation 5, quoted above, from the revised regulations promulgated in 1978,[5] and we shall now review public statements made by the principal parties involved as a means of determining authoritatively where the lines of ultimate responsibility and control actually lie.

In the course of a lecture delivered before the University of London in March 1950,[6] the then Director of Public Prosecutions, Sir Theobald Mathew, laid great stress on the ultimate accountability of the Director to Parliament for every prosecutorial decision that he made, whether to enforce the criminal law or to refrain from authorising a criminal prosecution to take place. Never one to equivocate on matters which concerned the office which he occupied with much distinction from 1944 to 1964, Sir Theobald Mathew explained his view of the constitutional position of the Director, which he said "is quite clear,"[7] as follows: "Parliament in this country is sovereign and the Executive, in whatever

elected London police authority on which representatives of the local authorities and the Home Office would serve—see *The Times*, March 17, 18 and 20, 1982. This latest debate repeats the concerns addressed by the 1960–62 Royal Commission on the Police, and which were partly dealt with in the Police Act, 1964. See further, the authorities referred to in fn. 4 below.

[4] For my analysis of this question in both the British and Canadian contexts, see Edwards, *Ministerial Responsibility for National Security*, 1980 (see fn. 26 below) at pp. 55–58, 72–76 and 89–109. See also Geoffrey Marshall, *Police and Government*, (1965), *passim*; T.A. Critchley, *A History of Police in England and Wales* (revised ed. 1978), pp. 278–290, 300–305; S. Atkins and A. Rutherford, "The Police and the Public: In Search of New Styles of Accountability" [1983] P.L. 241; P.C. Stenning, *The Legal Status of the Police in Canada*, (Law Reform Commission of Canada, 1981), especially Chapter 4, pp. 187–235.

[5] *Ante*, pp. 9–10.

[6] *The Office and Duties of the Director of Public Prosecutions*, (The Athlone Press, 1950).

[7] *Ibid*. p. 15.

capacity, is answerable to Parliament. When the office of the Director of Public Prosecutions was created in 1879 the Act laid down that he should act under the general superintendence of the Attorney General, thereby securing that there was a member of the Executive answerable to Parliament for the manner in which the Director carries out his duties. Any subsequent reference to the Director in legislation can, in my view, only mean the Director of Public Prosecutions as created by the Prosecution of Offences Acts 1879 and 1908, and the regulations made under those Acts. If the legislature had intended that, for some purposes, the Director should not be subject to the superintendence or the directions of the Attorney General, and thus not responsible to Parliament, it must surely have said that this was to be so notwithstanding the provisions of the 1879 Act. The Director, in my opinion, remains the servant—the proud servant possibly—of the public through Parliament which represents them, and of the Executive which, through Parliament, is responsible to them, and he is in no sense the master of either."[8]

Not one word of qualification is to be found in the above exposition of the ultimate authority that resides in the office of Attorney General, including, it should be noted, those situations in which it is the Director of Public Prosecutions who, by legislative edict, is empowered to grant or withhold consent to the institution of criminal proceedings for particular offences. The number of these statutory provisions has grown apace in the years since Sir Theobald Mathew occupied the office of the Director but the question remains the same. In those instances in which Parliament has given the Director of Public Prosecutions sole discretion with regard to the prosecution of certain offences, it can be argued that the Director is independent of the Attorney General and that he cannot be directed as to the exercise of his discretion. Support for this argument, it is claimed, is to be found in the occasional resort by the legislature to express language requiring that the Director be subject to the directions of the Attorney General in respect of particular duties imposed upon him as Director. An example of this kind of precedent is to be found in the Representation of the People Act 1949, s.159(4),[9] which declares that in carrying out his duties under that statute the Director is to act in accordance with the directions, if any, given to him by the Attorney General. Absent such a clear manifestation of the legislature's intention, so it is argued, the Director is free to exercise his discretionary authority untrammelled by any possible intervention and direction on the part of the senior Law Officer of the Crown. Mathew lent no support to such a doctrine.[10]

The foundation stone upon which all subsequent legislative provisions rests, according to the former Director, is the 1879 statute. Furthermore, Sir Theobald Mathew was clearly not disposed to draw fine distinctions

---

[8] *Ibid.*

[9] 11 & 12 Geo. 6, c. 65, re-enacting the Corrupt and Illegal Practices Prevention Act 1883 (46 & 47 Vict. c. 51), s.57(1).

[10] Mathew, *op. cit.* pp. 14–15.

between the concepts of "superintendence" and "direction" as explaining the true nature of the constitutional relationship between the Attorney General and the Director of Public Prosecutions.[11] I shall have more to say later on the significance of the distinctions that, at least in some other contexts,[12] are derived from Parliament's adoption of the language of supervision rather than that of control and direction. At that time we shall do well to recall the confidence with which Sir Theobald Mathew eschewed any distinction, in substance or in qualitative terms, between the Attorney General's position of superintendence and his powers of giving directions to the Director of Public Prosecutions.

Lest any misconceptions be allowed to arise by way of assimilating the position of the Director with that occupied by the permanent heads of other Government departments, Mathew was always at pains to emphasise that his actions were taken in his own name and in his own right as Director.[13] The theory and practice in government departments, in contrast, is exemplified by the language used to conduct official correspondence. Typical of the format resorted to would be letters emanating from, for example, the Home Office or the Treasury which start off by saying "I am directed by the Secretary of State to inform you, etc.," or from the Treasury, "I am directed by the Lords Commissioners of the Treasury . . . ."This formal language conceals the reality surrounding much of the day-to-day work in all government departments where the delegation of authority to make decisions is usually commensurate with the importance or difficulty of the issues concerned. Direct ministerial involvement is the exception rather than the rule and this is likely to be accentuated in the larger departments of State. By comparison the office of the Director of Public Prosecutions is miniscule in size. But this is not the basic explanation for the difference to which Sir Theobald Mathew adverted in another address which he delivered to the Law Society in 1952. "The decisions of my Department" Mathew explained "are announced as those of the Director. It follows that, if I prosecute, I do so as Director, not on behalf of the Attorney General, and that the Attorney General can give me directions to prosecute in a case in which I have announced a decision in the opposite sense."[14] The fact that no instance can be recalled in which the latter eventuality has occurred does not minimise the point of principle that was being emphasised. After all, situations would have to be quite exceptional in which the Attorney would be disposed to publicly renounce a decision that the Director had formally announced either in court or in some other public forum. Customarily, informal consultations will have taken place between the two officers, with or without their respective staff,

---

[11] *Ibid.*

[12] See *post*, Chap. 5, and *ante*, p. 38, fn. 2.

[13] Mathew, *The Department of the Director of Public Prosecutions*, a lecture published in pamphlet form by the Law Society, 1952, at p. 12. The main outlines of the same lecture had previously appeared in (1948) 16 *Medico-Legal Jo.* 50–57.

[14] *Loc. cit.*

and differences ironed out prior to any public announcement. Mathew's statement is concerned with the vital principle involved and this must govern the disposition of difficult decisions.

THE SKELHORN AND HETHERINGTON INTERPRETATIONS

What has been said so far describes the outer parameters of the constitutional status associated with the offices of Attorney General and Director of Public Prosecutions, in their dealings with each other. Within these extreme limits there are, of course, ample opportunities for the resolution of potential conflicts in the respective approaches to individual circumstances. Let us now take a close look at more recent expositions of the constitutional status accorded to the office of the Director of Public Prosecutions. Mathew's successor, Sir Norman Skelhorn, felt it necessary to explain to his public audiences that although the Home Secretary made the appointment he, as Director, had nothing more to do with him nor did he have any sanction over the actions of the Director.[15] As to the Attorney General "I am responsible to him and he is responsible for me in answering to Parliament with regard to the performance of my functions."[16] Skelhorn, like his predecessor, rejected the analogy of the relationship that exists between a Permanent Under Secretary and his Minister when describing the connection between the Director and the Attorney General. "The Attorney General" said Skelhorn, "is not in any full sense a Minister—[he] does not, for example, run the Director of Public Prosecutions' Department."[17] The most appropriate term "subtle,"[18] invoked by Skelhorn to describe his position vis-à-vis the Attorney General, was not intended to qualify his acceptance of the ultimate power of the Attorney General, and he alone, to give directions to the Director in matters concerning the overall control of the enforcement of the criminal law in England and Wales.[19]

Of all the holders of the office of Director of Public Prosecutions none has been so sedulous as the present incumbent, Sir Thomas Hetherington, in his endeavours to explain to all and sundry the true character of the Director's position in criminal law matters. Furthermore, unlike all of the

---

[15] Skelhorn: "The Machinery of Prosecution," Chapter 4 of a series of lectures published under the title *English Criminal Law: The Way a Briton Would Explain it to an American*, pp.32–36.

[16] *Ibid.* p. 32.

[17] "Between the Devil and the D.P.P.," an interview with Sir Norman Skelhorn, *Punch*, November 24, 1976, pp. 958–959.

[18] *Loc. cit.*

[19] On the related subject of improper pressures, Skelhorn has written: "I was responsible to four different Attorneys [General]—Hobson, Elwyn Jones, Rawlinson and Silkin, two Conservative and two Labour—and never once was any pressure put on me to exercise my discretion in a particular way, not even when the activities of the Home Secretary himself came under review" *Public Prosecutor: Memoirs of Sir Norman Skelhorn, D.P.P. 1964–1977* (London, Harrap, 1982), p. 73. For his handling of the allegations of possible corrupt involvement of Mr. Reginald Maudling, then Home Secretary, with the Poulson affair, see *ibid.* pp. 82–83.

earlier holders of that office, Hetherington came to his new responsibilities after many years' service in the Law Officers' Department including that of Legal Secretary, the permanent head of the Department,[20] in which capacity he served as the right hand man to Attorneys General of different political persuasions. Whenever the occasion has presented itself in which he has been called upon to articulate the Director's place in the English constitution Hetherington has consistently followed the same doctrinal path. Speaking in 1979, as part of his Upjohn Memorial Lecture in the University of London,[21] Hetherington acknowledged that the type of person who has over 100 years of its existence been appointed to the post of Director has altered with the changing society. "Changes in the standards of society" Hetherington declared "materially affects the nature of the work of the Department . . . and this factor clearly reflects the characteristics which those who have responsibility for appointing a Director are seeking in him. So the type of man appointed to the office is illustrative of the society in which he is serving."[22] Nevertheless, Hetherington was quick to remind his audience that one of the unchanging

[20] Details of Hetherington's legal and personal background were given by the Director himself in the course of his Upjohn Lecture. The lecture "A Changing Society and the Director of Public Prosecutions" was subsequently published in (1981) 14 *The Law Teacher* 92. Variations on the same theme are contained in Hetherington's address to the Gray's Inn Moots (April 24, 1980), under the title "The Role of the D.P.P." The latter title was again chosen by Hetherington in his talk to The Media Society on May 22, 1980. In each lecture the Director commented on the considerable degree of ignorance, outside the rather close circle of criminal law practitioners, which surrounds the office of D.P.P. and its functions.

[21] See fn. 20 *ante*.

[22] Upjohn Lecture *op. cit.* p. 2. In his talk Hetherington made an interesting comparison between the personalities and habits of work of two of his predecessors, *i.e.* Sir Archibald Bodkin (1920–30) and Sir Theobald Mathew (1944–64). As an example of the great lengths to which Bodkin was accustomed to go in pursuing a case personally, Hetherington recounts the steps taken by the former D.P.P. to have the book *The Well of Loneliness* (Jonathan Cape, 1928) banned as obscene and copies of the work destroyed by order of 35 J.P.'s sitting at the London Sessions. Following the court's order, according to Hetherington, Bodkin "set about personally recovering every copy of the book which had been distributed to defence lawyers and others for the purpose of the case. After a good deal of toing and froing (*sic*) he succeeded. There still remained the question of the books within the Director's own Department. Here Bodkin collected, so he believed, every copy and personally witnessed their destruction by burning" (*op. cit.* p. 11). With pardonable glee Hetherington informed his audience that, when he began to make enquiries about the case for the purpose of his lecture, one copy of the banned work was discovered in the Director's Library. When Bodkin died it was said of him that his conduct of the D.P.P.'s office was neither in advance nor behind the average public opinion at the time. "To my mind" Hetherington charitably observed "the case illustrates the man but does not in any way condemn him" (*op. cit.* p. 12). As for Sir Theobald Mathew, in Hetherington's view, he was in many ways ahead of his times in his own thinking. There are indications that Mathew was very hesitant about instituting criminal proceedings in 1960 against Penguin Books Ltd. with respect to the unexpurgated edition of D.H. Lawrence's *Lady Chatterley's Lover*. There is evidence that his colleagues in the Department regarded the book as eminently deserving of prosecution. As is well known, the jury acquitted the accused. Hetherington's verdict on his predecessor's handling of the case is that "he may have misjudged the climate of opinion, [but] he did what he did in prosecuting because he genuinely believed that the public interest required that action" (*op. cit.* p. 20). On the more general plane Hetherington described Sir Theobald's task, in succeeding Bodkin and Tindal Atkinson (1930–44), as that of "converting an organization based on Victorian lines, and influenced by Victorian standards, into a modern Department,

features of the role of the Director is its constitutional position. That, he declared, remains the same today as when it was first created in 1879.[23]

Since Sir Thomas Hetherington's interpretation of the constitutional relationship between the Director of Public Prosecutions and the Attorney General has been challenged as leading to the creation of "the unaccountable prosecutor,"[24] it is well to first set the record straight in terms of the present Director's own enunciation of his status in English constitutional law. In the course of his Upjohn Lecture, referred to earlier, Hetherington explained his understanding of the Director's constitutional position in these terms: "He is, by statute, appointed by the Home Secretary. He is under the superintendence of the Attorney General and the Attorney General may give him directions in a special case, although in practice he has never done so in my experience. There is frequent consultation, but the Attorney does not exercise control over the majority of the Director's decisions and the Attorney is not, and never has been, responsible for the Director to the extent that a Minister is responsible for his officials. On the other hand, because of his general superintending role, the Attorney is answerable to Parliament for the way in which the Director carries out his duties. That was the position in 1879 and it remains precisely the same under the consolidating Act of 1979."[25] There are, it is submitted, solid grounds for challenging the validity of Hetherington's attempt (in line with that advanced by his predecessors Theobald Mathew and Norman Skelhorn) to distinguish the nature of the Attorney's responsibility for the Department of Public Prosecutions from that which, it is said, normally reflects every other minister's responsibility for the acts of his departmental officials.

No modern exposition of the doctrine of ministerial responsibility goes so far as to extend the ambit of its application, with the ensuing sanction of resignation in appropriate circumstances, to each and every act of the departmental officials.[26] The sheer size of modern government departments and the complexities of the matters that fall within a Minister's portfolio are such as to impose major constraints on the expected level of ministerial oversight of departmental actions and decisions. For a variety of historical reasons the composition of the Law Officers' Department, over which the Attorney General presides, is small, in contrast to the

capable of applying modern doctrines to a much greater variety of cases than hitherto . . . In this he succeeded very well. In effect, it is his legacy which I have inherited in my present post. In my view the foundations and structure are sound. Modernisation and some refurbishing is required" (*op. cit.* pp. 15–16).

[23] Upjohn Lecture, p.8.

[24] In an article bearing this title in *The New Statesman*, October 19, 1979, Professor J.A.G. Griffith sought to establish, from the legislative and Parliamentary record of the previous 12 months, that a calculated attempt was afoot to formally detach the office of D.P.P. as far as possible from the Attorney General.

[25] *Op. cit.* p. 3.

[26] This concept of the doctrine is developed further in my monograph *Ministerial Responsibility for National Security* at pp. 77–87. The study was prepared in connection with the McDonald Commission of Inquiry into the Security Service of Canada (see *ante*, fn.2).

substantial complement of lawyers and support staff that man the Department of the Director of Public Prosecutions. So that in practical terms alone it would be totally unrealistic, in the absence of any major expansion of the Law Officers' Department, to contemplate the level of monitoring which Parliament has the right to expect of other Ministers of the Crown with respect to their individual departments. If we are to gain an accurate understanding of the respective status of the Attorney and the Director, in their dealings with one another, it will be better to concentrate our attention on aspects of the relationship that do not make false comparisons with the organisation of the major departments of government.

To this end, regard must be had to the Director's written evidence submitted in 1978 to the Royal Commission on Criminal Procedure which probably represents the fullest and most authoritative account that exists of the Department in its present form. After tracing the historical background to the office of Director of Public Prosecutions, and reviewing the statutory provisions that govern the functions of the Director, Hetherington described his constitutional position in the following extensive analysis[27]: "As section 2 of the 1979 Act clearly shows, I act under the general superintendence of the Attorney General. I should perhaps mention here that Regulation 5 of the 1946 Regulations states that: 'The Director of Public Prosecutions shall in all matters, including the nomination of counsel, be subject to the direction of the Attorney General.' This Regulation is somewhat superfluous, as it is already contained in section 2 of the 1879 Act, and therefore has not been included in the 1978 Regulations. However, although I exercise my functions under the general superintendence of the Attorney General, I think it is important to stress that the decisions that I make are my own and are not those of the Attorney. As will be seen . . . prosecutions under many statutes require my consent, which I am entitled to give or withhold without reference to the Attorney General. It is right to say that the majority of cases dealt with by my Department are never seen or heard of by the Attorney General. I believe that my independence from political influence is a factor of considerable importance in maintaining public confidence in the fair and impartial administration of the criminal law."

"Nevertheless, it is also right to say that there is a close and regular relationship of consultation between the Attorney General and myself. It is my practice to consult the Attorney General in cases of special importance or difficulty even where there is no legal requirement for the Attorney to be involved. It is, for example, customary for me to consult the Attorney General in cases involving possible contraventions of the Rhodesia sanctions. Cases in which the Attorney's fiat is required are considered by me, and the Attorney takes his decision only after my advice has been received. If the Attorney General gives his consent to criminal proceed-

---

[27] *Op. cit.* pp. 27–28, paras. 71–74.

ings, I have the conduct of the case. This position has two practical results. On the one hand, the Attorney's 'superintendence' does not require him to exercise control in detail over my work. On the other hand, I and my Department have to be perceptive enough to identify the type of case about which the Attorney General is likely to be concerned in the public interest."

Several observations are called for in estimating the importance and accuracy of Hetherington's analysis of the Director's status in the British constitution. It is written from the perspective of the Director and the Department of Public Prosecutions, so that it is not surprising to discern, in part of the analysis, a strong assertion of the *de facto* independence enjoyed by the Director in fulfilling his statutory duties. Emphasis is placed on the process of consultation or on the initiative taken by the Director in seeking the views of the Attorney upon cases that may have possible political repercussions and, therefore, should involve the Law Officers as the final arbiter of the public interest. At times, however, the Director's evidence to the Royal Commission is apt to be misleading, more by way of omission than by a positive distortion of the legal realities. A few points in particular will exemplify the concerns I have with respect to Hetherington's exposition. Thus, to revert to a subject already touched upon,[28] the present Director's dogmatic assertion that regulation 5 of the 1946 Regulations was superfluous "as it is already contained in section 2 of the 1879 Act" is, at least, debatable. What the Prosecution of Offences Act 1879, s.2 states is that the Director acts "under the superintendence of the Attorney General" or as "may be directed *in a special case* by the Attorney General."[29] Given a narrow perception of the Attorney General's involvement in matters of criminal prosecution, the 1879 Act would confirm the expectation that only in special cases would the Attorney be empowered to intervene and give specific direction to the Director. In short, intervention would be exceptional and would not be seen as a power that is exercisable as a normal ingredient in the Attorney General's functions. In the 1886 Regulations, however, the language is more expansive and unequivocal in that it is there stated: "The action of the Director of Public Prosecutions shall *in all matters*, including the selection and instruction of counsel, be subject to the directions of the Attorney General."[30] The same principle is enshrined in the 1946 consolidated regulations which provide that "The Director of Public Prosecutions shall *in all matters*, including the nomination of counsel, be subject to the directions of the Attorney General."[31]

According to the 1886 and 1946 "charters" governing the office of the Director there is no suggestion of restricting the Attorney's intervention to

---

[28] *Ante*, pp. 9–10, 39.
[29] Author's italics.
[30] Reg. 10, author's italics.
[31] Reg. 5, author's italics.

"a special case," whatever meaning might be given to such a criterion. Rather the Attorney General's power of intervention and of giving directions to the Director is unrestricted and does not have to meet any predetermined conditions. Such was the understanding of Sir Theobald Mathew when speaking of the office of Director and no suggestion emanated from his lips to the effect that the foundational "regulation 5" was superfluous in that it merely duplicated the principle contained in section 2 of the 1879 Act.[32] Given the elimination of the express language contained in the earlier charters, conferring an absolute right of intervention and direction upon the Attorney General in all matters pertaining to the exercise of the Director's responsibilities, when occasion arises to give meaning to the remaining repository of the constitutional connection between the two offices, *i.e.* section 2 of the 1879 Act, it is of the greatest importance that the elucidation formerly contained in the 1886 and 1946 Regulations not be forgotten.

Another item in Hetherington's submission to the Royal Commission which calls for comment is the statement that "it is important to stress that the decisions that I make are my own and not those of the Attorney,"[33] for which the illustrations provided are prosecutions under the many statutes which require the consent of the Director of Public Prosecutions. As to these Director's "consent" prosecutions, Hetherington claims "I am entitled to give or withhold consent without reference to the Attorney General."[33] It is undoubtedly true, as the present Director claims, that the majority of cases dealt with by his Department are never seen or heard of by the Attorney General. What is open to objection, if that indeed were intended, is the assertion that in cases subject by statute to the Director's fiat the Attorney General is *functus officio* since the Director is entitled to give or withhold his consent without reference to the Attorney General. It does not contribute to an accurate understanding of the Attorney General's powers in these situations to claim that the vast majority of cases dealt with in the Director of Public Prosecutions' Department are never brought before the Attorney for his attention. What is important to recognise, as Theobald Mathew publicly acknowledged,[34] is the supreme authority vested in the Attorney General to intervene and countermand any preliminary decision reached by the Director in a consent case, notwithstanding the apparent exclusive jurisdiction conferred by statute on the Director in his own right by the pertinent statute.

THE SILKIN AND HAVERS APPROACHES TO THE ATTORNEY'S SUPREME AUTHORITY AND ACCOUNTABILITY

Following in the wake of the Director's evidence to the Royal Commission on Criminal Procedure, the promulgation of the new

[32] Upjohn Memorial Lecture, p. 15, quoted *ante*, p. 43.
[33] *Op. cit.* para. 72.
[34] See *ante*, pp. 39–40.

consolidated Regulations in 1979, and a combination of what were described as "other recent straws in the wind," a strong attack was launched by Professor J.A.G. Griffith, in the columns of *The New Statesman*,[35] on what he perceived to be a concerted attempt to formally detach the Director of Public Prosecutions as far as possible from the Attorney General. "While this would have no effect on the closeness of their working relationship" according to Professor Griffith "it would greatly reduce the responsibility of the Attorney General for the Director of Public Prosecutions' actions; and so remove the Director of Public Prosecutions from Parliamentary scrutiny. The dangers need no stressing."[36] The result of the legislative changes enacted on January 1, 1979, according to the writer, was to render the Attorney General in law accountable to the House of Commons for a much more limited range of decisions of the Director than he was during the period since 1886. As a corollary, the article concluded, "the Director of Public Prosecutions is on many important matters accountable neither to the Attorney General nor to Parliament."[37] Such conclusions in my view are unwarranted. I have endeavoured to show in the first couple of chapters that the fundamental relationship established in 1879 between the Director of Public Prosecutions and the Attorney General remains exactly the same today as it was when the Director's office was first created. The alarm bells set ringing by Professor Griffith's controversial article did not pass unheeded in the two offices primarily interested in its contents, though it required not much difficulty to refute the interpretations placed on the strands of evidence which the author had used to substantiate the claim that a significant shift was afoot in the constitutional balance of power as between the first Law Officer of the Crown and the Director of Public Prosecutions.

The most useful result to emanate from the ensuing public debate was the opportunity taken by the Attorney General, Sir Michael Havers, to correct the mistaken impressions created through the medium of *The New Statesman* article on "The unaccountable prosecutor." In a written answer prepared in response to a private question tabled in the House of Commons, the Attorney General set forth authoritatively his interpretation of the nature and extent of the Attorney's continuing responsibilities for the Director of Public Prosecutions.[38] Speaking in general terms of the working relationship between himself and the Director, Sir Michael Havers declared: "My responsibility for superintendence of the duties of the Director does not require me to exercise a day-to-day control and specific approval of every decision he takes. The Director makes many decisions in the course of his duties which he does not refer to me but nevertheless I am still responsible for his actions in the sense that I am answerable in the House for what he does. Superintendence means that I

[35] See *ante*. fn.24.
[36] *Ibid.*
[37] *Ibid.*
[38] H.C. Deb. Vol. 976, Written Answers, cols. 187–188, December 13, 1979.

must have regard to the overall prosecution policy which he pursues. My relationship with him is such that I require to be told in advance of the major, difficult, and, from the public interest point of view, the more important matters so that should the need arise I am in the position to exercise my ultimate power of direction."[39] Adverting to the changes incorporated in the Prosecution of Offences Act 1979 and the new consolidated regulations of 1978, the Attorney General claimed that the current statutory position involved no departure from the previous law. "Under Regulations made under the primary legislation" (*i.e.* the Prosecution of Offences Acts 1879 to 1908) Havers maintained that "provision has been made to prescribe the areas in which it is his duty to give advice to chief officers of police. The Regulations made to that effect in 1946 provided that the Director was to be in all matters subject to the direction of the Attorney General. That provision was not repeated in the recent Prosecution of Offences Regulations 1978, which replace the 1946 Regulations, because the view was taken that it added nothing to the statutory position set out in the primary legislation and accordingly was unnecessary. Any contention that the subordinate Regulations altered the statutory position referred to above is mistaken because such Regulations would be *ultra vires* if they purported to alter the position set out in the Statute itself. The omission, therefore, of the 1946 provision in the current Regulations has in no way affected the statutory relationship between the Director and myself. The Director still carries out his duties under my superintendence and I still have the power to direct in particular cases."[40]

This parliamentary statement was intended to rectify any misconceptions that could be read into the description afforded of his legal status by the present Director of Public Prosecutions, Sir Thomas Hetherington, in his evidence before the Royal Commission on Criminal Procedure. Two aspects of the Attorney General's statement to the House of Commons need to be emphasised. The first is the expectation that the Director regularly bring to the Law Officers' attention those cases which are likely to engender questions as to the correctness of the action taken. Defining the circumstances in which such questions may be raised with any degree of particularity is well nigh impossible. Past experience, the exercise of judgment and a sense of what is likely to arouse public reaction are the ingredients by which the Director is expected to comply with the Attorney General's policy that he "be told in advance of the major, difficult, and, from the public interest point of view, the more important decisions" concerning the institution of criminal proceedings. There must be consultation in advance of making a decision in such cases. Otherwise the Attorney General is placed in the vulnerable position of having to defend the exercise of discretionary power without having been apprised beforehand of the facts and issues involved in such a manner that he can

[39] *Ibid.*
[40] *Ibid.*

determine himself whether to approve or reject the Director's advice and recommendations.

Entirely consonant with this policy is the other crucial aspect of the Attorney's most recent elaboration of his responsibilities wherein he described his need to be kept informed "so that should the need arise I am in a position to exercise my ultimate power of direction." This affirmation that the source of the ultimate power of direction is vested in the office of the Attorney General remains the fundamental proposition to remember when defining the constitutional status of the Director of Public Prosecutions in England and Wales. The practical caveat "should the need arise" is of equal relevance, emphasising as it does that the Attorney General's intervention by way of issuing directions to the Director is not envisaged as a normal or regular occurrence. There might not arise a single instance in which the first Law Officer of the Crown and the Director of Public Prosecutions would disagree as to the proper course to take in a particular case. It will be recalled that Hetherington, in his Upjohn Lecture, stated that in his experience the Attorney General had never issued a formal direction to him as Director, in the sense of overriding the Director's own formal recommendation.[41] Given the ultimate authority of the Attorney General in such a situation it would be foolhardy on the part of any Director to press his objections to the brink unless he was prepared to simultaneously tender his resignation as the only remaining sanction to achieve his wishes in the matter.

Documented evidence of disputes between the Attorney General and the Director of the day are unlikely to surface in the normal course of events. It is true that Sir Hartley Shawcross, when he was the Attorney General, made reference to his having experienced some differences of opinion with Sir Theobald Mathew when he was the incumbent Director. Referring to the advice that he had had recourse to both from the Director of Public Prosecutions and "very often of Treasury Counsel," Shawcross informed the House of Commons "I have hardly ever, if ever, refused to prosecute when they have advised prosecution. I have sometimes ordered prosecution when the advice was against it."[42] On this specific question Theobald Mathew also declined to give any specific illustrations, though he went so far as to declare that "the Attorney General can give me directions to prosecute in a case in which I have announced a decision in the opposite sense."[43] Relationships between the holders of the respective offices would surely deteriorate rapidly in the event of a public renunciation of the Director's actions by the Attorney General of the day.

What, it may be asked, is the policy where extremely sensitive cases arise such as those involving someone known to the Law Officers of the Crown personally, colleagues in the Government, or a fellow Member of

[41] *Ante*, p. 44.
[42] See *Law Officers of the Crown*, p. 223, fn. 72.
[43] *Ante*, p. 41.

Parliament? In the event of the decision being made, and announced publicly, that no prosecution is to be brought, there is every likelihood that there will ensue imputations of bias and favouritism in which it will be difficult for the Attorney General to rebut the allegation that his decision was taken for the wrong reasons. Two conflicting philosophies can be expected to find adherents among those who bear the burden of making such a delicate decision. Faced with the kind of sensitive circumstances described above there are those who would maintain it is preferable that the Director of Public Prosecutions be authorised to take the decision without specific guidance from the Attorney General or his colleague the Solicitor General. By doing so, the perception in the public's mind of independence and impartiality in resolving the dilemma would be measurably enhanced. Any express relinquishment of authority along these lines would in no way diminish or absolve the Attorney General of his constitutional responsibility for the Director's actions. Ranged against this point of view is the belief, tenaciously given expression to by several former incumbents, that however embarrassing it may be to discharge the duties and responsibilities enforced upon the Attorney General by statute there should be no withdrawal when the political pressures are at their most intense level. Rather, it is argued, it is in the really sensitive cases that the essential qualities associated with the Law Officers of the Crown should be publicly demonstrated.

These views evoke the division of opinion that has surrounded the participation of the Attorney General before tribunals of inquiry set up to investigate, for example, allegations of corruption on the part of certain Ministers of the Crown and government officials, or allegations impugning the integrity of the Chancellor of the Exchequer or the deputy chairman of the political party to which the Law Officers for the time being themselves belonged.[44] Both Lord Shawcross and Viscount Dilhorne, when serving as Attorney General, took the position that they should lead the government's team of counsel before the respective tribunals set up to investigate these matters.[45] This action entailed the introduction of incriminating evidence and the conduct of a rigorous cross examination against their ministerial and political colleagues in an endeavour to assist the tribunal in ascertaining the truth. The philosophy that guided those Attorneys General was expressed forcefully in these words used by Shawcross when addressing the Lynskey Tribunal on the opening day of its inquiry: "As the tribunal knows very well, but is not always understood elsewhere, although the Attorney General is a member of the government he has certain duties which he cannot abdicate in connection with the administration of the law, especially of the criminal law and more particularly that branch of it which is concerned with the prevention of corruption. These duties are sometimes said to be of a quasi-judicial nature. The Attorney General has

---

[44] See Edwards *op. cit.*, pp. 300–301.
[45] *Ibid.* and see *post*, Chap. 7.

to discharge them with complete independence of the government. . . . In these matters . . . the Attorney General's duty (and it is his duty) is to concern himself, and to concern himself only, with the representation and protection of the public interest."[46]

The contrary position, argued before, and adopted by, the Salmon Commission on Tribunals of Inquiry concluded in 1966 that the present practice whereby the Attorney General, or in Scotland the Lord Advocate or Solicitor General, and counsel nominated by him, represent the tribunal should be discontinued.[47] Instead, the Commission recommended "that the tribunal should select its own counsel and should not be represented by a Law Officer of the Crown or other counsel who has any connection with the Government of the day or with any political party."[48] The Commission felt that not only was it desirable to remove the public's difficulty in distinguishing between the political and legal roles of the Law Officers but to protect them from the criticism that their impartiality was affected by their political loyalties. The subject of the Law Officers' role in tribunals of inquiry will be explored further later on[49] but it is useful at this point to note the parallels that exist with the exercise of prosecutorial discretion in which the involvement of the Attorney General in the decision making process is such as to unavoidably call into question the Law Officer's political affiliations and independence.

THE JEREMY THORPE CASE

Judging by recent precedents in the area of criminal prosecutions it is noticeable that there is an increasing tendency for the Attorney General, in the kind of sensitive circumstances we have been alluding to, to seek the formal opinion of leading counsel experienced in the criminal law. This is an addition to the advice he expects to receive from the Director of Public Prosecutions. Normally this procedure can be expected to provide a substantial measure of protection for both the Attorney General and the Director of Public Prosecutions against imputations of partiality. But there can be no absolute guarantee of immunity from public criticism or questioning of the Attorney's decision before the House of Commons. The handling of the *Jeremy Thorpe* case provides a rare exposure to the behind the scenes discussions that preceded the decision to prosecute the former Leader of the Parliamentary Liberal Party. Thorpe, it will be recalled, was eventually acquitted by a jury at the Central Criminal Court after a trial in which he, and others, were charged with incitement to murder and conspiracy to murder. When interviewed later on the BBC Radio 4 programme, Sir Thomas Hetherington, Director of Public Prosecutions, disclosed that the decision to prosecute Thorpe had been taken by himself,

[46] *Ibid.* pp. 301–302.
[47] *Report* (Cmnd. 3121 of 1966), pp. 34–36.
[48] *Ibid.* para. 94.
[49] See *post*, pp. 197–206.

after internal discussions with his own staff.[50] After explaining the difficulties in getting across to the general public the relationship that exists between his office and that of the Law Officers of the Crown, Hetherington informed his audience: "The Attorney General . . . can give me general directions about how to behave in a particular type of case but in practice he does not give us directions in particular cases. Just to clarify the issue, the former Attorney General, who was in office at the time the decision was taken to prosecute in this case, did not in fact give me any directions whatsoever."[51] The Attorney General in question was Mr. Sam Silkin who, also in the course of a radio interview that reviewed his five turbulent years in office, disclosed that the *Jeremy Thorpe* case "was one that I had nothing whatever to do with."[52]

Mr. Silkin's policy of non-involvement in the actual decision making process was not confined to the *Thorpe* case. As he revealed in the course of an address to the American Bar Association at its centenary meeting[53]: "As Attorney I have the power to direct the Director to institute or not to institute proceedings. I have never done so. We consult and work together in harmony. Indeed some cases are so sensitive or embarrassing to a political figure that I prefer to distance myself from decisions and merely keep myself informed of events." Mr. Silkin recalled that in the four and a half years since he took office he had the ultimate ministerial responsibility for decisions on possible prosecutions involving five of his Parliamentary colleagues, three of them fellow members of Her Majesty's Privy Council, three of them members of his own party, and one a Minister. "In all five cases" Silkin disclosed "the decision whether to prosecute has effectively been that of the Director of Public Prosecutions, advised by experienced counsel. But that has not relieved me either of deep embarrassment or of misrepresentation, wilful or innocent."[54] Speaking with obvious reference to the *Thorpe* prosecution, the Attorney General bemoaned the ugly rumours that were circulating in the British Press attacking his integrity. On the one hand, he pointed out, before the decision was announced that criminal proceedings were to be instituted against Jeremy Thorpe it was alleged that there was a cover-up on the grounds that the Labour Government was anxious to promote harmony with the Liberals so as to

[50] Transcript of an interview broadcast on June 22, 1979, and reported in the *Daily Telegraph*, June 23, 1979. This revelation cannot have surprised many listeners, since the Director, in a letter to *The Times*, November 18, 1978, had previously sought to dispel misapprehensions as to where responsibility lay for the decisions taken in the *Thorpe* case. After explaining his statutory relationship to the Attorney General, Hetherington stressed that "I have in this particular case, with the approval of the Attorney General, acted independently throughout. Accordingly, responsibility for all decisions, including that to grant an immunity to Mr. Bessell, has rested solely with me."

[51] *Ibid.*

[52] *The Listener*, July 3, 1980.

[53] On April 8, 1978 in New York. Quotations are from the text of Mr. Silkin's speech which, so far as I have been able to discover, was never published. Extracts did appear in (1978) New L.J. 942.

[54] *Ibid.*

damage the Conservatives at the forthcoming General Election. Then, following the announcement of the charges against the former Leader of the Liberal Party, there were further ugly rumours that events were skilfully timed in order to destroy the Liberal Party at the ensuing election. Mr. Silkin's response to this no-win situation, a by no means unique experience for any Attorney General of modern times, was to confirm to his United States audience that "In fact, I have had no influence on either the decision or the timing."[55]

Whilst it is true that the eventual decision to go ahead with the Thorpe prosecution was made by the Director of Public Prosecutions none of the cryptic accounts given above adequately portray the roles adopted by the Attorney General and the Director, respectively. In the course of an interview I had with Mr. Silkin,[56] the former Attorney revealed that he had nominated a leading Queen's Counsel from the Western circuit, where the case would have to be tried, to act as counsel advising the Director of Public Prosecutions. Whilst intending that the Director be given independence in reaching a decision on the merits the Attorney General did not, and indeed could not, relieve himself of his ministerial responsibility to "superintend" the Director's decision making process. This inescapable duty was discharged by requiring that the Attorney be kept informed of progress in the case. Mr. Thorpe and Mr. Silkin, it should be noted, were not only fellow Members of Parliament but both served as members of the House of Commons' Committee on Privileges. At one point thought was given to delegating to the Solicitor General the "superintendence" of the Director but, for much the same reasons as those which prompted Mr. Silkin to transfer the decision out of his own hands, the Solicitor General solution was rejected. It should also be remembered that the offences with which Mr. Thorpe was charged, serious as they were, did not require the Attorney General's consent by virtue of some express statutory provision. Had the situation been otherwise the Attorney could not have opted out from the responsibility imposed upon his office by Parliament, of making the actual decision whether or not criminal proceedings should go forward. In both situations the Attorney General is the Minister of the Crown accountable to the House of Commons but in the *Thorpe* case Mr. Silkin elected, as he was entitled to, to leave the decision in the hands of the Director of Public Prosecutions.

In seeking the formal opinion of leading counsel the Attorney General was following a wise precedent that has become increasingly common in cases likely to engender strong public interest. What was unusual in the *Thorpe* case was the strange twist to this outward manifestation of the Attorney General's attempt to distance himself from the crucial decision. Having elected to transfer that burden on to the shoulders of the Director of Public Prosecutions with the assistance of advice by independent

[55] *Ibid.*
[56] In the House of Commons on July 8, 1980.

counsel, Mr. Silkin approached the Leader of the Western Circuit, Sir Peter Rawlinson Q.C. (as he then was) expecting, as Mr. Silkin subsequently recounted, that Rawlinson would readily agree to the leader of another circuit being called upon to review the case and give his opinion to the Director. Such expectations may not have been seen in the same light by the Leader of the Western Circuit who, notwithstanding his political position as a leading member of the then main opposition party, could understandably have viewed the Attorney General's invitation as imposing a duty upon him to assume the difficult assignment. This perception of where his duty lay would have been reinforced by the fact that Sir Peter Rawlinson had occupied the office of Attorney General in the previous administration. Rawlinson's acceptance may well have caused more than a ripple of surprise on the part of Mr. Silkin but there remains the difficulty in reconciling the Attorney General's decision, first, in removing himself from direct involvement in the Director of Public Prosecutions' decision making and, next, in approaching his predecessor in the previous Conservative Government to become involved, albeit in his different capacity as leader of the pertinent circuit.

Sir Peter Rawlinson's position in this cause célèbre needs some further elaboration. In earlier related proceedings, involving the shooting of a dog, Rawlinson, as the most senior Q.C. on the Western Circuit, had been nominated by Mr. Silkin to prosecute. The potential seriousness of the surrounding circumstances concerning this charge explains the Attorney General's adherence to the traditional practice governing the nomination of counsel to take charge of the prosecution. After studying the papers and engaging in consultations it became clear that the case indirectly involved Jeremy Thorpe. In addition to being a fellow member of the House of Commons, Thorpe was also a member of the Western Circuit. Rawlinson returned the brief and another senior member of that circuit took over the case on behalf of the Crown. When, subsequently, Attorney General Silkin again nominated his Conservative predecessor to prosecute in the more serious case that involved charges of incitement and conspiracy to murder, no arrests had taken place. According to Sir Peter Rawlinson,[57] when it became clear, following further inquiries which he instigated on the part of the police, that Mr. Thorpe was directly involved he immediately returned the brief to the Attorney General and advised Mr. Silkin to instruct the leader of another circuit to prosecute. As we now know, this suggestion was adopted.

There appears, however, to be a conflict in the recollections of the principal parties involved. As noted earlier, Mr. Silkin confirmed to this writer his considerable surprise that Sir Peter Rawlinson had originally accepted the brief in the case that led to Mr. Thorpe standing trial as one of the co-accused. For his part, Rawlinson recalls the several consultations that he had with his successor when the matter was still under

---

[57] Personal communication to the author, August 1, 1983.

investigation. According to Rawlinson,[58] in each of the occasions he made his position clear that, if the further police inquiries revealed a prima facie case against Jeremy Thorpe and if he was to be indicted as a defendant, there would be no question of his (Rawlinson) taking part in the trial. Moreover, Rawlinson recalls, his position was wholly accepted and understood by Mr. Silkin, the Attorney General. In the absence of any further, independent evidence it would be inappropriate to draw firm conclusions as to what understandings or misunderstandings eventuated from these meetings. The questions raised in the preceding paragraphs are still relevant, qualified only by the importance that appears to be accorded the prevailing custom of the Attorney General nominating the leader of the circuit to prosecute the most serious cases in each particular circuit. Given the exceptional set of circumstances surrounding the handling of the *Thorpe* case, undue importance appears to have been accorded this aspect of the Attorney General's prerogative in nominating counsel to lead for the Crown.

Another feature that is worth noting, typifying as it does the trust and confidence exchanged between the existing and former Law Officers of the Crown, relates to the action taken by Mr. Silkin in consulting with the then Shadow Attorney General, Sir Michael Havers, as to the course of action that he proposed to take in the handling of the *Thorpe* case.[59] Such consultation does not impose any sense of joint responsibility for the eventual decision, or of expectations that criticism will be stifled by virtue of the sharing of confidences. Whether Mr. Silkin's successor, or any of his immediate predecessors in office, would have taken the same stance in delegating to the Director of Public Prosecutions control over the decision to prosecute can only be a matter of conjecture. Reference, however, to the views expressed by Sir Michael Havers on the working relationship that he has established with the Director suggests that, in parallel circumstances, a much tighter rein would be retained in the hands of the Attorney General.

What is at issue here is the precise nature of the responsibility that rests on the Attorney General's shoulders concomitant with his ultimate authority to decide whether a prosecution shall be instituted. There is available to the Law Officers of the Crown a large body of advice both on substantive matters of criminal law and evidence, and also in estimating the public repercussions that might ensue in the wake of a particular decision. This advice includes the entire resources of the office of Director of Public Prosecutions, the small but dedicated legal staff in the Law Officers' Department, Treasury Counsel and also from among the ranks of leading counsel engaged in criminal practice. There is, in truth, no restriction on the ambit of those, including his ministerial colleagues, to whom the

---

[58] *Ibid.*
[59] Entirely distinct from this consultative process was the action taken by Mr. Silkin in advising the Prime Minister, and the new Leader of the Liberal Party, of the D.P.P.'s decision to institute criminal proceedings against Mr. Thorpe.

Attorney General may properly turn for their opinions on the alternative options open to him. At the end of all the consultations and opinion gathering, however, the final decision rests squarely in the hands of the State official in whom the constitution has reposed the ultimate authority for making prosecutorial decisions.

In those situations that create the greatest controversy it is preferable that the Attorney General be able to face the House of Commons, when discharging his public accountability, with a full mastery of all the various factors that led to his making the crucial decision. There is no reason to question the integrity of Attorney General Silkin in electing to leave the final responsibility for the *Thorpe* decision in the competent hands of Sir Thomas Hetherington, the Director of Public Prosecutions. If, however, real substance is to be accorded to the proud title of "protector of the public interest" there should be no escaping the harsh criticisms that may accompany the actions taken in the discharge of that responsibility. The fulfilment of the many invidious functions associated with the position of Attorney General demands that the occupant of this historic office accept the praise or condemnation that will emerge as public reaction to his decisions become known. The office of the Attorney General has been no sinecure throughout its long history, but its constitutional importance has been strengthened by the intestinal fortitude of those incumbents who have manifested their commitment to the widest interpretation of the public interest, at whatever cost it might be to their personal or party's fortunes.

3

Philosophic Differences in Approach to the Office of Attorney General

Among the many inquests convened in the aftermath of the Watergate affair[1] few, if any, approached the potential significance associated with an unpublicised conference convened in 1980, under the joint auspices of the United States Department of Justice and the University of Virginia.[2] Its purpose was simply to examine the relationship between the President of the United States and the Attorney General, as the executive head of the federal Department of Justice. The groundwork for this meeting had been laid two years earlier by Attorney General Griffin Bell in commissioning a study to explore ways and means of making the office of Attorney General non-political and more independent.[3] The model chosen as exemplifying the qualities that might be emulated in the United States was the office of Attorney General for England and Wales, itself the original root from

---

[1] See especially the *Report of the Watergate Special Prosecution Force* (United States Govt. Printing Office, 1975), Appendix L, which contains an excellent bibliography of Watergate source materials, including the 25 volumes of testimony before the Senate Select Committee on Presidential Campaign Activities, and 43 volumes of evidentiary material and testimony released by the House of Representatives Impeachment Inquiry Staff; see also the *Report of the American Bar Association's Special Committee on Preventing Improper Influence on Federal Law Enforcement Agencies* (1976, Washington, D.C.). For a review of the major recommendations that emanated from these two bodies see Edwards, "The Integrity of Criminal Prosecutions—Watergate Echoes beyond the shores of the United States" in P. Glazebrook (Ed.), *Reshaping the Criminal Law: Essays in honour of Glanville Williams*, (London, Stevens & Sons Ltd., 1978), pp. 364–390.

[2] The Conference was held at the White Burkett Miller Center of Public Affairs, University of Virginia, January 4–5, 1980, and its proceedings published under the title *The President, The Attorney General and the Department of Justice*. British readers will be surprised at the readiness with which former U.S. Attorneys General and Solicitors General discussed details of cases with which they had been directly involved in very recent memory and of their discussions pertaining thereto within the Department of Justice and with White House officials.

[3] The results of this study were embodied in the major paper presented for discussion and written by Professor Daniel J. Meador, University of Virginia Law School (*ibid.* pp. 1–71). The author, when commissioned by Attorney General Bell to undertake the study, was serving as head of the Office for Improvements in the Administration of Justice, U.S. Department of Justice.

which the American counterpart, the Attorney General of the United States, had sprung into existence by an Act of Congress in 1789.[4] The Judiciary Act of that year provided for the appointment of a "meet person, learned in the law, to act as Attorney General for the United States."[5] To this office was assigned responsibility to "prosecute and conduct all suits in the Supreme Court in which the United States shall be concerned" and to give opinions on questions of law, when requested, to the President and heads of departments.[6] This initiative was no great surprise since the office of Attorney General was already a familiar aspect of the early colonial government in those parts of that vast country that fell within British jurisdiction. Thus, Virginia appointed its first Attorney General in 1643, Rhode Island in 1650 and Massachusetts in 1680, each being clothed with the common law powers and duties of the parent office of Attorney General of England and Wales, except as changed by the constitution of the individual colony or its local statutes.[7] A fuller account of both the early history of the office and the comparative lessons to be gained from the United States experience is not possible within the compass of this work, but occasional references will be made whenever it is appropriate.

The appointment of Mr. Edward Levi as Attorney General of the United States in late 1974 was generally viewed as a move towards reinvesting the office with professional detachment, an opinion that was amply confirmed by the record of Mr. Levi's accomplishments during his tenure of office.[8] High among these was the successful execution of a campaign to bring the Federal Bureau of Investigation back within the doctrine of ministerial control and accountability.[9] And his successor, Mr.

---

[4] Act of September 24, 1789, ch. 20, 1 Stat. 73. It is of interest to note that the first Congress did not deal with the office of Attorney General in the general context of creating the executive departments of the new federal government. Instead, it established the office as part of the new provisions setting up the Supreme Court, the circuit and district courts, and a district attorney and marshal for each federal judicial district.

[5] *Ibid.*

[6] *Ibid.* Edmund Randolph, the first appointee, attended a meeting of the Cabinet for the first time in 1792. The Attorney General of the day has attended regularly ever since. By Congressional legislation in 1886 the office was ranked fourth among the members of the federal Cabinet. For a fuller account of the origin and evolution of the U.S. Attorney Generalship, see H. Cummings and C. Macfarland, *Federal Justice*, (New York, Macmillan Co., 1937); J.S. Easby Smith, *The Department of Justice: Its History and Functions*, (Washington, W.H. Lowdermilk & Co., 1904); and A. Langeluttig, *The Department of Justice of the United States*, (Baltimore, John Hopkins Press, 1927).

[7] See O.W. Hammonds, "The Attorney General in the American Colonies" (1939) 2 *Anglo-American Legal History Series* pp. 1–24. For a current review of the role and powers of the States' Attorneys General see *The Office of Attorney General*, 1971 which contains the findings of a two-year study commissioned by the National Association of Attorneys General.

[8] For a succinct account of Edward Levi's approach to the Attorney General's responsibilities see his article "The Justice Department: Some Thoughts on its Past, Present and Future" (1975) 64 *Illinois Bar Journal* 216. Prior to his appointment as the Attorney General of the United States Levi had served as Dean of the Law School and, subsequently, as President of the University of Chicago.

[9] See particularly, John T. Elliff, *The Reform of FBI Intelligence Operations*, (Princeton Univ. Press, 1979).

Griffin Bell, during his sojourn as head of the Department of Justice, repeatedly spoke of his ambition to take the Justice Department out of politics by creating a "neutral zone" within the department where the law would be administered in an objective, non-partisan fashion.[10]

As the author of the study commissioned by Attorney General Bell fully recognised, however, the fundamental problem that gave rise to Watergate is compounded by the plethora of responsibilities attached to the office of Attorney General of the United States.[11] From the inception of the office in 1789 the Attorney General was considered to be the principal legal adviser to the federal government, giving legal advice to the President and also to his ministerial colleagues who are members of the Cabinet. As the government's chief lawyer, the Attorney General continues to be responsible through a network of United States Attorneys for the prosecution of federal crimes and for representing the United States Government in most of its civil litigation. In all of these respects it is easy to discern the common features shared by the Attorney General of the United States with his counterpart in England and Wales. At the same time, however, the United States' Attorney General presides over what has grown since 1870[12] to become an enormous executive department, including a large array of bureaus, agencies and services, the best known of which are the Federal Bureau of Investigation, the Federal Bureau of Prisons, the short-lived Law Enforcement Assistance Administration, and the Immigration and Naturalisation Service. Commenting on this bewildering amalgam of lawyering and bureaucratic functions, Professor Daniel Meador, the author of the inhouse study referred to earlier, has written: "Some able lawyers who become Attorney Generals (sic) tend to think of the Department of Justice primarily in relation to its lawyering functions; that is their major interest in its work. They may have too little concern for the management of the non-lawyering elements of the Department. But whether or not they are concerned about those aspects of the job, those non-lawyering responsibilities thrust themselves upon the office. If, however, an Attorney General has a primary interest in management and administration, he will have little time to devote to being a lawyer, and

---

[10] Address before Department of Justice lawyers, September 6, 1978. See also Meador, *op. cit.* pp. 33, 43–49, 58–60, and M. Rogovin, "Reorganising Politics out of the Department of Justice" (1978) 64 A.B.A.J. 855, 857. For an expanded account of Griffin Bell's chequered tenure of the Attorney-Generalship see his memoirs, *Taking Care of the Law* (New York, 1982), esp. pp. 173–186, 208–214.

[11] Meador, *op. cit.* pp. 24–43. In the euphoria that immediately followed the Watergate hearings in the U.S. Congress, the Senate Judiciary Committee held extensive sessions examining the question of removing politics from the administration of justice. Of the 17 witnesses who appeared in these hearings, 14 opposed legislation designed to make the Attorney General independent of the President. Meador concluded that "it is becoming clearer that efforts to establish a genuinely independent Attorney General or Department of Justice are likely to be illusory, unrealistic, unworkable, and inconsistent with the constitutional framework" *ibid.* p. 25. For the views of the experienced participants at the Virginia conference see *ibid.* pp. 77–149.

[12] Act of the Congress, June 22, 1870, ch. 150, 16 Stat. 162.

there is no one else in position to serve as the government's top legal officer responsible directly to the President."[13]

"Although the head of every executive department," Meador continued, "is heavily burdened, the Attorney General is unique. In addition to carrying a vast array of administrative responsibilities, he must also perform as a lawyer. No other cabinet officer fills such a dual role, with the special professional obligations which attach to the lawyer, as an officer of the courts, as a member of the Bar, and as a representative of a client. At the heart of all this is the need to rethink the role of the Attorney General of the United States and the institutional position of that office within the government."[14]

We shall have occasion later to consider in more detail the proposals for institutional rearrangements within the Justice Department that were discussed at the Virginia conference in 1980. In essence, the proposal that was seriously contemplated, but rejected, envisaged the separation of the "lawyering" functions of the Attorney General from the other administrative responsibilities which would be assigned instead to a new portfolio of Minister of Justice, so designated.[15] What is strikingly similar is the philosophic debate as to the proper constitutional character of the Attorney General's functions that was being engaged in simultaneously in the United States and in Great Britain. In this country the focus of the debate was necessarily somewhat narrower than that which has occupied the attention of the former establishment figures in Washington. The central theme, however, of the public debate in both countries has been the necessity of ensuring to the maximum extent possible the independent and impartial exercise of the very considerable powers associated with the State's Law Officers. To this end, the view has been expressed in England that it is time to seriously consider transforming the office of Attorney General to that of a non-political appointment, in which the holder would be a public servant rather than a politician who is a member of the government.[16] Another major point of difference, embodied in the public statements of recent Attorneys General, is the question of membership in the Cabinet and the extent to which the Attorney General and the Solicitor General as Law Officers of the Crown should be actively involved in the government's policy discussions. Each of the contrary points of view has its adherents among the ranks of present and past holders of these offices, ranging from that of unqualified participation in policy making to the more conservative stance of non-involvement until called upon to give a legal opinion on a matter of legal interpretation or constitutional authority.

These same issues have also occupied the attention of Law Ministers and Attorneys General throughout the Commonwealth, each of whom has inherited, to a lesser or greater degree, a governmental position bearing

---

[13] Meador, *op. cit.* p. 3.   [14] *Ibid.*   [15] *Ibid.* pp. 57–58.
[16] The most significant voice raised in support of this fundamental change is that of Lord Shawcross, in a letter to *The Times*, August 3, 1977. See further, *post*, pp. 63–70.

the hallmarks of the ancient office of the English Attorney General.[17] Notwithstanding the varied nature of the constitutional arrangements defining the relationship of the Attorney General to the Minister of Justice or, where pertinent, to the Head of Government or executive President of the State, it is noteworthy that everyone present at the Winnipeg meeting of Commonwealth Law Ministers in 1977 agreed that the essential role of the Attorney General was the same. In the words of the communique issued at the close of that meeting: "In recent years, both outside and within the Commonwealth, public attention has frequently focused on the function of law enforcement. Ministers endorsed the principles already observed in their jurisdiction that the discretion in these matters should always be exercised in accordance with wide considerations of the public interest, and without regard to considerations of a party political nature, and that it should be free from any direction or control whatsoever. They considered, however, that the maintenance of these principles depended ultimately upon the unimpeachable integrity of the holder of the office whatever the precise constitutional arrangements in the State concerned."[18] This acknowledgment of the realities of the practical application of constitutional power must not be allowed to obscure the fact that there have been occasions in the past when adherence to the above principles has been sullied to the point that suggests either a total lack of understanding of the fundamental tenets surrounding the office of Attorney General or a cavalier determination to let party or personal considerations prevail in the disposition of a particular case. In this chapter it is proposed to confine the discussion of the philosophical differences to the publicly expressed views of those who presently occupy or who have once occupied the position of Attorney General or Solicitor General in this country or in other parts of the Commonwealth, and whose contributions to the ongoing debate on these questions has done much to sharpen public perception of the divergent philosophies.

SHOULD THE OFFICE OF ATTORNEY GENERAL BECOME A NON-POLITICAL APPOINTMENT?

As the epitome of the doctrine of independent aloofness that, it is said, should permeate the Attorney General's relations with the Prime Minister, the Cabinet and every other ministerial member of the Administration, Lord Rawlinson has best expressed the conception of non-political involvement by the Law Officers in the shaping of government policies.[19]

---

[17] An analysis of the variety of solutions followed in different Commonwealth countries is contained in the paper that I prepared for the 1977 Meeting of Commonwealth Attorneys General and Law Ministers—see *Proceedings*, pp. 196–204, and also the ensuing discussion among the Ministers with respect to the advantages and disadvantages of the public servant concept of the office of Attorney General, *ibid.* pp. 39–51.

[18] *Ibid.* p. 138.

[19] See "A Vital Link in the Machinery of Justice" (1977) 74 *Guardian Gazette* 798, the official publication of the Law Society of England and Wales.

As Sir Peter Rawlinson he served first as Solicitor-General (1962–64) and subsequently as Attorney General (1971–74) in the Conservative Governments led by Mr. Harold Macmillan and Mr. Edward Heath, respectively. What prompted the former Law Officer's exposition of the Attorney General's proper role in the constitution was the case of *Gouriet* v. *Union of Post Office Workers*.[20] As Lord Rawlinson described it, the Court of Appeal had given the Attorney General "a bloody nose."[21] The fact that the House of Lords had later declared in categorical terms that the Court of Appeal had wrongly interpreted the pertinent law, and so unfairly knocked about Mr. Sam Silkin, was unfortunately likely to be forgotten but the case, according to Rawlinson, had the salutary effect of emphasising contemporary concerns about the dual role associated with the Law Officers of the Crown. For those advocating a change in the status of the Attorney General, he explained, the situation could no longer be tolerated whereby the Attorney General's decisions with respect to the enforcement of the law, civil and criminal, in his capacity as protector of the public interest, were beyond the jurisdiction of the courts to question and control. Rawlinson also acknowledged the existence of critics who felt that the enforcement of public rights should no longer lie exclusively within the discretion of a person who is a member of a political Ministry. As the former Attorney General explained: "The case of *Gouriet* v. *H.M. Attorney General and others* brought to the surface the doubts which lurk in some minds that no person can, or no person nowadays appears to, carry out the quasi-judicial duties of Law Officer while at the same time serving in a modern Ministry. The system, according to this view, which was acceptable in the 19th century is no longer acceptable in the second half of the 20th [century]."[22]

No doubt Lord Rawlinson had in mind the opinions which Lord Shawcross had expressed in an extensive letter to *The Times*, also by way of commenting on the decision of the House of Lords in the *Gouriet* case. The special consideration due to the views of any former Attorney General is heightened in this instance by virtue of what have come to be regarded as the classical statements of principle relating to the independence of the Law Officers of the Crown made, and acted upon, by Sir Hartley Shawcross in his capacity as Attorney General during the post-war Labour Administration.[23] With respect to Mr. Silkin's action in refusing to grant his fiat for a relator action in the *Gouriet* case Lord Shawcross drew attention to the fact that the number of such applications which had been turned down during the ten years preceding *Gouriet* was in fact under five per cent.[24] Although, therefore, the Attorney General's decision was "very exceptional," Shawcross added "it is quite possible that had it been

---

[20] [1977] 3 All E.R. 71.
[21] Rawlinson, *op. cit.* p. 799.
[22] *Ibid.*
[23] See Edwards, *op. cit.* pp. 220–225.
[24] *The Times*, Letters to the Editor, August 3, 1977.

my responsibility I might have reached a similar conclusion."[25] The former Labour Attorney General was, however, more concerned with the wider implications of the House of Lords decision. On the subject of ministerial accountability, for example, he drew attention to the realities as well as the applicable constitutional theory, saying: "the theory that the Attorney General is answerable to Parliament may have been true enough in the days of Dicey although its application has (consider, for instance, the famous *Campbell* case) by no means always been that which is sometimes complacently assumed."[26]

According to Lord Shawcross the House of Commons had signally failed to make the Attorney General answer for his omission to refute publicly and authoritatively the misrepresentations aired publicly on the BBC, by the General Secretary of the Union of Post Office Workers, as to the legality of the workers' actions. Mr. Silkin, according to his Labour predecessor, was delinquent in not stating publicly the erroneous nature of the General Secretary's interpretation of the law. As the Attorney General, Mr. Silkin should have made it clear to all and sundry that the Telegraph Act 1893 and the Post Office Act 1953, forbidding any wilful delay in the appropriate services, represented the law of the land and must be obeyed. Had the Attorney General done so, Shawcross maintained, the issues that occupied the attention of the Court of Appeal and the House of Lords in *Gouriet* might well have been avoided. Such conjecturing can never be refuted with any absolute conviction and, moreover, fly in the face of repeated statements by other Attorneys General, including Sir Hartley Shawcross in his day, that the timing of any possible intervention by the Law Officers has to keep in mind the exacerbation of the industrial dispute that can result from a too rigid and inflexible adherence to the enforcement of the criminal law.

In his analysis of the *Gouriet* case—with which he sought to tie the House of Commons' ineffectual reaction to the *Grunwick* affair, the *Clay Cross* situation[27] and the so-called *Shrewsbury martyrs* case—Lord Shawcross developed a forbidding scenario of what may be in store if no thought is given to the problems attendant upon a highly politicised Attorney General and a compliant Parliament. "The fact is," he stated, "we have moved away from Dicey's age of reasoned democracy into the age of power. Responsibility to Parliament means in practice at the most responsibility to the party commanding the majority there which is the party to which the Attorney General of the day must belong. . . . That the present Attorney General has acted in the utmost good faith is not the question. But it requires no great stretch of the imagination to assume that at some future date we might have a majority in Parliament of extreme left or extreme right persuasion with an Attorney General of similar views.

---

[25] *Ibid.*

[26] *Ibid.*

[27] The impact of this particular episode and its handling by Mr. Silkin is dealt with later, see *post*, pp. 342–353.

True to the well known Leninist (which was also the Fascist) strategy, such a Law Officer might well consider it his duty to manipulate the law so as to further the philosophy in which he believed or at least decline to enforce it in a way which would be thought inappropriate by his political colleagues."[28]

Out of the depths of such a pessimistic appraisal Lord Shawcross questioned whether "the once great office of Attorney General should now become one wholly outside the political arena and enjoying in the task of law enforcement the status and independence of a Judge. Of course the Government would still require Law Officers to supervise and conduct Government litigation, although court appearances nowadays seem to be far less frequent than before. But the enforcement of the rights of the public and the rule of law would then be given not only the reality (which I hope it still has) but also the appearance (which it now lacks) of complete detachment from party politics. And the holder would be entitled to consider without fear or favour the effect which, *e.g.*, a prosecution might have 'upon public morale and order.' Be it noted that when I used that phrase long ago I said and meant public and not party or trade union morale."[29]

What Lord Shawcross appears to be advocating is the adoption in England and Wales of a non-elected, non-political, public servant model for the office of Attorney General. A survey of the constitutions of other Commonwealth countries reveals that India, Kenya, Singapore, Sri Lanka, Malta, Cyprus, Botswana, the Bahamas and the Seychelles already subscribe to this interpretation of the role of the Attorney General.[30] The office, in effect, is combined with that of the Director of Public Prosecutions and is not subject to the directions or control of any other person or authority. In other member States of the Commonwealth, it is the Director of Public Prosecutions, not the Attorney General, who is a public servant and who is not amenable to the direction or control of any other person or authority.[31] The latter model will be recognised as the classic Commonwealth Office pattern which the United Kingdom Government consistently sought to incorporate into the independence

---

[28] *Loc. cit.* Referring to public criticism of Silkin's handling of the *Gouriet* case, Shawcross described as "naive" the distinction which purports to justify the Attorney General having regard to political considerations but "not of course acting for party political reasons." According to the former Labour Law Officer: "It is 'of course' exactly the present appearance and the future possibility that he might so act which endangers both existing respect for, and the future effectiveness of, the rule of law, already eroded in many fields" *loc. cit.*

[29] See *ante*, fn. 16.

[30] See S.A. de Smith, *The New Commonwealth and its Constitutions*, (London, Stevens & Sons, 1964), pp. 74–75, 143–145 and W. Dale, *The Modern Commonwealth*, (London, Butterworths, 1983), pp. 117–121.

[31] Unfortunate personal differences between the holders of the offices of Attorney General and D.P.P. in Fiji around 1979 led to that country's Supreme Court being asked by its D.P.P. to declare as "unconstitutional" a direction by the Governor General assigning responsibility to the Attorney General for the administration of the department of the D.P.P. The dispute finally reached the Judicial Committee of the Privy Council which, in its review of the Fiji

constitutions.[32] In many instances, however, after a short interval following the attainment of independence, the relevant constitution has been amended to bring the Director of Public Prosecutions under the direct control of the Attorney General. The Federal Constitution of Nigeria was one of the first to follow this course of action.[33] Jamaica and Guyana, on the other hand, have retained the total independence of the office of Director of Public Prosecutions.[34] The Republic of Ireland is the latest state to adopt a similar philosophy.[35]

Whether the publicly appointed official envisaged by Lord Shawcross is described as the Attorney General or the Director of Public Prosecutions the same fundamental weakness is inherent in the proposal. It is also noteworthy that Lord Shawcross chose to ignore its existence. I refer, of course, to the question as to who is to be ultimately accountable to Parliament for the decisions that are made concerning public rights or the

Constitution, distinguished between (i) those areas (*e.g.* matters of supply from public funds, communications with the Cabinet and Parliament regarding the estimates for the office, and the provision of appropriate facilities) with respect to which the D.P.P.'s department could properly be made subject to the direction and control of the Attorney General as the relevant Minister, and (ii) those specified areas wherein the Constitution conferred complete independence upon the D.P.P. (see s.85(7)). The latter categories extend to the D.P.P.'s power: (a) to institute and undertake criminal proceedings before any court of law; (b) to take over and continue any such criminal proceedings that may have been instituted by any other person or authority; and (c) to discontinue, at any stage before judgment is delivered, any such criminal proceedings instituted or undertaken by himself or any other person or authority (Constitution, s.85(4)). Reversing the Fiji Court of Appeal, the Judicial Committee held that the Governor General's direction was validly executed within the prescribed terms of the Constitution—see *Attorney General of Fiji* v. *D.P.P. of Fiji* [1983] 2 W.L.R. 275, and (1981) 7 *Commonwealth Law Bulletin* 1236 (containing a full account of the judgments rendered by the Supreme Court and Court of Appeal).

[32] Not all of the newly independent countries of the Commonwealth have adopted this model. Alternative solutions resorted to include rendering the D.P.P. subject to the directions of the country's executive President but to no other person. This is the situation that exists in Tanzania and which prevailed in Ghana during the latter years of the first Republic from 1962 to 1966. For some illustrations of the effects of this system as it was practised in Ghana during the Kwame Nkrumah regime, when Geoffrey Bing was Attorney General, see my essay in *Reshaping the Criminal Law*, p. 380, fn. 55. For the present constitutional position in Ghana see A.N.E. Amissah, *Criminal Procedure in Ghana* (1982), pp. 18–28. In Zambia the D.P.P. is not subject to control by any other person but, if in his judgment, a case involves general considerations of public policy the D.P.P. must bring the case to the attention of the Attorney General who is then empowered to give directions to the Director. See further W. Dale, *op. cit.* (fn. 30), p. 120.

[33] de Smith, *op. cit.* pp. 145 and 298. In my discussions with the Federal Attorney General of Nigeria in 1968, Dr. T.O. Elias (as he then was) described the increasing frustration that he experienced in being unable, for the purposes of responding to questions by members of the Legislative Assembly, to secure sufficient information from the D.P.P. as to decisions that that official had taken with respect to the enforcement or non-enforcement of the criminal law. The final straw had been instances in which the D.P.P. had refused to have any communication with Dr. Elias, in the latter's capacity as the federal Attorney General and Minister of Justice.

[34] Doubts as to the justification for continuing such an arrangement under the Jamaican constitution were expressed by that country's Minister of Justice and Attorney General, a political appointee, during the 1977 Meeting of Commonwealth Law Ministers—see *Proceedings*, pp. 47–48.

[35] A fuller account of this recent development in the Republic of Ireland is contained in Chapter 9, *post*, pp. 262–268.

institution or withdrawal of criminal proceedings. Unless the total elimination from Parliament is envisaged of the right to scrutinise controversial prosecutorial decisions, or actions to enforce or not enforce public rights, there will remain the necessity of having a Minister of Justice, with a seat in the House of Commons, and of defining the nature of his relationship to the Attorney General and the Director of Public Prosecutions.[36] The unhappy experiences of those Commonwealth countries which have attempted to totally isolate the responsible Minister from independent public officials will be ignored at our peril.

The other fallacy that is obscured, in the simplistic contrast drawn by Lord Shawcross between an avidly political Attorney General and the dispassionate public servant serving the state as Attorney General or Director of Public Prosecutions, is alluded to in a paper that I prepared for the meeting of Commonwealth Law Ministers in 1977.[37] Based on my examination of the administration of justice in a broad sample of Commonwealth countries, conducted between 1966 and 1968, I am convinced that, no matter how entrenched constitutional safeguards may be, in the final analysis it is the strength of character, personal integrity and depth of commitment to the principles of independence and the impartial representation of the public interest, on the part of holders of the office of Attorney General, which is of supreme importance. Such qualities are by no means associated exclusively with either the political or non-political nature of the office of Attorney General. Instances of indefensible distortion of the Attorney General's powers can be documented in countries which have subscribed to the public servant model of the offices of Attorney General and Director of Public Prosecutions, equally with the occupancy of the political portfolios of Minister of Justice and Attorney General in other countries.[38] It is these kinds of situations that induce widespread disillusionment with the ideals associated with democratic government.

THE DOCTRINE OF INDEPENDENT ALOOFNESS

To revert to Lord Rawlinson's philosophy of what is required of the modern Attorney General in British political life, the remedy is not to be found in the creation of new constitutional machinery but rather in

[36] The same inherent flaw in Shawcross' argument was adverted to by Rawlinson, *op. cit.* p. 799, and by Silkin, (1978) 59 *The Parliamentarian* 157. In Silkin's words: "To whom would the independent, non-political Law Officer be accountable? . . . If there were no Minister through whom he could be accountable we should have to invent one. And if there were, we have returned full circle; for accountability without control is meaningless, and whatever Minister were answerable for the independent Law Officer would in practice have to control him; else we should have the semblance of accountability and not the reality. And in my experience there is no more potent weapon in a democratic society than the reality of accountability to Parliament," *loc. cit.*

[37] See *ante*, fn. 17.

[38] See Edwards, "The Integrity of Criminal Prosecutions," in P. Glazebrook (Ed.) *Reshaping the Criminal Law*, at pp. 375–380; A.N.E. Amissah, *Criminal Procedure in Ghana*, p. 23.

underlining the priorities that ought to govern the Law Officers' response to the ever growing demands upon their time and energies. An English Attorney General, according to Rawlinson, "ought to be aloof from his colleagues in the Ministry to a quite formidable extent. Even in ordinary matters of law affecting the Government he should attend upon Cabinet, give his opinion and leave. With prosecutions it should be even more formal."[39] By way of emphasising the same approach, Rawlinson pointed to the fact that the Attorney General's base of operations is located within the Royal Courts of Justice in London. Its presence there, he claimed, underscored the dual role of the Law Officers and he strongly counselled against any move that would locate the Law Officers' Department elsewhere in Whitehall.[40] Much of the same thinking is reflected in the choice of title used to describe the modest establishment that serves both the Attorney General and the Solicitor General as the principal legal advisers to the government and as chief counsel representing the Crown in its broadest application. To those who wish to highlight the litigation and prosecutorial roles of the Attorney General, the offices in question are properly described as "The Attorney General's Chambers." For those, on the other hand, who espouse the more ministerial features of the work undertaken in the same offices, the appropriate description is "The Law Officers' Department."

Such symbols are not to be dismissed as of no significance. Likewise they should not be allowed to divert attention from the more substantial aspects of the divergent approaches to the discharge of the Attorney General's responsibilities. Two formulations of the political side to the Law Officers' functions help to understand what is really at stake. According to Lord Rawlinson the modern problem is to demonstrate the separation of the political and legal roles inherent in the present day Attorney General. "Certainly," he explained, "dangers will arise if, during his term of office, a Law Officer is seen to be or thought to be too overtly 'political,' too much the Minister and too little counsel to the Crown and to Parliament. Like the Lord Chancellor he should not, in my opinion, engage in extravagant party political debate."[41] It would be hard to find a more diametrically opposed explanation of how to approach the inherent conflict of roles than that advanced by Lord Elwyn Jones, a former Attorney General and former Lord Chancellor. Speaking to the Cambridge University Law Society in 1969, before his elevation to the Woolsack, Sir Elwyn Jones (as

---

[39] Rawlinson, *op. cit.* p. 799. Some clues to the former Conservative Law Officer's ideology are contained in the account he gives of being invited in 1962 to become Solicitor General when Harold Macmillan, the Prime Minister, reminded him that the Law Officers were the last of the professional servants of the Crown who still remain M.P.s. "He said that my obligations were first to the Crown, second to the House of Commons; and only then to his Ministry."

[40] *Op. cit.*

[41] *Op. cit.* Not everyone will agree with Rawlinson's identification of the Lord Chancellor's office as one that necessarily eschews participation in "extravagant party political debate."

he then was) stated: "You may think by now that the Attorney General is some sort of detached creature who has nothing to do with politics. But that would be highly disingenuous. In fact, the Attorney General, when he is acting in political matters, is a highly political animal entitled to engage in contentious politics. I suppose the only thing one can say is that some Attorneys General are more contentious than others as politicians. But the basic requirement of our constitution is that however much of a political animal he may be when he is dealing with political matters, he must not allow political considerations to affect his actions in those matters in which he has to act in an impartial and even quasi-judicial way."[42]

The terms "politics" and "political matters," it is well to recognise, bear several connotations and their use, without elaboration of the precise meaning intended by the writer, can readily lead to misunderstanding.[43] In adopting Lord Elwyn Jones' language and describing himself as a "political animal" when he appeared before the Court of Appeal in the *Gouriet* case, Mr. Silkin can hardly have been surprised at the line of questioning that followed on the part of the Master of the Rolls and the other members of the Court.[44] In the present debate it matters greatly where the emphasis is placed by those who seek to explain and describe the roles ascribed to the Law Officers of the Crown. Fortunately for us, Mr. Silkin saw fit to elaborate his own views in an article prepared for *The Parliamentarian*,[45] after much of the dust generated by the *Gouriet* confrontation had settled down. Of the many addresses given by Mr. Silkin during his tenure of

[42] "The Office of Attorney General," [1969] Cambridge L.J. 43, at p. 50.

[43] For a useful discussion of the imprecise distinctions embedded in these phrases, seen in the context of the relationship between the Attorney General and the President of the United States, see Meador, *op. cit.* pp. 41–43. Some striking illustrations of the conflicts of expectation on the part of the Executive members concerned are also contained in the section of Professor Meador's background paper which is devoted to "Law, Policy and Politics," *ibid.* pp. 25–41. He concludes: "The insistence by many that the Justice Department be free of White House interference is basically sound, so long as it is realised that the Attorney General [under the U.S. Constitution] is accountable to the President and that there is a permissible play of policy concerns in the administration of the Department of Justice. Since 'policy' usually involves what the public considers 'political,' it is misleading to say that 'politics' should play no part in the legal work of the Attorney General and the Department of Justice. At the same time it is equally true that certain kinds of political considerations [*e.g.* personal friendships or the politically influential position of individuals or groups] are inappropriate in the administration of justice . . . Making this distinction is one of the most difficult tasks confronting the Attorney General and the President"—*ibid.* pp. 41–42. A prominent illustration of this inherent conflict is contained in the statements made by President Carter and Attorney General Bell regarding the decision making process leading up to the disposition of the *Richard Helms* case in 1977—see *New York Times*, September 30, November 1, 3, 4, 5, 1977. Helms, the former Director of the U.S. Central Intelligence Agency, was eventually convicted of withholding information from a Congressional Committee in 1973 concerning covert operations in Chile. See, too, the confusion surrounding the handling of the case involving *Ramsey Clark*, a former U.S. Attorney General, who travelled to Iran during the hostage crisis in 1980 in violation of a widely publicised Presidential ban on travel to that country—*New York Times*, June 9, 11, 18, 1980, and *Washington Post*, June 12, 1980.

[44] *The Times*, January 18 and 19, 1977.

[45] "The Functions and Position of the Attorney General in the United Kingdom" (1978) 59 *The Parliamentarian* 149–158.

office as Attorney General,[46] this essay represents by far the most cogent exposition of his particular interpretation of the functions associated with the Law Officers of the Crown.

The Doctrine of Intimate but Independent Involvement

Commenting specifically on Lord Rawlinson's article in the *The Guardian Gazette*, Mr. Silkin said that he "would not seek to alter one word of nine-tenths of what he wrote."[47] This included Rawlinson's treatment of the *Gouriet* case and his strong refutation of the view that the day of the political Law Officer was coming to an end. That said, the gulf in their respective approaches became very evident as Silkin explained his own approach to his relationship with colleagues in the Government. "My own philosophy" he wrote "is wholly different on this aspect from that of my predecessor. I regard it as almost my prime duty to keep my colleagues out of the court rather than to represent them in the courts. I do not believe that I could have done that even with such moderate success as I may have achieved if I had held myself aloof from them 'to a quite formidable extent,' or if I had conceived it as my duty to attend upon Cabinet, give my opinion, and leave, as Lord Rawlinson would have it. On the contrary, I regard it as the Law Officer's duty to learn as much as he can of his colleagues' policies, their intentions, their wishes, their methods, indeed their very temperaments and characters. I believe that only so can he give them the best possible advice, not merely as to what they cannot lawfully do, or should not with propriety do, but also as to how they can achieve their aims by means which are both lawful and proper. I cannot accept that a formidable aloofness is likely to assist such an achievement. The Law Officer must know the colleague he is dealing with, and the colleague he is dealing with must know the Law Officer, and know him well enough to be able to place his trust in his experience, his wisdom, and his full-hearted desire to achieve the governmental objectives which unite them in a common Ministry."[48]

"I would, indeed, go further," Silkin went on to say, "and add that for my part I regret—and I know how strongly Lord Rawlinson would disagree—that the Attorney General in this country does not, unless invited, sit at the Cabinet table. I regret it because I am convinced that the more intimately the government's principal legal adviser is aware of the battles and the arguments and the stresses and the strains that eventually result in policy, the better able he is to assist in ensuring that if there is a lawful and a proper way of achieving its objectives, that way will be found. I do not crave for either a vote or a voice in Cabinet; I do not desire a share in Cabinet responsibility. Like the Chief Whip I would be content to listen

---

[46] Not all of these were published. Reference, however, should also be made to Silkin's paper "The Attorney General's Dilemma" (1979) Malayan L.J. xxvi–xxx, delivered earlier as the George Bean Memorial Lecture in Manchester on October 19, 1978.

[47] (1978) 59 *The Parliamentarian* 149 at p. 156.

[48] *Loc. cit.*

and to speak only when asked to do so. In saying this I record a personal, not a governmental view: I am well aware of the arguments based on half a century's tradition to the contrary. But they are arguments which do not prevail in many Commonwealth countries and which, I find, cause considerable surprise in some."[49]

SOME COMMONWEALTH PARALLELS

For whatever reason, unlike their United States and British counterparts, Attorneys General throughout the Commonwealth have been notably reticent in speaking of their ministerial experience or in expressing their individual conception of the office they once held. It must be, therefore, that Mr. Silkin was basing his remarks on personal discussions with his Law Officer colleagues or perhaps on the exchange of views that took place at the meeting of Commonwealth Law Ministers which was held in Canada in 1977.[50] Subsequent to this gathering, the legal profession and the general public in New Zealand were afforded a rare but refreshing insight into the reflections of their former Attorney General, Mr. Peter Wilkinson, on stepping down from office.[51] After a somewhat tempestuous tenure of the portfolios of Minister of Justice and Attorney General, in the course of which he entered stays in a series of politically contentious cases,[52] Mr. Wilkinson reaffirmed his strong conviction that the Attorney General in New Zealand should function within, not outside, the Cabinet. Such has been the situation since 1967, though it is important to bear in mind that, during the whole of this period, the office of Solicitor General in New Zealand has been a permanent non-political appointment, in charge of the Crown Law Office, to which senior members of the legal profession have frequently been appointed.[53] A not inappropriate parallel that helps to illuminate the New Zealand constitutional system is to regard its Solicitor General as encompassing the functions of the Director of Public Prosecutions in England and Wales. The two offices are by no means identical but the non-political character of the respective appointments will serve to underline the relevance of the opinions advanced by Mr. Wilkinson on relinquishing his seals of office.

In accepting that the position of the Attorney General as a member of the New Zealand Cabinet can indeed be invidious at times, he concluded that it was not insurmountably so. "It is not hard to envisage a situation,"

---

[49] *Loc. cit.* p. 157

[50] See *ante*, fn. 17. A list of the Commonwealth countries in which the Attorney General (sometimes designated also as the Minister of Justice or similar title) is normally a Cabinet Minister includes Australia (in both the States and Commonwealth Governments), Canada (likewise in both the Provinces and the Federal Government), Nigeria, New Zealand, Malaysia, Trinidad and Tobago, and Sierra Leone. See W. Dale, *The Modern Commonwealth* (*ante*) fn. 30).

[51] [1979] N.Z.L.J. 116.

[52] See *post*, pp. 396–402.

[53] A brief account of the evolution of the Law Officerships in New Zealand is given in Chapter 12, *post*, pp. 388–391.

Mr. Wilkinson wrote, "in which the Attorney General's sitting in Cabinet might place him in a difficult position in the exercise of his law officer powers where his decision will have political flow-on effects. Difficult, but not impossible. Such a difficult situation could well arise where, for example, an Attorney General's independent decision to stay a criminal prosecution happens to coincide with the political advantage of the Government of which he is a member. As I see it, if the Attorney General has sustainable arguments on grounds of public interest and the interests of justice which can stand on their own, independent of any political consideration, . . . he should be able to live with any 'difficulty' arising from that situation. There will undoubtedly be times when a situation would be easier for an Attorney General if he was not a member of Cabinet. This is in my view, however, substantially outweighed by the fact that, as a member of the Cabinet, he is much better equipped to make assessments on matters of public interest. Only in Cabinet can he obtain the 'over-view' needed to make fully informed and properly balanced decisions."[54] Speaking of the controversial decisions which prompted accusations of government interference in pursuit of political expediency, the former New Zealand Attorney General asserted that the Government had had no part in the decisions which had been made by him and him alone. To reinforce, as it were, his commitment to the constitutional philosophy expressed above, Mr. Wilkinson concluded: "With the perspective of hindsight I would say of those decisions that they cost me dear in personal political terms but—faced with exactly the same circumstances again in each case—I would make the same decision again."[55]

New Zealand critics might not be disposed so readily to accept the inevitable correctness of all the Attorney General's decisions, or the desirability of a political Attorney, and member of the Cabinet, having the ultimate say in deciding whether or not to enter a stay of summary proceedings,[56] a statutory power that is not available to the Attorney General of England and Wales. A more careful study of these contentious cases, and the New Zealand law pertaining to the entry of stays in criminal proceedings, must be deferred to Chapter 12 when we shall take a look at

[54] [1979] N.Z.L.J. 118.

[55] *Loc. cit.*

[56] This power was conferred by the Summary Proceedings Amdt. Act (N.Z.) 1967, s.2, the passage of which through the New Zealand Parliament was expedited in order to overcome the obstacle to the extradition from the U.K. of one Robert Gardner who was wanted by the New Zealand Police on 37 charges of fraud involving a sum of $120,000. In presenting the Bill, the Attorney General (Mr. J.R. Hanan) explained that only if it was passed into law would it be possible for the New Zealand Government to guarantee to the U.K. Government that when Gardner was extradited he would not be charged with any other offence. I have good reason to believe, based on my subsequent discussion with the then Permanent Under Secretary of State, that the undertaking requested by the Home Office referred to the possibility of the accused person being rendered liable to prosecution for an offence carrying the death penalty, but this implicit assumption somehow did not filter through to the New Zealand authorities. See, too, *post*, p. 398, fn. 80 and p. 449, fn. 24.

recent Commonwealth experience in sustaining the independent role of the Law Officers.

It is undoubtedly true that the British practice—constitutional convention might not be too strong a description—since 1928 has been to exclude the Attorney General, and perforce the Solicitor General, from the ranks of ministers given Cabinet rank and thus entitled to a seat and vote in meetings of the Government's chief policy making body. The reasons for this reversal of the comparatively short practice of according the senior Law Officer a seat in the Cabinet are fully set forth in my earlier work on the *Law Officers of the Crown*.[57] A review of the history of this subject suggests that the appointment of Sir Rufus Isaacs as the first Attorney General to receive Cabinet rank in 1912 was in no way a deliberate break with tradition. The new practice, moreover, was short lived, terminating in 1928 when Sir Thomas Inskip, the new Attorney General, was excluded from the list of Cabinet ministers. This latter policy has been followed without exception ever since. In this connexion, perhaps I may be permitted to repeat the conclusion expressed in my earlier study where I stated: "On the question of membership of the Cabinet itself, . . . it is the outward manifestation of the Attorney General's dissociation from the inner council of the government that assumes the greatest importance in underlining his independence in the enforcement of the criminal law. By excluding the Attorney General from actual membership of the Cabinet the tradition may well have been enhanced that the subject of criminal prosecution is outside the purview of the Cabinet's decision making functions."[58] I remain of the same persuasion today.

There is nothing particularly new in the current dispute regarding the propriety of including the Attorney General within the Cabinet. Sir John Coleridge, in 1872, saw the omission in terms of disparagement of the office.[59] A more substantial examination of the underlying issues had earlier been undertaken in some of the older colonies where the inclusion of the Attorney General within the Executive Council was regarded as mandatory. The reasons for doing so were ably stated in 1862 in a memorandum prepared by Mr. Justice Boothby of the Supreme Court of South Australia in support of his view that a clause, contained in a Bill to establish a Legislature in the colony, compelling the Crown to receive into its Executive Council the Attorney and the Solicitor General, was unconstitutional.[60] The restricted context within which those views were expressed should not diminish the pertinence of Mr. Justice Boothby's analysis in which he stated: "To compel the Crown to receive its Law Officers among its Cabinet Ministers is exposed to most important objections, founded on the nature of such offices. The Crown cannot be compelled to seek legal advice from law officers who, after the advice is

[57] *Op. cit.* Chapter 9.
[58] *Ibid.* p. 175.
[59] *Ibid.* pp. 158–159.
[60] *Ibid.* pp. 167–168.

given, have the power, it may be, by casting vote to compel that advice to be adopted . . . Such a position would unfit the Law Officers of the Crown for the impartial consideration of questions necessarily requiring their decision, and so lessen their power of efficient service to the Crown. The wish, as Cabinet Ministers, that a certain course should be pursued, would become 'father to the thought' that the law would permit it. The Attorney and Solicitor General were never Cabinet Ministers in the whole course of English constitutional government. That these officers have been made members of the Executive Councils of Colonies has only arisen from this, that constitutional government has not existed, and the Law Officers so situated had only the right to offer advice, without any power to compel that advice being adopted."[61]

With the exception of those countries, such as India and Cyprus, which have elected to make the office of Attorney General a non-political appointment, the nearly universal practice throughout the Commonwealth is to include the Attorney General within the Cabinet. In Canada, for example, the Attorney General of Canada is invariably also the federal Minister of Justice and it is by virtue of the latter appointment that his inclusion within the Cabinet is assured. It has been thus since Canada achieved self-government in 1867.[62] And the majority of the provinces have followed the same pattern,[63] continuing the two portfolios, with different responsibilities, in the one minister. The observation, in Mr. Silkin's paper in *The Parliamentarian*, that the arguments opposed to the inclusion of the Attorney General in the British Cabinet do not prevail in many Commonwealth countries, and in fact cause considerable surprise when the constitutional positions are set side by side, should not be pressed too far.

AN ASSESSMENT OF THE CONFLICTING PHILOSOPHIES

There is, after all, a strong legacy of colonial history exhibiting an unbroken record in including the Attorney General as an *ex-officio* member of the Executive Council, the colonial equivalent to the British Cabinet.[64] So that a formidable body of precedent and prerogatives of status and influence have always surrounded the office of Attorney General in Commonwealth countries outside of the United Kingdom. These considerations are unlikely to be readily set aside no matter how cogent the theoretical arguments for change may be. A more pertinent question that should be asked is the extent to which public confidence in the independence of the Attorney General is enhanced or diminished by the continuance in Britain of the political claims to a senior seat around the

---

[61] *Ibid.*
[62] See Edwards, *Ministerial Responsibility for National Security as it relates to the offices of Prime Minister, Attorney General and Solicitor of Canada*, (Ottawa, 1980), pp. 5–9.
[63] *Ibid.* pp. 11–19.
[64] *Ibid.* pp. 15–16. For the early history of the office in the Australian colonies see *post*, Chapter 12, pp. 367–372.

Cabinet table. Speaking of recent Canadian and Australian experience in these matters, it can be stated that the perpetuation of the long standing convention of Cabinet rank for every Attorney General has not passed unchallenged. In these countries, and other Commonwealth states that will be looked at later, there exists widespread sceptism, as no doubt can be said of opinion within the United Kingdom, as to the ability of present day Law Officers to demonstrate publicly their determination to separate the political and quasi-judicial roles inherent in their offices.

As Mr. Silkin has pointed out, the Attorney General in this country does not, unless invited, sit at the Cabinet table. His arguments were addressed not to exercising a vote and thereby sharing in Cabinet responsibility but to the recognition of a right in the principal Law Officer of the day to attend meetings of the Cabinet, to receive all Cabinet papers and to be afforded the opportunity of hearing at first hand, "the battles and the arguments and the stresses and strains that eventually result in policy."[65] The analogy with the position occupied by the Chief Whip at the Cabinet table, which Mr. Silkin invoked in support of his argument,[66] is a rather inappropriate one embracing as it does a political figure whose major preoccupation is to ensure the continued existence in power of the current Administration. A more pertinent parallel might be that of the secretary of a large corporation, a lawyer, whose attendance at meetings of the board of directors is taken for granted and whose function could well be described in the language used by Mr. Silkin apropos the Attorney General in Cabinet, viz. the better able he is to ensure that if there is a lawful and a proper way of achieving the corporation's objectives, that way will be found.[67]

Perceptions so often conflict with the realities of any situation. There is admittedly much force in the case developed by Mr. Silkin in defence of a more active involvement by the Attorney General in the preliminary discussions amongst his ministerial colleagues preceding the formal adoption of government policies by the Cabinet. What is missing in the Silkin excursus is an acknowledgment of the costs attendant upon this philosophy. Those costs would assuredly involve a further erosion in the public's perception of an independent Attorney General. That perception, to the extent that it does exist, rests on the belief that, being outside the innermost political discussions of the government at their highest and most sensitive levels, the Attorney General can more readily demonstrate the independence of his legal advice and decisions, and his capacity to withstand political pressures savouring of party advantage. It cannot be denied that there exists a measure of consistency in the former Attorney General's philosophy, on the one hand, of wishing to be very much involved in Cabinet deliberations and, on the other hand, of forsaking

---

[65] (1978) 59 *The Parliamentarian* 149 at p. 157.

[66] "I do not crave" wrote Mr. Silkin "for either a vote or a voice in Cabinet; I do not desire a share in Cabinet responsibility. Like the Chief Whip I would be content to listen and to speak only when asked to do so"—*loc. cit.*

[67] *Ibid.* p. 156.

responsibility in favour of the Director of Public Prosecutions when faced with the necessity of making prosecutorial decisions that have strong political overtones. Mr. Silkin's handling of the *Jeremy Thorpe* case in 1977, referred to earlier,[68] can readily be interpreted as a sincere determination by the Attorney General to exclude political considerations from the judgments that had to be made before deciding to institute criminal proceedings against the former leader of the Liberal Party. As Mr. Silkin, however, himself later acknowledged, the perception in the public mind of how the prosecution process functioned in that case was complicated by its failure to separate the participation of the Attorney General from that of the Director of Public Prosecutions in reaching the final decision. Only much later was this transfer of responsibility by the Attorney General made publicly known and even then it is doubtful if all of Mr. Silkin's critics were silenced by his protestations of non-involvement.

How the Attorney General's actions are perceived in particular cases is a matter of much consequence to the characterisation of the office as independent or highly political. It can well be argued that the closer and more intense the Attorney General's involvement in the politics of government, even as counsellor, the greater becomes the uphill task facing any Law Officer of demonstrating his non-partisan approach to his other responsibilities in the field of criminal prosecutions and the protection of public rights where the government may be an interested party. In my view, the high price that must be paid for the adoption of Mr. Silkin's philosophy is disproportionate to the benefits described as flowing from the doctrinaire approach so close to Mr. Silkin's heart. It would almost certainly accelerate the movement toward further questioning the validity of the much vaunted independence of the Law Officers of the Crown.

A further point of difference in approach advanced by Lord Rawlinson, in explanation of the shift towards the predominantly ministerial role that he associated with the Silkin era, was "the decline, or apparent decline in very recent years, of the Law Officers' regular appearances in the civil or criminal courts."[69] Added to which was a scarcely veiled rebuke to Mr. Silkin and his colleague, Mr. Peter Archer, the Solicitor General, for rejecting the traditional knighthood given to Law Officers of the Crown on

---

[68] *Ante*, pp. 52–57.

[69] (1977) 74 *The Guardian Gazette* 799. Against this assertion should be placed the account given by Mr. Silkin's colleague as Solicitor General, Mr. Peter Archer, of the more notable cases in which the Labour Attorney General appeared in accordance with the criteria "where the weightiest Government interests are at stake or the repercussions widest." These included "the Crossman Diaries case, the Steadman case relating to official secrets, the contempt proceedings against Mr. Paul Foot, the references from Northern Ireland relating to the criminal liability of a soldier who shoots a civilian believing him to be a terrorist, the Laker Airways case, the Gouriet case, the Icelandic fisheries case before the International Court of Justice, the Anglo-French arbitration as to the respective rights to minerals on the continental shelf, and before the European Court of Human Rights on the Irish State case relating to methods of interrogation. For the Solicitor General, the most demanding subject in terms of days spent in court consists of disputes between taxpayers and the Revenue."—see fn. 77 *post*.

appointment.[70] It would not be difficult to estimate the reasons, a mixture of political and personal credo, for this break with an established convention that had remained inviolate over the previous 400 years. At the same time it is well to remember that resistance in the past to the acceptance of the accolade of knighthood included such doughty figures as Samuel Romilly and John Scott, the future Lord Eldon.[71] In 1873, also, Mr. Gladstone was faced with a recalcitrant Attorney General and Solicitor General, in the persons of William Harcourt and Henry James, who were unsuccessful in their attempt to be excused from accepting knighthoods.[72] And we have only to look back to 1910 to discover the sentiments of John Simon who balked at the prospect of becoming Sir John because it would "stamp the holder as a mere government lawyer and nothing more."[73]

It is idle to deny the importance that attaches to symbols but it is questionable whether the action of the Labour Law Officers in 1974, in the words of Lord Rawlinson, "served to emphasise a political rather than the legal approach to the offices."[74] What, after all, is "the legal approach?" Presumably, the writer was adverting to his earlier observation that regular appearances in the courts, on behalf of the Crown and the Government, had visibly diminished during the period of Labour Administrations. No statistical evidence was advanced in support of Lord Rawlinson's claim and a review of the instances in which Mr. Silkin appeared in court suggests, at the very least, an acceptance of the "legal" responsibilities associated with the Attorney General's office and a weighing, in each situation, of the relative priorities that should attach to the ministerial and counsel functions facing an extremely busy Law Officer. The daily agenda facing the modern Attorney General as described by Mr. Silkin "is intensive, wide ranging and never ending."[75] He went on to explain that "with the ever growing problems connected with our membership of the European Economic Community, the Commission and Court of Human Rights at Strasbourg, the resources of the continental shelf, the general growth of administration, and the special difficulties in Northern Ireland, the work grows and will grow rather than diminish. If it were not so fascinating in its scope, it would be oppressive in its demands. Even so, I am conscious that the necessarily rigid system of priorities to which the Attorney General must submit if he is always to be available at short notice when required (as indeed he must be) inevitably means that some aspects of the Attorney General's traditional work, such as travelling the circuits and becoming

---

[70] *Loc. cit.* For a fuller account of the historical background to the conferment of the accolade of knighthood upon the Attorney General and Solicitor General and of the earlier attempts to evade this honour see Edwards, *op. cit.* pp. 282–285.

[71] Edwards, *op. cit.* p. 283.

[72] *Ibid.* p. 284.

[73] *Ibid.*

[74] Rawlinson, *op. cit.* p. 799.

[75] (1978) 59 *The Parliamentarian* 149 at p. 158.

familiar from personal experience with the members of his profession, have to take second place."[76]

Mr. Silkin's unwillingness to accept the strictures offered by his Conservative predecessor was expanded upon by Mr. Peter Archer, the Solicitor General from 1974 to 1979 in the Wilson and Callaghan Ministries. In an elaborately argued pamphlet on "The Role of the Law Officers" published in 1978 by the Fabian Society,[77] Mr. Archer claimed that the criticism, however valid, was more properly directed to the record of Law Officers since World War II, as opposed to the practice of their forerunners in earlier generations. "If it is implied" the pamphlet read "that the process has accelerated since Labour took office in 1974 and that Labour Law Officers spend so much time in controversial activities of government that they have grown away from the courts it is worth recording that the number of days spent in court by Law Officers has varied little over the last eight years, and that one of my predecessors, Sir Geoffrey Howe, was closely involved in the Parliamentary debates on two of the most controversial bills of the decade, the Industrial Relations Bill of 1971 and the European Communities Bill of 1972."[78] It would be a sad day if the attributes of particular Law Officers came to be judged in statistical terms. Random illustrations, on the other hand, can be equally misleading, so that the special pressures that confront the Attorney General and Solicitor General of a particular Administration, and their responses to those same challenges, should properly be placed in the broader context of what I have described as philosophical interpretations of the Law Officers' functions within the British constitution. It is within this framework that judgment should be exercised with regard to the rejoinder, attributed to Mr. Silkin, that "Law Officers are primarily responsible for ensuring that Ministers generally act on the best legal advice and so are best enabled to uphold the rule of law and it is, therefore, not surprising that Law Officers, like all good lawyers, concentrate on keeping their clients out of court, in preference to representing them there."[79]

Alleviation for some of the burdens of parliamentary work was forthcoming in the early 1970s when the prospects of the United Kingdom's entry into Europe seemed destined to create a raft of new problems for the Law Officers' Department. Events have confirmed the anticipated projections of a much expanded agenda calling for the attention of both the Attorney General and the Solicitor General.[80] With it

[76] *Ibid.*
[77] Fabian Research Series no. 339.
[78] *Ibid.* p. 30.
[79] *Ibid.* p. 31.
[80] Appearances of one or other of the Law Officers before the European Commission of Human Rights and the European Court of Human Rights, since the inception of these institutions, show no obvious disparity as between Conservative and Labour Attorneys General and Solicitors General. Thus, Mr. Silkin, as Attorney General appeared on several occasions on behalf of the U.K. Government in the *Irish State* case before both the Commission and the Court (see (1978) 2 E.H.R.R. 25), and Mr. Archer, the Labour Solicitor General, led the Government's team of lawyers before the European Court of Human Rights

has come the establishment of a Parliamentary Secretary to the Department, thereby providing a welcome source of relief from some of the parliamentary obligations shouldered by the Law Officers. How far this expedient will provide a permanent reallocation of functions must remain for further examination in Chapter 7, when we shall look at the role of the Law Officers as the chief legal advisers to the Government.

in the *Sunday Times* (the Thalidomide) case (see (1979) 2 E.H.R.R. 245). Mr. Archer also took part in the *Krugerrand* case before the European Court of Justice in *R. v. Thompson, Johnson & Woodiwiss* (Case 7/78), but there appears to be no record of Mr. Silkin having made any appearance before the European Court of Justice. The present Attorney General, Sir Michael Havers, argued the Government's case in *R. v. Henn & Darby* (Case 232/78) (importation of obscene publications) before the European Court of Justice but has yet to lead for the Government in a case before the European Court of Human Rights. Havers has, however, acted in this capacity before the European Commission of Human Rights in the *Malone* case (involving the legitimacy of telephone tapping). The former Conservative Solicitor General, Sir Ian Percival, heads the list in terms of frequency of appearance, arguing the Government's position in the *Closed Shop* case (*Young, James & Webster* v. *U.K.*) before both the European Commission (see (1980) 3 E.H.R.R. 20) and the European Court of Human Rights ((1981) Series A, no. 44). He also acted in the same capacity before the European Court of Justice in *Commission* v. *Belgium* (Case 149/79) and *Commission* v. *U.K.* (Case 40/82). An interesting development is the trend towards the Lord Advocate, on the nomination of the Attorney General, appearing on behalf of the U.K. Government in European proceedings. Most of these cases have been before the European Court of Justice and have involved disputes over fisheries jurisdiction and fisheries conservation measures. Other instances, involving issues of wider import, include *France, Italy and U.K.* v. *Commission* (Cases 188–190/80) and *Staple Dairy Products* v. *I.B.A.P.* (Case 84/81). The Lord Advocate was the principal Government's lawyer in *Campbell and Cosans* v. *U.K.*, heard before the European Court of Human Rights, involving the issue of corporal punishment in schools (see (1982) Series A, Vol. 48). I am indebted for the information contained in this footnote to Mr. Henry Steel, Legal Secretary, Law Officers' Department.

4

Police Investigations and Prosecutions—Proposals for Change

Prior to the setting up of the Royal Commission on Criminal Procedure in 1978 there had been renewed expressions of dissatisfaction with the system wherein the vast majority of prosecutions are brought at the instigation of the police who are also responsible, earlier in the process, for the investigation of the self same crimes. The principal grounds for criticism of this state of affairs, unique to England and Wales, were the doubts entertained as to the ability of the police to maintain an impartial, dispassionate approach to the decision whether or not to prosecute. Such a model approach, it was argued, is unattainable having regard to the degree of commitment to each case that derives from the police function of investigating the circumstances in the first instance and seeing the investigation through to the point of charging the accused with the relevant offence. Objection to the integration of both investigating and prosecution roles in the same body of officials has been voiced over a long period of our political history, commencing with the evidence tendered before the various Parliamentary Committees into the subject of public prosecutors in the nineteenth century[1] and reiterated in the reports of the Royal Commission on Police Powers and Procedure in 1929[2] and, later, the Royal Commission on the Police in 1962.[3]

As Sir Archibald Bodkin, the then Director of Public Prosecutions, testified before the 1929 Commission,[4] it was important to keep distinct, on the one hand, the duty which lies upon the police of preventing and detecting crime, and, on the other, the duty of bringing to justice persons who have broken the law. In Bodkin's opinion it was undesirable that investigators into crime should also act as advocates who present to the court, as prosecutors, the circumstances of the crime. By the same token, it was regarded as outside the normal functions of the Director of Public

---

[1] Edwards, *Law Officers of the Crown*, pp. 342–344.
[2] Cmnd. 3297, paras. 226–228.
[3] Cmnd. 1728, p. 114, paras. 380–381.
[4] See Edwards, *op. cit.* p. 395.

Prosecutions, and his staff, to engage in the actual investigation of alleged crimes.[5] That role, the 1929 Royal Commission declared, should continue to be the responsibility of the police. "The only ground for withdrawal in any particular instance" the same report observed, "should be that the police are not competent for the task, whether on account of the intricacy or complexity of the case, or on account of their inexperience, as occasionally happens in a small county force. In all ordinary circumstances we consider that the present practice should be maintained."[6] The major changes in organisation that in the 1960s and 1970s effectively reduced the multiplicity of local police forces to the network of regional police forces[7] has, if anything, served to reinforce the reluctance of the Director of Public Prosecutions to encroach upon the division of functions as expressed by Sir Archibald Bodkin in 1929.

NEW PRECEDENTS SET IN THE POULSON AFFAIR

Before we move on to examine the converse claims of the police that their exercise of prosecutorial discretion is an integral part of their duties of law enforcement and should be retained, it is worthy of particular note that in recent years situations have arisen in the course of which, to meet exceptional circumstances, the Attorney General has been actively involved in the development and execution of investigative strategies. The office of the Director of Public Prosecutions has also been involved but I can think of no prior precedent to the extraordinary participation in the early 1970s of the principal Law Officer of the Crown in guiding and controlling the choice of targets in a major police investigation of corruption among public officials. This role arose in connection with the *Poulson* affair, a large scale conspiracy involving a considerable number of persons occupying prominent positions in public life, including at least one senior Minister of the Crown. The allegations of corruption associated with the Poulson disclosures were largely instrumental in the setting up in 1974 of the Royal Commission on Standards of Conduct in Public Life, under the chairmanship of Lord Salmon.[8] The evidence tendered to the Commission showed that, over the years, Mr. Poulson had succeeded in corruptly penetrating high levels of the civil service, the national health service, two nationalised industries and a number of local authorities including, in one case, the chairman of a police authority. The network of corruption also extended downwards to implicate some 300 persons, most of them in subordinate positions, whose activities were deemed to be of a

---

[5] *Ibid.*
[6] *Ibid.*
[7] As a result of the amalgamations executed in 1966 and 1974 the number of police forces outside London was reduced from 117 to 41. These now range from an establishment of about 6,000 in Greater Manchester and the West Midlands to 800 in Northamptonshire—see T.A. Critchley *op. cit.* pp. 298–301.
[8] Details of the "Poulson affair" are given in Chapter 2 of the Royal Commission's [the Salmon] Report, Cmnd. 6524 of 1976, pp. 5–9.

relatively minor character.[9] The sheer scale of the potential police investigation, diverting the scarce ranks of trained fraud investigators in the Metropolitan and City of London police forces, compelled the setting of limits to the investigation. From the moment when the Attorney General, Sir Peter Rawlinson, gave his formal consent in June 1973 to the prosecution of the principal figures in the conspiracy and it was apparent that the continuation of the investigation was inevitable, the same Law Officer appointed a team of senior counsel to be committed full time to the case and to represent the Attorney in such investigations.[10] By May 1974, further consideration was given to the scope of the ongoing inquiry and the new Attorney General, Mr. Silkin, gave his approval to the guidelines that both controlled the investigative boundaries and the ensuing selection of persons against whom charges of corruption would be brought.[11] These guidelines were designed to concentrate the prosecutions, and thereby the scope of the police investigations, to major cases of public importance. In the result, six further individuals, the majority of these being public servants, were charged with criminal offences under the Prevention of Corruption Acts.[12]

Exceptional as the circumstances in the *Poulson* affair turned out to be, the policies followed in that investigation were consistent with that resorted to at the higher reaches of the prosecution machinery in which the Director of Public Prosecutions is required to, and the Law Officers may elect to, play an active part. In such situations it is abundantly clear that decisions of prosecution policy are made at the Director's or Attorney General's level of authority. "It is they who decide whether great resources in time and skill should be deployed in bringing home to a man or group of men the consequences of their criminal actions."[13] Describing the handling of the *Poulson* case in retrospect, Mr. Silkin, the Attorney General, filled in some of the gaps contained in the briefest of accounts provided by the Salmon Commission in its report.[14] The investigators, he explained, were consulted, advised, said what they thought was practicable and what was not, and made suggestions as to how essential evidence might be

[9] *Loc. cit.*
[10] Heading the team of counsel committed full time to the case were Mr. John Cobb, Q.C. (later the Hon. Mr. Justice Cobb, deceased 1977) and Mr. Peter Taylor, Q.C. (now the Hon. Mr. Justice Taylor).
[11] Salmon Report, p. 7.
[12] In its report the Salmon Commission confessed to the doubts it entertained whether Mr. Poulson would ever have been prosecuted but for his bankruptcy (and the ensuing cross examination as to his financial affairs) and his habit of meticulously preserving copies of everything that he wrote or that was written to him—however incriminating these pieces of paper might be. Had it not been for the combination of these two factors, the Commission concluded, Poulson and his country-wide network of accomplices might well still be carrying on their corrupt practices today—*ibid.* para. 24. The recommendations of the Royal Commission are not directly germane to the present work but were intended to make it much more difficult for anything resembling the Poulson affair to recur.
[13] Attorney General Silkin, in a speech to the Somerset and South Avon Magistrates at Bath, February 23, 1979—unpublished.
[14] *Loc. cit.*

established. In short, the role of the police investigators was not purely mechanical. Mr. Silkin continued: " . . . in the end the decision whether to prosecute, or whether to continue a prosecution or to close the file is the Director's or the Law Officer's. And for that decision the Law Officer is, directly or indirectly, responsible to Parliament. This division of function has never, to my knowledge, created any real problem. I came closest to it in the *Poulson* series of cases. Because of the widespread corruption associated with Mr. Poulson my predecessor created, and I inherited, a closely knit system, in which Law Officers, the Director, counsel, a carefully picked police team and accountants, worked together under my general supervision until we were able to say 'the policy of law enforcement does not require us to go further.' We could indeed have gone another two years if we had thought it right to scoop up all the minnows or those who had unwisely accepted some stupid little benefit as an investment in future possibilities rather than current advantages. The system worked well. At the meeting when we finally decided to draw the line, that was a decision with which we all agreed."[15]

What distinguished the *Poulson* trials was the frank recognition that, as a matter of everyday practice in the English administration of justice, it is often extremely difficult to abide by a strict demarcation of functions. In theory, the investigative strategy and decision making are said to be wholly within the police domain, whilst the subsequent decisions as to prosecution, if made by the Director of Public Prosecutions or the Attorney General, are said to be discharged in an atmosphere of insulation and objectivity.[16] After studying the system in place in other countries,

---

[15] *Loc. cit.*

[16] A more recent illustration of the consequences attendant upon the direct involvement of a representative of the D.P.P.'s office in a major crime investigation that turned sour is the series of allegations and counter-allegations surrounding the handling of "Operation Countryman." This prolonged inquiry into allegations of corruption involving members of the Metropolitan London Police was originally headed by Mr. Arthur Hambleton, Chief Constable of Dorset. In the course of a Granada television programme on August 3, 1982 Mr. Hambleton, by then retired, accused the D.P.P. of failing to support the investigation. This charge appears to have been based on the Director's refusal to sanction a number of prosecutions that the police investigators felt were warranted. In assigning a member of his Department to full time duties with the police investigators in Operation Countryman, there is no suggestion that the D.P.P. was thereby divesting himself of the final responsibility for deciding whether to approve the institution of criminal proceedings. In a statement refuting Mr. Hambleton's accusations, Sir Thomas Hetherington said that he refused throughout Countryman to abuse his office by starting prosecutions where the evidence did not justify action, adding "it is to be regretted that Mr. Hambleton has now seen fit to stigmatize this adherence to principle as obstruction." The temptation for the police, who have invested much time and energy in criminal investigations, to view decisions by the prosecuting authority not to proceed with criminal charges as irrefutable evidence of non-cooperation, if nothing more, is again demonstrated by the recent furor surrounding the Countryman affair. The episode underlines the importance of emphasising the separate roles of the police and the D.P.P. The maintenance of this dividing line should not be prejudiced by making available to the investigators the legal resources of an experienced prosecutor. The practice appears not to have created any problems in the handling of the Poulson affair but Operation Countryman involved the investigation of alleged criminal acts by members of Britain's largest police force and thus created additional problems of its own. See *The Times*, August 4 and 5, 1982, and

including those involving the United States district attorneys, Crown attorneys in the Canadian provinces, and the Scottish procurators fiscal, the Royal Commission on Criminal Procedure in 1981 concluded that "the two roles overlap and intertwine. This is partly because the decision to prosecute is not a single intellectual act of a single person at an identifiable moment in the pre-trial process but it is made up of a series of decisions of a widely different kind made by many people at various stages in the process."[17] Accurate as this portrayal is of the comparative systems referred to, the description contains within it the very essence of the debate that continues to surround the separation issue. Unless the various participants have before them a clear understanding of the different considerations that must govern a decision to prosecute, as opposed to pursuing investigative leads and accumulating relevant evidence, the natural tendency is to accord increasing significance to the investment of time, money and human energy that has preceded each stage of the process.

It is precisely this awareness of the human inclination that hitherto has strengthened the resolve in the English system to maintain a functional separation of duties and which makes the handling of the *Poulson* affair so exceptional. In saying this, it is recognised that the Director of Public Prosecutions and his Assistant Directors, in discharging their statutory mandate with respect to those offences reportable to the Director's office by chiefs of police, are entitled to call upon the police to provide the fullest information they deem necessary. These powers provide a natural vehicle for controlling the scope and direction of police investigations, if such action becomes necessary. Normally, the process is one of consultation and exchange of views, each side bringing a particular body of expertise to the resolution of problems as they arise. Within the statutory categories of offences calling for involvement by the Director the directing hand behind the investigative activities is the professional staff in the office of Public Prosecutions. This situation prevails irrespective of the size and resources of the police force concerned. In the field of crimes specifically included within the Prosecution of Offences Regulations the Director's edicts have the force of law. This is not true, however, in the much larger area of crimes not encompassed within the Regulations and this is so notwithstanding the existence of a prosecuting solicitor's department associated with a

---

the *Sunday Times*, August 8, 1982. Speaking later in the House of Commons, the Attorney General criticised some of the investigative procedures followed by the police assigned to Operation Countryman and rejected complaints that the team's investigators had been obstructed by the D.P.P. Sir Michael Havers described his meeting with Mr. Hambleton and Sir Peter Mathews, who took over direction of the Countryman investigation, as follows: "We went through everything that was there. In the end the only obstruction I could identify was, for example, that the D.P.P. could not agree to a general immunity against anybody that he [Hambleton] wanted to call as a witness, even when it might be in a serious armed robbery. Directors have for years refused to give blanket immunities of that sort"—*Daily Telegraph*, October 26, 1982.

[17] Cmnd. 8092, p. 133, para. 6.30.

police force. To the problems that have emerged from this kind of relationship we will return shortly and we shall see how prosecution policy is determined by the investigators, the police. They may take the lawyer's advice but the decision is that of the local chief constable. There remains the power of the Director of Public Prosecutions to intervene if he is disposed to "take over" the prosecution but this power is rarely exercised.

DECISION MAKING AND AUTHORITY IN POLICE PROSECUTIONS

At this stage of my analysis we can identify two distinct sectors in the criminal prosecution process, as it applies within England and Wales. In the first of these, at the apex of the organisation and wielding the supreme legal authority is the Attorney General, with the Director of Public Prosecutions immediately subordinate to him but effectively making most of the prosecutorial decisions. The boundaries of this sector are to be found in the list of crimes contained in the latest set of regulations to be promulgated under the authority of the Prosecution of Offences Act 1879 to 1979. Within this sphere of investigative activity and the making of decisions whether or not to prosecute there may well be a substantial measure of input by the police but the final word rests in the hands of the Law Officers of the Crown or the Director of Public Prosecutions, as the situation demands. In the other sector to which we will next turn, there is no national organisation comparable to that just described and presided over by the Attorney General. What we see instead is a series of police fiefdoms in which the ultimate say, both with respect to the allocation of investigative resources and the ensuing prosecution decision making, is, according to present English constitutional law, vested in the local chief constable.[18]

The extent of the power exercised by chief constables in this regard is vividly demonstrated by the fact that, even at the Central Criminal Court in London, where it is generally believed the most serious criminal trials are conducted, some 80 per cent. of these prosecutions are police prosecutions, the remainder being under the control of the Director of Public Prosecutions.[19] The frustrations of one Attorney General in this regard were described in these terms: " . . . I have no standing to advise Chief Constables that police resources, and indeed court resources, might in certain areas be better employed than in the pursuit of colourful magazines or over insolent youths . . . My Parliamentary colleagues, or opponents, may and do get very hot under the collar when I play with a dead bat their calls upon me to secure the arrest, trial, sometimes even impeachment of pickets, city sharks or racial bigots—or should I say sturdy

[18] For a discussion of the historical background to the present legal position of chief constables, see the ancillary report by the Phillips Commission "*The Investigation and Prosecution of Criminal Offences in England and Wales—The Law and Procedure*," 1981, Cmnd. 8092—1, Chapters 1 and 5.

[19] *Per* Mr. Silkin in his address to the Somerset and South Avon Magistrates, *ante*, fn. 13.

trade unionists, influential businessmen and lovers of free speech. I may, and in some cases do, refer such questions to the Director, who then asks the police to investigate and report to him. In matters of considerable importance, as where my consent to a prosecution would be required, I may take that course. But it is certainly not for me to advise Chief Constables to station officers on picket lines or to send out panda cars in search of football hooligans. Those are matters within their own responsibility. They must make the decisions. Unlike myself, they are not answerable to Parliament for them."[20] Our present concern is less with the accountability of chief constables for every administrative decision taken in discharge of their responsibilities for preventing crime and maintaining law and order, but rather with the specific questions of control and accountability in relation to prosecutorial decisions made by the force without reference to the Director or the Law Officers of the Crown.

After the active debate on this subject that preceded the 1978–81 Royal Commission on Criminal Procedure it is satisfying to read the Commission's perceptive evaluation of the present law and to note its specific recommendations which are designed to trim the existing unlimited authority of chief constables within that sector of the prosecution process which is our present concern.[21] We can expect the police lobbying against the Commission's recommendations to continue, since their basic premise rests on the fundamental assumption that the discretion to prosecute is an integral part of law enforcement. To remove that discretion from the police, to deprive them of the final say in whether a particular offender is brought before the courts, as the Commission interpreted the police evidence to be saying, would be to seriously hamper them in their primary function of maintaining law and order, because it would be likely to diminish the constable's authority. Stated in a slightly different form, the police submissions argued that there was no strong evidence that the police have fulfilled their functions as prosecutors less than adequately. Removing the decision from them would be an arbitrary and doctrinaire expression of the public's lack of confidence in their competence and integrity and would likely be damaging to morale and hence to effectiveness in law enforcement.[22] A majority of the Royal Commission members were unwilling to accept the force of this line of reasoning[23] though the report makes one particularly telling point on the question of innate bias prompted by the earlier police involvement in investigating a case. "It may perhaps be true" the Commission acknowledged "that the investigator is psychologically committed to a belief in the guilt of the subject and is therefore incapable of making a dispassionate decision on whether or not to prosecute. His decision to proceed may be influenced by factors which

---

[20] *Loc. cit.*
[21] Phillips Commission Report, *op. cit.* Chapter 7, pp. 144–170.
[22] *Ibid.* para. 7.12, p. 148.
[23] *Ibid.*

can never be put in evidence (perhaps information from an informer). But we have not been made aware of any systematic empirical evidence that supports it in relation to investigators as a group. It may be equally true that lawyers who spend their professional lives working in a prosecution agency become just as committed to securing convictions as police officers are said to do."[24] In the same vein the Commission noted that "cases that have been handled from an early point by the Director of Public Prosecutions are among those which some have criticised as displaying bad judgment in the decision to prosecute."[25] All of these observations contain elements of subjectivity. There does not exist, nor is there likely to be created in the foreseeable future, with all the resources claimed by computer technology, an infallible set of discretionary yardsticks that, in their application to particular cases, will result in universal approbation.

PROSECUTING SOLICITORS AND THEIR RELATIONSHIP TO CHIEF CONSTABLES

What disturbed the Royal Commission on the Police in 1962 was the inadequacy of legal advice available to the police in making decisions as to possible criminal prosecutions and also their assumption of the prosecutor's role at the trial. It recommended that consideration be given to the appointment of a prosecuting solicitor for every force where this is not already the practice.[26] On the subject of police advocacy the 1962 Commission recommended that " . . . the employment in England and Wales of police officers as advocates for the prosecution be reviewed. The practice in this respect varies from place to place. In some large cities salaried lawyers are employed to undertake police prosecutions, but elsewhere we understand that full-time police prosecutors undertake this duty. There is also much variety in the type of offence which is regarded as appropriate for police advocacy. In general, we think it is undesirable that police officers should appear as prosecutors except for minor cases. In particular, we deplore the regular employment of the same police officers as advocates for the prosecution. Anything which tends to suggest to the public mind the suspicion of alliance between the court and the police cannot but be prejudicial."[27] The impetus provided by this statement of policy has wrought significant changes to the point where, as the Phillips Commission reported in 1981, at the present time 31 of the 41 police forces scattered across the length and breadth of England and Wales have prosecuting solicitors' departments of varying establishments.[28] The

---

[24] *Ibid.* para. 6.29, p. 133.
[25] *Ibid.* para. 6.27, p. 133.
[26] Final Report, Cmnd. 1728, paras. 380–381.
[27] *Ibid.*
[28] Cmnd. 8092–1, para. 141. For an authoritative survey and analysis of the prosecuting solicitors' departments in existence at the time of the recent Royal Commission on Criminal Procedure, see the reports prepared by M. Weatheritt and D.R. Kaye: *The Prosecution System—Organisational Implications of Change*, Research Studies Nos. 11 and 12 (H.M.S.O., 1980).

number of legally qualified staff now available to a chief constable and the members of his force, both to render legal advice before the trial and to represent the police in any ensuing criminal proceedings, varies in accordance with the size of the force concerned. Greater Manchester, for example, has 59 lawyers on staff, Merseyside 37, South Wales 29, down to the more modest complements of 8 in Durham, 10 in Devon and Cornwall and 5 in Gloucestershire.[29] The Metropolitan London Police has for a long time had a solicitor's department of its own, whereas the City of London Police uses the resources of the legal department of the Common Council.[30] To round off this brief survey it should be noted that in several of the police forces presently without a legal department of any kind a request for such an establishment has been made by the local chief constable. As a substitute arrangement the services of local private firms of solicitors are resorted to on an ad hoc basis.

With the growth in numbers and influence represented by the body of prosecuting solicitors in the closest contact with the police it is not surprising that there surfaced in the late 1970s a well orchestrated campaign to increase the authority of the legal advisers and correspondingly make inroads into the unfettered discretion of chief constables.[31] Leading the way in this exercise has been the Prosecuting Solicitors' Society representing the 660 qualified lawyers who want a greater say in the making of decisions by the police as to prosecution. The Society ensured that the recent Royal Commission on Criminal Procedure had a comprehensive appreciation of the system as it presently exists.[32] This is conveniently summarised in the Commission's report as follows: "There are no nationally prescribed standards for the organizational arrangements of prosecuting solicitors' departments. The prosecuting solicitor and his staff may be employed by the police authority itself, or they may be on the staff of the local authority (perhaps with other duties to perform on behalf of that authority). There is little uniformity in their terms and conditions of service and no unified career structure throughout the country. Similarly, there are wide variations in the type and amount of work done by the prosecuting solicitors' departments and the way the work is handled. Some are highly centralised, with solicitors going out from one office to the various courts; others are decentralised, with one or two solicitors permanently attached to one area of the force. In some cases the prosecuting solicitor is employed full time on police work, in others he may

---

[29] Cmnd. 8092–1, App. 22.

[30] As of August 31, 1980, the number of legally qualified staff totalled 62—*loc. cit.*

[31] See, *e.g.* the Law Society's memorandum: "The Office of Prosecuting Solicitor," 1972; J.A. Sigler: "Public Prosecution in England and Wales" [1974] Crim. L.R. 642–651, and P.K.L. Danks: "The Public Prosecutor" *The Magistrate*, October 1970, pp. 148–149. For the contrary position, see A.S. Bowley: "Prosecution—A Matter for the Police" [1975] Crim. L.R. 442–447, and J.D. Devlin: "Police Prosecutors," (1970) *Police Review* 1245.

[32] See *Written Evidence and Minutes of Oral Evidence by the Prosecuting Solicitors' Society of England and Wales*, and Appendix A to the Home Office memorandum no. 8 on "The Prosecution Process," pp. 32–35, submitted to the Phillips Commission.

also occasionally prosecute on behalf of the local authority or agencies such as the British Transport Police; and the police may also make use of private firms of solicitors. The kind and proportion of cases in which the prosecuting solicitor is asked for advice, the stage at which he is called in, and the proportion of summary cases in which he conducts the prosecution case also vary. But broadly, the functions of prosecuting solicitors may be summarized as the conduct of prosecutions in magistrates' courts, briefing counsel in trials on indictment and advising the police on prosecution matters. They have no responsibility for investigations."[33]

Such broad variations in the practice followed in individual forces should not obscure the one fundamental-aspect of the relationship between each chief constable and the local prosecuting solicitor, whether employed full time or ad hoc as a solicitor in private practice. It is always that of a client and solicitor relationship. The solicitor may tender advice to the chief constable or subordinate police officer and the degree of mutual confidence that has built up between them over a period of time may result in the solicitor's opinion being invariably followed. Nevertheless, the final decision on whether a prosecution should be brought, for what offences and against which individuals, rests in the hands of the police.[34]

The Director of Public Prosecutions' Overriding Discretion to Intervene and its Implications

As will be readily appreciated this relationship differs markedly from that which obtains in the sector of criminal prosecutions described earlier, where the final word is by law vested in the Director of Public Prosecutions. For purposes of comparison it will be recalled that the paramountcy of the Director of Public Prosecutions extends beyond those offences which by statute require his formal consent. It also includes the list of specific crimes in which, if there is a prima facie case, the chief constable must send the police file to the Director for his decision. And, since the enactment of the Prosecution of Offences Regulations 1978, the Director is further empowered to specify, from time to time, such other cases as appear to him to be of importance or difficulty or for any other reason require his intervention.[35] Such discretionary specifications also impose a mandatory duty upon each chief constable to comply,[36] thus transferring effective control over the disposition of individual cases to the Director of Public Prosecutions.

Theoretically, the most powerful discretion available to the Director is that presently contained in the Prosecution of Offences Act 1979, s.4.

[33] Cmnd. 8092–1, para. 142, p. 52.
[34] *Ibid*. para. 143.
[35] See reg. 6(2).
[36] *Ibid*.

Repeating the language of earlier enactments it provides that "Nothing in this Act shall preclude any person from instituting or carrying on any criminal proceedings; but the Director may undertake, at any stage, the conduct of those proceedings, if he thinks fit." Although the above language is silent on the matter it is hardly open to question that in taking over proceedings the Director may elect to continue with the prosecution or to discontinue the case against the accused by offering no further evidence.

The enormous breadth of this statutory power has been approached with circumspection by successive Directors, preferring to limit its invocation to extraordinary circumstances[37] of which, as we have already seen, the recent cases of *D.P.P.* v. *Turner*[38] and *Raymond* v. *Attorney General*[39] provide unprecedented illustrations. In both instances the Director of Public Prosecutions intervened to take over a private prosecution launched by a convicted person against his erstwhile accomplice who had elected to give evidence for the Crown and eventually contributed to the guilty verdict. In *D.P.P.* v. *Turner* a formal undertaking to confer immunity from criminal proceedings had been negotiated between the police, the accomplice's solicitor and the Department of Public Prosecutions. The immunity implications of this case will be postponed until Chapter 14, but it should be recalled that the challenge to the exercise of the Director's statutory power under section 2(3) of the Prosecution of Offences Act 1908 (now embodied in section 4 of the Prosecution of Offences Act 1979) was dismissed, there being no evidence of *mala fides* and the *ultra vires* argument being unsupportable in the light of the statutory provision under which the Director had purported to act.[40]

In *Raymond* v. *Attorney General* the Director intervened at a much later stage of the proceedings, and then only when his attention was drawn by the justices' clerk to the dilemma created by the original accused laying

---

[37] *D.P.P.'s Written Evidence* to the Royal Commission on Criminal Procedure, December 1978, para. 214, p. 76. In his memorandum, Hetherington wrote: "The protection against unjustified prosecution lies, in my view, with the courts. Justices have a discretion whether to grant process under s.1 of the Magistrates Court Act 1952. If process is granted to a private prosecutor, the case should, in my view, be allowed to proceed subject to the normal rules of evidence and procedure." Commenting on the apparent change of attitude towards the right of private prosecution that has taken place in the past fifty years the D.P.P. recalled that in 1972, during the passage through Parliament of the Criminal Justice Act, "at one stage a clause was proposed which would have excluded private prosecutions except where the prosecutor had statutory authority or where the offence was such that on conviction the court could have made an order of compensation or restitution," (para. 215, p. 77). Adhering to the departmental practice referred to in the text above, the D.P.P. declined to intervene in a case where the West Midlands Regional Health Authority had initiated criminal proceedings, under the Midwives Act 1951, against a father who delivered his wife's baby without medical supervision—*The Times*, June 19, 1982.
[38] (1978) 68 Cr.App. R. 70.
[39] [1982] 2 W.L.R. 849. An earlier application by Raymond for an order of mandamus directed against the D.P.P. was summarily dismissed by the C.A.—see (1979) 70 Cr.App.R. 233.
[40] See *ante*, pp. 26–27 and *post*, pp. 91–93.

informations against his confederate, *inter alia*, for alleged perjury committed at the preliminary hearing of the original charges against Raymond. After some initial hesitation the Director intervened in the private prosecution commenced by Raymond, being persuaded that the informant's action was vexatious, designed to discredit the witness who had turned Queen's evidence and not aimed at bringing him to justice.[41] Counsel representing the Director offered no evidence against the defendant who was accordingly discharged. Dissatisfied with the outcome of his efforts to invoke the criminal law in pursuit of his goal to exact vengeance, Raymond met further obstacles in his attempt to obtain an order of mandamus requiring the Director to pursue the charges laid against his former accomplice. The same results were forthcoming in his subsequent proceedings seeking an injunction and a series of declarations against the Director of Public Prosecutions and his senior colleagues.[42]

The true significance of *Raymond* v. *Attorney General* lies in the pronouncements of the Court of Appeal, defining the limits of the Director's discretion under section 4 of the Prosecution of Offences Act 1979 to undertake "the conduct" of a prosecution commenced privately. Delivering the judgment of the court Sir Sebag Shaw drew attention to the distinction embedded in the statute law and which has remained unchanged since it was first enacted in the Prosecution of Offences Act 1908, s.2(3). Thus, while any private citizen may institute or "carry on" any criminal prosecution the Director's power is defined in terms of the right to undertake, at any stage, the "conduct" of the proceedings. In the opinion of the Court of Appeal, Parliament intended to confer a more expansive discretionary authority upon the Director of Public Prosecutions than that reaffirmed with respect to the private citizen. "The word 'conduct' " it was stated, "appears to be wider than the phrase 'carry on' and suggests to our minds that when the Director intervenes in a prosecution which has been privately instituted he may do so not exclusively for the purpose of pursuing it by carrying it on, but also with the object of aborting it; that is to say he may 'conduct' the proceedings in whatever manner may appear expedient in the public interest. The Director will thus intervene in a private prosecution where the issues in the public interest are so grave that the expertise and the resources of the Director's office should be brought to bear in order to ensure that the proceedings are properly conducted from the point of view of the prosecution. On the other hand there may be what appears to the Director substantial reasons in the public interest for not pursuing a prosecution privately commenced."[43]

Reverting to the administrative policies within the Department of Public Prosecutions, as explained by the present Director to the Royal Commis-

[41] See [1982] 2 W.L.R. 852.
[42] See *ante*, fn. 39.
[43] [1982] 2 W.L.R. 854.

sion on Criminal Procedure,[44] the practice appears to have evolved that the statutory "take-over" power under what is now section 4 of the Prosecution of Offences Act 1979 should only be exercised with respect to truly private prosecutions in contradistinction to what are generally described as police prosecutions. In support of this interpretation it can be argued that the special relationship between chiefs of police and the Director of Public Prosecutions is precisely defined in the Prosecution of Offences Regulations, and that the Director is thereby confined to operating within the specific limitations on the chief constables' prosecutorial discretion provided for in those regulations. The fact remains, however, that the language of the enabling Act of Parliament is unconditional and unequivocal. The Director has the legal authority to undertake, at any stage, the conduct of proceedings instituted by a private prosecutor, if the Director thinks that he should do so. This statutory provision, first enacted in 1908, has the potential for controlling *any* police prosecution, there being no authority that I know of which makes "private prosecutions" and "police prosecutions" mutually exclusive.

Resort to the Director's overriding discretion, it might be argued, has been diminished by the terms of regulation 6(2) of the 1979 Regulations which states: "The chief officer of every police area shall give to the Director of Public Prosecutions such information as he may require with respect to such other cases as the Director of Public Prosecutions may from time to time specify as appearing to him to be of importance or difficulty or for any other reason requiring his intervention." The obligation of the chief constable, it will be noted, is to supply information. The regulation clearly visualises the possibility of intervention by the Director but does not expressly authorise the substitution of the Director's discretion for that of the chief constable. The legal authority for any such intervention by the Director of Public Prosecutions, displacing the police prosecutor, rests in the long line of statutory provisions culminating in the present section 4 of the Prosecution of Offences Act 1979. Its shadow pervades every communication between the office of the Director of Public Prosecutions and the police forces of this country. And behind the shadow of the Director of Public Prosecutions and his overriding powers of control lies the Attorney General with his superintendence over the Director and ultimate accountability to Parliament.

If the conclusions advanced here are constitutionally valid it may seem strange to note the reluctance of the present Director of Public Prosecutions to assert any claim to a universal, dominant role in any new system of prosecutions that might have been recommended by the Royal Commission on Procedure. In his written submission to the Commission, Sir Thomas Hetherington rejected any argument that the office he occupied has become largely superfluous. This suggestion derived from the fact that one of the principal reasons for the office's creation in 1879, *viz.*,

---

[44] *D.P.P.'s Written Evidence, op. cit.* pp. 76–77.

the provision of legal advice and general guidance to the police, was now adequately dealt with at the local level by the network of prosecuting solicitors. On the contrary, the Director argued " . . . there is still a need, and perhaps a growing need, for a central prosecuting agency, responsible for advising the police and undertaking the conduct of cases of importance or difficulty."[45] The emphasis, it will be noted, was on the Director's *advisory* role, a theme that is consistently adhered to in all of Sir Thomas Hetherington's statements on this subject. This principal function is not looked upon as disqualifying the Director from direct intervention, but such intervention is viewed as confined to cases of particular complexity or difficulty, either because of the nature of the case itself or because of the type of offence which is involved. This policy reflects the approach adopted in the 1978 Regulations with its accent on flexibility in the categories of offence which have to be reported to the Director of Public Prosecutions.

PROPOSALS FOR REFORM—DO WE NEED A NATIONAL PROSECUTING SERVICE?

Earlier I referred to the proposals for reform advanced by the Prosecuting Solicitors' Society, the essential characteristics of which will suffice for the present.[46] We shall examine the full ramifications of the Society's propositions later. These envisage the removal of the power presently exercised by the chief constables of deciding whether or not there should be criminal proceedings and its transfer to the local prosecuting solicitors. In effect, the prosecuting solicitor would cease to be the legal adviser to the police and instead would assume a position of independence qua the local chief constable. Such a radical change in functions and responsibility received no support from the present Director of Public Prosecutions. Several objections to the proposal were identified in the Director's submission to the Royal Commission. First, Hetherington stated, "For well over a century, the responsibility for bringing the majority of criminal proceedings in England and Wales has rested with the police, and in my view such a radical change as that suggested by the Prosecuting Solicitors' Society, which would also entail the virtual abolition of the right to private prosecution, could only be justified by evidence of public disquiet with the existing arrangement or of more than isolated examples of their abuse. I am aware of no such evidence and am therefore unable to support the proposition."[47] Secondly, he continued, "In reaching this conclusion, I also have it in mind that any such switch of responsibility would not result in any greater accountability to either Parliament or the public, it being envisaged that the prosecuting solicitor would be subject, not to the control of the Attorney General, but only his 'influence.' "[48] The present Director, however, stepped back from

[45] *Written Evidence, op. cit.* p. 94, paras. 251–252.
[46] See *ante*, fn. 32.
[47] *Written Evidence, op. cit.* p. 95, para. 255.
[48] *Ibid.*

recognising the logical consequences of his analysis, and declined to accept that his objections to the proposed scheme "could be overcome by making the prosecuting solicitor subject to my directions, both generally, by way of code of practice and procedure . . . and specifically in such individual cases as I thought fit."[49] "I have come to the conclusion" said Hetherington "that such an arrangement would create a structure which, in the context of England and Wales, would be unwieldy and difficult to operate efficiently . . . "[50] The main thrust of the Director's opposition to expanding his responsibilities, either directly or through area directors reporting to him, to include both the tendering of advice and the conduct of the prosecution in all those cases, or all indictable crimes, which currently fall outside his jurisdiction, was an aversion to the massive organisational changes that would ensue. In other words, the objection stemmed from the practical implications of the proposed changes and not from any theoretical grounds. Hetherington's position can be summed up in his final statement that "if the value of the office of the Director of Public Prosecutions is to be maintained, it is important to restrict 'Director's cases,' both in the advisory and prosecuting roles, to cases of real importance or difficulty with national significance."[51] If a degree of uniformity in the application of the criminal law was a desirable goal "the better way of achieving this is by improving the arrangements for liaison on policy relating to the prosecution of offenders, perhaps by making more precise arrangements for the issue of guidance or general policy from my Department, and the acceptance of it by local prosecutors."[52]

The same general position of advocating the continuance of the Director's advisory role in all cases falling outside the Director's consent or Attorney General's consent crimes is confirmed in Sir Thomas Hetherington's oral testimony before the Phillips Commission. The Director's preference for maintaining a guiding but hidden presence in the making of prosecutorial decisions reached its zenith when he declared that "general guidance in cases not requiring [my] consent should not be made public, as it might be tantamount to altering the law or be an encouragement to commit offences."[53] The same official stance has been adopted in other jurisdictions when the argument is advanced that public accountability requires more, rather than less, disclosure of the discretionary factors that govern the making of prosecution decisions. The problem is certainly not a straightforward one[54] but it is doubtful if the reasons put forward by the present Director of Public Prosecutions carry with them any innate persuasive value.

[49] *Ibid*. This situation would be analogous to that presently in place in Northern Ireland, the Area Assistant Directors being directly subject to the instructions of the D.P.P. in that province.
[50] *Written Evidence, op. cit.* p. 96, para. 258.
[51] *Ibid*. p. 97, para. 260.
[52] *Ibid*.
[53] *Minutes of Oral Evidence*, February 13, 1980, para. 4.
[54] For a full discussion, see *post*, Chapter 14.

Hetherington's preference for maintaining the *status quo* in the relationship of the chief constable to the local prosecuting solicitor, with the ultimate power of decision making resting with the police, saw one important qualification introduced in the course of the Director's oral evidence before the Commission. In the event that the chief constable's legal adviser, *i.e.* the prosecuting solicitor, disagreed with the police instructions to proceed or not to proceed, it should be open to the prosecuting solicitor to have recourse to the Director of Public Prosecutions for a "second opinion," it being supposed that the Director's opinion would bind the chief constable and be followed.[55] The alternative, of giving the prosecuting solicitor authority not to proceed on legal or evidentiary grounds, with the chief constable having a right of appeal to the Director, was described as an unattractive proposal.[56] No explanation was advanced, however, for the distinction which was drawn between the separate rights of appeal in terms of the likelihood of ill-feeling being generated.

Support for nearly every argument advanced by the Director was forthcoming in the evidence of Sir Michael Havers, the Attorney General who assumed office in the closing stages of the Royal Commission on Criminal Procedure. "I am not" he stated "in favour of a comprehensive public prosecution service responsible for all criminal proceedings; still less do I incline towards a system in which the prosecuting and investigative functions are under the control of the one group of officials."[57] Havers' support for the development of the existing system in preference to the introduction of a national prosecuting service was based on a mixture of practical and theoretical considerations. "A fully developed Prosecuting Solicitor service" he maintained "will provide a fully adequate service, probably at lower cost, with a smaller administrative tail and, above all, one attuned and conscious to local needs. A local Prosecuting Solicitor's Department is also more likely to be aware of and respond to local criminal trends which may mean that an offence, which causes little concern nationally, is of local importance and calls for a stricter prosecution policy inconsistent with overall national requirements."[58] It might be thought that the Attorney General was according an exaggerated interpretation to the concepts of "consistency" and "uniformity" in relation to a nationally organised prosecution service, as espoused by its supporters. In those jurisdictions, outside of England and Wales, where a national or provincial model obtains, the kind of flexibility, about which Sir Michael Havers expressed concern, does not appear to be ignored. It is rather a question of degree, on which individual judgments may well differ.

[55] *Op. cit.* para. 5.
[56] *Ibid.*
[57] *Minutes of Oral Evidence*, January 26, 1980, para. 3.
[58] *Ibid.* paras. 18 and 22. The Attorney General had in mind particularly cases involving moral issues. Citing the attitudes towards pornography as an illustration, Havers explained the difficulties that faced the D.P.P. in applying a consistent prosecution policy without ignoring the genuine feelings of a local community—*ibid.* para. 20.

The Attorney General's approach to the question of ultimate authority as between the police and the prosecuting solicitor was somewhat less than crystal clear. The basic relationship, he believed, should continue to be that of legal adviser and client leaving the ultimate decision of what charges should be preferred to the police.[59] The prosecuting solicitor should play no part in the conduct of police enquiries although he would advise on evidence and the final decision as to which witnesses should be called ought to be his, or counsel's if instructed. Decisions as to the acceptance of pleas to some charges only, according to the Attorney General, ought only to be taken after consultation with the police if circumstances allow. Evidence of the practical results that flow from the solicitor-client relationship, to which reference has been made earlier, lie uncomfortably alongside Sir Michael Havers' description of the same relationship in which, he stated, "It is . . . important that every police force should have available to it a body of skilled and experienced legal advisers who are not dependent on maintaining the goodwill of their client, the police, to assure the flow of work and who can advise as independent legal advisers applying consistent principles to every case."[60] This description would seem to contain an inherent contradiction which, other witnesses before the Commission argued, will only be resolved if the solicitor-client relationship is abolished and the independent power of decision making conferred on the prosecuting solicitor. Havers' solution to the possibility of a serious disagreement arising between the prosecuting solicitor and the police, within the existing relationship, would be to seek counsel's advice, if appropriate, or by referring the matter to the Director of Public Prosecutions who could then consult with the Attorney General if he wanted.[61]

A very different philosophy was enunciated by the former Labour Law Officers, Mr. Sam Silkin and Mr. Peter Archer, who had been largely instrumental in ensuring that the country's prosecution arrangements were included within the Royal Commission's terms of reference. "Whatever arrangements were ultimately adopted" according to Mr. Silkin "it was essential to rationalize the present ramshackle arrangements."[62] Excluded from this severe judgment was the Solicitor's Department in the Metropolitan London Police, which Mr. Silkin conceded worked well. What he wished to see was a series of such departments across the country organised as a national prosecuting service responsible to the Attorney General.[63] He dissociated himself from the submissions made to the Commission, including particularly that by the Director of Public Prosecutions, which suggested that the present arrangements were, generally speaking, working satisfactorily. According to the former

---

[59] *Ibid.* paras. 7 and 8.
[60] *Ibid.* para. 6.
[61] *Ibid.* para. 9.
[62] *Minutes of Oral Evidence* by Mr. Silkin and Mr. Archer, November 14, 1979, para. 2.
[63] *Ibid.* paras. 7 and 8.

Attorney General, that had not been the impression he gained during his five years in office from 1974 to 1979.[64] He referred to criticisms voiced within the legal profession about the working of the present system and especially the operation outside of London of the Director of Public Prosecutions' office.[65] Sir Michael Havers, in the course of his testimony, corroborated Mr. Silkin's observations on the latter aspect of the Director of Public Prosecutions' record.[66] References by both prosecuting solicitors and members of the Bar to occasional attempts by the police to pressure them to pursue a case, or to pursue it in a particular manner, against their professional tenets, were so frequent, according to Mr. Silkin, that he assumed some of them must be justified.[67] He described the gradual transformation in his thinking which led him to the view that in the long term some form of national system was the only viable solution. A visit, when serving as the Attorney General, to study the Crown attorneys system in the Canadian provinces appears to have been particularly influential in shaping Mr. Silkin's judgment of what was needed in England and Wales. In Canada, he explained, the police accepted the situation in which the Crown attorney, a full time prosecutor responsible to the provincial Attorney General, was the final arbiter whether a prosecution should be initiated or continued and for the conduct of the proceedings at the trial on behalf of the Crown. The police acceptance of the Crown prosecutor's role was consistent with the great importance attached by the police to their unfettered right to determine who should be charged and for what offences.[68]

Both of the former Labour Law Officers favoured the separation of the investigation and prosecution functions. Reference was made to ill advised

[64] *Ibid.* para. 2.
[65] *Ibid.*
[66] Havers, *op. cit.* para. 12.
[67] Silkin, *op. cit.* para. 10.
[68] Silkin, *op. cit.* paras. 2 and 8. Those members of the Phillips Commission who visited Canada confined their observations to the prosecution arrangements in the provinces of Ontario and British Columbia. The Royal Commission's conclusions corroborated those of Mr. Silkin, stating: "In both [jurisdictions] the police have full authority for the investigation of crime and for the initial decision to bring a person to court for trial. They it is who lay the charge in the first instance . . . Once the case is in the court system, the conduct of the prosecution is vested entirely in the Crown Counsel or Attorney. He may amend, extend or drop the charges at any stage and cannot be required to proceed by the police:" *Report*, Cmnd. 8092, p. 136. This description, whilst theoretically accurate, gives insufficient recognition to the inherent pressures that derive from the continuous contacts between the Crown attorney or assistant Crown attorney (often with little experience behind him) and the investigating police officer (possibly with many years seniority). To expect automatic deference to the views of the legally qualified prosecutor in such a relationship is to ignore the realities of human interaction—see R.V. Ericson, *Making Crime—A Study of Detective Work*, (Butterworths, Toronto, 1981). Interestingly, in speaking of the United States district attorney and the Scottish procurator fiscal, as they observed these comparative offices, the Phillips Commission concluded that [in the U.S.A.] "the threads of investigation and prosecution are often difficult to disentangle" (*op. cit.* para. 6.34) and [in Scotland] "the line between investigator and prosecutor is not quite as sharp as some of those who gave evidence to us suggested" (*op. cit.*, para. 6.37). Similar conclusions are no less apposite in describing the Canadian system of prosecutions.

prosecutions, albeit not very often, where no proceedings or different charges would have been brought had the criteria used by the Director been applied. In cases where the Director became involved, it was claimed that he frequently found his options limited or effectively closed by earlier action on the part of the police or delay in submitting a case. The model championed by both Mr. Silkin and Mr. Archer would involve the creation of a national prosecution system, the nucleus for which would be the office of the Director of Public Prosecutions.[69] It would be organised on a regional basis outside London, and thus, could offer improved career prospects and tend to attract more and better qualified staff. The Director's office, it was claimed, failed to do that at present because it was too small to offer attractive promotion prospects, an interesting range of work and the opportunity to specialise in particular fields. A decentralised, autonomous system of local prosecuting solicitors, it was argued, could better take account of local conditions but this objective was not seen as paramount to the goals of a co-ordinated prosecution policy and a degree of political and ministerial accountability that was not possible under a series of autonomous local prosecutors.[70]

RECOMMENDATIONS OF THE ROYAL COMMISSION ON CRIMINAL PROCEDURE

When the Report of the Royal Commission on Criminal Procedure was finally made public it soon became evident that the Commissioners were inclined "to secure change with the minimum of upheaval and at the lowest cost possible" and not to ignore "the strength, resilience and complexity of the existing arrangements and institutions."[71] Given this pragmatic approach to the series of problems adverted to by the principal witnesses before the Commission the reader may be forgiven for feeling at times that its recommendations shy away from resolving some of the more controversial issues and, moreover, that its specific proposals do not always relate to the Commission's own exposition of the proper principles that should govern the country's refurbished prosecution system. Briefly, these are greater conformity of general prosecution policies, enhanced efficiency and a higher degree of accountability for the efficient use of resources and for the execution of those policies.[72]

As a first step in the process towards the attainment of these objectives the Phillips Commission recommended that a statutory based prosecution service be established to cover all police forces in England and Wales.[73] In addition to filling the gap left by the incomplete adoption of recommendations made by the Royal Commission on the Police in 1962, it is proposed that the legislation should set out the functions of the prosecution agency in

[69] Silkin & Archer, *Oral Evidence, op. cit.* para. 7.
[70] *Ibid.*
[71] Cmnd. 8092, paras. 7.1 and 7.3, pp. 144–145.
[72] *Ibid.* pp. 127–143.
[73] *Ibid.* p. 145.

fairly precise terms. These would be: "(a) the conduct of all criminal cases once the initial decision to proceed has been taken by the police, (b) the provision of legal advice to the police, as and when requested, on matters relating to the prosecution of offences, and (c) the provision of advocates in the magistrates courts in all cases where proceedings are commenced by the police (apart from guilty pleas by letter under section 1 of the Magistrates Courts Act 1957 which only require someone to read out the statement of facts), and the briefing of counsel in all cases tried on indictment which are not the province of the Director of Public Prosecutions."[74] It will be noted that the Commission, in (a) above, proposes to leave untouched the common law prerogative of the police, as indeed is the case with every private citizen, of deciding whether to lay the original information before a Justice of the Peace charging the accused with a criminal offence. Responsibility for the *conduct* of a case is separated from responsibility for making the *initial decision to proceed*.

This distinction, the Commission emphasised, is a central feature of its proposals that there be a division of functions between the police and the prosecutor. The demarcation of responsibilities is explained in a key paragraph which states: " . . . we would leave with the police complete responsibility for investigating offences and for making the initial decision whether to bring the matter before a court (that is, under present procedures, whether to charge or to apply to the court for issue of a summons or warrant of arrest), or to take no proceedings. It also includes the decision whether to caution as an alternative to prosecution, which in our view should continue to be the responsibility of the police. Once that initial decision has been taken the case is within the jurisdiction of the court. This seems to us to be the clearest point, which, for the purpose of legislation, can be used to mark the division in responsibilities of the police and the prosecutor. After that point the case should become the responsibility of the latter—he may then on the information before him decide to proceed as charged, or to modify or withdraw the charges. In practice there is, of course, a variety of decisions taken as a case is being prepared for trial and is being tried. Those decisions will be for the prosecutor; and it is in that sense that he will have responsibility for the conduct of the case once the initial decision to proceed has been taken . . . In essence what we are proposing is a system in which the local prosecutor will have similar responsibilities locally to those which the Director of Public Prosecutions now has nationally."[75] What this projected system envisages is a major restriction on the existing independence of the police to control throughout the handling of their own prosecutions, including that of presently overriding the prosecuting solicitor's advice. By the same token, it is contemplated that the prosecuting solicitor's status in the later stages of the process will be significantly enhanced by virtue of his

[74] *Ibid.*
[75] *Ibid.* p. 146, paras. 7.7 and 7.8.

independence to decide whether to proceed as charged by the police, or to modify or withdraw the charges.

At one stage in their deliberations, the Commission's report reveals,[76] consideration was given to drawing a different demarcation line between the respective responsibilities of the prosecutor and the police. This would have given the prosecutor the final word in respect of the legal elements in the decision to prosecute, especially the evidentiary issues, leaving with the police the final determination on what were described as social and policy grounds. In the end, this distinction was rejected in favour of that already described, in the hope that both sides will work in partnership and keep unresolvable disputes to a minimum. "If they occur" the Commission concludes "the arrangements we propose for local and national accounta-bility and supervision and for the Director of Public Prosecutions to act as final arbiter should provide the remedy."[77]

It is my intention to deal with the subject of police accountability in the next chapter when consideration will be directed to the choice of forum—the courts or the legislature—for manifesting ultimate control over the machinery of criminal prosecutions and giving effect to the doctrine of ministerial responsibility. I hope to demonstrate at that time the inappropriateness and inadequacy of this aspect of the Commission's solution to situations where both the police and the prosecutor dig their heels in and adopt positions of intransigence. Calls for collaboration and working in partnership are in themselves admirable sentiments but, if the testimony tendered before the Phillips Commission is to be taken seriously, the prospects of differences of opinion arising as to how prosecutorial discretion should be exercised are inevitable. This is likely both in terms of broad policy considerations and in their application to individual cases. The Commission has no views to contribute on the extent to which the Director of Public Prosecutions should act as the final arbiter of disputes at the local level between the chief constable and the Crown prosecutor.

It will be recalled that the present Director, Sir Thomas Hetherington, in giving evidence before the Commission, distinguished between two sets of circumstances.[78] Where the prosecuting solicitor disagreed with the police decision to proceed or not to proceed, Sir Thomas proposed that it should be open to the prosecutor to have recourse to the Director of Public Prosecutions for a second opinion, it being assumed that the Director's ruling would be followed by the chief constable involved. According to the Commission's recommendations, once the initial step of laying an information has been taken by the police their jurisdiction will come to an end and the prosecutor will be free to terminate the proceedings by withdrawing the prosecution's case when it comes before the magistrates'

[76] *Ibid.* p. 149, para. 7.17.
[77] *Ibid.* p. 150.
[78] See *ante,* p. 95, fn. 55 and 56.

court.[79] If this recommendation is adopted, there would be no room for the police to challenge the prosecutor's decision in an appeal to the Director of Public Prosecutions. What would be left is the right of the prosecutor to challenge the police decision *not* to proceed, a situation that clearly exhibits a serious lacuna in the enhanced independent status that, the Commission claims, its proposals represent for the new ranks of Crown prosecutors. If this is indeed what the Commissioners had in mind they should have said so, instead of leaving such a vital question of jurisdiction to be negotiated afresh when the provisions of the proposed new Bill are being developed.[80]

Given the vagueness of the Commission's reference to the Director of Public Prosecutions as final arbiter in disputes between the police and the local prosecutor it would not be surprising if a chief constable felt entitled to appeal to the Director of Public Prosecutions for his advisory ruling in those instances where the police are unhappy with the prosecutor's proposal to undo the results of police investigation by terminating the criminal proceedings launched earlier by the police themselves. However unattractive the present Director may assess this kind of role for himself, we may yet see the police preferring an ultimate right of recourse to the Director of Public Prosecutions over the conferring upon the prosecutor of an unconditional veto over the police decision to proceed with a case.[81] This variation in the scope of the prosecuting solicitor's veto powers is bound to cause difficulties. Moreover, it demonstrates the inappropriateness of the analogy drawn by the Royal Commission in describing its proposed scheme as one in which the local prosecutor will have similar responsibilities locally to those which the Director of Public Prosecutions now has nationally.[82] By virtue of the Director's extensive powers of calling for police files and his duty to institute, undertake or carry on criminal proceedings in any case which appears to him to require his intervention the final say in situations of conflict between the chief

---

[79] Cmnd. 8092, para. 7.7, p. 146.

[80] Speaking in the House of Lords on July 26, 1982, Lord Elton, Under-Secretary for Home Affairs, confirmed that the Government has reservations about the Royal Commission's recommendations regarding the appointment of local Crown prosecutors and wishes to explore alternative systems "which would avoid the dangers both of over-centralisation and of the kind of local accountability which the Commission proposed"—see H.L. Deb., Vol. 434, cols. 112–117. With this purpose in mind the Government has reappointed the inter-departmental working party which carried out a preliminary assessment of the Royal Commission's proposals following the release of the Commission's report in 1981. In December 1982 the working party issued a discussion paper outlining three possible forms of an independent prosecution service. These in-house deliberations are continuing—see [1983] Crim.L.R. 1.

[81] It is worth noting that, in a letter dated January 1983 which had the prior approval of the Attorney General, the D.P.P. has *requested* chief officers of police to consult with him in any case where the police wish to institute or continue criminal proceedings contrary to the advice of the local prosecuting solicitor. And see, too, Home Office Circular No. 26 of 1983 to the like effect.

[82] *Report*, Cmnd. 8092, para. 7.8, p. 146.

constable and the Director is not open to question. The Director's ruling is paramount. No such expansive powers are recommended for the local prosecutors. Consequently, serious doubts must remain in defining the position of the Crown prosecutor, vis-à-vis the police where the latter's decision is not to initiate criminal proceedings.

Among the fundamental objectives set by the Commission for its proposed new prosecution system, it will be recalled, was the establishing of greater conformity of general prosecution policies and accountability for the execution of such policies.[83] Although these two objectives go naturally hand in hand I propose to defer the subject of accountability to a special chapter devoted entirely to this large question. How then, it may be asked, is it proposed that greater conformity of general prosecuting policies will be achieved? The Commission's response can best be described as an expression of faith that, after an initial period in which the guiding hand of the Director of Public Prosecutions would be very much in evidence, the Director's role in local cases would gradually diminish to the point where his involvement would be quite exceptional.[84] The main general criticism of the present arrangements was the delay in handling cases by the Director's office, which was attributed to a lack of resources to meet the substantial pressure of work which has been associated with the general increase in crime. The Commission's answer to this state of affairs, reflecting the sense of reluctance exhibited by the present Attorney General and Director of Public Prosecutions towards an expansion of the Director's office, was against an infusion of new resources to handle the increased volume of cases. "We consider" the report states "that the service we propose will, in time, remove the need for the Director to be brought in by local prosecutors to decide or advise on prosecutions to anything like the extent that he is required to do now, and will thus reduce the pressure upon him and delay in consultation . . . For the time being he will have a key part to play in the development and promulgation of national guidelines on matters of prosecution policy and practice. Once that stage is passed, the need for the Director to be involved in local cases will be diminished. He will retain a major involvement in the maintenance of national consistency of policy and practice. We would see his operational role, however, as being likely to be concentrated on dealing with all allegations of serious criminal offences committed by the police or Crown prosecutor and with other locally sensitive cases; to acting as an arbiter and final authority in the event of a chief constable being dissatisfied with a Crown prosecutor's decision not to proceed in a particular case; to continue to be able to take over the conduct of proceedings in any case, for example, where it became apparent that the local decision had been improperly taken; and to making the decision to prosecute and advising the Attorney General upon the exercise of his

[83] *Ibid.* pp. 138, 145.
[84] *Ibid.* pp. 162–163.

discretion in those classes of case which Parliament considers should be reserved to him."[85]

What is at stake here, as we have seen elsewhere, is a definition of the basic philosophy underlining the role and functions of the Director of Public Prosecutions. If by an operational role is meant the actual direction and handling of a criminal prosecution by a member of the Director of Public Prosecutions' office, or counsel representing the Director, it is easy to comprehend that such occasions would not constitute the run of the mill cases brought before the magistrates' courts. It will also be noted that the Director's operational role as arbiter is envisaged as being confined to appeals by the police against a prosecutor's decision not to proceed, and does not include the converse situation. The other criteria tend to circumscribe the Director's intervention to cases having a particularly local sensitivity and fail to recognise the more expansive interpretation of his role advanced by the Director himself in describing "Director's cases" as those of "real importance or difficulty with national significance," the determination of which would be entirely in the hands of the Director and, if necessary, the Attorney General. The Commission's own projection of a severely limited scope for the Director's intervention is not likely to commend itself to Parliament.

There remains the question of maintaining consistency of prosecution policy and practice. Resort to such phrases as "consistency," "conformity," and "uniformity" is calculated to arouse opposition if what is contemplated is rigid adherence to a detailed set of formal policy statements. It matters not whether these are described as rules, regulations or guidelines, unless a common understanding prevails that any departure from the set norms is not intended to invoke an elaborate machinery for the review of every individual decision. Both from on high and on the local scene there appears to be acceptance of the position that local circumstances will dictate variations in the application of nationally determined guidelines. Whether and when a "variation" becomes a "questionable departure" from nationally set guidelines established by the Director of Public Prosecutions will depend on the circumstances and the perspective of the parties involved. Here again the important question to be resolved in advance of promulgating any such policy guidelines is who has the final word in interpreting the policy and whose decision must prevail in the application of that policy to an individual case.

Speaking to this question of conformity in the application of the criminal law, it will be recalled that Sir Thomas Hetherington eschewed any direct supervisory function on his part with respect to the network of local Crown prosecutors. "The better way of achieving such a goal," he argued before the Phillips Commission, is "by improving the arrangements for liaison or policy relating to the prosecution of offenders, perhaps by making more precise arrangements for the issue of guidance or general policy from my

[85] *Ibid*. para. 7.55, pp. 162–163.

Department, and the acceptance of it by local prosecutors."[86] The key words are acceptance of the Director's policy direction by local prosecutors. Unless, however, the statutory scheme proposed by the Commission makes it clear that such directions have a mandatory character, either expressed in explicit language or indirectly, in the manner contained in the Prosecution of Offences Act empowering the Director to take over any case which he thinks fit, there can be no assurance that the complement of Crown prosecutors, scattered across the length and breadth of the country, will view the Director's policy guidelines and advice as having the force of law. Sheltering behind the paternal image of sage and counsellor will not avert the clash as to the boundaries of responsibility between the Director of Public Prosecutions and the local prosecutors. This question has to be determined first and with it the parallel question of control and accountability. To this subject we next turn.

Update: The Government's Response

In the Queen's Speech on June 22, 1983, the government announced its intention to bring forward legislation that will establish a single national prosecution service for England and Wales, controlled and directed by the Director of Public Prosecutions. The new service, which may take several more years to become a reality, will be based on the principle of independence of the local prosecutors from the local chief of police. The idea of a joint police and prosecutions authority in each area, recommended by the Phillips Commission, has been totally rejected. So has the notion of a police and prosecutions inspectorate. The Attorney General, not the Home Secretary, will be the minister responsible to Parliament for the new prosecution service. Although an expansion of the present D.P.P.'s Department is accepted as inevitable, with a single line of accountability to the Director for resource management, it is expected that the great majority of prosecution decisions will be taken locally in accordance with guidelines issued under the authority of the Attorney General. Prosecution policy and the handling of important or difficult cases will remain the primary responsibility of the Director of Public Prosecutions. The reassembled inter-departmental working party, on whose conclusions the government's legislative plans are based,[87] did its work well in recognising the basic weaknesses in the Royal Commission's report. And the Director has presumably come to terms with his augmented responsibilities. In a word, the nineteenth century campaign for a system of public prosecutions in England and Wales, analogous to that in Scotland, is about to come to fruition.

---

[86] Hetherington, *Written Evidence*, para. 260, p. 98.
[87] The Government's plans, with the working party's report, are contained in a White Paper presented to Parliament to October 1983, Cmnd. 9074.

5

Fundamental Issues of Control and Accountability

During the first quarter of this century the Home Secretary considered it his prerogative to instruct both the Attorney General and the Director of Public Prosecutions on the necessity for prosecuting offences involving interests of state or public security. Particularly in the field of prosecutions that involved considerations of policy relating to matters of internal security we find the Permanent Under-Secretary of State for Home Affairs expressing the firm opinion in 1925 that a distinction had to be drawn between the legal aspects of a case and the question of policy that might be at stake.[1] As to the former, Sir Edward Troup wrote " . . . the Home Secretary would almost always regard the opinion of the Law Officers as final."[2] Within the ambit of policy considerations Troup included the determination whether, in the prevailing circumstances, it would best serve the public interest to prosecute a man or to ignore the offence and avoid giving advertisement to the offenders. As to the resolution of this policy question, Troup asserted, "it is one which the Home Secretary must either decide or, if the matter be of first importance, bring it before the Prime Minister or the Cabinet."[3] Strange as this exposition of constitutional principles governing ministerial responsibility for criminal prosecutions may sound to present day parliamentarians it is an undoubted fact that, on a number of occasions both during and immediately following the First World War, both the government and the notable occupants of the Attorney General's office participated in decisions that effectively transferred the ultimate responsibility for prosecutorial decisions from the Attorney General to the Home Secretary or, beyond him, to the Cabinet of the day.[4]

To understand these deviations from the modern conception of where ministerial control and accountability are said to reside it is necessary to

[1] Edwards, *Law Officers of the Crown.* p. 186, fn. 31.
[2] *Ibid.*
[3] *Ibid.*
[4] *Ibid.* pp. 192–198.

refer to the relevant legislation, at the time, governing the areas of responsibility of the Attorney General and the Home Secretary in the enforcement of the criminal law. Thus, under the Prosecution of Offences Act 1879, s.2, it was provided that "It shall be the duty of the Director of Public Prosecutions under the superintendence of the Attorney General to institute, undertake or carry on such criminal proceedings . . . as may be for the time being prescribed by regulations under this Act or may be directed in a special case by the Attorney General." Among the cases prescribed by the prevailing regulations of 1886 as incumbent upon the Director to institute was the category "where an order in that behalf is given to the Director by the Secretary of State (for Home Affairs) or the Attorney General."[5] No further elaboration was provided in the regulations delineating the specific areas within which the Home Secretary and the Attorney General were to be responsible for assuming the initiative or exercising the final decision whether or not to instruct the Director of Public Prosecutions to proceed.

   Left in this indeterminate position, conflicting claims to exercise ultimate "jurisdiction" might have been expected to arise. All the evidence, however, suggests the contrary and lends support for the view propounded in a memorandum to the Cabinet in 1924 prepared by the then Home Secretary, Sir William Joynson-Hicks, which stated that: "For many years it has been recognized by successive Home Secretaries and Attorneys General that as regards offences involving no question of public security or state interest the decision whether a prosecution in a particular case should be instituted or not was one entirely for the Director and the Attorney General, but that where a prosecution might involve any consideration of public security or any interest of state it was the bounden duty of the Attorney General or the Director before deciding upon a prosecution to ascertain the views of the Ministerial Department best qualified to pronounce upon the public interest involved—the Department in ordinary 'political' cases being the Home Office."[6]

   It will be noted that the Secretary of State was claiming no more than the existence of a duty on the part of the principal Law Officer "to ascertain the view of the Ministerial Department best qualified to pronounce upon the public interest involved." The cases examined in *The Law Officers of the Crown*[7] convey a very different impression as to the practical relationship between the Home Secretary and the Attorney General in the matter of criminal prosecutions. In those cases in which either Sir F.E. Smith or Sir Gordon Hewart was involved, as the Attorney General of the day, there is no indication that the incumbent merely "ascertained the views" of the executive, whether represented in the person of the Home Secretary or of the Cabinet as a whole. The impression, rather, is of the first Law Officer of the Crown concerning himself primarily with the

[5] Reg. 1(c).
[6] Quoted in Edwards, *op. cit.* p. 197.
[7] *Ibid.* pp. 185–198.

technicalities of the criminal law and abdicating the assessment of the policy considerations, which ultimately dictate the course of action to be taken, completely to the executive.[8] There had to be close co-operation in giving effect to the statutory provisions, but the *Campbell* case in 1924 was to focus public and Parliamentary attention on the very delicately adjusted relationship between the Law Officers and the executive branch of government.[9]

The task of comprehending and defining the respective areas of authority exercisable by the Home Secretary and the Attorney General in the administration of criminal justice continued to engage the attention of Parliamentary Select Committees up to 1946. Central to this ambivalence was the responsibility for superintending the work and decisions of the Director of Public Prosecutions.[10] Until 1946 the exact nature of this superintendence was somewhat uncertain, for although the Regulations of 1886 had stated explicitly that "the action of the Director of Public Prosecutions shall, in all matters, including the selection and instruction of counsel, be subject to the directions of the Attorney General," the same regulations made it mandatory for the Director to prosecute any case "when an order in that behalf is given to the Director by the Secretary of State . . . " It is not known when the Home Office's policy of desisting from any interference in the conduct of criminal prosecutions was instituted, though the reverberations of the *Campbell* case must have contributed to the final decision. Certainly, as both the Director of Public Prosecutions and the Permanent Under-Secretary of State of the Home Office testified before the Select Committee on the Obscene Publications Bill in 1958,[11] the Home Secretary's power under the 1886 Regulations had been abandoned in practice long before 1946. It was removed altogether when the departmental regulations were revised in 1946, the constitutional position of the Director of Public Prosecutions being laid down as subject, in all matters including the nomination of counsel, to the directions of the Attorney General.[12] This doctrine, as we saw in the opening chapter, has been left untouched by the Prosecution of Offences Act 1979 and the related Regulations of the previous year.

Political Accountability for Local Prosecutions—A New Role for the Home Office?

A new dimension, however, to the question of political accountability has been opened up by the recommendations of the recent Royal

[8] See, particularly, the handling of the *Rees* (1916), *Morris* (1916), *The Morning Post* (1917), *Ramsay* (1919) and *Diamond* (1920) cases—Edwards, *op. cit.* pp. 192–196.

[9] The details of this all important case, and the subsequent debates in the House of Commons, are recounted in Edwards, *op. cit.* Chap. 11. See further, *post*, pp. 310 *et seq.* and F. H. Newark "The *Campbell* case and the First Labour Government" (1969) 20 N.I.L.Q. 19–42.

[10] Edwards, *op. cit.* pp. 367–389.

[11] *Ibid.* p. 389.

[12] S.R. & O. 1946 No. 1467, L. 17, reg. 5.

Commission on Criminal Procedure. If adopted, the Home Secretary and the Home Office will once again protrude into the constitutional machinery of prosecutions. I hope to show that the Commission's approach and specific proposals are misconceived insomuch as they contribute to a serious weakening of the separation between investigative and prosecutorial functions in relation to the criminal law. A lively concern for the maintenance of this division of functions is what prompted the 1962 Royal Commission on the Police, and also the latest Commission, to urge that the conduct of the prosecution's case in court be the responsibility of someone who is legally qualified and is not identified with the investigative process. Considerations of fairness and the avoidance of even the perception of bias that attaches to the police conducting their own prosecutions, or controlling police prosecutions, are at the root of the proposals discussed in the preceding chapter. Yet, in its approach to the organisation and supervision of the new proposed prosecuting service the Phillips Commission at times exhibits a lack of sensitivity to the implications of its approach. There is no suggestion, I hasten to add, that the well established responsibility of the Attorney General for the actions of the Director of Public Prosecutions be changed in any way that would restore to the Home Secretary some of the powers that once prevailed under the 1886 Regulations. No reference, surprisingly, was made to the anomaly that is regrettably perpetuated in the Prosecution of Offences Act 1979, and which continues to place the appointment of the Director of Public Prosecutions in the hands of the Secretary of State for Home Affairs.[13] Effectively, as is well known, it is the Attorney General who controls the choice of appointee and it would be sensible if the legislation conformed to the long standing practice in this matter. The main thrust of the Commission's concern is with respect to the organisational framework for the new prosecution service and the responsibility at successive levels of government for its management and operational decisions. What we are discussing here, it should be made clear, is the system of *local* prosecutions conducted primarily in the magistrates' courts.

The Royal Commission on Criminal Procedure opposed the establishment of a centrally directed national prosecution system for England and Wales for a combination of reasons. "In order to transmit policies from the centre into effective practice at the local level and to ensure adequate accountability to the Minister" its Report states, "elaborate reporting and other supervisory systems would be required; this might create pressure for management to be in the hands of professional administrators rather than of solicitors. All would be at the cost of substantial resources and, perhaps, of the morale of solicitors who would be operating on the ground. Furthermore, there would be powerful forces at work tending to promote the interests of those at the centre rather than those on the periphery whom the organisation is, in fact, there to serve and to work with in the

[13] 1979 c. 31, s.1(1).

local police, courts and the community."[14] Repeating a sentiment distressingly heard whenever there is resistance to emulating the example of another country, the Commission observed that "we believe it to be hazardous to argue from the experience of other jurisdictions that a national prosecutions service would be workable in England and Wales."[15]

Instead, the Commission's blessings were conferred on a modification of the existing system of police authorities. "We see some difficulty" the Commissioners declared "in simply tacking responsibility for the Crown prosecutor's department on to those of the existing police authority and to do no more than that. Such an arrangement would not indicate clearly enough that the responsibilities of the Crown prosecutor and of the chief constable are distinct."[16] Several alternative models were explored. A separate prosecutions authority was rejected on the ground that "it would have little to do and, as a committee within the larger framework of the local governmental authority, it would be likely to have less prestige and therefore carry less weight than the other spending committees. As a result it might provide the Crown prosecutor with less support than he will require in order to play a full and independent part in the administration of justice."[17]

The solution finally chosen was to develop the existing police authority in such a way as to represent the interests, and supervise the activities, both of the police and of the prosecution service. To mark its different functions from that of the present police authority it is proposed to call it "the police and prosecutions authority."[18] As to its constitution it is envisaged that it have two-thirds of its membership drawn from elected councillors but have the remaining third comprised of local magistrates, solicitors in private practice who regularly do criminal defence work and others with relevant interests. The chief constable and the Crown prosecutor would be of equal but independent status before the joint authority. According to the majority of the Commission "having both chief officers answerable to the same authority would help to maintain the balance of interest between each, serving in the last resort to assist in the resolution of differences of view between the chief constable and the Crown prosecutor on matters which they have found it difficult to resolve."[19]

The assimilation of the two offices in terms of their independent status before the joint authority requires closer examination. In this, a distinction

---

[14] Phillips Commission Report, Cmnd. 8092, p. 152, para. 7.22.

[15] *Ibid.* para. 7.23.

[16] *Ibid.* p. 153, para. 7.27.

[17] *Ibid.* para. 7.28, adding the debatable proposition that "An ineffective authority could be as damaging to the independence of the Crown prosecutor as a stronger one which has failed adequately to recognise it", *loc. cit.*

[18] *Ibid.* p. 154, para. 7.29.

[19] *Loc. cit.* The Commission proposed that the joint authority have responsibility for a jurisdiction co-terminous with existing police areas. Separate arrangements were envisaged for London having regard to the long standing responsibilities of the Home Secretary (for the Metropolitan force) and the Common Council of the City of London (for the City force), *ibid.* pp. 154–157.

must quickly be drawn between the generally recognised independence of the chief constable in matters of prosecution policy (apart from prosecutions subject to statutory consent or intervention by the Director of Public Prosecutions) and his position vis-à-vis the police authority and the Home Office on questions of crime prevention and the maintenance of law and order.[20] Much the same line of distinction is followed when the Commission elaborates on the relationship it proposes between the Crown prosecutor and the local police and prosecutions authority. Thus, the report states, the prosecutor "must be answerable for the efficient operation of his department, that is for how he uses his resources (of buildings, equipment and manpower) to achieve the objectives of his department. These we would assume to be, in general terms, the preparation of cases for trial (or other disposal) without unreasonable and inexplicable delay and the achievement of a level of convictions which does not differ greatly and inexplicably from the national norm. We do not suggest by the latter criterion that the function of the prosecutor is to gain convictions at all costs; it is his job to put the prosecution's case proficiently and dispassionately before the court. Nonetheless a significant divergence from the norm should cause the Crown prosecutor at least to consider whether his advocates are competent, whether their cases are being properly prepared, whether the decisions of the prosecutor to continue with proceedings or of the police to initiate are being carefully taken, or whether there is some other explanation."[21] Presumably, in the event that the prosecutor's explanations for any inefficiency in his managerial role are found unsatisfactory the joint committee of the local authority may, in serious cases, resort to the same disciplinary measures as those which apply to other professionals in local government.

There is more circumspection and more compromise in the Commission's approach to supervision of the prosecutor's discretion in the handling of criminal cases. "If the prosecutor is to exercise his discretion to prosecute within national policy guidelines in a way that takes account of local conditions (and we believe that he should do so) there should continue to be some formal channel of explanatory accountability to a local body to ensure that his discretion is not arbitrarily exercised."[22] This, it is intended, should cover both the general policies of the prosecutor and his decisions in individual cases.[23] If this recommendation evokes feelings of unease with its prospect of pressures and interference by the elected or appointed members of the joint police and prosecution authority, the additional factor of generally closed meetings which regulate the proceedings of a police authority should ensure that much more thought is accorded to this question before Parliament is asked to give its approval. If it is argued that what is contemplated is but a natural extension of the

[20] See *ante*, pp. 38–39, fn. 2–4.
[21] *Ibid.* p. 153, para. 7.25; see, too, *ibid.* p. 139, para. 6.51.
[22] *Ibid.* p. 141, para. 6.55.
[23] *Ibid.* p. 141, para. 6.59.

principle that the Attorney General can be held accountable for the actions of the Director of Public Prosecutions, and counsel representing the Crown, it must also be remembered that the boundaries within which the Attorney can be questioned in the House of Commons with respect to individual cases are constrained in large part by the highly public nature of the forum. There is also a universal recognition shared by all political parties of the quasi-judicial role which the Attorney General must assume and be seen to have discharged when exercising his level of prosecutorial discretion.[24]

It would be a big leap in public faith to accord a similar degree of confidence in the understanding on the part of the proposed joint authorities as to what the present independence of the chief constable and the proposed independence of the local Crown prosecutor is really all about. The Commission acknowledges that, so far as they are aware, few police governing bodies interest themselves in the chief constable's exercise of his prosecutorial discretion. This, they surmise, is partly to be explained by the doubts that exist, and over which there is currently much debate, about the extent of the accountability of the chief constable to the police authority for the general policy of the area force.[25] Notwithstanding the absence of any reliable empirical evidence to clarify the practical workings of this crucial relationship it would be foolhardy to ignore the pitfalls that would be inherent in the system of local accountability as defined in the Commission's Report.

RELATIONSHIPS BETWEEN LOCAL CROWN PROSECUTORS AND THE CENTRAL PROSECUTING AUTHORITIES

In addition to the problems attendant on the degree of control and accountability exercisable at the field level, thought has to be given to the nature of the relationship between the prosecuting solicitors and the central prosecuting authorities in the persons of the Director of Public Prosecutions and the Attorney General. Involved in this relationship is the generally accepted goal of consistency in prosecution policies. As explained earlier, such consistency is not to be equated with uniformity in any absolute sense of the word. A useful parallel to bear in mind is the role expected of the Criminal Division of the Court of Appeal in eliminating gross disparities in sentencing on the part of trial judges and in developing a body of consistent sentencing principles. These are attainable objectives. Rigid adherence to some kind of precise measurements would fail to allow for special circumstances and local conditions. The same considerations must govern the actions of the Director in fulfilling his legislative duty to give advice to chief constables in accordance with the statutes and regulations governing his office. In the opinion of the present Director such

[24] See Edwards, *op. cit.* pp. 224–225.
[25] Phillips Report, p. 141, para. 6.59.

statutory duties do not include the giving of unsolicited advice to chiefs of police on general prosecuting policy.[26] At the same time Sir Thomas Hetherington saw no particular difficulty, if that duty were placed upon the Director, in discharging the function of providing prosecution guidelines that would have nationwide application.[27]

An examination of the relevant legislation suggests that perhaps this disinclination to assume the larger role of head of a national prosecution agency explains the conservative approach, by Hetherington and his predecessors, towards their interpretation of the Prosecution of Offences Acts and the more detailed Regulations. In an explanatory note submitted to the Phillips Commission, Hetherington pointed out that section 2(1)(*b*) of the 1979 Act placed on him the duty "to give such advice and assistance to chief officers of police, justices clerks and other persons . . . concerned in any criminal proceedings respecting the conduct of these proceedings."[28] The view of the Director of Public Prosecutions has been to regard general prosecuting policy as falling outside the ambit of "criminal proceedings" and hence to disqualify the Director from engaging in general aspects of prosecutions.[29] The 1978 Regulations, on the other hand, speak of the Director of Public Prosecutions giving advice, whether on application or by his own initiative "in any criminal matter which appears to him to be of importance or difficulty or which for any other reason appears to him to require his intervention by way of advice . . . ."[30] This is the language used in the former consolidated regulations of 1946[31] and contrasts with the phrase "in any case which appears to him to be of importance or difficulty" which was the criterion inserted in the earlier set of regulations promulgated in 1886.[32]

What do these variations in language mean? It could be argued that to speak of "any criminal matter" or "any case" permits of the most general application of the Director's initiative and that the self imposed restraints said to derive from the test of "any criminal proceeding" is not in accord with the expectations associated with the original conception of the office of Director of Public Prosecutions and its responsibilities. Even weaker is the argument that the Director's advice in an individual case must be strictly confined to the particular issue and the particular circumstances. Such is not the approach of an appellate court when enunciating the

[26] See the Director's separate memorandum on "Consistency of prosecution policy and practice," Appendix 26 to the *Law and Procedure* Report of the Commission, Cmnd. 8092–1, pp. 216–217.
[27] *Ibid.* Such guidelines have since been prepared and, bearing the imprimatur of the Attorney General, a memorandum containing the recommended "Criteria for Prosecution" was distributed to all chief officers of police in Home Office Circular No. 26 of 1983. Access to the criteria is readily available, the Att. Gen's memorandum having been published in (1983) 147 J.P. 227 and [1983] *Commonwealth Law Bulletin* 607. See further *post*, Chapter 14.
[28] *Ibid.*
[29] *Ibid.*
[30] S.I. 1978 No. 1357 (L. 33), reg. 4.
[31] S.R. & O. 1946 No. 1467, (L. 17), reg. 2.
[32] Reg. 3.

principles of law. Its decisions are viewed by both the lower courts and the legal profession as having general application subject to new variables arising in other circumstances that call for further requirements of the basic doctrines. This is what should be expected of the Director's office if it is to perform the unifying function of developing and promulgating directives with respect to general prosecuting policies. The occasion for doing so may be an individual case or it may be in anticipation of new problems that may arise. The universality and force of such directives will derive from acceptance of that responsibility, both on the part of the Director of Public Prosecutions and those who are subject to his advisory statements of policy. The present Director has stated publicly, in a written submission to the Royal Commission, that he can see no particular difficulty about offering such general advice, if that duty were placed upon him.[33]

PARLIAMENTARY ACCOUNTABILITY—THE VIEWS OF THE ROYAL COMMISSION ON CRIMINAL PROCEDURE

Present arrangements for accounting to Parliament for all levels of criminal prosecutions in this country, in the Commission's judgment, are unsatisfactory in many respects and require strengthening, especially at the centre of national government.[34] It did not question the opinion of Sir Thomas Hetherington that he presently lacks the legal power to issue general advice on prosecution policy. As a consequence, the Commission concluded, the Director's role is limited to securing consistency of practice in those cases for which he is responsible. "This means that Parliament is able by questioning the Attorney General to explore the Director's and the Attorney's policies only in respect of a very limited number and range of cases."[35] The comparison was usefully drawn with the Lord Advocate's responsibility for the procurator fiscal service in Scotland covering the whole field of crime, which enables the House of Commons to enquire both into general policies and particular decisions.[36] Far from accepting, however, the logical conclusion inherent in the comparison, the Phillips Commission continued to speak of a strictly limited definition of the Director's future responsibilities. These can best be described as the enunciation of guidelines seeking national consistency of prosecution

---

[33] See *ante*, fn. 27.

[34] Phillips Report, p. 141, para. 6.56. The Commission stressed that it was not passing judgment on "whether the system was efficiently run, whether general prosecution policies are sound or whether individual decisions are generally good" but rather to suggest ways and means of improving the standards of accountability.

[35] *Ibid.* para. 6.58.

[36] *Ibid.* As to Parliamentary questions and debates pertaining to the actions of the Law Officers and their agents, the Phillips Commission correctly observed that these enquiries "do not seem to be regular or frequent and replies on specific cases are normally couched in general terms." This seems to miss the essential point that the door to full and detailed accountability is constantly open and can be pressed as far as members of the House of Commons choose to pursue the handling of individual cases. Examples of such intensive examination are referred to in succeeding chapters of this work.

policies and practice but without the clout necessary to ensure adherence to the standards set by the Director of Public Prosecutions.

My dissatisfaction with the Commission's proposals for the future extends into its advocacy of increased involvement by the Home Secretary and the Home Office in this country's machinery of criminal prosecutions. I have earlier described the historical background against which the recommendations of the Royal Commission in Criminal Procedure should be viewed.[37] In the light of the constitutional relationship between chief constables and the Secretary of State for Home Affairs, as it has been interpreted consistently by successive holders of that appointment, the role of the Home Office in matters of police prosecutions is indeed peripheral. In a word, "The Home Secretary has no authority to direct a chief constable to a particular course of action, and chief constables are under no obligation to justify their decision to him."[38] Whether viewed from the perspective of the Director of Public Prosecutions or that of the Home Office, according to the Commissioners, effective machinery for achieving conformity in prosecution policies is lacking.[39]

Under the new system proposed by the Phillips Commission "the police, as the initiators of prosecutions, will have a vitally important part to play in the development of the system; we would regard it as essential that the Home Office and the inspectorate of constabulary should in future be more actively concerned with general questions of police practice in regard to the prosecution process . . . . We see no danger that if the Home Office adopts a more positive role on general policies this would conflict with the principle, which we would wish to maintain, that the Home Secretary should not be concerned with individual decisions to prosecute."[40] Attempts to keep distinct, on the one hand, general policy guidance and, on the other, interference with the actual outcome of an individual case may seem to the Royal Commissioners to be a straightforward delineation of separate issues. If so, they live in an unreal world, one that prefers not to comprehend how the potential integration of functions can arise— sometimes it may occur in the individual disposition of a case, at other times it may derive from developing a policy to deal with the instant situation and others of a similar nature. Hard and fast boundary lines of the kind envisaged for the future Home Office role in the prosecutions system are dangerously misleading insofar as they are called upon to support a

[37] *Ante*, pp. 105–107.
[38] Cmnd. 8092, p. 137, para. 6.44.
[39] Over the past 20 years only two Home Office circulars were identified in which advice had been tendered to chief constables as to their exercise of prosecutorial discretion, and this advice has largely been confined to procedural matters. At regional levels, agreement has been reached among chief officers about when to prosecute for speeding offences and on cautioning for certain other traffic offences. These questions, and the broader application of uniformity in prosecution policies, are rarely discussed in the national conferences of the Association of Chief Police Officers, even on those unsystematic occasions when the D.P.P. or senior members of his staff are in attendance—see Phillips Report, p. 137, para. 6.43.
[40] *Ibid.* p. 164, paras. 7.58 and 7.59.

fundamental shift in approach that would substantially enlarge the Home Secretary's involvement in prosecution matters and almost certainly set the Home Office on a collision course with the Director of Public Prosecutions and his ministerial superior, the Attorney General.

In fairness to the Commission its report does purport to evaluate the pros and cons of placing ministerial responsibility for the new organisation in the hands of the respective ministers, *i.e.* the Home Secretary or the Attorney General.[41] The arguments, it claims, are evenly balanced but this may amount to no more than a reluctance to state explicitly what the Commission's analysis suggests with but a thinly disguised emphasis as to its own preference. Ministerial control, it is stated, should embrace the management of the new service. "The Minister's function would be to set national standards for the staffing of Crown prosecutor's departments and to ensure that minimum standards of performance are being achieved. The appointment of the Crown prosecutor and his deputy by the police and prosecutions authority should be from a short list approved by the Minister, and the Minister would be involved if the Crown prosecutor or his deputy were to perform their duties so inefficiently as to warrant dismissal."[42] The model for this form of ministerial control is that which presently governs the appointment and dismissal of chief constables and other senior officers. Local police authorities cannot act under their own auspices but are subject to the Home Secretary's final decision.[43] As an extension of the same analogy, the Commission recommends that funding arrangements similar to those for the police would be appropriate. Thus the ultimate sanction for an inefficient local operation would be the central's government's withholding of its contribution from the national exchequer.[44] Any remaining doubts as to the Commission's preference for locating ministerial control in the Home Office is dispelled by its further recommendation that "The Minister (Home Secretary) should also establish a prosecutions inspectorate within his department. This would inspect and report to the Minister and to the police and prosecutions authority on the organization and policies of, and the discharge of their functions by, individual Crown prosecutor's departments, and advise Crown prosecutors."[45] One can almost hear the plans being developed for merging the existing Inspectorate of Constabulary into an expanded service of Her Majesty's Inspectors of Police and Prosecutions.

In rather more explicit terms the Commission argues that the Home Secretary's ministerial responsibility for most other aspects of the criminal justice system qualifies him, in a number of ways, to take responsibility for this important part of the overall organisation. The Crown prosecutor would join the police in controlling the burden of business that the courts,

---

[41] *Ibid.* pp. 165–166, paras. 7.62–7.66.
[42] *Ibid.* p. 164, para. 7.60.
[43] T.A. Critchley, *op. cit.* pp. 286, 294.
[44] Phillips Report, p. 164, para. 7.60.
[45] *Ibid.* p. 165, para. 7.61.

and ultimately the penal institutions, are required to bear. This attention to cost effectiveness is evident throughout the Report with its emphasis on a total systems approach and measuring the prospects of future productivity levels.[46] Not that a nagging concern for the prosecutor's independence is altogether ignored by the Phillips Commission, but its general philosophy is captured in the following extract from its report: "Although the Crown prosecutor will be independent of the police in the sense that he will not be subject to their instructions, there will need to be a close working relationship between the police service and the Crown prosecutors; and the police will have to develop in close consultation with the Crown prosecutor their policies in relation to the decision to institute proceedings in which the Home Secretary, because of his general role in respect of the police, will have a part to play. Tensions can be relieved and disputes more readily resolved, if they occur, through a single department rather than two inspectorates reporting to separate Ministers . . . The Home Office could absorb most of the proposed functions quite naturally, as they are analogous to others it performs in respect of the police and probation and after care services for example."[47]

This kind of thinking epitomises the Commission's lack of sensitivity as to the essential conditions necessary to both maintain and exhibit publicly the independent quality of prosecution decisions, balancing as they must the interests of the State and those of the individual, particularly his liberty. Prosecutions are not instituted at the behest of government and there should be no suggestion that prosecution policies are determined with the interests of the central or local governments being uppermost in the minds of the decision makers. That may be so with respect to the other parts of the criminal justice system for which the Home Office is responsible. It would be fatal to public confidence in any new system if its organisational place in the structure of government lent substance to the suggestion that prosecution policies were subject to the direction of the central government as represented by the Home Secretary. In the light of the earlier advocacy by the Royal Commission on Criminal Procedure of a more active role by the Home Office and its inspectorate of constabulary with respect to future prosecuting policies something less than unquestioned confidence should be extended to its assurance that "even if the Home Secretary were to be designated as the responsible Minister, his responsibility should be limited to the administrative aspect of the service (staffing matters, training and funding); general questions relating to prosecutions policy (and in particular to the role of the Director of Public Prosecutions) would be a matter for the Attorney General."[48]

Many of the Commission's witnesses, understandably, had argued that ministerial responsibility should rest with the Attorney General in order to mark the prosecution service's independence of the police which, in turn,

[46] *Ibid.* p. 165, para. 7.65.
[47] *Ibid.*   [48] *Ibid.*

was recognised to be within the Home Secretary's bailiwick. Since the creation of the office of Director of Public Prosecutions in 1879 it is the Attorney General who has been looked to by the House of Commons for answers concerning the actions and decisions of the Director. These arguments, however, carried little weight in the Commission's assessment of the obstacles to any expansion of the Attorney General's responsibilities to include prosecutions in the lower courts. As to these the Phillips report states: " . . . the Law Officers' Department in its present form could not deal with the proposed functions of the responsible department. The Attorney General's office is not that of a spending Minister. Nor is the Attorney General a member of the Cabinet, but rather he is the legal adviser to it, to the Government and, if required, to the House of Commons. Additionally he is the Crown's Attorney with, essentially, only an operational role himself as a prosecutor. He is the head of the Bar and as such is identified with the barristers' profession than with that of the solicitors, who will staff the new service to a great extent. Historically, his interests and activity have been with the Crown Court, which deals only with a small proportion of all prosecutions."[49] Many of these arguments make no sense whatsoever. The Attorney General is indeed the State's chief prosecutor. This, it is contended, disqualifies him from bearing the final responsibility for the ranks of prosecuting solicitors who, elsewhere in the same report, the Commission recommends be given the title of "Crown prosecutors."[50] As the minister responsible for the office of Director of Public Prosecutions the Attorney General already exercises supervisory functions over the complement of lawyers, both barristers and solicitors, who staff that office, and the same officials are wont to appear on behalf of the Director in the magistrates' court, as well as the Crown Court or other superior courts, according to the nature of the case and the stage of the proceedings. No legal or historical barrier, of the kind suggested by the Commission, confines the Attorney General, or counsel representing him, to particular levels of the criminal courts. Furthermore, as has been shown elsewhere, the exclusion of the Attorney General from the Cabinet, far from being the handicap suggested by the Commission, is one of the

---

[49] *Ibid.* p. 165, para. 7.63.

[50] *Ibid.* p. 147, para. 7.8. A major pre-occupation of the Royal Commission was the scope of the new responsibilities to be accorded Crown prosecutors when acting on behalf of police forces maintained by local authorities and grant-aided by the Home Office under the Police Act 1964. As to other statutory police forces (*e.g.* the British Transport Police (by far the largest), the British Airports Authority Police, the Ministry of Defence Police, and the Atomic Energy Authority Constabulary) the Commission recommended that all their prosecutions should become the responsibility of the local Crown prosecutor on the same footing as the handling of civil police prosecutions. Resource limitations, rather than any argument of principle, persuaded the Commission to recommend against a similar transfer of responsibility for prosecutions initiated by non-police agencies, *i.e.* government departments, local authorities and voluntary societies, which account for approximately a quarter of all prosecutions of persons over 17 for offences other than motoring offences—see Report, Cmnd. 8092, pp. 158–160, paras. 7.40 to 7.45, and Research Study no. 10, Chapters 7 and 8. See also B. M. Dickens: "Discretion in Local Authority Prosecutions" [1970] Crim.L.R. 618.

cornerstones of the philosophy that protects the quasi-judicial independence of the Law Officers of the Crown.[51]

There is far more substance to the claim that the Law Officers' Department in its present form could not deal with the proposed functions of the responsible department. It makes sense to conclude that, if the Attorney General were to be given ministerial charge of the new prosecutions service, the necessary administrative arm would be provided by enlarging the Department of the Director of Public Prosecutions.[52] How far this would alter the nature of the Director's role, as the Commission perceived to be inevitable, may be more a matter of degree than substance.[53] There would have to be some devolution of the Director's (or area directors) expanded functions with the possible appointment of regional deputy directors exercising a large measure of autonomy but subject to general guidelines laid down by the Director in consultation with the Attorney General. Devolution of functions and decision making should mean a minimum of interference from above. The same principle should apply in relation to the exercise of prosecutorial discretion by the prosecutor on the spot, the recourse to higher authority being normally at the initiative of the prosecutor in charge of a case who is in need of a second opinion. Such a system should not entail the creation of a large bureaucracy. This is not the case in the Canadian provinces to whose experience and existing prosecution machinery the Commission turned for the model it recommended.

It is time now to turn our attention to the subject of existing accountability to Parliament, leaving for the moment the major controversy generated in the *Gouriet* case by the Court of Appeal with its vigorous canvassing of the novel theory that the Law Officers are accountable to the courts for the manner in which they discharge their prerogative authority.[54] Parliament, in the present context, essentially means the House of Commons, for it is in that chamber that the Attorney General and Solicitor General sit as Members of Parliament. The range of the discretionary powers inherent in, or attached by statute to, the office of Attorney General include both criminal and civil proceedings, of which "consent" offences, and the prerogative power of entering a *nolle prosequi* or granting a fiat in relator proceedings are prominent examples. Recent years have also produced a significant increase in the number of parliamentary questions and ad hoc debates concerning the actions of the Director of Public Prosecutions, an experience with which the earliest incumbents of that office were quite familiar.

---

[51] See Edwards, *op. cit.* pp. 158–176.

[52] Phillips Report, p. 165, para. 7.64.

[53] The effects of any such institutional changes were the subject of discussion between the Commission and the D.P.P. "who took the view that he could take on this additional responsibility were it to be required"—*loc. cit.* See also *Minutes of Oral Evidence* to the Phillips Commission, February 13, 1980.

[54] See *post*, pp. 129–137.

What seems extremely unlikely is acceptance by the House of Commons of the recommendation, made in the report of the Royal Commission on Criminal Procedure, that neither the Home Secretary nor the Attorney General should have any responsibility to Parliament for the conduct of individual cases.[55] Their powers to make enquiries about such cases, according to the Commission, should be limited to requiring the chief constable or the Crown prosecutor to explain the reasons for their actions.[56] A review of the House of Commons' precedents, however, provides ample authority for the proposition that a Law Officer may be questioned, after the case is closed, with respect to the institution, non-institution or withdrawal of individual criminal proceedings.[57] This makes good sense, since it is invariably the particular application of a law or discretionary power that creates public concern for both the power and its exercise. It also reflects a wise balance between non-interference during the actual process of reaching a decision and an obligation subsequently to present an explanation for the decision, which may have been by the Attorney General himself, the Director of Public Prosecutions or by another official for whose actions the minister is accountable to Parliament.

There are several features that exert powerful constraints on the lengths to which the principle of ministerial accountability should be pressed publicly on the floor of the Commons. Among these are the dangers of allowing the questioning to degenerate into what could amount to a retrial or, alternatively, calling into question a decision not to proceed in such a way as to assail the reputation of a suspect without the customary procedural safeguards of a trial. Stonewalling or the resorting to uninformative answers on the part of the Law Officers are unlikely to satisfy an aroused Commons. What Parliament has the right to call for is an explanation that avoids the dangers just described whilst at the same time demonstrating that the Attorney General, the Solicitor General, or the Director of Public Prosecutions, as the case may be, has considered all the relevant legal and policy factors and has reached his decision with that impartiality of judgment which is the ultimate protection of the constitutional independence of the Law Officers of the Crown. I see no reason why the same principles should not be extended to embrace the accountability of the Attorney General to the House of Commons for decisions made at the level of local prosecutors.

[55] Phillips Report, p. 166, para. 7.67. In its final position the Commission appears to have come out in favour of an indeterminate system of divided accountability: "As regards prosecution policy the Home Secretary's main concern will be with the principles on which the police should initiate prosecutions and the consideration and development of possible alternatives to prosecution. The Attorney General will be concerned with the ethical and professional standards required of Crown prosecutors and questions of public policy relating to the use of criminal proceedings."
[56] Ibid.
[57] Edwards, op. cit. pp. 260–261.

JUDICIAL CONTROL OVER THE INHERENT POWERS OF THE ATTORNEY
GENERAL—COMMONWEALTH RULINGS

Echoes of the English Court of Appeal's dramatic confrontation in 1977 with the Attorney General, Mr. Sam Silkin, in the *Gouriet* case, still reverberate around the Commonwealth where the search for a solution to the problem of controlling prosecutorial conduct that is viewed as an abuse of the criminal process remains a lively issue. In Canada, for example, large numbers of trial judges in the provincial courts gave practical effect to the abuse of process principle, associated with Lord Devlin's judgment in *Connelly* v. *D.P.P.*,[58] by staying proceedings in which the handling of the case by the police or the Crown prosecutor before the trial offended the presiding judge's subjective sense of fair play.[59] Notwithstanding the decision of the Supreme Court of Canada in *Rourke* v. *R.*[60] that there does not exist any jurisdiction under the Criminal Code to stay proceedings because the prosecution is considered oppressive, judicial ingenuity to keep alive the abuse of process principle shows no sign of abating in the years following the *Rourke* decision.[61] Sustenance for this movement was provided in the approval given, by the majority of the Supreme Court Justices in *Rourke*, to the views expressed by Viscount Dilhorne in *D.P.P.* v. *Humphrys*.[62] In that case the former Lord Chancellor stated: "If there is the power . . . to stop a prosecution or indictment *in limine* it is in my view a power that should only be exercised in the most exceptional circumstances."[63] What is often overlooked, at times with suspicious deviousness, is the same judge's warning of the considerable dangers inherent in an undefined power of controlling prosecutions that are looked upon as an abuse of process.[64]

The High Court of Australia has now had an opportunity to express its views on the highly sensitive question of how far judicial control is exercisable with respect to the powers inherent in the office of the Attorney General. The appellant in *Barton* v. *the Queen*[65] challenged the

---

[58] [1964] A.C. 1254, 1347 *per* Lord Devlin who stated that " . . . *the judges of the High Court* [emphasis added] have in their inherent jurisdiction, both in civil and criminal matters, power (subject of course to any statutory rules) to make and enforce rules of practice in order to ensure that the court's process is used fairly and conveniently by both sides."

[59] A full review of the pre-*Rourke* decisions by the lower courts in Canada is contained in (1976) 25 C.C.C. (2d) 555.

[60] (1977) 33 C.R.N.S. 268; 35 C.C.C. (2d) 129. For the present writer's comments on this case see *Reshaping of the Criminal Law*, pp. 381–382.

[61] See the cases reviewed in Stanley A. Cohen, "Observations on the Re-Emergence of the Doctrine of Abuse of Process" (1981) 19 C.R.(3d), pp. 310–326. Moreover, the recently enacted Canadian Charter of Rights and Freedoms gives every indication of providing an alternative, but no less fertile, avenue for challenging the prosecution's handling of a case before trial.

[62] [1977] A.C. 1.   [63] *Ibid*. p. 26.

[64] See *post*, p. 127, fn. 91. The former Lord Chancellor and Attorney General may have overlooked the role of the judiciary in authorising the preferment of an indictment and the possibility of conflict between the bench and executive that such a statutory responsibility may yet engender—see *post*, pp. 434–442.

[65] (1980) 32 A.L.R. 449.

grounds on which the Attorney General of New South Wales had filed an
ex officio indictment thereby depriving him of his right to a preliminary
hearing. The High Court declined to examine the appellant's further
allegations that the Attorney General's actions had been at the direction of
the State Premier and involved no genuine exercise of discretion on the
Attorney's own part. These allegations were denied but evidence to test
the allegations was not taken because it was considered convenient to first
decide whether there was any legal foundation for the challenge to the
Attorney General's filing of an *ex officio* indictment. The High Court
unanimously held that the Attorney General's decision, under the
Australian Courts Act 1828, s.5,[66] was not subject to judicial review. The
purpose of the above statutory provision, the High Court declared, was to
arm the Attorney General for New South Wales, and Crown prosecutors
appointed by him, with a power in all respects similar to that formerly
enjoyed by the Attorney General for England and Wales.[67] "The provision
does not limit or restrict the Attorney General in any way in the
consideration which he may give to a particular case. And because the
language leaves the Attorney General at large in deciding what course he
shall take, it makes his decision immune from judicial review."[68] In a later
passage, reminiscent of Viscount Dilhorne's concern to leave the door at
least ajar for possible judicial intervention, Gibbs and Mason JJ., in the
leading judgment of the court, declared: "It would be surprising if
Parliament intended to make the Attorney's information subject to review.
It has generally been considered to be undesirable that the court, whose
ultimate function it is to determine the accused's guilt or innocence, should
become too closely involved in the question whether a prosecution should
be commenced—though it may be that in exercising its power to prevent an
abuse of process the court will on rare occasions be required to consider
whether a prosecution should be permitted to continue."[69] They went
on[70]: "It is one thing to say that the filing of an *ex officio* indictment is not
examinable by the courts; it is quite another thing to say that the courts are
powerless to prevent an abuse of process or the prosecution of a criminal
proceeding in a manner which will result in a trial which is unfair when
judged by reference to accepted standards of justice. The courts exercise
no control over the Attorney-General's decision to commence criminal
proceedings, but once he does so, the courts will control those proceedings
so as to ensure that the accused receives a fair trial. The distinction

---

[66] 9 Geo. IV, c. 83.

[67] (1980) 32 A.L.R. 449 at p. 457. *Cf.* the Commonwealth Judiciary Act 1903, s.71A of
which empowers the federal Attorney General to file an indictment for any indictable offence
against the law of the Commonwealth in the High Court of the Supreme Court of a State
without examination or commitment for trial. The former prerogative power of the English
Attorney General to file *ex-officio* informations was abolished by the Criminal Law Act 1967,
s.6(6)—see further *post*, pp. 438–439 and Edwards, *op. cit.* pp. 262–267.

[68] (1980) 32 A.L.R. 449, *per* Gibbs and Mason JJ., at p. 458.

[69] *Ibid.*

[70] *Ibid.* p. 459.

between the court's lack of power to review the Attorney's decision whether to commence proceedings or not and the court's power to control its proceedings was central to the judgment of Lord Langdale in *R* v. *Prosser*.[71]"

"There is ample authority for the proposition that the courts possess all the necessary powers to prevent an abuse of process and to ensure a fair trial. The exercise of this power extends in an appropriate case to the grant of a stay of proceedings so as to permit a preliminary examination to take place. As a result of the speeches in *Connelly* v. *Director of Public Prosecutions* and *Director of Public Prosecutions* v. *Humphrys*, it is now established in the United Kingdom that although a judge has no power to refuse to allow a prosecution to proceed merely because he considers that, as a matter of policy, it ought not to have been brought, the courts have a general power to prevent unfairness to the accused, even to the extent of preventing an abuse of process resulting from the prosecution of proceedings brought without reasonable grounds . . . The view that there can be no injustice or unfairness to an accused in putting him on trial without reasonable grounds merely because he will be ultimately acquitted and because he can bring an action for damages for malicious prosecution has been emphatically rejected, as it should be."[72]

"It is for the courts, not the Attorney-General, to decide in the last resort whether the justice of the case requires that a trial should proceed in the absence of committal proceedings. It is not for the courts to abdicate that function to the Attorney-General, let alone to Crown prosecutors whom he may appoint. We need to recall that the commencement of prosecutions is in very many cases left to Crown prosecutors. It is quite impossible for an Attorney General to deal personally with the question except in a minority of cases and then in accordance with advice tendered to him by officers who are acquainted with the materials. If the courts were to abdicate the function, there is the distinct possibility that the *ex officio* indictment, so recently awakened from its long slumber, would become an active instrument, even in cases in which it has not been employed in the past, notwithstanding the vigorous criticism which has been directed to it and the assertions of commentators that it was appropriate for use only in a very limited category of cases."[73]

Counsel for the Attorney General of New South Wales did not contest the existence of a power in the courts to stay criminal proceedings in those very exceptional cases where it may transpire that there has been an abuse of process, but he vigorously disputed the proposition that the mere absence of committal proceedings gives rise to such an abuse. The High Court of Australia, by a majority of 3 to 2, was of a different mind and declared that a trial held without antecedent committal proceedings, unless

---

[71] (1848) 11 Beav. 306; 50 E.R. 384.
[72] (1980) 32 A.L.R. 449 at pp. 459–460.
[73] *Ibid*. p. 463.

justified on strong and powerful grounds, must necessarily be considered unfair. This ruling in effect, as was pointed out by Stephen J., places a significant practical qualification upon the Attorney General's unexaminable power to file *ex officio* indictments. "It is one thing" he stated "freely to acknowledge that power while retaining for the courts the not inconsistent duty of ensuring that in each individual case the accused has a fair trial; it is quite another to treat the Attorney General's power as never properly exercised in the absence of prior committal proceedings."[74] It is difficult for an outsider, accustomed to the movement towards restricting or abolishing committal proceedings[75] to comprehend the high importance accorded to preliminary hearings in 1981 by the High Court of Australia.[75]

To look beyond the immediate decision in *Barton* v. *The Queen*,[76] it will be noted that the High Court did not resolve the problem of where the line is to be drawn between the judges' disclaimer of interference with the executive's control over its discretion in bringing a case before the court and judicial insistence on its inherent right to stay proceedings because they constitute an abuse of the criminal process. Possibly there cannot be any definitive answer to this legal conundrum given the amplitude of meanings which can be read into both concepts. For example, in the New Zealand case of *Moevao* v. *Department of Labour*[77] each of the members of the Court of Appeal resorted to different interpretations as to the ambit of the abuse of process doctrine. Woodhouse, J., after stressing the court's

---

[74] *Ibid.* p. 466. Adoption of the latter proposition, Stephen J. reminded his colleagues, "would place a significant practical qualification upon the Attorney General's unexaminable power to file *ex officio* indictments."

[75] In England the movement towards restricting the availability of preliminary hearings was substantially advanced by the new procedure of "paper committals" introduced under s.1 of the Criminal Justice Act 1967—see *post*, p. 435. In Canada, the Federal Law Reform Commission in 1974 recommended the abolition of committal proceedings describing such a procedure as a cumbersome and expensive vehicle for obtaining discovery. That goal was attainable by procedures specifically designed for that purpose—see Working Paper No. 4, *Criminal Procedure—Discovery*, containing specific proposals for reform. Further impetus towards reform is contained in the 1982 report of the Special Committee of the Ontario Bench and Bar chaired by Mr. Justice G.A. Martin, Ontario Court of Appeal. That committee, in urging the curtailment of committal proceedings, cautioned against any modification that failed to provide for a screening mechanism to protect an accused against being required to stand trial unless a judicial officer is satisfied of the existence of a prima facie case against him.

[76] In *Barton*, it should be carefully noted, the High Court was concerned primarily with the special situation in New South Wales which, alone of all the Australian States, adheres to the necessity for preliminary hearings in indictable cases. According to Murphy J., the N.S.W. system, as it presently operates, is a "disgrace to the administration of criminal justice . . ." *ibid.* p. 469. Another Australian observer has written: "It does seem a little late in the day to proclaim the indispensability of the oral hearing. In each jurisdiction except New South Wales it is possible for a defendant to be committed for trial on the basis of written statements. In four states this can be achieved without magisterial consideration of the sufficiency of the evidence. The view that all cases should be screened before a jury trial takes place commands less support than it did"—see J. Seymour, *Committal for Trial, an Analysis of Australian Law Together with an Outline of British and American Procedures*, Australian Institute of Criminology, (1978).

[77] [1980] 1 N.Z.L.R. 464. Each of the judgments delivered by the Court of Appeal canvass thoroughly the pertinent English and Canadian decisions in this relatively uncharted territory.

obligation to avoid confusing its own role with the executive's responsibility for deciding upon a prosecution, maintained that the basic consideration was "the process of law." "It is not something" he said "limited to the controversial practices or procedures of the court system. It is the function and purpose of the courts as a separate part of the constitutional machinery that must be protected from abuse rather than the particular processes that are used within the machine. It may be that the shorthand phrase 'abuse of process' by itself does not give sufficient emphasis to the principle that in this context the courts must react not so much against an abuse of the procedure that has been built up to enable the determination of a criminal charge, as against the much wider and more serious abuse of the criminal jurisdiction in general."[78] By way of illustration, Woodhouse, J., indicated that, in his opinion, the trial judge in another case would have been entirely justified in stopping the prosecution against the accused who, while he was in Australia on lawful business, was illegally abducted by the police and returned unwillingly to New Zealand so that he could be interviewed and charged.[79]

According to Richardson, J., on the other hand, "criminal proceedings are not an appropriate vehicle for a separate review of the decision to prosecute. . . . The twin problems of objectively ascertainable standards and the relative unfamiliarity of the courts with the weighing of all the considerations which may bear on this exercise of prosecutorial responsibility require the courts to tread with the utmost circumspection. While the court must be the master and have the last word, it is only where to countenance the continuation of the prosecution would be contrary to the recognized purposes of the administration of criminal justice that a Court would ever be justified in intervening."[80] The same judge clearly perceived that while the respective questions were, in a sense, legal issues, they also raise questions of considerable constitutional significance concerning the relationship between the three branches of government.[81] In the judgment of Richardson, J., "It is not a matter of the Courts usurping or intruding on the functions of another organ of government . . . It is simply that the existence of other sanctions cannot justify the abdication by the Court of responsibility for control over its own processes. When it comes to actual or threatened abuse of the Court's processes the Crown's position is no different in principle from that of any other litigant."[82] The confidence of

[78] *Ibid.* p. 476. *Cf.* the conclusion advanced by Richmond P. that "It must be quite clear that the case is truly one of abuse of process and not merely one involving elements of oppression, illegality or abuse of authority in some way which falls short of establishing that the process of the Court is itself being wrongly made use of"—*ibid.* pp. 470–471.

[79] See *R. v. Hartley* [1978] 2 N.Z.L.R. 199 and also *R. v. Moore* [1974] 1 N.Z.L.R. 417.

[80] [1980] 1 N.Z.L.R. 464 at p. 482.

[81] *Ibid.* p. 479.

[82] *Ibid.* p. 481. The extreme step of the court staying a prosecution is justified, according to Richardson J., " . . . if it concludes from the conduct of the prosecutor in relation to the prosecution that the Court processes are being employed for ulterior purposes or in such a way (for example, through multiple or successive proceedings) as to cause improper vexation and oppression. The yardstick is not simply fairness to the particular accused. It is not

these resounding assertions rests in large part on the subjective interpretation of the judiciary's role in defending the public interest. Contrary statements by those occupying the position of the Law Officers of the Crown have been expressed with an equal degree of righteousness. Time may bring about a reconciliation as to the proper jurisdictional boundaries on the part of all three branches of government. All that can be said is that such a prospect is not imminent. Given the level of strong animadversion that is capable of being generated by competing claims to review the exercise of discretionary power by the Attorney General, and by agents of the Attorney General, on the part of the courts and by Parliament, we can look forward to continuing outbursts of the jurisdictional tug-of-war.

ENGLISH DECISIONS ON ABUSE OF PROCESS—A MATTER FOR THE COURTS OR THE CROWN?

The seeds of this controversy were originally planted in the form of certain pronouncements by members of the Appellate Committee of the House of Lords, commencing with the case of *Connelly* v. *D.P.P.* in 1964.[83] The appellant had been indicted for murder and acquitted. He was later indicted for a robbery committed at the same time and place as the murder. It was held that a plea of *autrefois acquit* was not available to the appellant. At issue on that occasion was the extent of the court's discretion, outside the normal pleas of *autrefois acquit* and *autrefois convict*, to stay an indictment that contained charges founded on the same facts as those on which a previous indictment was based. It fell to Lord Devlin to focus attention on what he regarded as a point of great constitutional importance. After reciting the various ways in which the Crown could, unless restrained by the courts, reopen again and again what is in effect the same matter against an accused, Lord Devlin turned his attention to the position taken by the Solicitor General, Sir Peter Rawlinson, in the course of arguing the appeal before the House of Lords. The Solicitor General did not dispute that, if the prosecution were in fact

---

whether the initiation and continuation of the particular process seems in the circumstances to be unfair to him. That may be an important consideration. But the focus is on the misuse of the Court process by those responsible for law enforcement. It is whether the continuation of the prosecution is inconsistent with the recognised purposes of the administration of crimial justice and so constitutes an abuse of the process of the Court." *Ibid.* p. 482.

[83] [1964] A.C. 1254; and note also the same judge's interpretation of Lord Goddard C.J.'s landmark decision in *R.* v. *Chairman, County of London Quarter Sessions, ex p. Downes* [1954] 1 Q.B. 1 which is invariably relied upon as setting the limits within which an indictment can be challenged once it is before the court. To the four grounds enumerated in that case, *i.e.* if the indictment is defective, if matter in bar is pleaded, if a *nolle prosequi* is entered or if the court has no jurisdiction, Lord Devlin argued the existence of a fifth ground, *viz.*, where there is a gross abuse of process and the court refuses to allow the indictment to go to trial. *Ex p. Downes*, he maintained, falls far short of an authority for the view that a vexatious use of process by the prosecution . . . can be dealt with only by means of a *nolle prosequi*—*ibid.* at p. 1355. The Solicitor General *arguendo* had claimed that the four exceptions were complete and comprehensive in themselves. The views of Lord Morris and Lord Hodson in *Connelly* on this point were opposed to those of Lord Devlin—*ibid.* pp. 1300, 1336.

to behave in all ways in which according to his argument they could legally behave, there could be abuses which ought to be corrected. In Rawlinson's submission the danger of abuse is exclusively a matter for the Crown. The Crown itself, he claimed, could be trusted not to abuse its powers and if a private prosecutor were to be the cause of all the trouble the Attorney General could interfere and terminate the proceedings by entering a *nolle prosequi*. Such a solution was totally unacceptable to Lord Devlin who responded by saying: "The fact that the Crown has, as is to be expected, and that private prosecutions have (as is also to be expected for they are usually public authorities), generally behaved with great propriety in the conduct of prosecutions has up till now avoided the need for any consideration of this point. Now that it emerges, it is seen to be one of great constitutional importance. Are the courts to rely on the executive to protect their process from abuse? Have they not themselves an inescapable duty to secure fair treatment for those who come or are brought before them? To questions of this sort there is only one possible answer. The courts cannot contemplate for a moment the transference to the executive of the responsibility for seeing that the process of law is not abused."[84]

Support for Lord Devlin's basic principle, that there exists in English criminal law a general power in the judiciary to stop a prosecution that creates injustice or unfairness to the accused, was accorded in the judgments of Lord Reid and Lord Pearce, both of whom saw the ancient pleas of *autrefois* as emanating from the larger doctrine of an inherent power to protect the court's process from abuse.[85] "Instead of attempting to enlarge the pleas beyond their proper scope" said Lord Pearce, "it is better that the courts should apply to such cases an avowed judicial discretion based on the broader principles which underlie the plea."[86] It was left to Lord Hodson to stress the difficulties involved in defining "unfairness" within the inherent discretion claimed for the criminal courts by the majority in *Connelly* v. *D.P.P.* "I cannot concede" he stated "that there ought to be given to the judge a discretion, which, in my opinion, he has not hitherto been allowed, to interfere with anything that he personally thinks is unfair. If one disclaims such a proposal but seeks to substitute a discretion to determine, in accordance with principle, whether or not a prosecution should be stopped, I do not know what principle can be applied. In the case now under consideration different judges will, as the history of the cases shows, have different views as to what is unfair, and I should find the discretion, if there is one, immensely difficult to exercise at all, nor should I know how to exercise it judicially."[87] Standing alongside

---

[84] *Ibid.* p. 1354.
[85] *Ibid.* p. 1296 *per* Lord Reid and p. 1364 *per* Lord Pearce.
[86] *Ibid.*
[87] *Ibid.* p. 1337. In the New Zealand case of *Moevao* v. *Department of Labour* one member of the Court of Appeal rejected the force of Lord Hodson's argument, saying " . . . the real question as to whether a particular prosecution is actually oppressive must be answered, like any serious issue for the Courts, by some kind of judicial evaluation, and the fact that all the relevant tests cannot be supplied at once with absolute assurance, or their practical

Lord Hodson we find Lord Morris of Borth-y-Gest uttering words of caution as to the ambit of the court's power to prevent a prosecution from going ahead.[88]

If the post-*Connelly* experience in the Canadian courts is of any significance, the law reports of the 1960s and 1970s provide ample testimony to the enthusiasm with which members of the judiciary at the provincial courts level embraced a new found power to control the process of criminal prosecutions.[89] That this has proved to be short lived in terms of the more extreme applications of the doctrine of abuse of process owes its restraining influence to the views expressed by the House of Lords in the later case of *Director of Public Prosecutions* v. *Humphrys*.[90] In deciding that the doctrine of issue estoppel did not apply in the criminal law, several of their Lordships took advantage of the opportunity to comment on the earlier expositions in *Connelly* as to the court's inherent authority to protect its process from abuse. The later opinions are important insomuch as they serve to emphasise the distinction between an inherent power to ensure that the process of the court is itself not being put to wrongful use and any general right that is asserted on behalf of the judiciary to review the propriety of individual prosecution decisions.

Leading the way in forcefully resisting any claims couched in the latter terms was Viscount Dilhorne, a former Attorney General of many years experience. He stated: "If there is the power . . . to stop a prosecution on indictment *in limine*, it is in my view a power that should only be exercised in the most exceptional circumstances—a judge must keep out of the arena. He should not have to appear to have any responsibility for the institution of a prosecution. The functions of prosecutors and of judges must not be blurred. If a judge has power to decline to hear a case because he does not think it should be brought, then it soon may be thought that the cases he allows to proceed are cases brought with his consent or approval."[91]

Lord Salmon, alone of the other Lords of Appeal sitting in the *Humphrys* case, saw fit to recognise the considerable dangers attached to too broad an interpretation of the abuse of process jurisdiction. Agreeing explicitly with the caveat enunciated by Viscount Dilhorne, Lord Salmon stated: " . . . a judge has not and should not appear to have any responsibility for the institution of prosecutions nor has he any power to refuse to allow a prosecution to proceed merely because he considers that, as a matter of policy, it ought not to have been brought. It is only if the prosecution amounts to an abuse of the process of the court and is

application may seem difficult or the answer that should be produced may be hard to find, could be no reason for ignoring the important need for it—*per* Richardson J., [1980] N.Z.L.R. 464 at p. 474.
[88] [1964] A.C. 1254 at pp. 1300, 1304.
[89] See *ante*, fn. 59.
[90] [1977] A.C. 1.
[91] *Ibid.* p. 25.

oppressive and vexatious that the judge has the power to intervene. Fortunately, such prosecutions are hardly ever brought but the power of the court to prevent them is, in my view, of great constitutional importance and should be jealously preserved. For a man to be harassed and put to the expense of perhaps a long trial and then given an absolute discharge is hardly from any point of view an effective substitute for the exercise by the court of the power to which I have referred."[92]

The policy considerations behind a particular prosecution may, of course, range widely to include such factors as the perceived harm to the public, the prevalence of the particular offence, the likelihood of repetition and the attitude of the local community or society at large. Any attempt by a court to substitute its views of a piece of legislation, the breach of which forms the subject of an indictment, by declining to proceed with the trial would, as Lord Edmund Davies stressed in *D.P.P.* v. *Humphrys*, be unacceptable in any country acknowledging the supremacy of the rule of law.[93] This kind of intolerable interference by a court is in sharp contrast to the other illustration invoked by the same judge to demonstrate the applicability of the abuse of process principle. "While judges should pause long before staying proceedings which on their face are perfectly regular" he stated "it would indeed be bad for justice if in such fortunately rare cases as *R* v. *Riebold*[94] their hands were tied and they were obliged to allow the further trial to proceed."[95] After conviction of the accused on a charge of conspiracy, the remaining 27 counts of larceny and obtaining by false pretences were ordered to remain on the file and not to be proceeded with unless the court granted leave. According to the Crown's contention the prosecution can thereafter proceed with the indictment even if the judge in a proper exercise of his discretion refuses leave. In the particular circumstances of *Riebold*, the presiding judge, though satisfied that the prosecution did not desire to be oppressive, looked at the matter in the light of the results that would accrue if he were to grant the application by

---

[92] *Ibid.* p. 46. In similar vein, Lord Scarman in *R.* v. *Sang* [1979] 2 All E.R. 1222 lent support to the view that the inherent power of the court to stop a prosecution is confined to situations which can properly be classified as cases of abuse of process. "The role of the judge" Lord Scarman observed "is confined to the forensic process. He controls neither the police nor the prosecuting authority. He neither initiates nor stifles a prosecution. Save in the very rare situation, which is not this case, of an abuse of the process of the Court (against which every Court is duly bound to protect itself) the judge is concerned only with the conduct of the trial"—*ibid.* at p. 1245. Recent cases, in which the *Humphrys* principle has been put to the test in situations exhibiting excessive delay, include *R.* v. *Horsham Justices, ex p. Reeves* [1981] Crim.L.R. 566 and *R.* v. *Grays Justices, ex p. Graham* [1982] 3 All E.R. 653.

[93] [1977] A.C. 1 at p. 53.

[94] [1967] 1 W.L.R. 674.

[95] [1977] A.C. 1 at p. 55. The same judge had delivered the more cautious judgment of the Court of Criminal Appeal in *Connelly* v. *D.P.P.* [1963] 3 All E.R. 510. In the House of Lords Lord Edmund Davies cast aside all equivocations in declaring: "I am now satisfied that, in the words of Lord Parker C.J., in *Mills* v. *Cooper* [1967] 2 Q.B. 456, 467; ' . . . every court has undoubtedly a right in its discretion to decline to hear proceedings on the ground that they are oppressive and an abuse of the process of the court.' " [1977] A.C. 1 at pp. 52–53.

the Crown. Following the principle set forth in *Connelly*, Barry J., refused to allow the remaining counts on the file to be tried on the grounds that any retrial of the outstanding charges would amount to a complete reproduction of the previous trial. This would be bad and oppressive to the accused.

My reading of the two English leading cases, *Connelly* and *Humphrys*, lends no colour to the proposition that there exists a general accountability to the courts rather than to Parliament for the manner in which the Law Officers of the Crown and their agents exercise their discretionary powers in the field of prosecutions. No such claim can reasonably be deduced from the very broad statements attributed to those Lords of Appeal who have espoused the abuse of process principle as a natural corollary to the inherent power of a judge to control the procedure of his court. The illustrations used to exemplify the principle, as well as the results of its application in the cases concerned, mark the very exceptional circumstances in which it would be constitutionally proper for the court to impose its discretion over that of the Crown and its representatives. In retrospect, it may be thought to be unfortunate that the Solicitor General in *Connelly* v. *D.P.P.* advanced the extreme claim that questions of possible abuse in the handling of criminal prosecutions were exclusively a matter for the representatives of the Crown. Although not expressed at the time, it can be assumed that the Solicitor General's claim was founded on the tacit assumption that the House of Commons was the proper forum in which to challenge the actions of the Attorney General and his colleague the Solicitor General. In rejecting Sir Peter Rawlinson's unqualified stance on the subject of control of possible abuses by the Crown's prosecutors, Lord Devlin in *Connelly* did no more than lay the foundation for a strictly limited jurisdiction to protect the court's own responsibilities. This is designed to ensure that in those circumstances where the justice and fairness of the court's procedures are placed in jeopardy it should not be left to the executive branch of government alone to police any abuses that are perpetrated by the prosecuting arm of government. At the same time it must be recognised that to the extent that the abuse of process touchstone is invoked by any court to express its condemnation of police practices or the policy aspects of prosecutorial discretion there exists the potential for a growing conflict as to the constitutional division of powers.

THE GOURIET CASE AND ITS CONSTITUTIONAL IMPLICATIONS

The country has already witnessed one such major confrontation, spearheaded by Lord Denning M.R., in the now famous case of *Gouriet* v. *Union of Post Office Workers et al.* in 1977.[96] At issue in those proceedings

---

[96] [1977] 1 Q.B. 729 (C.A.); [1977] 1 All E.R. 696. For academic reviews of this case and its manifold implications, see R.W.M. Dias: "Götterdämmerung: gods of the law in decline" (1981) 1 *Legal Studies* 3; D.G.T. Williams: "The Prerogative and Preventive Justice" (1977) 36 C.L.J. 201 and (by the same writer) "Preventive Justice and the Courts" [1977] Crim. L.R. 703–709; H.W.R. Wade: "The Attorney General and the Trade Union" (1978) 94 L.Q.R. 4; "Gouriet: The Constitutional Issue and Labour Law Aspects" (1978) 41 M.L.R. 58, and P.P.

was the power of the court to review decisions made by the Attorney General in granting or refusing his consent to the institution of relator proceedings.[97] The factual situation that gave rise to the *Gouriet* case can be simply stated. As a political protest against apartheid the executive of the Union of Post Office Workers had resolved to call upon its members not to handle mail in the course of transmission between England and Wales and the Republic of South Africa. If acted upon, such conduct would have been in clear violation of the Post Office Act 1953, ss.58 and 68.[97a] John Gouriet, secretary of an organisation called The National Association of Freedom, sought to bring a relator action to obtain an injunction against the Union's proposed embargo. The Attorney General, "having considered all the circumstances including the public interest relating to the application for my consent,"refused his fiat, whereupon the plaintiff issued a writ in his own name and applied to the court for an interim injunction against the Postal Workers' Union. Stocker J. dismissed the application on the ground that he had no power to make the order requested. The Court of Appeal was more receptive to Gouriet's pleading. Aware of the fact that the union's order to halt the mail was due to take effect on the Sunday following the applicant's abortive approach to secure the Attorney General's fiat, the Court of Appeal convened on the Saturday for a special sitting. In an earlier relator action, *Attorney General ex rel. McWhirter* v. *Independent Broadcasting Authority*,[98] Lord Denning M.R. (with the support of Lawton L.J.) had advanced the view that "in the last resort, if the Attorney General refuses leave in a proper case or improperly or unreasonably delays in giving leave, or his machinery works too slowly, then a member of the public, who has a sufficient interest, can himself apply to the court itself. He can apply for a declaration and, in a proper case, for an injunction, joining the Attorney General, if need be, as defendant."[99] At the Saturday hearing, doubts were expressed as to whether the Attorney General had directed himself properly, Lawton L.J. being prompted to remark, in the course of argument, that he could see no good legal reason for the Attorney General's refusal of consent though he

---

Mercer: "The Gouriet Case: Public Interest Litigation in Britain and Canada" [1979] *Public Law* 214. For a sample of the intensive coverage and debate conducted in the Press, see also *The Sunday Times*, January 23 & 30, 1977, *The Observer*, January 23 & 30, 1977, *The Times*, January 21 & 24, 1977 & February 3, 1977, *The Guardian*, January 19, 26 & 31, 1977.

[97] See, generally, Edwards *op. cit.*, pp. 286–295; S.A. de Smith, *Judicial Review of Administrative Action* (3rd ed.) pp. 385–388; (4th ed.), pp. 431–434.

[97a] At the time of Mr. Gouriet's intervention, seeking the assistance of the Attorney General and the courts, it is debatable whether the Post Office workers had actually perpetrated any criminal act under the statute—see *per* Lord Wilberforce [1978] A.C. 435 at p. 475 and *per* Lord Fraser *ibid.* at p. 520.

[98] [1973] Q.B. 629.

[99] *Ibid.* pp. 649 (per Denning M.R.) and 657 (*per* Lawton L.J.). As was pointed out by the Attorney General in his argument in the *Gouriet* case, the Court of Appeal had reaffirmed the principle that in relator proceedings the discretion of the Attorney General is absolute and as a matter of law his decision is not to be reviewed or questioned by the court—*per* Denning M.R. (at p. 648) and Cairns L.J. (at p. 653).

could conceive of many political reasons for his decision.[1] Such an observation is regretfully suggestive of the same kind of bias that was itself being condemned and calls into question the objectivity of the court. In fairness, it should be added that, subsequently, Mr. Silkin, in expressing his surprise at Lawton L.J.'s remark, generously acknowledged that the term "political" had more than one meaning.[2]

Intervening in the case, a few days later, at the request of the Court of Appeal, Mr. Silkin explained that the decision whether or not to sanction the bringing of relator proceedings was one of many functions exercised by the Attorney General, not in a ministerial capacity, but in a special jurisdiction divorced from the collective responsibility of other ministers. Some of these functions are statutory, such as the granting or withholding of the Attorney General's consent in certain types of prosecution. Others are of ancient origin such as the power to come before the court *ex officio*; the relator function which was in issue directly in the present case; and the power to bring before the court matters which the Attorney General asks the court to say are in contempt of court. The common thread running through all these discretionary powers is the Attorney General's answerability to Parliament and not to the courts. In support of his position Mr Silkin quoted the classic exposition of the law in the much cited passage from Lord Halsbury L.C.'s judgment in *London County Council* v. *Attorney General*,[3] viz., "My Lords, one question has been raised . . . which I confess I do not understand. I mean the suggestion that the courts have any power over the jurisdiction of the Attorney General when he is suing on behalf of a relator in a matter in which he is the only person who has to decide those questions. It may well be that it is true that the Attorney General ought not to put into operation the whole machinery of the first Law Officer of the Crown in order to bring into court some trifling matter. But if he did, it would not go to his jurisdiction, it would go, I think, to the conduct of his office, and it might be made, perhaps in Parliament, the subject of adverse comment; but what right has a court of law to intervene? It there is excess of power claimed by a particular public body, and it is a matter that concerns the public, it seems to me that it is for the Attorney General and not for the courts to determine whether he ought to initiate litigation in that respect or not . . . In a case where as part of his public duty he has a right to intervene, that which the courts can decide is whether there is excess of power which he, the Attorney General, alleges. Those are the functions of the court; but the initiation of the litigation, and the determination of the question whether it is a proper case for the Attorney General to proceed in, is a matter entirely beyond the jurisdiction of this or any other court. It is a question which the law of this country has made to reside exclusively in the Attorney General. I make

[1] [1977] 1 Q.B. 729 at p. 739; [1977] 1 All E.R. 696 at p. 705.
[2] See *The Times* Law Report, January 18 and 19, 1977.
[3] [1902] A.C. 165.

this observation upon it, though the thing has not been urged here at all, because it seems to me very undesirable to throw any doubt upon the jurisdiction, or the independent exercise of it by the first Law Officer of the Crown."[4] Lord Macnaghten, in the same case, said that he entirely concurred in the above observations.[5]

In making his decision in the *Gouriet* case, the Attorney General told the Court of Appeal that he took into account nothing that was not proper to be considered in exercising his discretion. In refusing his consent he had followed the normal, though not necessarily invariable, practice of giving no specific reasons. Denying that his conduct was that of a dictator who is not subject to challenge, the Attorney General stood firm by his position that if he had acted wrongly he was answerable to Parliament and to Parliament alone, not to the courts.[6] Nevertheless, the Attorney General canvassed openly before the Court of Appeal the range of factors that would operate in his mind when deciding which option to adopt in particular circumstances.[7] It was not, Mr. Silkin explained, simply a matter of whether there was a prima facie case in which the court could act. He had to have regard to the balance of the public interest. He was not simply a lawyer applying a lawyer's knowledge and standards. The Attorney General adopted the language used by Lord Shawcross, when Attorney General, in explaining his reasons for not taking action against various groups of unofficial strikers during the turbulent postwar years.[8] According to Mr. Silkin, though upholding the law was a very important matter, he should also consider whether taking criminal proceedings to uphold the law was likely to produce a situation in which there would be more widespread breakdown in the criminal law than if another course was taken. Precipitate action might produce consequences exactly opposite to those desired. In responding to his own hypothetical question, the Attorney perhaps came closest to imparting the explanation for his refusal to grant his fiat in the *Gouriet* application.[9] If the Attorney General was aware that a union having issued an instruction it was nevertheless, on the best

---

[4] *Ibid*. pp. 167–168.
[5] *Ibid*. p. 170.
[6] [1977] 1 Q.B. 729, *arguendo*, pp. 741–742; 707. A clear distinction, the Attorney argued, should be made between the court's jurisdiction in relation to his special functions and powers when acting as *parens patriae* indirectly on behalf of the Crown and in the exercise of a prerogative power, and the court's exercise of greater control over the executive than in the past in cases such as *Padfield* v. *Min. of Agriculture, Fisheries and Food* [1968] A.C. 997, and *Laker Airways Ltd.* v. *Dept. of Trade* [1977] Q.B. 643. With respect to relator proceedings the Attorney General makes his decisions as representative of the Crown. "It is he alone who has to balance competing interests, however unpopular that may make him. If he acts irresponsibly the Prime Minister may relieve him of his office ex post facto; if the court intervenes, it will be sapping away his independence which decades of authority have not questioned; and it would be wrong for *a* court of law looking at *a* case in *a* particular set of circumstances to change the law and thereby take to itself an important function of Parliament" (Mr. Silkin's emphasis)—[1977] 1 Q.B. 729, p. 745.
[7] *Ibid*. pp. 743–744.
[8] Quoted in Edwards, *op. cit.* pp. 222–223.
[9] See especially [1977] 1 Q.B. 729 at pp. 743–744.

information available, highly unlikely that that instruction would be obeyed, and that the thing most calculated to cause it to be obeyed would be precipitate action against the union, was it to be said, Mr. Silkin argued, that such action was nevertheless to be taken? In discharging his thankless task of deciding where the delicate balance of the public interest should come to rest, the Attorney General was entitled to have recourse to the opinions of his ministerial colleagues but in the final crunch he and he alone must make the ultimate decision. "The Attorney General," Mr. Silkin concluded "has a delicate balance of public interest to perform on the Sovereign's behalf. It is very easy for him to be wrong, and if he is wrong he can be taken to task by Parliament, which controls the actions of the Sovereign. This is a far, far different thing from saying he can be taken to task here, and it is a far, far different thing from saying that, because the law may appear to have inconsistencies and anomalies, it is for the courts to take the great leap either forwards or backwards as the case may be, and treat the law as having been changed when the proper authority to do so is Parliament."[10]

The Master of the Rolls was not persuaded by the Attorney General's assertions as to the absence of any power in the judiciary to review the Law Officers' exercise of their prerogative discretion. In a familiar burst of rhetoric he castigated the Attorney's conduct as "contrary to the whole spirit of the law of England"[11] adding, for good measure, that by refusing to disclose his reasons for not issuing his consent to the relator application the Attorney General had made "a direct challenge to the rule of law."[12] Lord Denning ultimately conceded, however, that the court could not enquire into the giving of consent by the Attorney General to the institution of a relator action but he stoutly maintained that a refusal to grant the necessary fiat could be reviewed by the courts.[13] The Master of the Rolls repeated the position he had taken in the case of *Attorney General, ex rel. McWhirter* v. *Independent Broadcasting Authority*[14] and sought again to elicit support for his views in the pronouncement of Lord Halsbury in *L.C.C.* v. *Attorney General*, quoted above. According to Lord Denning, the Lord Chancellor's statement of the law governing relator actions did not cover a case where the Attorney General has refused his consent. "I am sure" said the Master of the Rolls "that Lord Halsbury

---

[10] *The Guardian*, January 20, 1977.

[11] [1977] 1 Q.B. 729 at p. 753; [1977] 1 All E.R. 696 at p. 710.

[12] *Ibid.* p. 758. The Master of the Rolls said that Mr. Silkin's claim meant that the Attorney General, together with his predecessors and successors, "can, one after another, suspend or dispense with the execution of the law of England." Lord Denning's reminder of the fate that befell James II was put in perspective by Lord Edmund-Davies when, in the course of his judgment in the House of Lords, he stated: "This sounds most alarming, but it has to be said that the Attorney General has for generations possessed and exercised that very power in relation to criminal prosecutions, notwithstanding which the heavens have not fallen and the stars stay in their courses"—[1978] A.C. 435 at p. 507.

[13] *Loc. cit.*

[14] [1973] Q.B. 629 at p. 649.

L.C. did not have such a case in mind for the simple reason that it had never arisen since until now."[15] As a careful reading of the much quoted passage instantly reveals, however, the former Lord Chancellor encompassed both situations in his declaration of the governing principle, saying " . . . the initiation of the litigation and the determination of the question whether it is a proper case for the Attorney General to proceed in, is a matter entirely beyond the jurisdiction of this or any other court" and " . . . it is for the Attorney General and not the courts to determine whether he ought to initiate litigation . . . or not."[16] Lord Denning's colleagues in the Court of Appeal refused to follow his lead, neither Lawton L.J. nor Ormrod L.J. being prepared to subscribe to the Master of the Rolls' claim that the courts have the right to review the Attorney's decision and, if necessary, to substitute its views for those of the senior Law Officer.[17] All three members of the Court of Appeal, however, joined in upholding the plaintiff's claim to a declaration and an interim injunction in the face of a threatened breach of the criminal law.[18]

Even this salvage operation was rejected when the case reached the House of Lords.[19] In sharp contrast to the expansive interpretation advocated by the Master of the Rolls in recent years on the ambit of declarations at the instance of aggrieved citizens, and subscribed to by all the members of the Court of Appeal in *Gouriet* v. *Union of Post Office Workers*, the Lords of Appeal could find no legal basis for the lower court's attempt to outflank the Attorney General's refusal to grant his fiat to Mr. Gouriet. Declaratory relief, Lord Wilberforce stated, can be granted only if "the plaintiff, in proper proceedings in which there is a dispute between the plaintiff and the defendant concerning their respective legal rights, asserts a legal right which is denied or threatened, or claims immunity from

---

[15] [1977] 1 Q.B. 729 at p. 758. Although the question of a refusal by the Attorney General in a relator application had not been considered previously by the courts, the same principle had been addressed in a case where the Attorney had refused to grant his fiat for a writ of error, a discretion that, in its time, was indistinguishable from that exercised in the areas of *nolle prosequi* and relator actions. In *Ex p. Newton* (1855) 4 E & B 869, strong exception was taken to the view expressed by Lord Mansfield C.J. in *R.* v. *Wilkes* (1770) 4 Burr. 2527 at p. 2550 that in the event of a refusal by the Attorney General to issue his fiat in misdemeanour cases he could be directed to do so by the court. Lord Campbell C.J. supported by Wightman, Erle and Crompton JJ., in *Ex p. Newton*, held that it was for the Attorney to determine whether or not each case was proper and that the court could not review his decision. The Attorney General's responsibility was to Parliament. Reference to *Ex p. Newton* was made by Mr. Silkin in the course of his argument before the Court of Appeal, but strangely not one member of the court adverted to its significance. The importance of *Ex p. Newton* was expressly recognised by the House of Lords—see [1978] A.C. 435, at p. 479 *per* Lord Wilberforce, and at p. 506 *per* Lord Edmund-Davies.
[16] [1902] A.C. 165 at pp. 167–168.
[17] *per* Lawton L.J. [1977] 1 Q.B. 729 at pp. 766, 768: "I accept that the courts have no jurisdiction over the discretion of the Attorney General as to when, and when not, he should seek to enforce the law having public consequences. The courts cannot make him act if he does not wish to do so; nor can they, as of right, call upon him to explain why he has not acted;" and *per* Ormrod L.J. at p. 772.
[18] [1977] 1 Q.B. 729 at p. 762 *per* Denning M.R., pp. 770–771 *per* Lawton L.J. and pp. 777–778 *per* Ormrod L.J.
[19] [1978] A.C. 435.

some claim of the defendant against him or that the defendant is infringing or threatens to infringe some public right so as to inflict special damage on the plaintiff. The present proceedings do not possess the required characteristic . . . In my opinion the law is clear, and rightly so, that only the Attorney General—either *ex officio* or *ex relatione*—can apply to the civil courts for the injunctive relief against threatened breaches of the law."[20] The other members of the Appellate Committee expressed themselves in similar terms. Although the larger constitutional issue of accountability to the courts by the Law Officers of the Crown had been abandoned by the plaintiff before the case reached the House of Lords,[21] it is important to note that each of their Lordships rejected any jurisdiction on the part of the courts to review and control the Attorney General's decisions in matters affecting public rights and the public interest generally. Delivering the leading judgment Lord Wilberforce declared it to be "a fundamental principle of English law that private rights can be asserted by individuals, but that public rights can only be asserted by the Attorney General as representing the public. In terms of constitutional law, the rights of the public are vested in the Crown, and the Attorney General enforces them as an officer of the Crown . . . That it is the exclusive right of the Attorney General to represent the public interest— even where individals might be interested in a larger view of the matter is not technical, not procedural, not fictional. It is constitutional . . . it is also wise."[22] Lord Wilberforce went on to explain why, in his opinion, the courts should abstain from staking a claim to substitute their judgment for that of the Attorney General in matters affecting the public interest generally. "The decisions to be made as to the public interest" he argued "are not such as courts are fitted or equipped to make. The very fact that, as the present case very well shows, decisions are of the type to attract political criticism and controversy, shows that they are outside the range of discretionary problems which the courts can resolve. Judges are equipped to find legal rights and administer, on well known principles, discretionary remedies. These matters are widely outside those areas."[23]

Much the same kind of approach was expressed by Lord Edmund Davies. After comparing the stern condemnation of the Attorney General's conduct by the three members of the Court of Appeal with the opinion of Viscount Dilhorne (a former Law Officer) that Mr. Silkin may well have acted in the public interest in withholding his consent,[24] Lord

---

[20] *Ibid.* p. 483. [21] *Ibid.* p. 475.

[22] *Ibid.* pp. 477, 481.

[23] *Ibid.* p. 482. Speaking extra-judicially in his Child Lecture in 1978, Lord Hailsham stated his belief that his father (who was Attorney General between 1924 and 1928) would have taken the same stand as Mr. Silkin did *vis-à-vis* the C.A., adding "I myself have never had any doubt that the decision of the H.L. was right in law"—see *post* p. 281, fn. 38 at p. 9.

[24] *Ibid.* p. 491. " . . . any suggestions that [the Attorney General's] refusal constitutes a challenge to the rule of law appears to me to be entirely misconceived, and though views may differ as to where the balance of public interest lies, it should not be lightly assumed that his refusal of consent in a particular case was unjustified and not grounded on considerations of public interest"—[1977] 3 All E.R. 70 at p. 94.

Edmund Davies declared: "This highlights the undesirability of making the matter one of disputation in the courts, instead of in Parliament."[25] Consistent with these views is the conclusion advanced by Lord Fraser of Tullybelton who stated: "If the Attorney General were to commit a serious error of judgment by withholding consent to relator proceedings in a case where he ought to have given it, the remedy must in my opinion lie in the political field by enforcing his responsibility to Parliament and not in the legal field through the courts. That is appropriate because his error would not be an error of law but would be one of political judgment, using the expression of course not in a party sense but in the sense of weighing the relative importance of different aspects of the public interest. Such matters are not appropriate for decision in the courts."[26]

On the very day that the Court of Appeal handed down its judgment the Attorney General was on his feet in the House of Commons explaining and defending his decision in refusing Mr. Gouriet's application for consent to bring relator proceedings.[27] Mr. Silkin informed the House that before reaching his decision he had sought the advice of Treasury Counsel and had confirmed, through the solicitor to the applicant, that Mr. Gouriet had no special interest beyond that of any other member of the public in seeking the Attorney's fiat. Furthermore he had not been approached for his advice or his fiat by the Post Office Corporation. The crux of the Attorney's defence of his negative decision is contained in the following passage: "On the face of information available to me and in my judgment, the taking of injunction proceedings in my name had the inherent risk, at this early stage, of inflaming the situation before the need for it was demonstrated and might well result in breaches of the law and inconvenience to the public over a much wider area than the two sections of Post Office employees affected by the circular."[28]

"This possible reaction to court proceedings based on a criminal offence" Mr. Silkin continued, "was all the more real in the light of the fact that the Conservative Government in the Industrial Relations Act, 1971, had, for very good reasons which were fully stated by the Solicitor General of the day, deliberately removed from the criminal law the principal

---

[25] *Ibid.* p. 512.
[26] *Ibid.* p. 524. The same Lord of Appeal showed his understanding of the difficult task facing the Attorney General when he stated: "Enforcement of the criminal law is of course a very important public interest, but it is not the only one, and may not always be the predominant one. There may be even more important reasons of public policy why such procedure should not be taken at a particular moment, and it must be proper for the Attorney General (acting of course not for party political advantage) to have regard to them. He may have information that there is a good prospect of averting the threatened illegal conduct by negotiation. Or he may know that the time would be particularly inopportune for a confrontation. Or he may regard it as essential to leave the way clear for subsequent prosecution before a jury. The information before him may be confidential and, even if it is not, it may not be widely available to the public. For reasons of that sort I would be against stretching the law to allow a member of the public to launch preventive proceedings without the consent of the Attorney General"—[1978] A.C. 435 at p. 524.
[27] H.C. Deb., Vol. 924, cols. 1699–1715, January 27, 1977.
[28] *Ibid.*

existing provisions making industrial action a crime. And whether for that reason or not, it had not taken action in the virtually identical circumstances prior to the French nuclear tests in 1973. Whether the wording of section 58 (of the Post Office Act), whose origin was in the Act of 1710, was deliberately excluded from the 1971 amendment, and, if so, why, I do not know, but when originally enacted it was certainly not intended to deal with trade union activity in industrial relations. In all these circumstances and giving full weight to the importance of enforcing the law I concluded, and I am confident that I was right, that the balance of public interest was against giving consent to Mr. Gouriet's application on the Friday to take in my name immediate injunctive proceedings to enforce the criminal law."[29]

Subjected to intensive pressuring from both sides of the House of Commons, Mr. Silkin reminded the Opposition that the Law Officers of previous Conservative Administrations had discharged their prerogative duties in exactly the same manner as he had done. Accusations of political partiality were confined to the expression of a suspicion that political use had been made of the Attorney General's discretion, a suspicion that cynics will instinctively embrace but experience the greatest difficulty in substantiating. In this connexion, amidst all the virulent criticisms generated by the *Gouriet* affair, Mr. Silkin must have gained quiet satisfaction in the comments made by Lord Devlin when reviewing the *Gouriet* proceedings in an article in *The Sunday Times*.[30] The former Lord of Appeal in Ordinary wrote: "Nothing can be more obvious than that a decision to act would have affected Mr. Silkin's political fortunes. While on the one hand he had to be trusted to put that out of his mind, he could not on the other hand be expected to reject a decision which he believed to be in the country's interest because it would also suit himself, and his party too, down to the ground. But the delicacy of his position raises the question whether a decision of this sort should not be taken by someone aloof from party politics. But who else is there? It must be someone with a political sense, someone who knows or can ascertain what the law enforcement resources of government are, and someone who can be questioned in Parliament. Moreover respect for the Attorney-General's independence in this sphere is now established. Nothing in Mr. Silkin's conduct of this case, can be said to have diminished it." The passage of time is likely to reinforce the accuracy and justice of that independent evaluation of the Attorney General's actions in the *Gouriet* case.

---

[29] *Ibid.*

[30] Under the arresting title "Don't Shoot the Attorney," *The Sunday Times*, July 31, 1977. On the issue of enforcing the law, Lord Devlin adopted the realistic stance of recognising that "where there is likely to be resentment which may lead to disorder or industrial unrest, the Attorney General has to estimate the price of law enforcement and decide whether the State should afford it. This is regrettable but in Britain today it is a political fact. This is how fear of the consequences becomes a legitimate consideration. But it must be a fear in the public interest"—*loc. cit.* The former Lord of Appeal in Ordinary also expressed his opposition to licensing the general public to apply for an injunction to prevent crime.

6

Leading Role but no Monopoly as Guardian of the Public Interest*

The resounding reaffirmation by the House of Lords in *Gouriet* of the Attorney General's position as the Crown's principal agent for enforcing public rights was received with less than general acclamation.[1] This body of negative reaction, moreover, has not been confined to England and Wales. In several of the Commonwealth countries proposals are emerging that would enhance the prospects of a private citizen seeking recourse to the courts and their authority, notwithstanding the refusal of the Law Officers to intervene in their capacity as guardians of the public interest.[2] The

* In presenting the Crown's appeal before the House of Lords in *Gouriet*, the Attorney General described the wide range of functions possessed by the Attorney General when acting in his special capacity as "guardian of the public interest." Mr. Silkin continued: "Some might express the view that that was a somewhat dramatic, or even pompous, expression. It is not for one moment asserted that the Attorney is the sole guardian of the public interest. All who are concerned with the administration of justice have a role to play as guardians of the public interest. So indeed do many others. But the Attorney has a particular role and a particular responsibility": [1978] A.C. 435 at p. 442.

In a comprehensive survey of English civil proceedings,—see (1982) 1 *Civil Justice Quarterly* 312–347—Master Sir Jack Jacob helpfully identifies the specialised public officials and agencies which have been assigned responsibility, in their respective spheres, for taking action in the public interest through court proceedings. Among these bodies are: (1) the Director General of Fair Trading with respect to monopolies and mergers, restrictive trading agreements, resale price maintenance, and consumer protection; (2) the Commission for Racial Equality (replacing the former Race Relations Board and the Community Relations Commission); (3) the Equality Opportunities Commission (in relation to the enforcement of the Sex Discrimination Act, 1975); (4) the Official Solicitor of the Supreme Court with extensive duties to assist the court in ensuring that both the liberty of the subject and the public interest are adequately represented; (5) the Comptroller-General of Patents, Designs and Trade Marks with a combination of judicial duties and representation of the public interest in proceedings before the Patents Court, a branch of the Chancery Division; (6) the Criminal Injuries Compensation Board; (7) the Official Receiver in bankruptcy and liquidation proceedings; and (8) the Parliamentary Commissioner and other Ombudsmen. If any reminder is necessary, the cases to be discussed in this chapter will serve as a constant reminder that the judiciary, too, have an abiding responsibility, parallel to that exercised by the Law Officers of the Crown, in safeguarding the public interest in legal proceedings brought before the courts.

[1] For commentaries on the H.L. decision see *post* Chapter 5, fn. 96, and see also *post*, fn. 29.

[2] See, *e.g.* the Australian Law Reform Commission's Working Paper No. 7(1977), pp. 99–134 and Discussion Paper No. 4 (1977), pp. 8–18. Both papers bear the same title: *Access*

reasons for this dissatisfaction with the Attorney General's exclusive authority to determine whether any particular public right should be enforced derives from the perceptions entertained of the Law Officers as members of the government and their proven record as the repository of the public conscience. The broad scope of the Attorney General's position as representative of the Sovereign in the role of *parens patriae* includes both controversial and non-controversial issues.[3] Examples of the latter would normally include the Attorney General's obligation to enforce charitable and public interests, either *ex officio* or *ex relatione* at the instigation of some private person who considers, for example, that a particular charity is being abused. Another instance of more frequent occurrence, as to which little that is controversial is ever heard, inheres in the Crown Proceedings Act 1947, to the effect that proceedings against the Crown are to be instituted against the appropriate government department but, if there is none, or where there is any doubt, then the claim must be made against the Attorney General.[4]

When the public rights, however, are associated with activities that enjoy a certain level of notoriety, either locally or nationally, the degree of satisfaction with the Attorney General's decision will tend to reflect the public's judgment as to whether the government department, public corporation, trade union, or other body concerned should be brought before the court to account for its actions. Above all, the major source of disenchantment with the existing law derives from diminished confidence in the principle of parliamentary accountability and the readiness of the House of Commons to demonstrate its ability to place the public interest above the political fortunes of the respective parties. These extrinsic pressures must not be lost sight of as we proceed to examine further the current status of the Attorney General and Solicitor General as custodians of the public interest and to evaluate the alternative avenues open to a private citizen to achieve his objective of enforcing compliance with the law. Given the most recent and authoritative examination of this subject by the House of Lords in *Gouriet* v. *Union of Post Office Workers*[5] we should commence this chapter by reviewing the principles reaffirmed in that case and the criticisms to which the judgment of the final appellate court has been subjected.

---

to the Courts–I, Standing: Public Interest Suits. Whatever the desirable position might be the Commission "is of the view that the time has come in Australia to provide an alternative to the relator action so as to permit private individuals to approach the court in public interest cases. The procedure should be such as to enable the Attorney General to intervene and put relevant public interest matters. The courts would, of course, retain their present discretion as to the granting of relief and their present cautious policy in respect of injunctions to restrain anticipated criminal offences"—Discussion Paper No. 4, p. 14, and see editorial comment in (1981) Aust. L.J. pp. 247–248.

[3] Edwards, *Law Officers of the Crown*, pp. 286–287, 291–292; S.A. de Smith, *Judicial Review of Administrative Action*, (1st ed.), pp. 236–328, 343.

[4] Edwards, *op. cit.* pp. 153–154, 156.

[5] [1978] A.C. 435.

LOCUS STANDI IN ENFORCING COMPLIANCE WITH THE LAW: THE GOURIET
CASE

The heart of the matter in *Gouriet*—leaving aside altogether the
question of reviewability of the Attorney General's discretion in relator
actions[6]—was the exceptional nature of the civil remedy of injunction in
aid of the criminal law and the extent to which a private citizen, in the
absence of any' special interest in the subject matter concerned, can
activate the Attorney General's powers in a preventative action before the
crime has been committed. Hitherto, as such cases as *Attorney General* v.
Harris[7] and *Attorney General* v. *Bastow*[8] have shown, resort to injunctive
proceedings, in a special application of the relator procedure, has been
restricted to situations in which a public or private body has deliberately
and continuously flouted the criminal law and it has become apparent that
the sanctions available are totally inadequate to ensure that the relevant
legislation is obeyed.[9] Another recognised category is where the defendant's disobedience to the statutory prohibition may cause grave and
irreparable harm, as in *Attorney General* v. *Chaudry*.[10] The Attorney
General's intervention in such cases, *ex officio* on his own initiative, or *ex
relatione* at the instigation of an aggrieved citizen, is as the representative
of the community at large. As Devlin J. explained in *Attorney General* v.
Bastow: "The Attorney General . . . is the officer of the Crown, who is
entrusted with the enforcement of the law. . . . If he, having surveyed the
different ways that are open to him for seeing that the law is enforced and
that it is not defied, has come to the conclusion that the most effective way
is to ask this court for a mandatory injunction—and I am satisfied that the
very nature of a relator action means that he has surveyed those ways and
has come to that conclusion—then I think that this court, once a clear
breach of the right has been shown, should only refuse the application in
exceptional circumstances."[11] The final word, it is emphasised, rests with
the court which can with equal propriety reject the Attorney's assessment
of the situation and deny him its assistance. Such an eventuality, as Devlin
J. stated above, would only arise in such extraordinary circumstances as
where: first, bad faith on the part of the relator was disclosed; secondly, it
was shown that an injunction was likely to prove ineffective or would cause
injustice; or, finally, the evidence adduced at the hearing was not within
the knowledge or contemplation of the Attorney General when granting
his fiat and which might place a different complexion on the whole
situation.[12]

---

[6] This is dealt with in the previous chapter, pp. 129–137.
[7] [1961] 1 Q.B. 74.
[8] [1957] 1 Q.B. 514.
[9] See Edwards, *op. cit.* pp. 289–293.
[10] [1971] 1 W.L.R. 1614.
[11] [1957] 1 Q.B. 514 at p. 522. This is precisely what the Supreme Court of Jamaica did in
Attorney General v. *National Workers Union*, noted in [1982] C.L.B. 1334.
[12] Edwards, *op. cit.* p. 293 and the authorities cited in the accompanying footnotes.

What the House of Lords in *Gouriet* was not prepared to accede to was the argument, accepted by the Court of Appeal, that every member of the public has *locus standi* to apply for declaratory relief through his public interest in having the criminal law enforced.[13] The Appellate Committee rejected unanimously the claim advanced by Mr. Gouriet that, in the event of the Attorney General refusing his fiat to the bringing of relator proceedings with the aim of obtaining the court's injunction to prevent a threatened breach of the criminal law, a private citizen with no special interest at stake could nevertheless invoke the court's jurisdiction to make declarations as to any public rights that might be endangered. Mr. Gouriet's unwillingness to rest his claim on the basis of special damage is readily explained by reason of the wide exemption from tortious liability conferred upon trade unions by section 14 of the Trade Union and Labour Relations Act 1974 and likewise with respect to the Post Office, its officers and servants under sections 9(4) and 29(1) of the Post Office Act 1969.[14] On the question of *locus standi* the Court of Appeal's line of reasoning was discussed by the House of Lords in a series of painstaking judgments the essence of which is captured in Lord Wilberforce's words stating: "The Attorney General's right to seek, in the civil courts, anticipatory prevention of a breach of the law, is a part or aspect of his general power to enforce, in the public interest, public rights. The distinction between public rights, which the Attorney General can and the individual (absent special interest) cannot seek to enforce, and private rights is fundamental in our law. To break it, as the plaintiff's counsel frankly invited us to do, is not a development of the law, but a destruction of one of its pillars. Nor, in my opinion, at least in this particular field, would removal of the distinction be desirable. More than in any other field of public rights, the decision to be taken before embarking on a claim for injunctive relief, involving as it does the interests of the public over a broad horizon, is a decision which the Attorney General alone is suited to make."[15] The other members of the

---

[13] [1977] 1 Q.B. 729, at p. 762 *per* Lord Denning M.R., pp. 770–771 *per* Lawton L.J., and pp. 776–778 *per* Ormrod L.J.

[14] None of these exemptive provisions would have any relevance to proceedings for alleged breaches of the criminal law.

[15] [1978] A.C. 435 at p. 482. Without in any way adverting to the suggested reform of *locus standi* contained in the Australian Law Reform Commission's papers (referred to above), Lord Wilberforce's later observations seem pertinent thereto, especially the following: "It is said that the Attorney-General can always be joined as a party—as he was here—and so can represent the public interest. There are clear objections to making him a defendant: if he were so joined, he, and through him all members of the public, would be bound by the decision. But even if he appears as *amicus curiae*, what is gained? His presence as, presumably, a hostile or at least a non-supporting party cannot legitimize the plaintiff's otherwise illegitimate claim to represent the public. Moreover, when he is there, either he objects to the proceeding in the public interest without giving reasons, in which case (unless the court overrules him) nothing has been achieved beyond his refusal to allow relator proceedings or he is obliged to state his reasons for objection and the court is able to review them. But this is contrary to the whole nature of his office and to the general principle that the court cannot review." *Ibid*. p. 82.

House of Lords adhered closely to the basic differentiation made between the enforcement of public rights and the provision of redress to citizens whose rights in private law have been infringed or are threatened.[16]

Several alternative procedures were referred to by various members of the Appellate Committee as being available to citizens dissatisfied with the uncooperative stance adopted by the Attorney General. None, it might be concluded, provide an adequate answer to the present disinclination to confer *locus standi* upon any private citizen who seeks to enforce public rights.[17] Thus, to the argument that the courts have allowed liberal access to the prerogative writs of mandamus, certiorari and prohibition under a generous conception of *locus standi*, Lord Wilberforce rejected the analogy advanced by the plaintiff in support of his application, declaring: "The correct comparison is not between the court to which application is made for the writ and a court before which an individual seeks to enforce a

---

[16] *Per* Viscount Dilhorne at pp. 492–495; *per* Lord Diplock at pp. 499–501, 502; *per* Lord Edmund Davies at pp. 508–510; and *per* Lord Fraser of Tullybelton at pp. 518–519. The sole qualification to the distinction was said to reside in the Local Government Act 1972, (c.70), s.222(1)(*a*) of which gives local authorities a limited statutory power to sue on behalf of the public for the purpose of preventing public wrongs. For an unsuccessful attempt to limit the operation of this statutory provision by reference to the *Gouriet* decision, see *Kent County Council* v. *Batchelor* [1978] 3 All E.R. 980.

[17] Often cited as illustrative of a more liberal approach to the question of standing is the decision of the Supreme Court of Canada in *Thorson* v. *Attorney General of Canada (No. 2)* (1974) 43 D.L.R. (3d) 1, in which a federal taxpayer (incidentally a former Justice of the Exchequer Court of Canada) sought a declaration as to the unconstitutionality of certain federal statutes. Delivering the majority judgment Laskin J. (as he then was) stated " . . . where all members of the public are affected alike . . . the Court must be able to say that as between allowing a taxpayer's action and denying any standing at all where the Attorney General refuses to act, it may choose to hear the case on its merits"—*ibid.* p. 18. This approach was cited approvingly by the English Law Commission (see below) and by Lord Denning M.R. in *Gouriet* [1977] 1 Q.B. 729 at pp. 759–760. It was dismissed by the House of Lords as "unimpressive support" for the position taken by the Court of Appeal, on the ground that it was concerned with the enforcement of public rights in the special context of the constitutionality of legislation.—*per* Lord Wilberforce [1978] A.C. 435 at p. 480. In a more recent decision *Min. of Justice of Canada et al.* v. *Borowski et al.* (1982) 24 C.R.(3d) 352, the Supreme Court of Canada again divided with Chief Justice Laskin in the dissenting minority. The respondent sought a declaration that the exculpatory provisions of the abortion section of the Criminal Code (s.251(4)(5) and (6)) were invalid by reason of the Canadian Bill of Rights declaration as to the human right to life. The respondent did not fall within any of the special classes encompassed by the Code's exculpatory language (*e.g.* doctors, nurses and hospitals) but was rather opposed on religious grounds to the legislation. Laskin C.J., in rejecting the respondent's claim to standing, reaffirmed the "prevailing policy . . . that a challenger must show some special interest in the operation of the legislation beyond the general interest that is common to all members of the relevant society" and ascribed a limited application only to the decision in *Thorson*—(1982) 24 C.R.(3d) 352 at p. 355. The majority of the Supreme Court of Canada, however, ruled that to establish status as a plaintiff in a suit seeking a declaration that legislation is invalid, where there is a serious issue as to its validity, a person need only show that he is affected by it directly or that "he has a genuine interest as a citizen in the validity of the legislation and that there is no other reasonable and effective manner in which the issue may be brought before the courts." *Ibid.* p. 372. The respondent was awarded standing and allowed to proceed with his action. For developments in other Commonwealth countries see the useful review by G. L. Peiris: "The Doctrine of Locus Standi in Commonwealth Administrative Law" [1983] *Public Law* 52.

public right, but between the court exercising the prerogative power of controlling an abuse of authority or jurisdiction and the Attorney General under prerogative power considering whether the public interest will be served by a relator action. To allow unrestricted access of individuals to any judge of the High Court—seeking enforcement of a public right—would be to depart from analogy not to apply it."[18]

Several academic commentators have bemoaned what they consider to be the reactionary philosophy of the House of Lords. No real surprise was entertained at the rejection of the concept of an *actio popularis* by which any citizen, however remotely concerned, might obtain an injunction to prevent any other citizen from infringing the criminal law. As Professor H.W.R. Wade described it: " . . . in the mood of euphoria that followed the decision of the Court of Appeal it seemed that this door had indeed been opened. The question now, on the other hand, is whether the House of Lords have shut it with too resounding a slam, with repercussions for the disinterested citizen who may legitimately concern himself with the legality of acts of government, if not with those of his private neighbour."[19] Adopting a phrase coined in a New York case by Judge Frank[20] the same writer extolled the advantages of the prerogative remedies whereby "private Attorney Generals" enjoy generous standing in proceedings brought against public authorities.[21]

Of rather less practical significance are the other choices of action that were said to be available to a private individual, the first of which is commencing a criminal prosecution after the event. This right, often overlooked and equally often exaggerated as to its effectiveness as "a valuable constitutional safeguard against inertia or partiality on the part of

---

[18] [1978] A.C. 435 at pp. 482–483, and see S.M. Thio, *Locus Standi and Judicial Review*, (Singapore Univ. Press, 1971) *passim*.

[19] (1978) 94 L.Q.R. 1 at pp. 4–9. The same writer bemoans the absence of any signs that the House of Lords was conscious of the movement towards relaxing the restrictive rules about standing with respect to the prerogative remedies "in the face of otherwise uncontrollable government power." Mentioning Lord Wilberforce and Lord Dilhorne as having acknowledged "without disapproval" the liberal approach to prerogative remedies, Professor Wade ignores Lord Wilberforce's express rejection of any analogy between such proceedings and the status of the private citizen in seeking to enforce public rights by the relator procedure. *Ante*, fn. 18.

[20] In *Associated Industries of New York State Inc.* v. *Ickes* (1943) 134 F. 2d 694.

[21] In considering possible directions for the reform of English law pertaining to standing not much help is provided by the recommendation of the English Law Commission in its *Report on Remedies: Administrative Law* (No. 73) Cmnd. 6407 of 1976, *viz.*, "that the standing necessary to make an application for judicial review should be such interest as the Court considers sufficient in the matter to which the application relates"—*ibid.* para. 48, p. 22. This test was subsequently adopted in the Rules of the Supreme Court, Ord. 53, r. 3(5), prompting the comment by the Master of the Rolls: "The rule committee must have thought it represented the existing law: else the rule would have been *ultra vires*. I also think it represents the existing law. This leaves open the question . . . what is a 'sufficient interest' . . . " [1980] 2 All E.R. 378 and p. 389. The issue of *ultra vires* has now been effectively put to rest with the incorporation of the "sufficient interest" formula into section 31 of the Supreme Court Act 1981 (c.54). In *Gouriet* the defendant trade union, not being a public authority, was outside the scope of the prerogative remedies.

authority,"[22] it must always be remembered is subject to the pervasive intervention of the Director of Public Prosecutions if he thinks fit. By offering no evidence or, in cases triable on indictment, by entering a *nolle prosequi* on the authority of the Attorney General, the citizen's right can be effectively nullified.[23] Lord Diplock, alone among the House of Lords, adverted to yet another option that might have been invoked in anticipation of the commission of a crime. This is the power exercisable by any court of criminal jurisdiction to require that a person enter into recognizances, with or without sureties, to be of good behaviour and to keep the peace.[24] The origins of this preventive justice jurisdiction are rooted in the Justice of the Peace Act 1361 and one writer has advanced the view that its existence might have been used in *Gouriet* as a basis for questioning the allegedly exclusive jurisdiction of the Attorney General to vindicate the public interest in the enforcement of the criminal law.[25]

What has been written so far in this book belies any claim attributed to the Attorney General to exclusive jurisdiction in the enforcement of the criminal law, as part of his prerogative powers as the Crown's chief Law Officer and chief prosecutor. The fact that the Attorney, when intervening in criminal cases, does act on the basis of his prerogative power in no way justifies ascribing to the first Law Officer any exclusive authority that, by definition, must exclude other potential prosecutors from gaining access to the courts without his fiat. This is not so. As we have seen, the vast number of prosecutions initiated by, and conducted on behalf of, the police and other non-police agencies is ample testament to the sharing of prosecutorial responsibility in England and Wales.[26] And to the extent that the position of the private individual who seeks to set the criminal law machinery in motion is more nominal than might be wished,[27] this should

---

[22] *Per* Lord Wilberforce, [1978] A.C. 435 at p. 477; and Lord Diplock spoke of it as being "a useful constitutional safeguard against capricious, corrupt or biased failure or refusal of those authorities [the D.P.P. and the police] to prosecute offenders against the criminal law" (at p. 498). For a less enthusiastic view of private prosecutions see the comments of Edmund Davies L.J. (as he then was) in *Metropolitan Police Commissioner, ex. p. Blackburn* [1968] 2 Q.B. 118 at p. 149, and also those of the Royal Commission on Criminal Procedure, *Report* (Cmnd. 8092) at p. 160.

[23] See Edwards, *op. cit.* pp. 227–237, 398–399. These major limitations to the right of private prosecution were fully recognised by the House of Lords—see, *e.g.* [1978] A.C. 435, *per* Lord Edmund Davies at p. 510, and *per* Lord Fraser of Tullybelton at pp. 520–521, who also distinguished the position under Scottish law pertaining to private prosecutions.

[24] [1978] A.C. at p. 498. Lord Diplock described as inaccurate the description of this procedure as "preventive justice," preferring to label it as "deterrent and punitive" like the ordinary processes of the criminal law (*loc. cit.*).

[25] D.G.T. Williams, (1977) 36 C.L.J. pp. 201–205 and by the same writer in [1977] Crim. L.R., pp. 703–709.

[26] See *ante*, p. 117, fn. 50, and research study No. 10 *"Prosecutions by Private Individuals and Non-Police Agencies"* by K.W. Lidstone, R. Hogg and F. Sutcliffe, (H.M.S.O. 1980).

[27] In *The Law Officers of the Crown* (at pp. 399–400) I drew attention to the misguided repeal in 1908 of the provision in the Prosecution of Offences Act 1879, s.6, conferring on private prosecutors a right of appeal against the action of the D.P.P. who had intervened and stayed the proceedings. This right was exercisable before the High Court which could reinstate the prosecution and order that it be continued either by the Director or the private

direct public concern to methods of overcoming its present limitations.[28] The principal ruling of the House of Lords in *Gouriet*, it should be emphasised again, was not concerned with the general role of the Attorney General in the criminal law but with the more limited question of how may the civil remedies of injunction and declaration be resorted to, by means of relator proceedings, in those circumstances where a crime is apprehended but has not yet been perpetrated. In the unanimous opinion of the House of Lords these particular civil remedies were subordinate to the public rights at stake and in this sphere the Attorney General's prerogative paramountcy could not be displaced by any ordinary citizen without a special interest to protect.[29]

LOCUS STANDI—THE HOUSE OF LORDS AND COURT OF APPEAL AT ODDS AGAIN

Since the decision in *Gouriet* other opportunities have arisen in which to consider the exact boundaries of the House of Lords' ruling regarding the availability of the declaratory remedy. Undaunted by the caustic rebuffs accorded by the Lords to his interpretation of the appropriate qualifying conditions in such cases as *ex parte McWhirter*[30] and *R.* v. *Greater London Council ex p. Blackburn*,[31] the Master of the Rolls, supported by Ackner L.J., was quick to point out in *R.* v. *Inland Revenue Commissioners, ex p. National Federation of Self Employed and Small Businesses Ltd.*,[32] that the *Gouriet* decision was concerned only with relator actions and that the

---

prosecutor. Restoration of this right would do more than confer upon the private citizen in England and Wales the same essential privilege that his counterpart in Scotland may invoke in appropriate circumstances—see *post*, Chapter 10.

[28] If the recommendations of the Phillips Commission are adopted, the private citizen may well experience relief from the financial burden of launching a prosecution, it being envisaged that application to proceed would be channelled initially through the Crown prosecutor. If satisfied that it is a proper case to undertake, the conduct of the proceedings, and the derivative costs, would be assumed entirely by the Crown prosecutor. If not satisfied, the private citizen would have to persuade a magistrates' court (of at least two justices) to grant leave to proceed with the understanding that the prosecutor's reasonable costs would then be met out of central funds but that he would be obliged to undertake the case with the aid of his own solicitor.—*op. cit.* pp. 160–162. In thus emphasising the element of accountability and control over the expenditure of public funds it might be thought that the Commission signally failed to comprehend the possibility of a private prosecutor who desires to exercise his constitutional right without the control of a magistrates' court.

[29] Lord Scarman, in his Sulzbacher Memorial Lecture delivered at Columbia University School of Law on March 31, 1978, thought it significant that public reaction to the *Gouriet* case, including that of *The Times*, the *Guardian*, and most of the legal press, had been strongly against the House of Lords and in favour of the Court of Appeal. "This reaction" he observed "indicates the strength of the tide moving in support of the citizen against the modern engines of power—in this case a formidable pair—a trade union and a law officer acting in parallel, though, I hasten to add, not in combination"—(1975) 78 Col L.R. 1575 at p. 1584. For further evaluations of the *Gouriet* decisions by the Court of Appeal and House of Lords see (1978) 41 M.L.R. 58; [1979] *Public Law* 214; (1978) 12 U.B.C.L.R. 320; (1978) 5 Monash L.R. 133; (1982) 13 Melb. Univ. L.R. 468.

[30] *Sub. nom. Att. Gen. ex. rel McWhirter* v. *Independent Broadcasting Authority* [1973] Q.B. 629 at p. 649, sometimes referred to as "the Andy Warhol" case.

[31] [1976] 3 All E.R. 184 at p. 192.

[32] [1980] 2 All E.R. 378.

House of Lords' rejection of his views on standing did not apply to the prerogative writs such as mandamus and prohibition.[33] Furthermore, there was the added distinction to be made that the *Gouriet* case involved trade unions not public authorities and it was with respect to the latter only that the prerogative remedies are available.[34] As might be expected in view of the large issues at stake the Inland Revenue Commissioners pressed their suit before the House of Lords. In a series of major judgments exploring both the niceties and fundamentals of the law on *locus standi* with respect to judicial review of administrative decisions the Appellate Committee reaffirmed the separate nature of the principles enunciated in *Gouriet* with respect to the enforcement of public rights by way of relator proceedings.

The facts in the *Inland Revenue Commissioners* case were simple. It became publicly known that the Commissioners, faced with the possibility of large scale industrial action, had reached an agreement with the Fleet Street newspapers and their 6000 casual workers that they would be granted an amnesty in relation to their past failure to disclose their proper names on their pay-cheques, thus enabling them to avoid paying income tax, in return for an undertaking to comply with the law in the future. The applicants, riled at what they perceived to be special treatment not accorded to taxpayers in general, sought a declaration under Rules of the Supreme Court, Order 53 that the Board of Inland Revenue had acted unlawfully in granting the amnesty. To establish standing the federation, representing a large body of taxpayers, either self employed or with small businesses, had to show a "sufficient interest" in the subject of the application. Earlier cases had distinguished between the position of ratepayers and taxpayers, the most authoritative judgments, recognising the former class and excluding the latter, being those of the House of Lords in the *Arsenal Football Club Ltd.* v. *Ende*.[35] In the present case the Divisional Court was not prepared to depart from the demarcation line drawn by the House of Lords.[36] It refused to apply the very wide test invoked by the Court of Appeal in *R.* v. *Greater London Council, ex p. Blackburn*,[37] in which the indefatigable Mr. Blackburn succeeded, as a

---

[33] *Ibid.* at pp. 389–390, 398. It should be noted that the Master of the Rolls wanted the best of both worlds. In one breath, the *Gouriet* decision (rejecting his views in *McWhirter* and *Blackburn*) was said to have been concerned with relator proceedings not the procedures by way of the prerogative writs. In another part of his judgment, however, he persisted in arguing that standing in pursuit of injunctions or declarations against public authorities should be governed by exactly the same test as in prerogative writ actions—*ibid.* p. 390.

[34] *Ibid.* p. 389.

[35] [1979] A.C. 1.

[36] *Coram* Lord Widgery C.J., and Griffiths J., the latter being strongly critical of Lord Denning's views on *locus standi*—[1980] 2 All E.R. 378, at pp. 386–387.

[37] *Supra*, fn. 31. *Cf. R.* v. *Metropolitan Police Commissioner, ex parte Blackburn* (1980) *The Times*, March 6, 1980, in which the C.A., whilst recognising the irrepressible plaintiff as having a "sufficient interest," within R.S.C., Ord. 53, r. 3(5), to enforce the laws regulating obscene material, refused to issue an order of mandamus on the ground that there was no justification for the courts meddling with the way the police commissioner performs his duties. The law report contains the following footnote: "Mr. Blackburn while addressing the court on costs and leave to appeal, referred to Lord Denning as the 'greatest living Englishman.' Lord Denning retorted: 'Tell that to the House of Lords'."

resident and citizen of London, in obtaining a writ of prohibition against the Greater London Council to prevent it from exceeding its censorship powers by allowing pornographic films to be shown openly in London.

In the Court of Appeal Lawton L.J. took a conservative position,[38] refusing to follow the bold approach favoured by Lord Denning and Ackner L.J. who were in favour of opening the doors wide to any taxpayer, or group of taxpayers, who have a genuine grievance and seek to challenge what was castigated as the Board's exercise of a dispensing power not given to them by Parliament. "Rather than grant the [Inland] Revenue [Commissioners] such a dispensing power," Lord Denning declaimed "I would allow the body of taxpayers a *locus standi* to complain. Assuredly the Attorney General will not complain on their behalf. He never does complain against a government department."[39] Sweet as the victory may have seemed to the federation representing the self-employed and small businesses it was shortlived, the Lords unanimously reversing the Court of Appeal's decision to grant standing.[40] The Appellate Committee did so by a notably different approach that permitted some, but not all, of their Lordships to subscribe to the general philosophy propounded by the Master of the Rolls[41] and at the same time to reject its application in the particular circumstances before the court.

Based on their review of all the evidence that had been placed before it, the House of Lords could find no support for the allegations that the Inland Revenue Board had failed to do its statutory duty or that its administrative discretion with respect to the Fleet Street casuals was ultra vires and

---

[38] [1980] 2 All E.R. 378 at p. 305.

[39] *Ibid.* at p. 392. In his support, the Master of the Rolls cited the general principle advanced by Prof. H.W.R. Wade in his *Administrative Law* (4th ed., 1977), p. 608 that " . . . in suitable cases, *subject always to discretion*, the court should be able to award the remedy on the application of a public-spirited citizen who has no other interest than a regard for the due observance of the law" (my italics). Missing, of course, from this expansive test are the pertinent factors that will govern the exercise of the court's discretion in determining the original question, *viz.*, what constitutes a "sufficient interest"? See, now, the elucidation provided by the House of Lords in *Inland Revenue Commissioners* v. *National Federation of Self-Employed and Small Businesses Ltd.* [1981] 2 W.L.R. 722, discussed below.

[40] *Supra*, fn. 39. Apart from its substantive importance the case will also be remembered as the occasion in which the Lord Advocate (Lord Mackay of Clashfern Q.C.), rather than one of the English Law Officers, led the team of counsel representing the Inland Revenue Commissioners. No aspect of Scottish law was involved.

[41] See *per* Lord Diplock: "I agree in substance with what Lord Denning said [in *R.* v. *G.L.C., ex parte Blackburn* [1976] 1 W.L.R. 550 at p. 559] though in language more eloquent than it would be my normal style to use. . . . The reference here is to flagrant serious breaches of the law by persons and authorities exercising governmental functions which are continuing unchecked. To revert to technical restrictions on *locus standi* to prevent this, that were current 30 years ago or more, would be to reverse that progress towards a comprehensive system of administrative law that I regard as having been the greatest achievement of the English courts in my judicial lifetime" [1981] 2 W.L.R. 722 at p. 737. *Cf.* the opinion of Lord Roskill: "—the view of the learned Lord Denning M.R., if applied to all applications for judicial review, would extend the individual's right of application for that relief far beyond any acceptable limit, and would give a meaning so wide to a "sufficient interest" in R.S.C. Ord. 53, r.3(5) that they would in practice cease to be, as they were clearly intended to be, words of limitation upon that right of application." *Ibid.* p. 755.

unlawful. Since this was the crux of the application for a declaration it was impossible for the national federation to establish that it had "a sufficient interest in the matter to which the application related" as required by R.S.C., Ord. 53, r. 3(5). The yardstick of "sufficient interest," the House of Lords has decided, must not be isolated from the legal and factual context of the application. Apart from isolated instances of applications by readily identifiable busybodies, cranks and other mischief makers, the court must now have regard to the substantive merits of the application even at the earlier stage of determining whether to grant standing to an applicant in search of a declaration or one of the prerogative remedies. If at that preliminary step in the process the plaintiff fails to establish a prima facie case that the public body concerned has breached or failed to perform its public duty, the court would be in error if it grants leave to proceed.[42]

These considerations, it was explained, pertain only to the pursuit of public law remedies, Lord Diplock pointing out that the Lords' decision in *Gouriet* v. *Union of Post Office Workers* was irrelevant to the questions to be decided in the *Inland Revenue* case.[43] Lord Scarman, likewise, emphasised that the *Gouriet* decision had nothing to do with the prerogative jurisdiction of the High Court.[44] Admittedly the scope of the declaratory remedy has been widened by virtue of the new procedural rules governing standing, as incorporated in R.S.C., Ord. 53, but as Lord Scarman again underlined: "The new Order has made the remedy available as an alternative, or an addition, to the prerogative order. Its availability has, therefore, been extended, but only in the field of public law where a prerogative order may be granted."[45]

These distinctions may well strike more than the ordinary layman as deserving of the strong criticism resorted to by Lord Diplock when he stated: "It would, in my view, be a grave lacuna in our system of public law if a pressure group, like the federation, or even a single public-spirited taxpayer, were prevented by outdated technical rules of *locus standi* from bringing the matter to the attention of the court to vindicate the rule of law and get the unlawful conduct stopped. The Attorney General, although he occasionally applies for prerogative orders against public authorities that do not form part of central government, in practice never does so against government departments. It is not, in my view, a sufficient answer to say that judicial review of the actions of officers or departments of central government is unnecessary because they are accountable to Parliament for the way in which they carry on their functions. They are accountable to Parliament for what they do so far as regards efficiency and policy, and of that Parliament is the only judge; they are responsible to a court of justice

---

[42] For academic assessments of this leading case see J.A. Jolowicz, "Civil Proceedings in the Public Interest" (1982) 13 Cambrian L.R. 32; D. Feldman, "Standing in the Lords: A Matter of Interest" (1982) 45 M.L.R. 92; J. Griffiths, "Mickey Mouse and Standing in Administrative Law" [1982] C.L.J. 6.

[43] [1981] 2 W.L.R. 722.

[44] *Ibid.* at p. 745.

[45] *Ibid.* and see *per* Lord Roskill at p. 752.

for the lawfulness of what they do, and of that the court is the only judge."[46]

This purported division of accountability with respect to adjudicating the conduct of government departments or other public bodies for which Ministers of the Crown are responsible is, I suggest, of dubious validity. As we shall see shortly, the House of Commons has frequently evinced its concern as to the legality of proposed measures that might infringe on this country's international commitments as a member of the European Community.[47] Once enacted, the execution of the same laws becomes the duty of the appropriate divisions of government. Failure to do so, or any excess that steps beyond the statutory powers imposed by Parliament, may be challenged in a court of law by any citizen to whom standing is accorded. The same citizen, or others of like persuasion, may elect instead to publicise the issue in Parliament itself and that assembly is not likely to feel constrained in the range of its debate by the claims to exclusive jurisdiction advanced by Lord Diplock on the question of lawfulness. Any Attorney General who, in deflecting away questions as to the legality of the Government's conduct, sought to take refuge in the argument that such matters were justiciable only before the courts and not in the House of Commons would quickly be made to realise the vulnerability of his interpretation of the office he occupies.

Questions of legality, whenever they arise in government, should normally be disposed of through the channels of the departmental legal advisers in conjunction with the Law Officers, a subject to which we will turn in the next chapter. Applications by the Attorney General for prerogative orders against departments of the central government should not be necessary in view of the binding nature of the Law Officers' rulings on questions of law that are submitted for their determination. Resort to a court of law would be tantamount to acknowledging the lack of authority in the Attorney General to enforce his rulings as the Government's chief legal adviser. It is wrong to equate the functions of the Attorney General with the initiatives available to the ordinary litigant. The private citizen may pursue his remedial rights through the courts or he can avail himself of the parliamentary system in which to air his grievances. The level of parliamentary accountability at present may well be inadequate though there are signs of a more effective use of the Commons' procedures in the form of Select Committee hearings. Judicial claims to expand the courts' jurisdiction at the expense of parliamentary scrutiny of ministerial power should be viewed with circumspection.

The strong commitment of the Court of Appeal to an extensive application of the declaratory procedure produced another major clash between the Master of the Rolls and, in turn, the Law Officers of the Crown and the House of Lords in the case of *Imperial Tobacco Ltd.* v.

[46] *Ibid.* p. 740.
[47] See *post*, pp. 211–213.

Attorney General.[48] In October 1978 Imperial Tobacco Ltd., embarked on a sales promotion campaign known as "Spot Cash." Each packet of cigarettes contained a ticket with spaces covered by silver foil. Rubbing these spaces revealed whether or not the purchaser was entitled to claim a variety of prizes ranging from another free packet of cigarettes to the sum of £5000. Concerned about the potential sales advantage of their rival's enterprising campaign, and informed by counsel's opinion that the scheme was illegal, British American Tobacco Ltd. applied to the Attorney General for his consent to the institution of relator proceedings against Imperial Tobacco. The Attorney General[49] refused and sent the papers to the Director of Public Prosecutions who gave instructions to the police to lay informations in the magistrates' court charging the firm and some of its senior management with various offences under the Lotteries & Amusement Act 1976, ss.2 and 14.[50] Without much ado Imperial Tobacco Ltd. sought a declaration in the Commercial Court that their "Spot Cash" scheme was lawful. In response, the Attorney General and the Director of Public Prosecutions applied to have the proceedings struck out as an abuse of the process of the court, saying that the Commercial Court, if it possessed jurisdiction to entertain the application, should decline to grant the declaration since the issue of legality was now before the Crown Court, a criminal court of coordinate jurisdiction. Donaldson J. (as he then was) ruled that he would have issued the declaration if he had been persuaded, which he was not, that the scheme was lawful.[51] Before the Court of Appeal, the Solicitor General argued that the court should not grant a declaration when simultaneous proceedings were pending for an indictable offence and especially when the proceedings were instituted at the behest of the Director of Public Prosecutions. The Master of the Rolls, joined by the other members of the court, took a very different view maintaining that "in those cases where there is a really debatable question of construction on which it is desirable that an authoritative ruling should be speedily obtained, no barrier should be raised to prevent an action for a declaration against the Attorney General even though criminal proceedings have already been commenced. The Director of Public Prosecutions should not be able to deprive a party of this opportunity by rushing in with a prosecution beforehand. By the very nature of things in the criminal courts it will take a very long time before a ruling can be obtained. And there is a serious risk to an innocent party. He may be convicted on an erroneous interpretation by a lower court and sentenced to imprisonment, with no redress even though it be reversed on appeal. Much better, in a

---

[48] [1980] 1 All E.R. 866.

[49] For Lord Denning's conjecturing on the reasons for the Attorney General's decision to refuse his consent in this case see [1979] 2 All E.R. 592 at p. 597, and for the observations of Viscount Dilhorne on the same subject see [1980] 1 All E.R. 866 at p. 869.

[50] c.32.

[51] [1979] 2 All E.R. 592 at p. 595.

commercial case such as this, for the matter to be decided quickly in an action for a declaration."[52]

If there is any validity to this reasoning, with its wholly negative characterisation of the criminal law process, every defendant in a criminal case can resort to the civil courts for an independent ruling as to the law before the criminal trial has even begun. Commercial firms, in principle and in status, are no different from other persons accused of criminal offences. Attractive as Lord Denning's thesis was to the Court of Appeal, his approach received short shrift from the House of Lords. Describing the Court of Appeal's decision as unprecedented, no previous case having been cited where a civil court, after the commencement of a prosecution, had granted a declaration that no offence had been committed, Viscount Dilhorne declared "I think the administration of justice would become chaotic if, after the start of a prosecution, declarations of innocence could be obtained from a civil court."[53] Lord Lane expressed the unanimous opinion of the Appellate Committee in this statement of the law: "Where criminal proceedings have been properly instituted and are not vexatious or an abuse of the process of the court it is not a proper exercise of the court's discretion to grant to the defendant in those proceedings a declaration that the facts to be alleged by the prosecution do not in law prove the offence charged."[54]

This was not the end of the matter, for the conduct of the Director of Public Prosecutions in his handling of the criminal proceedings against Imperial Tobacco came in for strongly expressed censure from several members of the House of Lords. Lord Lane, subsequently appointed Lord Chief Justice of England and Wales, described the Director's handling of the prosecution as "a maladroit performance."[55] "It seems" Lord Lane said "as though everything was being done to inject venom into a situation where plainly no venom was necessary or justified."[56] Objection was voiced on several points, including the Director's decision to proceed by way of indictment in the Crown Court rather than before the justices, the disproportionate relationship between the minimal harm occasioned by the lottery and the prosecution of individual defendants in addition to the company, and the threats by the Director to charge "the small fry," wholesale and retail tobacconists. Viscount Dilhorne, speaking with the added authority of having served as Attorney General for many years, endeavoured to distance the Director from what he described as the personal views of the principal assistant director in whose name the letters

---

[52] *Ibid.* at p. 599.

[53] [1980] 1 All E.R. 866 at p. 875. The interesting possibility was canvassed and accepted *obiter* that in "a very exceptional case" it would be proper for a civil court to issue a declaration as to the criminality or otherwise of future conduct. In *Att.Gen.* v. *Voluntary Euthanasia Society, The Times*, April 19, 1983, Woolf J., refused an application by the Attorney General for a declaration that the distribution of the Society's booklet, "A Guide to Self-Deliverance" was an offence under the Suicide Act 1961 (9 & 10 Eliz. 2, c. 60).

[54] [1980] 1 All E.R. 866 at p. 884.

[55] *Ibid.* at p. 882.

[56] *Ibid.*

to Imperial Tobacco had been sent. In the absence of any explanation that might be forthcoming, Dilhorne said, the Director of Public Prosecutions' handling of the case "appears difficult, if not impossible, to justify."[57] Such magisterial rebukes are all the more potent because of their infrequency. They also illustrate a form of effective accountability that evades the jurisdictional disputes surrounding judicial control of prosecutorial discretion.

Issues of jurisdiction, as we have seen, have loomed large in the leading cases so far discussed in this chapter. Where these questions are brought together in a cluster it might be expected that much judicial debate would be engendered in the attempt to disentangle and resolve the separate issues. On the contrary, the recent case of the *Royal College of Nursing of the United Kingdom* v. *Department of Health and Social Security*[58] illustrates in a sensible fashion the ability of the judiciary and the Law Officers to discover means whereby urgent questions of public policy can be disposed of expeditiously and without rancour. A fundamental difference of opinion existed between the Royal College of Nurses and the Department of Health and Social Security about the true construction of the Abortion Act 1967,[59] section 1 of which created a new defence when a pregnancy is terminated by a registered medical practitioner in accordance with certain prescribed criteria. In actual practice, hospital nurses are the most visible participants in the procedure, known as medical induction, by the use of the drug prostaglandin for terminating pregnancies. According to a circular issued by the department the nurses' actions were perfectly lawful but the College of Nurses was less confident of the legality of the special degree of participation expected of its nurses. The college accordingly sought clarification of the law by way of a declaration. As Lord Edmund Davies aptly described the college's initiative before the case reached the House of Lords, the nurses "must ruefully regard such judicial illumination as has hitherto been vouchsafed them."[60] The trial judge, Woolf J. having pronounced "without any doubt at all" that the nurses' part in the induction procedure was within the terms of the Act,[61] the Court of Appeal unanimously held that it was not.[62] The same divergence of judicial opinion became evident in the House of Lords which decided, by a majority, to restore Woolf J.'s declaration.[63]

---

[57] *Ibid.* at p. 870. Before the Court of Appeal, the Solicitor General (Mr. Peter Archer, Q.C.) disclosed that "the Director's decision to proceed by way of indictment was because he thought that the magistrates could only inflict a comparatively small fine; whereas on indictment there would be a large fine such as would discourage even this great firm." [1979] 2 All E.R. 592 at p. 598.

[58] [1981] 1 All E.R. 545.

[59] c. 87.

[60] [1981] 1 All E.R. 545 at p. 571.

[61] *Ibid.* at p. 553.

[62] *Ibid.* at pp. 554–563.

[63] *Ibid.* p. 578. The House of Lords announced their decision immediately following the conclusion of counsel's arguments "in the interests of the health service" and "the urgency of the matter." This unusual course, it was emphasised, was not to be taken as a precedent. Written judgments followed two months later.

It was at the initial stage of the case that the jurisdictional obstacles were surmounted with the active cooperation of the Law Officers of the Crown. In the first place it was emphasised that although problems of *locus standi* could not be overcome by consent of the parties, the decision of the House of Lords in the *Imperial Tobacco* case could be distinguished on the ground that the present application for a declaration did not involve existing criminal proceedings. In fact, the House of Lords expressly reserved the question whether a declaration as to the criminality or otherwise of future conduct can ever properly be made by a civil court. More difficulty was encountered in overcoming the similarity between the present application and that presented in *Gouriet* v. *Union of Post Office Workers*. Mr. Gouriet, it will be recalled, was denied standing by the House of Lords on the basis that, in the absence of any special interest on his part, he was not entitled to seek a declaration, let alone an injunction, to enforce public rights. In those circumstances, as Woolf J. reminded himself, the court has jurisdiction to grant a declaration at the suit of the Attorney General alone.[64] The Solicitor General, to facilitate matters, refrained from pressing the Law Officers' prerogative authority, and chose to treat the case as exceptional because of the special responsibilities that the college has in providing not only advice but also insurance for its members.[65] That Woolf J. was somewhat less than totally comfortable with the resolution resorted to is apparent from his references to the alternative procedure for judicial review under R.S.C., Ord. 53, where the jurisdiction of the court is the same as that which previously existed with regard to the prerogative writs and where the requirements as to *locus standi* are more easily satisfied.[66]

The Attorney General as "Amicus Curiae" and "Intervener"

Occasionally the law reports contain references to the Attorney General "intervening" in a private suit or appearing as an *amicus curiae*. In what respects are these roles distinguishable from the standing accorded to the Attorney General or the Solicitor General when either of the Law Officers appears *ex officio* as "guardian of the public interest" to protect or enforce public rights? The role of an *amicus curiae* or friend of the court is by no means restricted to participation by the Law Officers of the Crown, it being open to the presiding judge in any case to grant leave to a person, not necessarily a member of the Bar who is not engaged in the case being litigated, to assist the court in the capacity of an adviser by drawing to its

---

[64] *Ibid.* at p. 551.

[65] *Ibid.*

[66] *Ibid.* pp. 551–552. For a lively review of the later organisational changes in the deployment of the High Court judiciary effectuated under the "new, new Order 53" which came into force on January 12, 1981 (S.I. 1980 No. 2000) see Louis Blom Cooper "The New Face of Judicial Review: Administrative Changes in Order 53" [1982] *Public Law* 250 and also the useful commentary by Andrew Grubb [1983] *Public Law* 190.

attention legal authorities that might otherwise be overlooked.[67] By its very definition an *amicus curiae* is not an adversary in the proceedings. In sharp contrast, where standing is granted to a person who is accepted as an intervener in the proceedings before the court, the intervener becomes a party to those proceedings in the fullest sense of the word. When the Attorney General sees fit to intervene in his official capacity he is entitled to tender evidence, cross examine witnesses, and appeal the judgment in the same manner as if he were an original party to the suit. What then dictates which of the roles, intervener or *amicus curiae*, is properly assumed by the Attorney General?

This question arose directly in 1970 in the case of *Adams* v. *Adams*[68] where the substantive issue was whether English law would recognise a decree of divorce pronounced in the Rhodesian courts, during the period following that country's unilateral declaration of independence, by a judge who had failed to take the oath of allegiance and judicial oath required by the 1961–64 Constitution. Following the decision of (as he then was) Sir Jocelyn Simon, President of the Probate, Divorce and Admiralty Division, reluctantly dismissing the plaintiff's petition, the Secretary of State for Foreign and Commonwealth Affairs announced that the government intended to introduce legislation that would remove the disability reflected in the present case. Ample warning of the impending divorce petition had been communicated by the plaintiff's solicitors to both the Queen's Proctor and the Attorney General, inviting them to assume the role of *amicus curiae* in the proceedings. When the case did come before the President, counsel for the Attorney General claimed a right of intervention on the ground that constitutional issues were involved in which the Sovereign's interests might be affected. In an authoritative statement of the pertinent law, Sir Jocelyn Simon, himself a former Solicitor General, declared[69]: "In my view the Attorney General has a right of intervention in a private suit whenever it may affect the prerogatives of the Crown, including its relations with foreign States (see *Duff Development Co. Ltd.* v. *Kelantan Government*)[70]; and he certainly has in such circumstances a *locus standi* at

---

[67] See, *e.g. Williams* v. *Butlers Ltd.* [1975] 1 W.L.R. 946. The growing reliance on the *amicus* procedure by pressure groups seeking to achieve standing before the Supreme Court of the United States and the Supreme Court of Canada is well documented by M.L. Friedland in his essay on "Pressure Groups and the Development of the Criminal Law" in Glazebrook (Ed.), *Reshaping the Criminal Law* 202 at pp. 226–229. Appearances by the Attorney General, or counsel on his behalf, as *amicus curiae* in the House of Lords are listed in Blom Cooper & Drewry's *Final Appeal*, 1972, O.U.P., pp. 249–250. For the functions of the Queen's Proctor as *amicus* in divorce cases see *Halsbury's Laws of England* (4th ed.) Vol. 13, paras. 1001–1002, and as intervener, *ibid.* paras. 1003–1005. Recognition of the role traditionally performed in English courts by *amici curiae* led the European Court of Human Rights to amend its Rules of Court in 1982 to permit representation from parties other than the Commission and the States involved in the particular dispute. See [1983] *Public Law* 32–33.

[68] [1971] P. 188.

[69] *Ibid.* at pp. 197–198.

[70] [1924] A.C. 797 at p. 802; and see also *The Fagernes* [1927] P. 311 at pp. 323–325, 329–330.

the invitation of the court (*The Parlement Belge*,[71] in which the Attorney General appealed the instant decision) or with the leave of the court (*Engelke* v. *Musmann*).[72] I think that the Attorney General also has the right of intervention at the invitation or with the permission of the court where the suit raises any question of public policy on which the executive may have a view which it may desire to bring to the notice of the court. . . . Of course, if clear law is expressly based on considerations of public policy the executive must accept it and them unless and until the law is changed by the Queen in Parliament. But where the law is doubtful or the considerations of public policy may be in dispute, the view of the executive may be of value to the courts—if only in indicating that this may be a sphere better left for the direct determination of the constitutional Sovereign, the Queen in Parliament. Several issues in the instant case were based or turned on considerations of public policy."

"Although in later stages of the instant case counsel for the Attorney General claimed to be doing no more than drawing relevant legal considerations to the attention of the court," the President continued, "he intervened by wish as a party rather than be heard as *amicus curiae*; and I was left clearly under the impression that there were matters here, not merely affecting prerogative power in the narrower legal sense, but extending to matters of policy, on which the Crown wished to express a view. . . . I would, in any event, have wished to hear an argument on behalf of the Crown. Counsel for the wife expressed the preference that the Attorney General should be an intervener, rather than merely address the court as *amicus curiae*. There seemed to me to be manifest advantages in having the Attorney General a party, so that my judgment can, if so desired, be tested on appeal in all events. I therefore readily allowed the intervention of the Attorney General, who is now a proper party to the suit. . . . "[73]

Rare as the occasions may be when such action becomes necessary, the legitimacy of the Attorney General's claim to intervene, if necessary in private litigation, to make representations as to the policies of Her Majesty's Government is undisputed. The court is, of course, not bound in any way to adopt the administration's view of how the public interest should direct the resolution of the instant dispute. Changing judicial attitudes towards questions of Crown privilege amply demonstrate the proper demarcation of functions by the government's representatives and the courts.[74] Within the narrow sphere of recognising the Law Officers' right to be heard, however, the House of Lords in *Re Westinghouse Uranium Contracts*[75] readily granted the Attorney General leave to

---

[71] (1879) 4 P.D. 129 at pp. 130, 145; and (1880) 5 P.D. 197.

[72] [1928] A.C. 433 at pp. 435–437.

[73] *Ibid*. p. 198.

[74] See *R.* v. *Lewes Justices, ex p. S. of S. for the Home Dept.* [1973] A.C. 388 at pp. 400, 405–6, 407 and 412.

[75] *Sub. nom. Rio Tinto Zinc Corp. et al* v. *Westinghouse Electric Corp.* [1978] A.C. 547.

intervene so that he might convey the strong disapproval of the United Kingdom Government to interference by the United States Department of Justice in a matter beyond its jurisdiction. Private litigation for breach of contract having been instituted before the United States federal courts, objection was taken by certain English companies to the production of documents and the examination of their staff before a United States consular officer in London, pursuant to letters rogatory addressed by the trial judge in Virginia to the High Court of Justice in London.

A plea of self incrimination having been successfully argued before the United States court on the basis of the Fifth Amendment, and in this country on the grounds of possible liability for fines under the EEC Treaty which is part of English law, the United States Department of Justice informed the District Court judge that it required the evidence of the British violations of the United States anti-trust laws by members of an alleged uranium cartel. Involved in the appeal to the House of Lords from the order of MacKenna J., and the Court of Appeal accepting the revised letters rogatory, were complex questions concerning the interpretation of the governing United Kingdom statutes,[76] which need not concern us. Our interest is only with the response of the Appellate Committee to the Attorney General's submissions that consistently strong objections had been registered, through diplomatic channels, against the Justice Department's attempts to extend its anti-trust investigating procedures to include the activities of United Kingdom companies which took place outside United States territory.

Such action, Mr. Silkin asserted was an unacceptable infringement of United Kingdom sovereignty and should be rejected by the courts when exercising their discretion whether or not to give effect to the letters rogatory.[77] The Attorney General's intervention, in Viscount Dilhorne's words, "was . . . not only his right but also his duty to make on the ground that, despite the representations made by Her Majesty's Government, the sovereignty of this country had been prejudiced and that there had been an 'excess of sovereignty or an excess of jurisdiction' on the part of the U.S."[78] The convention binding the two countries to assist each other's courts by way of letters rogatory relates only to evidence required for civil or commercial proceedings. Moreover, the grand jury's anti-trust investigations were not regarded, in the instant case, as the institution of criminal proceedings which might have justified recourse to the Evidence (Proceedings in Other Jurisdictions) Act 1975.[79] Reversing the Court of Appeal, the Appellate Committee acceded to the representations made by

---

[76] Including the Civil Evidence Act 1968 (c. 64), s.14; and the Evidence (Proceedings in Other Jurisdictions) Act 1975 (c. 34), ss.1, 2 and 3; Treaty of Rome, Arts. 85–86 and EEC Regulation 17/62.

[77] *Ibid.* at pp. 589–595. See the comprehensive treatment of this subject by P. F. Sutherland, "The Use of the Letter of Request (or Letter Rogatory) for the purpose of obtaining Evidence for Proceedings in England and abroad" (1983) 31 I.C.L.Q. 784.

[78] *Ibid.* at p. 630.

[79] *Supra*, fn. 76.

the Attorney General and declined to give effect to the unacceptable demands made by his counterpart in the United States.

We have seen already that in relator proceedings, if he consents to the issue of his fiat, the Attorney General's involvement *ex relatione* is only nominal. Once the action is under way the Attorney General virtually drops out of the proceedings, the actual conduct of the case being entirely in the hands of the relator who becomes responsible for the costs of the action and for fulfilling such undertakings as may be imposed by the court. If, however, the Attorney General initiates the proceedings in his *ex officio* capacity for the purpose of enforcing the law, the consensus of judicial opinion still favours according a privileged position to the Law Officer representing the Crown.[80] Rarely does the situation arise, as it did in the unusual circumstances portrayed in the case of *Attorney General ex rel. McWhirter* v. *Independent Broadcasting Authority*,[81] in which the Attorney General assumed different roles in the same case, first as *amicus curiae* and later as the nominal plaintiff in the relator action before the Court of Appeal. The applicant, Ross McWhirter, a member of the public, sought an injunction to restrain the Independent Broadcasting Authority from broadcasting, on the same evening that he appeared before the court, a controversial programme concerning the mentality of an American film producer named Andy Warhol. According to McWhirter the film was in breach of the authority's statutory duty under the Television Act 1964.[82] The applicant claimed that, as time was so short, it was not possible to proceed by way of obtaining the Attorney General's consent to relator proceedings. So as to keep open the issues raised by the extraordinary application brought before it, the Court of Appeal, by a majority, granted an interim injunction.[83] At the subsequent hearing the Attorney General appeared as *amicus curiae* on the preliminary question of the applicant's *locus standi* and intimated that, in view of the importance of the main issue as to the scope of the authority's statutory duty with respect to its

[80] See especially in this regard *Hoffman-LaRoche & Co.* v. *S. of S. for Trade and Industry* [1974] 2 All E.R. 1128. In that case Lord Diplock explained that one of the principal reasons for adopting the device of relator proceedings in the 19th century was that orders for costs could not be made for or against the Crown. Lord Diplock continued: "The Attorney General had an undoubted right to sue alone *ex officio* in a law enforcement action . . . but in that event the expense incurred by him in doing so would have to be met out of public funds win or lose; while the defendant if he lost was out of pocket for the costs of his successful defence. So instead of going *ex officio* it became the practice for the Attorney General to sue on the relation of a subject so that orders for costs could be made for or against the relator (*Attorney General* v. *Cockermouth Local Board* (1874) L.R. 18 Eq. 172)." *Ibid.* at p. 1153. The special position of the Crown with respect to costs was abolished in 1933 (see the Administration of Justice (Misc. Provs.) Act 1933, s.7) but no change was made in the practice of requiring an undertaking in damages from the relator as a condition of the grant of an interlocutory injunction but never requiring a similar undertaking from the Attorney General. The Crown Proceedings Act 1947 has not changed the situation in this regard, thus leading Lord Diplock to criticise the absolute nature of the privilege enjoyed by the Crown, a view also shared by Buckley L.J. in the Court of Appeal [1973] 3 All E.R. 945 at p. 958.
[81] [1973] 2 W.L.R. 344.
[82] c. 21.
[83] *Ibid.* pp. 347–352.

programmes, he would give his consent to relator proceedings properly instituted by the applicant. The applicant's writ having been suitably amended by joining the Attorney General as nominal plaintiff the Attorney withdrew from the case and the appeal proceeded on the substantive issue.

The appearance of the Attorney General in person as *amicus curiae*, as illustrated in the *McWhirter* case above, is most unusual. The occasions, however, in which the authority of the first Law Officer is sought to instruct counsel to assist the court as *amicus curiae* are increasing in frequency and acceptance. This is especially true in the Divisional Court where questions of law may arise in an action between private individuals but which may have direct importance to a government department with its concern to protect the policy which led to the legislation in question being enacted by Parliament. The department may choose to instruct counsel to intervene in the case on its own behalf or it may seek the assistance of the Attorney General.[84] In a Practice Note, issued in April 1975, Lord Widgery C.J. outlined the conditions in which a Divisional Court can properly seek the assistance of an *amicus*.[85] This was followed by the Attorney General, Mr. Silkin, setting down for the benefit of the Court of Appeal and the Industrial Tribunals, respectively, the general principles that guide his decisions to instruct counsel as *amici* in appropriate cases. Foremost among these principles was the view that a court can properly seek the assistance of an *amicus* when it considers that an important point of law falls for decision, and that it would be seriously handicapped in reaching its conclusions without such assistance. The quality of the assistance which an *amicus* can give to the court depends in large measure on the extent to which its difficulties are made clear to those instructing the *amicus*. "As the authority to instruct an *amicus* comes from me," the Attorney General wrote, "the Treasury Solicitor and I feel that it is most convenient if an approach from the court is made to me in the first instance, so that I can make the decision in principle whether to instruct an *amicus* and then make any necessary arrangements with the Treasury Solicitor. If I am in doubt, I might wish to discuss the request myself with the court, although in the normal case I would of course accept the court's request without question."[86]

---

[84] For a striking example see *S. of S. for Trade & Industry* v. *F. Hoffman-La Roche & Co.* [1973] 3 All E.R. 945 and [1974] 2 All E.R. 1128 (H.L.).

[85] Two such situations were predicated—(a) when an important point of law is in danger of being decided without the court hearing argument on both sides; (b) when a point of law which affects a government department is being argued by individuals and the department is not represented. Under (b), the Practice Note suggested, the Department might prefer to instruct counsel on its own behalf in which case counsel will have no special obligation to the court.

[86] Law Officers' Department files, ref. 400/75/0080 dated December 4, 1975. Apart altogether from the possibility of appointing counsel to act as an *amicus* in the circumstances outlined in paragraphs (a) and (b) *supra*, the Attorney General adverted to the other possibility where he might deem it necessary to intervene in his capacity as representative of the public interest. Keeping these separate roles distinct from one another is of prime importance.

Attorney General's References to the Court of Appeal: A New Co-operative Venture

The courts are not the only legal institution which can seek outside assistance in fulfilling their appointed task of resolving important questions of law. Since the Criminal Justice Act 1972,[87] the Attorney General has been empowered to have recourse to the Criminal Division of the Court of Appeal, in a kind of co-operative venture similar to the *amicus* procedure, when the law is in need of speedy clarification and no other immediate procedure is available for securing an authoritative judicial ruling on the point of law in question. According to section 36(1) of the 1972 statute: "Where a person tried on indictment has been acquitted (whether in respect of the whole or part of the indictment) the Attorney General may, if he desires the opinion of the Court of Appeal on a point of law which has arisen in the case, refer that point to the court, and the court shall, in accordance with this section, consider the point and give their opinion on it." It will be noted that the reference is not intended to be addressed in the abstract but in relation to the particular case in which the point of law has arisen. Resort to this provision has been frequent and generally beneficial,[88] particularly in the circumstances that prevail under English law whereby no appeal against the acquittal of an accused can be brought at the instigation of the Crown. Such a right of appeal has long been exercisable by the prosecution in cases heard before a magistrate's court.[89] This is not so in cases tried on indictment in the Crown Court.

In the first reference heard by the Court of Appeal, Criminal Division, in 1974[90] the Lord Chief Justice described the new procedure as conferring upon the prosecution for the first time a limited right of appeal on a point of law following an acquittal on indictment. This description is apt to be seriously misleading since, as Lord Widgery himself was quick to emphasise,[91] both the 1972 Act and the rules made under it go to great lengths to ensure that the person acquitted shall not be prejudiced by the fact that the Attorney General seeks the opinion of the appellate court on a point of law that arises from the original trial. Put shortly, there can be no reversal of the acquittal in the court below. The former accused is given the opportunity, if he wishes, to be represented by counsel before the Court of Appeal without any obligation as to the payment of the legal costs involved.[92] Furthermore, the new law provides that the identity of the

---

[87] c. 71.

[88] For initial appraisals of the new procedure see [1981] Crim. L.R., pp. 543–551 and (1980) 32 *King's Counsel*. Other instances where the executive branch is empowered to seek judicial rulings from the courts by way of a direct reference include: section 4 of the Judicial Committee Act 1833 (3 & 4 Will. 4, c. 41) (in constitutional matters) and section 17 of the Criminal Appeal Act 1968 (c. 19) (at the behest of the Home Secretary, following a conviction on indictment, either (a) the whole case may be referred to the Court of Appeal or (b) if the assistance of the court is desired on any point arising in the case. See, *e.g. R. v. Podola* [1960] 1 Q.B. 325).

[89] See Magistrates Courts Act 1952, s.87.

[90] *Re Attorney General's Reference (No. 1 of 1974)* [1974] 2 All E.R. 899.

[91] *Ibid.* p. 901.   [92] Criminal Justice Act 1972, s.36(5).

respondent, the person acquitted in the Crown Court, is not to be disclosed during the reference proceedings except where the respondent has given his consent in that regard.[93] An example of this is found in the *Attorney General's Reference (No. 2 of 1975)*[94] when the United Artists Corporation Ltd. consented to the disclosure of its name in a criminal case that turned on the interpretation of the Obscene Publications Acts 1959 and 1964. Another unusual feature in the same case was that the Attorney General did not seek to question the ruling of the trial judge in which he directed the acquittal of the respondent company. At an earlier date, in a different court, on a motion for an order to quash the indictment, Lord Widgery C.J. had taken a contrary view as to the interpretation of the relevant sections involved.[95] The private prosecutor having persuaded the Attorney General to exercise his power under section 36 of the Criminal Justice Act 1972, so that the conflict of judicial views might be conclusively resolved, the Court of Appeal found itself in the unfamiliar position of not having the Attorney General contesting the interpretation of the law adopted in the lower court. Instead, the Court of Appeal sought the Attorney's assistance in appointing an *amicus curiae* to present the arguments in favour of a construction contrary to that of the trial judge which led to the company's acquittal.[96] This was done, thus illustrating the complementary nature of both procedures in clarifying an important question of law.

 Enthusiastic judicial support for the new process was made known in one of the earliest references when the Lord Chief Justice declared: "It would be a mistake to think, and we hope people will not think, that references by the Attorney General are confined to cases where heavy questions of law arise and they should not be used in other cases. On the contrary, we hope to see this procedure used extensively for short but important points which require a quick ruling of this court before a potentially false decision of law has too wide circulation in the courts."[97] Some instances of the points of law dealt with under the Attorney General's reference procedure may help to give an appreciation of its usefulness. Among these are: the meaning of the term "conditional intention" in relation to attempted burglary under the Theft Act 1968, s.9(1)[98]; whether sex education is in the "interests of learning" within the defence of public good under the Obscene Publications Act 1959, s.4(1)[99]; the legality of breath tests under the Road Traffic Act 1972, s.9(3), conducted *bona fide* by the police but in ignorance of the

[93] Rule 6 of the Criminal Appeal (Reference of Points of Law) Rules, 1973, (S.I. 1973 No. 1114 (L. 15)).
[94] [1976] 2 All E.R. 763.
[95] *Ibid.* at p. 764.
[96] *Ibid.* Amici counsel before the Court of Appeal had represented the Crown at the original trial before Kenneth Jones J.
[97] *Attorney General's Reference (No. 1 of 1975)* [1975] 2 All E.R. 684 at p. 685.
[98] *Attorney General's Reference (Nos. 1 & 2 of 1979)* [1979] 1 All E.R. 143. In another pioneering move, the Law Commission was permitted to submit a detailed memorandum of the legal problem involved, for the assistance of the Court of Appeal, and received the court's plaudits for the quality of its submission.
[99] *Attorney General's Reference (No. 3 of 1977)* [1978] 3 All E.R. 1166.

manufacturer's instructions[1]; and the significance of the resumption of possession by the true owner to a charge of handling stolen goods under the Theft Act 1968, ss.21(1) and 24(3).[2] Mention should also be made of the possibility for a further reference to the House of Lords either on the motion of the Court of Appeal itself or in pursuance of an application to that end, presumably, by the Attorney General or the respondent.[3] Up to the present time there has been only one such reference to the highest court, the subject being that of the ambit of self defence and the degree of force that can be said to support such a plea.[4] The reference emanated from Northern Ireland at the instigation of the Attorney General in his capacity as Attorney General for Northern Ireland and under parallel legislation to that contained in the Criminal Justice Act 1972, s.36.[5]

CONTEMPT OF COURT AND THE ATTORNEY GENERAL'S ROLE: THE PHILLIMORE REPORT AND DIVERGENT JUDICIAL OPINIONS

If only by virtue of the major attention given to the subject of contempt of court in recent years by the Phillimore Committee, the Court of Appeal and the House of Lords in several important cases involving the news media, and, finally, by Parliament with the enactment of the Contempt of Court Act 1981,[6] we must next direct our minds to the functions associated with the office of the Attorney General in this branch of the law. The alleged contempt may arise in connection with civil or criminal proceedings, its essential characteristic being that of conduct which tends to

[1] *Attorney General's Reference (No. 2 of 1974)* [1975] 1 All E.R. 658.
[2] *Re Attorney General's Reference (No. 1 of 1974)* [1974] 2 All E.R. 899.
[3] Criminal Justice Act 1972, s.36(3).
[4] *Reference under s.48A of the Criminal Appeal (Northern Ireland) Act 1968 (No. 1 of 1975)* [1976] 2 All E.R. 937. The marked unhappiness of the House of Lords with the manner in which the Northern Ireland reference had been drawn up, and the possibility of the appellate court rejecting an Attorney General's reference, were dealt with in the final paragraphs of Lord Edmund Davies' judgment where he stated: "In the result, it appears to me that the public advantage intended to be obtained by s.48A of the 1968 Act will not be secured unless it is throughout borne in mind that only in respect of a point of law which has arisen in the case tried and ending in an acquittal can a reference under that section properly be instituted. Only then would the Attorney-General be correct in saying that 'his decision [to refer] is not a matter for the courts; it may be challenged elsewhere.' For his decision does not relieve the appellate court from their duty of deciding whether what is presented as a point of law 'has arisen in the case,' nor from their duty of rejecting the reference if in their clear view it has not. What I do not think is permissible is to refer (as in the present instance) a case consisting of a mosaic of 'facts,' only some of them arising from any actual case, the rest being not only hypothetical but, indeed, in direct conflict with those of that same actual case. Whether or not we would favour it, neither s.36 of the Criminal Justice Act 1972, nor s.48A of the Criminal Appeal (Northern Ireland) Act 1968, has created a system for referring mere 'moots' to appellate courts for their adjudication. Nevertheless, that is precisely what has unfortunately happened in this case." *Ibid.* at pp. 961–962. See, too, the comments by Viscount Dilhorne (at pp. 953–954) and Lord Russell of Killowen (at p. 962).
[5] See s.63(3) and Sched. 4, conferring jurisdiction upon the Northern Ireland Court of Criminal Appeal corresponding to that exercisable by the English Court of Appeal, Criminal Division. For the parallel provisions in Scottish law, exercisable by the Lord Advocate, see the Criminal Justice (Scotland) Act 1980 (c. 62), s.37.
[6] c. 49.

obstruct, prejudice or otherwise interfere with the administration of justice either generally or in relation to a particular case. The diversity of behaviour that is potentially covered by this broad definition includes disobedience to court orders, contemptuous conduct in the face of the court, reprisals or the intimidation of witnesses or parties to a suit, and conduct out of court that is aimed at, or has the potential for, interfering with the course of justice in particular proceedings.[7] It is with the last of these categories that recent holders of the office of Attorney General have become involved and, in turn, been praised or condemned for their intervention.

Some of the criticism derives from a misconception of the term "contempt of court," it being often thought that it has something to do with protecting the dignity of the judges or those who are associated with the smooth functioning of the courts. This "petty and misleading"[8] interpretation misses the core essentials of the law of contempt. In theory, it is concerned to ensure that the courts of justice function without being subjected to extraneous pressures that might imperil the impartial and objective determination of the issues, which are the critical hallmarks of our courts of justice. Increasingly, however, the realities of the situation have impinged on any exclusive emphasis upon the need to protect the court's processes. Adherence by equally determined proponents of the principles of freedom of speech has demonstrated, in several recent *causes célèbre*, the irreconcilable conflict of values that can arise if either philosophy is pressed to the elimination of the other. Into the very heart of this controversy the Attorney General's office has been injected by virtue of his traditional responsibilities as guardian of the public interest. These interventions by the Attorney General of the day have contributed to the subject of contempt of court being examined by the Appellate Committee of the House of Lords for the first time in its history.[9] If there existed any previous doubts as to the uncertainty and inadequacy of the law of contempt in relation to the press the successive rulings of the House of Lords in *The Sunday Times (Thalidomide)*,[10] *Colonel B*,[11] and the *Exclusive Brethren* cases,[12] served to impel Parliament to deal with the important questions of policy inherent in this branch of the law and to

---

[7] See, generally, C.J. Miller, *Contempt of Court* 1976, and the *Report of the [Phillimore] Committee on Contempt of Court* (1974) Cmnd. 5794, Chapters 1 & 2.

[8] *Johnson* v. *Grant* 1923 S.C. 789 at p. 790 *per* Lord President Clyde, who maintained that the offence of contempt "challenged the fundamental supremacy of the law." More recently, in *Attorney General* v. *B.B.C.* (see below) Lord Scarman declared: "It is high time . . . that we rearranged our law so that the ancient but misleading term 'contempt of court' disappeared from the law's vocabulary" [1980] 3 All E.R. 161 at p. 184. For the Phillimore Committee's response see its *Report*, para. 12.

[9] See the statement by Lord Reid in *Attorney General* v. *Times Newspapers*, (see below) at p. 303.

[10] *Attorney General* v. *Times Newspapers Ltd.* [1974] A.C. 273.

[11] *Attorney General* v. *Leveller Magazine Ltd.* [1979] 1 All E.R. 745.

[12] *Attorney General* v. *British Broadcasting Corporation* [1980] 3 All E.R. 161.

declare its legislative position in the terms of the Contempt of Court Act
1981.

Before turning to the Act's specific provisions we should take stock of
the various judicial statements that concern the Attorney General's
intervention in contempt cases. These represent the fertile ground from
which the new law of contempt has emerged. Theoretically, proceedings to
restrain or punish conduct described as contempt of court, other than
disobedience to court orders, can be brought at the instigation of a private
individual who claims to be adversely affected by the contempt.[13] For all
practical purposes, however, the levers of control over contempt proceedings appear to rest in the hands of the Attorney General. With one notable
exception this policy has enjoyed universal support since 1954 when, in
relation to proceedings for a writ of attachment against the editor of
Lilliput magazine for criminal contempt, the former Lord Chief Justice,
Lord Goddard declared: "In this class of case I have always taken the view
that it would be a good change if these actions were moved only by a Law
Officer or on the instructions of the Attorney General because the object is
to punish an editor who has committed contempt, not to assist the
defence."[14] Proceedings for contempt instituted for the sole purpose of
winning costs, according to Lord Goddard, were previously not uncommon
and, to obviate the possibility of similar objectives being pursued, it
became the accepted practice in the Queen's Bench Division to follow the
guidance proffered by the former Chief Justice.[15] Commenting on the
restriction, in its report on contempt of court in 1959, *Justice*, the British
section of the International Commission of Jurists, described the innovation as most salutary because "it has put an end to proceedings for
contempt by the unworthy and malicious simply for the purpose of winning
costs which had been so common hitherto."[16] The same body's recommendation that no proceedings for criminal contempt outside the court
should be allowed except by the authority of the Attorney General was
rejected by the government when the Administration of Justice Act 1960
was in contemplation.[17]

That the private citizen's right to initiate criminal proceedings without
the prior sanction of the Attorney General was by no means defunct is
illustrated by the two cases of *R. v. Duffy ex p. Nash*[18] and *R. v.
Metropolitan Police, ex p. Blackburn* (No. 2).[19] Exceptional as these
instances may be regarded, it must be emphasised that they arose in

[13] A recent example is *Schering Chemicals Ltd. v. Falkman Ltd.* [1981] 2 W.L.R. 848—see
post, pp. 170–171. Conversely, certain forms of contempt proceedings may only be instituted
by or with the consent of the Attorney General, *e.g.* under the Judicial Proceedings
(Regulation of Reports) Act 1926 (16 & 17 Geo. 5, c. 61), s.1(3).
[14] *R. v. Hargreaves, ex parte Dill, The Times*, November 4, 1953; [1954] Crim L.R. 54.
[15] See Edwards, *op. cit.* p. 242.
[16] *Contempt of Court*, 1959, p. 34. The *Justice* committee was presided over by Sir Hartley
Shawcross (as he then was).
[17] Communication from the Law Officers' Dept.
[18] [1960] 2 Q.B. 188.
[19] [1968] 2 Q.B. 150.

connection with criminal not civil proceedings. Until the enactment of the 1981 Act there was a body of judicial opinion that favoured the reinstitution of the policy that placed the responsibility for instituting contempt proceedings upon the party to a civil suit who claimed that his case was prejudiced by the conduct complained of. This question was widely canvassed in both the Court of Appeal and the House of Lords in what has become known as the *Thalidomide case, Attorney General* v. *Times Newspapers Ltd.*[20] The story began in 1958 when Distillers began to market a drug containing thalidomide. About 450 children were born with gross deformities to mothers who, under medical prescription, had taken the drug during pregnancy. The drug was withdrawn in 1961. Writs were issued later on behalf of a number of children claiming damages against Distillers on the grounds of their alleged negligence. These initial claims were settled in 1968 on the basis of an *ex gratia* payment of £1 million which was conditional on the allegations of negligence against the company being withdrawn. Leave to issue writs out of time was subsequently granted *ex parte* to the parents of a further 266 children. The litigation process dragged on until 1971 when Distillers proposed to set up a charitable trust fund of £3 million for those children who fell outside the original settlement. The proposal was subject to all the parents agreeing to its terms. Five parents refused and resisted an unsuccessful application to have them replaced, as "next friend" of the children, by the Official Solicitor. While the negotiations for an overall settlement continued, the *Sunday Times* published the first in what was intended to be a series of articles drawing public attention to the plight of the children affected by thalidomide. Distillers complained to the Attorney General that the article was in contempt of court since it was prejudicial to the ongoing negotiations. The Attorney decided to take no action, leaving it to the company to take the matter to the Divisional Court if it so wished. Distillers did nothing. The doughty editor of the *Sunday Times* responded by sending the Attorney General a draft copy of a further article which purported to describe in detail the testing, manufacture and marketing of the drug, the factual accuracy of which was confidently asserted by the newspaper and which included evidence that related to the issue of liability in pending thalidomide actions against Distillers. At this point the Attorney intervened and, acting in accordance with the practice established following *Ex parte Dill*, sought an injunction before the Divisional Court restraining the owners of the newspapers from publishing the proposed article. The Divisional Court granted the injunction[21] but this

---

[20] [1973] 1 All E.R. 815 (C.A.); [1973] 3 W.L.R. 298 (H.L.).

[21] [1972] 3 All E.R. 1136. In parallel proceedings for contempt initiated by the Attorney General with respect to a current affairs television programme, the Divisional Court refused to find the respondents guilty because it had not been established that they were deliberately intending to influence the pending proceedings and, in the circumstances, a single showing of the programme did not create a serious risk that the course of justice might be interfered with—see *Attorney General* v. *London Weekend Television Ltd.* [1972] 3 All E.R. 1146.

was discharged by the Court of Appeal, consisting of Lord Denning M.R., Phillimore and Scarman L.JJ.[22]

In the opinion of the Master of the Rolls, a distinction should be maintained with respect to contempt proceedings arising out of a civil suit and a criminal trial, respectively. As he put it: "When a man is on trial in a criminal court, the Crown itself is a party. . . . It is only right and proper that the Attorney General should take the responsibility of proceeding for contempt of court. But a civil action is different. The Attorney General will, as a rule, have no knowledge of the course of a civil action—or of any interference with it—unless it is brought to his knowledge by one of the parties to it. If the Attorney General then himself takes proceedings for contempt, it means that he is putting the authority of the Crown behind the complaint. No doubt he can do so if he thinks it proper to do so. But I venture to suggest that he should not do so except in a plain case. When the case is open to controversy or to argument, it would be better to follow the previous practice. The complainant should be left to take proceedings himself at his own expense and risk as to costs."[23] Phillimore L.J. expressed his views in similar terms stating that, in a civil case, the Attorney General should only move in some quite unusual situation when he thinks that he should do so in the public interest. As for criminal cases, in the event that the Attorney General refused to intervene, Phillimore L.J. was in favour of according the accused the privilege of seeking the protection of the court in his own right.[24] This opinion might have helped to sustain the position taken by the Court of Appeal in the *Gouriet* case but, as we have seen, it was categorically rejected by the House of Lords. Phillimore L.J. was to adhere to his views, and gather support from his fellow members, in the Report of the Departmental Committee on Contempt of Court published in 1974 which bears the chairman's name.[25] According to the Phillimore Report, although the Attorney General must retain his right to act in the public interest where he thinks fit to do so, his prerogative power should not be an exclusive jurisdiction. "If for one reason or another" the Committee recommended "the Attorney General decides not to act the individual should have the right to test the matter in the courts. There are special reasons for such exceptions as exist to the general principle that prosecutions may be privately brought. We do not consider that the reasons here suffice to make contempt a further exception."[26] At the same time, the Phillimore Committee added, the normal practice should be, especially where the alleged contempt is in relation to criminal proceedings, that the attention of the Attorney General should be drawn to the matter before any private proceedings are

---

[22] [1973] 1 All E.R. 815.
[23] *Ibid.* pp. 820–821.
[24] *Ibid.* p. 824.
[25] Cmnd. 5794 of 1974; reprinted in 1977.
[26] *Ibid.* p. 80, para. 187.

begun.[27] And reference was made to the additional safeguard that the leave of the court must be obtained before an application can be made.[28]

To revert to the *Thalidomide* case, it is noteworthy that 12 days after the Divisional Court had granted an injunction to the Attorney General the House of Commons debated a motion concerning the plight of the thalidomide children. No inhibitions were evident on the part of the Lower House in discussing the self same questions that were to be covered in the projected *Sunday Times* article, and the House's own *sub judice* rule was not seen as being infringed.[29] Because of the extraordinary circumstances surrounding the dispute between the thalidomide parents and Distillers, the inordinate delay in bringing the proceedings to finality and the national interest in discussing the matters at issue, the Court of Appeal was unanimous in vacating the injunction. The Attorney General appealed to the House of Lords which, by a majority, reversed the ruling of the lower court and remitted the case to the Divisional Court with a direction to grant an injunction.[30] Various grounds were relied upon in justification of the decision, the broadest principle being that advanced by Lord Diplock and Lord Simon of Glaisdale. According to the former, contempt of court in a civil action is not restricted to conduct calculated to prejudice a fair trial by influencing the tribunal or the witnesses but extends to conduct calculated to inhibit suitors from availing themselves of their constitutional rights to have their legal rights determined by the courts by holding them up to public obloquy for doing so or exposing them to public and prejudicial discussion of the merits of the facts of the case before the action had been disposed of in due course of law.[31] Other members of the House of Lords were content to base their decision on the serious danger that the article in question would induce public prejudgment of the issue of negligence which was the central question in the pending civil proceedings before the court.[32]

Although the members of the Appellate Committee were divided on the question of how far the public interest of maintaining freedom of

---

[27] *Ibid.* For the current procedure in Scottish law and the role of the Lord Advocate, see *ibid.* pp. 82–83.

[28] R.S.C., Ord. 52, r. 2.

[29] H.C. Deb., Vol. 847, cols. 432–510, November 29, 1972. For the parliamentary rules governing discussion of *sub judice* matters, see Erskine May, *Parliamentary Practice* (18th ed. 1971) pp. 416–417; see also C.J. Miller, *Contempt of Court*, pp. 154–157 and G. Drewry, "Parliament and the Sub-Judice Convention," (1972) 122 New L.J. 1158. The parliamentary rule, in respect of pending civil proceedings, forbids all reference to matters under adjudication from the time when the case has been set down for trial or otherwise brought before the court. In the *Thalidomide* case, as Denning M.R. pointed out, all that had happened was that writs had been issued in 266 out of 389 cases and nothing more, *ibid.* p. 823.

[30] [1973] 3 W.L.R. 298.

[31] *Per* Lord Diplock at p. 318; *per* Lord Simon of Glaisdale at p. 325.

[32] See, *e.g.* Lord Reid's judgment, at p. 305, and at p. 308 where he stated: "The crucial question on this point of the case is whether it can even be permissible to urge a party to a litigation to forego his legal rights in whole or in part. . . . In my view it is permissible so long as it is done in a fair and temperate way and without any oblique motive."

discussion on matters of public concern can legitimately outweigh the incidental effects of such discussion in bringing pressure to bear upon a particular litigant to abandon his action, there was unanimous agreement as to the proper role to be fulfilled by the Attorney General in contempt of court proceedings. "Unlike the Court of Appeal" said Lord Diplock "so far from criticizing I commend the practice which has been adopted since 1954 as a result of the observations of Lord Goddard C.J. in *R.* v. *Hargreaves, ex parte Dill,*—whereby the Attorney General accepts the responsibility of receiving complaints of alleged contempt of court from parties to litigation and of making an application in his official capacity for committal of the offender if he thinks this course to be justified in the public interest. He is the appropriate public officer to represent the public interest in the administration of justice. In doing so he acts in constitutional theory on behalf of the Crown, as do Her Majesty's judges themselves; but he acts on behalf of the Crown as 'the fountain of justice' and not in the exercise of its executive functions. It is in a similar capacity that he is available to assist the court as *amicus curiae* and as a nominal party to relator actions. Where it becomes manifest, as it had by 1954, that there is a need that the public interest should be represented in a class of proceedings before courts of justice which have hitherto been conducted by those representing private interests only, we are fortunate in having a constitution flexible enough to permit of this extension of the historic role of the Attorney General."[33]

In the same vein, Lord Cross of Chelsea expressed his disagreement with the views expressed by Lord Denning M.R. and Phillimore L.J. as to the role of the Attorney General in cases of alleged contempt of court. "If the Attorney takes them up" Lord Cross declared "he does not do so as a Minister of the Crown—'putting the authority of the Crown behind the complaint'[34]—but as *amicus curiae* bringing to the notice of the courts one matter of which he considers that the court shall be informed in the interests of the administration of justice.[35] It is, I think, most desirable that in civil as well as in criminal cases anyone who thinks that a criminal contempt of court has been or is about to be committed should, if possible, place the facts before the Attorney General for him to consider whether or not those facts appear to disclose contempt of court of sufficient gravity to warrant his bringing the matter to the notice of the court. Of course, in some cases it may be essential if an application is to be made at all for it to be made promptly and there may be no time for the person affected by the 'contempt' to put the facts before the Attorney before moving himself. Again the fact that the Attorney declines to take up the case will not prevent the complainant from seeking to persuade the court that

[33] *Ibid.* p. 319.
[34] Quoting Lord Denning M.R. in the C.A., [1973] 1 All E.R. 815 at p. 820.
[35] Issue may be taken with Lord Cross's characterisation of the Attorney General's intervention as that of an *amicus curiae*—see *ante*, pp. 153–158.

notwithstanding the refusal of the Attorney to act the matter complained of does in fact constitute a contempt of which the court should take notice."[36]

What emerges from this review of recent judicial opinion in the Court of Appeal and the House of Lords is a strong inclination towards maintaining that delicate balance which identifies the protection of the public interest as the proper function of the Attorney General whilst also asserting the residual right of the subject to move the court on his own behalf if the Attorney General declines to act. Apart from Lord Diplock who saw the Attorney General's role in contempt cases as analogous to that of the first Law Officer's functions in relator actions, thus suggesting exclusive control over the bringing of contempt proceedings, the other judicial opinions which have been quoted above lean strongly in the opposite direction with different degrees of emphasis as to the circumstances that should dictate the Attorney General's intervention. References were made to "some quite unusual situation" and to contempts "of sufficient gravity" to warrant the Attorney General interceding and assuming control over the application to the court. Only the Master of the Rolls saw fit to choose criteria that modern holders of the office of Attorney General can be counted upon to reject as a total distortion of the constitutional responsibilities attaching to that office. According to Lord Denning, it will be recalled, in civil proceedings when the case is "open to controversy or argument" it would be preferable if the Attorney General remained silent and left the complainant to his own resources to seek the protection of the court.[37] If the character of the alleged contempt properly raises important questions of public interest, over and beyond the immediate concerns of one of the parties to a civil suit, it would surely reflect adversely on the incumbent Attorney General if his sole reason for declining to respond to the litigant's call for help was a desire to avoid public controversy or argument. The assessment of what is and what is not a matter of genuine public interest may frequently call for the exercising of a balanced judgment, based on past and contemporary experience, but it would be intolerable if the responsibilities of the office were to be abdicated out of a desire to escape public criticism.

Where the respondent to an application by the Attorney General in contempt proceedings is one of the major organs of the press or of the other news media the likelihood of controversy is heightened by allegations of interference with freedom of speech. It matters not whether the

---

[36] *Ibid.* p. 333. According to Lord Reid: " . . . the Attorney General is not obliged to bring before the court every prima facie case of contempt reported to him. It is entirely for him to judge whether it is in the public interest that he should act"—*ibid.* p. 303. Lord Morris of Borth-y-Gest made the further point: "I do not consider that when an Attorney General decides that he ought to bring a matter to the attention of, and consideration of, a court, he is in any way identifying himself or his office with the interests of a party to litigation"—*ibid.* p. 314.
[37] [1973] 1 All E.R. 815 at pp. 820–821.

objective is that of an injunction or an order for committal until the contempt is discharged. Contempt, even in respect of a civil action, is ostensibly a criminal offence punishable, in an extreme case, by imprisonment. And even the less severe but extremely potent sanction of a temporary injunction can evoke strong language from the court when responding to the Attorney General's appearance in contempt proceedings. A vivid illustration of this is to be found in the recent case of *Attorney General* v. *B.B.C.*,[38] in which the Attorney General sought to restrain the defendants from televising a programme that was extremely critical of a religious sect called the "Exclusive Brethren," including the fact that it was receiving rate relief for its meeting houses under the General Rate Act 1967. A further hearing to secure exemption was destined to take place before a local valuation court shortly after the date of the projected programme, but the B.B.C. refused to cancel the programme. As in other similar cases involving the news media, great expedition was shown in trying the issue of contempt before the Divisional Court, the principal issue being whether the local valuation court was protected as an "inferior court" within the Rules of the Supreme Court, Ord. 52, r. 1(2).[39] As it turned out, the contempt motion was unnecessary because the Exclusive Brethren were granted relief without any hearing, but news of this action did not reach the Court of Appeal before it entertained the Attorney General's motion. By a majority, its members affirmed the decision of the Divisional Court that the valuation court enjoyed the protection of the law of contempt.[40] Counsel for the Attorney General had argued that it was in the public interest and in accordance with sound principle that the decision of the Divisional Court be upheld. In resolving the conflict between the two vital aspects of public interest that always arise in this kind of case, *viz.*, maintaining freedom of speech and, at the same time, protecting the courts from unwarranted interference by public discussion of the issues to be tried, the majority tilted the balance in favour of the latter precept. As the avowed champion of freedom of the press, Lord Denning M.R., dissenting, described the Attorney General's intervention as using the authority of his office to seek a "gagging injunction" at the instance of a party to the case.[41] All such requests that seek to prevent true and fair comment on matters of public interest, he maintained, should be rejected.

Although the House of Lords reversed the Court of Appeal on the question of interpretation, holding that a valuation court was not a court of law and thus outside the ambit of contempt of court, none of their Lordships was disposed to diminish the difficulties of conducting the balancing exercise between the competing considerations alluded to earlier. In rejecting the Attorney General's interpretation of what the

[38] [1980] 3 All E.R. 161 (H.L.).
[39] *Attorney General* v. *B.B.C.* [1978] 2 All E.R. 731 (Div. Ct.).
[40] [1979] 3 All E.R. 45 (C.A.).
[41] *Ibid.* p. 51.

public interest demanded in the instant case, the House of Lords gave a clear indication to Parliament that, if any extension of the scope of contempt was to be entertained, it was for the legislative body, not the court, to make the necessary changes in the law.[42] Referring to the case propounded by the Attorney General, Lord Edmund Davies rejected any suggestion that the courts should rely on the Attorney's *ipse dixit*.[43] To do so in the confidence that all holders of that office will always be both wise and just about instituting proceedings for contempt, it was said, would involve a denial of justice to those who on occasion are bold enough to challenge that a particular holder has been either wise or just. With respect to questions of jurisdiction and recourse to the courts, Lord Edmund Davies declared it to be unacceptable to leave it to the Attorney General ultimately to decide when and where proceedings will lie.

Predictably, in another recent contempt case *Schering Chemicals* v. *Falkman Ltd.*,[44] Lord Denning fastened on to the above summary of Lord Edmund Davies' judgment in the *Exclusive Brethren* case, describing it as an occasion when the Attorney General was "cut down to size."[45] Resort to such language may be excused as the exaggerations of a judge who gets carried away sometimes by the cause he espouses. What is unacceptable is the conclusion advanced by the Master of the Rolls as derived from the House of Lords' decision in the *Exclusive Brethren* case, according to which, he said, "It is not for the Attorney General but for the judges to be the guardians of the public interest."[46] Too much should certainly not be read into this observation, confined as the remark was to the situation in which decisions have to be made with respect to the bringing of contempt applications before the court. What is objectionable is the implied suggestion that the Attorney General of the day is avid for the expansion of his prerogative powers and in his claims to control the ordinary citizen's access to the courts by means of his discretionary fiat. We have already reviewed the wide range of circumstances in which the Attorney General is clothed with authority to represent the public interest. Acceptance of the

---

[42] Examples of such parliamentary action to extend the scope of the law of contempt include the Tribunals of Inquiry (Evidence) Act 1921 (11 & 12 Geo. 5, c.7), s.1(2); Parliamentary Commissioner Act 1967 (c.13), s.9(1); Nuclear Installations Act 1965 (c.57), s.22(5); Restrictive Trade Practices Act 1956 (4 & 5 Eliz. 2, c.68), s.2(3), see, further, Miller, *op. cit.* pp. 33–35.

[43] [1980] 3 All E.R. 161 at pp. 171–172. Lord Edmund Davies was particularly critical of a passage in the Attorney General's printed case, submitted to the House of Lords, which read: "The exercise of the contempt jurisdiction of the High Court is within the discretion and under the control of the court (*and in practice the Attorney General*) as the guardian of the public interest" (my italics). Such a claim was rejected as a "nonchalant" approach to the exercise of balancing the relevant competing interests.

[44] [1981] 2 W.L.R. 848.

[45] *Ibid.* at p. 863. In Lord Denning's colourful language, the *Sunday Times* case, (*ante*, p. 164, fn. 20), by contrast, had "elevated the Attorney General to an exceptional height," (*ibid.* p. 862) a reference to the opinions of all the Law Lords that in civil and criminal cases the Attorney General should first be approached to determine whether he wished to "take over" the projected contempt proceedings.

[46] *Ibid.*

responsibilities constitutionally associated with the Law Officers of the Crown has generally produced a prompt awareness of the invidious position occupied by the Attorney General or the Solicitor General when discharging these responsibilities. An Attorney General who cultivates the pursuit of additional burdens by way of new fields in which to administer his fiat will quickly realise that his decisions activate no wave of popularity. A strong sense of public duty should not be confused with a false attribution of personal aggrandisement on the part of the Law Officers of the Crown.

In the context of applications for the protection of the court in contempt proceedings the overwhelming balance of judicial opinion, and the recommendations of the Phillimore report,[47] incline towards restricting intervention in criminal contempt cases to the Attorney General as the appropriate public officer to represent the public interest in the administration of justice. Conversely, in cases of civil contempt there is widespread support for the view that a residual right of access to the Divisional Court should be exercisable by a private litigant in the event that time constraints preclude a preliminary reference to the Attorney General, or in those cases where the Attorney refuses to intervene in his capacity as the custodian of the public interest. In either of these latter situations, it is considered that the court should be the final arbiter not only with respect to granting standing to the applicant but also with respect to the appropriate sanction to impose if the alleged contempt has been established to its satisfaction.

THE CONTEMPT OF COURT ACT 1981—NEW BURDENS FOR THE ATTORNEY GENERAL

What of the future? The Contempt of Court Act 1981, incorporated into the statute book after a lively passage through the parliamentary machine, is now the benchmark that transcends the recommendations of the Phillimore report and divergence of judicial opinions that we analysed in the preceding pages. All future disputes as to the ambit of criminal contempt of court and the functions of the Attorney General in such cases must begin by referring to the measure hammered out by Parliament. In certain key aspects of the law, substantial changes were introduced from the language of the original Bill. Some of these vitally affect the future responsibility of the Law Officers of the Crown, but before adverting to

---

[47] Cmnd. 5794, para. 187 and recommendations 26 and 27 (pp. 94–95) which read as follows: "The right of private individuals to initiate proceedings for contempt both in England and Wales and in Scotland should continue, without prejudice to the powers of either the Attorney General or Lord Advocate to take proceedings at his own instance should he consider it proper to do so in the public interest. In all contempt proceedings which a private individual seeks to institute, other than those for the enforcement of a court order made in his favour, he should be required to serve notice of these proceedings on the Attorney General or Lord Advocate as the case may be."

these provisions a brief synopsis of the core elements of the new statute may be advisable.[48]

The main terms of the 1981 enactment concern the introduction into English law of the strict liability rule under which an intent to interfere with the court in particular legal proceedings does not have to be established to create liability for a criminal contempt of court. Much of the debate in both Houses touched on the criteria by which contempts will be judged in future cases, the final compromise being embedded in section 2(2) of the Act which states that the strict liability rule applies only to "a publication which creates a substantial risk that the course of justice in the proceedings in question will be seriously impeded or prejudiced."[49] It is also to be noted that the strict liability foundation of contempt of court is confined to publications "by means of speech, writing, broadcast or other modes of communication,"[50] thus excluding forms of conduct such as tampering with witnesses or a newspaper entering into an arrangement to pay money to a witness the amount of which will vary according to whether the accused is convicted. The latter kind of circumstances may well be included within other bases of contempt liability that embrace conduct intended to impede or prejudice the administration of justice.[51] Special provisions deal with fair and accurate reports of legal proceedings,[52] and the defence of innocent publication or distribution is also provided for.[53] In the first major case to be appealed to the House of Lords in connection with the new legislation, *Attorney General* v. *English et al.*,[54] the court ruled that a publication made as part of a discussion in good faith of public affairs or a matter of general public interest is not to be treated as a contempt of court under the strict liability rule if the risk of impediment or prejudice to particular legal proceedings is merely incidental to the discussion. Furthermore, the strict liability rule only applies if the proceedings in question are "active" as defined in Schedule 1, the most significant

---

[48] For instructive commentaries on the entire provisions of the Act, see C.J. Miller, [1982] Crim L.R. 71; and S.H. Bailey (1982) 45 M.L.R. 301.

[49] This test displaces that part of the House of Lords decision in the *Sunday Times* (*Thalidomide*) case [1974] A.C. 273; [1973] 3 All E.R. 54, which held that any prejudgment of the issues in a pending case might constitute a contempt irrespective of its likely effect. The language of section 2(2) was intended to bring English law into line with the European Convention on Human Rights concerning the right of freedom of expression, the European Court of Human Rights having ruled in April 1979, by a majority decision (11 votes to 9) that the House of Lords judgment in the *Sunday Times* case was inconsistent with the fundamental precepts contained in Article 10 of the Convention—see (1979) 2 E.H.R.R. 245. For statements of the Government's spokesmen on the intention behind the main provisions of the 1981 Act see *per* Lord Hailsham, H.L. Deb., Vol. 415, col. 657–660, December 9, 1980, and *per* the Attorney General, Sir Michael Havers, H.C. Deb., Vol. 1000, cols. 28–30, March 2, 1981. For commentaries see D.J. Harris, (1979) 50 B.Y.I.L. 257–260, and F.A. Mann, (1979) 95 L.Q.R. 348.

[50] Contempt of Court Act 1981, s.2(1).

[51] *Ibid.* s.6(*c*) and note also s.6(*a*) which preserves any defence available at common law to a charge of contempt of court under the strict liability rule.

[52] *Ibid.* s.4(1).

[53] *Ibid.* s.3(1) and (2).

[54] [1982] 3 W.L.R. 278; [1982] 2 All E.R. 903 (H.L.).

legislative change in terms of the criminal law being the extention of the scope of the *sub judice* net. Thus, whereas the Phillimore report had recommended that, for England and Wales, the strict liability rule should apply from the time the accused is charged or a summons is served on him[55] the 1981 statute specifies instead the earlier stage involving the arrest of the person suspected.[56] Objections by the news media to such an extention of the *sub judice* rule collapsed in the light of the extraordinary publicity that followed the arrest of the person dubbed as "the Yorkshire Ripper" and before he was actually charged with the multiple murders. There was much conjecture at the time as to why the Attorney General had refrained from instituting contempt proceedings in such flagrant circumstances, it being readily recognised that the widespread violation by Fleet Street of the previously understood *sub judice* rules had already been ignored by the police themselves in convening an unprecedented press conference to announce the successful end to their months old manhunt of the wanted killer.[57] The Attorney General's explanation offered to the House of Commons, during the debates on the Contempt of Court Bill, was that it was customary for a final decision on whether to institute contempt proceedings to be deferred until after the actual trial in which the contempt has been involved, because to do otherwise would "hit the headlines all over again."[58] His predecessor, Mr. Silkin, confirmed that such had been the practice during his period in office, added to which was

---

[55] *Op. cit.* recommendation 10, para. 123.

[56] Sched. 1, para. 4. See, too, the criteria governing strict liability pertaining to contempt arising out of civil proceedings, *ibid.* cls. 12–14, and appellate proceedings, *ibid.* cls. 15 and 16.

[57] For the immediate reaction of the Attorney General to what was described in the Commons as the "well publicised junketing" of the investigating police force, see H.C. Deb., Vol. 996, cols. 745–746 January 12, 1981. A halt to the unbridled reports, broadcasts and commentaries by the Press and other media was apparently effected by a letter, circulated within a few days of Mr. Sutcliffe's arrest, under the signature of the Solicitor General, reminding its recipients of the permissible limits of coverage of an impending prosecution and the penalties associated with a criminal contempt of court, *loc. cit.* After the trial of Peter Sutcliffe had concluded, resulting in his conviction for murder, the Attorney General announced in the House of Commons that he had decided it would not be in the public interest to bring contempt proceedings against the offending media (H.C. Deb., Vol. 6 (6s.), Written Answers, col. 123, June 10, 1981). His reasons for not doing so were later conveyed in a letter to the Chairman of the Press Council (Mr. Patrick Neill Q.C.) who had written to the Attorney General expressing concern about the extent of pre-trial publicity in the case and the widespread breaches of reporting restrictions. With less than obvious confidence Sir Michael Havers informed Mr. Neill that, as a result of the Solicitor General's warning, "I formed the opinion that the lesson had been learned and that it was not in the public interest that a very large number of editors and others should be paraded in front of the Divisional Court"—see *The Times*, February 4, 1983 and the Press Council's report, *Press conduct in the Sutcliffe Case*, 1983. The effects of such exhortations on Fleet Street appear to have been shortlived—see the later proceedings instituted by the Attorney General against five national newspapers for alleged violations of the Contempt of Court Act 1981, s.2 in publishing details of the man charged with burglary following his audacious incursions into Buckingham Palace. The Queen's Bench Division found the publishers of the *Sunday Times* and the *Daily Star* guilty but acquitted the other newspapers *Attorney General* v. *Times Newspapers Ltd., et al., The Times*, February 12, 1983.

[58] H.C. Deb., Vol. 1000, col. 33, March 2, 1981.

the imminence of the new legislation and the certainty it would bring to some of the grey areas in the law of contempt of court.[59]

Amongst these is the clear definition of in whose hands lies the future control over the institution of contempt proceedings that fall within the strict liability rule. Such proceedings, by the terms of section 7 of the 1981 enactment, "shall not be instituted except by or with the consent of the Attorney General or on the motion of a court having jurisdiction to deal with it." Opinion on the merits of such a consent restriction was sharply divided in the House of Lords but generally welcomed by the House of Commons. The former Lord Chancellors, Lord Elwyn Jones and Lord Gardiner, were in favour of rendering strict liability prosecutions for contempt subject to the fiat of the Attorney General,[60] only to be reminded by Lord Hailsham that such a veto was in sharp conflict with the recommendation of the Phillimore Committee which had expressed its opposition to conferring exclusive jurisdiction upon the Attorney General to institute contempt proceedings.[61] The Lord Chancellor based his opposition on two grounds, first, the further encroachment on the private individual's right to bring criminal proceedings and, secondly, the possibility of a conflict of interest arising. Where the Crown, represented by the Attorney General, is one of the parties to a civil or criminal case, the Lord Chancellor argued, to debar the other party from instituting proceedings for a contempt that might substantially prejudice his case is an incompatible duty for the Attorney General to have to perform.[62] At the same time, the Lord Chancellor recognised the force of the arguments in favour of controlling frivolous or vexatious litigants and protecting the reputation and integrity of a person who is being wrongfully and unfairly harassed. At the end of the Lords' consideration of the Bill, Lord Hailsham and those of a like mind accepted the fact that the balance of argument justified the additional powers entrusted to the Attorney General under section 7 of the Act.

There was stronger resistance to the insertion, at a later stage in the passage of the enactment through the Commons, of the Attorney General's consent as a precondition of contempt proceedings that derived from a breach of confidentiality of a jury's deliberations. The original purpose of section 8 of the Act was to reverse the decision of the Divisional

---

[59] *Ibid.*

[60] H.L. Deb., Vol. 415, cols. 666 (*per* Lord Elwyn Jones), 693 (Lord Gardiner), December 9, 1980 (2nd reading); and Vol. 416, cols. 205–206, (*per* Lord Elwyn Jones), January 15, 1981 (Committee Stage). Another former Attorney General, Lord Rawlinson of Ewell, was opposed to making the contempt proceedings subject to the consent of the senior Law Officer, expressing his "very personal embarrassment" in having been forced to bring the *Sunday Times* (*Thalidomide*) case before the court. *Ibid.* col. 207.

[61] See *ante*, p. 171, fn. 47.

[62] For Lord Hailsham's views see H.L. Deb., Vol. 415, col. 694, December 9, 1980, in the course of which the Lord Chancellor also invoked Article 6 of the European Convention on Human Rights in support of the principle that no restriction be placed on the right of the individual to have access to a court of competent jurisdiction; see also H.L. Deb., Vol. 416, cols. 208–210, January 15, 1981 and H.L. Deb., Vol. 422, cols. 236–237, July 1, 1981.

Court in *Attorney General* v. *New Statesman Ltd.*[63] That case arose out of an article published in the *New Statesman* which contained the revelation by a juror in the *Thorpe* trial that one of the chief prosecution witnesses had been discredited following the disclosure of his financial arrangements with another newspaper. The juror in question had not received any inducement or reward for his unsolicited disclosure. The controversial article, the Divisional Court ruled, did not constitute a contempt of court in that it was not likely to either imperil the finality of the verdict in the *Thorpe* case itself or affect the attitude of future jurors.

In its original form, the pertinent clause in the Contempt of Court Bill was designed to close the door opened by the *New Statesman* decision by prohibiting the publication of details of jury deliberations in identified cases. Exempted from this ban were the results of bona fide research into the jury process provided it did not identify individual cases. This safeguard for legitimate research came in for scathing criticism by several Law Lords who descended into the parliamentary forum to argue passionately against any tampering whatsoever with the secrecy of the jury room. To avoid the dangers of trivial, stupid prosecutions arising on account of the breadth of the statutory prohibition resort was had instead to the Attorney General's fiat as the sanctioning mechanism for bringing criminal proceedings.[64]

As the former Attorney General, Mr. Silkin, pointed out, however, the consent clause in section 8 "substitutes for something which ought to be the subject of a general expressed exception . . . the discretion of the Attorney General which ought to be exercised not generally but in relation only to particular cases, as it always has been. It may be said that those who want to indulge in research can go to the Attorney General in advance and ask him to undertake that he will not enable proceedings to be taken against them if they are guilty of contempt of court. But no Attorney General could give such an undertaking on his own account or on his successor's account. That will not do. Therefore, we are either introducing a liability on the Attorney General which he ought not to bear or we are saying that the sanctity of the jury is so great that not even legitimate research ought to be allowed in any circumstances."[65] Despite this eloquent plea to resist the

---

[63] [1982] Q.B. 1. The article in question appeared on July 27, 1982. Also relevant in establishing the origins of section 8 is the *Tenth Report of the Criminal Law Revision Committee: Secrecy of the Jury Room*, Cmnd. 3750 (1968), which recommended that no change be made in the law governing the secrets of the jury room "unless serious mischief has been established or there are other compelling reasons." For the views of Lord Lane C.J., communicated in a letter to the Lord Chancellor, see H.L. Deb., Vol. 422, cols. 248–252, July 1, 1981, and that of Lord Edmund Davies, formerly the Chairman of the C.L.R.C. when the above report was issued, *ibid*. cols. 243–244, 250. The tenor of these remarks was directed to the implications of the facts revealed in the *New Statesman* case and the "serious mischief" inherent in the climate portrayed on that occasion. For a review of the law and practice in the United States see "Public Disclosures of Jury Deliberations" (1983) 96 Harv.L.Rev. 886–906.

[64] For the discussion of these late amendments see H.L. Deb., Vol. 422, cols. 239–254, July 1, 1981, and H.C. Deb., Vol. 1216, cols. 410–438, July 22, 1981.

[65] H.C. Deb., Vol. 1216, cols. 418–419, July 22, 1981.

amendment that had originated in the House of Lords,[66] and the clear distaste exhibited by the present Attorney General for controlling the enforcement of the catch-all offence,[67] the House of Commons excused the imperfections of the legislation by simply transferring the basic problem of discretion to the Law Officers of the Crown. This example of undisguised political expediency should not be forgotten when consideration is given to reintroducing the Consents to Prosecution Bill, discussed in the opening chapter, and to.conducting a major overhaul of the statutory responsibilities imposed upon the office of Attorney General.

[66] For Lord Hailsham's pungent denunciation of the new section—"I think they are going too far in an anti-liberal direction. If the House wants to do that, I shall not complain that I have been beaten, and at least my honour will remain intact"—see H.L. Deb., Vol. 422, col. 253, July 1, 1981.

[67] H.C. Deb., Vol. 1216, cols. 410–412, July 22, 1981. It is, of course, unnecessary to obtain the Attorney General's fiat if the contempt proceedings are initiated on the motion of a court of record having jurisdiction to deal with such a matter—see the language of the 1981 Act, s.8(3).

7

Chief Legal Adviser to the Government and Counsel to Tribunals of Inquiry

In 1973 the United Kingdom became a member of the European Economic Community, an historic step that has entailed important legal and constitutional consequences for all three branches of government. Even before the European Communities Act 1972,[1] was safely on the statute book, there were renewed calls for the appointment of a third Law Officer[2] to assist in handling the host of legal questions that were expected to derive from the interpretation of the Community treaties as well as the implications that derive from the supremacy of Community Law within the Community's legal system. Moreover, by its acceptance of the compulsory jurisdiction of the European Court of Human Rights and its recognition of the right of individual citizens to petition that court,[3] the United Kingdom Government opened the gates to what, in retrospect, may be seen as the forerunner to a full blown, indigenous Bill of Rights with all its ramifications.[4]

Experience since 1972 has confirmed the predictions that the decision to join the European Community would lead to a major expansion of the Law Officers' advisory functions. It has been said that instruments emerging from the European Economic Community lack the precision of enactments

---

[1] c.68. For the uninitiated reader anxious to learn more about the law and institutions of the European Communities reference should be made to D. Lasok & J.W. Bridge's introductory work, under the same title, (3rd ed., 1982, Butterworths), also D. Wyatt & A. Dashwood, *The Substantive Law of the E.E.C.* (1980, Sweet & Maxwell).

[2] See P. Archer, *Fabian Research Series*, pamphlet no. 339 (November 1978) at p. 23.

[3] For the text of the 1950 Convention see Cmnd. 8969, esp. Art. 25 which authorises a petition "by any person, non-governmental organisation or group of individuals claiming to be the victim or a violation . . . of the rights set forth in this Convention." The United Kingdom's acceptance of the compulsory jurisdiction of the European Court under Art. 25 was first made in 1966—see Cmnd. 2894. For instances of recourse to the court involving the United Kingdom see *Ireland* v. *U.K.*, E.C.H.R., Series A, judgment of January 18, 1978 and *The Golder Case* E.C.H.R., Series A, Vol. 18, judgment of February 21, 1975.

[4] See, *e.g.* Lord Scarman's Hamlyn Lectures: *English Law—the New Dimension*, (1974), esp. Part VII. With the enactment of the Constitution Act 1981, by the Westminster Parliament, Canada now has an entrenched Charter of Rights and Freedoms.

prepared by the British parliamentary draftsman's office.[5] Compromise between the member States as to the meaning to be accorded to existing and new treaties and to Community "legislation" is said to be preferable to having resort to the European Court of Justice for an authoritative ruling.[6] This option may not exist where the conflict in interpretation is brought before the British domestic courts for resolution and where adherence to the English doctrine of parliamentary supremacy is assured of its proper place in the arguments placed before the court.[7] In all of these situations the legal position of the United Kingdom Government may require the presence of one or other of the Law Officers of the Crown to argue the government's case. Despite the most pessimistic assessment of the burdens that would be imposed on the Attorney General and Solicitor General following entry into the European Common Market serious objections were raised in opposition to the proposed resurrection of a third Law Officership. Instead, the solution adopted by the Prime Minister at that time was the appointment of a Parliamentary Secretary to the Law Officers' Department,[8] an innovation that has generally been regarded as highly successful in relieving the Attorney General and Solicitor General of much parliamentary work. Speaking in Committees of the House, meeting with outside bodies, and handling much of the parliamentary correspondence have all been discharged without impinging upon the expectations of members of the House of Commons that their problems can only be adequately considered by one of the Law Officers.

Problems Associated with the Resuscitation of a Third Law Officer of the Crown

Some indications of the lukewarm response accorded the idea of a third Law Officer are to be found in studying the background documents relating to the creation in 1964, long before the EEC problems had surfaced, of a ministerial post tailored to the special attributes of its first and only occupant, Sir Eric Fletcher.[9] Described in the first Wilson Government as the Minister without Portfolio, Fletcher's principal duties were to answer questions in the House of Commons relating to certain matters falling within the departmental responsibilities of the Lord Chancellor.[10] These would normally fall within the Attorney General's standard functions in

---

[5] S.C. Silkin: "The Attorney General's Dilemma" (1979) 24 Malayan L.J. xxix.

[6] *Ibid.*

[7] See Lasok and Bridge, *op. cit.* pp. 346–352.

[8] See S.C. Silkin, (1978) 59 *The Parliamentarian*, 149 at p. 158, for an insight into the circumstances surrounding this event. In retrospect Mr. Silkin writes: " . . . I suspect that future thought may well, in the not very distant future, be given to the possibility of a second assistant Law Officer joining the Solicitor General to provide some further relief to the Attorney General's arduous duties."

[9] For the contrary expression of an enthusiastic welcome to Fletcher's appointment as a "Third Law Officer" see (1964) 108 S.J. (November 20, 1964) and (1965) 3 *Law Guardian* 33 (which contains a biographical summary of Dr. Fletcher's career). The only occupant of this new office went on to become Deputy Speaker and, later, Lord Fletcher.

[10] See the Prime Minister's statement in H.C. Deb., Vol. 703, col. 151, December 7, 1964.

the Lower House. The matters specially assigned to the Minister without Portfolio included legal aid, land registration, the Public Trustee, the Public Records Office and the Lands Tribunal. To this meagre fare was added the incumbent's long standing attachment to the cause of law reform and, in particular, the work of the Law Commission.

The appointee in question had wished to be given the status of a third Law Officer with the title of Queen's Solicitor, in recognition of his membership in the solicitors' branch of the profession.[11] It was pointed out, however, in the gentlest of minutes addressed to the new Attorney General, that the office of Solicitor General was originally known as the Queen's Solicitor rendering it historically inappropriate to use the former title alongside its present day successor.[12] Dr. Fletcher's earlier submission, that he should be given the title of Solicitor General, was accompanied by the suggestion that all the customary functions associated with that office should continue to be exercised by the deputy to the Attorney General but under another title.[13] Constitutional objections to each of these ambitious proposals were quickly forthcoming. Added to which it was argued that the appointee, as a solicitor, would not enjoy the privileges of audience. Such privileges continue to be substantially restricted, so far as the higher courts are concerned, to counsel who have been called to the Bar.[14] And a Law Officer of the Crown is, by definition, one of the Crown's counsel.

Substantial as this final argument is in the light of existing circumstances, it may be seriously questioned whether it constituted insurmountable grounds for excluding from appointment an otherwise highly qualified candidate. The movement towards relaxing the rules governing audience before the superior courts is unlikely to diminish and we may well see the day come when a solicitor is accorded the status of a Law Officer of the Crown. Other jurisdictions, which have opted for a unified legal profession, have been able to avoid the predicament that in Britain derives from the bifurcation of the profession. The recommendations of the Royal Commission on Legal Services, however, contain little promise for change in this regard[15] and consequently any push in the direction of opening one

[11] Law Officers' Department files. In his autobiography *In My Time* (1983, Wiedenfeld & Nicholson) Lord Elwyn Jones describes how the new Prime Minister was persuaded to change his original intention of appointing a solicitor as Solicitor General, resulting in the eventual appointment of Dingle Foot, not Fletcher, to that office—*ibid.* p. 195.

[12] See Edwards, *op. cit.* Chapter 7.

[13] Law Officers' Department files. In his minute to the Prime Minister, Fletcher did not balk at the prospect of legislation becoming necessary to achieve his proposed submission.

[14] The detailed rules governing the rights of audience exercisable by barristers and solicitors, respectively, are conveniently set out in Annex 18·1 to the *Final Report of the Royal Commission on Legal Services*, Vol. 1, Cmnd. 7648 of 1979.

[15] *Op. cit.* recommendation 18·4., "Subject to the exercise of the Lord Chancellor's power [under the Courts Act 1971] to extend the rights of audience of solicitors in specific areas, there should be no extension of such rights in Crown business"; "There should be no general extension of the rights of audience of solicitors" *ibid.* 18·5; and "A solicitor should have a right of audience to enable him to deal with formal or unopposed matters in any court" *ibid.* 18·6. For the proposals of the Law Society, and the reactions of the Bar and Bench as submitted to the Royal Commission, see *ibid.* pp. 208–219.

of the Law Officerships to a solicitor Member of Parliament must first overcome the restrictions on the right of audience before the courts.

No theoretical difficulties of a similar nature exist with respect to the discharge of the parliamentary duties associated with the offices of Attorney General and Solicitor General.[16] The division of labour in regard to the House of Commons work must, in practical terms, be a matter for the Attorney General to decide as the senior Law Officer. Each holder of the senior office may have his own predilections, such as wanting to maintain control over answering parliamentary questions. Since a substantial proportion of these are regularly concerned with matters falling within the departmental responsibilities of the Lord Chancellor,[17] experience would suggest the advisability of dividing up the territory in some order of personal preferences. The same comment applies to the division of labour respecting new legislative measures that have legal questions buried within their provisions.[18] The lessons derived from the precedent set in 1964 with the appointment of a Minister without Portfolio, and the recent expedient of having a Parliamentary Secretary attached to the Law Officers' Department, should afford ample guidance in this regard. More substantial obstacles exist in contemplating the assistance that a third Law Officer might bring to the task of advising the government and individual ministers, added to which are the prerogative and statutory restrictions associated with the Attorney General's powers in the area of the criminal law. Should it ever be considered necessary to contemplate the delegation of any of these statutory responsibilities, or to make provision for emergency situations when neither the Attorney General nor the Solicitor General is available to give the necessary authorisation, suitable amend-

[16] Among the Parliamentary tasks envisaged as suitable for transfer from the Solicitor General's shoulders on to those of the Minister without Portfolio was the legal work connected with the passage of the annual Finance Bill through the House of Commons—see Edwards, *op. cit.* p. 47, fn. 73. To this suggestion a departmental minute responded "three rousing cheers." It is not known whether this sentiment was repeated when the proposal reached the Treasury.

[17] It is estimated that an Attorney General answers on average somewhere around 60 parliamentary questions in each session. Of these about a third are on matters falling within the departmental responsibilities of the Lord Chancellor. When fulfilling the latter obligations the position of the Attorney General has been aptly described as really that of "a Parliamentary Secretary to a Ministry whose Minister is a member of the House of Lords"—Law Officers' Department files.

[18] Writing to the Attorney General on October 29, 1964, Dingle Foot, Solicitor General at the time, observed: "During my twenty broken years of parliamentary experience it has seemed to me that the Law Officers have been called on far too often to act as supervisory Ministers. This was particularly noticeable during the thirties when there were several incompetent Ministers. The practice appeared to be growing of bringing in a Law Officer to steer any complicated measure through the House of Commons. In my view this practice did not add to, and indeed even derogated from, the status of the Law Officers. I therefore welcome the appointment of a Minister who will take over, in part at least, this form of parliamentary devilling. At the same time it should be clear at the outset that the division of parliamentary labour between the Law Officers and the Minister without Portfolio is to be decided by the Attorney General"—Law Officers' Department files.

ments to the Law Officers Act 1944,[19] will have to be steered through Parliament.

Arguments surrounding the need for a third Law Officer should not overlook the history surrounding the former office of the Queen's Advocate General. In the specialised fields of international, maritime and ecclesiastical law, the Queen's Advocate (as the holder was generally known) occupied a position equivalent to that of a third Law Officer of the Crown from the beginning of the seventeenth century until the office's eventual demise in 1872. A full account of this ancient office is contained in my earlier study,[20] from which it will be gathered that the appointment of a standing adviser to the Crown on questions of international law was drawn from the ranks of "Doctors Commons," a society of professors and advocates concerned with the practice of civil and common law. With the abolition of that august body in the wake of the Court of Probate Act 1857 and the retirement of the last Queen's Advocate in 1872, there emerged a gradual realisation that a resident full-time legal adviser was necessary to handle the vast increase in the amount of legal work associated with the Foreign Office's international responsibilities.[21] In its third report, tabled in December 1875, the Jessel Committee on the Legal Business of Government recommended the establishment of a Legal Assistant-Under Secretary of State in the Foreign Office.[22] In support of its proposal the committee cited the earlier precedent, in 1867, when the appointment of a similar officer in the Colonial Office was authorised and "whose services the Law Officers have recognised as a material assistance to them."[23]

RESISTANCE TO MAJOR RESTRUCTURING OF THE GOVERNMENT LEGAL SERVICE

Later redesignated as Legal Advisers, respectively, to the Foreign Office and Colonial Office (itself subsequently changed to the Commonwealth Office in tune with the changing times) the occupants of these positions are essentially in-house specialists on all legal questions that fall within the aegis of their particular department. The special status associated with the office of Queen's Advocate General ceased to exist from the time when the last holder of that office retired and the appointment was never renewed.[24] In my earlier work the conclusion was advanced that, notwithstanding the status and authority generally accorded the position of Legal Adviser to the Foreign Office, as the modern descendant from the erstwhile office of Queen's Advocate, it is the Law Officers of the Crown who constitute the government's highest legal advisers and, in cases of dispute, represent the

---

[19] 7 & 8 Geo. 6, c.25.
[20] Edwards, *op. cit.* pp. 131–140.
[21] *Ibid.* pp. 137–138.
[22] *Ibid* p. 139. For additional information as to how the Foreign Office legal staff came into being see the 39 *Transactions of the Grotius Society* 198, 204–206, and D.H.N. Johnson, "The English Tradition in International Law" (1962) 11 I.C.L.Q. 416, at pp. 433–437.
[23] *Ibid.*
[24] *Ibid.* p. 137.

ultimate advisory authority on matters of international and constitutional law.[25] In a recent pamphlet written by a former Solicitor General the position of the Legal Adviser to the Foreign Office is described as "a full time official whose relationship to the Law Officers in matters of international law is similar to that of the Treasury Solicitor and departmental solicitors in domestic law."[26] How appropriate is this analogy? What, it might be asked, is the nature of the day-to-day relationship between the Law Officers, at the apex of the government's hierarchy of legal advisers, and the network of approximately 1,000 lawyers who are members of the so-called "government legal service"? These lawyers, scattered throughout the departments and agencies of the central government, are generally organised into tight cells serving the individual ministries under the guiding hand of the department's senior legal adviser, who may be described as "The Solicitor" even though barristers are eligible for the post.[27]

The most senior of these offices, both in terms of its history and centralising role, is that of the Treasury Solicitor whose existence (under one title or another) can be traced back to around 1655.[28] By 1877 the Treasury Solicitor was acting for 16 departments besides the Treasury. For a short period the office of Director of Public Prosecutions was amalgamated with that of the Treasury Solicitor, a move best explained by the insatiable appetite of the redoubtable Sir Augustus Stephenson for more and more administrative responsibilities in the field of government litigation, civil and criminal.[29] In testimony before the Harcourt Select Committee into the Office of Public Prosecutions in 1884 Stephenson, then the Treasury Solicitor, was in a position to state that with the exception of the Departments of Inland Revenue, Customs, the Board of Trade and the Post Office, he was responsible for the whole of the legal business of government.[30] This trend towards centralisation was very much in tune with the recommendations of the earlier departmental committee, presided over by Sir George Jessel, which conducted a major examination into every aspect of the legal business of government and which was instrumental in bringing about a substantial reorganisation of the functions of departmental solicitors.[31] Whilst not prepared to recommend the establishment of a central office in which all the legal business of government might be conducted the Jessel Committee went on record as

[25] Ibid. p. 140.

[26] P. Archer, "The Role of the Law Officers" (1978) 339 Fabian Research Series 23. Mr. Archer served as Solicitor General from 1974 to 1979.

[27] The most accessible and up to date account of the Government Legal Service is by Gavin Drewry, "Lawyers in the U.K. Civil Service" (1981) 59 Public Administration 15. I am indebted to him for much of the contemporary material contained in the pages that follow.

[28] Edwards, op. cit. pp. 371–372.

[29] Ibid. pp. 371–375.

[30] Ibid. pp. 372–373.

[31] See the Third Report of the Jessel Departmental Committee appointed to inquire into the Legal Business of Government, H.C. Paper 199 of 1877.

stating that it considered it "both possible and desirable that the departmental solicitors should have a common head and, to a certain extent, form a single body."[32] The natural candidate for this role was the Treasury Solicitor, and the committee so recommended. With due sensitivity, however, to departmental independence and the prerogatives claimed by the permanent heads of the departments of State, the Jessel Committee declared: "We do not contemplate that the Solicitor to the Treasury would in any degree interfere between the departmental solicitors and the chiefs of their several offices, but simply that he would be the head of their class, who would act as a referee in all matters of practice, and would be the adviser of the Government in all that concerned the organisation of the legal departments of its offices."[33] In the years that have elapsed since that report was delivered not much has changed. The bulk of departmental litigation and conveyancing has been centralised in the office of the Treasury Solicitor and the same senior official is viewed as the central coordinator of recruitment, promotion and training policies with respect to the vast majority of legal members in the civil service. The principal exceptions in which the Treasury Solicitor's career management functions can be said not to run are the Lord Chancellor's Department, the Foreign and Commonwealth Office (where the Legal Adviser and his 22 professional lawyers are part of the diplomatic service), and the 21 lawyers who are employed in the highly specialised task of legislative drafting in the office of Parliamentary Counsel.[34]

There appears to be little prospect of realising a major reorganisation of the entire legal service within government along the lines adopted in Canada following the recommendations of the Glassco Commission in the 1960s.[35] The Canadian inquiry favoured the concept of a centralised body of lawyers acting within the establishment of the federal Department of Justice and exercising their professional duties from a position of detachment.[36] The benefits of diverse experience drawn from postings to

[32] Op. cit. p. 62, quoted in Drewry op. cit. pp.19–20.

[33] Ibid.

[34] Drewry, op. cit. pp. 28–29. Also listed as exceptions, because the Treasury Solicitor's parish does not extend north of the Tweed, are the professional staff of the Lord Advocate (7 members of the Scottish Bar and 4 solicitors, and the 195 members of the procurator fiscal service attached to the Crown Office in Edinburgh).

[35] Report of the Royal Commission on Government Organisation, (1962, 4 vols. Queen's Printer, Ottawa); see esp. Vol. 2, pp. 367 et seq.

[36] Ibid. pp. 412–414 and 419–421. According to the Glassco Commission: "Among the more important tasks of the lawyer in public service, the initial framing of bills and regulations and advising on their application in individual cases, demand a special degree of independence for the lawyer, setting him somewhat apart from the 'line' activities of his department. Lawyers often find themselves drawn into the policy-making machinery of their departments, thereby becoming so closely identified with departmental management that their capacity to provide impartial advice becomes impaired. At the other end of the scale, some lawyers perform duties of such routine nature that they could be performed adequately and more economically by clerical employees. When this happens, professional skill tends to deteriorate. Isolated from members of his own profession, the sole lawyer in a department is usually further handicapped by lack of access to that indispensable tool of a lawyer—a good legal library. The integration of isolated departmental lawyers into a common legal service,

the various divisions of the department were joined to arguments based on economy in the disposition of legal manpower and on more attractive career possibilities. These are not new arguments by any stretch of the imagination, but the prospect of their being adopted in the United Kingdom has made little headway in the past 100 years. Inquiries galore, from Jessel in 1877[37] to Barlow in 1944[38] and Fulton in 1968[39] have been confronted with what has been aptly described as the "deep rooted departmentalism of the legal service [that] remains its most obvious and enduring characteristic."[40] No perceptible change of attitude was evident either on the part of those who constitute the backbone of the government legal service or in the latest inquiry conducted into this subject in 1971. Like its predecessors, the Compton report[41] endorsed the principle that, in those government departments where law and policy considerations are highly intermingled and where legal advice must reflect this body of

revolving around the Department of Justice, appears to your Commissioners to offer the most practicable remedy—if not the sovereign solution—for many of the present afflictions." *Ibid* pp. 412–413. The same Commissioners favoured exclusion from the proposed integrated service of the legal branches in the Judge Advocate General's office, the legal division in the Department of External Affairs, the legal branch in the Taxation Division of the Department of National Revenue, and the legal branch in the Royal Canadian Mounted Police (*ibid*. p. 413). One result of the McDonald Commission of Inquiry into the activities of the R.C.M.P. Security Service was the elimination of the last exception favoured by the Glassco Commission.

[37] *Departmental Committee on the System upon which the Legal Business of the Government is conducted: First, Second, and Third Reports* (H.C. Paper 199 of 1877, Parl. Papers, Vol. 27, pp. 1 *et seq.*).

[38] The Barlow Committee on Legal Departments of the Civil Service was set up within the Treasury in 1944 in response to a letter from the Attorney General, Sir Donald Somervell, expressing anxiety about the recruitment of legal staff. The committee's report was never published but is referred to extensively in Drewry, *op. cit.* pp. 23–24. Four legal posts—those of Treasury Solicitor, Director of Public Prosecutions, First Parliamentary Counsel and Permanent Secretary to the Lord Chancellor—rank as permanent secretaries in the civil service hierarchy.

[39] *Departmental Committee on the Civil Service, Report*, Cmnd. 3638 (1968), esp. Vol. 1, pp. 152–154 and Vol. 4, Chapter 27 "The Legal Class." In his valuable study (*supra*) Drewry provides a useful lexicon for distinguishing the various expressions used when referring to lawyer civil servants, amongst which may be found—"The Government Legal Service" (in the annual *Bar List*); "The Legal Groups" (superceding the term "Legal Class" and used to describe civil servants with appropriate professional qualifications and experience, recruited on a government wide basis); "The Legal Civil Service" and "Lawyer Civil Servants" (an even wider group that describes all lawyers employed in a professional capacity whether or not they are members of the Legal Group); and "The Legal Career Service" (management machinery headed by the Treasury Solicitor that was instituted following the Compton review of legal services in 1971.

[40] Drewry, *op. cit.* p. 28.

[41] The report itself was never published but Drewry (*ante.* fn. 27) points out that a summary of its main recommendations, and the steps taken to implement them, appears in the 47th annual report of the Civil Service Legal Society, October 1972, pp. 4–8. One part of the Compton report was devoted entirely to the Law Officers' Department (L.O.D.) and its problems. "Identifying suitable staff for posting to the L.O.D., the report underlined, should be a specific function of the Treasury Solicitor in his capacity as Head of the Legal Career Service. The significance of this recommendation is heightened by the realisation that the Law Officers' Department is generally regarded as an important source for 'fliers' in the legal civil service, analogous in that respect to a Minister's private office or to the Cabinet Secretariat."

experience, it is essential that the departmental lawyer regard himself, and be viewed as such, as a fully integrated member of the departmental team.

Recognition of this philosophy, however, should not depend on the sense of permanence of the lawyer's attachment to the department. The passage of time may well reinforce the depth of that identification with the ministry's outlook but so it can be said of all the other public servants whose career may be exclusively centred within the same division of the central government. It is noticeable that transfers within the senior ranks of the public service is commonplace and is seen as contributing to the exercise of a better informed judgment no matter in which department the official happens to be serving at the time. An appreciation of the essential inter-relationship between policy considerations and the application of legal rules is what should imbue the lawyer's approach to his departmental functions. Adoption of this principle should not depend on whether the legal adviser is an entrenched member of the particular ministry or on detachment from a centralised body of government lawyers with experience of serving in other parts of the central administration. The professional detachment of the trained lawyer should be capable of being maintained alongside his readiness to share in the common goal of implementing the department's objectives.

THE LAW OFFICERS' RELATIONSHIP TO DEPARTMENTAL LEGAL ADVISERS IN GOVERNMENT

There can be little doubt that this goal of detachment reflects the approach of most departmental legal advisers who nevertheless regard themselves primarily as members of the parent government department. If asked, they would probably state that their authority to tender advice to the presiding Minister, or to the permanent head and other members of the department, derives from the essential character of their appointment and not by way of delegated authority from the Law Officers of the Crown as the government's chief legal advisers. The precise nature of this relationship deserves close analysis. If the senior members among the ranks of current legal advisers were to be canvassed as to their conception of this relationship it is likely that they would describe the Attorney General as occupying a position analogous to that of the "final Court of Appeal" on matters of strictly legal advice. This means that the Attorney General is available to be called upon if the issue is such that the interests of other departments may be affected, or is of a kind that is likely to call for resolution by ministers acting collectively in Cabinet or in the appropriate committee of Cabinet. Less frequent will be those troublesome occasions when a department's legal adviser turns to the Attorney General as a refuge and tower of strength in time of need, as where a major confrontation erupts between departments or the adviser's legal opinion is rejected by his own minister and the feeling is entertained that serious consequences will follow if the department refuses to heed the legal opinion placed before it. Further examination of the ongoing contacts between the network of departmental lawyers and the Law Officers may help to clarify the perception of that relationship as seen from both perspectives.[42]

Recourse to the Law Officers, and the small band of professional lawyers who serve the Attorney General and Solicitor General in the Law Officers' Department,[43] varies in frequency according to the range of the responsibilities encompassed by the individual department. At the highest level of frequency of contact is a group that includes the Director of Public Prosecutions, the Lord Chancellor's Office, the Home Office, the Foreign and Commonwealth Office, and the Northern Ireland authorities, particularly the Director of Public Prosecutions for Northern Ireland whose office is situated in Belfast. Within this group the level of communication is on a day to day basis, initially at the official level between senior legal advisers in Whitehall and the appropriate staff member in the Law Officers' Department. The latter must be sufficient of a generalist to know well the work of the department concerned, the policy implications of the issues raised, and the likely response of the Attorney General, so that he can best determine when and how to present the problem for the advisory opinion of one or other of the Law Officers. The normal situation in which resort to the Attorney General or the Solicitor General is called for presents little time in which to prepare a formal brief. Whether it be another minister, the Director of Public Prosecutions, or one of the departmental legal advisers, the need is to secure a ruling and the guidance of one of the Law Officers in person without submitting full, or indeed any, papers.

At a rather lower level of frequency than the group of departments identified above are the regular communications exchanged between the Law Officers and the Parliamentary Counsel's office in the routine consideration of Bills with respect to which, in their form and quality, the Attorney General, in conjunction with the Lord Chancellor, has a special responsibility. As standing members of the Legislation Committee of Cabinet the Law Officers are continuously engaged in the review of measures that initially originate in one or other of the government departments. This supervisory task may have begun much earlier during

[42] My treatment of this subject was considerably assisted by being allowed access to the L.O.D.'s detailed submission to the Compton inquiry in 1971.

[43] The number of professional staff has increased from 3 (in 1966–67) to the present 7. Since the mid-1960s the practice has been followed, with respect to all but the two or three mid-senior posts, of filling the established positions by secondment from other departments. Some of the inadequacies and haphazard nature of the present organisation in the Law Officers' Department are highlighted in the memorandum referred to in the previous footnote, where it is stated: " . . . much of the allocation of work has to be on the basis of who can best cope with matters as they arise from day to day. The small number of professional staff means that they are fully occupied with immediate matters, and some of those they are unable to process thoroughly. There is no time for detailed research or to study long term topics. Particularly on matters such as prosecutions, where there is a specific statutory function placed on the Attorney General to superintend the work of the Director of Public Prosecutions, there is never the time with the manpower available to concentrate on major questions of prosecution policy or the criminal law" (op. cit. para. 32).

the embryonic stages of a Bill. On a par with the office of Parliamentary Counsel, in terms of the regularity of contact, is the Cabinet office. This line of communication will include legal advice to the staff of the Cabinet office itself and with respect to matters arising out of official and ministerial committees. To these two major coordinating agencies of government must be added the Privy Council office, the Departments of Trade and Industry, and, as might be expected, the Treasury Solicitor's Department. Civil litigation involving the Crown necessitates close liaison between the Treasury Solicitor and the Law Officers and this will rise and fall according to whether the Attorney General or the Solicitor General elects to lead the team of counsel representing the Crown.

Ministerial Consultations with the Law Officers

If the bulk of the Law Officers' staple work derives from these two groups of departments, it must also be recognised that, from time to time, they will be called upon to advise every ministry and governmental agency. Furthermore, the taking of initiative in this regard is not left to the personal inclination of the senior legal adviser in the department concerned. Fledgling and experienced ministers alike are expected to familiarise themselves with the arrangements for consulting the Law Officers that have been developed over the years and been sanctioned by successive Prime Ministers.[44] In the ultimate analysis it is the individual minister's responsibility to ensure that these arrangements are followed by the senior administrators and departmental legal advisers in his particular ministry.

The basic principle is straightforward enough. The Law Officers must be consulted in good time before the government is committed to critical decisions involving legal considerations. An elaboration of this principle cannot be exhaustive in the sense of defining the exact circumstances which should prompt a minister or his departmental staff to seek the advice of the Law Officers. Past experience, however, has demonstrated that certain categories of situations render it appropriate to take such initiative. Thus, the Law Officers should be consulted where the legal consequences of proposed action by the Government might have important repercussions in the foreign or domestic fields. The same obligation would arise where the resolution of a particular legal problem might raise political aspects of a given policy. A vivid illustration of the political consequences that can flow from ignoring this particular guideline will be discussed in a later chapter, where we shall see the first Thatcher Government being obliged to introduce an indemnity Bill of its own. The object of this exceptional treatment was the Secretary of State for Social Services who, presumably under the advice of his own departmental legal staff, had exceeded his powers in dismissing the members of an area health authority. The purpose

---

[44] The general principles governing the duties of departments to refer to the Law Officers are set forth in the *Code of Procedure for Ministers*, para. 28.

of the Bill was to relieve the minister and his officials from the legal penalties that would have ensued from the unlawful dismissal. Despite valiant attempts by the minister concerned, during the second reading of the indemnity Bill, to assume the entire responsibility for what had happened and to protect his officials by invoking the parliamentary practice of not disclosing upon whose advice he had acted, the pages of *Hansard* leave little doubt that no reference at all was made to the Law Officers before the controversial decision was taken.[45] If this interpretation of what occurred is valid, and given the existence of the standard guidelines we are presently examining, the omission on the part of both the department's legal advisers and the minister himself to refer the implications of the proposed dismissal to the Attorney General for his advice can only be described as monumental blunders.

Presumably, the omission is explained by the absence of any doubts that were entertained at the time as to the legal powers under which the Secretary of State was proposing to execute his policy of eliminating the recalcitrant members of the area health authority.[46] In this example of misplaced legal confidence is to be found the explanation for the specific policy that requires a departmental legal adviser to consult the Law Officers if he is in doubt concerning the legality or constitutional propriety of legislation which the Government propose to introduce, the *vires* of subordinate legislation or the legality of administrative actions. The same philosophy underlines the wisdom of ministers and their officials seeking the advice of the Attorney General or the Solicitor General on questions involving legal considerations and which are destined, in due course, to surface before the Cabinet or one of its committees. This eventuality may arise in connection with proposed legislation but that in no way exhausts the range of situations in which law and policy are intermingled and Cabinet decisions must be taken in the light of both considerations.

To avoid the embarrassment of a minister discovering for the first time the legal uncertainties or objections to the course of action that he brings before the Cabinet for its collective approval it makes eminent good sense that he first clear away any potential legal objections by consulting beforehand the Law Officers. This may give the false impression that the Attorney General and Solicitor General, with their small coterie of legal officials, are themselves fully equipped to handle the infinite range of legal questions that are brought to their attention in this way. This is not so. What is clear is the unlimited extent to which the Law Officers' Department can mobilise at short notice the full range of legal and other expertise within the government itself, from outside counsel and academic lawyers, which may be demanded in dealing with a complex situation. It is the same breadth of approach that explains the resistance within the Law

[45] *Post*, pp. 350–353. The legal issues arising out of this situation are featured in the decision of Woolf J., in *R. v. Secretary of State for Social Services, ex parte Lewisham, Lambeth and Southwark Borough Councils*, *The Times*, February 26, 1980.
[46] *Post*, p. 351, fn. 63.

Officers' Department to permitting the briefing of the Attorney General and Solicitor General, on legal points that may arise in ministerial meetings, to be undertaken by the departmental legal adviser directly concerned.[47] This task, it is rightly felt, must be undertaken by lawyers who are constantly available and responsible to the Law Officers and whose outlook is not coloured by the narrowly conceived needs of each ministry. Furthermore, as previously mentioned, the possibility is a very real one of two or more departments disagreeing on legal questions and the proper solution out of such an impasse is to seek the opinion of the Law Officers.

It is natural that the primary emphasis in these ministerial guidelines should be accorded to the taking of initiatives by officials and ministers in individual departments. There can, of course, be no guarantee that the deep rooted departmentalism of the government's legal service will not produce other embarrassing situations, similar to that arising out of the Lewisham health authority affair in 1980.[48] A parallel responsibility may therefore be considered necessary whereby the staff of the Cabinet office, the repository of the government's central liaison mechanism, maintain close contact with the staff of the Law Officers' Department on general legal policy questions. Such advice is especially necessary with respect to what might be described as "Law Officers' points" such as definitions, onus of proof, the form and quality of a Bill, indemnities and retrospective legislation. By resort to a system of giving advance warning the chances are measurably improved of ensuring that careful consideration will be given by the Attorney General and Solicitor General to the legal problems that beset every government in modern times.

So far I have been concerned to describe the range of circumstances in which a reference to the Law Officers can be said to be a normal expectation, as part of the regular machinery of government. No less important is the appreciation by everyone concerned as to the scope of the Law Officers' authority and the degree of independence with which the Attorney General and the Solicitor General discharge their advisory functions. These questions assume major importance when law and policy issues are seen to be intertwined in the reference to the Law Officers. Thus, policy considerations may well have been in the forefront of the thinking among a department's own legal advisers, especially if they have been involved from the start in the internal discussions leading up to the preparation of a Bill for presentation to Cabinet and, hopefully, for passage through Parliament. When the legal aspects of a reference to the Law Officers reach the desk of the Attorney General or Solicitor General he may defer to the policy position taken by the referring department. This, however, will be by choice and not by any constitutional obligations imposed upon the Law Officers to confine themselves to expressing a legal

[47] This position is strongly argued in the Law Officers' Department response to the Compton inquiry, para. 13, and submitted to the Treasury.
[48] *Ante*, fn. 45.

opinion in the narrowest sense of that expression. There will be times when the Attorney General, perceiving the legal implications of a department's proposed course of action, will find it necessary to oppose the minister's declared policy and to do so, if informal persuasion fails, within the appropriate Cabinet committee, or in Cabinet itself. Such opposition must derive from the legal implications of the proposed policy if it is to carry the full weight of the Law Officer's position. For the government to reject such advice would be quite exceptional and might reasonably be expected to lead to serious questioning by the Attorney General of his continuing to serve as the government's chief legal adviser.

As such, the Attorney General, together with his colleague the Solicitor General, occupies the same degree of constitutional independence as that associated with his position as the State's chief prosecutor responsible for, and ultimately in control of, all prosecutions. It is by virtue of this unique measure of constitutional independence that the Law Officers are enabled to insist on their being the "court of last resort" to which the ranks of departmental legal advisers must defer. In some instances, the reference to the Law Officers may be initiated early in a department's own considera-tion of a projected course of action. Such an informal sounding-out of the legal implications may help to prepare the legal adviser for the stand he takes within the department's own councils. Whether the approach is at such a preliminary stage or in the final stage of a department's internal deliberations, when the legal adviser is facing a major confrontation with the ministry's senior administrators, the opinion of the Law Officers cannot be circumvented or controverted and must be adhered to by the senior legal adviser. In a controversial policy question that has legal implications there may be differences of opinion as to the significance of such implications. Here again the Attorney General's ruling must be accepted by the ministry's legal advisers. A minister who elects to do battle with the Attorney General on this kind of issue may discover that he has backed a losing horse, unless he can persuade his ministerial colleagues that the Attorney's legal opinion should receive minimal importance in their overall balancing of the policy considerations involved. Even in cases of conflict of this nature much will depend on the kind of policy issues that are involved. In such matters as international litigation involving problems associated with the seabed and the continental shelf, or in the interpreta-tion of the law relating to legal picketing or human rights under EEC law, the paramountcy of the Law Officer's opinion may be less readily questioned than in such other areas as trade, employment, social security, environment and defence where the aspects of legal policy would tend to be viewed as more peripheral than central.

THE GOVERNMENT LEGAL SERVICE—COMPARISON WITH FOREIGN MODELS

To gain a better appreciation of the links that exist between the Attorney General of England and Wales and the widely dispersed members of the

Government Legal Service it may be useful to draw comparisons with the corresponding officers in the United States and Canada. In these countries the Attorney General is also the Minister of Justice and in that capacity presides over, and is responsible for, the entire operations of the Department of Justice of the federal government.[49] Thus the Justice Department building in Ottawa houses the headquarters of nearly all the legal services of the federal government with sections devoted to civil litigation, criminal prosecutions, legislation, constitutional and international law as well as counsel engaged in servicing the legal needs of individual departments, agencies and crown corporations.[50] Excluded from this list are the legal counsel in the Department of External Affairs and the Judge Advocate's office in the Ministry of Defence. Until the government reorganisation in 1966 the Department of Justice was also responsible for the federal police force, the Royal Canadian Mounted Police, the penitentiaries and the national parole system. In that year, the new Department of the Solicitor General was created to which were assigned the law enforcement and correctional services previously within the portfolio of the Minister of Justice.[51]

There have been rumblings in recent years that a similar bifurcation of the United States Department of Justice might be advantageously effected so as to restrict the Attorney General's duties to the strictly lawyering functions of advising the President of the United States and the other executive departments of the federal government, as well as conducting litigation and prosecutions on behalf of the Government of the United States.[52] The litigating responsibilities are carried out through the Office of the Solicitor General, the five pertinent divisions of the Department of Justice (criminal, civil, civil rights, antitrust, and natural tax resources) and the 95 United States Attorneys' offices scattered across the vast continent. The statistics pertaining to the Justice Department's personnel and budget provide a further appreciation of that giant organisation which has approximately 54,000 persons on its payroll.[53] Of these the numbers of lawyers involved in the lawyering functions, for which the United States

---

[49] Space forbids extending the comparison to the office of Attorney General in the respective States and Provinces of these two countries.

[50] The current number of lawyers on the establishment of the federal Department of Justice, including those on secondment to other departments, is 569. Non-lawyers and support staff constitute a further body of 700 personnel.

[51] For an account of the 1966 reorganisation and the current responsibilities of the Department of Justice and the Department of the Solicitor General of Canada see Edwards, *Ministerial Responsibility for National Security*, Government Publishing Centre, (1980), Chapters 2 to 5.

[52] See *ante*, pp. 58–61. A comprehensive review of the past and present organisation of the United States Department of Justice is contained in D.J. Meador, *The President, the Attorney General and the Department of Justice*, (1980, University of Virginia). The same volume contains a prospective view of possible changes in the responsibilities of the Attorney General of the United States and the reactions thereto by some of the previous holders of that office. The detailed information contained in the text above is derived from Professor Meador's description of the present Justice Department—see *ante*, p. 58, fn. 2 and 3.

[53] D. J. Meador, *op. cit.* p. 18.

[handwritten marginalia: funding ... annual intake ... record]

Attorney General has ultimate responsibility, is 3,600, representing only 6·7 per cent. of the department's total work force. With the ancillary personnel engaged in the divisions devoted to the litigation and legal counselling work of the Department of Justice, this percentage is increased to 13 per cent. Viewed from a different perspective, 87 per cent. of the Justice Department's personnel and 90 per cent. of its annual budget are committed to activities beyond those of the traditional legal responsibilities of the Attorney General.[53] Foremost among the non-lawyering functions are supervision and control of the Federal Bureau of Investigation,[54] and the Bureau of Prisons which operates all federal correctional institutions throughout the United States. To complete this cursory description of an office that is in stark contrast to the miniscule department headed by the Attorney General of England and Wales, his United States counterpart also presides over the Immigration and Administration Service, the former Law Enforcement Assistance Administration,[55] the United States Marshals Service together with a variety of offices concerned with pardons, professional responsibility, legislative affairs, and improvements in the administration of justice.

The English Attorney General, it is quite apparent, is no ministerial colossus of the kind epitomised by the above summaries of what prevails in the governments of Canada and the United States, or in those other countries that have adopted a Ministry of Justice model with the Attorney General as its ministerial head. In this country the Attorney General exercises no direct control over the lawyers who serve in the legal advisory sections of the various departments that together constitute the Government of the United Kingdom.[56] If any future Attorney General were to be so minded as to lay claim to overall ministerial responsibility for the Government Legal Service he would without question reopen the

[54] From a force of 23 men in 1908 the F.B.I. has grown to 18, 452 employees in 1979. It is by far the largest single unit within the Justice Department occupying, in Meador's words, "one of the most expensive government structures yet erected—larger than the main Justice Department building." The Director of the F.B.I. is appointed by the President, with the advice and consent of the Senate, for a term of 10 years—D. J. Meador, *op. cit.* p. 24.

[55] After 12 years' existence as a semi-independent agency funding criminal justice research with, in comparison with British standards, enormous resources at its disposal, L.E.A.A. was officially terminated in April 1982—see 13 *C.J. Newsletter* (No. 2), 4. Its functions are now exercised under the Office of Justice Assistance, Research and Statistics as an integral part of the federal Dept. of Justice. For a review of the former organisation's work and its persistent problems, see M. Feeley and A.D. Sarat, *The Policy Dilemma: Crime Policy and the L.E.A.A., 1968–1978*, (Univ. of Minnesota Press, 1980). For an even franker assessment of the expendability of L.E.A.A., a "notorious example of porkbarrel politics," and the intrigues that accompanied its eventual demise, see the former Att. Gen. Griffin Bell's memoirs, *Taking Care of the Law*, 1982, pp. 86–89, 153–154.

[56] In his essay on "The Office of Attorney General" (1978) 59 *The Parliamentarian* 149, Mr. Silkin described his advisory role as follows: "Whilst the Attorney General is at the apex of the government legal hierarchy, he is not the solicitor to the Government and is not responsible for the actions of the government legal service . . . [The Attorney's] advising functions, little known and rarely visible to the public, are certainly the most time-consuming, probably the most important and possibly the most interesting of his responsibilities"—*ibid.* p. 153.

long-standing debate as to the desirability of a major reorganisation leading to the establishment of a Ministry of Justice.[57] At present, the Attorney General occupies a distinctive position derived from his constitutional role as the chief legal adviser to the government.[58] No second opinion is permitted in search of a more favourable ruling supporting the purposes of the departmental client. In this sense the more detached stance taken by the Attorney General is likely to be strengthened by a Law Officers' Department that has its own independent establishment with control over the estimates it submits for parliamentary approval. Against this position is the argument that the department is too small to be

[57] The prospects of unifying all the component parts of the criminal justice system in a Ministry of Justice were reviewed in 1981 by the Home Affairs Select Committee. In its Fourth Report the Committee recognised the advantages that would accrue in terms of setting priorities, allocating resources and reconciling conflicting goals. The deep rooted constitutional objections to any such integration, however, were expressed by Lord Hailsham L.C., who stated: "I regard myself as the Minister of Justice but I would not desire to have either the prosecuting process or the penal treatment process under my responsibility because I think they are incompatible." In the opinion of the Select Committee "the temper of public and Parliamentary opinion could not in the foreseeable future be harnessed to such a change." See [1981] C.L.B. 1602. The long history of proposals to create a Ministry of Justice in this country is documented in R.M. Jackson, *The Machinery of Justice in England*, (6th ed., 1972), pp. 546–549. Among the more recent discussions of this controversial subject are: the *Justice* colloquium "Do we need a Ministry of Justice?" under the chairmanship of Mr. Justice Scarman (as he then was), February 7, 1970: 2nd interim report of the Percival Committee, Society of Conservative Lawyers, 1971 (both the present Attorney General and former Solicitor General were members of this committee) entitled "Ministerial responsibility for the Law"; and Gavin Drewry's "Lord Haldane's Ministry of Justice—Abortion, Stillbirth or Infanticide," (1981), an unpublished paper which draws on the official files from the Lord Chancellor's Department pertaining to various proposals to reconstitute that office as a Ministry of Justice, particularly the responses to the recommendations of the Haldane Committee on the Machinery of Government—Cd. 9230 (1918). For the views of another recent Lord Chancellor, Lord Elwyn Jones, see (1983) 8 Holdsworth L.R. 12 at pp. 17–20.

[58] Occasionally, the error is perpetrated of mistakenly describing the Lord Chancellor as the senior legal adviser to the government, see, *e.g.* Shimon Shetreet, *Judges on Trial* (1976), at p. 49. For the correct constitutional position see the lecture given to the Cambridge University Law Society by the then Attorney General, Sir Elwyn Jones, where he stated: "Naturally the Lord Chancellor sometimes expresses his opinion about legal matters which come before the Cabinet. Sometimes he is asked by the Prime Minister to advise on some problem of particular difficulty or weight, but it is not his role to advise government departments. Indeed, it would be inconsistent with his office as head of the judiciary if he were to do so. . . . As I say, his function in advising on legal matters is limited to those special occasions I mentioned. It falls to the Law Officers of the Crown to be the Government's legal advisers." [1969] C.L.J. 43 at p. 46. To the same effect see S.C. Silkin *op. cit.* (fn. 56) at p. 153. In my talk with the former Attorney General, Mr. Silkin stressed his appreciation of the way Lord Elwyn Jones, as Lord Chancellor, repeatedly reminded his Cabinet colleagues that it was to the Attorney General the government must turn as its chief legal adviser. A similar tribute to Lord Gardiner's meticulous care, when he was Lord Chancellor, in sustaining the Attorney General's position, is contained in Lord Elwyn Jones's autobiography, *In My Time* (1983) p. 196. Whether all modern Lord Chancellors exhibit a similar reticence in expressing themselves on legal or constitutional questions that may surface unexpectedly around the Cabinet table is doubtful. In which event, the invidious situation might arise where the Law Officers, after careful study of the relevant law, might be forced into the embarrassing position of repudiating their senior colleague. Another difficult position, which can readily be apprehended in the light of recent experience, is where the Law Officers disagree in their legal opinions and the Prime Minister preferring that of the Solicitor General, seeks to bolster that preference by invoking the advice of the Lord Chancellor.

independent so far as establishment matters, such as promotional opportunities, pay and pension scales, are concerned. For the small enclave of full time professional lawyers belonging to the Law Officers' Department loyalty to the serving Attorney General and Solicitor General in no way conflicts with the advantages that are seen to accrue from integration, on the establishment side, with either the Lord Chancellors' Department or the Treasury Solicitors' Department. Outright fusion, however, between the Law Officers' Department and one of the above larger departments has been consistently resisted, never more strongly than in 1949 when, at the insistence of Sir Hartley Shawcross, then the Attorney General, it was decided that the integrity and independence of the Law Officers' Department must be preserved, and the overtures of Sir Thomas Barnes, the Treasury Solicitor, to bring about an integration of the two legal staffs was summarily rejected.[59] A few years later a new round of negotiations were begun, with a view this time to arranging a fusion with the staff of the Lord Chancellor's Department.[60] Although this objective was again discarded, the intervening years have witnessed an increasing inclination to develop informal working relationships, falling short of complete integration, with the Treasury Solicitor assuming *de facto* responsibilities for finding suitable lawyers to man the professional positions in the Law Officers' Department.[61] This task has been accomplished by secondment from other government departments including, for example, the offices of the Director of Public Prosecutions, the Treasury Solicitor and the Lord Chancellor.

When, therefore, it is claimed that the Treasury Solicitor nowadays occupies the same refereeing position within the legal career service as that described in the Jessel Report of 1875,[62] it is important to recognise the limits of this kind of adjudicative responsibility. In matters of staffing, involving such issues as recruitment, promotion, secondment, pay and pensions, the Treasury Solicitor occupies a central role in the career management councils of government.[63] This has nothing to do with the "refereeing" of legal and policy questions, that relate to substantive issues of legislative or executive action, which flow from the desks of the

[59] Law Officers' Department files.

[60] *Ibid.* When the matter was reviewed in 1965 it was again agreed that, whilst outright fusion was unacceptable, the staff of the L.O.D. should be treated as though they were incorporated in the Lord Chancellor's Department. No adjustment in the respective votes was involved, only an arrangement whereby the Permanent Secretary to the Lord Chancellor assumed a general oversight over the staffing positions of both departments.

[61] The re-emergence of the Treasury Solicitor's role in this regard derived from the recommendations of the Compton Report, (LC(MC)(72)2).

[62] Drewry, *op. cit.* p. 28.

[63] *Ibid* pp. 27–28. In matters of accountability to the House of Commons it is the Chancellor of the Exchequer, as head of the Treasury Department, and not the Attorney General who is the responsible minister—*per* Sir Elwyn Jones in his testimony when Attorney General before the Salmon Commission on Tribunals of Inquiry (see *post* fn. 82), p. 141. The contrary statement (in Wade & Phillips, *Constitutional and Administrative Law* (9th ed.) p. 334) that the senior Law Officer is responsible for the work of the Treasury Solicitor is misleading.

departmental legal advisers for resolution by the Attorney General or the Solicitor General. Whether the disputed questions are channelled unilaterally from a single department or involve inter-departmental conflicts of jurisdiction or interpretations of the law, the Attorney General occupies the seat of final authority. Recognition of this unchallengeable position contributes greatly to the smooth functioning of the government's legal advisory machinery and has enabled the system to operate with such small resources at the apex of the organisation.

One of the costs of continuing to perform the multiple duties associated with the office of Attorney General with such limited manpower resources is the imposition of a burden that has consistently been described as being as onerous as that of the most heavily engaged minister.[64] And there can be no disputing the disparate burden that attaches to the senior Law Officership in comparison with the responsibilities of the Solicitor General. In its report to the Prime Minister in 1964 the independent Committee on the Remuneration of Ministers and Members of Parliament went out of its way to recognise that the total burden of work discharged by the Law Officers of the Crown is different from that which rests on other ministers, because the Attorney General and Solicitor General have additional duties which are not part of the normal work of ministers.[65] Foremost among the additional responsibilities identified by the committee were appearances in court on behalf of the Crown in important civil and criminal cases and the provision of professional legal advice. Concern was expressed by the Lawrence Committee in 1964 that failure to maintain an appropriate level of emoluments, whereby the salaries of the Law Officers bore some reasonable relationship to the earnings of the leaders of the profession, would jeopardise the availability of men of the highest quality to fill these vitally important positions.[66] This message has been echoed by each committee that in the past was charged with the invidious task of recommending the appropriate salaries to be paid to Ministers of the Crown.[67] What is significant is the testimony adduced before the 1964 Committee that for some years there has been a serious contraction in the

---

[64] See the *Report of the Committee on the Remuneration of Ministers and Members of Parliament*, Cmnd. 2516 (1964), p. 38. The earlier history of the Law Officers' remuneration in respect of the legal business of Government is examined in Edwards, *op. cit.* Chapters 5 and 6, where much evidence is adduced in support of the repeated claims as to the especially onerous nature of combining the political and professional duties associated with the offices of Attorney General and Solicitor General. In more recent times, the case for special treatment of the Law Officers' salaries was urgently argued in a memorandum by the Solicitor General (Rawlinson) to the Attorney General (Hobson) in June 1964, and repeated in a letter from the Attorney General to Sir Geoffrey Lawrence, Chairman of the Departmental Committee—L.O.D. files. It is not without significance that serious reservations were expressed by the Legal Secretary of the L.O.D. at the time who recalled the contrary impressions registered by Sir Hartley Shawcross (when comparing the burdens of office as Attorney General and, later, as President of the Board of Trade) and by Viscount Dilhorne (Hobson's immediate predecessor as Attorney General) following his elevation to the Woolsack—*ibid.*

[65] *Ibid.* para. 140, p. 38.

[66] *Ibid.* para. 142, p. 38.

[67] See Edwards, *op. cit.* Chapters 5 and 6, *passim.*

number of eligible candidates for the Law Officerships, insofar as the essential qualifications include membership of the House of Commons and high attainment among the ranks of the Bar.[68] The Committee spent little time in canvassing possible alternative paths to these appointments. The only option referred to, that of appointing a Queen's Counsel who has had no prior experience of politics in the Lower House and then of finding a "safe" constituency for him to represent, was summarily dismissed. "It would be more than unfortunate," the Committee declared, "if the time should come when the candidates available for selection were those who had been unsuccessful in their profession."[69] The Committee's report went on: "It is difficult to determine what motives lie behind a barrister's entry into the House of Commons but if the possibility of appointment as a Law Officer may be an incentive to the best men to become Members of the House of Commons, we think that it is essential that the attraction of this possibility should not be removed by the extent of the financial sacrifice entailed in accepting the office."[70] This did not mean, Sir Geoffrey Lawrence and his colleagues concluded, that the Law Officers' salaries should be set at a level commensurate with the highest earnings of the leaders of the Bar "because no doubt there will rightly be a readiness to accept a reduction of income on the assumption of public duty."[71]

Translated into actual figures, the Committee in 1964 was conscious of the fact that the existing salaries of the Attorney General (£10,000) and the Solicitor General (£7,000) were those fixed in 1946, and reflected the decision on the part of the then Law Officers to accept the abolition of their long established right to receive fees for contentious business on behalf of the Crown.[72] This drastic change in the method of calculating the emoluments of the Attorney General and Solicitor General had greatly reduced their total incomes. Taking into account the interval of time between 1946 and 1964, and adhering to the principle that a marked difference in salary between the Attorney General and other Ministers had been accepted without question for a great many years, the Lawrence Committee recommended that the salaries be increased to £16,000 for the Attorney General and £11,000 for the Solicitor General.[73] In addition, both of the Law Officers, like other Ministers of the Crown, should be permitted to draw the parliamentary allowance in respect of their

[68] *Ibid.* No abatement of this situation is discernible in the observations of Lord Hailsham L.C., speaking in 1978—see his Child Lecture, *post* (p. 218, fn. 38) at p. 11.
[69] *Ibid.*
[70] *Report of the Committee on the Remuneration of Ministers and Members of Parliament,* para. 143, p. 39.
[71] *Ibid.* para. 144, p. 39.
[72] See Edwards, *op. cit.* pp. 117–118.
[73] *Op. cit.* para. 145, p. 39. With respect to the Scottish Law Officers, it was recognised that professional earnings at the Scottish Bar are not at the same level as those of the English Bar. Nevertheless, having regard to the fact that the Lord Advocate's salary (£5,000 p.a.) was fixed as long ago as 1894, and, since 1946, he was precluded from engaging in private practice, the Committee recommended that the salary of the Lord Advocate be raised to £11,000 and that of the Solicitor General of Scotland be increased from £3,750 (set in 1957) to £7,500.

membership of the House of Commons.[74] In 1980 the Boyle Committee on the salaries of Ministers, Members of Parliament and senior positions in the public service recommended that the Law Officers receive salaries amounting to £30,500 for the Attorney General and £24,000 for the Solicitor General.[75] Parliamentary salaries of £8,000 would be payable in addition to these amounts. In the event, a slight reduction from these levels was sanctioned by Mrs. Thatcher, the Prime Minister. With respect to the Scottish Law Officers the review body proposed that the Lord Advocate receive a salary of £24,000 and the Solicitor General for Scotland the slightly lower figure of £20,500.[76] These salaries might usefully be compared with those awarded to the Lord Chancellor (£44,000), the Prime Minister (£38,000), the Master of the Rolls and Lords of Appeal in Ordinary (£40,000), the Secretary to the Cabinet and Permanent Secretary to the Treasury (£35,845), a Cabinet Minister (£37,000), and a High Court Judge (£28,500).[77]

ROLE OF THE ATTORNEY GENERAL BEFORE TRIBUNALS OF INQUIRY

The impartial detachment expected of the Attorney General in fulfilling his responsibilities as the chief legal adviser to the Government is paralleled in those situations where he is expected to act as protector of the public interest. Most of these situations have been referred to in earlier chapters. The outstanding topic, as yet unexamined in this work, concerns the role of the Attorney General in relation to public inquiries set up under the authority of the Tribunals of Inquiry (Evidence) Act 1921.[78] The Act provides that if both Houses of Parliament resolve that it is expedient that a tribunal be established for inquiring into a definite matter of urgent public importance, and in pursuance of such resolution a tribunal is appointed either by the Crown or by a Secretary of State, then the tribunal for certain purposes has all the powers, rights and privileges that are vested in the High Court or, in Scotland, the Court of Session.[79] The historical background to the 1921 statute, and a review of the more important and contentious tribunals that were convened between 1921 and 1964, were contained in my earlier study of *The Law Officers of the Crown*, particularly with reference to the participation of the Attorney General as counsel to the tribunal.[80] Most of the tribunals of inquiry set up during this period came into existence as the result of highly charged accusations of

---

[74] *Ibid.* para. 145 and 147.
[75] *Report No. 14 of the Review Body on Top Salaries*, Cmnd. 7952 (1980).
[76] *Ibid.*
[77] *Report No. 15 of the Review Body on Top Salaries*, Cmnd. 7953 (1980). In the latest notification of Government pay increases, the Attorney General becomes the highest paid member of the Government, surpassing the Prime Minister and the Lord Chancellor, both of whom have elected to receive lower salaries than they would be entitled to under the new scales. *The Times*, July 22, 1983.
[78] 11 Geo. 5, c.7.
[79] s.1(1).
[80] *Op. cit.* pp. 295–308.

political and other public misdoings. Although none of the findings of the respective inquiries have given rise to widespread dissatisfaction, certain procedural aspects of the machinery set up in 1921 were, from time to time, the subject of public criticism.

Questions concerning the hardship caused to innocent individuals by the nature of the proceedings were coupled with doubts as to the desirability of seeing the Attorney General, a member of the government, assume the leading role as counsel to the tribunal which was assigned the task of getting to the bottom of public suspicion about the conduct of fellow members of the government or other prominent persons. In 1966 a Royal Commission under the chairmanship of Lord Justice Salmon (as he then was) was set up to consider whether the Tribunals of Inquiry (Evidence) Act 1921 should be replaced by some other procedure or retained with such desirable changes as might be necessary.[81] After hearing an impressive array of legal heavyweights, including a representative group of Conservative and Labour ex-Law Officers of the Crown,[82] the Commission concluded that the former practice should be discontinued and counsel to the tribunal chosen from the senior ranks of the Bar who had no connection whatsoever with the government of the day or with any political party.[83]

On the role of the Attorney General, the Salmon Commission considered it difficult for the public to understand the distinction between the Attorney as the chief Law Officer of the Crown and his position as a member of the government, particularly when applied to a tribunal of inquiry that was investigating the conduct of ministerial colleagues of the same Attorney General.[84] Conversely, it was said that witnesses, whose interests were inimical to those of the minister or ministers concerned, might gain the impression, however wrongly, that the odds had been weighted against them. Whatever line of approach the Attorney General might take, the Salmon Commission argued, he was likely to be criticised, either because he cross-examined too vigorously or not vigorously enough.[85] However groundless such criticisms might have been with respect to past Attorneys General and however slight the risk of bias in the future, the Salmon Commission concluded that the confidence of the public in the conclusions of the investigation would be enhanced if the Attorney General were never to act as counsel for the tribunal.[86] "It seems to us undesirable and unnecessary that Law Officers of the Crown should be exposed to such criticisms," the Commission wrote in its final report.[87]

---

[81] Its report, Cmnd. 3121 (1966), reviews the shortcomings of the 1921 statute in its application to the most controversial inquiries convened under its authority. A full list is provided in Appendix C to the Report.

[82] See Salmon Commission, *Minutes of Oral Evidence*, (H.M.S.O. 1966).

[83] Cmnd. 3121, paras. 94 and 96.

[84] *Ibid*. para. 94, p. 35.

[85] *Ibid*.

[86] *Ibid*. para. 95, p. 35.

[87] *Ibid*. para. 94, p. 35.

History, however, has shown abundantly the impossibility of an Attorney General ever fully satisfying all shades of opinion, political or otherwise, if he is guided in his conduct by what he considers to be in the best interests of society at large. To remove the special duty, that we are presently considering, from the range of responsibilities that attach to the office of the Attorney General as the protector of the public interest would in no way diminish the Attorney's exposure to public criticism on other fronts. Should we then seriously consider depriving the Law Officers of all their traditional duties qua Law Officers because of their complementary responsibilities as members of the government? This larger question has surfaced in recent years, in the wake of the *Gouriet* case, when the argument was propounded for transforming the office of Attorney General into an exclusively public office, the principal ground being that public confidence in the impartiality and non-partisan nature of the office would be better ensured if the holder was not drawn from the ranks of political ministers.[88] Attractive as this argument might be in strict theory, it conceals one inherent weakness that derives from the belief that the qualities of integrity and impartiality can be secured through the instrumentality of constitutional change. Experience in several Commonwealth countries during the post-war period has demonstrated the vital importance of the personal qualities of the Attorney General as the surest indicator of his ability to fulfil the essential attributes of the office, it being equally possible to find these qualifications in either model of the office, political minister or public servant.[89]

Reading the evidence tendered before the Salmon Commission, by those witnesses upon whose judgment the commission ultimately rested its case, it is noteworthy that nowhere is there the slightest suggestion that any Attorney General, of whichever political party happened to be in power at the time, has ever been found wanting in the full and proper discharge of his duty to the public and in his representation and protection of the public interest. The Salmon Commission itself had no reservations as to "the admirable way in which all Attorneys General appearing before tribunals in the past have performed their onerous and self-imposed task. We have nothing but admiration for their impartiality and high sense of duty."[90] This conception of the duty of the Attorney General first surfaced in connection with the Lynskey Tribunal in 1948.[91] The task of that tribunal was to inquire into allegations of corruption against certain members of the Attlee Government. As Lord Shawcross, who appeared as Attorney General, has subsequently disclosed there were many, both in his own, the

---

[88] *Per* Lord Shawcross in his letter to *The Times*, August 3, 1977. The former Attorney General's views are discussed more fully *ante*, pp. 63–70.

[89] I endeavoured to develop this thesis more fully in a paper "Emerging problems in defining the Modern Role of the office of Attorney General in Commonwealth countries" contained in the *Minutes of Meeting and Memoranda*, Commonwealth Law Ministers meeting in Winnipeg, 1977–Annex to LMM (77) 10.

[90] Cmnd. 3121, para. 93, p. 34.

[91] Cmnd. 7616 (1948).

Labour, party and in the ranks of the Conservative Opposition, who argued strongly that in the circumstances the Attorney General should not take part in the proceedings.[92] Memories of the handling of the *J.H. Thomas* case before the Budget Disclosure Inquiry in 1936[93] were still fresh in the minds of both critics and supporters of the stance adopted by Shawcross before the Lynskey Tribunal. Shawcross's thinking as he approached the conflict is worth noting for its enunciation of the "high sense of duty" associated with the office of Attorney General. "I felt myself," Shawcross subsequently wrote, " . . . that it was of the utmost importance from the public point of view to maintain the position that it was the duty (however personally unpleasant) of His Majesty's Attorney General to represent the public interest with complete objectivity and detachment, and that to refuse to discharge that duty in a particular case in which the public interest might be suspected to conflict with the interests of certain of his friends or of his political colleagues would be tantamount to saying that the office itself was inadequate to represent and protect the public interest against whosoever might challenge it. It was in many ways a very distasteful decision to have to make, but I hoped it helped to consolidate the Attorney General's right and duty—and that is what I emphasise in these matters is the duty—to be wholly detached, wholly independent and to accept the implications of an obligation to protect what he conceives to be the public interest whatever the political results may be."[94]

Without exception every former Attorney General who testified before the Salmon Commission in 1966 subscribed to this resounding exposition of the Law Officers' public duty.[95] According to Lord Dilhorne, the former Lord Chancellor, who appeared as Attorney General before the Tribunal of Inquiry in 1957 into the alleged Bank Rate Leak involving two prominent Conservative colleagues,[96] a Law Officer should, unless he is personally involved, appear to conduct the proceedings before every major inquiry. "Every Attorney is used to wearing two hats," Dilhorne emphasised, "and accustomed to keeping his political and legal duties distinct. If the public interest is so involved as to necessitate the appointment of a tribunal it is right that the Attorney should appear. He is,

---

[92] Edwards, *op. cit.* pp. 297, 300–301.

[93] Cmnd. 5148 (1936); and see Edwards, *op. cit.* p. 299.

[94] *The Office of Attorney General*, The Law Society, (1953), p. 16.

[95] Report, para. 92, p. 34. In acknowledging the unanimity of the views expressed by the former Attorneys General, the Salmon Commission also drew attention to the "even larger body of evidence, including that of the Lord Chief Justice of England, Lord Radcliffe, Lord Devlin, the Bar Council, the Council of the Law Society, and the Treasury Solicitor, to the effect that it would be better if the tribunal were to instruct independent counsel of the highest standing to represent them."

[96] Cmnd. 350 (1958). Addressing the tribunal, Sir Reginald Manningham Buller (as he then was) stated: "It is my duty to act here, as in some other fields, without any regard to political considerations of any kind, and in discharging this duty I am not in the least concerned with—indeed I am completely indifferent to—political or personal results"—quoted in Edwards, *op. cit.* p. 301.

of course, liable to be criticised, but his shoulders are usually broad. If it is once recognized, as it would be, by saying that he should not appear when any of his political colleagues may be concerned, then that will go far to undermine the position of the Attorney and his reputation for fairness and impartiality in the conduct of legal proceedings. It would next be suggested that he should not conduct a prosecution if there were political implications."[97]

At the time when the Salmon Commission was conducting its investigation the Attorney General, Sir Elwyn Jones, had no first hand experience of the working of tribunals of inquiry. His views, however, echoed those of his predecessors in stating that he regarded his duties as the independent protector of the public interest to be the foremost aspect of his office.[98] Within a day of the Royal Commission's report being made public, including the recommendation that independent counsel take the place of the Law Officers as counsel to tribunals of inquiry, Sir Elwyn Jones appeared in his capacity as Attorney General before the tribunal appointed to inquire into the Aberfan Disaster.[99] The circumstances were somewhat unprecedented. As the chairman of the Aberfan Tribunal of Inquiry, Lord Justice Edmund Davies (as he then was), explained at the outset, the incumbent Attorney General, because of his close ties with South Wales and his great knowledge of its coalfields and mining valleys, would be able to assist the inquiry to an extent which, in the nature of things, could not normally be expected of the Head of the Bar however zealous. Lord Justice Edmund Davies emphasised that it was at his personal request that the Attorney General was leading the senior and junior counsel who would act for the tribunal.[1] As events transpired the Attorney General was

---

[97] *Minutes of Oral Evidence*, p. 88, and see, too, pp. 90–91, 94.

[98] *Ibid.* pp. 137–138, 140.

[99] H.L. 316, H.C. 553 of 1967. Before announcing his decision to appear as counsel for the tribunal, the Attorney General, with the full knowledge and approval of the tribunal's chairman, issued a public warning against the possible infringement of the contempt laws by the examination of potential witnesses on television and in the other news media. Because of the widespread misunderstanding accorded to Sir Elwyn Jones' statement in the Commons (H.C. Deb., Vol. 734, cols. 1315–20, October 27, 1966), the Prime Minister made a further statement in the course of which Mr. Wilson elaborated on "the unique position of the Attorney General" which included that of acting "as adviser on matters of law to this House and through this House to the country" (H.C. Deb., Vols. 735, cols. 254–264, November 1, 1966). For Lord Elwyn Jones's further reflections on this episode, including an acknowledgment that the public warning was badly drafted, see his autobiography, *In My Time* (1983), pp. 234–235.

[1] *Ibid.* p 8. Referring, at the preliminary meeting of the Aberfan Disaster Tribunal, to the publication a day earlier of the Salmon Commission Report the chairman (Lord Justice Edmund-Davies) accepted the fact that the Royal Commission "had, of necessity, to make its recommendations in the light of the type of inquiries hitherto held under the Act," adding that the present inquiry "was of a totally different character." What appears from the circumstances which resulted in the setting up of the various inquiries since 1921 is a fairly clear line of demarcation between (1) highly political inquiries in which the Government, or some of its members, are directly involved, and (2) inquiries that concern matters of urgent public importance and where the political ramifications or government involvement is less obvious. In strictly quantitative terms, by far the larger proportion of the inquiries held since 1921 have exemplified the second category above—see Cmnd. 3121, App. C.

unable to participate in the tribunal's hearings beyond making his opening address. Notwithstanding this curtailment of the Attorney's involvement in the Aberfan Tribunal of Inquiry its members saw fit in their report to state: " . . . we are unanimously of the opinion that he made so valuable a contribution that we take leave to doubt the wisdom of adopting any general rule which might hereafter totally exclude the participation of the Law Officers of the Crown in proceedings such as the present."[2]

In two subsequent tribunals of inquiry convened in Northern Ireland in 1969 and 1972, both concerned with the handling of large scale civil disturbances in Londonderry, independent counsel to represent the tribunal were nominated by Lord Widgery C.J., and Mr. Justice Scarman (as he then was), the English judges appointed to conduct the respective inquiries.[3] The procedure in the Republic of Ireland, where resort to the Tribunals of Inquiry (Evidence) Act 1921 is still in vogue, varies from the appointment of senior and junior counsel, instructed by the Chief State Solicitor, representing the Attorney General, to the occasional instance where counsel are nominated by the tribunal itself.[4] It has never been the practice for the Irish Attorney General to appear in person.[5] The same situation describes the experience in those countries, such as Australia and Canada, where similar legislation governs the procedures of commissions of inquiry set up to examine matters of vital public importance and for which no other method of investigation is considered adequate.[6] In these Commonwealth jurisdictions it must be remembered that the Attorney General is, and always has been, a member of the Cabinet and the problem of demonstrating his independence from his ministerial colleagues is correspondingly more acute than in the United Kingdom. The Salmon Commission's view that each tribunal should nominate counsel other than a Law Officer of the Crown to act on its behalf was rejected by the Heath Government. In a White Paper, released in 1973,[7] setting forth the administration's position with respect to the various recommendations of the Royal Commission on Tribunals of Inquiry, published 7 years earlier, it was stated that "The Government considers that the Tribunal should be free to choose its own counsel, and should neither be restricted in its choice to counsel other than a Law Officer of the Crown, nor be obliged to select a Law Officer. The Tribunal should consult the Attorney-General or the Lord Advocate before deciding whether or not a Law Officer should appear, and also about the choice of other counsel for the Tribunal. It it is decided that a Law Officer should appear, he might take a full part in the

---

[2] *Ibid.* p. 9.
[3] See H.L. 101, H.C. 220 of 1972 (The "Bloody Sunday" Inquiry) and Cmd. 566 (1972) Belfast (Scarman Inquiry into Violence and Civil Disturbances in Northern Ireland in 1969).
[4] J.P. Casey, *The Office of the Attorney General in Ireland* (Dublin, 1980), pp. 162–165.
[5] *Ibid.*
[6] See the memorandum, containing a comparative survey of the legislation and practice in Canada, India and Australia, submitted to the Salmon Royal Commission by Mr. Justice Scarman (as he then was), *Documentary Evidence*, pp. 62–65.
[7] Cmnd. 5313.

proceedings, or he might in appropriate cases confine his appearance to opening the particular issues involved in the terms of reference, and thereafter being available to the Tribunal to deal with specific matters such as contempt, waiver of Crown privilege and the grant of immunity from prosecution. Accordingly, the Government does not accept the Commission's recommendation in this matter."[8] The White Paper also made reference to the role of the Treasury Solicitor, agreeing with the Salmon Commission that in England and Wales the government's chief solicitor should continue to be appointed as the solicitor acting for the tribunal.[9] No conflict of interest appears to have been experienced in discharging this responsible function, the general tenor of all the evidence tendered before the Royal Commission exhibiting unqualified satisfaction with the work of the Treasury Solicitor's Department in assisting the various tribunals of inquiry set up under the 1921 legislation.[10] To maintain consistency of practice within the government, the White Paper suggested that in Scotland it would be preferable for the tribunal to be represented officially rather than by a private firm of solicitors. The choice would normally lie between the Crown Agent and the Solicitor to the Secretary of State for Scotland,[11] public officials as to whose duties further reference will be made in a subsequent chapter.[12]

It will be noted that the Government's White Paper envisages consultation between the tribunal of inquiry and, in England and Wales, the Attorney General, or the Lord Advocate if the subject matter of the inquiry is Scottish in origin. The ultimate determination would rest in the hands of the tribunal itself, though it is difficult to contemplate a tribunal ignoring the express wishes of the Law Officer concerned that he should assume the duty of representing the same public interest that underlies the original appointment of the tribunal in question. In seeking to reach an accommodation between the conflicting views advanced before the Salmon

---

[8] *Ibid*. para. 16, p. 8.

[9] *Ibid*. para. 15, p. 8.

[10] *Ibid*. pp. 32–33. On the problem of public perceptions of the independence of the Treasury Solicitor the Salmon Commission, with somewhat exaggerated confidence, observed: "The Treasury Solicitor no doubt comes into close contact with the Government of the day. But Governments come and go. The Treasury Solicitor and his staff . . . like all civil servants, go on impartially carrying out their duties whatever Government happens to be in power; the work of the Civil Service is in no way affected by political influences, and this fact without doubt is well recognised by the public." For a more sceptical view of the Civil Service see, *e.g.* Richard Crossman's *The Diaries of a Cabinet Minister* (2 vols.) (London, 1975). The unequivocal position of the Treasury Solicitor was spelt out, in his written memorandum to the Salmon Commission, as follows: "The Treasury Solicitor's function is to act as solicitor to the Tribunal . . . notwithstanding the fact that there may be Government Departments or Ministers for whom the Treasury Solicitor normally acts, who are concerned directly with the inquiry. . . . It is clearly, however, impossible for the Treasury Solicitor to serve two masters. He is the solicitor to the Tribunal and it is from the Tribunal he must receive instructions"—*op. cit.* p. 45.

[11] *Ibid*. para. 15, p. 8, and see memorandum of evidence submitted to the Salmon Commission by the Scottish Crown Office and Home Department—*Documentary Evidence*, pp. 19–20.

[12] *Post*, Chapter 10.

Commission, the Government's White Paper has wisely avoided the
position adopted by the Commission in rejecting unconditionally any role
for the Attorney General of the day. Without any legislative amendments
to the 1921 Act which would control the options available to the parties
concerned, we may confidently expect future Law Officers for England and
Scotland to interpret their role as protectors of the public interest by
appearing in person if the circumstances warrant their personal involvement in the tribunal's proceedings or, if not, appointing senior counsel to
represent them. Thus, if the nature of the inquiry's terms of reference were
to involve the Law Officers personally or the activities of the Law Officers'
Department it would be highly improper for either the Attorney or the
Solicitor to take part in the proceedings. Where, on the other hand, the
subject-matter of the inquiry or the cross-examination of a particular
witness lends itself to the delegation of the Attorney's role to counsel, it
should be a matter for the Attorney General to decide in the exercise of his
well established prerogative to nominate counsel where a question of the
general public interest is involved. This discretion, in the opinion of the
Salmon Commission, should be removed from the Attorney General so far
as tribunals of inquiry are concerned. "To leave the choice with him," the
Commission concluded, "would be to put him in a most inviduous position.
If he decided not to appear, he might feel that he was shirking an
unpleasant duty or that some sinister implication might be read into his
decision. . . . The Tribunal should select its own counsel to be instructed
by the Treasury Solicitor."[13]

The Salmon Commission's perceptions of the public's misconception of
the hybrid responsibilities of the Law Officers is regrettably all too well
founded. Much more effort is going to be necessary, by example and by
education, to engender public awareness of the distinctions that are
supposedly well understood by lawyers and parliamentarians.[14] By
deciding to adhere to the conception of the Law Officers' public
responsibilities, as explained and practised by Shawcross and Dilhorne, we
may confidently expect to find the Attorney General in future administrations following in their footsteps and not shirking his inherent duty to
represent the public interest no matter how embarrassing this might be to
his political colleagues in the government. Nothing, it might be thought,
could be more calculated to identify the Law Officers as mere "legal hacks
advising a ministerial department"[15] than the Salmon Commission's view
that "there is no reason why a Law Officer, if he considered it right to do
so, should not represent any minister or Government Department
concerned in such proceedings."[16] This interpretation of the Law Officers'
functions would tend to eliminate in the public mind any association of the

[13] *Op. cit.* para. 96, p. 36.
[14] For my suggestions in this regard see the paper referred to in fn. 89 *ante.*
[15] *Per* Sir Elwyn Jones, Attorney General, in the course of his oral evidence before the
Salmon Royal Commission—see *Minutes*, p. 138.
[16] *Report*, para. 96, p. 36.

Attorney General or the Solicitor General with the general public interest. History has imposed that special responsibility upon the Law Officers of the Crown. Its abdication or withdrawal by parliamentary action would surely herald the transformation of the offices of the Attorney General and the Solicitor General into predominantly political creatures with no independence and no obligation to act impartially.

There is one further aspect of the Salmon Commission's report that must be confronted. It concerns the resolution of a possible conflict between the Attorney General and the tribunal itself as to what in fact constitutes "the public interest" in the circumstances being investigated. Such a possibility may be remote in actual practice but it needs to be addressed and resolved in the calm of reasoned debate rather than in the highly charged political atmosphere surrounding an ongoing inquiry. This question surfaced repeatedly in the course of the Commission's examination of the witnesses who appeared before it, most of whom were inclined to regard the issue as of academic interest.[17] Lord Salmon and his fellow members likewise were disposed to regard as unlikely the possibility of a major clash on the determination of where the public interest should lie but, in the event of its occurring, they maintained that "it is the tribunal which is the guardian of the public interest and which alone is charged by Parliament to investigate and report in the interest of the public."[18] Having regard to the traditional attributes associated with the Attorney's role as protector of the public weal it is to be expected that, at times, the Attorney's views might well differ from those of the tribunal as to the lines of inquiry to be pursued or the conclusions that follow from such investigation. In the opinion of the Salmon Commission such conflicts were undesirable.[19]

It seems to have escaped the Commission's attention that the possibility of such a conflict in the resolution of what represents the public interest is an ever-present feature of the respective roles performed by the judiciary and the Attorney General whenever the latter appears before the court in his representative capacity as guardian of the public interest. Motions for contempt, questions of state privilege, the exercise of the Attorney's fiat in relator proceedings, appearances as *amicus curiae*, all involve considerations of what is in the public interest and as to which the presiding or appellate judge may have different views from those advanced by the Attorney General or counsel representing him. The Attorney is not thereby disqualified from expressing publicly his views of the matter. Not to do so would be a dereliction of his duty as the acknowledged representative of the wider public interest that would otherwise not be heard. The jurisdiction of the court imposes a parallel and deciding responsibility on the judge to decide which view he will take having regard

---

[17] See, *e.g.* the exchanges between Lord Shawcross and members of the Royal Commission. *Minutes of Oral Evidence*, pp. 125–126, and likewise during Sir Elwyn Jones' testimony, *ibid.* p. 141.

[18] *Report*, para. 96, pp. 35–36.

[19] *Ibid.*

to the representations of the Attorney General and any other parties to the dispute. So, it is suggested, should the tribunal of inquiry approach the discharge of its duties. This should not be seen as displacing the traditional functions of the Attorney General. His views do not represent the last word, that position is rightly accorded to the tribunal of inquiry. In this analysis, there is no conflict of the kind invoked by the Salmon Commission in support of its recommendation that the Attorney General be excluded altogether from future tribunals of inquiry. On the contrary, it is to be hoped that the Law Officers of the Crown will continue to fulfil their duty of representing the public interest conscientiously, impartially and vigorously and in so doing measurably increase public awareness of their role as the appointed champions of the public good.

8

Legal Advisers to Parliament

Among the functions associated with the Attorney General and Solicitor General for England and Wales that have experienced difficulty in taking root in other Commonwealth countries is their role as legal advisers to Parliament. More precisely, this concerns the Law Officers' duties as legal advisers to the House of Commons. The mandatory enjoinder embodied in the ancient language of the Writ of Attendance, issued on appointment to the Attorney General and the Solicitor General along with the patents of their respective offices, to attend upon the House of Lords "to treat and give your advice—and this you may in no wise omit . . . " has not been obeyed or taken seriously by any Law Officer since 1742.[1] The situation is very different with respect to the Lower House which continues to exhibit its expectations that one or other of the Law Officers of the Crown should make himself available to guide the Commons on legal questions pertaining, for example, to the meaning and legal implications of proposed legislation, the privileges of the House or the conduct and discipline of Members of Parliament.

When the volume of parliamentary business was markedly less than is customary in modern times, such demands for the participation of the Attorney General or the Solicitor General in the daily business of the House of Commons were accommodated with varying degrees of dedication and ability. Some insight into the parliamentary reputations in this regard of the more noteworthy Law Officers during the Victorian era, many of whom went on to become Lord Chancellors, are to be found in contemporary biographies of that period.[2] What the pages of *Hansard* and various parliamentary papers reveal is the growing sense of dissatisfaction with the unavailability of the Law Officers when their services were required to give authoritative legal opinions on measures before the

---

[1] See Edwards, *Law Officers of the Crown,* Chapter 3, esp. at pp. 33–34. As Lord Elwyn Jones has pointed out, an Attorney General who has been made a Privy Councillor may sit on the steps of the Throne during proceedings in the House of Lords, and occasionally does so. Such appearances, however, would not be in the Attorney's capacity as legal adviser to the Upper House—[1969] C.L.J. 43 at p. 44.

[2] Edwards, *op. cit.* pp. 48–49.

Commons.[3] Thus, in the course of a debate on the adjournment which took place in 1872, the view was advanced, and rejected in an elaborate reply by Sir John Coleridge, then the senior Law Officer, that the first duty of the Attorney General and Solicitor General ought to be to attend to legislation in the House of Commons.[4] This move was part of a proposal for restructuring the Law Officers' functions so as to secure for the public the undivided attention of those who were responsible for tendering legal advice to Her Majesty's Government. Underlying the members' dissatisfaction was the controversial question of the Law Officers being permitted to continue in private practice, it being felt that too much of their time and energies were devoted to the financially rewarding side of their professional work. The case for transforming the offices of Attorney General and Solicitor General into full time salaried Ministers of the Crown was to be pressed at great length in a series of departmental and select committees, and on the floor of the House of Commons, for the ensuing 60 odd years.[5]

The clearest enunciation of the dilemma surrounding the appropriate mode and level of remuneration of the Crown's Law Officers was that advanced by Sir Stafford Cripps in 1937, during the passage of the Ministers of the Crown Bill. Speaking as a former Solicitor General in the Labour Government of 1930–31, Cripps reminded the House of Commons that "Until a decision has been arrived at as to whether a Law Officer is really a Minister, and is to be paid and regarded as a Minister, or whether he is half Minister and half practising lawyer, no satisfactory conclusion will be arrived at as regards to his salary. . . . we cannot deal with the Law Officers as though they occupy positions carrying ministerial responsibilities similar to that which appertains to ordinary Ministers . . . The function of the Law Officers is to advise the government and respective Ministers, and to take charge of various cases in the Courts."[6] Eventually, in 1946, the solution to this perennial and embarrassing problem was implemented by means of a Treasury Minute. The hybrid character of the Attorney General and Solicitor General was formally recognised in a scheme of remuneration that embodied both of the major constitutional roles associated with these offices, as ministerial members of the executive branch of Government and as chief counsel for the Crown before the courts. Thus, the Treasury Minute of 1946[7] provided, first, for the payment of a single all-inclusive salary to cover all business of whatever sort done by the Law Officers for or on the instructions of any department of the Government, and secondly, for the payment of fees for briefs delivered to the Law Officers in contentious business when they appeared on behalf of the Crown, with this important qualification that the fees so paid should be set off against the salaries receivable by them. By this imaginative formula,

[3] *Ibid.* pp. 49–50.
[4] Hansard Debates (3s), Vol. 211, cols. 250–251, May 3, 1872.
[5] Edwards, *op. cit.* pp. 50–51 and Chapters 5 and 6.
[6] H.C. Deb., Vol. 324, cols. 1200–1201, June 3, 1937.
[7] See Edwards, *op. cit.* pp. 117–118.

criticism of the allegedly inordinate remuneration paid by the State to the Law Officers was effectively neutralised, at the same time preserving the professional standing of the Attorney General and Solicitor General when either incumbent appeared as the Crown's chief counsel in criminal or civil proceedings.[8]

This essential duality in the Law Officers' functions has been subjected in recent times to changes that are more a matter of degree than of fundamental substance. Demands on the Attorney General and his political colleague the Solicitor General, on the ministerial side of their respective offices, continue to absorb the greater proportion of the Law Officers' time and energy. As we have seen earlier, the distinguishing characteristic that is said to divide individual holders of the office of Attorney General is the degree of their commitment to the original role of the King's Attorney in conducting cases in the courts on behalf of the Crown.[9] This differential is, however, of marginal significance in terms of the distribution of actual time devoted to the discharge of the Law Officers' ministerial duties. Whatever the personal inclination of the Attorney General may be towards taking a leading role in major criminal trials or in important civil, constitutional and international cases he cannot escape the pervasive responsibility of advising his ministerial colleagues on matters of law and policy and in fulfilling his parliamentary obligations. It is doubtful whether the process of conversion, culminating in the Treasury Minute of 1946, to renumerating the Law Officers by fixed, all inclusive salaries exerted any dramatic changes in the approach of the Attorney General or the Solicitor General to their parliamentary duties. What is perhaps more evident is the level of expectation fostered by members of the House of Commons who, when the occasion demands, are inclined to stress the importance of the Law Officers attending to what are conceived to be their primary obligations to the House and its Committees.

RECENT PRECEDENTS AND CONFUSION IN DEFINING THE SCOPE OF THE ADVISORY ROLE

It may be noted, in passing, that even before the new policy of remuneration was introduced in 1946 the post-war Labour Prime Minister, Mr. Clement Attlee, had issued a directive to the Law Officers that they should give priority to their parliamentary duties.[10] Even so, some years later the same Prime Minister was to issue a warning to the House of Commons that limits must be set on the demands imposed upon the Attorney General and the Solicitor General.[11] This was in reply to the complaint voiced by some Members of Parliament that the efficiency of the

---

[8] For the current position regarding the salaries of the Law Officers in England and Scotland, see *ante,* pp. 196–197.
[9] *Ante,* Chapter 3.
[10] Edwards, *op. cit.* p. 51, fn. 86.
[11] *Ibid.*

Standing Committees, set up by the Lower House to accelerate the passage of legislation, was being prejudiced by "an insufficient number of Law Officers to attend all the meetings of these Committees."[12] Mr. Attlee's response was typically succinct: "It has never been the practice" the Prime Minister stated "for a Law Officer to attend meetings of all Standing Committees. Although the burden of work now imposed upon the Law Officers is substantially heavier than hitherto, I understand that a Law Officer has been present on all occasions where the Minister in charge of the Bill concerned has indicated that their attendance in connection with particular clauses might be of assistance to the Committee. Law Officers have other important public duties in connection with litigation and other matters but they give precedence to parliamentary work and I hope that Committees will not find it necessary to require their constant attendance."[13]

Reinforcement of this general understanding was voiced by another former Prime Minister, speaking when out of office as Leader of the Opposition. The occasion for this intervention was the heated controversy engendered in 1963 by the Conservative Government's refusal to grant political asylum to Chief Enahoro of Nigeria. The motion being debated sought to condemn the Home Secretary and the Attorney General, Sir John Hobson, for misleading the House in not revealing that the Government had good reason to believe that Enahoro would be refused representation by English counsel of his choice at the subsequent trial in Nigeria.[14] Speaking in the course of the censure debate Sir Harold Wilson reminded the House of Commons that "The Attorney General, whoever he may be, is not only the legal adviser to the Crown and to the government. He is also a servant of this House. It is, from time to time, his duty to advise the House on legal matters—a duty going beyond his responsibility to this government and the Crown—and [the present Attorney General] like his predecessors has frequently accepted this duty and has told us that it was his duty to advise the House in a particular legal sense."[15] No exception to this brief exposition of the Attorney General's advisory role in the House of Commons was expressed by either the first Law Officer of the day, Sir John Hobson, who was present in the House at the time Sir Harold was speaking, or the Prime Minister, Mr. Harold Macmillan, who wound up the debate on behalf of the Conservative Government.

---

[12] *Ibid.*

[13] H.C. Deb., Vol. 419, col. 2098, February 28, 1946; quoted in Edwards, *loc. cit.*

[14] This episode subsequently resulted in unprecedented proceedings before the Masters of the Inner Temple Bench, who were required to adjudicate charges against Sir John Hobson of unprofessional conduct in the handling of the *Enahoro* case. After a private hearing, at which the Attorney General appeared in his own defence, the 30 Masters of the Bench found that the charges, initiated by Mr. R. T. Paget, Q.C., a well-known Labour M.P., were unfounded and that there were no grounds for criticising the Attorney's conduct—see *The Times,* October 22 and 23, 1963 and Edwards, *op. cit.* p. 52.

[15] H.C. Deb., Vol. 678, col. 994, May 27, 1963; quoted in Edwards, *op. cit.* p. 52, fn. 89.

Whether such silence should be construed as constituting unqualified acceptance of all the propositions contained in the Wilson statements is, I suggest, arguable. Indeed, it may seem remarkable that so much emphasis appears to have been attached to the Opposition Leader's interpretation of the relationship between the Law Officers and the House of Commons, made without that careful consideration of all its implications that would normally precede the formal declaration of a constitutional convention by the Prime Minister of the day. Resort to the Standing Orders for Public Business is not particularly helpful either, the only relevant provision (S.O. 63) being that which ordains that the Law Officers for England and Wales and for Scotland, "though not members of a Standing Committee, may take part in the deliberations of the committee, but shall not vote or make any motion or move any amendment or be counted in the quorum." This language is consistent with according a right only to address any of the House's Standing Committees. It in no way embodies a convention that every committee of the House of Commons, whether it be a Standing Committee concerned with reviewing the individual provisions of a proposed piece of legislation or a Select Committee charged with inquiring into a specific area of parliamentary concern, has the right to demand the attendance before it of a Law Officer to provide the necessary legal guidance with respect to its particular affairs. Nevertheless, as we shall see later, considerable importance is attached to the distinguishing features of a Standing Committee in contradistinction to those of Select Committees, when consideration is given by the Attorney General to requests that he appear before a particular committee as its ad hoc legal adviser.

The expansion in recent years in the number of Select Committees, created as part of the movement towards reforming the procedures of the House of Commons, and the growing importance of the reports emanating from these committees, have all contributed to a heightening awareness of the wide implications that surround the proper scope of the Law Officers' advisory role to the House and its committees. Few, if any, other recent developments in defining the responsibilities of the Attorney General and the Solicitor General have the practical significance that would attach to an expanded interpretation of the Commons' expectations in this area of its activities. It is not surprising, therefore, to discover a distinct lack of enthusiasm in the response of recent Attorneys General to invitations that they become actively involved in the work of the Select Committees. Before examining this newly emergent problem it may be useful to review the recent parliamentary record of intervention by the Law Officers in the proceedings of the House of Commons, either on their own initiative or in response to a call for assistance.

On the second reading of the Customs (Import Deposits) Bill in 1968 a question arose as to the irreconcilability of certain provisions in the Bill with the United Kingdom's obligations under the European Free Trade Agreement (EFTA). The Minister, piloting the measure through the Commons, suggested that the House defer debate on the issue until the tribunal (the EFTA Council), seized with jurisdiction to make such pronouncements, had formally considered the matter. Furthermore, the Minister declared that having taken the best advice available to it the Government was persuaded that the pertinent convention contained no specific prohibitions that might nullify the Bill's provisions. In a move designed to test the matter on the floor of the Commons and to clarify the United Kingdom's treaty obligations the shadow Attorney General, Sir Peter Rawlinson, asked the Attorney General during the committee stage for a categorical statement as to the legal position on the dispute that had arisen. In requesting the Attorney's intervention in the debate, Rawlinson cited the 1963 statement of principles enunciated by Sir Harold Wilson, which was quoted earlier.[16] The Attorney General of the day, Sir Elwyn Jones, responding to the Opposition's call, provided the Committee of the whole House with an elaborate legal opinion as to the meaning and effect of the controversial clause in the Bill.[17]

Several points deserve notice in interpreting this precedent. Although striking, both in the source of the request and the nature of the response by the Attorney then in office, it should not be unduly exaggerated. On at least two subsequent occasions a request by members of the House of Commons for the attendance of a Law Officer to explain the legal effects of a clause, in the context of the country's treaty obligations, was not complied with. In the first of these instances, in 1978, the clause formed part of the European Assembly Election Bill under the terms of which it was proposed that no treaty increasing the powers of the European Assembly should be ratified by the United Kingdom Government unless specifically approved by the Westminister Parliament. Questions were raised as to the meaning and effectiveness of the pertinent clause having regard especially to Articles 235 and 236 of the European Economic Community Treaty. Neither the Attorney General nor the Solicitor General being in the House at the time, the questions were answered by the Minister of State for Foreign Affairs. Several members called for the attendance of a Law Officer to express his opinion on the question as legal adviser to the House, but on this occasion no Law Officer responded.[18] It is of no significance that, subsequent to the Commons exchange on this issue, clarification in writing was provided by the Attorney General to Sir Ian Percival, the Shadow Solicitor General. This could not be construed, however, as advice tendered to the Lower House as a whole.

In December 1979 the House was debating the Government's White Paper containing the proposed new immigration rules, in the course of which a former Attorney General, Mr. Sam Silkin, and a former Home Secretary, Mr. Merlyn Rees, called attention to the possibility that the rules were in violation of the provision in the European Convention on

---

[16] H.C. Deb., Vol. 774, cols. 1269–1274, December 3, 1968 (at the Committee stage).
[17] *Ibid.* cols. 1274–1281.
[18] H.C. Deb., Vol. 943, cols. 793–831, 833–835, esp. cols. 821 and 827, February 2, 1977.

Human Rights regarding discrimination based on race. Both former Ministers called for the presentation of a Law Officer's considered opinion on the legality of the new immigration regulations.[19] Moreover, the request was not made on the spur of the moment, since Mr. Rees had previously advised the Home Secretary, Mr. William Whitelaw, of his intention to call for the views of the Law Officers of the Crown before the formal regulations were introduced in the House.[20] Replying to the Opposition's demand, the Home Secretary declared that the Government had collectively considered the full implications of its immigration proposals, including the question that had been raised by the chief Opposition spokesmen about the country's international obligations under the European Convention on Human Rights. Mr. Whitelaw expressed the Administration's confidence that if its proposals were challenged before the European Human Rights Commission and the European Human Rights Court there would be strong arguments to justify the proposed new law.[21] Be that as it may, the Home Secretary's response to the Opposition's call that the opinion of the Attorney General be placed before the Commons was simply to divert the thrust of the invitation by invoking "the tradition that the Government do not disclose any advice that they may receive from the Law Officers."[22] A request to the Speaker for clarification of the House's entitlement to require the attendance of a Law Officer to explain the international legal implications of the proposed immigration rules got nowhere, the Speaker declining to add anything to what the Home Secretary had said in his carefully worded reply.[23]

The confidentiality of the legal opinions sought from the Law Officers by other ministers or government departments underscores the parallel position of the Attorney General and Solicitor General as the Crown's chief legal advisers. In the immigration rules debate referred to above, what we are witnessing is a clash of conflicting principles. Where the duty of the Law Officers is to advise the Crown, meaning the government in its collective sense and in its several parts, the crucial question is what practical expectations can be sustained by the House of Commons in its determination to look for objective legal opinions from the Law Officers acting as legal advisers to Parliament? I shall return to this fundamental problem later in this chapter.

Continuing this review of the sparse collection of parliamentary precedents in which the question of the Law Officers' advisory role in the Commons has been raised, there is the further need to distinguish those

---

[19] H.C. Deb., Vol. 975, cols. 256–257, per Mr. Silkin; and cols. 351–352 per Mr. Rees, December 4, 1979.

[20] Ibid. col. 352.

[21] Ibid.

[22] Ibid. In truth, no such unqualified convention exists. For a review of the precedents on this question, illustrating the readiness of governments of different political persuasion to invoke the convention or to disregard it, if found expedient to do so, see Edwards, op. cit. pp. 256–261.

[23] Ibid. col. 353.

other occasions in which the Attorney General or the Solicitor General
may be directly involved in carrying measures through all stages of the
House of Commons. Recent examples that come to mind include the
Administration of Justice Act 1972,[24] the Domicile and Matrimonial
Proceedings Act 1973,[25] and the Contempt of Court Act 1981,[26] the
contents of which statutes are relatively devoid of partisan implications. In
some of these measures the Home Secretary was also very much involved
as the minister to whom the reports of the Criminal Law Revision
Committee are submitted for the Government's consideration. In the
House of Lords the piloting of legal measures of this sort is the
responsibility of the Lord Chancellor, it being a matter of parliamentary
time-tabling as to whether such a Bill originates in one House rather than
the other.

   Not that the responsibilities of the Attorney General and the Solicitor
General are confined to actively participating in debates that are concerned
with Bills having a predominantly legal flavour. Rather more difficulty, as
we have seen, is experienced in determining the role of the Law Officers in
the carriage of Bills that are concerned with the implementation of
international legal obligations. As the government's chief legal advisers it
can be assumed that the legal aspects of such Bills will, as a matter of
course, have been carefully examined by the Law Officers and their legal
staff in the Law Officers' Department during the preparatory steps that
precede the introduction of new legislative measures. Among the questions
likely to be considered would be the effect of a Bill's provisions in
implementing the country's external obligations, as well as the consistency
of the proposed measure with existing international treaties or conventions. This is part and parcel of the functions of the Law Officers as the
principal source of legal judgment and advice available to the
government.[27] Access to such legal advice is always available to the Law
Officers' ministerial colleagues who preside over the various departments
of State. In the same vein, the assistance of the Attorney General or the
Solicitor General may be sought by a minister charged with the burden of
securing the passage of a departmental Bill through the Commons. In so
acting, a Law Officer would be performing in his capacity as a ministerial
colleague with special competence and authority to deal with any legal
questions that may arise in interpreting the provisions of a new measure.
Examples of this latter kind of participation by the Law Officers in the
House's proceedings, leading up to the enactment of statutes or subordinate legislation, are scattered throughout the annual volumes of *Hansard*.
As illustrations of what this involves special reference might be drawn to
the debates preceding the final approval given to the Rhodesia Sanctions

[24] c. 59.
[25] c. 45.
[26] c. 49. For a useful discussion of this aspect of the Attorney General's parliamentary
responsibilities see Lord Elwyn Jones, *In My Time* (1983), pp. 201–206.
[27] *Ante*, Chapter 7.

Order 1968,[28] and the European Communities Act 1972,[29] in both of which instances questions of international obligations and consistency with the domestic law of the United Kingdom were canvassed and dealt with by the Attorney General or the Solicitor General on the floor of the House of Commons.

In none of the distinctive situations just described is there any suggestion that what is involved is the Law Officers' role as servants and general legal advisers to the House of Commons. Understandably, the task of separating the different roles expected of the Attorney General and Solicitor General as, first, the government's chief legal advisers, secondly, as ministerial colleagues assisting in piloting measures through the House of Commons, and thirdly, as servants of the House in their capacity as legal advisers to Parliament, is apt to confuse parliamentarians and non-parliamentarians alike, to say nothing of the ability of the Law Officers themselves to maintain the essential qualities attached to the respective roles. Despite all these difficulties it is of the greatest importance that there be a proper understanding of the dividing lines that mark out the various capacities in which the Attorney General and the Solicitor General participate in the House of Commons debates and in the proceedings of its committees.

There have been a few notable occasions in the last decade in which the Attorney General has sought the leave of the House to make a prepared statement on the legal ramifications of a contentious subject that was occupying the attention of Parliament and the country at large. Of special significance, it might be thought, is the initiative taken in this regard by several recent Attorneys General who were serving as members, respectively, of the Conservative and Labour Governments in power at the time. Thus, during the industrial troubles that consumed the attention of every sector of the community during the winter of 1979, Mr. Sam Silkin, the Labour Attorney General, in response to the Opposition's pressure upon the Government to introduce more effective legislation, as well as more vigorous enforcement of the existing law, made a lengthy statement on the law regarding picketing and answered a variety of questions in connection with his opinions as to the relevant provisions of the criminal and civil law.[30] Within a short period of time, during which the Conservative Party under Mrs. Margaret Thatcher had assumed office, the new Attorney General, Sir Michael Havers, repeated his predecessor's performance in

---

[28] See H.C. Deb., Vols. 766, cols. 728–746, June 17, 1968.

[29] For examples of the burden assumed by the Solicitor General of the day in carrying this epoch making measure through the Commons, see Vol. 831, cols. 648–651, 652–656 (February 17, 1972); Vols. 832, cols. 1152–60, 1161–6, 1335–43 (March 6, 1972); Vol. 839, cols. 258–268 (June 20, 1972).

[30] H.C. Deb., Vol. 962, cols. 706–721, January 25, 1979. The Attorney General confirmed that his statement had previously been shown to, and approved by, the Lord Advocate as an accurate statement of the law of Scotland with respect to the same subject. An unusual aspect of this precedent was the similar exposition made in the House of Lords, of which he was a member, by the Solicitor General for Scotland. Commenting on this kind of unusual situation

affording the differently constituted House of Commons an opportunity to hear a straightforward explanation of English law relating to picketing.[31] The Attorney's statement had been precipitated by widespread secondary picketing in the steel industry.

The criminal law of the land, the Attorney General explained, applies to pickets as much as to any other citizen. The law permits picketing solely for the purpose of peacefully obtaining or communicating information or of peacefully persuading another person to work or not to work. The immunity from civil proceedings, he further stated, given by the Trade Union and Labour Relations Act 1974,[32] s.5, does not extend to any wrongful act such as violence, or threats of violence or similar intimidation—whether by excessive numbers of pickets or molestation amounting to a civil trespass or assault. The Attorney General went on to declare that the freedom to picket does not confer or imply any right to stop vehicles—still less do pickets have the right to stop people going about their lawful business. Pickets have no right to link arms or otherwise prevent access to the place they are picketing. Resort to large numbers of pickets, it was pointed out, may constitute an affray or an unlawful assembly or even a riot. At the same time, there was a realistic appreciation of the difficulties facing chief officers of police in deciding how order can best be maintained and, in particular, when and when not to invoke the criminal law.

Reading the exchanges that followed in the wake of the Attorney General's exposition it cannot be said that the atmosphere of unbiased analysis of the law, reflected in Sir Michael Havers' statement, was cultivated by spokesmen on either side of the House. In this respect, some of the Attorney General's own contributions were no different from the partisan speeches indulged in by other members of all parties who took part in the ensuing debate. Essentially, however, readers of the *Hansard* report could entertain no doubt as to which particular mantle the Attorney General was wearing when he spoke on this highly charged subject. In reply to an Opposition member's suggestion that it would have been more to the benefit of the whole country if a statement on the steel industry's pay dispute had been made by another member of the Government, Sir Michael Havers replied without hesitation: "The Law Officers owe a duty to the House to express a view on the law. Clearly there is some doubt in various areas about the law. If one looks at the newspapers over the past

---

Lord Elwyn Jones has stated: "Nowadays, if the Law Officers are not members of the House [of Commons] when they are appointed, efforts are made to find a seat for them. Unhappily, this has not been so successful north of the border as in the south, so we only rarely have the privilege of having a Lord Advocate in the House of Commons, thereby increasing the responsibilities of the Attorney General who occasionally has to endeavour to explain the mysteries of the law of Scotland to an unbelieving House of Commons"—[1969] C.L.J. 44. See, too, *post*, Chapter 10.

[31] H.C. Deb., Vol. 978, cols. 238–259, February 9, 1980.
[32] c. 52.

few days one finds that that is amply demonstrated. I thought it would be helpful to the House and to the public if a clear, simple exposition was given of the law as it relates to secondary picketing."[33]

This kind of initiative, exemplifying the impartial role expected of the Attorney General by his parliamentary colleagues, is not without some real problems of its own. Following Sir Michael Havers' intervention on the floor of the House he was invited to give evidence before the Select Committee on Employment, the committee assigned the responsibility of supervising the activities of the Department of Employment, it being rather obvious that the committee's purposes included the opportunity to question the Attorney General on the legal immunities of trade unions.[34] The invitation was refused for reasons that will be examined later and which underline the significance of the choice of parliamentary forum in which the Law Officers are prepared to assist the House of Commons.

What seems undeniable, having regard to the explanations put forward in the passages quoted in the text above, is the continued existence of the constitutional practice expressed in Sir Harold Wilson's statement in 1963. The general outlines of this advisory role as an independent, impartial servant of the House of Commons have been reiterated sufficiently to brook no further doubts as to its validity. What is rather remarkable is the realisation that an elaboration of its exact parameters has never been the subject of public debate in Parliament or elsewhere. Outside of Parliament itself, it is true that there has been a number of occasions in which equally inadequate explanations have been offered by those in a position to speak from first hand experience of the advisory responsibility. Thus, in an address to the Law Society in 1953, Lord Shawcross, speaking as a former Attorney General, stated: "In relation to Parliament, the Law Officers have other and wider duties. They may, for instance, be called upon by the House to advise on any legal problem which arises. If they do, they advise the House in an entirely non-party way. They may be asked to act for the House in some matter—it does not often happen nowadays—which the Commons wish to pursue, or possibly to prosecute somebody for contempt of Parliament, or something of that kind. Every evening after court hours they are to be found in their rooms in the House of Commons supposed to be ready to go into the Chamber if any need for their attendance arises."[35] In somewhat the same vein, Lord Dilhorne, formerly Sir Reginald Manningham Buller, revealed a little of the complexities surrounding the Attorney General's advisory role in relation to the House of Commons. Addressing the Canadian Bar Association in 1956 he contented himself with referring to the "somewhat odd position" in which the Law Officers found themselves occupied. He went on, "we have . . . to answer as best we can any legal questions which arise in the course of debate. We have to

---

[33] *Ibid.* col. 243.

[34] The intentions of the committee were made very apparent in the same sitting of the House of Commons as that referred to above, see *ibid.* col. 248.

[35] *The Office of the Attorney General*, The Law Society, 1953.

make ourselves familiar with all the Bills which come before the House and be ready to express our view on any legal point arising in the course of the discussion of these Bills."[36] Lord Elwyn Jones, in an address on the office of Attorney General which appeared in the *Cambridge Law Journal* in 1969, was even less informative on the subject.[37] We must turn to the present Lord Chancellor, Lord Hailsham, who never served as a Law Officer of the Crown, for the fullest synthesis of the possible conflict of roles that constantly confronts the Law Officers in Parliament. In the course of delivering the Child Lecture in 1978 Lord Hailsham explained the situation in these terms: "The Attorney-General or the Solicitor-General is expected to perform a dual, or at least a hybrid, role. He is the spokesman for the government on legal matters, and he is often employed, in addition, in a purely political role to defend or put questions of policy, including some which he has had no part in framing. But on purely legal questions, the meaning or effect of a clause for instance, or a proposed amendment of a Bill, he is expected to place his legal expertise at the disposal of the House and not at the disposal of his colleagues."[38] Reference to the standard works on constitutional law and parliamentary procedure are inexplicably silent on the nature and scope of the Law Officers' duty to advise the House, being content to allude only to the right of the Attorney General and the Solicitor General to attend meetings of Standing Committees.[39]

LIMITATIONS ON THE LAW OFFICERS' RESPONSIBILITIES

If further clarification is to be sought, reference must be made to official correspondence between the most recent holders of the office of the

---

[36] *Proceedings of the C.B.A., 1956*, Vol. 39, pp. 138–143. In the course of his address the former Attorney General recalled the occasion many years ago, when a private Bill was introduced to deal with local matters in a Borough. It was a long Bill with a long Schedule. Tucked away in a long paragraph in the Schedule was a sentence inserted by the Town Clerk who did not get on too well with his wife. That sentence read "The Town Clerk . . . is hereby divorced from his wife." It is said that this escaped detection. Confessing that he had not found time to verify the matter, Manningham Buller tantalisingly wondered aloud whether the provision only applied to the Town Clerk or to his successors as well.

[37] For sheer compression it is hardly likely to be surpassed. According to the speaker: "[The Law Officers] are invariably members of the House [of Commons] and there they answer questions in regard to legal issues which may arise in the course of government."

[38] The Child Lecture was given in the Middle Temple Hall on March 9, 1978. This lecture series was inaugurated in 1973 to mark the 300th anniversary of the bank's establishment at No. 1, Fleet Street and its close association with the legal profession.

[39] *e.g.* there is no reference to the Law Officers' duty to advise the Commons in Erskine May's *Parliamentary Practice,* Ivor Jennings' *Parliament* (2nd ed., 1957) or de Smith's *Constitutional & Administrative Law* (2nd ed., 1973). What is repeatedly mentioned is the Law Officers' right to attend Standing Committees and take part in their deliberations. As to this exercise de Smith states: "their presence is often important for obscurities in drafting need to be clarified and the implications of proposed amendments made clear"—*op. cit.* pp. 279–280. *Cf.* Wade & Phillips, *Constitutional and Administrative Law* (9th ed., 1977), which makes passing reference to the parliamentary responsibilities of the Law Officers in "helping to see legal and fiscal Bills through the Commons and giving advice to the Committee of Privileges"—*op. cit.* p. 334.

Attorney General.[40] This exchange of letters will be examined, first, with respect to the general character of the Law Officers' relationship to Parliament and then in relation to their steadfast refusal to accept a mandatory duty to act as advisory counsel to the expanding number of Select Committees which have sprung into existence in recent years. In a carefully worded reply to a request in early 1978 from the chairman of the Select Committee on Trade and Industry that the Attorney General assist the committee with respect to the existing state of the law on various aspects of fish farming, Mr. Silkin, the Attorney General at the time, set forth what he described as the well understood limits of the Law Officers' responsibilities to Parliament. According to Mr. Silkin: "when legislation is passing through Parliament the Law Officers explain to the House and to Committees their views of the meaning and legal implications of the legislation; they carry out that task in the capacity as Ministers of the Crown having a special departmental responsibility for the legal aspects of legislation which is being promoted. This is . . . a wholly different function from that of advising upon the existing state of the law, and I can find no occasion when a request for such advice has been made. Certainly it is not a recognized departmental responsibility of the Law Officers to give such advice."[41] Not persuaded by the Attorney General's refusal to accede to the committee's request, its chairman, Dr. Edmund Marshall, approached Mr. Silkin a second time. In doing so a series of specific precedents was cited involving the Attorney General and earlier Select Committees, of which more will be said shortly.[42] The Attorney General's response was more specific than his previous communication, in the course of which he sought to justify the earlier precedents as falling within a set of categories that together encompass the full extent of the advisory role. "The Law Officers," Mr. Silkin wrote, "have indeed customarily undertaken certain duties to provide legal advice to the House, but, so far as I am aware, these duties do not extend beyond the giving of legal advice in relation to (a) the constitution of and conduct of proceedings in the House, (b) the conduct and discipline of members, and (c) the effect of proposed legislation. . . . Law Officers also give evidence to committees of the House, and give advice, in relation to matters which fall within the responsibilities of their office, whether as a matter of tradition, usage or by virtue of some particular statutory provisions; examples of such matters are the Official Secrets Acts, the legal position of the Crown, criminal investigations by the Director of Public Prosecutions and charity matters."[43]

---

[40] Acknowledgment is readily made of the assistance afforded by the present Attorney General, Sir Michael Havers, and the officials in the Law Officers' Department in granting me access to this correspondence. It provides invaluable insights into the divergent approaches adopted by M.P.s and the Law Officers, respectively, as to the scope of the latter's advisory duties.

[41] Law Officers' Department files, letter dated March 9, 1978.

[42] See *post*, pp. 230–231.

[43] L.O.D. files, letter dated April 13, 1978.

In his original letter of enquiry the chairman of the Select Committee had placed considerable emphasis on the views expressed by former Prime Minister Harold Wilson in the course of the Enahoro deportation debate in 1963, to which reference has been made earlier in this chapter.[44] Adverting to Sir Harold Wilson's views, the Attorney General was disinclined to read too much into the oft quoted passage, saying that "I think Sir Harold's purpose was to point out that in giving advice to the House the Attorney General owed a special duty, over and above his general duty to the Crown. I find it hard to believe that Sir Harold Wilson intended to convey the impression that the House had the right to demand the Attorney General's advice on any question of law. Indeed, such an interpretation would conflict with the well established practice of Law Officers refusing to disclose to the House the advice which they had given to their ministerial colleagues. . . . I am reluctant to allow the Law Officers to be drawn into a position where they are required to act as standing counsel to the House, under a duty to provide advice on any issue of law which may arise."[45] The matter was not to lie dormant for long. According to Dr. Marshall, the chairman of the Trade and Industry Select Committee, the gloss placed by Mr. Silkin on Sir Harold Wilson's remarks in the House of Commons was not in accord with the former Prime Minister's views.[46] Mr. Silkin's final word in the correspondence was magisterial in both tone and substance. "Since it appeared that Sir Harold takes a different view of the duties of my office," he concluded, "from that which I hold myself and which, so I believe, my predecessors have taken, the Prime Minister has authorised me to say that he confirms that the position is that which I have set out in my letters to you."[47]

This official seal of approval given by Prime Minister Callaghan to the Attorney General's exposition of his duties as legal adviser to the House of Commons does not conclude the matter. However weighty any pronouncement by the Prime Minister of the day must be on questions of constitutional practice, the opinion attributed to Mr. Callaghan certainly lacks something of the authoritative qualities that would attach to statements by the Attorney General and the Prime Minister if they had been made on the floor of the Commons. In his final letter to Dr. Marshall, it will be noted that Mr. Silkin claimed that his views as to the duties of the Attorney General were in accord with those of his predecessors. As we have seen, however, the public record is noticeably thin in its collection of statements made by former holders of the office on the nature of their advisory relationship to Parliament. Prior to the Silkin-Marshall correspondence no comparable exposition of this important function existed in either the public domain or in the official papers housed in the Law

---

[44] *Ante,* p. 210.
[45] *Loc. cit.*
[46] These views had been confirmed in the course of an exchange of letters between Dr. Marshall and Sir Harold Wilson—L.O.D. files.
[47] *Ibid.* letter dated May 23, 1978.

Officers' Department. The explanation is simple, in that most of the questions discussed in this chapter have surfaced only recently and never before with that degree of urgency that compels a close assessment of the implications underlying whatever policies are eventually agreed upon between the Law Officers and the House of Commons.

As mentioned earlier, the attempt by the Select Committee on Employment in 1980 to compel the attendance of the Attorney General to answer a wide ranging series of questions concerning picketing and the legal immunities of trade unions was strongly resisted for the same reasons as those invoked by Mr. Silkin in his brush with the Select Committee on Trade and Industry two years earlier. In the case of the Employment Committee the ostensible purpose behind the invitation was to examine the Attorney General on the effect in criminal law of the clause in the Government's Employment Bill dealing with peaceful picketing, and as to which Sir Michael Havers had earlier given the House a lengthy discourse, the gist of which was summarised earlier in this chapter.[48] Furthermore, there were clear indications that the members of the committee were unlikely to restrain themselves from engaging in a free wheeling exercise that might go well beyond the terms of the Employment Bill and cover the whole field of legal immunities of trade unions, both civil and criminal.

There was the further important consideration that the Standing Committee, to which the Bill had been referred, was already seized of the controversial issues associated with the Bill's provisions. No invitation, it seems, had been extended to the Law Officers to appear before the pertinent Standing Committee which would have created a very different situation. In declining the invitation by the Select Committee on Employment the Attorney General adhered to the position taken by his predecessor when he rejected a call for help from the Select Committee on Trade and Industry. The duty to give advice to the House, it was stated, has well defined limits. With reference to the meaning and effect of proposed legislation, that duty was to be discharged by intervening in debate on the floor of the House or in Standing Committee, to which Bills are normally referred for detailed consideration. The attendance of a Law Officer before a Standing Committee might be by invitation of the committee or, alternatively, in his *ex officio* capacity in accordance with the Commons Standing Order 63 which confers a right on any of the Law Officers to take part in the deliberations of the committee. Much play was made, in Sir Michael Havers' response to the Employment Select Committee,[49] as to the nature of his participation before a Standing Committee in which, he claimed, the Attorney would be speaking in debate and not attending as a witness subject to cross examination. The latter characterisation of the proceedings before a Select Committee may be somewhat exaggerated. It nevertheless emphasises a difference in

[48] See *ante*, pp. 215–216.
[49] L.O.D. files, letter dated March 10, 1980.

degree rather than in principle, and may not be seen as providing the most substantial grounds on which to take refuge from a House of Commons that is determined to extract the maximum amount of information from the Law Officers in the course of their duty to advise the Lower House.

Judged by their responses to the invitations extended by the Select Committees in the past few years it would be reasonable to conclude that the recent bevy of Attorneys General adhered to a common philosophy in delineating the boundaries that govern the Law Officers' duties to the House of Commons. This identity of views, however, is not absolute. To better understand the divergences in interpreting these responsibilities we must have regard to another important exchange of letters, this time between Mr. Silkin and his immediate successor as Attorney General, Sir Michael Havers. The occasion that triggered the dispute has already been referred to. It centred around the Government's White Paper on Immigration and the call in the House of Commons for the Law Officers' opinion on the apparent conflict between the proposed new immigration rules and the pertinent provisions of the European Convention on Human Rights relating to race discrimination.[50] In his letter to the Attorney General following the Commons debate, Mr. Silkin expressed his concern about the Home Secretary's rejection, given after advance notice and consideration of the Opposition's insistence that the impartial opinion of one of the Law Officers be made known to the House before its members voted on the subject under debate. Conceding at the outset that "it is not the function of the Law Officers to act as general legal advisers to the House or its Committees" Mr. Silkin continued: " . . . my understanding is that where the House, or a Committee, is required to make a decision on proposed legislation, primary or secondary, it is entitled to the impartial advice of the Law Officers on the meaning and effect of that proposed legislation. For this reason Law Officers do periodically attend Committees of the House and tender legal advice on the wording of Bills and amendments."[51] In thus interpreting the general understanding of the Law Officers' advisory duties, the former Attorney General was reiterating principles that enjoy universal support. A more debatable proposition was then advanced in Mr. Silkin's letter, it being stated that "When the House is concerned to approve or disapprove proposed rules which have the effect of secondary legislation . . . and there is genuine doubt as to whether those rules are in accordance with, or would occasion a breach of, our obligations under international law or covenant, it seems to me that the House is entitled to the impartial opinion of the Law Officers and is severely handicapped if it is not given that view."[52]

---

[50] See *ante*, pp. 212–213.

[51] L.O.D. files, letter dated December 6, 1979. Mr. Silkin reminded his successor that, following the practice of consulting with the Shadow Attorney General of the day, he had been shown and approved of the position taken earlier in the Attorney's correspondence with the chairman of the Select Committee on Trade and Industry (*ante*, fns. 41 and 43).

[52] *Ibid.*

Little time was wasted in discussing the Home Secretary's attempt to justify the Government's refusal to allow the Law Officers to be heard on the ground that their opinions were confidential and that traditionally those opinions were not disclosed to Parliament. As Mr. Silkin rightly pointed out, this rule is not an absolute one, citing the publication by the Heath Government of the full text of the Law Officers' opinion on the United Kingdom's international obligations concerning the export of arms to South Africa.[53] Many other precedents could be referred to as confirming the correctness of the statement contained in Erskine May's *Parliamentary Practice* that: "The opinions of the Law Officers of the Crown, being confidential, are not usually laid before Parliament or cited in debate; and their production has frequently been refused; but if a Minister deems it expedient that such opinions should be made known for the information of the House, he is entitled to cite them in debate."[54] In short, disclosure is discretionary at the behest of the responsible minister or the government, to whom the considered opinion of one of the Law Officers has been addressed. It is not within the purview of the Attorney General or the Solicitor General, on their own initiative and in the exercise of their personal judgment, to make public the contents of legal opinions prepared in their capacity as the government's chief legal advisers. This fundamental restriction, by its very definition, engenders a potential conflict of interest whenever the House or its committees seek to draw upon the advisory services of the Law Officers. Moreover, the dilemma is likely to manifest itself with growing regularity.

Following the Government's apparent unwillingness to lift the veil on the Law Officers' opinion as to the legality of the new immigration rules, Mr. Silkin wrote to his successor inviting him to state exactly where the boundary line should be drawn where questions arose as to the compatibility of proposed legislation with the United Kingdom's obligations and rights in international law. In his reply, the Attorney General addressed himself to the general question involved rather than the particular case for the immigration rules, thus enhancing the significance of his statement as to the scope of the constitutional convention.[55] Sir Michael Havers expressed his agreement with the threefold description of the Law Officers' duty contained in Mr. Silkin's letter to Dr. Edmund Marshall in 1978, referred to earlier. That duty, according to the present Attorney General, does not extend beyond the giving of legal advice in relation to (a) the constitution of, and conduct of proceedings in, the House of Commons, (b) the conduct and discipline of members, and (c) the meaning and effect of proposed legislation. The first two items were not pursued further. Attention instead was concentrated on amplifying the

---

[53] Cmnd. 4589 (1971). The formal opinion expressed the substance of the advice tendered to the government over the previous six months and was signed by the Attorney General (Sir Peter Rawlinson) and the Solicitor General (Sir Geoffrey Howe).
[54] *Op. cit.* 19th ed., p. 432.
[55] L.O.D. files, letter dated January 29, 1980.

proper ambit of the last category. "Proposed legislation," it was agreed, should include, "proposed secondary legislation," at least where the measure was before the House or a Committee of the whole House.[56] It will be noted, however, that the Attorney General declined to accept the wider definition of the Law Officers' advisory duties that would include appearing before Standing Committees of the House when requested to do so. It has already been observed that under the Commons' Standing Orders any of the Law Officers are entitled to appear and participate in the proceedings of a Standing Committee.[57] So far as secondary legislative measures are concerned the most likely forum in which legal questions might arise is the Joint Select Committee on Statutory Instruments which, in any case, already has available to it the expert legal services of the Speaker's Counsel.[58] Since the Statutory Instruments Committee was first established in the session of 1943–44 it is understood that no Attorney General has attended its meetings.[59] Unlike other Select Committees, the Committee on Statutory Instruments is directly concerned with proposed legislation, albeit of a delegated nature. The need for calling upon one of the Law Officers is likely to be remote, given the ready availability of Counsel to the Speaker. Should the occasion ever arise, however, adherence to the principles set forth in both the Silkin and Havers interpretations of the constitutional convention indicate that it would be the Law Officers' duty to respond affirmatively to a request for their legal advice.

On the international aspects of proposed legislation, Sir Michael Havers departed fundamentally from the position adopted by his predecessor. An examination of *Hansard* over the past 20 years, according to the Attorney General, indicated that there has been no course of conduct by the Law Officers in that period which would substantiate the existence of an accepted constitutional practice to give legal advice to the House of Commons on the question whether a proposed legislative measure would occasion a breach of the country's international obligations.[60] The Attorney General further maintained that the needs of the House, to be reassured as to the consistency of the government's legislative or executive measures with prior international commitments, should best be fulfilled by the responsible minister in the course of debate.[61]

[56] *Ibid.*
[57] *Ante,* p. 211. Judged by the records kept in the Law Officers' Department the prevailing tendency has been to confine such attendance to Standing Committees that deal with the Lord Chancellor's Bills, some criminal law Bills, some trade measures of a technical character (*e.g.* patents and the protection of trading interests) and an oil pollution Bill. No case was tracked down prior to the precedent established by Sir Elwyn Jones in the debates on the Customs (Import) Deposits Bill of 1968, in which a Law Officer had attended a Standing Committee to advise on the question of consistency of a clause in a Bill with a concurrent international obligation—L.O.D. files.
[58] See Erskine May, *Parliamentary Practice* (19th ed.), p. 586.
[59] A similar approach has been taken with respect to the question of attendance at meetings of the Select Committee on European Community secondary legislation.
[60] *Op. cit.* letter dated January 29, 1980.
[61] *Loc. cit.*

As to where the boundary line should be drawn, the Attorney General favoured a demarcation that separated questions according to their impact on domestic law as opposed to international law. The constitutional duty of the Law Officers, according to Sir Michael Havers, "does not extend beyond advising the House on the meaning and effect in domestic law of proposed legislative provisions. A duty to advise the House on the consequences of a proposed legislative measure for our international legal obligations would raise conflicts with the primary duty of the Law Officers to advise the Crown on legal questions. . . . "[62] The Attorney readily acknowledged that there have been occasions when a Law Officer has, with the agreement of his colleagues, disclosed to the House his advice to the Crown on the consequences in international law of proposed measures. Presumably, though Sir Michael Havers was not specific on this point, he was referring to such precedents as those mentioned earlier in this chapter. They include the Heath Government's publication of the White Paper containing the Law Officers' legal opinion on the effects of the Simonstown Agreement relating to the sale of arms to South Africa,[63] and the positive response of the Labour Attorney General, Sir Elwyn Jones, to a request by Sir Peter Rawlinson for the Law Officers' opinion on the legality of the Customs (Import) Deposits Bill of 1968.[64] These comparatively recent precedents certainly fall within the flexible rule governing the confidentiality of the Law Officers' opinions. Talk of an absolute prohibition against such disclosure is totally unsupportable. Expressed in realistic terms, the rule enables considerations of political advantage or embarrassment to the government to govern the decision whether to reveal what advice the Law Officers have given a ministerial colleague or the government as a whole.

In my previous study several instances drawn from the domestic law context were cited in which the Prime Minister or another Minister had seen fit to disclose to the House of Commons the nature of the advice they had received from the Law Officers.[65] The proper explanation for the discretionary approach was enunciated as long ago as 1865 by Lord Palmerston, the then Prime Minister, speaking with a long parliamentary experience behind him. According to Palmerston: "I do not apprehend that there is anything contrary to the Rules of the House in reading or quoting any opinion of the Law Officers. It is a question of discretion on the part of the government, not one bearing on the Orders of the House. There may be occasions when they may be properly read. As a general rule, no doubt, they are not laid before Parliament, and for this reason, not because it would be against an Order of the House, but because the Law Officers would be more cautious in expressing an opinion if they knew that it was to be laid before Parliament and the public. But as I have said, there may be occasions, like the present, when it is convenient and proper for the

---

[62] *Loc. cit.*
[63] *Ante*, fn.53.
[64] *Ante*, p. 212.
[65] Edwards, *op. cit.* pp. 256–261.

convenience of the House that such opinions should be made known."[66] This view has not been consistently adhered to by subsequent Prime Ministers[67] but there is support in modern times for the reversal of constitutional practice and the imposition of an impregnable moat around the Law Officers' opinions. Furthermore, it is questionable whether any significance should be attached to the executive or legislative character of the government's proposed action, to which the opinion of the Attorney General is directed. The advice to the Crown may originate in a wide variety of circumstances and it would be unrealistic to attempt to develop a series of categories according to which an automatic rule of disclosure or exclusion would be applied.

In terms of potential embarrassment it may well be that disclosure of a Law Officer's opinion may have international repercussions that exceed anything which could be envisaged as arising on the domestic political scene. If the effect of divulging the Law Officers' legal advice to the Crown would be to discredit claims made by the government's representatives before international bodies such as the European Assembly, the European Court of Justice or the United Nations, adherence to the theory of a compelling duty to disclose the Law Officers' opinions to the House might well prove counter-productive. On the other hand, a dividing line that seeks to separate domestic and international matters in any finite sense is likely to prove unworkable as, for example, if negotiations with the Irish Government relating to the Northern Ireland question were involved and the question arose of disclosing the contents of a Law Officer's opinion as to the legality of informal extradition arrangements between Belfast and Dublin.

What this analysis suggests is the desirability of a much more stringent standard of proof in international situations when attempts are made to justify a departure from the normal rule of non-disclosure of the Law Officers' opinions. It further suggests that a hard and fast line cannot be drawn between domestic law and international law situations as suggested in Sir Michael Havers' considered reply to Mr. Silkin's original question on this subject. It might be argued that in the international sphere a valid distinction could be drawn between questions of "pure law" in the interpretation of treaties and conventions with respect to a possible conflict with proposed domestic legislation, as to which it would be entirely appropriate for the House of Commons to expect guidance from the Law Officers, and questions of government policies involving particular decisions in the international area which could be categorised as "political" rather than legal questions. However attractive initially this distinction might appear to be it must be remembered that the execution of government policies in such European areas as trade, industry and commerce or in the matter of international maritime boundaries will

---

[66] Parl. Debates (3s) H.C., Vol. 177, col. 354, February 17, 1865, quoted in Edwards, *op. cit.* p. 257.
[67] Edwards, *op. cit.* pp. 258–259.

frequently surface in the form of a Bill introduced by the government. In these situations the suggested distinction between questions of "pure law" and "policies of the executive" will be untenable. Policy considerations and their legal implications cannot be readily disentangled. The price to be paid for unrestricted disclosure of the Law Officers' opinions on international questions might well prove too high for even the Opposition to press its case for the intervention of the Attorney General as the legal adviser to the Commons. Each situation will have to be assessed individually. One important consideration remains to be stressed in this discussion. It is this. The readiness of the Attorney General or the Solicitor General of the day to fulfil the expectations of the members of the Lower House, unless some overriding considerations are clearly evident, must enhance those independent qualities of their offices to which attention is properly drawn. This important concern must not be overlooked whenever the question of disclosure or non-disclosure is at stake.

THE SPECIAL PROBLEM OF SELECT COMMITTEES

Uncertainty also surrounds the obligation of the Law Officers to assist Select Committees[68] of the House of Commons in their appointed tasks. Invitations to provide such committees with legal advice and background information on the exercise of statutory powers have been strongly resisted by each Attorney General who has faced this problem. This, in turn, has met with public criticism[69] much of which is uninformed and lacks an appreciation of the grounds upon which the Law Officers have resisted parliamentary and media pressures to make themselves available for examination as witnesses before the committees. Familiarity with the nature of Select Committees, therefore, is essential to an understanding of the Law Officers' intransigence in this matter. Unlike Standing Committees of the House of Commons to which legislative measures are normally remitted at the Committee stage of a Bill for clause by clause debate, the underlying purpose of a Select Committee is to examine in depth a specific subject or subject area referred to it by delegation from the House.[70]

---

[68] On the role and expansion of Select Committees in the Westminister Parliament see, generally, Wade & Phillips, *Constitutional and Administrative Law* (9th ed., 1977), pp. 195–197; S.A. de Smith, *Constitutional and Administrative Law* (2nd ed., 1973), pp. 280, 288–295, 678. R. S. Arora, "Parliamentary Scrutiny: The Select Committee Device" [1967] P.L. 30–40.

[69] See, *e.g.* the criticisms directed against Sir Michael Havers following his refusal to appear before the Select Committee on Employment in 1980—*The Times, Daily Telegraph* and *Financial Times*, March 13, 1980.

[70] The mechanism of a Select Committee to investigate social, economic or administrative problems was resorted to with considerable frequency in the 19th century and the early part of the present century, usually with a specific issue as the committee's terms of reference. Some early examples include the Select Committee on Public Business (1847–48), Parl. Papers, Vol. xvi, (No. 644); the Select Committee on Capital Punishment (1930–33), Parl. Papers, Vols. 6 (No. 15); and the Select Committee on Nationalised Industries (1952–53) H.C. Paper 235 and (1966–67) H.C. Paper 340.

As such, Select Committees have come to be seen as possessing the potential for informed criticism and scrutiny of the actions of the executive branch on a continuing basis. It is no wonder, therefore, that the House of Commons has shown a growing inclination to extend the number of its "subject" Select Committees which specialise in particular areas of governmental activity or with specific reference to the activities of individual departments of State. Among the Select Committees appointed during the fertile period from 1964 to 1970[71] were those devoted to agriculture, education and science, and overseas aid. The subject of race relations and immigration followed. Public sessions in which ministers and senior public servants appeared as witnesses became commonplace. Specialist assistance was employed on a regular basis. This aggressive interpretation of their respective "charters" has continued with the blessings of the House and a corresponding lack of enthusiasm on the part of the government. Under the active leadership of the then Leader of the House, Mr. Norman St. John Stevas, the House of Commons resolved in 1979 to set up 13 Select Committees covering the following subject areas—agriculture, defence, education, science and the arts, employment, energy, environment, foreign affairs, home affairs, industry and trade, social services, transport, the Treasury and the civil service, and the reports of the Parliamentary Commissioner for Administration and the Health Service Commissioner. According to the Leader of the House the new Select Committee structure constituted "the most important parliamentary reform of this century."[72] Time alone will confirm the accuracy or otherwise of that assessment.[73]

This major expansion derived from the recommendations of the Select Committee on Procedure which, in its report to the House of Commons in 1965,[74] singled out the lack of knowledge of how the executive operates on a day-to-day basis as the principal source of weakness in the House of Commons. No thought seems to have been given at that time to dissociating the Lord Chancellor's Department and the Law Officers' Department from the terms of reference assigned to the committee that was to oversee the activities of the Home Affairs portfolio. Significantly, however, both these departments have been excluded from the purview

---

[71] Much of the impetus for the expansion in this form of parliamentary investigation is traceable to a series of reports that emanated from the House's Select Committee on Procedure—see H.C. 92–1 (1958–59) para. 47. Later expansionary activities by additional select committees were heralded in H.C. 410 (1968–69) and Cmnd. 4507 of 1970. For a critical appraisal of these developments see A. Morris (Ed.) The *Growth of Parliamentary Scrutiny by Committee* (1970), pp. 1–13, 125–131 and Wade & Phillips, *Constitutional & Administrative Law* (9th ed., 1977) pp. 195–197.

[72] H.C. Deb., Vol. 969, col. 35, June 25, 1979.

[73] For initial assessments see Anne Davies, *Reformed Select Committees: The First Year*, 1980, Outer Circle Policy Unit, London, and D. Pring (Clerk of Committees in the House of Commons), "The New Select Committee System at Westminster" (1983) 64 *The Parliamentarian* 57. *Cf.* the inside evaluation by the House of Commons' Liaison Committee in its *First Report on the Select Committee system, session 1982–83—The Times*, February 8, 1983.

[74] H.C. Paper 303 (1964–5).

of the presently constituted Select Committee on Home Affairs. Explaining the transformation in the Government's thinking on this sensitive matter the Leader of the House in 1979 explained: "I am sure that the House will agree that the new Committee should not be allowed to threaten the independence of the judiciary or the judicial process. In the Government's view there would be a real danger of that if a Select Committee were to investigate such matters as the appointment and conduct of the judiciary and its part in legal administration, or matters such as confidential communications between the judiciary and the Lord Chancellor and the responsibility of the Law Officers with regard to prosecutions and civil proceedings. The Law Officers have no administrative functions and the legal advice given by them to Government Departments is confidential and, by definition, is not disclosed outside the Government. . . . For those reasons, the Government consider that the most appropriate course is to exclude those two small Departments from scrutiny by the new Select Committees. There will, however, be no change in the existing answerability of the Law Officers to the House, both for themselves and on behalf of the Lord Chancellor."[75]

This deliberate exclusion of the Law Officers' Department from the functions of the Select Committee on Home Affairs has provided a haven of refuge into which the Attorney General has retreated in the face of repeated and vociferous demands that the committee be allowed to examine the Director of Public Prosecutions and the policies that govern his exercise of prosecutorial discretion. Approval by the House of the government's restrictive recommendations has not been allowed to go unchallenged.[76] To assess the merits of this dispute we must endeavour to place the problem in its wider constitutional context.

Reference has already been made to the unsuccessful attempt, launched in 1978 by the Select Committee on Trade and Industry, to secure the advisory services of Attorney General Silkin.[77] Apart from the theoretical arguments based on the conflict of interest principle, very practical objections were raised by Mr. Silkin in explaining his rejection of the committee's request. These relate to the impossibility of providing the degree of specialist advice required by a Select Committee from within the resources of the Law Officers' Department and its small coterie of professional legal staff. Compliance, it was said, would set a precedent that

[75] *Ante*, fn. 72, cols. 38–39 and see also cols. 52, 120–122.

[76] An amendment, designed to expand the terms of reference of the Home Affairs Select Committee to include the Lord Chancellor's office and the Law Officers' Department was defeated by the Commons, *ibid.* cols. 229–230. One of the chief Opposition spokesmen, Mr. Peter Archer (a former Solicitor General), not surprisingly, did not object to the government's proposal as it related to the Law Officers' Department—*ibid.* cols. 118–121. For the final order of the House see *ibid.* cols. 249–252. In their latest report (1983) to the Commons on the working of the various select committees (*ante*, fn. 73) the 23 chairmen (who constitute the Liaison Committee) again recommend the inclusion of the Law Officers' Department and the Lord Chancellor's Department in the terms of reference of the Select Committee on Home Affairs—*The Times*, December 14, 1982.

[77] *Ante*, pp. 219–220.

would have far reaching repercussions if it became established that among the duties expected of the Law Officers was the provision to Select Committees of advice as to the current state of the law. Instead, the Trade and Industry Committee was urged to utilise its own powers of obtaining assistance of a professional or technical character.[78]

With the proliferation in the number of Select Committees and an energetic approach to their duties there is no denying the valid nature of the practical objections raised by Mr. Silkin in his correspondence with the chairman of the Trade and Industry Committee. There is, however, nothing sacroscanct about the size of the Law Officers' Department so that if convincing arguments can be made for extending the ambit of the Law Officers' duty to the House and its committees presumably a solution could readily be found to the question of legal manpower. As the chairman of the Trade and Industry Committee was quick to point out in 1978 there were a number of earlier precedents in which either the Attorney General or the Solicitor General, having been summoned to appear before various Select Committees, raised no objection in public to giving evidence on matters of current law.[79] What, the chairman inquired, distinguished those occasions from the request of his committee? He might well have added to his list the forceful contributions of Attorney General Cockburn to the Select Committee on Public Prosecutors in 1854.[80] In that earlier situation the subject matter of the committee's deliberations was central to the Law Officers' traditional responsibilities and the testimony proffered was not that of an adviser but more in the nature of an advocate commenting upon proposals for reform in the administration of justice. Modern precedents that illustrate the same obligation of the Attorney General to cooperate with a Select Committee derive from the Attorney's "consent" powers under such statutes as the Obscene Publications Act 1959,[81] and the Official Secrets Act 1911.[82] In this kind of situation, it is customary for the Attorney General to provide both a written memorandum on the strengths and deficiencies of the existing law and to follow this up with an appearance before the committee to answer questions and to defend the government's position on possible changes in the relevant legislation.

In two modern instances, where the Law Officers cooperated with a Select Committee, questions concerning the constitution of, and conduct of proceedings in, the House of Commons were involved. Thus, the Attorney General was asked to advise as *amicus curiae* the Select

---

[78] L.O.D. files, letter dated March 9, 1978.

[79] L.O.D. files, letter dated March 23, 1978.

[80] See Edwards, *op. cit.* pp. 239–240, 341–346.

[81] *Ibid.* pp. 240–241. Reference has been made earlier to the testimony and memorandum submitted by the Attorney General to the Select Committee on the Obscene Publications Bill, 1958—see *Report,* H.C. Paper 123–1, esp. App. I, pp. 23–24.

[82] See H.C. 173 of 1938 containing the evidence of the then Attorney General, Sir Donald Somervell, given before the Select Committee appointed to inquire into the Attorney's exercise of his consent powers under the Official Secrets Act 1911, s.8, in the *Duncan Sandys* case—this is examined in Edwards, *op. cit.* pp. 244–245.

Committee appointed in 1950 to examine the legitimacy of the election of the Reverend MacManaway, a clergyman of the Church of Ireland. An explanation of the state of the relevant law was provided orally by Sir Hartley Shawcross, the then Attorney General.[83] It was the Solicitor General's turn in 1967 to appear as a witness before the Joint Committee on the Sound Broadcasting of Parliamentary Proceedings and to give evidence as to the current state of the law relating to copyright and the privileges of Parliament.[84] Both of these precedents fall squarely within a well recognised duty on the part of the Law Officers to serve as legal advisers to the Commons. A similar basis exists and explains the affirmative response of the Law Officers to the order of the House of Commons that they attend the Select Committees appointed in the 1939–40 and 1976–77 Sessions to inquire into the conduct of individual Members of Parliament "to present evidence relevant to the subject matter of the inquiry" and "to give such further assistance to the Committee as may be appropriate."[85] With respect to the latter of these committees Mr. Silkin, as Attorney General, attended on three separate occasions to lend his assistance. It requires little imagination to conceive of circumstances in which the range of a committee's inquiries may extend into activities that trespass well beyond the narrow purview of the House's own proceedings. What, for example, would the Attorney General's response be if the committee sought to question him on the exercise of his prosecutorial discretion with regard to a member's criminal activities or to examine the Director of Public Prosecutions and his possible involvement in the case, as to which the Attorney General is ministerially accountable?

Some idea of the attitude likely to be adopted by the Law Officers in such an eventuality was provided a short while ago in the much publicised confrontation between the Select Committee on Home Affairs and Sir Michael Havers, the Attorney General, on the question of deaths in police custody. Over a period of 10 years a total of 26 deaths had occurred of persons while in the custody of various police forces across the country. In some of these instances, *e.g.* the deaths of Liddle Towers, Blair Peach and James Kelly, a great deal of public controversy had been generated by allegations of police brutality, added to which was a growing concern with the unexplained fact that in none of these cases had criminal proceedings against a police officer been authorised by the Director of Public Prosecutions. The newly created Select Committee on Home Affairs undertook to look into the whole situation and with this objective in mind

---

[83] H.C. Paper 68 of 1950, p. viii. An earlier illustration occurred in the 1940–41 Session, when the Select Committee on Offices of Profit under the Crown received both oral and written evidence from the Attorney General on the current law and practice relating to the Committee's subject of inquiry—see H.C. 120.

[84] H.C. 284 of 1976–77.

[85] See H.C. Paper 177 of 1939–40; H.C. Paper 5 of 1940–41; and H.C. Paper 490 of 1976–77. The Commons "directive" to the Attorney General is contained in the Votes and Proceedings of the Lower House, Vol. 176, p. 1007, November 1, 1976.

sought to require the attendance before it of Sir Thomas Hetherington, the Director of Public Prosecutions.[86]

Consent for the Director's participation in the committee's proceedings was, of course, subject to the approval of the Attorney General as the responsible minister. And as Sir Michael Havers correctly explained,[86] although the Attorney is answerable generally to the House for all the activities of the Director of Public Prosecutions, including the Director's responsibilities under the Police Act 1964, it was the House of Commons itself which in 1979 had approved the exclusion of the Law Officers' Department from the list of departments answerable to Select Committees. This exclusion is total and covers all functions in respect of criminal prosecutions, including those carried out by the Director. It was further emphasised to the committee that the Director of Public Prosecutions has no administrative responsibilities with respect to the police and any information that he might have received in connection with deaths in police custody would be directed towards making a quasi-judicial decision regarding the institution of criminal proceedings. It was for precisely this reason that the House had agreed to exclude the Law Officers' Department from the scrutiny of the Select Committee on Home Affairs.

Undeterred by the Attorney's refusal to cooperate, the committee accepted the fact that the Director could not be expected to answer questions about individual decisions but expressed their continued desire to receive evidence from Sir Thomas Hetherington on the procedures which are carried out in his department following deaths in police custody and the criteria by which decisions are made.[87] The Attorney General, convinced that the committee was attempting to circumvent by a back-door stratagem the House's earlier decision on the limited jurisdiction of the Home Affairs Committee, sought to meet its needs by providing it with a written statement, prepared by the Director, setting out the principles on which he considers cases involving police officers and which are referred to him by chief officers of police under the Police Act 1964.[88]

The Director, in his written memorandum,[89] explained that under section 49 of the 1964 statute a chief constable, who has received a complaint from a member of the public against a member of his force, must have the complaint investigated. On receiving the internal report, the chief constable must send it forward to the Director of Public Prosecutions unless he is satisfied that no criminal offence has been committed. In practice, the Director's memorandum revealed, most chief officers of police send a report to the Director whenever there is a suspicion that an

[86] L.O.D. files; letter dated January 25, 1980.

[87] L.O.D. files; letter dated January 29, 1980.

[88] L.O.D. files; letters dated February 1 and 4, 1980. In addition, it was stressed that the police reports submitted to the D.P.P. were not even shown to the Home Office.

[89] The D.P.P.'s memorandum is published in full in the *Minutes of Evidence* taken before the Home Affairs Select Committee investigating deaths in police custody, February 14, 1980—H.C. Paper 401–iii.

officer may have committed a crime, regardless of whether or not there has been a complaint from a member of the public. Sir Thomas Hetherington stressed to the Home Affairs Committee that his department's decision whether or not to prosecute was determined in accordance with exactly the same criteria as those applied in all other cases reported to him under whatever circumstances. First, on the evidentiary side, the question to be answered was whether the totality of the available evidence is of such quality that a reasonable jury (or magistrate in the case of summary offences) is more likely than not to be satisfied beyond reasonable doubt that the accused is guilty of the offence charged. If the evidence before the Director fails that test, no prosecution would be instituted. If it satisfied the test, consideration was given to whether in all the circumstances of the case it is in the public interest to prosecute. The nebulousness of the "public interest" criterion was not overcome by substituting a formula based on the "interests of justice." It would only be in exceptional circumstances that no prosecution would ensue if there was sufficient evidence to support a serious charge against the officer in question such as assault occasioning bodily harm. With lesser offences, it was explained, the choice of some other course such as a caution or other disciplinary action would be taken into account.

This review of the general principles that govern the exercise of the Director's absolute discretion failed to assuage the Home Affairs Committee with its sensitivity towards the high visibility cases that had prompted it, in the first place, to investigate the cluster of unexplained deaths in police custody. When the Director appeared on BBC Television[90] to discuss the nature of his office and his accountability for the decisions he made, the Select Committee on Home Affairs renewed its pressures upon the Attorney General to give his consent to the Director's appearance as a witness.[91] Eventually, an accommodation was reached whereby the Select Committee gave two undertakings viz., that the attendance of the Director of Public Prosecutions to give evidence would not be treated as a precedent for further requests and, moreover, that there would be no questioning of Sir Thomas Hetherington directed towards individual cases.[92] In the event,

[90] The Director was interviewed on "Newsnight" on BBC 2 Television on February 4, 1980. As a matter of courtesy the Attorney General had given the chairman of the Select Committee advance notice of the planned broadcast.

[91] It is my understanding that pressure, to concede to the Select Committee's invitation that the D.P.P. appear before it, was also exerted upon the Attorney General by the Leader of the House of Commons, Mr. Norman St. John Stevas. The discomfiture of Sir Michael Havers at this strange turn of events must have been marked, in view of the House Leader's role in arguing earlier that the Law Officers' Department should be exempt from the scrutiny of any Select Committee—ante, fnn. 72 and 75.

[92] The impasse appears to have been resolved at a meeting in the House of Commons on the evening of February 7, 1980 between the Attorney General and Sir Graham Page, chairman of the Home Affairs Select Committee. The assurances noted in the text above were confirmed in an exchange of letters the following day. The D.P.P. was authorised to appear before the Select Committee on February 14, 1980 and a press release followed announcing the conditions under which the Attorney General had agreed to the Director giving evidence on the subject of deaths in police custody.

the Committee was unable effectively to penetrate the discreet curtain drawn in the exposition contained in the Director's written memorandum.[93] The exercise was not altogether fruitless, insomuch as the Director was able to explain his position with regard to providing the complainant with what amounts to a pro-forma justification for not invoking the criminal law in a particular case. According to Hetherington, it was in the greater public interest that the confidential nature of police reports and statements taken from potential witnesses not be breached. Likewise, it would be unjust to disclose the detailed considerations that led to a decision not to prosecute which might include the grounds for not believing some witnesses, or details about the prospective defendant's background and previous record, without the safeguards that the accused would have in court.[94] The failure of the Director to persuade the members of the Home Affairs Committee as to the correctness of his philosophy in making decisions was made manifest in the Committee's final report to the House of Commons.[95] It recommended that the Director of Public Prosecutions make it his normal practice to supply a complainant with at least a summary of the considerations which led him to decide against prosecution.[96] Later, in a statement made to the House of Commons, the Home Secretary indicated that the Attorney General had rejected the Committee's recommendation for the same reasons as those put forward by the Director when he testified before the Select Committee.[97] There the matter rests for the moment.

Exactly the same dilemma confronts the Attorney General wherever he is questioned on the floor of the Commons with respect to a particular criminal case, either on the basis that he or the Director had authorised a prosecution to be launched or, alternatively, that he had withheld the necessary consent. Even more acute is the dilemma of explaining to the satisfaction of the House the reasons for terminating a criminal prosecution by way of entering a *nolle prosequi* or by offering no evidence when the Crown is about to open its case at the actual trial. As the minister responsible to Parliament the Attorney General must tread the delicate line between making full disclosure to the Commons with its attendant dangers of prejudice to the accused, on the one hand, and, on the other, adhering to the principle of confidentiality surrounding police documents. Every Attorney runs the risk of sacrificing his credibility and the House's confidence in him if he fails to make sufficient disclosure of the reasons that prompted the decision that is under question. The inherent conflict of principle that is involved in these kinds of situation is generally resolved by mutual understanding between the Law Officers and the members of the House as to the outside limits within which the examination of the minister

---

[93] See *Minutes of Evidence* (fn. 90 above) pp. 30–40.
[94] *Ibid.* pp. 36–38.
[95] H.C. Paper 631 of 1980, pp. xii–xiv.
[96] *Ibid.* p. xvi.
[97] H.C. Deb., Vol. 992, Written Answers, cols. 150–152, November 11, 1980.

can properly be conducted. Any Attorney General who refuses to fulfil the minimum expectations of Parliament in this regard, which relate to individual decisions as well as general policies, must be prepared to suffer the political consequences that may be mild or harsh according to the current political climate.

9

New Responsibilities as Attorney General for Northern Ireland

As of March 30, 1972, the Attorney General for England and Wales assumed the duties associated with the office of Attorney General for Northern Ireland. On that date the Northern Ireland (Temporary Provisions) Act 1972[1] came into force, under which legislation the Westminster Parliament assumed direct responsibility for the government of the province. The possibility, however remote, of such an exceptional intervention had been anticipated in 1920 and provided for in the Government of Ireland Act of that year,[2] the constitutional statute that sanctioned the separation of the six counties, known as Ulster, from what is now known as the Republic of Ireland. Supreme authority in relation to the government of Northern Ireland, although rarely invoked during the years of devolutionary rule, was expressly reserved to the United Kingdom Parliament and it was under the terms of section 75 of the statute of 1920 that the political decision was taken to reactivate direct legislative sovereignty.[3] The Northern Ireland Parliament at Stormont was prorogued, its powers being suspended and transferred to Westminster. Parallel to these arrangements, the United Kingdom Government assumed direct executive power over the administration of Northern Ireland, a responsibility that was initially assumed by the Secretary of State for Home Affairs and later assigned to the Secretary of State for Northern Ireland. Although the 1972 Act was originally conceived as a temporary measure the political turmoil in that unhappy island necessitated the emergency legislation being extended indefinitely.[4]

[1] c.22.

[2] 10 & 11 Geo. 5, c.67.

[3] In addition, by virtue of section 6 of the Government of Ireland Act 1920, the Parliament of Northern Ireland has no power to repeal or alter the 1920 statute or any Act passed by the United Kingdom Parliament and extending to Northern Ireland, notwithstanding that any such provision deals with a matter with respect to which the Northern Ireland Parliament was empowered to make laws.

[4] See the Northern Ireland Constitution Act 1973 (c.36), *post*, fn. 63. The most recent enactment, the Northern Ireland Act 1982 (c.38) continues the arrangement contained in the 1973 legislation but it anticipates the eventual resumption of devolutionary government

As an essential part of the transfer of executive authority to London, the Northern Ireland (Temporary Provisions) Act 1972, s.1(2) declared that, so long as the emergency legislation has effect, " . . . the Attorney General for England and Wales shall by virtue of that office be Attorney General for Northern Ireland also, and he and the Solicitor General shall by virtue of membership of the Bar of England and Wales have in Northern Ireland the same rights of audience as members of the Bar of Northern Ireland." The role of the Solicitor General for England and Wales, which office has known no counterpart in Northern Ireland's history,[5] was indirectly alluded to in the above provision. More explicit arrangements were included in the consequential provisions contained in the Schedule to the 1972 Act which enlarged on the functions exercisable by the Secretary of State[6] and the Attorney General in London. As to the latter office, in the event that it is vacant all the functions authorised or required to be discharged by the Attorney General for Northern Ireland may be discharged by the Solicitor General for England and Wales as his deputy. The same arrangements will prevail in the event that the Attorney General is unable to act owing to absence or illness, or if the Attorney General authorises the Solicitor General to act in any particular case.[7] The last of these contingencies enables the additional burdens to be shared between the two Law Officers of the Crown in a manner best suited to their

through a new Northern Ireland Assembly. No immediate change in the "law and order" arrangements, including those pertaining to the office of Attorney General, is envisaged in the new measure. For an analysis of its provisions see [1982] *Public Law* 518.

[5] The creation of the office of Solicitor General was considered and rejected by the newly formed Government of Northern Ireland in 1923—see H.C. Deb., (N.I.) Vol. 3, col. 1191–92. Instead, provision was made for the appointment of a deputy to act for the Attorney General in the case of a vacancy or if, for any other reason, the Attorney was unable to act—see Office of the Attorney General Act (N.I.) 1923 (13 & 14 Geo. 5, c.18 (N.I.)) and the Ministers (Temporary Exercise of Power) Act (N.I.) 1924 (14 & 15 Geo. 5, c.11 (N.I.)). This arrangement would not affect in any way matters that were within the competence of the Westminster Parliament but which applied to Northern Ireland. Although no inconvenience appears to have been experienced during the intervening years, the opportunity was taken in the Law Officers Act 1944, s.3 to ensure that the same emergency arrangements obtained irrespective of the source of the relevant legislation requiring the Attorney General to act.

[6] By cl. (2)(1)(a) of the Schedule, the Secretary of State is empowered to appoint such person(s) as he sees fit to discharge any functions exercisable by him by virtue of section 1(1) of the 1972 Act, with the sole exception of the power to make regulations with respect to the preservation of peace and the maintenance of order under the authority of the Civil Authorities (Special Powers) Act, Northern Ireland 1922. As originally enacted the Act was renewable every year. In 1933 it was made a permanent part of the continuing legislation in force in Northern Ireland. For a review of the exceptional powers exercisable under the Special Powers legislation before the introduction of direct rule, see Edwards, "Special Powers in Northern Ireland" [1956] Crim.L.R. 7. The terms of the 1922 Act and the regulations made under it are conveniently set forth in the Cameron Report *post*, fn. 12 at pp. 104–107. For the Commissioners' views on the "Special Powers Act" see *op. cit.* pp. 12–13.

[7] Sched., cl. 3 (1) and (2). These provisions were re-enacted in the Northern Ireland Constitution Act 1973, c.36, s.10, a measure designed to give effect to the constitutional proposals embodied in the Government's White Paper, Cmnd. 5259 (1973), one of many abortive attempts during the intervening years to find a solution to the government of that province that would prove acceptable to all shades of political opinion—see, too, *ante*, fn. 4.

individual inclinations and changing pressures. In this respect the statutory arrangements for conducting the business of the Northern Ireland Attorney General follow the enabling provisions contained in the Law Officers Act 1944 which provide for continuity in the functional aspects of the Attorney General's office if the incumbent becomes incapacitated or leaves the country on other business.[8]

Whatever administrative problems were to be encountered following the transfer of authority from the Attorney General for Northern Ireland to the Attorney General for England and Wales, the legislative instrument for effectuating the integration was simple and straightforward. The same could not be said for the first piece of legislation that was introduced in Westminster following the assumption of direct rule by the United Kingdom Parliament. That legislative measure, an Order in Council promulgated on the same day that direct rule took effect,[9] was concerned with the machinery of criminal prosecutions in Northern Ireland and, in particular, the establishment of the new office of Director of Public Prosecutions with responsibility for practically all indictable and summary offences committed in any part of the province.[10] A Bill to achieve these same purposes had nearly concluded all its legislative stages in the Northern Ireland Parliament when the British Government made its decision to assume direct responsibility for administering the six counties. That Bill had emerged from a background of dissatisfaction with the prevailing system in which the conduct of prosecutions in the lower courts had been regularly discharged by officers of the Royal Ulster Constabulary.

Process of Change Instigated by the Civil Disturbances of the 1960s and 1970s

As noted earlier in this work,[11] the blurring of the lines of responsibility between the investigation of crime and the conduct of ensuing prosecutions, where both functions are discharged by police officers, is a problem that extends beyond the boundaries of Northern Ireland. The fact remained that, however unsubstantiated the grounds upon which these beliefs were fostered, large numbers of the Northern Ireland population of one-and-a-half million (of these about two-thirds may be described as Protestants and one-third as Roman Catholics) perceived a dominant bias against their interests on the part of those associated with the administration of the criminal law. If the system was to recover public confidence reforms were inevitable. It is to this process of change in the 1960s and early 1970s that we must advert as the best means of gaining an

---

[8] See Edwards, *Law Officers of the Crown*, pp. 120, 155, 230–231.
[9] Prosecution of Offences (N.I.) Order 1972, S.I. 1972 No. 538 (N.I. 1).
[10] Art. 5(1).
[11] *Ante*, Chapter 4.

understanding of the law and practice that presently govern the relationship between the Director of Public Prosecutions for Northern Ireland and the members of the Royal Ulster Constabulary, and, no less importantly, between the Director and his political superior, the Attorney General for England and Wales in his capacity as the Attorney General for Northern Ireland.

Large scale demonstrations, leading to violent confrontrations with the police in the streets of Dungannon, Londonderry, Belfast and Armagh between June 1968 and May 1969, were the harbingers of worse things to come. The police handling of some of these events came in for strong criticism by the Cameron Commission which was appointed in March 1969 to inquire into the immediate causes of the civil disturbances in Northern Ireland and to assess the composition, conduct and aims of those bodies involved in the current agitation. According to the Commission's report,[12] referring to the largest of these demonstrations in Londonderry on October 5, 1968, there was unnecessary and ill-controlled force used by members of the Royal Ulster Constabulary and the Ulster Special Constabulary in the dispersal of the demonstrators.[13] Mention was also made of a "breakdown of discipline" by the police in the handling of later disturbances in the same city.[14] The wide publicity given by the press, radio and television to particular episodes inflamed and exacerbated feelings of resentment against the police which had earlier been aroused by their enforcement of an ill advised ministerial ban on the holding of the civil rights demonstrations. The subsequent failure of the police to provide adequate protection to marchers, and police violence towards persons in no way associated with the rioting in Londonderry, provoked serious hostility towards the police among the Catholic population in that city, and an increasing disbelief in their impartiality towards the non-Unionists.[15]

These violent events were symptomatic of a much deeper malaise in the body politic of Northern Ireland, as the Cameron Commission noted in its frank appraisal of the underlying causes of the 1968–69 civil disturbances. "It is plain from what we have heard, read and observed," the Commission concluded, "that the train of events and incidents which began in Londonderry on October 5, 1968 has had as its background, on the one hand, a widespread sense of political and social grievance for long unadmitted and therefore unredressed by successive Governments of Northern Ireland and, on the other, sentiments of fear and apprehension, sincerely and tenaciously felt and believed, of risks to the integrity and

---

[12] *Disturbances in Northern Ireland*, Cmd. 532 (1969), (Belfast, H.M.S.O.).

[13] *Ibid.* p. 31.

[14] *Ibid.* p. 71. In making these criticisms, the Cameron Commission recognised that the task of the police throughout all the demonstrations was an extremely difficult one. "We think it right to record" its *Report* added "that the police were stretched to the utmost limit both in numbers and endurance in endeavouring to carry out their very difficult task. In the majority of cases we find that the police acted with commendable discipline and restraint under very great strain and provocation from many quarters."

[15] *Ibid.* Chapter 4, pp. 24–31.

indeed continued existence of the state."[16] In such an atmosphere of latent, simmering hostility it is not surprising that incidents comparatively small in themselves could readily lead to explosions of violence of a dangerous and serious character.

THE HUNT AND MACDERMOTT REPORTS—HARBINGERS OF MAJOR REFORMS

The calling in of the military, at a later stage when conditions had deteriorated to a point that was beyond the ability of the civil police to contain, served only to further inflame the deep-rooted schism that divides the Protestant-Unionist and Roman Catholic-Nationalist segments of the population. It must also be remembered that, since the setting up of the Government of Northern Ireland under the Government of Ireland Act 1920, the Unionist political party has been continuously in power and, as the Cameron Commission noted, "the possibility of any organised opposition becoming the alternative government has not so far been one which was in any sense a reality."[17] Most of the early demonstrations were organised under the auspices of the Northern Ireland Civil Rights Association, a body ostensibly committed to rectifying civil rights issues in the province. Events were to demonstrate that, in actuality, the Association's activities tended to polarise the Northern Ireland community in traditional directions.[18] The political situation was deteriorating so rapidly that even before the Cameron Commission had tabled its report the Government was prompted, in August 1969, to announce the urgent appointment of a small advisory committee to examine the organisation, training and functions of the Royal Ulster Constabulary and its affiliate institution, the Ulster Special Constabulary. The Advisory Committee's report was submitted to the Minister of Home Affairs within one month of its appointment, a remarkable achievement by normal standards.[19] This expeditious dispatch of its business owed much to the wealth of experience represented in the small task force which consisted of Lord Hunt as the chairman, Mr. (now Sir) Robert Mark, later to become the Commissioner of the Metropolitan London Police, and Sir James Robertson, the Chief

---

[16] *Ibid.* p. 11. For a fuller assessment by the Cameron Commission as to the causative effect of such grievances on the ensuing violence and civil disturbances, see its *Report*, Chapter 12, pp. 55–67. As a sample of the Commission's findings, it concluded that in certain areas, notably those in which disorders had occurred, the arrangements of ward boundaries for local government had produced in the local authority a permanent Unionist (and therefore Protestant) majority which bore little or no resemblance to the relative numerical strength of Unionists and non-Unionists in the area. "There is very good reason to believe" the Commission said "that these arrangements were deliberately made, and maintained, with the consequence that the Unionists used and have continued to use the electoral majority thus created to favour Protestant or Unionist supporters in making public appointments—particularly those of senior officials—and in manipulating housing allocations for political and sectarian ends." *Ibid.* pp. 13–14.

[17] *Ibid.* p. 12, para. 7.

[18] *Ibid.* pp. 77–79.

[19] *Report of the Advisory Committee on Police in Northern Ireland*, Cmnd. 535 (1969), (Belfast, H.M.S.O.).

Constable of Glasgow. In its unanimous report the group stated its conviction that "nothing less than the full implementation of their proposals, within the shortest time possible, could suffice to restore public confidence and to lay a sound foundation for the good order and security of the Province."[20]

The recommended changes were equally swift in their execution, notwithstanding the fundamental nature of some of the Advisory Committee's proposals. Our concern must be restricted to selected areas of the changes introduced in the wake of the Hunt Report, but it remains important to bear in mind something of the police force's historical antecedents. Its roots derive from those of the Royal Irish Constabulary and the events in 1836 when the decision was made to unite all the constabulary forces then existing in Ireland and place them under a single police authority.[21] The same policy was adopted following Ulster's separation in 1920 from the rest of Ireland.[22] Like its predecessor, the Royal Ulster Constabulary has always been expected to fulfil a military as well as a civilian role, and this responsibility was reflected in the force's training, uniform and equipment. Among the Hunt Report's foremost recommendations was that the Royal Ulster Constabulary be relieved of all duties of a military nature and that its contribution to the security of the State from subversion be limited to the gathering of intelligence, the protection of important persons and the enforcement of the relevant laws.[23] Other proposals directed towards establishing police accountability to a representative body and thence to the responsible minister, and changes in recruitment, training and complaint procedures, were clearly designed to transform the province's police force into an organisation similar in character to that of the police forces in England and Wales.[24]

[20] *Ibid.* p. 3.

[21] *Ibid.* p. 13.

[22] To facilitate the transition, the legislation that established the Royal Ulster Constabulary as Northern Ireland's police force provided that existing enactments relating to the Royal Irish Constabulary, as modified, would be equally applicable to the Royal Ulster Constabulary—see Constabulary Act (N.I.) 1922, s.1(3). It is also of interest to note that the departmental committee which was set up following the separation in 1920 recommended that one-third of the new police force should be recruited from the Roman Catholic faith, a goal that has never been attained—*Hunt Report*, pp. 13, 29. Present figures indicate that no more than 11 per cent. of the force are Roman Catholic.

[23] *Ibid.* p. 21.

[24] The statutory relationship between the Royal Ulster Constabulary and the Government of Northern Ireland is described in the *Cameron Report*, pp. 102–104. In the opinion of the Hunt Committee that relationship was "vague and unsatisfactory." The Police Authority, recommended by the committee, would consist of representatives of local authorities, the universities, the legal profession, management and labour, and the Ministry of Home Affairs. The responsible minister, it was also recommended, should be empowered to (a) require the chief officer of police to submit an annual report on the policing of the Province to both the Police Authority and the Minister; (b) require the chief officer of police to submit to the Minister a report on any matter connected with the policing of the area; and (c) call upon the Police Authority to exercise its power of retiring senior officers in the interest of efficiency. The influence of the reforms instituted in England and Wales by the Police Act 1964 are evident throughout the above proposals—see Cmnd. 535, pp. 21–23. For the full list of the Hunt Committee's recommendations see *ibid.* pp. 44–46.

This led the Hunt Committee to a very short excursus on the subject of the use of police officers as prosecutors, a digression that was to produce remarkable results for such a cursory examination of the problem. After the briefest of statements describing the prevailing practice in Northern Ireland in which prosecutions in the lower courts were undertaken by police officers and the same police force decided, sometimes after taking legal advice, when and which prosecutions should be undertaken, the Hunt Report recommended that this deeply entrenched system be discontinued.[25] Otherwise, it was stated, the impartiality of the police would continue to be questioned and there would also exist a mistaken impression of the relationship between the courts and the police. In its place, in what appears to have been an uncritical acceptance by the English members of the superior features of the Scottish system of independent public prosecutors, explained and advocated by their colleague, the Chief Constable of Glasgow, the Hunt Advisory Committee recommended the adoption of the Scottish system in Northern Ireland.[26] "Under this system," the committee's Report explained, "the police are responsible only for the collection of information about offences, all subsequent action with regard to prosecution being undertaken by a solicitor in the public service. In Northern Ireland this might be the Chief Crown Solicitor, but further study than we have been able to give would be needed before the procedure could be precisely settled. Although the principal reason for proposing this change is the improvement in relations with the public, there would be a substantial secondary benefit in that a great deal of the time of District Inspectors and Head Constables is now taken up with court work, and this time could profitably be devoted to the leadership and administration of the police in their districts and to the development of good relations with the community."[27]

Having regard to the time pressures under which the committee was required to work it would be churlish to criticise the inadequacy of the Report's treatment of such a major issue. Understandably perhaps in the circumstances, the members chose to rely upon their experience and instincts and to avoid any examination of their proposal's implications for other aspects of the prosecution machinery in the province, especially the handling of indictable offences which are not triable summarily. Suitable words of caution, it will be noted, were inserted in the Hunt Report counselling further study before any new procedures could be precisely

[25] *Op. cit.* p. 34. A single paragraph (para. 142) is all that was devoted to this controversial topic. Speaking a few years later in the House of Lords, in the course of the debate on the Prosecution of Offences (N.I.) Order 1972, Lord Hunt admitted that he and his colleagues "were concerned more with effect than method and we had no time, as we made clear in the Report, to go into method. . . . Although I am not now, and certainly I was not then, an expert in these matters, Mr. Mark and I fell in very readily with Sir James's advocacy of the Scottish system, for the simple reason that it removed completely from the police any responsibility for prosecutions of any kind." H.L. Deb., Vol. 330, col. 627, May 1, 1972.

[26] *Ibid.*

[27] *Ibid.*

settled. This admonition was enough to prompt the Government of Northern Ireland to appoint a fresh Working Party in February, 1970, under the chairmanship of Mr. J.C. MacDermott, Q.C. (now Mr. Justice MacDermott of the High Court of Justice) to undertake an examination of the specific recommendation of the Hunt Committee that the Scottish system of independent public prosecutors should be adopted in respect to the initiation and presentation of summary prosecutions in Northern Ireland.[28]

At an early stage in its deliberations the MacDermott group decided to go beyond the prescribed terms of reference and later defended its actions by explaining that it was quite impossible to examine any one aspect of the criminal legal process in isolation.[29] Furthermore, it concluded that it would be quite impractical to graft the Scottish machinery on to the Northern Ireland system of criminal procedure and administration, noting in passing that nowhere in England or Wales has an effort been made to adopt the Scottish model of full-time public prosecutors.[30] One might be forgiven for observing that the rejection of the Scottish model by the MacDermott Working Party had much the same cavalier approach as that which prompted the earlier Advisory Committee to recommend its adoption. In fairness, it must be acknowledged that the MacDermott Committee had examined some of the existing literature which describes the functions and inter-relationships between the police, the procurators-fiscal, the advocates depute and the Lord Advocate in Scottish criminal law.[31] Whilst the absence of any attempt to elaborate the reasons for taking the respective positions is very evident, both advisory committees were of one mind in stressing their wholehearted support for the principle that prosecutions should be conducted by public prosecutors who are independent—in the sense of being untainted by any form of political influence and separated from the investigatory aspects of individual cases which are a police responsibility.[32] How to achieve these mutual goals became the major thrust of the MacDermott Working Party, which quickly subscribed to the basic premise that the police in Northern Ireland should be relieved of the burden of prosecuting in any but minor cases of a trifling nature.[33] At the same time, the representative group went out of its way to reject outright any imputations of former police unfairness or inefficiency that might be derived from its recommendation that the police and prosecution functions be separated. "It is our unanimous opinion," the

---

[28] See *Report of Working Party on Public Prosecutions*, Cmnd. 554 (1971), (Belfast, H.M.S.O.).

[29] *Ibid.* p. 10.

[30] *Ibid.* p. 4.

[31] See Appendix C to the report, which includes the following articles: Gerald H. Gordon, "Institution of Criminal Proceedings in Scotland" (1968) 19 N.I.L.Q. 249–276; Lord Normand, "The Public Prosecutor in Scotland" (1938) 54 L.Q.R. 345–357.

[32] *MacDermott Report*, pp. 4, 5.

[33] *Ibid.* p. 5. Indications of what the working party regarded as "serious" and "minor" cases are provided in its report at p. 6.

MacDermott Committee declared, "formed from a wide variety of personal experiences, that the Royal Ulster Constabulary have discharged this burden, which they have borne for so long, with absolute integrity and a degree of competence which has always been remarkably high."[34] This testimonial was further corroborated in the annual report of the Incorporated Law Society for Northern Ireland for 1969.[35]

Having satisfied themselves that a sufficient pool of lawyers was likely to be available and attracted by the prospect of serving as full time public prosecutors, the working party then turned its attention to the choice between grafting the proposed new organisation on to the existing system of Crown Solicitors or creating an entirely new body of public prosecutors headed by an official similar to the Director of Public Prosecutions in England. Just as in 1922 the Royal Ulster Constabulary emerged as the lineal descendant of the Royal Irish Constabulary, with the same organisational features as its forbears, so too the office of Crown Solicitor in Northern Ireland owes its origins to the indigenous machinery established in Ireland during the nineteenth century whereby Crown Solicitors and Crown Counsel were appointed in each county and made responsible to the Attorney General for Ireland for the conduct of all Crown business in the courts.[36] It has been noted elsewhere[37] that the basic model emulated in Ireland is that enjoyed for centuries by Scotland which entrusts the enforcement of the criminal law to its system of procurators fiscal and advocates depute acting under the general superintendence of the Lord Advocate. With the separation of Ireland in 1920 the northern counties simply continued the practice that previously embraced the entire country. Certain features deserve special mention. As already stated, the Attorney General for Northern Ireland is, and always has been, the sole Law Officer of the Crown.[38] Directly responsible to him and subject to his

[34] *Ibid.* p. 3.

[35] *Ibid.* Appendix A(1), p. 16.

[36] See Edwards, *Law Officers of the Crown*, p. 336 *et seq.* and J. P. Casey, *The Office of the Attorney General in Ireland*, pp. 23–24, 114.

[37] Edwards, "The Administration of Criminal Justice in Northern Ireland" [1956] Crim. L.R. 466 at 469–471.

[38] As with his English counterparts, an issue that repeatedly arises is the extent to which the Attorney General should appear in court as the chief counsel for the Crown—see Edwards, *op. cit.* pp. 306–308. In the background paper prepared for the MacDermott Working Party on Public Prosecutions it was stated: "The Attorney General . . . by tradition, only appears in person to lead for the Crown in murder cases; indeed since 1966 possibly only in capital murder cases [see Criminal Justice Act (N.I.) 1966, s.10]. This tradition was broken in the case of *R.* v. *Morgan* [Belfast City Commission, September 1966] who was charged with, and found guilty of, treason. Morgan had thrown a concrete block from the sixth floor of a building at a car in which H.M. the Queen . . . was travelling . . . . In these rather unusual circumstances the Attorney General led for the Crown"—Cmnd. 554, pp. 14–15. In 1970 Opposition speakers in the Northern Ireland Parliament criticised the Attorney General for his notable absence from all the controversial political cases that made their way through the courts in that troublesome period. Speaking in reply, Mr. Basil Kelly Q.C., the then Attorney General, explained that "the question of my prosecuting personally is a matter entirely for my discretion, and I follow precedent . . . my predecessors have set the pattern which I think is a wise one, that an Attorney General should prosecute only in cases which involve constitutional issues or cases of murder . . . ." From time to time Attorneys General appear

directions was the Chief Crown Solicitor for the whole of Northern Ireland, a permanent official, who also fulfilled the duties associated with the Treasury Solicitor in England and the Crown Agent in Scotland. In each of the province's six counties a part-time Crown Solicitor conducted the Crown's business in the criminal courts assisted by two Crown Counsel who received briefs to represent the Attorney General in the higher courts. The only other permanent position in the former system of criminal prosecutions was that of the Assistant Chief Crown Solicitor who combined with the duties of his title the role of Crown Solicitor for the City of Belfast.[39]

As part time appointments the county Crown Solicitors were free, subject to certain limitations, to engage in private practice, an aspect of the office that did not diminish the belief in some sections of the community that Crown Solicitors were part and parcel of the political machinery of government. The MacDermott Working Party, whilst expressing their own satisfaction that the duties of the office had been carried out fairly and impartially were forced to recognise the implications of a contrary perception that, whether justified or not, was deep-seated and widely held by the minority element of the population.[40] This belief, coupled with the part-time nature of the appointment outside of Belfast, persuaded the working party to take a strong stand against any attempt to graft the new body of public prosecutors on to the historic network of Crown Solicitors in the province.[41] Those among the existing appointees who wished to become full-time public prosecutors would be free to seek an appointment based on merit. To this end the committee urged that the new appointments not be made at a political level by the Minister for Home Affairs but by a body such as the Civil Service Commission.[42] Barristers and solicitors would be equally eligible to be appointed and, in order to emphasise the independent character of the new office, it was recommended that the prosecutors be referred to as Public Prosecutors, all forming part of a new Department of Public Prosecutions.[43]

This body would be responsible for the conduct of criminal proceedings in all courts and headed by a Director of Public Prosecutions. Unlike his English counterpart it was envisaged that the Director would be responsible for the day-to-day work of prosecution in all the criminal

---

in the House of Lords and sometimes in the Court of Criminal Appeal when important points of criminal law are canvassed—H.C. Deb. (N.I.) Vol. 75, col. 601, February 25, 1970. For an account of the approach to this question by Irish Attorneys General prior to the attainment of self rule in 1920 see J. P. Casey, *op. cit.*, p. 25.

[39] A full account of the former system in Northern Ireland, prior to the creation of the office of D.P.P., is contained in the paper "The Machinery of Prosecutions in Northern Ireland" prepared for the MacDermott Working Party by D. A. Haggan, the Asst. Chief Crown Solicitor—*op. cit.* App. A(1) pp. 13–16.

[40] *Ibid.* p. 8.

[41] *Ibid.* pp. 8–9.

[42] *Ibid.* p. 11.

[43] *Ibid.* p. 9.

courts throughout the province.[44] His authority and involvement through his deputies, the Public Prosecutors, would be all pervasive. To underline the dominant role of the Public Prosecutor the working party distinguished between the police powers of arrest and the formulation of charges which would remain unchanged, and the decision whether or not to institute a prosecution coupled with the handling of the ensuing proceedings which would be the exclusive responsibility of the independent Department of Public Prosecutions.[45] Only in the most minor offences, and then for administrative reasons of expedition and an avoidance of paperwork, would the initiation of criminal proceedings remain with the police.[46]

Pre-Direct Rule Initiatives in Establishing a New Department of Public Prosecutions

These are the essential rudiments of the system that is now in place in Northern Ireland. That it should have come into being with unusual rapidity owes much to the forceful language used by both the Hunt Committee in 1969 and the MacDermott Working Party in December 1970, the latter saying, "We would repeat as emphatically as is possible that we feel that the immediate establishment of a Department of Public Prosecutions is of the utmost importance. Fitting this Department into the present legal framework will however necessitate a review of existing establishments, offices and responsibilities. We feel that such a review should be undertaken as soon as possible but should not be allowed to delay the establishment of a Department of Public Prosecutions."[47] The note of extreme urgency struck by the two advisory bodies was heard and repeated by all the political parties represented in Stormont, the Parliament of Northern Ireland. In January 1972, prior to the imposition of direct rule, the Prosecution of Offences Bill (Northern Ireland) was introduced by the Prime Minister, Mr. Brian Faulkner.[48]

In supporting the Bill in the Northern Ireland House of Commons, the Attorney General described the measure as marking the end of an era.[49] Its provisions were intended to give effect to the recommendations of the MacDermott Working Party. The main outlines of these proposals have already been discussed but there were refinements in the Bill that deserve special attention. As we have seen, the MacDermott Committee had very little to say on the relationship that should exist between the proposed new

---

[44] *Ibid.* pp. 9–10.
[45] *Ibid.* p. 10.
[46] *Ibid.*
[47] *Ibid.*
[48] H.C. Deb., (N.I.) Vol. 83, cols. 1598–1603, January 13, 1972.
[49] *Ibid.* col. 1613. Drawing on his experience over 20 years as an advocate in the criminal courts, the Attorney General rejected any imputation that the reason for withdrawing from the Royal Ulster Constabulary their former powers of initiating and conducting prosecutions was their partiality or inefficiency. Its record in this field, he said, was untarnished. The Attorney added: "I have never known them to be unfair or sharp, to take any shortcuts or do anything improper in their handling of prosecutions"—*loc. cit.*

office of Director of Public Prosecutions and the Attorney General for Northern Ireland. The first draft of the Bill required the Director to perform his statutory duties "under the directions of the Attorney General."[50] As presented to the House of Commons in its revised form, however, clause 2(2) provided that "the Director shall be responsible to the Attorney General for the due performance of the functions of the Director under this Act."[51] To further underline the independent status of the Director the office was to be held "during good behaviour," the same condition of appointment as that pertaining to Her Majesty's judges. The assimilation stopped short, however, of following the model for the removal of a superior court judge and, instead, made the removal of the Director subject to the decision by the Governor "upon the advice of the Privy Council for Northern Ireland."[52] Much debate was centred upon this procedural clause, an assurance being given on the third reading of the Bill by the Attorney General that "if and when the Government's advice is sought on this matter our advice will always be to summon a Council in which judges and ex-judges will be in the majority. I make the assurance categorically here and now so that it can be recorded in Hansard for the benefit of posterity."[53]

The Attorney General emphasised that both with respect to summary prosecutions and prosecutions in indictable cases the new Bill was designed to afford the Department of Public Prosecutions virtual independence in the assessment of whether proceedings should or should not be brought.[54] The only exception would be those cases in which, by statute, the consent of the Attorney General was a prerequisite. Even in those circumstances, by virtue of clause 4(2), a consent provision would be deemed to have been complied with if the consent to the initiation or the carrying on of its proceedings was given by the Director of Public Prosecutions, unless the Attorney General directed otherwise.[55]

The proclaimed goal of the proposed legislation was to confer the maximum degree of independence on the corps of public prosecutors headed by its Director. As the Attorney General for Northern Ireland further explained: "If the Director of Public Prosecutions fails to prosecute in any case and on reading the papers the Attorney General decides otherwise then the Attorney General brings his own prosecution. But it will be evident that this is the situation: that the prosecution has been brought by the Attorney General and not by the Director of Public Prosecutions. Conversely, if the Director of Public Prosecutions decides to prosecute and the Attorney General feels that he is wrong and that no prosecution should be brought, then the Attorney General may, and has

---

[50] Draft No. 1, dated June 8, 1971, cl. 2.
[51] Bill no. 26, as amended in Committee, dated March 14, 1972.
[52] *Ibid.* cl. 1(2).
[53] H.C. Deb., (N.I.) Vol. 84, cols. 312–313, February 10, 1972.
[54] H.C. Deb., (N.I.) Vol. 83, cols. 1614–1616, January 13, 1972.
[55] *Ante*, fn. 51.

the right to, enter a *nolle prosequi* and stop that prosecution. But this, again, will be seen to be done. In all such situations the Attorney General will be answerable to Parliament for his actions in either starting a prosecution which the Director of Public Prosecutions refused to start or in terminating a prosecution which the Director of Public Prosecutions initiated. No doubt there will be cases of importance or difficulty in which the Director of Public Prosecutions or his deputy will want to consult with the Attorney General before deciding to prosecute or not, and no doubt the Attorney General will want to see, as a matter of duty, the papers in an important and serious case, but save in those cases where the consent of the Attorney General is required by statute, at the end of the day the decision to prosecute will be that of the Director of Public Prosecutions and his Department."[56]

As will have been observed, the doctrine of ministerial responsibility was rightly given a prominent place in the above account of the Bill's interlocking provisions and especially in defining the exact nature of the independent status envisaged for the new office of Director of Public Prosecutions. It must be remembered that such a step represented a dramatic reformulation of prosecutorial responsibilities in Northern Ireland which, by reason of its small geographical size, enabled the policy of centralisation to be effectively institutionalised. Much play was made of the statutory language used to define the subordinate position occupied by the Director of Public Prosecutions in England and Wales, as contrasted with his proposed counterpart in Northern Ireland. In the former jurisdiction, it will be recalled, the relevant legislation provided that "the Director of Public Prosecutions shall in all matters be subject to the directions of the Attorney General."[57] "No equivalent to this," the Northern Ireland Attorney General claimed, "appears in this Bill and it is not the intention of this Bill to create such a dominance."[58] No mention was made of the standard enshrined in the very first draft of the Government's Prosecution of Offences Bill which appears to have based itself on the prevailing English principles of responsibility and powers of direction.[59]

The revised Bill, that was to run its parliamentary course and stop just short of receiving the Royal Assent before direct rule was introduced by Westminster, spoke instead of the Director of Public Prosecutions being "responsible to the Attorney General for the due performance of his functions under this Act."[60] The ultimate accountability of the Attorney General to Parliament was subscribed to in eloquent terms. That accountability, it was declared, "has been an important constitutional and democratic doctrine in the United Kingdom for a very long time. The

[56] H.C. Deb., (N.I.) Vol. 83, cols. 1615 and 1616, January 13, 1972.
[57] Prosecution of Offences Regulations, 1946 (S.R. & O. 1946 No. 1467, L.17) reg. 5, and see discussion *ante*, pp. 9–11.
[58] H.C. Deb., (N.I.) Vol. 83, col. 1616, January 13, 1972.
[59] *Ante*, fn. 50.
[60] *Ante*, fn. 51, cl. 2(2).

setting up of a Department of Public Prosecutions should not disturb that doctrine, for one cannot give wide powers of prosecution to a Director of Public Prosecutions and leave him answerable to no one, and if the Attorney General is answerable to Parliament not only in respect of his own prosecutions but also for the Department of the Director of Public Prosecutions it must surely follow that the Director must be responsible to the Attorney General for the proper performance of his functions. This is just another aspect of ministerial responsibility."[61]

The Westminster Order Governing the Director of Public Prosecutions for Northern Ireland

This particular piece of unfinished business, hammered out in the Northern Ireland Parliament in conditions of extreme political and social upheaval, was to be transported across the Irish Sea and become the first measure to be enacted by the United Kingdom Government under the emergency powers conferred by section 1(3) of the Northern Ireland (Temporary Provisions) Act 1972. Entitled the Prosecution of Offences (Northern Ireland) Order 1972,[62] the statutory Order in Council received quick affirmation by both Houses of Parliament. Apart from additional provisions contained in the Northern Ireland Constitution Act 1973, extending indefinitely the arrangements made in the emergency Order the previous year,[63] it is to the terms of the 1972 Order that we must turn to comprehend the nature of the prosecution system that is now operating in Northern Ireland. Foremost among the significant changes which were introduced, in substitution for those contained in the Northern Ireland Parliament's own Bill, is that defining the relationship of the Director of Public Prosecutions to his political superior, the Attorney General. According to the Prosecution of Offences Bill (N.I.) the Director was to be responsible to the Attorney "for the due performance of his functions under the Act." In its place the emergency Order states that the Director "shall discharge his functions under the superintendence of the Attorney General and shall be subject to the directions of the Attorney General in all matters including the filing or withholding of any such consent as is mentioned in Article 7 of (the 1972) Order."[64] The revised formulation, it

---

[61] *Ante*, fn. 54, col. 1617.

[62] S.I. 1972 No. 538 (N.I. 1).

[63] c.36, ss.39–42. Other provisions, *e.g.* abolish the Northern Ireland Parliament (s.31) and also the office of Governor (s.32).

[64] Art. 3(2). Consent provisions, as referred to in Art. 7 of the 1972 Order, embrace those situations in which the consent of the Attorney General of N.I. is required (whether by itself or a an alternative to the consent of any other authority or person) to the initiation or carrying on of criminal proceedings but excluding offences under the Official Secrets Act 1911 (c.28), s.8, and the Official Secrets Act 1920 (c.75), s.8(2). Originally, offences under the Civil Authorities (Special Powers) Act (N.I.), 1922 (c.5(N.I.)) were also excluded but this provision was repealed by the Northern Ireland (Emergency Provisions) Act 1973, s.31 and Sched. 5. The exclusions are important having regard to Art. 7(2) which states that "unless the Attorney General otherwise directs a consent provision passed before the coming into operation of this Order shall be deemed to be complied with . . . if the consent to the

will be noted, is closely akin to that which describes the status of the Director of Public Prosecutions for England and Wales.[65]

Nevertheless, according to Sir Peter Rawlinson, the Attorney General, speaking during the debate on the emergency Order in the Westminster House of Commons: "Although the Director for Northern Ireland bears the same title as the Director for England and Wales, his duties and responsibilities are different, for, as befits an office covering an area much smaller in jurisdiction than England and Wales, his control over and supervision of prosecutions will be closer and more comprehensive than the Director of Public Prosecutions for England and Wales. But he will enjoy a degree of statutory independence in the exercise of his functions in excess of that enjoyed by the Director here."[66] In view of the language chosen to define the status of the Northern Ireland Director of Public Prosecutions it is difficult to see what basis exists for the opinion expressed by Sir Peter Rawlinson that the Director in Belfast will enjoy a degree of statutory independence in excess of that associated with the office of Director of Public Prosecutions in London. The significant criterion used in this comparison is the degree of independence conferred by statute and in this respect there is no difference between the two offices.

The true answer is to be found in the further elaboration by the Attorney General of the principal difference between the 1972 Northern Ireland Bill and the subsequent Order enacted in Westminster. This, he explained, is to be found in Article 3 of the Order which ordains that "during the currency of the Temporary Provisions Act, the Director in Northern Ireland shall discharge his functions under my superintendence and shall be subject to my directions in all matters. This arises from my new role as Attorney General for Northern Ireland and my answerability to this House in Westminster. I shall have superintendence, as I have in England and Wales, but the day-to-day conduct will be that of the Director."[67] To reinforce, as it were, the supreme authority of the Attorney General, section 34(2) of the Northern Ireland Constitution Act 1973,[68] confers

initiation or carrying on of those proceedings is given by the Director." This transfer of consent power to the Northern Ireland Director of Public Prosecutions was particularly important in cases brought under the Explosives Substances Act 1883 (46 & 47 Vict. c.3) and which previously required the Attorney's consent under s.7(1). Note, however, the possibly unforeseen consequences of paras. 67 and 68 of Sched. 1 to the Criminal Justice (N.I.) Order 1980 (S.I. 1980 No. 704 (N.I. 6)), whereby the consent of the Attorney General for Northern Ireland is once again required for continuing proceedings under the 1883 Act. This view was confirmed by the Northern Ireland Court of Appeal in *R.* v. *Marron et al.* [1981] N.I. 132.

[65] *Ante*, pp. 9–11.

[66] H.C. Deb., Vol. 836, cols. 1057–1058, May 9, 1972.

[67] *Ibid.* col. 1059. An informal understanding was reached in 1972, on the institution of direct rule, that the "old procedure pre-1972" would continue in effect. This means that the D.P.P. for Northern Ireland is authorised to enter a *nolle prosequi* on behalf of the Attorney General—oral communication to the author by Sir Barry Shaw, the Northern Ireland D.P.P.

[68] c.36. *Cf.* this provision with that incorporated in the 1972 Order, Art. 4(1) and (2) which, repeating the terms of the Bill which had passed through the N.I. Parliament shortly before direct rule was imposed, vested the power of appointment of the Director and Deputy Director in the Governor, and the power of removal in the Governor upon the advice of the Privy Council for Northern Ireland—see *ante*, p. 247.

upon the Attorney General the power of appointing the Director and his deputy, and, more importantly, authority to remove either of the officials on the grounds of inability or misbehaviour.

To confine this discussion to the unemotional language contained in the various legislative enactments is to run the danger of over reliance on the legal provisions in interpreting the extent of the Attorney General's involvement in the decision making process that daily calls for resolution by the Northern Ireland Director and his staff of public prosecutors. Due regard must be had to the confidence reposed in the Director, the initial choice having fallen on the shoulders of Mr. (now Sir) Barry Shaw Q.C., an experienced and senior member of the Bar of Northern Ireland. Mr. Shaw won the confidence of all sections of the population when acting as the leading counsel to the 1972 Tribunal of Inquiry into the Civil Disturbances in Northern Ireland, which was presided over by Mr. Justice Scarman (as he then was).[69] His appointment as the first Director of Public Prosecutions of Northern Ireland was widely welcomed in every quarter of the province, auguring well for the future.[70] The same degree of confidence was accorded to Mr. Bernard McCloskey, the first Deputy Director and a solicitor of wide experience who also served with impartial distinction as part of the Scarman Tribunal. Allowing for the speed of modern communication it remains necessary to take account of the geographical circumstances that surround Northern Ireland. Physical distance between London and Belfast reinforces the dependence of the Attorney General on the effective discharge by the Director and the Department of Public Prosecutions of their statutory functions. These remain as enumerated in the aborted Bill of 1972 and generally encompass responsibility, on behalf of the Crown, for initiating and undertaking proceedings in all indictable offences and such summary offences as the Director considers necessary.[71] The right of a private citizen to institute a criminal prosecution in his own name is preserved but, as in English law, this right is subject to the authority of the Director to undertake at any stage the conduct of those proceedings if he thinks fit.[72]

The consent of the Attorney General for prosecutions under the Official Secrets Acts will continue to be exercised in person by the holder of that

---

[69] See *Report of the Tribunal of Inquiry into Violence and Civil Disturbances in Northern Ireland in 1969*, Cmd. 566 (1972), (Belfast, H.M.S.O.), Vol. 2, App. VII.

[70] Among the tributes paid to the new Director was that of Reverend Ian Paisley who stated in the House of Commons: "I agree with the Attorney General that Mr. Shaw is a man of great integrity. As he got me five months in Crumlin Road prison, I am better able to say that than anyone in the House"—H.C. Deb., Vol. 836, col. 1080, May 8, 1972. Unless the Attorney General by order directs otherwise the D.P.P. holds office until he reaches the age of 65 years.—Northern Ireland Constitution Act 1973, s. 34(3) and Art. 4(2)(c) of the 1972 Order (S.I. 1972 No. 538) (N.I. 1). Persons eligible for appointment are a barrister or solicitor with appropriate years of experience in either of those capacities.

[71] S.I. 1972 No. 538 (N.I. 1), Art. 5(1)(c) and see Art. 5 generally for a comprehensive statement of the functions exercisable by the D.P.P. for Northern Ireland.

[72] *Ibid*. Art. 5(3).

office.[73] It is noteworthy, however, that with respect to the institution of proceedings for all other statutory offences which are subject to the Attorney General's fiat, unless the Attorney otherwise directs, such consent is exercisable in his name by the Director of Public Prosecutions for Northern Ireland.[74] This provision reflects the degree of delegation of authority that must be taken into account in assessing the measure of independence that surrounds the Director's office. All the essential controls for ensuring the ultimate authority of the Attorney General are enshrined in the legislation. Alongside this fact of constitutional reality, however, is a body of evidence that points unmistakably to a very substantial degree of *de facto* independence. Regular visits to the respective capital cities are a necessary burdensome part of the consultative process between the Director and his ministerial superior. Close liaison between the Law Officers' Department and the Northern Ireland Department of Public Prosecutions is also facilitated by the appointment to the professional staff in London of the former Assistant Chief Crown Solicitor in the province, that office having lapsed as part of the major reorganisation of the machinery of criminal prosecutions recommended by the MacDermott Committee.[75]

The Cobden Trust Report and Assessment of the Director of Public Prosecution's Impartiality

That Committee's proposals to abolish the system of part-time Crown Solicitors and police prosecutors having been implemented, Northern Ireland can now look back on over 10 years of solid experience in administering a centralised prosecutions department. Allegations of partiality in enforcing the criminal law have not disappeared from the public record and cannot be ignored when estimating the effects of creating a new independent office of public prosecutions. What is very noticeable is the effort made to refute such allegations, especially when the criticisms emanate from an apparently objective source, accompanied by statistical data in support of the allegations. In October 1973, a mere 18 months into the life of the new Department of Public Prosecutions, wide publicity was given to a report published by the Cobden Trust, entitled *"Justice in Northern Ireland. A Study in Social Confidence."*[76] It included imputations against the impartiality of the prosecuting authority, allegations that

---

[73] See *ante*, fn. 64.

[74] *Ibid.*

[75] Under Art. 8(1) of the Prosecution of Offences (N.I.) Order, 1972, provision was made for the abolition of the office of Crown Solicitor "for any county or place" and for the automatic transfer of all functions pertaining thereto, in connection with criminal proceedings, to the D.P.P. It should, however, be noted that the Northern Ireland Constitution Act 1973 (c.36), s.35, has created a *new* office of "Crown Solicitor for Northern Ireland" to be appointed by the Attorney General with duties similar to those associated with the Treasury Solicitor in England and Wales, *i.e.* in providing legal representation and advice in civil matters to ministers and departments of government.

[76] References, henceforth, will be to the Cobden Report.

carried additional weight in view of the positions held by the authors of the report, both being senior academics on the faculty of Queen's University, Belfast and the New University of Ulster, Coleraine. As soon as the Hadden-Hilliard report was published, the Attorney General, then Sir Peter Rawlinson, instructed the Director of Public Prosecutions in Belfast to undertake a detailed analysis of those parts of the study that related to his area of responsibility. The results of the Director's empirical analysis were released as a White Paper in February 1974 by the Law Officers' Department in London.[77]

It is impossible to do justice in this work to either the Cobden Report or the detailed refutations contained in the Rawlinson reply. What is important is the unprecedented attempt by the prosecution authorities to place the facts before the public and thereby allow an informed judgment to be reached on matters that, if allowed to pass unchallenged, could have seriously undermined the high expectations for objectivity with which the new system was inaugurated. Only some of the issues canvassed in the two documents can be singled out for attention here. The main theme of the Hadden-Hilliard conclusions was the cumulative measure of sympathy exhibited towards Protestant and Loyalist defendants and, conversely, the apparent discrimination practised against Roman Catholic members of the population, when charged with criminal offences. Partiality, it was alleged, was manifest in the absence of a uniform policy and practice on questions of bail, in the selection of charges, particularly with respect to firearms offences, and in comparisons concerning the withdrawal and reduction of charges.

The conclusions were based on two data sources, an observational study of selected magistrates' courts during the Spring and Summer of 1972, and a review of the Crown books and committal papers in relation to cases heard at the Belfast City Commission in the first half of 1973.[78] Both studies were based on inferences as to the religion of the accused, there being no express reference of this kind in any of the investigation files submitted by the police to the Director of Public Prosecutions or in the documents upon which the accused was committed for trial.[79] Nevertheless, as the Government's White Paper acknowledges, given the geographical distribution of the Northern Ireland population, regionally and locally, in the majority of cases the accused's religious affiliation is capable of deduction.[80] The extent of the margin of error on this question is open to question but cannot seriously affect the broad interpretation of the data.

On the subject of bail there were no reliable records available to determine the validity of the authors' criticisms. This is unfortunate since the existence of a clear statement of prosecutorial policies regarding bail, a

---

[77] *Prosecutions in Northern Ireland—A Study of Facts* (London, H.M.S.O. 1974)—henceforth this document will be referred to as the Rawlinson White Paper.
[78] Cobden Report, pp. 45–46.
[79] Rawlinson White Paper, p. 10.
[80] *Ibid.*

fact demonstrated in the Attorney General's reply, must lack some degree of conviction if the necessary empirical data is missing to demonstrate the even-handed administration of those policies. The scrutiny pursued by the Director's office with respect to the Belfast City Commission's committal papers produced figures that were substantially different from those derived and relied upon in the Cobden Trust study. This discrepancy was especially noticeable in relation to the selection of offences under the Firearms Act.[81] The same observation applies to the treatment of withdrawals by the Director of Public Prosecutions,[82] a vivid example of which derives from the handling of charges under section 14 of the Firearms Act (Northern Ireland) 1969, an offence that carries a greater maximum sentence of imprisonment than any other section of the Act. Of the 21 cases where Protestants were charged with this offence, and in which the charge was withdrawn on the instructions of the Director, what the Hadden-Hilliard study failed to point out was that all the accused were simultaneously charged with other serious crimes. These additional charges included murder (5 cases) and robbery (4 cases). Furthermore, in 20 out of the 21 cases the defendant either pleaded guilty to, or was found guilty by a jury, of the other offences.[83] The unbiased observer is left further confused by the respective conclusions reached with respect to the percentage of overall charges withdrawn by the prosecuting authority, the Cobden study claiming that the data confirms the preference shown towards Protestant defendants and the Attorney General's paper demonstrating the exact converse to be the truth.[84]

Most of the debate centres upon the correct analysis of the cases and the statistical inferences drawn from the accumulated data. A different tone altogether is adopted by the Attorney General in refuting specific allegations that arose out of the "Bloody Sunday" shootings in Londonderry on January 30, 1972. According to the authors of the Cobden Trust study possible prosecutions against members of the security forces had been blocked by a directive from the Attorney General.[85] This serious

---

[81] See Rawlinson, *op. cit.*, pp. 12–22, responding to allegations in the Cobden Report that (1) Roman Catholics have been charged with more serious offences than Protestants for broadly similar behaviour (*ibid.* p. 42) and (2) the prosecuting authorities have been rather more ready to withdraw charges against Protestant defendants than to press doubtful charges against Roman Catholics; it being acknowledged that the judges had gone some way to correct the balance (*ibid.* p. 55).

[82] Rawlinson, *op. cit.* pp. 22–27.

[83] *Ibid.* pp. 26, 28–29.

[84] Thus, the Cobden Report alleged (*ibid.* p. 55) that 31 per cent. of charges against Protestants were withdrawn by the D.P.P. as opposed to 24 per cent. of charges against Roman Catholics. According to Rawlinson, the figures derived from the Director's scrutiny of the same data revealed that the percentages of withdrawals should read 17·5 per cent. for Protestants as against 22 per cent. for Roman Catholics (*op. cit.* p. 28). For fuller details of the individual cases involving withdrawals and verdicts of not guilty being returned by direction of the trial judge, see Rawlinson *op. cit.* pp. 34–42.

[85] Cobden Report, pp. 38–39.

allegation was described as "false" by Sir Peter Rawlinson[86] who stated that the possibility of instituting criminal proceedings had been examined in the greatest detail by the Director of Public Prosecutions who concluded that the evidence was insufficient upon which to direct a prosecution. Having reviewed the same files the Attorney General agreed with the Director's recommendation.[87] In a parliamentary reply dealing with the same turbulent events the Attorney General stated: "I have also decided that it would not be in the public interest to proceed further with charges of riotous behaviour which have been brought against certain civilians in respect of their participation in the events of that day; and accordingly directions will be given that no evidence be offered in support of charges already preferred and that the necessary steps be taken to apply to the court to withdraw such summonses as have been issued."[88] The Attorney General's White Paper also drew attention to the fact that during approximately the same period as that chosen by the Cobden Trust researchers to judge the record of the newly established Department of Public Prosecutions there had been directions to prosecute 70 members of the security forces for assault and 19 in respect of shooting incidents, including six cases of manslaughter and three of attempted murder.[89]

In the absence of access to all the evidence that was available to the court, caution is called for when seeking to draw firm conclusions from the available partial record of the trials under study. The researchers, in all fairness, were sensitive to the less than comprehensive nature of the information at their disposal.[90] Such imperfections could easily be invoked as an excuse for not embarking at all on the kind of external evaluation of Northern Ireland's prosecution system represented by the Cobden Trust's publication. Were that to have happened the larger interests of the population would have been ill-served. With all its methodological weaknesses,[91] and doubts as to the researchers' own impartiality in interpreting the relevant information, the Hadden-Hilliard study has performed a public service in reminding the prosecution authorities in

[86] Rawlinson, *op. cit.* p. 5. The same adjective was used to rebut the assertion made by Dr. Hadden and Mr. Hilliard that "The results of police and army investigations of criminal complaints [against members of the security forces] are sent first to the Northern Ireland Office before being forwarded to the Director of Public Prosecutions"—Cobden Report, p. 38.

[87] Rawlinson, *loc. cit.*

[88] H.C. Deb., Vol. 842, Written Answers, col. 122, August 1, 1972.

[89] Rawlinson, *op. cit.* p. 6. On the further allegations concerning jury selection and resort to stand-by challenges by the Crown as a means of ensuring an all Protestant jury, and the response of the Attorney General to such criticism, see the Cobden Report, p. 58 and Rawlinson *op. cit.* p. 7.

[90] See, *e.g.* the Cobden Report, pp. 62–65.

[91] On questions of guilt or innocence, and of the correctness of particular decisions on bail or on sentence, the authors acknowledge that the decision making process is not amenable to objective or scientific analysis—*ibid.* p. 44. There is no reason to treat decisions involving the exercise of prosecutorial discretion any differently.

Northern Ireland and elsewhere that accountability is an essential part of society's mandate to prosecute on behalf of the Crown.

In normal circumstances the interested citizen has to rely in the main on questions being raised or debates being generated on the floor of the House of Commons. By the very nature of these proceedings Members of Parliament are at a disadvantage in getting to the heart of individual decisions made by the Attorney General or the Director of Public Prosecutions. This is not necessarily to be construed as a stubborn reluctance on the part of the Law Officers to unfold the full background to particular decisions. What is commendable, for example, is the degree of disclosure represented by those sections of the Northern Ireland White Paper that explain the reasons for the Director's withdrawal of charges that were brought against Protestant and Roman Catholic accused under the most serious offences of the Firearms Act.[92] Similar explanations are afforded with respect to the trial judge's direction to the jury to enter acquittals in other cases involving a variety of firearms offences and where the defendants were perceived to be Protestants or Roman Catholics.[93] Perfection in achieving full accountability is unrealistic to expect, but the precedent represented by Sir Peter Rawlinson's documented response to the Cobden Trust allegations should not be lost sight of when criticisms are heard as to the inadequacy of the entire system of parliamentary accountability with respect to the Law Officers of the Crown.

PARLIAMENTARY ACCOUNTABILITY—STORMONT STYLE

Debates illustrating the high importance attached to the principle of the Attorney General's accountability to Parliament were a regular feature of the Stormont House of Commons during the period of political turbulence leading up to the introduction of direct rule. These debates were indulged in with a passionate determination to score political points, an observation that could be applied equally to the Government members, representing the Unionist party, and the small coterie of Nationalist members representing the Opposition. It might be thought an impossible task, in such a highly charged atmosphere, to exhibit steadfast adherence to the doctrine of the Law Officers' constitutional independence. That task is compounded by the realisation that each holder of the Attorney General's office was an avowed political supporter of the ruling Unionist party. In times of acute political strife, therefore, it cannot be a surprise to find, throughout the pages of the Northern Ireland *Hansard*, contrary perceptions being expressed vociferously from the thinly manned Opposition benches in which allegations of political bias on the part of the Attorney General fuelled the attacks on the government.

Whilst the Second World War was still being fought in Europe, the Northern Ireland Parliament engaged in partisan debate on the decision

---

[92] *Op. cit.* pp. 34–42.
[93] *Ibid.*

taken by the Attorney General, Mr. MacDermott (later to become Chief Justice of the Province and a Lord of Appeal in Ordinary), to institute criminal proceedings arising out of an illegal strike at Short and Harlands, the big shipyard firm in Belfast.[94] Five of the illegal strike leaders were prosecuted for offences against the Northern Ireland Conditions of Employment and National Arbitration Order 1940, which is identical with the corresponding Order in Great Britain. On being convicted, sentences of three months' imprisonment with hard labour were imposed. Production in the shipyard came to a halt amid dire threats, voiced by members of the Opposition, of further industrial action if the five men were not released immediately. In this critical situation the Attorney General defended his decision to prosecute the shop stewards on the grounds that the defendants' actions constituted a challenge to constitutional methods and the rule of law. "So far as I am concerned," Mr. MacDermott proclaimed, "the matter for consideration is not the rights or wrongs of a trade dispute. The choice here was between letting things drift from bad to worse and refusing to countenance a deliberate breach of the law, fraught with grave consequences which were well known to those who were prosecuted. To have taken the first course would have meant encouraging mob law and putting a premium on anarchy. The course which was adopted may be used in an attempt to cause mc.e trouble by those who are ready and willing to reduce the national effort at this juncture. But in my view it was the only course open to .ne compatible with the discharge of my duty, and I venture to think that, viewed dispassionately and in perspective, that opinion will have the support of all reasonable citizens at this time."[95]

The exigencies of war and the nation's priorities no doubt help to explain this assessment of the need to invoke the criminal law in pursuit of industrial peace. It can usefully be contrasted with the philosophy that guided Sir Hartley Shawcross in October 1950 when, using the similar provisions of the English Conditions of Employment Order 1940, he decided to prosecute 10 of the 1,400 gas maintenance men in London who had joined an unofficial strike.[96] On that occasion, in remarkably similar language to that used by his Northern Ireland counterpart, Shawcross emphasised that "there was no question of politics in this . . . . The question simply was whether in this country we were to enforce the rule of law or were to allow complete anarchy in these matters."[97] The English Attorney General went on to explain that he had sought the opinion of the Minister of Labour as to the likely results of instituting criminal proceedings against the strikers at one time rather than another. We have no means of knowing the extent to which any such opinion may have influenced the ultimate decision to launch criminal proceedings, but Sir Hartley Shawcross went to some pains to stress the fact that there was no

[94] H.C. Deb., (N.I.) Vol. 27, cols. 1038 *et seq.*, April 5, 1944.
[95] *Ibid.* col. 1048.
[96] See Edwards, *Law Officers of the Crown*, pp. 220–221.
[97] *Ibid.* p. 221.

question of the Cabinet approving or disapproving of his decision.[98] In the corresponding situation in Northern Ireland in 1944 one prominent member of the Unionist party ventured the opinion that if the Attorney General had embarked on these prosecutions without the concurrence and without the sanction of his chief (the Prime Minister) he was adopting a very courageous and very venturesome attitude. To this Mr. MacDermott, the then Law Officer of the Crown, gave the following reply: " . . . may I say at once that the responsibility for this prosecution is mine and no one else's. The Executive, under our Constitution, has no right to direct a prosecution or to tell the Law Officer what to do, and in this case there was no effort on the part of . . . the Minister of Home Affairs, or on the part of anyone else, to tell me that pressure should be brought by way of prosecution to bear on any person who had gone on strike. In fact, the papers on which I was bound to act, and which came to me direct from the police, did not pass through the Ministry of Home Affairs or any other Ministry."[99]

The same constitutional lines defining the Attorney General's relationship to the Cabinet[1] in Northern Ireland were underscored in the public statement issued on May 6, 1969 announcing a general amnesty for all persons convicted of offences and for those against whom charges were pending arising out of the civil disturbances in 1968 and 1969. Among the persons released from the Crumlin Road Prison in Belfast, as a consequence of this amnesty, were the militant Protestant leaders, Reverend Ian Paisley and Major Ronald Bunting. Four members of the Northern Ireland Parliament, against whom proceedings were pending, likewise were beneficiaries of the amnesty. The Prime Minister's statement to the House of Commons declared: "The Attorney General has informed the Cabinet that, in the public interest and after taking into account all relevant current circumstances, he has concluded that no criminal proceedings should continue or be initiated in respect of events associated with or arising out of political protests, utterances, marches, meetings or demonstrations occurring between October 5, 1968 and today and is giving instructions accordingly. The Attorney General made it clear to the Cabinet, however, that proceedings would be taken against any of those persons concerned in any way in activities relating to acts of sabotage who could be brought to justice. In the light of the Attorney General's decision the Minister of Home Affairs has decided to recommend forthwith to his

---

[98] *Ibid.*

[99] H.C. Deb., (N.I.) Vol. 27, col. 1046, April 5, 1944.

[1] The Government of Ireland Act 1920, s.8(4) and (5), would appear not to provide any statutory obstacle to the Attorney General serving as a member of the Northern Ireland Cabinet, but none has been so appointed. In an unpublished but influential memorandum, dated June 17, 1946, J. F. Caldwell, then First Parliamentary Draftsman, counselled strongly against any departure from the practice followed in England and Wales since 1928—see Edwards, *op. cit.* p. 174. Mr. Caldwell also recommended against any joinder of the office of Attorney General with that of any Cabinet Minister, and in particular that of Minister for Home Affairs.

Excellency the Governor such remission of sentences as will enable all persons presently serving terms of imprisonment as a result of such prosecutions to be released."[2] No hint, it will be observed, is given in this carefully worded statement of prior consultations having taken place between the Attorney General and his ministerial colleagues. It would be stretching credulity, however, in the political setting already described as prevailing in Northern Ireland during the particular period referred to, to conclude that the Attorney General was moved to take unilateral action of this importance in the solitude of his own office.

Within a short few months the Law Officer of the day, Mr. Basil Kelly, Q.C., was being assailed in the Ulster House of Commons for his failure to prosecute two prominent members of the Unionist party, one of them a former Minister of Home Affairs, for inciting violence in the course of delivering public speeches to their political supporters.[3] Accusations of political expediency were levelled against the Attorney General whose attitude, it was said, did not inspire public confidence in the impartial administration of the law. The incumbent's failure to resign from membership in the Orange and Masonic Orders was also said to compromise the public's perception of him as an impartial Law Officer. For these and other reasons the chief Opposition spokesman called for the removal from the Attorney General of his discretionary powers to prosecute, urging that this power be conferred upon a Director of Public Prosecutions who was not responsible to the Attorney General or to the Government.[4]

In replying to the charges levelled against him, the Attorney General took the opportunity to explain at some length the nature of the office that he occupied and, in addition, provided legal and factual reasons for his decision not to act in the individual circumstances cited by his critics. Quoting the classic pronouncement by Sir Hartley Shawcross on the duties of an Attorney General, delivered in the British House of Commons in 1951, "to which I subscribe without reservation,"[5] Mr. Kelly went on: "All I can say is . . . that I have tried to carry out my duties with the strictest impartiality in these difficult times independent of Cabinet or Government or political party or religious pressure from any quarter or by popular clamour or public agitation for prosecutions where serious crime has been committed and unsolved and where culprits have not been detected or where sufficient evidence does not exist to justify a prosecution."[6] The

---

[2] H.C. Deb., (N.I.) Vol. 73, col. 42, May 6, 1969. This "amnesty" was to herald the appointment of the new Prime Minister (Mr. Chichester-Clarke) and to give him a clean start.

[3] H.C. Deb., (N.I.) Vol. 74, cols. 1315 et seq., November 13, 1969.

[4] Ibid. cols. 1332–1335.

[5] Ibid. col. 1347.

[6] Ibid. col. 1348. Against this claim to strict impartiality in the discharge of his functions the Attorney General bemoaned the "jaundiced and subjective eye" that prevailed in the community at large. "There are some people" he continued "who were formerly decent, objective and unbiased who could look at the whole matter of the enforcement of law and order and the administration of justice objectively and properly but who now, perhaps through the strife and disorder of this past year, have become vengeful, bitter and hopelessly

Northern Ireland Attorney General disclosed that he received a great deal of signed and anonymous correspondence and telephone calls, conveying threats and intimidation from both sides of the religious and political fences in the community, about public prosecutions, and proceeded to take comfort from the fact that so long as the subjective and uneven criticism came from both the Protestant and Roman Catholic strands of the population this was proof that he was discharging his duties absolutely fairly and impartially.[7]

Mr. Kelly's eloquence was short lived in its effort to assuage the suspicions of his critics on both sides of the House of Commons. In May 1971 the House debated at length a formal motion seeking to censure the Attorney General in relation to his handling of a long list of cases arising out of street disturbances and firearms offences.[8] The ulterior purpose of the debate, however, was to propound once more the arguments for introducing into Northern Ireland a system of public prosecutions. It soon became clear, however, that the political parties represented in Stormont had widely divergent views as to what such a system would achieve. The aim of the Opposition members, representing the minority element of Roman Catholics, was to rid the prosecution system of its perceived political bias. Somewhat ingenuously perhaps, the mover of the motion stated that whether or not there was substance in the charges of politically tainted prosecutions a vast number of people throughout the community honestly believed that the Attorney General was acting in many ways as a politician and not as the leader of the Bar.[9] Striking support for this perception was close to hand. For who should be seen launching a stout defence in support of the Attorney General's actions but the Government member who also functioned as the senior Crown Prosecutor in the City of Belfast, an appointment within the patronage of the Law Officer of the Crown.[10] Confidence in the unbiased exercise of the Attorney General's powers was expressed from an unexpected quarter in the person of the Protestant militant leader, Reverend Ian Paisley, who a few months earlier had languished in prison as a result of the same Law Officer's action in

---

involved and subjective. Some of them desire to have prosecuted persons whom they want to see prosecuted for political or other irrelevant reasons or for reasons of revenge or bitterness and they desire to have undetected and free from prosecution other persons for the same improper and irrelevant reasons. They react violently to acquittals or in some cases convictions by the courts. They are infuriated by penalties and sentences imposed on some persons no matter what the justice of the case may be. They criticise the police for investigating and detecting or for not detecting crime. They criticise the law officer for prosecuting or not prosecuting according to their bias. They criticise magistrates and judges in the same subjective and biased way for convicting or acquitting or for imposing or refraining from imposing penalties. They seek to compare the penalty of one court on one person with that of the penalty of another court on another person. All this is hopelessly subjective and unjustified." *Ibid*. cols. 1350–51.

[7] *Ibid*. col. 1351. One such correspondent conveyed the intensity of her feelings towards the Law Officer by addressing him: "Dear Attorney General for the Republicans."

[8] H.C. Deb., (N.I.) Vol. 80, cols. 1783 *et seq*., May 13, 1971.

[9] *Ibid*. cols. 1783–1810.

[10] *Ibid*. cols. 1811–1821.

enforcing the criminal law against him with respect to his political activities.[11]

Winding up the debate on the motion of censure against the Attorney General, the Prime Minister announced the Government's acceptance of the MacDermott Committee's recommendation that a Director of Public Prosecutions be appointed for Northern Ireland.[12] At the same time the Prime Minister rejected outright the suggestion mooted earlier in the debate that the holder of such office be wholly independent of the Attorney General.[13] On the contrary, it was stated that the proposed relationship would be exactly parallel to the basic constitutional position in England and Wales where the Director of Public Prosecutions remains responsible to the Attorney General who, in turn, is answerable to Parliament.[14] As to the involvement of the government in questions of criminal prosecutions the Prime-Minister commended to the attention of all members of the House of Commons the Shawcross exposition, made at Westminster in 1951, as containing the answer to practically all the charges directed against the Attorney General in the censure debate. The repercussions of a given decision upon the government's political fortunes, the Prime Minister repeated, is a consideration which never enters into account.[15] "Let me say very clearly," he went on, "that in no sense is the Attorney General the agent of the Government. The Government never gives any instructions or directions as to who shall or who shall not be prosecuted nor would the Attorney General receive any such direction. It is for the Attorney General alone to decide, not just on narrow legal grounds but also on grounds of public policy, what the public interest requires. So let it not be said with any authority in this House that the Attorney General must carry out instructions from the Government."[16]

---

[11] *Ibid.* cols. 1825–1835. The same speaker roundly condemned the system, in place at the time and ever since the Province separated from the rest of Ireland, whereby "Crown prosecutors can be members of the House or of any political party." *Ibid.* col. 1829. The necessary reforms, discussed earlier, abolishing the part-time office of county Crown solicitors, stemmed from the Report of the MacDermott Working Party—*ante*, p. 243, fn. 28. Another criticism levelled against the Law Officer of the Crown for Northern Ireland, and long since rectified with respect to the English Law Officers (see Edwards, *op. cit.* Chapter 6), was the part time nature of that appointment and the ability of the incumbent to engage concurrently in private practice on the civil side—see *ibid.* cols. 1836–37, and also H.C. Deb., (N.I.) Vol. 74, cols. 1339–1340, November 13, 1969. For the earlier background to this contentious issue see N.I. Estimates 1921–26, Law Charges and Criminal Prosecutions, Class II, No. 4, pp. 1–2; *Report of the Select Committee on Ministerial Salaries*, etc., 1963, H.C. (N.I.) 1557, pp. 41–44, 100–101, 153; and the arguments propounded (by a future Attorney General) in favour of retaining "the important right to practise privately"—H.C.Deb., (N.I.) Vol. 55, cols. 728–731. With the assumption by the Attorney General for England of the responsibilities attached to the Attorney General for Northern Ireland, the problem has disappeared for the time being. When direct rule is eventually lifted we may hopefully assume that the English model will prevail in any future appointments to the Northen Ireland office of Attorney General.

[12] *Ibid.* cols. 1872–1873.

[13] *Ibid.*

[14] *Ibid.*

[15] *Ibid.* col. 1873.

[16] *Ibid.* cols. 1874–75.

At the end of the debate the House divided along strict party lines, the censure motion being easily defeated. It would be easy to dismiss the long debate as an exercise in futility in view of the predictable outcome. That would be a dangerous conclusion to subscribe to, encouraging as it would the elimination of opportunities to subject the Attorney General, and the government of which he is a member, to the maximum degree of public attention in explaining and defending the criteria by which prosecutorial discretionary power is exercised and the even-handed impartiality of the individual decisions for which the Law Officer is accountable to Parliament. For the time being the legislative assembly at Stormont is silenced and the affairs of Northern Ireland, including the functions of its Attorney General and Director of Public Prosecutions, are the responsibility of the Westminster Parliament.

If the Cobden Trust Study, referred to earlier, is any indication of the community's current perceptions of prosecution decision-making in Northern Ireland we must conclude that the former deep seated suspicions of bias against the Roman Catholic minority have not been completely dissipated. It would be rather remarkable if the simple creation of a Director of Public Prosecutions and a corps of public prosecutors were to establish universal confidence where previously criticisms were commonplace. Public confidence has to be earned and maintained over a considerable period of time and in circumstances of varying pressures. And even then the possibility of a fall from normal high standards of integrity and impartiality is never to be discounted. It is to meet such contingencies that the floor of the House of Commons must remain the ready forum, open to public scrutiny, in which the system and those responsible for its administration must remain fully accountable.

SOME COMPARISONS WITH THE ATTORNEY GENERAL AND DIRECTOR OF PUBLIC
PROSECUTIONS IN THE REPUBLIC OF IRELAND

Whether by coincidence, a simultaneous recognition of the need for reform in the machinery of prosecutions or for other less theoretical reasons, it is worth noting that the Republic of Ireland in 1974 created its own office of Director of Public Prosecutions,[17] shortly after the initiatives taken by the Northern Ireland and Westminster Parliaments. With the two systems now operating in such close proximity and tracing the functions of their Law Officers to a common heritage, we may usefully take a closer look at the distinctive characteristics of the relationship between the Attorney General and the Director of Public Prosecutions in the neighbouring state of Ireland. The office of Attorney General had existed for many centuries prior to the achieving of independence in 1920.[18] Its

---

[17] Statute No. 22 of 1974.
[18] For the fullest treatment see J. P. Casey, *The Office of the Attorney General in Ireland*, (1980, Dublin), Chapters 1 and 2. A detailed account of the machinery of criminal prosecutions in nineteenth century Ireland was given to the Select Committee on Public

status as one of the great officers of State is formally recognised in the Constitution of Ireland, enacted in 1937,[19] Article 30.1 of which declares: "There shall be an Attorney General who shall be the adviser of the Government in matters of law and legal opinion, and shall exercise and perform all such powers, functions and duties as are conferred or enforced on him by this Constitution or by law." Two other provisions of the Constitution are relevant to our present discussion. Article 30.3 states that "all crimes and offences prosecuted in any court . . . other than a court of summary jurisdiction shall be prosecuted in the name of the People at the suit of the Attorney General or some other person authorized in accordance with law to act for that purpose." The immediate ensuing provision declares that "the Attorney General shall not be a member of the Government," the intention clearly being to distance the Law Officer from the executive branch of government[20] and to enhance the quasi-judicial qualities of impartiality and independence with which the holder is expected to discharge his constitutional duties.

Prior to 1974 the Irish Attorney General's control over all prosecutions was, theoretically speaking, complete. Save for a change in nomenclature that followed the separation of Ireland from the rest of Great Britain in 1920, the title "State Solicitor" being substituted for "Crown Solicitor," the system familiar to residents of Northern Ireland was identical with that governing the handling of criminal prosecutions in the rest of Ireland throughout the nineteenth century.[21] No steps had been taken in 1879, when the first Prosecution of Offences Act was enacted in Westminster, to extend the jurisdiction of the newly created Director of Public Prosecutions beyond England and Wales to include Ireland. Confirmation of this policy to leave the Irish system undisturbed is to be found in the Newspaper Libel and Registration Act 1881,[22] section 3 of which confines the institution of criminal proceedings under the Act to cases in which a written fiat is obtained from "the Director of Public Prosecutions in England or Her Majesty's Attorney General in Ireland." The sole responsibility of the Attorney General in criminal proceedings brought before the Irish courts is made explicit in the Criminal Justice (Administration) Act 1924, s.9 of which declared that "all criminal charges prosecuted

Prosecutors 1854–56, by Joseph Napier, a former Attorney General of Ireland—see Parl. Papers 1854–55, Vol. xii (481) pp. 141–154. Casey, referring to Napier's account in 1855, states that "with certain minor modifications this system continued in force until Independence; thereafter an almost identical one, save for changes in title such as State Solicitor for Crown Solicitor, was in operation"—op. cit. pp. 23–24.

[19] No such provision is to be found in the 1922 Constitution of the Irish Free State. Prior to the 1937 Constitution the only statute bearing upon the office of Attorney General is the Ministers and Secretaries Act 1924, s.6, as to which see post, p. 266.

[20] There can be no doubt, however, that the Attorney General serves "at the pleasure" of the Prime Minister. Thus, the Constitution provides: "The Taoiseach may, for reasons which to him seem sufficient, request the resignation of the Attorney General" (Art. 5.2), and "In the event of failure to comply with the request, the appointment of the Attorney General shall be terminated by the President if the Taoiseach so advises" (Art. 5.3).

[21] See the references cited ante, fn. 18.

[22] 44 & 45 Vict. c. 60.

upon indictment in any court shall be at the suit of the Attorney General"
and the same procedure extended to prosecutions in courts of summary
jurisdiction "save where the proceedings were instituted by a Minister,
Department of State or person authorized in that behalf by the law for the
time being in force."[23]

The net effect of the Prosecution of Offences Act 1974 is to transfer
virtually the whole of the Attorney General's prosecuting functions to the
new office of Director of Public Prosecutions the statute making it clear
that the Director "shall perform all the functions capable of being
performed in relation to criminal matters . . . by the Attorney General."[24]
Included within this statutory assignment of legal functions are the
exclusive right to prosecute on indictment, to enter a *nolle prosequi*[25] and
the authority to lay *ex-officio* informations.[26] There are, however, certain
exceptions within which the Attorney General's ultimate authority
prevails. These include the authorisation of proceedings under section 3 of
the Geneva Conventions Act 1962, the Official Secrets Act 1963 and the
Genocide Act 1973.[27] Responsibility for upholding the constitutional
validity of laws also continues to rest in the lap of the Attorney.[28]

---

[23] For many years doubts were entertained as to whether this provision had eliminated the
right to private prosecution or qualified the institution of criminal proceedings by the police.
As to the latter question see *State (Cronin)* v. *Circuit Court Judge, Western Circuit* [1937] I.R.
34 and the authorities reviewed by Casey, *op. cit.* pp. 96–100. As to "the valuable right of
private prosecution" the decision of the Supreme Court in *State (Ennis)* v. *District Justice
Farrell* set doubts at rest with its confirmation that this historic right was not curtailed by
either the 1924 Act or Art. 30.3 of the Constitution—[1966] I.R. 107 at p. 121 *per* O'Dalaigh
C.J. It is, however, a power to institute summary proceedings only, a restriction derived from
the combined effect of s.9(1) of the 1924 Act and the above provision in the Constitution. As
stated by the Chief Justice in the *Ennis* case (*supra*): "The only limitation on the right of the
private prosecutor is that a prosecution on indictment must be conducted by the Attorney
General . . . . As a consequence, the private prosecutor may conduct the prosecution thus
far, *i.e.* up to the receiving of informations and return for trial. Thereafter, the Attorney
General becomes *dominus litis.*"

[24] *Op. cit.* s.3(1).

[25] See Casey, *op. cit.* 101–109. Attention is particularly drawn to what the author regards as
the unsatisfactory ruling by the Supreme Court in *State (Killiam)* v. *Attorney General* (1958)
92 I.L.T.R. 182, precluding any judicial review of the Attorney's and, since 1974, the
D.P.P.'s, decision to enter a *nolle prosequi*. "If the basis of judicial reticence in this area is
ministerial responsibility to Parliament" Casey observes "this attitude requires re-
examination in the circumstances of modern Ireland." Few Irish Attorneys General have
served as deputies or senators in the Irish Parliament, added to which are the problems which
will arise even where the Attorney is in the Oireachtas. As will be noted later, under the terms
of the Prosecution of Offences Act 1974, the Attorney General is not responsible for decisions
taken by the D.P.P. and cannot, presumably, be questioned about them—Casey, *op. cit.* p.
103.

[26] See Casey, *op. cit.* pp. 125–128, and for the position under English law see *post*, pp.
434–442. In Ireland, the Criminal Procedure Act 1967 has considerably shortened preliminary
proceedings, making it unnecessary to circumvent the problem of delay by resort to ex-officio
informations. No case involving resort to this procedure in Ireland since 1921 has been
discovered and, in addition, section 62 of the Courts of Justice Act 1936 empowers the
Attorney General (now the D.P.P.) to proceed by way of direct indictment notwithstanding a
District Justice's refusal of an information.

[27] Prosecution of Offences Act 1974, s.3(5). Resort to the Attorney General is not required
for the purposes of remands or bail hearings.

[28] *Ibid.* s.3(3).

Moreover, the Prosecution of Offences Act 1974, empowers the government, whenever it is of the opinion that it is expedient to do so in the interests of national security, to transfer functions in criminal matters back to the Attorney General.[29] The establishment of the office of Director of Public Prosecutions and the execution by such an official of the criminal law responsibilities associated with the Attorney General appear to have been contemplated when the new constitution of 1937 was being drawn up and proclaimed. Article 30.3 of the Constitution[30] anticipates the very step taken in 1974. It is to the more recent enactment, however, that we must turn in defining the relationship of the Director to the Attorney General for Ireland.

Whether any significant differentiation can be discerned in the day to day functioning of the respective offices in Belfast and Dublin remains to be tested. What is abundantly clear is the language of the Prosecution of Offences Act 1974, section 2(5) of which states quite simply: "The Director shall be independent in the performance of his functions."[31] The same Act envisages that the Attorney General and the Director of Public Prosecutions "shall consult together from time to time in relation to matters pertaining to the functions of the Director"[32] but this is not designed in any way to diminish the latter's independence. Thus, according to the explanatory memorandum issued by the Department of the Prime Minister of Ireland in making public the terms of the Prosecution of Offences Bill: "The provision for consultation would not confer on the Attorney General any right to give directions to the Director as to how he will perform his functions in relation either to particular cases or generally."[33]

We have already seen that according a major degree of independence to the Director of Public Prosecutions in Northern Ireland has always been the intention of the responsible Government and Parliament. Nevertheless, the statutory law in force leaves no doubt as to the ultimate responsibility of the Attorney General to Parliament for every action of the Northern Ireland Director, and, under the Emergency Order of 1972, the authority of the Attorney General, if necessary, to control the exercise of the Director's functions.[34] No such powers are conferred upon the

[29] *Ibid.* s.5(1).

[30] See *ante*, p. 263.

[31] Other provisions that underscore the Director's special status include the appointments committee that is charged with the duty of recommending to the Prime Minister the most suitable appointee—it consists, *inter alia*, of the Chief Justice, the Chairman of the Bar Council, the President of the Incorporated Law Society and the Secretary to the Government—Prosecution of Offences Act 1974, s.2(7); the procedure for removal of the Director from office which necessitates prior consideration by the Government of a report by a committee consisting of the Chief Justice, a Judge of the High Court and the Attorney General—*ibid.* s.2(9); and, finally, the prohibition of certain communications addressed to the Director, or a member of his staff, for the purpose of influencing a decision in relation to criminal proceedings—*ibid.* s.6(1)(*a*).

[32] *Ibid.* s.2(6).

[33] Quoted in Casey, *op. cit.* p. 227, fn. 12.

[34] See *ante*, pp. 249–251.

Attorney General for Ireland. Moreover, the Director of Public Prosecutions for Ireland is not accountable to the Attorney, or so it would appear from the remarks made by the Parliamentary Secretary to the Prime Minister on the second reading of the Bill that created the office in 1974.[35] In Westminster it would be customary for one of the Law Officers to steer such a Bill through the Commons. That a similar practice was not resorted to in the Irish Legislature is readily explained. According to the Ministers and Secretaries Act 1924,[36] "The Attorney General may be or become a member of the Dâil Eireann [the Irish Parliament]," a provision that absolves any holder of that office from any legal obligation to secure a seat in the legislative assembly. Nor, it would appear, is there any parliamentary convention in Ireland to this effect. In the period since independence was attained only six holders of the Irish Attorney Generalship have been elected as deputies in the Dâil,[37] whereas prior to 1922 it was customary for one or other of the Irish Law Officers to have a seat in the House of Commons at Westminster.[38] And throughout the period of devolutionary government in Northern Ireland, prior to the imposition of direct rule in 1972, every Attorney General of that province, without exception, was also a member of the Northern Ireland Parliament in Stormont.[39]

The absence of any prerequisite condition that the Attorney General occupy an elected seat in the Dâil should not obscure the fact that the office is a political appointment, the holder being a member of the party currently in power.[40] This policy is confirmed by the 1937 Constitution which provides that the Attorney General is appointed by the Prime Minister and retires from office whenever there is a change in the leadership of the administration.[41] Despite this, Article 30.4 of the Constitution states clearly that "the Attorney General shall not be a member of the Government." This is generally assumed to mean that the Attorney General is excluded from membership in the Cabinet[42] and that the State's Law Officer occupies a position of independence in the discharge of his constitutional duties. This principle was accepted in

[35] 273 Dâil Debates, cols. 803–805, June 11, 1974.
[36] Statute no. 16 of 1924, s.6.
[37] Casey, *op. cit.* pp. 62–68, and p. 218, fn. 1 for individual details.
[38] *Ibid.* pp. 27–32. Two Irish Solicitors General became Speakers of the Lower House and, another interesting note, the persons concerned did not always represent Irish constituencies—*ibid.* p. 210, fns. 51, 56.
[39] The full list is given in Casey, *op. cit.* App. 3. Three of the Attorneys General had previously served as Minister of Home Affairs but relinquished this portfolio, and with it Cabinet membership, on assuming the duties of Law Officer. For biographical summaries of the Irish Attorneys General since 1923, see *ibid.* App. 2.
[40] See Casey, *op. cit.* pp. 44–45.
[41] Art. 5(4).
[42] Several reasons are advanced in support of this conclusion. Art. 28 of the Constitution uses the term "Government" in the sense of "Cabinet." It is also characteristic of members of the government that they administer departments of State, leading Casey to conclude that any statute placing the Attorney General at the head of the Department of Justice, for example, would be unconstitutional, *op. cit.* pp. 45–46. For the pre-1937 position in the Irish Free State see *ibid.* pp. 45, and 215 fn. 37.

Ireland before 1937. According to the author of the carefully researched study on *The Office of the Attorney General in Ireland*[43] the same principle is universally recognised today by politicians and judges alike.[44] The same author suggests that the provisions in the Irish Constitution, quoted above, may have been inspired by the practice followed in Northern Ireland since its separation.[45] And, of course, it is the same theory, that the Attorney General's independence of the executive is better maintained by his exclusion from membership in the Cabinet, which has been consistently maintained in England for the past 60 years. The problems of equating this theory with the practice of the Attorney's constant attendance at, and participation in, Cabinet meetings has been discussed at length elsewhere in this book. Recent writing on this subject in Ireland suggests that the same concerns are evident in that country also.

The basic difference between the two countries is the issue of ministerial accountability. Given the option contained in the Ministers and Secretaries Act 1924, which permits the office of Attorney General to be held by an incumbent who is or is not a member of the Irish Parliament,[46] it is nevertheless remarkable that under the current Standing Orders of its Lower House even if the Attorney is a member of the Dâil he cannot be questioned as to his actions.[47] With complete independence being conferred upon the Director of Public Prosecutions in Ireland and the elimination of any power of direction or control over the Director's actions

---

[43] See, too, the authorities reviewed in J. M. Kelly, *The Irish Constitution*, Dublin, 1980, pp. 158–162.

[44] *Op. cit.* pp. 39–44, and pp. 49–51. Among the many expressions of this understanding is the statement of O'Dalaigh J., a former Law Officer and later Chief Justice, that "the Attorney General is not in the discharge of his functions as public prosecutor subject to the directions of the Taioseach but is an independent constitutional officer. If the purpose of Article 30 of the Constitution were to place the power to commence and withdraw prosecutions in the control of the head of the Government, I should have expected that apt words would have been found to provide for such a novel and unusual feature of the government of the country"—*McLoughlin* v. *Minister for Social Welfare* [1958] I.R. 1 at p. 25. Speaking in the same case, Kingsmill Moore J., declared that: "The Attorney General is in no way the servant of the Government, but is put into an independent position. He is a great officer of State, with grave responsibilities of a quasi-judicial as well as of an executive nature. The provsions for his voluntary or forced resignation seem to recognise that it may be his business to adopt a line antagonistic to the Government, and such a difference of opinion has to be resolved by his ceasing to hold the post, probably with repercussions on the political plane." *Ibid.* at p. 17.

[45] Casey, *op. cit.* p. 46.

[46] *Op. cit.* s.6.

[47] S.O. 32 of 1974. By way of explanation, the Standing Orders require that questions be addressed only to a "member of the Government," which by the express terms of the Constitution excludes the Attorney General. As Casey describes the "curious half-world" in which the Irish Attorney General finds himself, "a political appointee, privy to government secrets and possibly a parliamentary spokesman for government, he is virtually indistinguishable from a minister. Yet unlike ministers he is not personally answerable to Parliament for the way he discharges his functions"—*op. cit.* p. 71. On the infrequent occasions when deputies have put down questions about prosecutions the Prime Minister, or his Parliamentary Secretary, has responded even though the Attorney himself may have been present in the Dâil and able to explain or defend his actions—see, *e.g.* 85 Dâil Debates, col. 1025–29, December 3, 1941; 136 Dâil Debates, col. 921, February 12, 1953.

by the Attorney General, who, it may well be asked, is accountable to the Irish Parliament for the decisions taken by the Director of Public Prosecutions?[48] If the experience of other Commonwealth countries, which have adopted into their constitutions a similar model of an unaccountable public prosecutor, is any pointer to what lies in store for the Republic of Ireland it is only a matter of time before the fundamental questions of control and accountability force themselves before its elected Parliament for intense debate. Among the most interested observers will be the members of the United Kingdom Parliament whose commitment to the constitutional doctrine of ministerial responsibility has always extended to include the Attorney General and his subordinate colleague, the Director of Public Prosecutions. No student of Northern Ireland's parliamentary history can doubt its adherence to the same principles. Some notable examples of its application were dealt with earlier in this chapter. That said, it would nonetheless be unrealistic to fail to recognise the limitations, evident in Stormont and Westminster, in making the principle of accountability convincing and dependable.

---

[48] In answering this question it is pertinent to bear in mind that whereas the principle of independence is given express recognition, thus investing the Director with the last word as to prosecutions and protecting his office from any political control or direction, the question of accountability to Parliament is by no means necessarily foreclosed. Normally, the two concepts, accountability and control, go hand in hand but in the exceptional situation that prevails under Irish constitutional law we may assume that the Prime Minister will answer for the D.P.P.'s actions in the same fashion as that which obtains with respect to questions concerning decisions by the Attorney General. Strong support for this conclusion is contained in section 1(i) of the Ministers and Secretaries Act 1924, which assigns to the Department of the President of the Executive Council (i.e. the Prime Minister) "the administrative control of and responsibility for such public services and the business, powers, duties, and functions thereof as may not for the time being be comprised in any of the Departments of State constituted by this Act."

10

The Role and Functions of the Scottish Law Officers

In his autobiography *A Man of Law's Tale* Lord Macmillan was compelled to acknowledge with regret that few of his English friends had any detailed knowledge of the nature of the Lord Advocate's office in Scottish law.[1] Writing in the same vein a hundred years ago, the author of the standard work on the history of the Lord Advocates of Scotland ruefully complained that "Scotsmen always know more about England than Englishmen know about Scotland."[2] Allowing for the existence of more than a grain of truth in both these statements it is also a fact that, for some years now, envious glances have been directed from many quarters to the Scottish integrated system of criminal prosecutions with the police acting under the superintendence of the procurators fiscal. This kind of principle, its admirers have argued, should be incorporated into English law as the surest means of overcoming the problems associated with a splintered chain of responsibilities. There is nothing new in this modern admiration of the Scottish devotion to exclusively public prosecutors acting under the direct control of its senior Law Officer of the Crown.[3] The case for importing into England and Wales a system of criminal prosecutions analogous to that experienced for centuries in Scotland was expounded with vigour before the House of Commons Select Committee on Public Prosecutors in 1854–56.[4] The strengths of the Scottish system had earlier been recognised in the Eighth Report of the Commissioners of the Criminal Law, which appeared in 1845.[5] All these exhortations, however, never achieved their

[1] London, Macmillan & Co. Ltd., 1933, at p. 84.
[2] Omond, *The Lord Advocates of Scotland*, (Edinburgh, 1883), cited by Macmillan, *op. cit.*
[3] For a careful but enthusiastic evaluation of the Scottish system, see Lord Normand (Lord President of the Court of Session and later a Lord of Appeal in Ordinary): "The Public Prosecutor in Scotland" (1938) 54 L.Q.R. 345 at pp. 354–355.
[4] Edwards, *op. cit.* pp. 339–345, 375–376.
[5] *Op. cit.* pp. 339–340. Earlier still, Denman, who was to become Attorney General (in 1830) and Chief Justice of the King's Bench (in 1832), had acknowledged as "a strange anomaly in the English criminal system . . . the entire want of a responsible public prosecutor" and drawn adverse comparisons with the Scottish system of prosecuting crime—(1824) 39 *The Edinburgh Review* 191 (see Edwards, *op. cit.* p. 340 fn. 22).

full potential, the ensuing results of the nineteenth century campaign in England for reform producing instead the Office of the Director of Public Prosecutions which cannot be equated in any true sense with the Crown Office responsibilities in Scotland.

Many of the original sources of dissatisfaction with the respective roles of the police and prosecutors in England and Wales have continued to fester, resulting, most recently, in the setting up of the Royal Commission on the Police in 1960 and the Royal Commission on Criminal Procedure in 1978. Quite independently of these inquiries various concerned bodies such as *Justice*,[6] the Commons' Select Committee on Home Affairs,[7] and the Inns of Court Conservative Lawyers Association[8] have expressed enthusiastic support for the incorporation into English criminal law of Scotland's prescription for handling criminal prosecutions.[9] Added support for this movement was provided in the report of the MacDermott Committee in Northern Ireland which recommended the adoption in that province of the Scottish procurator fiscal's overall responsibilities for the investigatory and prosecutorial functions in crime.[10] As we have already seen, however, these contemporary platforms urging the assimilation of English and Scottish procedures in matters of prosecution, up to now, have all failed in their objectives. Nevertheless, future concern for possible changes makes it imperative that we seek a thorough understanding of how the Scottish Law Officers and their agents, the advocates depute and procurators fiscal, function in close collaboration with the police in Scotland's legal system. As with the corresponding offices in England and Wales, the most fruitful insights are likely to be secured by examining the evolution of the ancient offices of Lord Advocate and the Solicitor General for Scotland.

THE LORD ADVOCATE AS PUBLIC PROSECUTOR

Although universally identified as the Lord Advocate, the senior Scottish Law Officer is otherwise described as "Her Majesty's Advocate" in the commission issued by the Sovereign to each new incumbent

---

[6] *The Prosecution Process in England and Wales*, 1970, at pp. 9–13.

[7] *Deaths in Police Custody*, H.C. Paper 631 of 1980, pp. xiii–xiv and see also pp. 104–115.

[8] See Memorandum of Evidence submitted to the Royal Commission on the Police in 1962 by the Inns of Court Conservative & Unionist Society, quoted by Professor T. B. Smith in his Hamlyn Trust Lectures: *British Justice: The Scottish Contribution*, pp. 119–120.

[9] In drawing attention to this chorus of praise it is well to remember the caveat expressed, also by Professor Smith, in *A Short Commentary of the Law of Scotland*, (Edinburgh, 1962), p. 208, that methods which work well in one country may be quite unsuitable for export. This opinion was echoed by another eminent Scottish scholar and now a practising judge, Sheriff G. H. Gordon, who wrote that the system works so remarkably well in Scotland because of "the unwritten tradition which controls the manner in which it is operated and the way in which the wide discretions which it permits are exercised"—(1968) 19 N.I.L.Q. 249. Much the same sentiments were voiced by Lord Normand writing in 1938, see 54 L.Q.R. 345 at p. 357.

[10] See *ante*, pp. 243–246.

appointed to the portfolio in the United Kingdom Government.[11] According to G.W.T. Omond's standard treatise on *The Lord Advocates of Scotland*, the exact date on which the office was instituted is unknown.[12] The earliest landmark appears to be the reference in the Acts of Parliament of Scotland in 1483 which records that, when the Duke of Albany failed to appear in answer to a summons of treason, "In the name and behalf of our Sovereign Lord (James II), Johne the Ross of Montgrenan, advocate to his hienes craved the judgment of Parliament, which was given against Albany."[13] Omond explains this event as a natural corollary to the practice which had by then developed in Scotland of private persons using advocates to represent their interests in legal suits.[14] Similar origins account for the emergence of special legal representatives in England to "speak for the King" in the eyres and in the Court of King's Bench. Of these, the earliest English records show that Lawrence del Brok, as early as 1247, was being paid a regular fee of £20 a year "for suing the King's affairs," thus laying strong claim to having been the first King's Attorney and the progenitor of the modern office of Attorney General for England and Wales.[15] Letters patent appointing the Sovereign's legal representatives before the English Courts of King's Bench and Common Bench originated in 1311, to be followed in 1315 by the first recorded instance of a specially designated *attornatus regis*.[16] Omond's further suggestion that the French office of Procureur du Roi may have been the model expressly replicated by the Scottish Sovereigns in appointing a King's Advocate[17] must be judged alongside the practice already well established in England, at least a century earlier, of appointing an advocate to be regularly employed in representing the King's affairs.[18]

Additional support for the argument that the appointment of a King's Advocate derived its roots from the same soil that gave sustenance to the English office of King's Attorney is to be found in the early custom in Scotland of nominating the King's Advocate to sit as one of the judges of the Court of Session, the country's highest judicial body. The practice appears to have begun at the time of the original establishment of the

---

[11] Thus, the Royal Warrant appointing a former Solicitor General to the position of Lord Advocate on April 6, 1960 read, in part, as follows:

"Our Sovereign Lady being well informed and taking into Her Royal consideration that the Right Honourable William Grant, one of Her Majesty's Counsel learned in the Law, is a person of unquestionable abilities, sufficiency and integrity and very fitly qualified to exercise and discharge the Office and place of Her Majesty's Advocate in Scotland."

[12] *Op. cit.* p. 3.

[13] Acts Parl. Scot. ii. 151. Sir John Ross was later to stand trial for treason before the High Court of Parliament. He did not appear. Nevertheless, he was condemned to death and all his lands forfeited to the Crown. His fortunes were later restored, due to the intercession of Pope Innocent the Eighth, and in 1490 he was appointed one of the Lords of Council and Session—see Omond, *op. cit.* pp. 1–3.

[14] *Ibid.* p. 4.

[15] Edwards, *op. cit.* pp. 15–16.

[16] *Ibid.* p. 19.

[17] Omond, *op. cit.* p. 4.

[18] Edwards, *op. cit.* pp. 16–18.

College of Justice in 1532.[19] This departure from the separation of the functions of advocacy and adjudication had been quite normal in England three centuries earlier,[20] though public criticism was forthcoming when the King's Attorney saw fit to adjudge the very same case in which he had earlier personally participated as the King's legal representative.[21] Claims that the original resort to the same policy in Scotland was by way of emulating French procedures is unsupportable historically. For, as Lord Medwyn pointed out in *King's Advocate* v. *Lord Dunglas* in 1836,[22] the Scottish precedents predate the decision to permit a similar conjunction of functions taken by the Parliament of Paris in June 1605.[23] Certainly the practice was very much in vogue in Scotland until the late seventeenth century, Sir John Nisbet in 1664 being the last Lord Advocate to combine that office with his appointment as a Lord of Session, the title accorded a Judge of the College of Justice.[24] What to modern eyes must seem an indefensible anomaly is explained differently by Lord Medwyn in his painstaking review of the early records when he observed: "The King's Advocate, from his office, was, of course, employed in conducting the processes in which the King was concerned; and the circumstances of his being a Judge also in the Civil Court, where . . . he could not judge in the King's causes, will not appear so anomalous, when it is recollected that criminal causes were the province of another Court; and the Parliament and Privy Council also disposed of many causes now belonging to the Supreme Civil Court."[25]

[19] Now better known as the Court of Session. See the Stair Society's *Introduction to Scottish Legal History*, (1958), p. 39, and Omond, *op. cit.* pp. 12, 15. The first King's Advocate to combine this office with that of a Lord of Session was Sir Adam Otterburn who took his seat on the bench at the first meeting of the court. When pleading as an advocate both for private clients and as counsel for the Sovereign the King's Advocate did not mingle with the ordinary advocates but had the privilege of standing within the Bar (Stat. 1532, cap. 67)—Omond, *op. cit.* p. 15.

[20] Edwards, *op. cit.* pp. 17–18. The practice of combining the duties of a member of the Bench with those of the King's Attorney is traceable back to as early as 1234—*ibid.* p. 17, fn. 31 and 32.

[21] *Ibid.* p. 18, fn. 38. This deplorable practice came to an end in 1290 with the appointment of the former marshal of the King's Bench, Richard de Brettiville, with the assigned duty of prosecuting the King's Pleas in the Court of King's Bench—*ibid.* fn. 39.

[22] 1836 Sess. Cas. (1st ser.) (XVs) 314.

[23] *Ibid.* p. 326. Lord Medwyn was correcting the interpretation advanced by Sir George Mackenzie (*Works*, Vol. ii, p. 541) that in France the King's Advocates were at the same time judges and this was so decided by the Parliament of Paris in June 1605 " . . . and from this we probably, in Scotland, took occasion, a little after that time, to make Sir William Oliphant, and of late Sir John Nisbet, both Advocates and Lords of Session." Medwyn, in his judgment, identified the practice as originating in 1532 coincident with the original constitution of Scotland's Court of Session.

[24] No particular surprise seems to have been registered when the President of the Court of Session, Sir George Lockhart, was ordered, by a letter from King James VII, to officiate as advocate in the Parliament of 1686. In another instance, the President of the same court disqualified himself from sitting as a judge in order that he might assume the role of advocate in pleading a case on behalf of his son-in-law—*per* Lord Medwyn *op. cit.* citing Fountainhall, Vol. i, pp. 416, 500, *Decisions of the Lords of Council and Session 1678–1712* (2 vols. 1759–61).

[25] 1836 Sess. Cas. (1st ser.) (XVs) 314 at p. 331.

Before leaving this subject it should be noted that there were times when the judges of the Court of Session did not take too kindly to the King's Advocate taking part in their adjudicative functions. This led to their exclusion of the Lord Advocate, Sir Thomas Hope, in 1628, an action that resulted in Charles I issuing a formal direction to the judges to rescind their decision so that the Sovereign's representative "may the better consider and understand of what shall concern us, our interest and service."[26] The Scottish judges dutifully complied, passing an Act of Sederunt, or rule of court, authorising the Lord Advocate to sit in the Inner House and assigned him "ane particular place to sitt in without thair awin benches and placit him thairin after they had taken the said Sir Thomas his aith to keep the secreits of the house and not to revile nor divulge the same in any sort."[27] To this day the Lord Advocate enjoys the privilege of having a special place assigned to him in the well of the court.

The Lord Advocate's modern role as the supreme officer of State in charge of all public prosecutions did not materialise simultaneously with his functions as the King's legal representative in civil litigation.[27a] Only by a slow process of adjustment did Scotland, like many other countries, move away from its early commitment to enforcing the criminal law by private arrangements, whether by way of exacting revenge or the payment of compensation to the victim or the victim's next of kin.[28] Not until the sixteenth century does the evidence point to the Lord Advocate assuming increasing responsibility for criminal prosecutions whether by way of concurring in many private prosecutions, or on his own authority in serious crimes by virtue of a special warrant from the Crown or the Privy Council.[29] At a meeting of the latter body in 1579, when the state of the criminal courts in Scotland was considered in conjunction with its implications for the royal treasury, direction was given to the Treasurer and the Advocate to "persew all slauchteris, convocationis and utheris odius crymes" notwithstanding the failure of the victim and his kin to do so.[30] The courts, however, refused to recognise this regal mandate as authorising the Lord Advocate to prosecute all crimes. Thus, in *H.M. Advocate* v. *Chapman* in 1583[31] the King's Advocate sought to intervene in

---

[26] Omond, Vol. i, pp. 104–105. Henry Lander, Advocate to James V, had been admitted to sit with the judges in 1538, *ibid.* p. 21.

[27] *Ibid.* Act of Sederunt dated November 19, 1628.

[27a] Although the position of the Lord Advocate in relation to civil litigation is in many respects similar to that of the English Attorney General, his right to intervene *ex proprio motu* in litigation to argue the public interest is more limited than that of the Attorney, and there is no equivalent in Scotland of the relator action in England. The Lord Advocate may intervene only where there is a statutory power to do so or where a proprietorial interest of the Crown is involved or perhaps where the interests of a public trust are involved—see *D. & J. Nichol* v. *Aberdeen Harbour Trustees* 1915 S.C. (H.L.) 7 at pp. 10 and 17.

[28] *Introduction to Scottish Legal History*, pp. 39–40, 432–433; Omond, *op. cit.* pp. 16–18; Normand, (1938) 54 L.Q.R. 345 at pp. 345–346.

[29] Stair Society, *op. cit.* pp. 434–435.

[30] Privy Council Minute, May 28, 1579, quoted in Omond, *op. cit.* p. 48 and in *The Register of the Privy Council of Scotland* (Ed. D. Masson), Vol. iii, p. 173 (Edinburgh, 1880).

[31] Mor. Dict. Dec. 7896, cited in Omond, *op. cit.* p. 49.

order to press a charge of forgery. The case had earlier been settled between the parties involved but the King's representative argued that forgery was an offence against the State and the concurrence of the victim was not a prerequisite to authorising the prosecution. The court, however, declined to recognise the Advocate's right to proceed *virtute officii*. And in *H.M. Advocate* v. *Forest* the following year[32] the court took the same position when faced with the argument that the King's interest was separate from that of the victim, because it was the duty of the State to see that crime did not go unpunished.

The seal of approval to the Lord Advocate's paramount right to invoke the criminal law unilaterally, despite the contrary wishes of any private citizen, is generally associated with the Act of 1587 which authorised the Treasurer (on account of his interests in escheats) and the Advocate to "persew slaughters and utheris crimes althoucht the parties be silent or wald utherwayes privily agree."[33] Speaking in the course of delivering his opinion in *King's Advocate* v. *Dunglas* Lord Medwyn traced the transformation in the status of the Lord Advocate as public prosecutor in these words[34]: "The King's advocate was authorised to act as public prosecutor of crimes in the time of James VI. This is implied in 1579, c. 78,[35] and still more expressly by 1587, c. 77,[36] which authorised the Thesaurer and Advocate to pursue, although the private party did not. He may have had power previously from the Sovereign to prosecute in the pleas of the Crown; but in that large class of crimes, then prosecuted at the instance of the private party, his power was confirmed and firmly recognised by these statutes; so that, since the date of the latter act, his right to prosecute all crimes has been unquestioned. For after the passing of the first of these, and prior to the date of the other, this Court had refused to sustain his instance in the crimen falsi, where the private party did not also concur. But immediately after this his title is sustained in such a case[37] and it has not been disputed since." Despite the unconditional nature of the Lord Advocate's mandate, as expressed in the statute of 1587, special warrants continued to emanate from the Privy Council directing the Lord Advocate to prosecute in particular cases.[38] Omond

[32] Omond, *op. cit.* p. 49.
[33] cap. 77; Acts of Parl. of Scot., 1584–1593, ff. 101r–102r. There is no record of the Treasurer ever acting alone as prosecutor—Hume, *Commentaries*, Vol. ii, 131. An earlier statute in 1579, cap. 78, by implication seemed to confer upon the King's Advocate the power of prosecuting without the concurrence of the private complainer—Omond, *op. cit.* p. 48. The statute, by imposing penalties on private persons who instituted "sakeless" (*i.e.* groundless) criminal pursuits, implied that discretion as to what constituted a good cause pertained to the King's Advocate.
[34] 1836 Sess. Cas. (1st ser.) (XVs) 314 at p. 327.
[35] *Ante*, fn. 33.
[36] *Ibid.*
[37] Citing *Chalmers* v. *Dick*, Spottiswood, p. 166 and *Thirlestane* v. *Durham*, February 1597.
[38] Stair Society, *op. cit.* p. 435 and p. 39 citing an instance in which the Privy Council "ordained and commanded" the King's Advocate to prosecute a priest for the saying of Mass, *Register of the Privy Council of Scotland*, 1545–1689. Vol. x, p. 126.

explains this resort to a special fiat as having been dictated by consideration for the safety of the King's representative. In the lawless state of the country, Omond argues, "the peasants of Scotland were as vindictive as the mountaineers of Corsica, and the position of the public prosecutor would often have been one of extreme danger, had he not been able to show clearly that he was acting under the direction of the Privy Council."[39]

Another aspect of the 1587 statute that needs emphasis, in view of the discussion that will later be devoted to the subject, and recent manifestations of its surrounding problems, is the absence of any provision in the enactment confirming the Lord Advocate's right to institute proceedings for any crime that would restrict the corresponding entitlement of a private citizen to prosecute in his own name and his own authority. The consensus among the institutional writers confirms that, except for cases of treason and blasphemy, it was very common procedure in Scotland well into the seventeenth century for the victim or his kin to prosecute by means of "criminal letters" authorised by the Court of Session, a function that was transferred to the High Court of Justiciary, Scotland's highest criminal court, when it was established in 1671.[40] Prosecution by indictment in the name of the Crown has always been reserved to the Lord Advocate, and we shall return shortly to the disputes surrounding the ambit of the long established rule whereby the concurrence of the Lord Advocate is said to be an indispensable requisite to the bringing of a private prosecution in the Scottish courts.[41]

PARLIAMENTARY AND GOVERNMENTAL ROLES

The growing importance of the office of Lord Advocate in the public life of Scotland during the sixteenth and seventeenth centuries is discernible in other ways than his omnipotence in the area of prosecuting crime. Like his English counterpart, the Lord Advocate's duties embraced both governmental and legal concerns, but with very different emphasis on the significance of their administrative and executive involvement. The first appearance of the King's Advocate in the Scottish Parliament as an Officer of State, where he was placed at the bottom of the list, seems to have occurred in 1540, prior to which he was only a servant of the Crown.[42] The emergence of Officers of State as a separate and recognised body in the

---

[39] Omond, op. cit. p. 51.

[40] Stair Society, op. cit. p. 433.

[41] See post, pp. 300–309. Writing in 1797, one of Scotland's foremost institutional writers, Baron Hume concluded that "Prosecution [by the private prosecutor] is attended with this peculiarity, that the libel [i.e. charge] cannot be raised at the pleasure of the individual; and bears, by ancient and invariable style, to be raised with the concourse of his Majesty's Advocate, for his Majesty's interest; and truly receives this concourse, by the subscription of that officer, or some one authorised for him, at the bill for criminal letters" [the writ instituting proceedings]—Commentaries on the Law of Scotland respecting Crimes, (1844), Vol. ii, p. 125.

[42] Lord Medwyn in King's Advocate v. Lord Dunglas 1836 Sess. Cas. (1st ser.) (XVs) 314 at p. 332, citing Thomson's Acts, Vol. ii, pp. 355 and 368.

Scottish constitution dates back to 1487, but the King's Advocate was not originally included within their ranks.[43] They sat in Parliament by virtue of their official positions and formed what nowadays would be described as the Cabinet ministers of the Scottish monarch.[44] Although distinguished from the lesser category of Crown servants by the importance of their duties and privileges it is recorded that the Lord Advocate, in his new official capacity, was required to attend the execution at the Cross in Edinburgh of a man convicted of treason and to verify before Parliament that the sentence had been carried out.[45] The salary of the King's Advocate in 1582 was a meagre £40 Scots.[46]

His rank and eminence, however, were to grow rapidly, some of the signs of this increasing stature being revealed in the privileges accorded the holder of the office of Lord Advocate. On the foundation of the College of Justice in 1532 the King's Advocate "had place to sit within the Inner House to hear all causes reasoned and voted by the Lords except those wherein he was an actual pleader himself."[47] This right to plead from within the Bar was confirmed by an Act of the Scottish Parliament in 1532.[48] Another privilege of ancient origin is the right, still extant, of the Lord Advocate to wear his hat when appearing in court. Different explanations have been advanced as to the origins of this practice, the most credible being derived from the Lord Advocate's privilege of wearing a hat in Parliament House, exercisable by virtue of his position as an Officer of State, a right, it was claimed, that extended to appearing covered before the judges.[49]

The Lord Advocate's responsibilities as one of the principal Officers of State and a member of the Scottish Privy Council expanded with the growth of government and the vacuum created by the lack of direction on the part of the central administration in London. This part of the history of the Lord Advocate's office is inextricably interwoven with the struggle in Scotland to achieve its own Secretary of State responsible for the administration of Scottish affairs.[50] This goal was finally achieved in 1885

---

[43] *Ibid.* p. 331, citing Thomson, *op. cit.* p. 175.

[44] See *post*, fn. 53.

[45] *King's Advocate* v. *Lord Dunglas* (fn. 42, *ante*), p. 332.

[46] *Ibid.*

[47] See *ante*, p. 273.

[48] Stat. 1532, cap. 67; Omond, Vol. i, p. 15.

[49] Macmillan *op. cit.* p. 85. Less credence is attached to the explanation advanced by Lord Justice MacKinnon who wrote: "This is supposed to have had its origin from the fact that Sir Thomas Hope, who became Lord Advocate in 1626, had three sons who were Lords of Session. Before them he appeared covered, and so came to be allowed to do so before the other Judges. On the other hand, . . . Lord Wrightlands, was a Lord of Session when his father, Sir Thomas Craig, was still practising at the Bar. When his father appeared before him Lord Wrightlands took his hat off"—*On Circuit* (1924–1937), (Cambridge University Press, 1941), pp. 136–137.

[50] The story of this political campaign and the resultant legislation is dealt with comprehensively in H.J. Hanham, "The Creation of the Scottish Office, 1881–1887" (1965) *Juridical Review* 205–244. For a more succinct account see the document referred to *post* (fn. 73) at pp. 47–49, 65–66.

with the reconstitution of the Secretaryship that had been abolished in 1746.[51] During the intervening years the Lord Advocate, to all intents and purposes, was *the* Minister for Scotland. Speaking in the House of Commons on June 22, 1804, Charles Hope, the then Lord Advocate, elaborated on the vast array of duties associated with his office. "They who judge the office of Lord Advocate for Scotland," he stated, "by comparison with the dry formal office of Attorney General in this country, have, indeed, formed a most erroneous opinion on the subject."[52] Prior to the Union of 1707, the members of the executive government charged by the King with managing the affairs of Scotland comprised the following Great Ministers of State—the Chancellor, High Treasurer, Justice-General, Privy Seal, Treasurer-Depute, Clerk-Register, King's Advocate and the Secretary, if in Scotland.[53] They called themselves the Secret Committee. Due to a variety of causes each of these officials in time disappeared from the ranks of the Scottish administration leaving the Lord Advocate in solitary control of the country's affairs.[54] "To him" Hope disclosed, "all inferior offices look for advice and decision, and with the greatest propriety it may be said that he possesses the whole of the executive government of Scotland under his particular care."[55] As a well informed writer observed in *The Edinburgh Review* in 1824: "It has been said advisedly and on the most solemn occasions, that the Lord Advocate is the Privy Council of Scotland, the Grand Jury of Scotland, the Commander in Chief of the Forces of Scotland, the guardian of the whole police of the country and that, in the absence of higher orders, the general management of the business of the Government is devolved upon him."[56] According to Lord Macmillan, it was during this period that the office reached its summit of influence and importance in Scotland.[57]

[51] Hanham, *op. cit.* p. 205.

[52] H.C. Deb., col. 801, June 22, 1804.

[53] The composition of this inner council of Great Ministers of State was dictated in a letter from the Sovereign to the Privy Council dated December 13, 1683—Fountainhall, Vol. i, p. 250. Moreover, the same influential members of the Privy Council sat and voted *ex officiis* in the Estates (the Scottish Parliament) and in the powerful executive committee of the Estates known as the Lords of the Articles.

[54] As Hope described the situation to the Commons—"The Lord high chancellor was no longer in existence. The Lord privy seal existed merely for the purpose of appending the seal of Scotland. The lord chief justice general is the mere nominal head of a court at which he never presides. By a special act of parliament the lord justice clerk can have no seat in the house, and is wholly confined to his own Court."

[55] H.C. Deb., col. 802, June 22, 1804. As an illustration, Hope stated that "since the passing of the acts for the defence of the country, I have given to the Lord Lieutenants and others employed in carrying these acts into effect, no less than eight hundred different opinions on the subject of military arrangements."

[56] (1824) 39 *The Edinburgh Review* 363 at p. 369. *Cf.* the much quoted newspaper paragraph contained in Lord Cockburn's *Memorials of his Time*, Chapter 3: "Arrived in Edinburgh—The Lord High Chancellor of Scotland, the Lord Justice General, the Lord Privy Seal, the Privy Council and the Lord Advocate, all in one post-chaise, containing only a single person."

[57] Macmillan, *op. cit.* p. 86.

The nineteenth century was to mark the passage from the halcyon days of the Lord Advocate as the Scottish "manager" to a growing determination on the part of Scottish public opinion to establish a greater sense of accountability through the devolution of power in the person of its own Secretary of State. Administrative inertia, rather than political hostility to the move, was said to have delayed the eventual reform, the Scottish Law Officers and pertinent departments of State in London, especially the Home Office,[58] exhibiting a constant aversion to any change from the status quo.[59] Reform was eventually achieved with the enactment as a non-partisan measure of the Secretary for Scotland Act 1885.[60] This established a ministerial office of Secretary for Scotland, and after 1892 he was always in the Cabinet, except during the period of the War Cabinets. Since 1926 he has been a full Secretary of State.[61] The steadfast opposition of the Scottish Law Officers to change, especially the prospect of having to work with a new Scottish Minister of the Crown in place of their long association as legal advisers to the Home Secretary and the Home Office, is reflected in the savings clause contained in the 1885 enactment which stated: "Nothing in this Act contained shall prejudice or interfere with any rights, powers, privileges or duties vested in or imposed on the Lord Advocate by virtue of any Act of Parliament or custom."[62] The net effect of this savings clause was to preclude any question of the Lord Advocate's subordination to the new Secretary for Scotland.

Not that the physical surroundings in which the Lord Advocate was expected to function inside the Home Office contributed anything to the depth of that attachment. As described to the House of Commons in 1885 during the debate on the Secretary for Scotland Bill: "Anyone who had seen the room in the Home Office in which the Lord Advocate sat would not doubt for a moment that his condition had of late been of a provisional kind. It was a small and dark apartment and he doubted if it were even wholesome. The room was typical of the way in which Scotchmen (*sic*) carried on their affairs throughout the world; they carried them on in spite of the most adverse circumstances."[63] With the establishment of the new

---

[58] Formal responsibility for Scottish affairs had been assigned to the Home Secretary in 1828—see *Written Evidence by the Scottish Office* to the Commission on the Constitution, (1969), p. 47.

[59] Hanham, *op. cit.* pp. 206–207. Describing the administration arrangements around 1881 the author writes: "The Domestic Department of the Home Office simply referred 'the whole of the Scotch papers' to the Lord Advocate, leaving his secretary to sort them out. The Criminal Branch corresponded direct with the Scottish criminal authorities, the judges, the Prison Department, the Inspector of Police, the Crown Agent, and the Lord Advocate, just as they did with their English counterparts." When Lord Rosebery was appointed Parliamentary Under Secretary of State at the Home Office with special responsibilities for Scotland there was nowhere for him to meet deputations or conduct business in Edinburgh, apart from the Lord Advocate's office which he could sometimes borrow or share. *Ibid.* p. 208.

[60] 48 & 49 Vict. c. 61.

[61] Milne, *The Scottish Office*, p. 16 and Appx. II.

[62] 48 & 49 Vict. c. 61, s. 9.

[63] H.C. Deb., ser. 3, cols. 953–954, August 3, 1885.

Scottish Office in Dover House the Lord Advocate was given spacious accommodation though continuing his advisory functions with the Home Office.[64] Accompanying the Lord Advocate to the new surroundings was a small staff that by tradition had long consisted of only a legal secretary and a clerk. The former was usually a political appointee, the latter being the Lord Advocate's private clerk who managed his, by normal professional standards, modest practice. The inadequacy of these arrangements was to be drawn attention to by Lord Rosebery who, writing to Sir William Harcourt in 1881, declared: "The only administrative Scottish staff of late years has been the Lord Advocate and the Lord Advocate's secretary. When the government goes out of office, the Lord Advocate and the secretary disappear leaving no trace behind them. The new Lord Advocate and his secretary make their appearance on the scene and find nothing but the official furniture of their apartments."[65]

The advent of a powerful political figure, in the person of A.J. Balfour, to the ministerial portfolio of Secretary for Scotland in 1886, was to swing the balance of power away from the Home Office, and the office of the Lord Advocate, into the hands of the Scottish Secretary. Acting on Balfour's advice, the Cabinet decided to transfer responsibility for law and order from the Home Secretary to the Scottish Secretary.[66] Effect to these changes was given statutory form in the Secretary for Scotland Act 1887.[67] It contained no special clause safeguarding the privileges and duties hitherto associated with the office of the Lord Advocate, so it comes as no surprise to learn that the Bill was drafted without the knowledge of the Scottish Law Officers.[68] In the course of preparing the 1887 Bill and spelling out the Lord Advocate's powers it was ascertained that, with the exception of his status and responsibilities as the public prosecutor, these all derived from the Secretary of State for Home Affairs and not from either Acts of Parliament or the ancient privileges so carefully safeguarded by the 1885 enactment.[69] The exact nature of the Lord Advocate's so-called "prerogatives" was categorised, in a paper prepared for the Cabinet, as follows: "(a) Excepting as Public Prosecutor, the Lord Advocate has no functions which are not derived from the Home Office; (b) the responsibility which attaches to him in legislative measures depends on the confidence which is accorded him by the Government under whom

---

[64] According to contemporary records the Lord Advocate took a boyish delight in seeing that the new quarters were properly equipped, notably with stationery "correct in the quarterings, etc. of the Royal Arms for a Scottish Office." Several months, however, were to lapse before the Home Office handed over its Scottish papers relating to the previous five years and a telephone was installed connecting the new offices to the Treasury switchboard—see the archive records quoted by Hanham, *op. cit.* p. 234.

[65] *Ibid.* p. 244.

[66] *Ibid.* pp. 223–234, 241–242.

[67] 50 & 51 Vict. c. 52.

[68] Hanham, *op. cit.* p. 243.

[69] *Ibid.* p. 242. The author also points out that this conclusion had already been suggested by Lord Moncrieff in 1870 (see *Report of the Commissioners appointed to inquire into certain Civil Departments in Scotland* [c. 64] H.C. Papers, 1870, XVIII, *passim*).

he serves; it is all a matter of arrangement; (c) the patronage which has practically been vested in him is the legal patronage, subject to the approval of the Secretary of State. This legal patronage should still be vested in the Lord Advocate subject, of course, to the approval of the Secretary for Scotland."[70] Despite this illuminating analysis nothing was done to formally regularise the new relationship between the Lord Advocate and the Scottish Secretary, though the Prime Minister, Lord Salisbury, retained in his own hands the nominations to the most senior and prestigious legal offices of Lord President of the Court of Session, Lord Justice Clerk, Lord Advocate and Solicitor General for Scotland.[71] What is undeniable is the transformation effected by the 1885 and 1887 Acts in forcing the Lord Advocate of the day to leave the political problems of Scotland to the new "managers" in the Scottish Office and to concentrate increasingly upon his role as legal adviser to the government, including the Secretary for Scotland, the preparation of Bills relating to Scotland and the administration of the department of criminal investigation and criminal prosecutions (i.e. the Crown Office). In short, the Lord Advocate's office is seen as reverting to its original, predominantly legal character with the once prominent combination of political functions being relegated to a subordinate place within the portfolio.[71a]

PRECEDENCE, PRIVILEGES AND JUDICIAL PREFERMENT

Echoes of the Lord Advocate's former glory persist, however, in the precedence accorded the office holder over all the Scottish judges including the Lord Justice Clerk and excepting only the Lord President of the Court of Session.[72] Invariably the newest incumbent is sworn as a Privy

---

[70] Ibid. pp. 242–243.

[71] Ibid. p. 243. Advice on the filling of these offices was invariably tendered to the Prime Minister by Lord Lothian, the Secretary for Scotland, but no doubts were allowed to be expressed as to where the ultimate decision was made. For the present system see post, pp. 283–284, 288–289.

[71a] The Lord Advocate, however, in 1972 acquired ministerial functions relating to law reform (including responsibility for the Scottish Law Commission) and adjectival (procedural) law. These functions were set out in an announcement made by Prime Minister Heath to Parliament on December 21, 1972: see Vol. 848 H.C. Deb. Written answers, cols. 456–457. Under the reallocation of legal functions in Scotland between the Secretary of State and the Lord Advocate the latter assumed ministerial responsibility for the general oversight of the following subjects: (a) the jurisdiction and procedure of Scottish courts in civil proceedings; (b) the law relating to the enforcement of the judgments of Scottish courts in civil matters and the recognition and enforcement of judgments of foreign courts, other than orders for the payment of maintenance; (c) the law of evidence; (d) the law relating to prescription and the limitation of actions; (e) the law relating to arbitration; (f) the law relating to fatal accident inquiries. According to the Prime Minister's statement "The Lord Advocate's responsibility will extend to the consideration of proposals for the reform of the law relating to any of the subjects mentioned above and to the promotion of any necessary legislation affecting them. The existing powers of the Court of Session are not affected by the reallocation."

[72] Macmillan, A Man of Law's Tale, p. 84.

Councillor.[73] The traditional practice has always been to select the Lord Advocate from among the ranks of the Scottish Bar but the senior Law Officer of the Crown in Scotland, unlike the recognition accorded the Attorney General in England, is not the titular head of the Scottish Bar. That dignity is accorded the Dean of the Faculty of Advocates who is elected by his peers.[74] When appearing in court, however, the Lord Advocate leads all the other members of the Bar, including the Dean of the Faculty of Advocates.[75] At one time, the sensitive question of precedence involved the respective status of the Scottish Law Officers vis-à-vis their English counterparts. It arose specifically in 1834 in *The Attorney General* v. *The Lord Advocate*.[76] On the authority of the Lord Chancellor's judgment in that case: "There is no doubt nor ought there ever to have been any question about it, that the Attorney General of England leads the Lord Advocate of Scotland in all cases, whether Scotch (*sic*) or English, in the House of Lords, or any other court in which the Lord Advocate can practice whether in the Privy Council Court, the Court of Delegates, the House of Commons (supposing them not to be members) or in the House of Lords; they lead according to rank, first the Attorney General, and next the Lord Advocate."[77] The proper place to be accorded the Solicitor General, for England and Scotland respectively, was not dealt with by the House of Lords on the same occasion. Nevertheless, on the analogy drawn with the principle incorporated in article xxiii of the Articles of Union of 1706, it seems reasonable to conclude that, whether appearing alone or in conjunction with his senior colleague, the Solicitor General for England and Wales would accord precedence to the Lord Advocate but take rank before the Solicitor General for Scotland.[78]

[73] *Written Evidence* submitted jointly by the Lord Advocate's Department and the Crown Office to the Royal Commission on the Constitution 1969, (H.M.S.O.), p. 65. This departmental submission described the tradition as one where the Lord Advocate is "regularly sworn." *Cf.* Lord Macmillan who wrote: " . . . he is almost invariably appointed a Privy Councillor"—*op. cit.* p. 85.

[74] As such, the Dean presides at all meetings of the Faculty of Advocates and officially represents the Scottish Bar at public ceremonies. An interesting account of the early evolution of the pre-eminence of the office of Dean is contained in *The Minute Book of the Faculty of Advocates*, Vol. 1 (1661–1712) edited by J.M. Pinkerton, Clerk of Faculty, and published by the Stair Society, 1976. Prior to 1633, in relation to the Bench, the King's Advocate appears to have been regarded as the leader of the Bar. Subsequent to that date, however, the Dean had come to be accepted by the Lords of Session as the head of the Bar "at any rate in the sense of being responsible for the discipline of the Bar"—*op. cit.* pp. ii–iv.

[75] See the note in (1922) 153 *Law Times* 223. Although there is nothing laid down in writing within the Faculty of Advocates on the question of precedence in court, there is no doubt as to the settled acceptance of the following ranking—the Lord Advocate, the Dean of Faculty, the Solicitor General for Scotland: letter to the present writer by Sheriff J.V.M. Shields, March 29, 1961.

[76] (1834) 2 Cl. & Fin. 481; 6 E.R. 1236.

[77] *Ibid.* p. 485. In preparing his judgment, the Lord Chancellor revealed that he had "conferred on it with learned persons who had materials to form a sound opinion."

[78] See Edwards, *op. cit.* pp. 280–281. The analogy was relied upon by Sir John Campbell, then the Attorney General. Article xxiii declared, " . . . that all peers of Scotland and their successors to their honours and dignities, shall, from and after the Union, be peers of Great Britain, and have rank and precedency next and immediately after the peers of the like orders and degrees in England at the time of the Union." See (1834) 2 Cl. & Fin. 482.

Difficulties were once encountered in adhering to the principle that the choice of persons to serve as the Law Officers must be confined to the ranks of those who are members of the Scottish Bar. The advent of the first Labour Government in 1924, with Mr. Ramsay MacDonald as Prime Minister, confronted the new administration with the unprecedented situation of trying to find senior nominees among the Scottish Bar who were ideologically supporters of the Socialist Government in Westminster.[79] The radical suggestion was broached that a Socialist solicitor might be appointed Lord Advocate. The Lord President of the Court of Session, Lord Clyde, was asked for his opinion as to whether such a course of action would be supportable constitutionally. Extracts from the Lord President's memorandum in reply were subsequently published,[80] in the course of which it was shown that since the Court of Session and the Faculty of Advocates were first established in 1532, the person appointed to the office of Lord Advocate has always been a member of the Bar of Scotland.[81] Lord Clyde cited the description of the office given in Forbes' *Institutes of the Law of Scotland*, first published in 1722 as being "as accurate now as it was 200 years ago."[82] It states: "The King names out of the Body of Advocates an eminent person called Lord Advocate, who gives advice in making and executing laws, defends the King's rights and interests, concurs in all suits before Sovereign Courts, for breaches of the peace, and also in all matters civil wherein the Sovereign or any claiming under His Majesty has interest."[83] To execute these functions, as the supreme representative of the Crown in all criminal and civil cases the Lord Advocate must have the right of audience in the Court of Session and the High Court of Justiciary, which right has never been enjoyed or accorded to a Scottish solicitor.

In an earlier chapter, we considered the implications of such restrictive

---

[79] The fullest account of this episode is contained in Lord Macmillan's reminiscences, *A Man of Law's Tale*, pp. 81–84. As one of the leading *dramatis personae* in that unprecedented situation, Macmillan was in an excellent position to describe how the first Labour Prime Minister resolved the dilemma.

[80] See 1924 S.L.T. 43.

[81] According to Lord Clyde, himself a former occupant of the office of Lord Advocate: "It is part of the unwritten constitutional law of the land that the Lord Advocate and the Solicitor-General for Scotland are appointed from among the members of the Scottish Bar. This springs—in the same way as the other parts of that law—from long custom." He continued: "The existing system of administering justice in Scotland dates from 1532, when James V and his Parliament founded the College of Justice by a long series of enactments (cited under the year 1537, caps. 36–68). The present Judges and Bar of Scotland are none other than the 'Lords of Council and Session' and the 'advocates' or 'General Procurators of the Council' mentioned in these enactments. These 'Advocates'—along with the party litigants—were given by express provision the sole right of audience, and the forms of admission, oaths, and duties of the 'Advocates' forming the 'General Procurators of the Council' are preserved in use with but little change to this day. 'The King's Advocate' was given by another special provision the privilege of standing to plead within the Bar—a privilege he still enjoys by virtue of the original enactment. Since 1532 the person appointed to the office of Lord Advocate has always been a member of the Bar of Scotland." *Ibid.*

[82] *Ibid.*

[83] *Ibid.*

rights of audience to the appointment of future Law Officers in England and Wales.[84] Under the existing laws in Scotland in 1924 Ramsay MacDonald was forced to resort to the expedient of finding a Lord Advocate who was prepared to accept the seals of office on a basis that was entirely non-political. That choice fell on Mr. Hugh Macmillan K.C., a former editor of *The Juridical Review* and subsequently to become a Lord of Appeal in Ordinary.[85] In addition to the non-political character of his appointment as Lord Advocate, it was agreed that Macmillan "should discharge the duties and enjoy the rights of the office without participation in policy and, of course, without a seat in the House."[86] Whilst the unusual terms of this appointment occasioned a positive reaction among the Scottish legal profession, Lord Macmillan in his autobiography recounts also the condemnation voiced by some of the stalwarts of the Scottish Labour Party.[87] This opposition stemmed from their rejection of the constitutional understanding that selection of the new Lord Advocate was confined to membership in the Faculty of Advocates. Perhaps the real truth behind the criticism was dissatisfaction with the inability to find supporters of the right political persuasion to appoint as Law Officers, "it being found necessary to select as Solicitor General another Conservative lawyer, Mr. J.C. Fenton K.C., who was then serving as the senior advocate depute in the Crown Office."[88]

Another matter of contrast with the English Law Officers of the Crown, both in the case of the Attorney General and the Solicitor General, is the expectation that they be serving members of Parliament. Adherence to this convention has been less than consistent in the appointments of Lord Advocate and Solicitor General for Scotland. We have seen that in the first Labour Government in 1924 two non-party Law Officers were appointed for Scotland and neither sat in the House of Commons. In 1962 the Conservative Administration under Mr. Harold Macmillan accepted the necessity of selecting its Scottish Law Officers without regard to their not having seats in the Lower House. As with the unprecedented step taken in 1924, the appointments in 1962 were made without any expectation that the incumbents would contest parliamentary seats in the next general

---

[84] *Ante.* pp. 179–180.

[85] See *supra,* fn. 79.

[86] Macmillan's letter to the Prime Minister, dated February 7, 1924. In his reply, the following day, Ramsay MacDonald confirmed that: "The conditions on which you state you are prepared to accept the post of Lord Advocate represent accurately the basis which was agreed between us." Both communications were published in full in *The Times*, February 9, 1924.

[87] Macmillan, *op. cit.* pp. 83–84. Macmillan's selection, in his own judgment, was due to the intervention of Lord Haldane. Certainly, the new Lord Advocate made no secret of the fact that prior to accepting the appointment he deliberately took soundings as to "the attitude of my own party and I sought the advice of Sir Stanley Jackson at the Central Conservative Office. He was emphatic in urging the acceptance of the office if it were made to me"—*ibid.* p. 82.

[88] *Ibid.* p. 83.

election.[89] As it transpired, the Lord Advocate, Mr. Ian Shearer Q.C., was elevated to the Bench in 1964 and assumed the title of Lord Avonside. In more recent times, the increasingly ministerial role of the Scottish Law Officers, and the importance of their answerability to Parliament, has been reflected in three instances where the Law Officers concerned, who were not members of the House of Commons, have been elevated to the House of Lords. Thus, Lord Wilson of Langside served as Lord Advocate from 1967 to 1970, Lord McCluskey of Churchill was Solicitor General for Scotland from 1974 to 1979, and the present Lord Advocate, Lord Mackay of Clashfern, who has held the office since 1979.

An allied source of controversy is the perpetuation of the understanding that the Lord Advocate and the Solicitor General for Scotland enjoy a right of preferment to judicial office. In my previous work on *The Law Officers of the Crown* the same question was examined in the context of the once strongly held belief that the Attorney General for England and Wales was entitled to succeed to the Lord Chief Justiceship or the Lord Chancellorship, if either of those positions became vacant during his term of ministerial office. The conclusion drawn from past precedents, and confirmed in more recent years, is that no inalienable right of preferment exists.[90] For whatever reason, the contrary Scottish tradition still runs deep and can be explained in part by the influential role that the Lord Advocate continues to play in making recommendations, through the instrumentality of the Secretary of State for Scotland, for appointments to the Court of Session.[91] Since the Second World War, for example, with only one exception, appointment to the most senior judicial posts in Scotland have consistently been drawn from the ranks of those who have served as Lord Advocate.[92] Whether it represents a harbinger of a change of policy in this regard only time will tell but Lord Emslie, the present Lord President and Lord Justice General, never served as a Scottish Law Officer. It is noteworthy that this break with precedent, made in 1972 and associated with Lord Advocate Wylie's tenure of office, was paralleled in the decision to cease making the office of advocate depute a political appointment which had to be vacated automatically on a change of government. Subsequent Lords Advocate appear to have accepted the change of policy without challenge. There is also a well-established tradition, however embarrassing in its application, that the Lord Advocate recommends himself or his colleague if the urge to change roles from Law Officer to the Bench is made manifest. This tradition was challenged in 1965[93] when it

---

[89] *The Times*, October 13, 1962. In other Administrations less concern appears to have been exhibited in appointing a Scottish Solicitor General who was not a member of the House of Commons. Most recently (see *post*, p. 305, fn. 97) the unusual combination was seen of the Lord Advocate serving as a member of the House of Lords with the junior Law Officer handling the responsibilities of the Lord Advocate in the Lower House.

[90] Edwards, *op. cit.* Chapter 15.

[91] See *post*, p. 292.

[92] As Lord Wylie, the former Scottish Law Officer was appointed to the Court of Session in 1974.

[93] *The Times*, June 23, 1965.

became apparent that consideration was being given to elevating the Solicitor General of the day to the Court of Session, it being alleged that his qualifications for judicial office and professional experience were inadequate. Criticism by the Bar was directed against the political bias that was seen as operating in making appointments to the Bench, to which was added the realisation that fewer of the best advocates were inclined to take an active part in the political arena, with the consequent decline in the professional standing of those appointed to the Law Officerships.

A few years later, in 1968, another constitutional storm erupted in Scotland following the announcement that Lord Avonside, a judge of the Court of Session and former Lord Advocate, had agreed to serve as a member of the committee set up by the Leader of the Conservative Party, Mr. Edward Heath, to consider that party's proposals for a Scottish Assembly.[94] The controversy was further exacerbated by the disclosure that his nomination to the committee had been proposed by Lord Clyde, the Lord President of the Court of Session and himself a former Lord Advocate who had served in the post-war Conservative Administration under Sir Winston Churchill.[95] When the appointment of Lord Avonside to the Heath Committee was made public, the Labour Lord Advocate, Mr. Henry Wilson, expressed strong disapproval on constitutional grounds of one of Her Majesty's judges undertaking a task with such patently political overtones.[96] There ensued an unseemly series of public statements by the principal protagonists containing accusations and counter-accusations. Lord Clyde sought to dispel the misapprehensions surrounding his nomination of Lord Avonside by asserting that the Heath Committee was not to engage in "the formulation of policy for a political party," but rather to "analyse the feasibility, from a legal and constitutional point of view, of carrying out a policy which has already been formulated."[97] On such legal and constitutional issues, Lord Clyde maintained that an experienced judge of the Supreme Court in Scotland had an obvious contribution to make. What the Lord President's statement did not explain was why, of all the members of the Court of Session, a former Lord Advocate in a Conservative government had been nominated to serve on the committee set up by the Leader of the Opposition. In the face of the growing body of public criticism Lord Avonside announced his resignation from the committee, coupled with a lengthy diatribe describing the Lord Advocate's original questioning of his decision to serve as "complete nonsense."[98]

---

[94] *The Times*, July 27, 1968.
[95] *Ibid.*   [96] *Ibid.*
[97] *The Times*, July 30, 1968.
[98] The full text was published in *The Times*, August 6, 1968. Among the accusations levelled against Lord Avonside's acceptance of membership in Mr. Heath's committee was that it was "in breach of a long-standing constitutional convention that members of the judiciary should . . . stand aloof from participation in the political activities of any party." Avonside, in his reply, stated: "the origin [of the convention] certainly cannot be Scottish since the Lords of Session could be, and many were, members of the Parliament of Scotland. So far as I am aware, and this parallels our own history before 1707, no member of the highest

Some idea of the flavour of Lord Avonside's public statement may be gleaned from the concluding paragraphs which stated: "When great issues are abroad, and I believe they now are, it would be a poor creature who would not assist as best he could because of fear of the noise created by those who sacrifice truth to publicity and attribute to others the meanness of their own minds. There is all the difference in the world between a party-political issue and a constitutional issue, for which there has been no precedent in our time. If the political spleen and venom of the last 10 days has taught me one thing, it is that in the past I have paid far too little attention to what is happening in this country and the actions of those among us who attempt to arrogate to themselves a monopoly of speech. In the future, I will exercise to the full my undoubted right to comment on those happenings and those people."[99]

The controversy closed with the release by the Crown Office in Edinburgh of a statement by the Lord Advocate in the course of which the Scottish Law Officer briefly dissociated himself from the views expressed by Lord Avonside on the constitutional position of judges. With regard to the impression conveyed in the judge's threat to indulge publicly in political controversy, the Lord Advocate expressed the hope that Lord Avonside would not carry out this threat. "If, unhappily, he does he will just have to take the consequences."[1] This unsavoury episode, in which the conflict of personalities at times tended to obscure the constitutional issues at stake, has now passed into the pages of Scottish political history. It nevertheless constitutes a pointer as to the choice of direction that must be made in seeking to determine the proper role for the modern Law Officers of the Crown in Scotland. For, in criticising the incursion of Lord Clyde and Lord Avonside into the political arena, the Lord Advocate was conveying the impression that it was equally incumbent upon both the Law Officers of Scotland, when discharging the quasi-judicial duties of their offices, to likewise stand aloof from any semblance of being influenced by party political considerations.

ORIGINS AND DEVELOPMENT OF THE OFFICE OF SOLICITOR GENERAL FOR SCOTLAND

Sporadic reference has already been made in this chapter to the junior Scottish Law Officer of the Crown. It is necessary now to give a brief account of the origins and subsequent development of the office of Solicitor General for Scotland, from which it will be seen that the holder continues to exercise certain historic functions that are peculiar to his position. These unique duties apart, just as the Law Officers Act 1944

court in the kingdom today could be bound against his will to eschew party politics."—*loc. cit.* See further the letters to the Editor engendered by this conflict in interpreting the constitutional convention, *The Times*, August 10 and 14, 1968.

[99] *The Times*, August 6, 1968.
[1] *The Times*, August 7, 1968.

makes provision with respect of carrying out the functions of the English Law Officers so, too, in Scotland in the event of the office of Lord Advocate being vacant or his being unable to act owing to absence or illness the Solicitor General is empowered to step into the breach and fulfil the responsibilities of the senior office. In addition, the Lord Advocate may delegate authority to the Solicitor General to act on his behalf in any particular case.[2] This interchangeability between the Scottish Law Officers was not always so.

The year 1587 marks the first appointment of a King's Solicitor,[3] a commission being granted to William Macartney "one of the King's Clerks, Writer and special agent, solicitor and attender upon the writing of letters, keeping the diets before the Lords of Session, Secret Council or Exchequer, and in setting forward all things concerning the King's casualties and office of treasury for life with a fee of £100 yearly."[4] His successor, William Hart, for reasons not made apparent in the warrant of appointment dated 1591, was awarded a yearly fee of £600 and was promoted some years later to the position of King's Advocate.[5] Not all of the early King's Solicitors were eligible for advancement to the senior appointment which, as noted earlier, since its inception has continuously been restricted to members of the Faculty of Advocates. Many of the earlier King's Solicitors were essentially skilled clerks, a lower breed of Crown servants, who were expected also to discharge the duties of Church Solicitor, an appointment made by the General Assembly but subject to confirmation by the Sovereign.[6] Both appointments were vitally concerned with the protection of the King's financial interests, the Sovereign being entitled to a surplus of certain dues payable by the citizenry to Church ministers. This association of the King's Solicitor with the Church of Scotland has been perpetuated to the present day but for very different reasons, the Royal Warrant for each new appointee using the same language as that resorted to in the sixteenth century in imposing upon the

[2] s.2. One important difference distinguishes the position of the Solicitor General for Scotland from that of his counterpart in England and Wales. Thus, whereas section 1(1) of the 1944 enactment enables the English Solicitor General to act in place of the Attorney General *only* with respect to the latter's statutory powers and functions, section 2(1) is more expansive in its provision that "any functions authorised or required, *by any enactment or otherwise*, to be discharged" by the Lord Advocate may be performed by the Solicitor General for Scotland if any of the emergency situations exists.

[3] Most of the historical account that follows is derived from the two-part study of the office of "The Solicitor General for Scotland" by C.A. Malcolm, published in (1942) 54 *Juridical Review* 67 at pp. 67–79 and 125–143. The author was prompted to embark on this work because, apart from Omond's standard work on the History of the Lord Advocates, the subject had previously been totally neglected. Malcolm observes "Neither the institutional writers nor modern textbooks refer to the origin and the development of the 'Solicitor,' probably because of the difficulty in ascertaining facts of his early history, which are hidden in the MS archives of the Register House [in Edinburgh]."

[4] Malcolm, *op. cit.* p. 69.

[5] *Ibid.* pp. 70–71.

[6] *Ibid.* pp. 67–69. The office of Church Solicitor is traceable back to 1564, thus predating the earliest appointment of a Solicitor to the Sovereign.

Solicitor General the duties of "soliciting and agenting all Her Majesty's affairs as well relating to Her Majesty's service in all Courts of Judicature as for the affairs of the Church" and "to be present at all debates concerning Her Majesty's affairs or the affairs of the Church."[7] This mandate explains the otherwise anomalous attendance, in modern practice this is of a ceremonial nature only, of the Solicitor General for Scotland at each annual session of the General Assembly of the Church of Scotland.[8]

As time went on the duties of the King's Solicitor were sometimes shared between "conjunct solicitors",[9] appointments to these offices from the seventeenth century onwards becoming increasingly reserved to members of the Faculty of Advocates having a right of audience in all courts up to and including the Court of Session. So that no impediment existed in 1684 when, for the first time, the King's Solicitor was authorised to prosecute with the same jurisdiction as the King's Advocate.[10] In his work on *The Scottish Office*, Sir David Milne includes a list of holders of the office of Solicitor General for Scotland from 1709 onwards, preferring in the text to state that the title of Solicitor General "seems to date from about 1725."[11] This coincides with the accession to the junior Law Officership of Charles Erskine, who ultimately rose to become Lord Advocate and, later still, Lord Justice Clerk. Hitherto, the only counsel allowed to plead within the Bar of the Court of Session was the Lord Advocate. This special mark of distinction was not automatically extended to Erskine, the new Solicitor, it being necessary for him to present to the court a warrant under the Sign-Manual, subscribed by the Secretary of State, stating: " . . . whereas we have appointed Mr. Charles Erskine, advocate, to be solicitor . . . for Scotland and we being pleased to show a further mark of our royal favour it is our will and pleasure that a seat may be placed for him within the Bar of your Court, where and from whence he may be at liberty to plead cases in your presence. And we do hereby direct you to cause such to be placed accordingly."[12] This privilege was refused by the judges in 1760 when the last of the "conjunct solicitors" were appointed, it being maintained that the 1725 precedent infringed the Statute of 1537 which recognised only the

---

[7] The Royal warrant, examined by the author through the courtesy of the Lord Advocate's office, is that appointing Wm. Grant as Solicitor General for Scotland on January 12, 1955.

[8] Malcolm, *op. cit.* p. 67. Latterly, this function of the Solicitor General has been regarded as the Minister in attendance on the Lord High Commissioner to the Church and has occasionally been performed by the Lord Advocate.

[9] *Ibid.* pp. 76, 126–127, 133.

[10] *Ibid.* p. 77.

[11] Milne, *The Scottish Office, and Other Scottish Govt. Depts.* (New Whitehall Series, 1957). Malcolm, citing Fountainhall's *Chronological Notes*, p. 174, refers to Robert Pittilo[ch], advocate, as having been appointed Solicitor General under Cromwell's Commonwealth rule, *op. cit.* p. 74. Pittilo[ch]'s name, however, is not included in the list of Solicitors General for Scotland (from 1587 to 1941) appended to Malcolm's two part study of the office in *The Juridical Review*. Following the Civil War in 1652 the former Lords of Session were constituted new judges and named "Commissioners for the Administration of Justice to the People of Scotland"—only to revert to their former titles on the restoration of the monarchy—see the *Minute Book of the Faculty of Advocates*, *ante*, fn. 74, pp. iv–vii.

[12] Books of Sederunt, June 10, 1725 and quoted in Omond, *op. cit.* Vol. 2, p. 2.

right of the Lord Advocate[13] and, in any case, "there was no room for two Solicitors within the Bar."[14]

Interestingly, in the correspondence engendered by this dispute Lord Bute consistently referred to the "joint Solicitors for Scotland" whereas Robert Dundas, Lord President of the Court of Session, spoke of the privilege of pleading within the Bar as never having been given "to any Solicitor-General till in 1725, (when) his then majesty King George I was pleased to give a Sign Manual for that purpose to Mr. Erskine then appointed Solicitor . . . and since that period the same Priviledge has been enjoyed by the Solicitor-General."[15] The request of the joint holders of that office in 1760 was refused. Henry Dundas, on the other hand, one of the most notable of Scottish Law Officers, who served as the junior Law Officer from 1766 to 1775 and as Lord Advocate from 1775 to 1783, enjoyed the privilege of pleading within the Bar by virtue of a Royal Warrant to the effect.[16] No serious questioning of the Solicitor General's equal status with the Lord Advocate with respect to this particular privilege has since been entertained.

The Solicitor's office has come to be regarded as the natural stepping stone to the senior position of Lord Advocate,[17] from which vantage point elevation to a judgeship of the Court of Session or to the more prestigious appointment as Lord President or Lord Justice Clerk, have generally been regarded as within the reasonable expectations of the Lord Advocate, if his political party happens to be in power when one of these vacancies occur. Despite rumblings to the contrary, of which mention has already been made, the probabilities of this kind of judicial preferment remain at a higher level in Scottish affairs than that which currently describes the fate that will likely befall any of the English Law Officers who have aspirations to high judicial office. In each jurisdiction the Law Officers of the Crown represent a body of unrivalled experience, derived from the special position they occupy astride the executive, legislative and judicial branches of government. It would be extraordinary, and highly regrettable, if partisan obstacles were ever to be invoked by the appointing authorities to

---

[13] Strangely, in the course of the 1750 dispute, no reference appears to have been drawn to the Acts of Sederunt of the Court of Session 1662, pp. 83–84, which state: "That no person enter within the inner-barr of the Outer-house, where the advocats abide . . . and in like manner the macers are authorised to remove all perfons, of whatfoever quality, who fhall be found within the innermoft barr, where the Lords and clerks do abide, except the keeper of the minutt-book, the King's Folicitor, and one fervant appointed by his Majesty's advocat . . . "

[14] The episode is described by Malcolm, op. cit. p. 133.

[15] The text of the letters exchanged between Bute and Dundas is quoted in full in Omond, op. cit. Vol. 2, pp. 74–75. Charles Erskine, who was the first Professor of Public Law in Edinburgh University, held the Solicitorship until 1737, when he was promoted Lord Advocate, which office he held until 1742. In 1744 he was raised to the Bench as Lord Tinwald, becoming Lord Justice Clerk in 1748.

[16] Malcolm, op. cit. p. 134.

[17] In his informative essay Malcolm discloses that "of the eighty-one holders of the office from 1707 to 1943, forty-four did not reach the rank of Lord Advocate, but the majority of these were later promoted to the Bench"—op. cit. p. 141.

prevent the elevation to the Bench of an outgoing Attorney General or Solicitor General whose legal qualifications and experience would otherwise justify such an appointment.

EMOLUMENTS AND THE RIGHT TO ENGAGE IN PRIVATE PRACTICE

Another point of distinction that occupied the repeated attention of the House of Commons from 1850 onwards was the debate surrounding the mode and size of the emoluments payable to the English and Scottish Law Officers.[18] Underlying the much criticised stance, particularly, of the English Law Officers, who were constantly accused of being avaricious, was the struggle to preserve vestiges of the professional aspects of their offices. In England and Wales the right to engage in private practice had been finally terminated in 1894,[19] but it was not until after the Second World War that the principle was ultimately established, and incorporated in a Treasury Minute of March 25, 1946, that a single, all inclusive salary should be paid to the Attorney General and the Solicitor General "to cover all business of whatever sort done by the Law Officers for or on the instructions of any department of government."[20] Briefs delivered to the Law Officers in contentious business, however, would continue to be on a strictly professional scale with the important qualification "that the fees so paid shall be set-off against the salaries receivable by them."[21] By this formula, criticism of the allegedly inordinate remuneration paid to the English Law Officers has been finally stilled, whilst at the same time preserving their professional standing when they appear on behalf of the Crown in the courts.

The peculiar circumstances surrounding the geographical separation of the Scottish Law Officers from their professional base in Scotland no doubt helps to explain in part the converse approach adopted by the British Government towards the same question as it affected the Lord Advocate and the Solicitor General for Scotland. Thus, the Treasury Minute of 1894, in addition to providing for single inclusive salaries "to cover all business of whatever sort done . . . by virtue of their offices or . . . on the instructions of any department of government including contentious business" also expressly entitled the Lord Advocate and the Solicitor General for Scotland "to undertake such business on behalf of private clients as may be consistent with the proper discharge of their public duties."[22] As to these, the same Minute ordained that "the Lord Advocate shall attend in London throughout the Parliamentary Session, and the Solicitor General shall attend when and as often as his official duties make his presence in London desirable."[23]

---

[18] See Edwards, *op. cit.* Chapters 5 and 6.   [20] *Ibid.* pp. 117–118.
[19] *Ibid.* p. 100.   [21] *Ibid.*
[22] "Law Officers of the Crown in Scotland (Remuneration)" Treasury Minute dated August 22, 1894, published in H.C. Paper No. 327 of 1894.
[23] *Ibid.*

Envious glances, it might be thought, would be cast by the English Law Officers on this special dispensation awarded their Scottish colleagues in being allowed to continue their private practices. In truth, as Reports of the 1920 and 1930 Select Committees on Ministerial Remuneration acknowledged, the amount of private work undertaken by the Scottish Law Officers during their tenure of office was negligible.[24] That this was not always so appears from the evidence of the Lord Justice Clerk, James Moncrieff of Tullibole, before the Camperdown Commission to inquire into certain Civil Departments in Scotland in 1870.[25] The witness had been Lord Advocate under every Liberal Government since 1851. According to Moncrieff, accepting office involved "very considerable risk to the holder. A man in large practice at the Bar here will make certainly double the salary of the Lord Advocate. Leaving practice of that kind, and going away for six months, is a very hazardous affair even for the best employed counsel, so that the risk which the Lord Advocate runs is not inconsiderable; but I am glad to say that men at the head of the Bar have always been found to take the office."[26]

Just how far things had changed since 1870 with respect to the right to engage in private practice is reflected in the evidence given before the 1930 Select Committee by Lord Hailsham, the Lord Chancellor, who found it incongruous that the current Lord Advocate was appearing as counsel before the House of Lords on behalf of a private citizen.[27] Neither the same volume of work nor the same possibilities of making money at the Bar, Hailsham claimed, existed at the Scottish Bar so that the magnitude of the problem that bedevilled the position of the English Law Officers had never surfaced with the same degree of urgency north of the Border.[28] The adoption of the principle of a single inclusive salary for the Scottish Law Officers from 1894 onwards was used to telling effect in 1937 by Sir Stafford Cripps, Solicitor General in the Labour Government of 1930–31, when advocating reform in the mode of remunerating the English Attorney General and Solicitor General.[29] Indeed, during the period between the two World Wars private practice on the part of the Scottish Law Officers had become more and more impracticable owing to the increase in their parliamentary and other official duties. By 1927 or thereabouts it had become impossible for the Lord Advocate and minimal so far as the Solicitor General for Scotland was concerned. Following an interchange of correspondence between the Lord Advocate and the Chancellor of the

---

[24] See H.C. Paper of 1920, pp. iv, v, 18 and 21; and *Minutes of Evidence* [of 1930 Select Committee] p. 4, February 18, 1930.

[25] H.C. Papers, 1870, XVIII, *Minutes of Evidence*, pp. 39–40. The same source is informative on the subject of patronage and the position of the Lord Advocate relating thereto. See, too, the evidence of E.S. Gordon Q.C., Dean of the Faculty of Advocates and a former Lord Advocate, *ibid.* p. 65.

[26] *Ibid.* p. 40.

[27] *Minutes of Evidence*, May 21, 1930, p. 43.

[28] *Ibid.*

[29] See Edwards, *op. cit.* pp. 116–117.

Exchequer in 1946, both of the Scottish Law Officers relinquished their right to engage in private practice in exchange for an increase in salary for the Solicitor General.[30] This increase was authorised by a Treasury Minute in 1946, from which time onwards it can be concluded that the emoluments payable to both pairs of Law Officers, in England and Scotland, are governed by the same set of principles.

MINISTERIAL ESTABLISHMENTS, FUNCTIONS AND PATRONAGE

Notable divergencies, however, mark the scope of patronage discretion associated with the office of Lord Advocate, in contrast to that exercisable by the Attorney General for England and Wales which is restricted to the nomination of counsel to represent him in the civil and criminal courts. Indications of the once exalted and powerful position occupied by the Lord Advocate in Scottish history are still to be seen in the range of political and legal appointments that are either subject to his decree or are made on the basis of recommendations that he submits to the Secretary of State for Scotland.[31] Appointments to the following offices are made directly by the senior Law Officer in Scotland: advocates depute; legal secretaries and parliamentary draftsmen in the Lord Advocate's Department; standing junior counsel to government departments; the Crown Agent and Crown Office staff; procurators fiscal, Scottish members of the Council on Tribunals and its Scottish Committees, and members of the Scottish Law Commission. Appointments, on the other hand, to the ranks of Lord Ordinary in the Court of Session as well as to the Scottish judicial posts of sheriff principal and sheriff are made by the Crown on the recommendation of the Secretary of State for Scotland. Even in these cases, whenever a vacancy arises, it is the practice for the Lord Advocate to submit the name of his nominee to the Secretary of State for consideration thus ensuring that the effective voice remains that of the senior Law Officer of the Crown.[32] If this practice seems anomalous to an outside observer, it should be pointed out that in England appointments to what would be generally regarded as the equivalent offices rest in the hands of the Lord Chancellor, not the Attorney General.

---

[30] This information was kindly provided to me in July 1960 by Sir Andrew Innes, then Parliamentary Draftsman and permanent head of the Lord Advocate's Chambers in Dean's Yard, Westminster.

[31] H.C. Deb., Vol. 623, cols. 172–173, Oral Answers, May 10, 1960—statement by Mr. Wm. Grant, Lord Advocate.

[32] H.C. Deb., Vol. 623, col. 173, May 10, 1960. The importance of distinguishing between "the right to recommend," "the right to nominate" and the "right to appoint" with reference to Scottish judicial appointments was explained, using past precedents and tradition, by Lord Dunedin when giving evidence before the 1915 Royal Commission on the Civil Service, *Minutes of Evidence*, Cd. 8130, pp. 550–555. The witness was extremely well qualified to speak on the subject having occupied, in succession, the offices of Senior Advocate Depute, Solicitor General for Scotland, Lord Advocate, Secretary of State for Scotland and Lord President of the Court of Session. From the latter office he was elevated to be a Lord of Appeal in Ordinary, sitting in the House of Lords.

Since Scotland has no equivalent to the office of Lord Chancellor and it is the Lord Advocate who most closely approximates the functions of a Minister of Justice, it is natural that the Secretary of State, normally a non-lawyer,[33] should place strong reliance on the judgment of his senior legal colleague. In England and Wales, the opinions of the Law Officers might well be sought regarding potential appointments to the Bench but there is no understanding similar to that which pertains to the making of judicial appointments in Scotland.

Two locations, the Crown Office in Edinburgh and the Lord Advocate's Chambers in London, constitute the administrative base wherein the Lord Advocate fulfils his ministerial duties and those associated with his position as head of the criminal prosecutions department in Scotland. Never large since the days between 1877 and 1885 when the Lord Advocate, his legal secretary and a clerk were housed in cramped conditions in the Home Office, the present quarters in Westminster can also properly be described as of modest proportions. These offices house the small bevy of lawyers[34] who constitute the equivalent to the Law Officers' Department which is located in the Royal Courts of Justice and within which the variegated needs of the English Law Officers are served. In the same capacity the lawyers in the Lord Advocate's Chambers act as permanent legal advisers on Scottish matters to any Government Department that has no Scottish legal adviser of its own.[35] In addition, after a series of power struggles that sought to retain control in the Parliamentary Counsel to the Treasury, the Lord Advocate's Department since 1925 has been responsible for the drafting of all Government Bills that apply exclusively to Scottish affairs as well as those parts of United Kingdom Bills that relate specifically to Scotland.[36] Sir David Milne in his standard work on *The Scottish Office*, published in 1957, gives a detailed account of the work of the Scottish Parliamentary Draftsman, which remains broadly applicable to present day

[33] Two Lord Advocates, A. Graham Murray and Robert Munro, later became Secretary of State for Scotland (in 1903 and 1906 respectively) before going to the Scottish Bench and finally to the House of Lords as Viscount Dunedin and Baron Alness, respectively.

[34] Up to 1919 the appointment of the Lord Advocate's legal secretary was a temporary and personal one, the holder being expected to retire when the Lord Advocate left office. The Royal Commission on the Civil Service in 1915 considered the advisability of changing the office to a permanent one but, following strong protestations by Robert Munro, the then Lord Advocate, concluded that the status quo should not be interfered with: "It was represented to us . . . that his duties were of a personal and confidential character and the analogy of the Lord Chancellor's Permanent Secretary hardly applies, since the Lord Advocate is not responsible for the administrative control of the Scottish Legal Departments"—Cd. 7832, p. 68. Notwithstanding this conclusion, the post was converted in 1919 to an established appointment but retained the same title of Legal Secretary to the Lord Advocate. There are now nine Scottish lawyers occupying permanent civil service positions in the Lord Advocate's Department in London.

[35] Sir David Milne, *The Scottish Office*, (London, 1957), pp. 204–205.

[36] The Lord Advocate is always a member of the Ministerial Committee which scrutinises proposed Bills. For the fullest description of the advisory and legislative roles of the Scottish Law Officers, see the Memorandum by the Lord Advocate's Department and the Crown Office, submitted to the Commission on the Constitution, 1969 *Written Evidence*, Vol. 2, pp. 68–71.

conditions. The pervading sense of intimacy and direct involvement of its permanent officials in the daily commitments of the Law Officers of Scotland is captured in the description which states: "(The Department) is very small and its structure is the reverse of the normal broad-based pyramid; there are actually fewer executive and clerical officers on its staff than there are professional members . . . it is unusual in that the work, whether the drafting of a Bill or the giving of advice on a particular point, is normally dealt with from start to finish wholly by the member of the Department to whom it has been allotted. This is not to say, however, that he is precluded from consulting the Legal Secretary or any other member of the Department, and this is indeed freely done for the purposes of co-ordination as well as for assistance on difficult or unusual points. Moreover, each member of the Department has direct access to the Lord Advocate or the Solicitor General if he wants their views on a problem and will always consult them if he foresees political implications or possible litigation."[37] It should be added that the Lord Advocate also exercises some of his ministerial functions through the Scottish Courts Administration, situated in Edinburgh.

THE CROWN AGENT, ADVOCATES DEPUTE AND PROCURATORS FISCAL

The central machinery responsible for the smooth functioning of Scotland's indigenous machinery of prosecutions and criminal law administration remains in Scotland and is located in the Crown Office in Edinburgh.[38] It too, reflects a sense of history, its professional staff being headed by the Crown Agent, a position that first emerged in the late eighteenth century.[39] Customarily, the occupant will be a solicitor and a former procurator fiscal of considerable experience. With the responsibility of the Crown Office for the entire fiscal service it is natural that some of the small staff of civil servants should be drawn from the same background. Indications of the modest establishment that until recently performed all the Crown Office functions, and its inherent weaknesses, are evident in the thoroughly researched *Report of the Inquiry into the Patrick Meehan affair*, published in 1982, and which was conducted under the chairmanship of Lord Hunter. Prior to 1945 the Crown Agent held his appointment at the pleasure of the Lord Advocate, moving in and out of office with the political Minister, but it is now a permanently established

---

[37] *Op. cit.* p. 206.

[38] For a more expanded treatment of this subject see Lionel Gordon's chapter on "The Lord Advocate and the Crown Office" in *A Source Book and History of Administrative Law in Scotland* (Eds. M. R. McLarty and G. Campbell Paton) Edinburgh, 1956, Chapter V, pp. 55–65, and G. H. Gordon's article on "The Institution of Criminal Proceedings in Scotland" (1968) 19 N.I.L.Q. 249 in the course of which he wrote " . . . the oral law of Crown Office practice is more important than the written law of statute or judicial decision."

[39] L. Gordon, *op. cit.* p. 61, identifies Mr. John Davidson W.S., who acted in 1786, as the first Crown Agent, notwithstanding Hume's reference to the Agent for the Crown in 1765—see *Commentaries*, Vol. ii, 535.

position in the Scottish civil service.[40] It is from the Crown Office that directions emanate continuously to the network of procurators fiscal who represent the Lord Advocate in the various Sheriff Court areas. These instructions, unless the case is one of exceptional importance or difficulty in which eventuality the Solicitor General or the Lord Advocate may become involved, originate from the 12 part-time advocates depute who are appointed from the ranks of the Scottish Bar and act as Crown counsel.[41]

The office of advocate depute first made its appearance in 1544.[42] A significant change in the nature of the appointment appears to have taken place in 1970 when, following the general election of that year, the advocates depute who had served during the previous administration did not, as a matter of course, resign their appointments. The practice has continued ever since, it now being recognized that appointment as an advocate depute, unlike that of the persons appointed in normal circumstances to the office of Lord Advocate or Solicitor General for Scotland, does not *per se* involve affiliation with any particular political party. This change has introduced a desirable degree of continuity in the Crown Office. At about the same time, due to the increase in the volume of serious crime and the consequential expansion in the amount of work passing through the Crown Office, it became necessary to double the establishment of advocates depute. Prior to the early 1970s each advocate depute was assigned responsibility for one of the judicial districts into which Scotland was divided. This arrangement no longer exists and nowadays the twelve advocates depute take on any work that is assigned to them by the Law Officers or the senior-ranking Crown counsel.[42a] There is

[40] *Ibid.* Describing the position in 1915 the *Report of the Royal Commission on the Civil Service* disclosed that "Neither the Crown Agent nor the Advocates Depute are required to relinquish their private practice"—L. Gordon, *op. cit.* p. 67. The Lord Advocate of the time, Robert Munro, made suggestions which, if adopted, would have transformed the office to a whole-time, permanent official responsible for the civil and criminal business. Another 30 years were to elapse before this recommendation was effectuated. In many respects, *e.g.* in civil litigation by or against the Crown or any public department, the Crown Agent acts in a manner corresponding to that of the Treasury Solicitor in England and Wales. Other functions of the Treasury Solicitor are carried out in Scotland by the Solicitor to the Secretary of State.

[41] G. H. Gordon, *op. cit.* p. 272 describes these officials as "part-time, one might almost say, amateur prosecutors. They are counsel who act as advocates depute usually only for fairly short periods, and who before coming into the Crown Office may have had no experience in criminal matters, or may have had considerable experience on the defence side." The same writer adds: "It is often urged in favour of this situation whereby a fairly inexperienced advocate depute issues instructions to experienced procurators fiscal that the presence of the advocates depute injects into the system at a vital point an outlook which is not in any danger of being 'prosecution minded' " quoting *Alison on Criminal Law of Scotland* (1832), Vol. ii, p. xix.

[42] Omond, Vol. 1, p. 20. *Cf.* L. Gordon, *op. cit.* p. 60 who states that the office was first noted in 1582, citing Hume's *Commentaries*, Vol. ii, 132. Evidence refuting Hume is contained in Omond, Vol. 1, p. 20, fn. 4.

[42a] The description of the changes introduced in the Crown Office in the early 1970s derives from the *Hunter Report of the Inquiry into the Patrick Meehan affair*, H.C. Paper 444 of 1982, Vol. 2, pp. 767–770.

no ban on continuing with their private practices, so long as such commitments do not create the obvious problems. Reports on criminal cases received from the procurators fiscal are reviewed by the pertinent advocate depute who decides whether proceedings should be instituted, on what charges, and whether the case should be tried summarily or by indictment.[43] An accused in Scotland, it should be noted, has no right to elect trial by jury.[44] That is a decision made by the advocate depute in the Crown Office. So, too, is the election in trials by indictment whether to proceed before a sheriff and jury, where the maximum sentence is two years imprisonment, or before the High Court of Justiciary.[45] If the latter course is adopted, the advocate depute concerned will lead for the Crown. Only in exceptional circumstances will one of the Law Officers lead the team of Crown counsel at a trial or in an appeal before the Justiciary Court.

The impression should not be drawn from this brief summary of the Crown Office activities that the office of procurator fiscal is lacking in any true discretionary authority. Any such suggestion would be contrary both to its ancient lineage and to the specific functions that are associated with the procurator fiscal in terms of his supervisory responsibilities for the investigation of crime, an essential role that distinguishes the Scottish public prosecutor from the system which presently obtains in England and Wales. As the name suggests, the office was originally concerned with the collection of fines imposed by the court.[46] Until 1747, judges of the inferior

---

[43] Criminal trials are divided into two categories—*solemn* proceedings on indictment before the High Court of Judiciary or the sheriff sitting with a jury, and *summary* proceedings on complaint before the sheriff or justice of the peace sitting without a jury. Trials on indictment cannot proceed without the authority of Crown counsel (*i.e.* one of the advocates depute).

[44] In the 1960s the Grant Committee on the Sheriff Courts, in recommending an increase in the sheriff's summary powers of punishment, emphasised that its proposals "are not conditional upon the introduction of a right of jury trial. On the contrary, we would rather that the sentencing powers were not increased than that the increases were accompanied by a right to opt for trial by jury." *Report* (Cmnd. 3248) para. 227. The matter was considered afresh in 1975 by the Thomson Committee on Criminal Procedure in Scotland. All of its witnesses were opposed to any such reform, pointing to the delays in disposing of criminal business that would ensue, as well as the additional staff and accommodation that would be required. The Thomson Committee reaffirmed the Grant Committee's rejection of the proposal—*Report* (Cmnd. 6218) pp. 205–206.

[45] See Thomson Report *supra*, pp. 64–65. The same committee recommended an increase in the sentencing powers of sheriffs to three years imprisonment, a view previously expressed by the Grant Committee—*ibid.* p. 66.

[46] *The Stair Society, op. cit.* pp. 436–437. The fullest, often tedious, account of the development of this office is to be found in (1877) 21 *Journal of Jurisprudence* at pp. 24–26, 67–70, 140–143, 203–207, 248–253, 317–326, 370–378, 424–430, 485–486, 606–610, 655–658. The anonymous author's attempt to keep the series going in Vol. 22 was terminated without any explanation—see *op. cit.* pp. 24–28, 68–75. Procurators fiscal were originally paid entirely by fees and various perquisites, but by a Treasury Minute of July 5, 1850 they were placed on salaries out of which they were required to pay their deputes and clerks. Edinburgh and Glasgow were excepted from this obligation. This situation continued up to 1915—see the *Report of the Royal Commission on the Civil Service*, Cd. 7832, p. 55. The same Commission recommended that, as far as possible, appointments to the office of procurator fiscal, in

courts received no official salary, having to secure remuneration for their services out of the fines imposed, an exercise in which the fiscal also participated. His close relationship with the Sheriff Court is witnessed by the accounts in the seventeenth century of private parties prosecuting in that court with the concurrence of the procurator fiscal, to whom the sheriff had delegated his functions as prosecutor.[47] Later, the procurator fiscal is described in cases heard in the Sheriff Court as the "Pursuer in place of His Majesty's Advocate."[48] Traces of the original association with the sheriff, however, persisted into the beginning of the present century. As late as the Sheriff Courts (Scotland) Act 1877, the appointment of a procurator fiscal in that court was reserved to the sheriff subject only to the Secretary of State's approval.[49] Earlier, when the Burgh police courts were established in 1833 the magistrates themselves were given authority to appoint the fiscal who would conduct criminal proceedings therein.[50] The final authority of the Lord Advocate throughout the entire prosecution machinery, including the appointment of the officials to carry out these duties as his direct representatives, was first recognised in the Sheriff Courts (Scotland) Act 1907.[51] The removal from office of a procurator fiscal, however, on grounds of inability or misbehaviour, was vested in the Secretary (later Secretary of State) for Scotland and then exercisable only on the basis of a recommendation by the Lord President of the Court of Session and the Lord Justice Clerk.[52] These safeguards were retained in the Sheriff Courts and Legal Officers (Scotland) Act 1927,[53] but with the substitution of the Lord Advocate for the Secretary of State. The same enactment gave statutory sanction to the Lord Advocate's right to issue such instructions to procurators fiscal as he may deem necessary.[54]

This part of the legislation was hardly necessary, the practice of the Lord Advocate in issuing directives through the Crown Office to his deputes being traceable back to 1765 when the subject matter was the taking and reporting of precognitions.[55] Standing policy directives of this kind ensure uniformity and consistency of practice throughout Scotland's system of public prosecutions. It is understood that certain cases must be referred to

conjunction with other legal appointments in the government service, should be made without any regard to political opinions or services—*ibid.* p. 62. Its influence is clearly seen in the terms of the Sheriff Courts and Legal Officers (Scotland) Act 1927—*post*, fn. 53.

[47] *The Stair Society, op. cit.* p. 436.

[48] *Ibid.* Official recognition of the fiscal as public prosecutor was given by statute in 1701, c. 6.

[49] *Ibid.* Another authority maintains that by about 1834, although still described as the sheriff's fiscal, the fiscal was also directly responsible to the Lord Advocate and took instructions from him even in relation to cases not reported by precognition—G.H. Gordon, *op. cit.* p. 253.

[50] *The Stair Society, op. cit.* p. 436.

[51] 7 Edw. 7, c. 51, s.22.

[52] *Ibid.* s.23.

[53] 17 & 18 Geo. 5, c. 35, s.1. Since the passing of this enactment procurators fiscal and their deputes, with only a few exceptions, have been whole-time civil servants.

[54] *Ibid.* s.8(1).

[55] See Hume, *Commentaries*, Vol. ii, p. 535.

the Crown Office by every procurator fiscal.[56] These include the following categories; first, where there is doubt as to whether proceedings should be instituted or not; secondly, if there is any question of principle or importance which is raised; thirdly, any case which is serious enough to justify being tried on indictment and, finally, in a serious case where an accused offers a plea of guilty to a lesser charge than that on which he has been indicted. In addition, if experience suggests the advisability of constituting any new directives these will be circulated in the form of a Crown Office circular, bearing the full authority of the Lord Advocate.[57] Where there are no formal instructions to the contrary the procurator fiscal is left to the best exercise of his own judgment, no doubt acting in consultation with his colleagues in those large districts which require a fraternity of fiscals to discharge the multiple duties of that office. Even so, the procurator fiscal's decision may be challenged and brought to the attention of the Crown Office and there reviewed by one of the advocates depute. Thus, for example, an interim decision to try on indictment may be overruled and an order issued to terminate the prosecution or to proceed summarily in either the Sheriff Summary Court or one of the District Courts that were established by the District Courts (Scotland) Act 1975.[58] In short, whilst the procurator fiscal has undoubted discretionary powers his discretion is limited and conditional, the ultimate authority residing in the Lord Advocate and his representatives sitting in the Crown Office in Edinburgh.

In the investigation of crime the procurator fiscal occupies a very different position from that of the English prosecuting solicitor. In Scotland the procurator fiscal is totally independent of the police.[59] All serious offences committed within his jurisdiction must be reported by the police to the fiscal's office. Subsequent control of the mode and lines of the police investigation,[60] including the engaging of experts, the interrogation

---

[56] See Thomson Committee *Report, op. cit.* pp. 51–54, 64, 97, 102–103, and see, too, the tests generally accepted as the guidelines that control the procurator fiscal in deciding whether or not to prosecute, as set out in Renton & Brown's *Criminal Procedure According to the Law of Scotland* (4th ed.) at p. 14. The tests are quoted in full in the *Justice* report on "The Prosecution Process in England and Wales," pp. 10–11.

[57] See *ante*, p. 294.

[58] c. 20.

[59] A useful summary of the position and duties of a present day procurator fiscal, based on an address to the [English] Prosecuting Solicitors Society, in September 1970 is contained in Appendix C(IV) of the *Report of the MacDermott Working Party on Public Prosecutions*, Cmd. 554, H.M.S.O. Belfast, pp. 62–66. (see *ante*, p. 243). Procurators fiscal may be either solicitors or members of the Bar. The whole-time fiscal, their deputes and staff, are civil servants. They prevail in the larger districts. In a few of the smaller and more remote districts the procurators fiscal are part-time and normally carry on, simultaneously, their private practice as solicitors.

[60] In particular, all unexplained deaths are investigated under the direction of the procurator fiscal—see the memorandum submitted by the Solicitor General for Scotland to the Select Committee on Home Affairs, *Deaths in Police Custody*, H.C. Paper 631 of 1980, pp. 102–103. The Fatal Accidents and Sudden Deaths Inquiry (Scotland) Act 1976 (c. 14) consolidated and amended the previous legislation, especially the 1906 statute which endowed the Lord Advocate with a discretion to order an inquiry in the public interest into any sudden,

of witnesses if deemed necessary, the taking of "precognitions" or witness statements in cases which are to be tried on indictment, and decisions as to whether or not to oppose bail, are all in the hands of the procurator fiscal.[61] This long standing relationship to the police was given statutory embodiment in the Police (Scotland) Act 1967, section 17 of which provides that " . . . In relation to the investigation of offences the Chief Constable shall comply with such lawful instructions as he may receive from the appropriate prosecutor."[62] This range of discretionary responsibilities emphasises the independence of the procurator fiscal from the police. It is he, not the police, who must decide whether the evidence justifies the launching of a criminal prosecution. This relationship of the fiscal and the local chief constable, moreover, is in no way qualified by any later decisions taken by the Crown Office, amending or overruling the initial course of action decided upon by the procurator fiscal. One further statutory provision should be noted. It is contained in section 9 of the Criminal Procedure (Scotland) Act 1975, and empowers the Lord Advocate to issue directions to chief constables with regard to the reporting of offences committed within their respective areas.[63] This authority is analogous to that conferred upon the Director of Public Prosecutions in England and Wales[64] and is likewise designed to ensure uniformity in the matters of reporting and prosecution of certain troublesome offences.

Besides the powers normally delegated by the Lord Advocate to his representatives, the advocates depute and the procurators fiscal, to decide whether or not to prosecute, in what court, and with respect to what charges, until very recently it was accepted in Scottish law that the presiding judge had no power to withdraw a case in the face of opposition by counsel representing the Lord Advocate who, in this and in other aspects of criminal trials, is "the master of the instance." Delivering the judgment of the Justiciary Court in *Kent* v. *H.M. Advocate* in 1950 the

suspicious death or unexplained death. In future cases of death while in legal custody the requirement to hold an inquiry is mandatory, unless criminal proceedings have been taken and the Lord Advocate is satisfied that the circumstances of the death have been sufficiently established in the course of those proceedings—*ibid.*, s.1(1)(*a*).

[61] For fuller details see the Thomson Committee Report, *op. cit.* Chapters 2–13, 16–18.

[62] c. 77, s.17.

[63] Because of the breadth of the powers conferred upon the Lord Advocate by virtue of this provision—enabling the Crown Office to ensure that no prosecutions are in fact taken for certain types of offence or are taken only in certain circumstances—G.H. Gordon (*op. cit.* pp. 273–277) concludes that the Lord Advocate exercises something like a dispensing power. Among the policy decisions cited in support of this proposition are the following: (1) a refusal to prosecute in cases of therapeutic abortions carried out by reputable doctors under hospital conditions—the case of *Bourne* ([1939] 1 K.B. 687) would have been marked "No Proceedings" in Scotland; (2) notwithstanding the ruling by the Full Bench of the High Court that psychopathic personality is not sufficient ground for the Scottish law defence of diminished responsibility (*Carraher* v. *H.M. Advocate* 1946 J.C. 108), the Crown Office is free to accept pleas of guilty to culpable homicide, rather than murder, from psychopaths (see *H.M. Advocate* v. *Gordon* (1967) 31 J. Crim. L. 270),—and see, further, G. H. Gordon's *Criminal Law* (2nd ed.), pp. 392–397.

[64] See *ante* Chapter 1.

Lord Justice General, Lord Cooper, declared: "If . . . a practice of [the presiding judge] withdrawing criminal charges prematurely has arisen, derived from a supposed analogy with civil jury practice, or with the very different practice in criminal trials in England, I hope that it will now be discarded as wholly unwarranted in Scottish criminal administration . . ."[65] A modification of the Crown's mastery of the instance, through the trial judge's right to entertain a plea by the accused of "no case to answer" at the conclusion of the Crown's evidence—a right long available under English law—was introduced in Scotland only in 1980.[66] The potential ambit of the Lord Advocate's control over the criminal process is such that if he, or his representative, decides not to move for sentence after a conviction is returned, the accused would have to be discharged and go free.[67] It is also competent for the Lord Advocate to "restrict the pains of the law" by moving for sentence on a lesser charge which has been proven. Some insight into this unique discretion was offered by Lord Justice General Clyde in *Noon* v. *H.M. Advocate*, according to whom it dates "from a time when owing to the depth of partisan feelings juries, even sometimes judges, might be perverse or unfair; and the right to withdraw a case was thus preserved to enable an impartial prosecutor to secure that justice was done."[68]

PRIVATE PROSECUTIONS

Perhaps it is the unwillingness to ascribe these same attributes exclusively to the Lord Advocate, whilst at the same time accepting the burden of demonstrating judicial impartiality, which explains the law of Scotland on the subject of private prosecutions.[69] Instances of criminal proceedings for serious crimes being successfully instituted by a private citizen are extremely rare in the Scottish experience.[70] Even more

[65] 1950 J.C. 38; 1950 S.L.T. 130.
[66] See Criminal Justice (Scotland) Act 1980 (c. 62), s. 19.
[67] T. B. Smith, *British Justice—The Scottish Contribution*, Hamlyn Lectures, (1961), pp. 116–117. For a practical application of this procedure see *H.M. Advocate* v. *Smith* (1842) 1 Broun's Justiciary Reports 221, in which the accused had pleaded guilty to a charge of culpable homicide.
[68] 1960 S.L.T. (Notes) 51. Leaving aside the question of possible unfairness or perversity on the part of modern trial judges, it cannot be denied that the Scottish judge has less discretion to bend the law than that exercisable by the Lord Advocate. In the opinion of one writer, disposed to engage in a little chauvinistic praise of his native country, "it says a great deal for a system of public prosecution that in many cases the mercy of the prosecution may be preferable to the justice of the law"—(1968) 19 N.I.L.Q. 249 at p. 277.
[69] See Lord Normand, "The Public Prosecutor in Scotland" (1938) 54 L.Q.R. 345 at pp. 347–349, quoting from Hume's *Commentaries on the Law of Scotland* (1844), Vol. ii, p. 125: See, too, the review article on "The Powers and Importance of the Lord Advocate of Scotland" (1824) 39 *Edinburgh Review* 363, which is generally attributed to Henry Cockburn, who later became Solicitor General for Scotland in 1830.
[70] In a case in 1887, *Alex Robertson*, 15 R.(J.)1; 1 White 468, it was stated that an application to the court to order the Lord Advocate to concur in a prosecution had not been granted since the Revolution, and that private prosecutions had almost ceased to exist. For a summary of the prevailing position in Scottish law see Gerald H. Gordon: "Institution of Criminal Proceedings in Scotland" (1968) 19 N.I.L.Q. 249 at pp. 250–252. Gordon

exceptional is the situation illustrated in dramatic terms by a recent case in which the Lord Advocate, having decided not to indict again (two previous indictments having had to be deserted) the persons suspected of a gang rape because of what was believed to be the inability of the victim to testify against her assailants, was effectively precluded from granting his concurrence to a private prosecution. Fortunately such obstacles or objections that might be raised by Scottish criminal procedure permits the ordinary citizen to circumvent the Lord Advocate and to make application directly to the High Court of Justiciary for its approval of a private prosecution.[71]

Prior to the Glasgow rape case in 1982 only one such application for a private criminal prosecution had been successful and that was in 1909 in the case of *J. & P. Coats Ltd.* v. *Brown*.[72] At the heart of this unusual episode in the history of Scottish criminal law were allegations of commercial fraud involving the substitution of a lower grade of coal than that contracted for by the injured private party, a well known Scottish manufacturer of Paisley thread. At the commencement of the hearing before the Justiciary Court the Lord Advocate, Alexander Ure K.C. (later Baron Strathclyde), argued that "No subject of His Majesty has any right to demand the concurrence of the public prosecutor. Primarily, by the law and constitution of Scotland the right and duty of criminal prosecution is in the hands of the public prosecutor. He must exercise his discretion in the first instance and withhold or grant his concurrence accordingly as he thinks that there is or is not a reasonable ground for criminal prosecution."[73] In the instant circumstances, the Lord Advocate stated that he based his decision upon the improbability of a conviction being secured. Nevertheless, he acknowledged that he was not supreme in this matter. "I am not the sole judge and master of the situation. To use the familiar words of Baron Hume: 'The Lord Advocate is not absolute and unaccountable on these occasions.'[74] I cannot deny that the right of private prosecution still

---

distinguishes, first, the group of prosecutors acting under statutory powers such as customs officers, education authorities, and factory inspectors and, secondly, persons with a private right to prosecute for statutory offences, *e.g.* landowners afflicted by day poachers, and chartered bodies prosecuting someone falsely claiming to be a registered member. The first group are entitled to proceed without the concurrence of the public prosecutor. The second group requires the concurrence of the appropriate public prosecutor or leave of the court except in a statutory offence where imprisonment without the option of a fine is not competent—Criminal Procedure (Scotland) Act 1975, s. 311(4).

[71] See Edwards, *op. cit.* pp. 356, 399–400, where the comparison is drawn with the provision that once existed in English law whereby a private prosecutor, in the event that the D.P.P. intervened and withdrew the prosecution, could apply to a High Court judge to have the prosecution reinstated and continued either by the Director or the private prosecutor himself—see s.6 of the Prosecution of Offences Act 1879. This right was summarily abolished by the Prosecution of Offences Act 1908, s.2(2) and Sched. In explaining the procedure in Scotland in 1938 Lord Normand concluded: "It may safely be said that private prosecution either before the High Court of Justiciary or before the Sheriff Courts . . . is virtually unknown, and is of little more than antiquarian interest"—*op. cit.* p. 349.

[72] 6 Adam's Reports 19; 1909 S.C. (J.) 29.

[73] Quoted verbatim in Macmillan, *A Man of Law's Tale*, p. 112.

[74] *Commentaries*, Vol. ii, p. 118.

remains in the criminal law of Scotland, although very seldom availed of—never, so far as I am aware, during the last 200 or 300 years[75]— . . . Unless in very exceptional and unusual circumstances, the Court might probably think that they ought not to override my discretionary powers; but . . . if it can be shown that I have failed in my public duty, if it can be shown that I have acted in this matter corruptly, oppressively, or wantonly I do not deny that there is a remedy open to the complainers and there ought to be."[76]

That remedy might take one of two forms. The private prosecution could be sanctioned by the court either without the concurrence of the Lord Advocate or by the court ordering the Lord Advocate to grant his concurrence. According to the Lord Justice Clerk, a view shared by his judicial colleagues, the more practical and least embarrassing course is that the court should authorise the private party to proceed, rather than that a prosecutor, unwilling in the exercise of his discretion to grant concurrence, should be directed to do so. "It seems to me," said the Lord Justice Clerk, "to be not a good mode of correcting an unsatisfactory exercise of a vested discretion that an official should be forced into a position of saying in words that he concurs, when his non-concurrence is overruled as not being in the circumstances right."[77] By a majority, the High Court affirmed that, in the case brought before them, no real reason had been shown why a prosecution should not be allowed. The lone dissenting voice of Lord M'Laren deprecated very strongly the notion that the Justiciary Court was to be a court of review of the work of the Lord Advocate's department "a task for which, by its constitution and means of informing itself, the Court

---

[75] In his evidence before the Select Committee on Public Prosecutors (1854–55) the Lord Advocate, James Moncrieff, recalled "one instance and one only, of a regular prosecution by a private party since I came to the Bar." Through the kindness of the late Sheriff J.V.M. Shields, then Senior Lecturer in Criminal Law and Criminology, Faculty of Law, University of Edinburgh, who examined the index of all the criminal cases brought before the Justiciary Court between March 9, 1833 (when Moncrieff was admitted Advocate) and June 12, 1855 (when he gave evidence before the Select Committee), it can be stated with confidence that Moncrieff's assertion was unfounded. When speaking in 1855, he may have been thinking of *Haggart* v. *Brown*, a private prosecution for perjury in which the Lord Advocate, Andrew Rutherford, had concurred. It was, however, never proceeded with because when the case was called the prosecutor did not appear. Since, therefore, there was in fact no true private prosecution in that case, the Lord Advocate's statement in the *J. & P. Coats* case (quoted in text above) is probably correct: letter by Shields to the author, March 29, 1961. Prior to the *Coats* case, the issuance of a bill of letters had been refused in *Mackintosh* (1872) 2 Couper 236 and 367, and *Robertson* (1887) 15 R. (J.) 1, 1 White 468. In the earlier cases, members of the High Court of Justiciary had differed sharply on the court's power to direct the public prosecutor to give his concurrence.

[76] Quoted in Macmillan, *op. cit.* pp. 112–113.

[77] 1909 S.C. (J.) 34. "There is not vested in the public prosecutor" the Lord Justice Clerk stated "an absolute right of veto. . . . He must, if called on, shew cause for his declinature, and the Court can consider the question whether the withholding of the concurrence in the circumstances may involve a wrong to the citizen complaining, and a failure of public justice. For the citizen desiring to prosecute is seeking to invoke the law not for reparation to himself, but *ad vindictam publicam*, and this is clearly expressed in the criminal letters granted to him."

is alike unfitted . . . ."[78] A similar repugnance was voiced by the other members of the court who readily admitted they could conceive of very few cases in which the court would so interfere.[79] The circumstances presented to them in *J. & P. Coats Ltd.* v. *Brown* being of that exceptional character, the order was issued allowing "criminal letters to be expeded at the instance of the complainers, and that without the concurrence of His Majesty's Advocate."[80] It only remains to record the fact that at the ensuing trial before the Lord Justice Clerk and a jury the verdict was "guilty as libelled."[81] Counsel for the private prosecutor, Lord Macmillan (as he subsequently became) hailed the verdict as "a notable forensic victory."[82] No one would question his other prediction that the case of *J. & P. Coats Ltd.* v. *Brown* was unlikely to be soon forgotten in the Crown Office.

This ancient right on the part of the private citizen was not to be invoked again until 1961 in *M'Bain* v. *Crichton*,[83] when the issue at stake was the legality or otherwise of selling "Lady Chatterley's Lover," a work that the complainer alleged was obscene. The instigator of the action to proceed by way of a bill of criminal letters, in the face of opposition by the Lord Advocate to the institution of a public prosecution, was a Glasgow chartered accountant and vice-president of a union of boys' clubs. This voluntary office, it was claimed, gave the petitioner a particular interest to prevent the corruption of Scottish youth. At the hearing before the High Court the Lord Advocate stated that he had investigated the matter more than once and had reached the conclusion that the prosecution would not be justified. No further reasons were disclosed, though it cannot have been irrelevant to his decision that the English prosecution in respect of the same book had been unsuccessful at the Central Criminal Court.[84] Rejecting the application for criminal letters, the Lord Justice General, adopting the view of the law expressed by Hume, stressed the need for "some substantial and peculiar interest in the issue of the trial" to be

[78] 1909 S.C. (J.) 39. Lord M'Laren recalled that he had been a member of the Court in *Robertson* (*ante*, fn. 75). In the present case, he also stated: "It is one thing to say that we may give redress against an arbitrary refusal of the Lord Advocate's concurrence, or a refusal on legal grounds which are disclosed to us; and it is quite a different proposition that we are to review the Lord Advocate's decision that the facts do not warrant a prosecution"—*ibid.* p. 38.
[79] *Ibid.* p. 40. The Lord Justice General described the court's ruling as a "disagreeable necessity."
[80] *Ibid.* p. 41.
[81] Macmillan, *op. cit.* p. 114. Strangely, this sequel to the proceedings in the High Court of Justiciary seems to have escaped Sheriff Gordon's eagle eye—see (1968) 19 N.I.L.Q. 249 at p. 251.
[82] *Op. cit.* p. 114.
[83] 1961 J.C. 25, S.L.T. 209. All the earlier authorities, including the principles as set forth in the institutional writers (*Hume on Crimes* Vol. ii, p. 118 *et seq.* and *Alison on Criminal Law of Scotland* (1832), Vol. ii, pp. 99 and 100), are reviewed in the judgment of Lord Clyde, Lord Justice General. Lord Guthrie described the procedure as "a branch of Scottish legal administration of which we have reason to be proud"—*ibid.* p. 31.
[84] The case is reported as *R* v. *Penguin Books Ltd.* (1961) Crim. L.R. 176—see, too, *ibid.* pp. 137–138, and 224–233 (containing a useful bibliography of contemporary writing on the case).

shown by the petitioner if the court was to accept the claim that the Lord Advocate's decision was not the last word on the subject of prosecution.[85] In Lord Guthrie's summary of the matter "the good intentions of the complainer, which we can all respect, are not sufficient to entitle him to the exceptional remedy which he claims."[86]

The same principle had been adopted by the court in *J. & P. Coats Ltd.* v. *Brown* and accepted as having been fulfilled in the circumstances of that case. In *McBain* v. *Crichton*, on the other hand, the High Court ruled that the wrong alleged was a purely public one. "The distinction," Lord Justice General Clyde stated, "is no mere technicality. It involves a clear and definite principle embedded in our law, stated in the institutional writers and referred to again and again in the decisions of this Court."[87] As in the earlier case of *J. & P. Coats Ltd.* v. *Brown* the members of the court were at pains to underline the fact that their role was not that of reviewing the Lord Advocate's exercise of his discretion. According to Lord Guthrie, "that would be to confuse the functions of a Court of law and of the Minister of the Crown charged with the duty of the prosecution of crime."[88] In a passage strikingly at variance with the opinions recently expressed by some of his English judicial colleagues on the same general subject,[89] Lord Clyde, the Lord Justice General, concluded that it is utterly inconsistent with the role of the Lord Advocate as the State's public prosecutor "that the Courts should examine, as it was suggested that it would be proper or competent for us to do, the reasons which have affected the Lord Advocate in deciding how to exercise his discretion, and it would be still more absurd for this Court to proceed to review that soundness. Any dicta indicating that such a course is open to any Court are, in my view, quite unsound."[90] This approach to non-reviewability of the Lord Advocate's discretion is granting his concurrence to a bill for criminal letters was reaffirmed by the High Court in 1975 in *Meehan* v. *Inglis, Struthers and Gall*.[91] In that case the court refused the petitioner's bid to secure its authority to the institution of a private prosecution for perjury allegedly committed at his trial for murder. Subsequent events, moreover, served to underline the *caveat* expressed in the *Meehan* case when, referring to Lord Clyde's dictum in *McBain*, the Justiciary Court stated: "We see no reason to differ from that expression of opinion in so far as it is directed to cases where the Lord Advocate's reasons for refusing concurrence are derived from an exercise of his impartial judgment after

---

[85] 1961 J.C. 25 at pp. 29–30.
[86] *Ibid*. p. 32.
[87] *Ibid*. p. 30.
[88] *Ibid*. p. 31.
[89] See *ante*, pp. 129–137, and 140.
[90] 1961 J.C. 25 at p. 29.
[91] The judgment is contained in the *Hunter Report* (*ante*, fn. 42a) Vol. 4, pp. 298–302. Other instances, equally unsuccessful, of the same applicant's repeated endeavours to secure the issuance of criminal letters are referred to in the same report, Vol. 3, pp. 898–899. See, too, 1974 S.L.T.(Notes) 61 and *Trapp* v. *M.*; *Trapp* v. *Y.* 1971 S.L.T.(Notes) 30.

exhaustive investigation of all sources of evidence."[91a] For the avoidance of doubt, the Justices referred specifically to the assurances they had received from the advocate depute, representing the Lord Advocate, that the fullest investigation had been made into the whole circumstances of the Meehan trial, and that both the Lord Advocate and two of his predecessors had previously examined the allegations of perjury and had decided against a public prosecution.

These assurances were later shown to lack total reliability. As viewed by Lord Hunter, who conducted the inquiry into the actions of the police and the Crown Office before and after the trial of Patrick Meehan, the information conveyed to the High Court of Justiciary in May 1975, concerning the extent of the investigations and precognition carried out by the Crown, was "restricted and in a number of respects incorrect. . . . That information was of material importance to issues which arose for decision by the Court, since it related to the reason or reasons of the Lord Advocate for refusing his concurrence to the bill [for criminal letters]."[91b] Whatever the limitations revealed in the course of the inquiry as to the shortage of legal manpower in the Crown Office, the rebuke administered by Lord Hunter could hardly be said to be unwarranted: "The Court" he stated "is entitled to assume that information on matters of fact given at the Bar by any counsel is given upon instructions. In the case of Crown Counsel, the position is one of particular trust. If information is given by Crown Counsel about matters which are within the knowledge of the Crown, for example about action taken or investigations or enquiries made by or on behalf of the Crown, the Court must be able to place absolute reliance on that information as being both accurate and objective. Any apparent mistake should be corrected at the first opportunity. . . . It does not appear that any such steps were taken."[91c]

In the invervening years between the decision in 1909 and that in 1975, mentioned above, the view was expressed that this residual right of private prosecution had fallen into such disuse that the right should be abolished. The Scottish Law Commission, in its first annual report in 1966,[92] noted that among the questions which it had under consideration was whether any change should be made in the law relating to private prosecutions. No report on the subject by that body has, as yet, been forthcoming. In 1975, the major report of the inter-departmental Committee on Criminal Procedure in Scotland, under the chairmanship of Lord Thomson, concluded that no change in the law was called for.[93] The Thomson report pointed out that in presenting a bill for criminal letters the applicant must aver that the Lord Advocate has not only refused to prosecute but has also

[91a] *Hunter Report, op. cit.*, Vol. 4, p. 300.
[91b] *Ibid.* Vol. 3, pp. 901–902.
[91c] *Ibid.* p. 901.
[92] H.M.S.O., Edinburgh, para. 36(e).
[93] *Criminal Procedure in Scotland (Second Report)* Cmnd. 6218 (H.M.S.O., Edinburgh), pp. 121–123.

refused to concur in a private prosecution. As regards summary cases, the same requirement for the concurrence of a public prosecutor is to be found in the Criminal Procedure (Scotland) Act 1975, s.311(4).[94] "We cannot conceive" said the Committee, "of circumstances today in which a Lord Advocate as public prosecutor could be expected properly to concur in a private prosecution which he was not prepared himself to instruct as the public prosecutor. We accordingly recommend that in no circumstances should the Lord Advocate or public prosecutor be required to concur in a private prosecution."[95]

The pitfalls of formulating such an unqualified recommendation was to be amply demonstrated a few years later, in 1982, in what has come to be known as the Glasgow rape case. No public record is available as to the reactions of the members of the Thomson Committee to the extraordinary circumstances surrounding this case and which were eventually brought to light in Parliament.[96] Indirectly, and through the misjudgment of the minister concerned in commenting to the press on the quality of the evidence in the case, the Solicitor General for Scotland was forced to resign.[97] At least one fundamental principle was underlined by the Commons' and Lords' debates on the handling of this case, namely, the accountability of the Scottish Law Officers, like their brethren in England and Wales, for every action or decision taken in their name and within the scope of their ministerial duties.[98] The case began in the normal fashion with the procurator fiscal, following a report by the police, charging four youths with rape and attempted murder. The alleged rape, in October 1980, had been committed with unusual ferocity, necessitating the victim to receive some 150 stitches as emergency treatment for the cuts inflicted upon her. Following consideration of the file in the Crown Office three of the youths were indicted for rape and assault with intent to cause permanent disfigurement and danger to life, the prosecution being set down for trial at the June 1981 sitting of the High Court in Glasgow. Before the case was called, Crown counsel in charge of the prosecution arranged for the complainant to be examined by a consultant psychiatrist, doubts being entertained as to whether the victim was in a fit state to give evidence. These doubts were confirmed by the psychiatrist's report which concluded that there was a hazard of suicide if she was required to appear in court and testify as to the horrible experience to which she had been

---

[94] The *Thomson Report* also contains a useful account of Scottish law pertaining to summary prosecutions brought by (1) public bodies and (2) landowners and others, for certain statutory offences. Among the Committee's specific recommendations all such possible prosecutions should be reported to and, if approved, be conducted by the procurator fiscal. *Op. cit.* paras. 31.04–31.07.

[95] *Thomson Report, op. cit.* p. 122.

[96] See *The Sunday Times*, January 24, 1982.

[97] See H.L. Deb., Vol. 426, cols. 697–705, January 21, 1982—statement by Lord Mackay of Clashfern, Lord Advocate, and H.C. Deb., Vol. 16 (6s.), cols. 423–434, January 21, 1982, statement by the Solicitor General for Scotland, Mr. Nicholas Fairbairn, who later resigned.

[98] For earlier instances of the application of the doctrine of ministerial accountability to the Scottish Law Officers, see Edwards, *op. cit.* p. 188, fn. 37.

subjected. Later, the psychiatrist was to point out that he had not stated that there could never be a prosecution because of the state of her health, introducing a further element of confusion in the public's mind as to what had transpired.[99]

Acting on the basis of his interpretation of the medical report, and consequent inability of the Crown to call its principal witness, together with a prognosis of limited improvement in the victim's health, the advocate depute representing the Lord Advocate decided that the indictment should be allowed to fall.[1] No reference was made to either of the Law Officers before Crown counsel gave his instructions that the case should be dropped and the court informed of his decision.[2] In a letter dated September 15, 1981 the procurator fiscal at Glasgow, acting on the instruction of the Crown Office, informed each of the accused that there would be no further criminal proceedings against them, it being subsequently explained that the letters were intended to relieve the strain upon the defendants caused by the fear of the charges hanging over them. The victim was not informed of the Crown Office decision. As we have already seen, authority to make this kind of decision is exclusively within the discretion of the Lord Advocate's representative and no leave of the presiding judge is required to withdraw the charge. Because of the public controversy engendered by the handling of the Glasgow rape case the Lord Advocate subsequently announced a change of policy in the handling of charges involving rape or murder. In future, no decision to drop proceedings before the hearing of the evidence at the trial has begun will be made by Crown counsel without the question being referred to the Lord Advocate personally for his ruling.[3] This directive has been added to those administered by the Crown Office and communicated to the procurators fiscal and advocates depute as the standing instructions for public prosecutions conducted in the name of the Lord Advocate.

Parliamentary debate surrounding the decision taken by the Crown counsel to discontinue the prosecution centred on a combination of revelations contained in the Scottish news media. These included a claim that the police had in their possession a signed confession by one of the original accused, a disclaimer by the psychiatrist denying that he had advised against a prosecution because it might damage the victim's mental health, and, most significantly, an assertion by the complainant that she was now, as she had always been, ready and willing to testify. No satisfactory explanation was tendered to the House of Commons as to why the irreversible step had been taken to discontinue the criminal prosecution rather than allow for the possibility of filing a fresh indictment at a

---

[99] *The Times*, January 23, 1982, and see also *H.* v. *Sweeney* 1983 S.L.T. 48 at p. 52.
[1] A full account of the various steps taken by Crown counsel leading up to the discontinuance of the prosecution is given in the Solicitor General's speech to the Commons and the similar statement made in the House of Lords by Lord Mackay of Clashfern, the Lord Advocate *ante*, fn. 97.
[2] *Ibid.*
[3] *Ante*, fn. 97 *per* Lord Mackay at col. 698.

subsequent sitting of the High Court of Justiciary. The effect of the Crown Office decision at that time, as demonstrated by the ruling in *Thom* v. *H.M. Advocate*,[3a] was to deprive the Lord Advocate of his right to prosecute the defendants at any time thereafter on the charges contained in the indictments which had fallen. After September 1981 public prosecution of the three youths ceased to be competent. Furthermore, by the same action the Lord Advocate was disabled from granting his concurrence to a public prosecution being undertaken by a private citizen. The doors having thus been effectively closed to the Lord Advocate for reindicting the accused, there remained only the avenue of private prosecution open to the victim and, ironically, to the public prosecutor who by now was sensitive to the possibility that precipitate action may have been taken in his name in abandoning the prosecution in September 1981. Assurances were given to Parliament that if a private prosecution was to be instituted the Crown Office would place no impediment in the way of the complainer.[4]

At the subsequent hearing before the High Court of Justiciary seeking criminal letters the rape victim was represented by the Dean of the Faculty of Advocates. The Lord Advocate, appearing in person, indicated that he would not oppose the application since medical evidence was now available indicating a marked improvement in the complainant's health and in her ability to give evidence on behalf of the prosecution. In addition, the court was informed that both the victim-complainant and the Lord Advocate proposed to grant immunity from prosecution to the accomplice who was prepared to testify against his companions.[5] Much was made of the massive publicity which had attended the case, after it became publicly known that the Crown was not going to continue the prosecution, and which, it was claimed, rendered it impossible to ensure a fair trial for the three accused youths by an unprejudiced jury. As summarised by Lord Emslie, the Lord Justice General, no fewer than 160 articles about the Glasgow rape case had appeared in the Scottish daily newspapers before and after the Lord Advocate's statement in the House of Lords on January 21, 1982. There was similar saturation coverage in the television and radio programmes including interviews with the rape victim and remarks attributed to sources in the police and procurator fiscal service expressing disquiet that the proceedings had been abandoned. A few days prior to the statements in Parliament suggesting the possibility of a private prosecution, one

---

[3a] 1976 J.C. 48.

[4] *Ante* (fn. 97), at col. 427. This assurance, made by the Solicitor General for Scotland (Mr. Fairbairn), was in response to a direct question by a member of the Opposition back benches. In the Upper House, the Lord Advocate was far more circumspect saying "the [victim] had an avenue open to her to make an application . . . but it would not be right for me to speculate on the chance of success."—*ibid.*, col. 701.

[5] Without identifying the victim's name the case is reported as *X* v. *Sweeney, Sweeney and Thomson* 1982 S.C.C.R. 161. Of particular interest is the inclusion within the report of the full texts of the complainer's bill for criminal letters (*ibid.* p. 163) and the criminal letters as issued by the High Court of Justiciary (*ibid.* pp. 178–179). The archaic, verbose nature of the language used in the latter instrument strikes a discordant note having regard to the reforms instituted generally in drafting indictments and other legal documents.

newspaper went so far as to publish parts of an alleged confession by one of the unidentified youths, and of statements by the other collaborators in the gang rape, including the youth who was to have been a Crown witness. In dealing with the issue of pre-trial publicity the Lord Justice General emphasised that "while the public interest in securing fair trial of accused persons is of the highest importance, so too is the public interest in the fair administration of justice and the detection and trial of alleged perpetrators of crime. Great weight must be given to this latter aspect of the public interest in this case, for the crimes alleged are of a particularly serious and horrible nature. In light of this consideration, and my assessment of the probable course which presentation of available evidence at a trial would follow, can I confidently affirm now that fair and impartial trial of the three respondents cannot be reasonably secured? I have come to be of opinion that I cannot so affirm."[6] This conclusion was subscribed to in separate judgments by Lord Cameron and Lord Avonside, the other members of the Justiciary Court.

On the substantive argument advanced on behalf of the defendants that all right of prosecution had been extinguished when the Lord Advocate's representatives had earlier dropped the Crown's charges, the entire Court was of one mind in rejecting this interpretation of the previous Scottish precedents. "Upon the whole issue of competency of this bill," the Lord Justice General concluded "I am not persuaded that there are any good reasons, in principle or authority, for holding that in the events which have happened this bill must be rejected as incompetent. In so doing I am content to record that the Lord Advocate, in addressing us, said that he was satisfied that the bill was competent and that had he entertained any doubt about the question he would have felt it his duty to so inform the court."[7] In approving the issuance of criminal letters the Court made no criticism of the Crown Office or the Crown counsel who had authorised the final discontinuance of the prosecution in September 1981. At the next sitting of the High Court in Edinburgh in May 1982 the first accused was convicted of rape and assault, and sentenced to 12 years' detention. The other defendants were convicted of indecent assault and placed on deferred sentence for a year.[8] Thus ended a remarkable chapter in the history of the Lord Advocate's office and of his role as Scotland's public prosecutor. The Glasgow rape case and the lessons attendant on its handling by the Crown's representatives will occupy a significant niche in the textbooks on Scottish criminal procedure. No clearer indication could be sought of the healthy existence in Scottish law of the residual right of private prosecution and with it a reaffirmation of the need to preserve intact for exceptional cases the constitutional right of the ordinary citizen to seek judicial redress by way of a bill of criminal letters when otherwise justice would be denied.

[6] *Ibid.* p. 171.
[7] *Ibid.* p. 170.
[8] *Ibid.* p. 181.

11

Political Pressures and Safeguarding the Independence of the Law Officers—Recent British Experience

At the height of the public debate surrounding the controversial decision in the *Gouriet* case a former Solicitor General was moved to write: "No one in any government or administrative machine either in this country or elsewhere has ever occupied a comparable position to that of the Law Officers of the Crown." Anyone at all familiar with the recent history of the United States or those Commonwealth jurisdictions which have incorporated the offices of Attorney General and Solicitor General into their constitutions might well register a mild note of reproof against this untypical claim to British uniqueness in this regard. As we shall see in the following chapter there have been episodes, no less captivating than the *Gouriet* decision in their political implications, in which the Law Officers of other countries have found it necessary to echo the message spread across *The Times*[1] article written by former Solicitor General Dingle Foot.[2] It read quite simply: "The Campbell case should have taught governments not to interfere with the Law Officers."[3]

An Addendum to the Campbell Case in 1924[4]

This, of course, is a reference to the ignominious handling by the first Labour Government in 1924 of the prosecution against John Ross Campbell, the acting editor of the "Workers Weekly," a Communist publication. In one of its issues that year there appeared an open letter exhorting the fighting forces not to turn their guns on their fellow workers in the event that war was declared or their services were called upon to quell an industrial dispute. After consultations between the Attorney

---

[1] *The Times*, January 27, 1977.
[2] Solicitor General, 1964–67, in the Wilson Administration.
[3] *Loc. cit.*
[4] The addendum should be related to my analysis of this case in *The Law Officers of the Crown*, Chapter 11.

General, Sir Patrick Hastings, and the Director of Public Prosecutions, Sir Archibald Bodkin, the decision was taken by Hastings to grant his consent to the institution of criminal proceedings against Campbell under section 1 of the Incitement to Mutiny Act 1797. After questions were raised in the House of Commons, drawing attention to Campbell's gallantry and war injuries, second thoughts as to the wisdom of pressing ahead with the charges led the Attorney General to communicate to the Assistant Director of Public Prosecutions (the Director being out of London at the time) his intention to apply for consent to the withdrawal of the prosecution when the case came up on remand in the Metropolitan Magistrates' Court.[5] Counsel appearing on behalf of the Director's office, in making the necessary application, conveyed the impression that the decision to terminate the proceedings had resulted from representations to the prosecution authorities, the nature and source of which were not disclosed.[6] Conjecture was rife and Opposition questioning of the Prime Minister, Mr. Ramsay MacDonald, and the Attorney General revealed a sorry tale of bungled mismanagement of the prosecution and a gross departure by Ramsay MacDonald from the standards of truthfulness which the House of Commons demands of all its members. Asked whether he had given any instructions to the Director of Public Prosecutions to withdraw the proceedings, in a reply that was to spell his doom and that of his Administration, the Prime Minister stated: "I was not consulted regarding either the institution or the subsequent withdrawal of these proceedings. The first notice of the prosecution which came to my knowledge was in the Press. I never advised its withdrawal, but left the whole matter to the discretion of the Law Officers, where that discretion properly rests."[7] By October 8, 1924 the Opposition was in full cry after its prey, convinced that the criminal law had been interfered with and the proceedings against Campbell stayed under pressure from the Government. Challenged to refer the whole matter to a Select Committee, to investigate and report on the abandonment of the Campbell prosecution, the Government refused.[8] The Opposition's subsequent motion of censure, defeating the Government and forcing its resignation, carried by 364 votes to 198, thus closing temporarily the political inquest into the Campbell affair.

Ramsay MacDonald's appalling lack of candour with the Commons was confirmed shortly after the change of government when Stanley Baldwin entered into possession of 10 Downing Street. Speaking in the Lower House in December 1924, when refusing to reopen the *Campbell* case, the new Prime Minister disclosed the contents of the Cabinet minute of August 6, 1924 which had been approved by the previous Labour Administration and the existence of which had long been suspected.[9] The Cabinet

[5] *Ibid.* pp.201–202.
[6] *Ibid.* pp.205–206.
[7] *Ibid.* p. 202, fn. 13.
[8] *Ibid.* pp. 211–212.
[9] *Ibid.* p. 213.

instruction declared that "no public prosecution of a political character should be undertaken without the prior sanction of the Cabinet being obtained."[10] Such an instruction, Mr. Baldwin asserted, "was unconstitutional, subversive of the administration of justice and derogatory to the office of the Attorney General. His Majesty's Government have therefore given directions that the instruction be excised."[11]

Supplementary questions addressed to the Prime Minister indicated that members of the former Labour Cabinet still harboured the view that they had acted constitutionally.[12] As the deposed Labour Prime Minister saw the problem when he was still in office: " . . . It is on record that the opinions of the Law Officers have been influenced to the extent of being altered and being reversed by the advice given to them by the executive. Is that improper? I am not a lawyer, but in my view there is nothing else that is possible. . . . Surely, every prosecution, especially of a political character, is undertaken in the interests of the State. Surely, every Law Officer who is undertaking a prosecution in the interests of the State must possess himself not only of guidance on technical law but must possess himself of guidance on this question, whether if a prosecution is instituted the effect of the prosecution will be harmful or beneficial to the State in whose interests it has been undertaken."[13] This formulation by Ramsay MacDonald of the dilemma facing an Attorney General is calculated to induce an affirmative answer. There is missing, however, one crucial element in the analysis, an element that could only be demonstrated after the fact by the disclosure of the express terms in which the Cabinet had couched its response to the Attorney General's handling of the *Campbell* prosecution. As Prime Minister Baldwin explained the constitutional position to the Opposition critics in December 1924: " . . . it is the duty of the Attorney General, in the discharge of his responsibilities so entrusted to him, to inform himself of all relevant circumstances which might properly affect his decision: when the proposed prosecution is of such a character that matters of public policy are, or may be, involved, it is the duty of the Attorney General to inform himself of the views of the Government or of the appropriate Minister before coming to a decision. It is because in the view of the Government the instructions referred to in the question went beyond this that these instructions were rescinded by the (present) Cabinet."[14]

[10] *Ibid.* p. 214.
[11] *Ibid.* p. 213.
[12] Were this question to have been answered by reference to the precedents established by former Conservative Governments, (see Edwards, *op. cit.* Chapter 10) the new Administration, headed by Mr. Baldwin, might have found themselves infinitely less capable of maintaining an air of constitutional rectitude in the Commons exchanges surrounding the handling of the *Campbell* case. See Edwards, *op. cit.* pp. 213–214.
[13] H.C. Deb., Vol. 177, col. 629, October 8, 1924, quoted in Edwards, *op. cit.* p. 212.
[14] H.C. Deb., Vol. 179, cols. 1213–1214, December 18, 1924, quoted in Edwards, *op. cit.* p. 214.

The full story of this notable case, with its fundamental constitutional implications, was set forth in the *The Law Officers of the Crown* to which the reader's attention is directed. Since that volume was published additional evidence has become accessible in the form of Cabinet minutes and papers of the period in question,[15] as well as the contents of the diary kept by the official who was Principal Assistant Secretary to the Cabinet in 1924 and whose verbatim notes of the Cabinet discussions throw additional light on the handling of the *Campbell* case by the leading participants.[16] Since its repercussions continue to reverberate through the corridors of Whitehall and Westminster, as well as further afield throughout the Commonwealth, it is important that the record of that case be fully documented.

The comprehensive notes recording the discussion at the August 6, 1924 meeting of the Cabinet reveal that each of the Service Ministers and the Home Secretary had previously seen the offending article and expressed their views to the Director of Public Prosecutions before the latter's consultation with the Attorney General which resulted in criminal proceedings being authorised against Campbell.[17] Prior to the Cabinet deliberations the Prime Minister had sent for the Attorney General and Assistant Director of Public Prosecutions at which meeting Ramsay MacDonald expressed the view that the prosecution had been ill advised from the beginning. Hastings informed the Prime Minister that he had come to the conclusion that the prosecution ought to be withdrawn.[18] Notwithstanding this understanding MacDonald instructed the Attorney General to attend the Cabinet meeting later the same day so that he could inform his ministerial colleagues what the fuss was all about.[19] Speaking later on the subject in the House of Commons, Sir Patrick Hastings said that if he were entitled to say what happened at the Cabinet meeting he would tell the House with pleasure. "All I can say," he went on, "is that I left the Cabinet meeting with a decision at which I had arrived interfered with by nobody . . . ."[20] Writing in 1964, and seeking to interpret the events in 1924, I concluded that whatever influence may have been exerted by the Prime Minister or by members of the Cabinet there was no reason to

---

[15] See the results of F. H. Newark's enterprising researches in "The Campbell case and the First Labour Government" (1969) 20 N.I.L.Q. 19. In addition to examining the relevant Cabinet papers in the Public Record office, when they became available for inspection, Professor Newark made a "special pilgrimage" to visit James Campbell in the Communist Party Headquarters, King Street, London. What he discovered suggests that James Maxton, the Clydeside Independent Labour Party member, in describing Campbell's war wounds to the House of Commons in 1924, indulged in considerable flights of fancy—*ibid.* pp.24–41. *Cf.* too, Maxton's false information conveyed to the Attorney General, Sir Patrick Hastings, which appears to have influenced the Attorney's subsequent decision to withdraw the prosecution against Campbell—Edwards, *op. cit.* pp. 201–202.

[16] See Thomas Jones, *Whitehall Diary*, (Ed. Keith Middlemas), (London, 1969), Vol. 1, pp. 286–301, *passim.*

[17] *Ibid.* pp. 287–288.

[18] Edwards, *op. cit.* p. 202.

[19] *Ibid.* p. 204.

[20] *Ibid.*

suppose that Hastings did not reach his decision to discontinue the prosecution by the exercise of his independent judgment.[21] Whether the decision of the Cabinet, later communicated to the Law Officers' Department as a Cabinet instruction, was reached in the presence of the Attorney General or following his retirement from the Cabinet room, I also observed, was not known and probably could no longer be ascertained.[22]

With the availability of the new evidence from the contemporary records of the Cabinet discussion on August 6 these doubts can now be fully resolved. My interpretation of Sir Patrick Hastings' stance appears to have been too charitable. The expanded record shows that he was a compliant Attorney General anxious to do the bidding of his political colleagues assembled in the Cabinet. Referring to the messages that emanated from the Service Ministries and the Home Office, which had viewed "The Workers Weekly" issue containing the open letter and had urged the advisability of prosecution, the Attorney General confirmed that if confronted with the same evidence he would again advise prosecution.[23] Significantly, however, Hastings continued: " . . . there is a possible way out if you desire it as against this man."[24] Ramsay MacDonald interjected that being a political case the circumstances should have been brought to his attention and "if put to me I should not have sanctioned it."[25] On the motion of J.H. Thomas that it be an instruction that no prosecution of a political character take place without the prior sanction of the Cabinet, the resolution was approved unanimously *in the presence* of Sir Patrick Hastings.[26]

There is no record of the then Attorney General having objected to the principle embodied in the Cabinet instruction. In effect, the Ramsay MacDonald Government, through the Cabinet, asserted its right to interfere with decisions to prosecute political cases and, by his silence, Hastings must be deemed to have conceded that right. His subsequent

---

[21] *Ibid.*

[22] *Ibid.* p. 205.

[23] Thomas Jones, *op. cit.* p. 289.

[24] Edwards, *op. cit.* p. 205. This intervention by Sir Patrick Hastings, however, is formally incorporated in the Cabinet Minute which states: "The Attorney General said he took full responsibility for proceeding with the case, which disclosed a bad criminal offence, but inasmuch as it transpired that the person charged was only acting temporarily as Editor and was prepared to write a letter to that effect steps could be taken not to press the prosecution in the circumstances against this particular offender, if the Cabinet so desired."—*ibid.* p. 287.

[25] Edwards, *op. cit.* and *cf.* the earlier intimation, attributed to the Prime Minister, during the circulation of the offending article through the Admiralty, the War Office and the Air Ministry, which recorded the fact that the "P.M. must be informed before action taken." The Secretary of State for War was in favour of prosecution. The Home Secretary was against criminal proceedings—*ibid.* p. 288. Newark, *op. cit.* p. 37, concluded that the Home Secretary was in favour of prosecution but this is not borne out by the notes of the Cabinet discussion—see Thomas Jones, *op. cit.* p. 288.

[26] Edwards, *op cit.* p. 289. Earlier in the course of the Cabinet discussion, and before the Attorney General entered the House of Commons room in which the meeting was taking place, the Colonial Secretary (J. H. Thomas) expressed his opinion that "nothing of this sort should happen without the P.M. and Cabinet knowing of it."

protestations to the contrary, conveyed to the Commons as stated above,[27] ring hollow in the light of his acquiescence in the formal decision of the Cabinet and recorded in the minutes of the executive body. Neither does it affect the basic issue of the Law Officers' independence that, since the Cabinet decided to adopt the same option as that which Hastings had chosen to follow, there was in fact no political interference in the *Campbell* case.[28]

Furthermore, as indicated in a subsequent note to the Prime Minister from Sir Maurice Hankey, Secretary to the Cabinet, neither of the Law Officers of the Crown, to whom the draft conclusions were circulated for possible corrections criticised the minute recording the decision reached at the August 6 meeting.[29] That official record states as follows:

"The attention of the Cabinet was called to a prosecution which had been instituted against John Ross Campbell. . . .

The Home Secretary stated that a letter of apology had been received from the printers.

The Attorney General said he took full responsibility for proceeding with the case which disclosed a bad criminal offence, but inasmuch as it transpired that the person charged was only acting temporarily as editor and was prepared to write a letter to that effect steps could be taken not to press the prosecution in the circumstances against this particular offender, if the Cabinet so desired.

After considerable discussion of the procedure which had led to the action being taken in the courts without the knowledge of the Cabinet or the Prime Minister, the Cabinet agreed:

(a) no public prosecution of a political character should be undertaken without the prior sanction of the Cabinet being obtained;

(b) that in the particular case under review the course indicated by the Attorney General should be adopted."

A challenge as to the accuracy of the above Cabinet minute having been voiced six weeks later by Ramsay MacDonald,[30] then still the Prime

---

[27] *Ante*, fn. 20.

[28] See Newark *op. cit.* p. 40.

[29] Nor did any member of the Cabinet see fit to question any aspect of the "Campbell affair" Minute.

[30] Sir Maurice Hankey (later Lord Hankey) prepared a statement, dated October 2, 1924, recording the circumstances in which this unusual challenge had taken place. Presumably, this action was taken in anticipation of a possible public inquiry. It read: "On 22 September 1924 the Prime Minister in the presence of a number of his Cabinet colleagues asked me to show him the Cabinet conclusion in regard to the prosecution of [Campbell] the Editor of the *Worker's Weekly* . . . On reading the Minute the Prime Minister at once challenged its accuracy, more particularly in regard to conclusion (B). I made no record of this at the time, nor of the reasons given by the Prime Minister for this challenge, but on returning to my office I mentioned to my private Secretary, Captain Burgis, that the Prime Minister had questioned the accuracy of the Minute, and I am asking Captain Burgis to initial this to bear out my statement." Thomas Jones, *op. cit.* p. 292. It will be observed that Ramsay Macdonald, even in retrospect, was not concerned to question the accuracy of conclusion (A) which embodies the principle that eventually contributed to the downfall of his Administration.

Minister, expansive notes as to the circumstances surrounding the famous meeting of August 6 and the consequent fall out were prepared by both the Secretary to the Cabinet and the Assistant Secretary.[31] These are printed in full in Thomas Jones' *Whitehall Diary*.[32] Before handing over the reins of office to his successor MacDonald instructed Hankey to ensure that if ever the controversial Cabinet minute of August 6 should be called for, there should also be made available the transcript of the notes made at that same meeting by the Assistant Secretary to the Cabinet.[33] Immediately on succeeding to the Prime Ministership, Stanley Baldwin asked to see the offensive Cabinet instruction and used its contents to good effect when the *Campbell* case surfaced once more in the House of Commons in December 1924.[34]

Had Ramsay MacDonald been as persistent in reviewing the record of previous administrations, in their handling of political cases, he might have been more successful in blunting much of the criticism levelled against the Labour Government's conduct in the *Campbell* case. Thus, on a number of occasions during and immediately following the First World War, the then holders of the office of Attorney General, the redoubtable Lord Hewart

---

[31] Prompting these fascinating insights into the daily workings of the Cabinet office at the time was the further conversation between the Prime Minister and Sir Maurice Hankey on October 2, 1924, at which the Lord Advocate (Hugh (later Lord) Macmillan) was present. On that occasion Ramsay MacDonald said that he could not recollect his having been shown the Minute of the Cabinet Meeting on August 6, 1924, in regard to the *Workers' Weekly*. From his detailed reconstruction of the events, commencing with the preparation of the draft Minutes on the morning of August 7, (based on the rough notes taken by Tom Jones, the Assistant Secretary), to the form in which the draft conclusions were circulated "by direction of the Prime Minister," Hankey wrote to the Prime Minister, "I do not think there is the smallest doubt that I did show you the Minute," adding "Mr. Tom Jones tells me that this entirely confirms his recollection, which is that at the time I definitely informed him that the Prime Minister approved this particular Minute"—Thomas Jones, *op. cit.* pp. 290–292.
[32] Tom Jones's recollections were penned on October 15, 1924. He recalled digging out his rough notes on which the famous Minute was based and showing them to Hankey. Because of Hankey's other commitments as Secretary General of the post-World War I Conference on Reparations, he was unable to attend the Cabinet meeting on August 6. Hankey expressed the opinion that, on the evidence of Jones's notes, the Minute was, if anything, an understatement. In particular, Tom Jones recalled, "I had down 'A.G. authorised,' whereas in the Minute I had used our usual formula 'The Cabinet agreed!' " With respect to Ramsay MacDonald's denial to the House of Commons of any involvement in the withdrawal of the proceedings (see *ante*, fn. 7), Jones recalls his own reactions and those of the Secretary to the Cabinet: "That, in Hankey's words, was 'a bloody lie.' When I heard it, as I did, in the House, a shiver went down my spine"—*ibid.* pp. 295–298. See, too, Jones's comments upon the Prime Minister's attempt (on October 8) to explain away his original inaccurate answer (on September 30) to the private notice question tabled by Sir Kingsley Wood—quoted in Edwards *op. cit.* p. 202, fn. 13. MacDonald, on the second occasion, had endeavoured to persuade the Commons that his answer on October 8 was made in the "heat of temper" and not carefully prepared in advance. According to Tom Jones, MacDonald had drafted the original reply in his own handwriting and had refused to change it notwithstanding his attention having been drawn to the existence of the Cabinet Minute of August 6, 1924—Thomas Jones, *op. cit.* p. 297.
[33] Thomas Jones, *op. cit.* p. 301.
[34] See Newark, *op. cit.* p. 337. Baldwin's request, and Hankey's compliance in providing the new P.M. access to a Cabinet Minute of a previous Administration, are documented in the papers available for consultation in the Public Records Office.

and Lord Birkenhead (as they subsequently became), participated actively in Cabinet deliberations that led to the Executive, not the Law Officers, making the final decision as to whether or not criminal proceedings should be instituted against particular defendants. In each of the cases reviewed in my earlier study of *The Law Officers of the Crown*[35] the record shows that the incumbent Attorney General concerned himself with the technicalities of the criminal law leaving the assessment of the relevant political considerations, and thereby the final determination of what course of action should be followed, to the Cabinet of the day. These instances, it must be stressed, were not cases in which the Attorney General was seeking the opinion of his Cabinet colleagues as a wise preliminary to making up his own mind whether to set the machinery of the criminal law in motion. Rather they represent a clear abdication of the Law Officers' ultimate responsibility to make such decisions as to which the constitution has clothed the office of the Attorney General with the greatest measure of independence from executive and parliamentary interference.

The pronouncements of a long line of Prime Ministers in defining this independence provides unquestioned authority for the constitutional convention to which Mr. Harold Macmillan gave expression in the House of Commons on February 16, 1959.[36] "It is an established principle of government in this country," the Prime Minister declared, "and a tradition long supported by all political parties, that the decision as to whether any citizen should be prosecuted, or whether any prosecution should be discontinued, should be a matter, where a public as opposed to a private prosecution is concerned, for the prosecuting authority to decide on the merits of the case without political or other pressure. It would be a most dangerous deviation from this sound principle if a prosecution were to be instituted or abandoned as a result of political pressure or popular clamour . . . I think that it would be the general view of the House that it would be a very bad thing if the House or the Cabinet of the day tried to influence the semi-judicial functions of the Law Officers in the institution or the dropping of prosecutions."[37]

---

[35] *Ibid*. pp. 191–196, and *cf.* the hypocritical views expressed in 1924 by F.E. Smith condemning Patrick Hastings' handling of the Campbell case, *ibid*. pp. 207–210.

[36] H.C. Deb., Vol. 600, col. 31.

[37] Macmillan's pronouncement, delivered from a prepared statement, arose out of the public controversy surrounding the Lord Advocate's decision not to institute criminal proceedings against two Caithness police officers who were alleged to have violently assaulted John Waters, a boy of 15. For the *Report of the Tribunal of Inquiry into the Waters case* see Cmnd. 718. The Prime Minister, in expounding the correct constitutional doctrine, assimilated the position of the Lord Advocate to that of the Attorney General for England and Wales. Moreover, there is ample evidence that Macmillan had the 1924 precedent very much in mind which he told the House of Commons: "I do not want a Campbell case in reverse"—H.C. Deb., Vol. 600, col. 33, February 16, 1959. On the following day he returned to the same theme saying that had he yielded and instructed the Lord Advocate to institute criminal proceedings he "would have erred against the first rule that the Prime Minister and the Cabinet owe to the Law Officers placed in their senior judicial position. They have neither the right to instruct a prosecution to begin nor for any reason whatever to instruct that it

The tradition, to which Mr. Macmillan addressed his prepared statement, is of considerable antiquity though there have been times when it has not enjoyed the same level of universal recognition claimed for it in 1959. Lord Eldon expressed the same philosophy in equally trenchant language in 1793,[38] and in 1903 we find Prime Minister A.J. Balfour adhering to the same principles in stating: "It is due to the Attorney General to say in the clearest manner, not only in the interests of the Attorney General but in the interest of all, that his position as the Director of Public Prosecutions (*sic*) is a position absolutely independent of any of his colleagues. It is not in the power of the Government to direct the Attorney General to direct a prosecution. No government would do such thing; no Attorney General would tolerate its being done."[39] Further corroboration of the acceptance of this doctrine and of the need to maintain a separation of functions between the government and the Law Officers in decisions affecting prosecutions is to be found in the parliamentary statements of Mr. Gladstone in 1873[40] and Lord Salisbury in 1896.[41] At the time they made these pronouncements each was occupying the position of Prime Minister. And reference has already been made to the important distinction drawn by Prime Minister Baldwin in 1924 between, on the one hand, the Attorney General's duty to inform himself of all relevant circumstances which might properly affect his decision including the views of the government or of the appropriate minister and, on the other hand, the rejection of the edict adopted by Ramsay MacDonald's administration to the effect that no prosecution of a political character should be undertaken without the prior sanction of the Cabinet having been first obtained.[42]

GENESIS AND BACKGROUND TO THE SHAWCROSS STATEMENT IN 1951

In more modern times the classic pronouncement on the role of the Attorney General in exercising his prerogative and statutory responsi-

should cease. I remember very well that I referred in passing yesterday to a great Parliamentary situation which arose from confusion about that. I will not put it higher than that"—*ibid*. col. 226.

[38] Twiss, *The Public and Private Life of Lord Chancellor Eldon*, (3rd ed. 1846), Vol. 1, p. 158, quoted in Edwards *op. cit.* p. 179.

[39] The Prime Minister was speaking at the close of the debate on a motion expressing regret that no prosecution had been instituted against the directors of the London & Globe Finance Corporation, among whom was the notorious financier, Whittaker Wright. Parl. Deb., Vol. 118, ser. 4, cols. 349–380, February 19, 1903. Balfour's remarks are reported *ibid*. col. 376–377. See, too, the speech of Sir Robert Finlay, the Attorney General, *ibid*. col. 359–361.

[40] Parl. Deb., H.C., Vol. 216, ser. 3, col. 1064–1065 and see Edwards, *op. cit.* pp. 184–185. The circumstances which occasioned Gladstone's remarks were the allegedly contemptuous comments on the *Tichborne* case made by several members of the House of Commons.

[41] Parl. Deb., H.L., Vol. 42, col. 519, July 2, 1896. In issue was the question whether the Attorney General, Sir Richard Webster, when demanding a trial at bar in the *Jameson Raid* case, was acting on his own absolute discretion or under the orders of the government. For the views of Lord Halsbury L.C., see *ibid*. col. 517, and Lord Herschell, see *ibid*. col. 518. As to this episode and for an examination of Herschell's experience as a Law Officer, see Edwards, *op. cit.* pp. 186–187.

[42] See *ante*, p. 312 and the general treatment of this subject in Edwards, *op. cit.* pp. 212–225.

bilities is that contained in Sir Hartley Shawcross's speech in 1951 in the
House of Commons when explaining his decision to prosecute in the *Gas
Strikers* case.[43] It deserves repetition. "The true doctrine" said Shawcross
"is that it is the duty of the Attorney General, in deciding whether or not to
authorise the prosecution, to acquaint himself with all the relevant facts,
including, for instance, the effect which the prosecution, successful or
unsuccessful as the case may be, would have upon public morale and order,
and with any other consideration affecting public policy. In order so to
inform himself, he may, although I do not think he is obliged to, consult
with any of his colleagues in the government, and indeed, as Lord Simon
once said, he would in some cases be a fool if he did not. On the other
hand, the assistance of his colleagues is confined to informing him of
particular considerations which might affect his own decision, and does not
consist, and must not consist, in telling him what that decision ought to be.
The responsibility for the eventual decision rests with the Attorney
General, and he is not be be put, and is not put, under pressure by his
colleagues in the matter. Nor, or course, can the Attorney General shift his
responsibility for making the decision on to the shoulders of his colleagues.
If political considerations which in the broad sense that I have indicated
affect government in the abstract arise it is the Attorney General, applying
his judicial mind, who has to be the sole judge of those considerations."[44]

This carefully phrased exposition of the proper approach to be followed
by the Attorney General, when faced with a situation in which questions of
national or international public policy may surround the exercise of his
prosecutorial discretion, was the result of a collaborative effort that serves
to further underline the major importance which has been accorded to
Shawcross's statement in the intervening years. For, as the files in the Law
Officers' Department reveal, the Attorney General went to infinite pains
to ensure, as he put it, "that the integrity of the office should be very fully
maintained since its position is, I am afraid, often widely
misunderstood."[45] Among the individuals to whom draft copies of
Shawcross's proposed statement had previously been circulated for
comment were Viscount Simon, Viscount Jowitt, and Lord Kilmuir, each
of them a former Law Officer of the Crown who subsequently rose to
become Lord Chancellor. In addition, Shawcross sought the views of Sir
Theobald Mathew, the Director of Public Prosecutions, and Mr. Herbert
Morrison, the Lord President of the Council and Deputy Prime Minister.
Viscount Simon, whose statements when he was the Attorney General

[43] For the background to this case see Edwards, *op. cit.* pp. 220–223.
[44] H.C. Deb., Vol. 483, cols. 683–684, January 29, 1951. In the course of his
comprehensive exposition of the Attorney General's responsibility for prosecutions (*ibid.*
cols. 679–690) Shawcross also stated that in deciding whether or not to prosecute in a
particular case "there is only one consideration which is altogether excluded and that is the
repercussion of a given decision upon my personal or my party's or the government's political
fortunes: that is a consideration which never enters into account"—*ibid.* col. 682.
[45] In a letter from Shawcross to Viscount Simon, December 1950—L.O.D. (Law Officers'
Dept.) files.

were incorporated into the proposed text, responded at length to Shawcross's invitation for his observations, explaining his zeal as being prompted by the realisation that Sir Hartley Shawcross would be "making a classical pronouncement which ought to stand for the future."[46] Sir Theobald Mathew likewise offered a series of criticisms each of which was incorporated in the final version delivered in the House of Commons.[47] All the correspondents were in total agreement with the principles enshrined in the Attorney General's speech, which must have been a source of considerable strength knowing that the opinions reflected the broadest spectrum of political opinion in Parliament at the time.

Another interesting item of background information disclosed in the departmental files is the genesis of the Shawcross statement delivered in the House of Commons in January 1951. A few months earlier, as the Attorney General, Shawcross had submitted a memorandum to the Attlee Cabinet[48] seeking the opinions of his ministerial colleagues with regard to the institution of criminal proceedings "should the necessary evidence be available in connection with the strike of meat lorry drivers which is at present taking place." This subject had been canvassed earlier in the Emergencies Committee of Cabinet in the course of which, according to Shawcross, some misunderstanding had been evinced as to the constitutional position of the Attorney General in relation to his political colleagues in such matters. Reading between the lines, it would seem that the lessons of the *Campbell* case had not permeated the thinking of every member of the post-war Labour Administration, so much so that Shawcross felt it necessary to repeat what he had written in a letter to the Colonial Secretary on January 11, 1949 in connection with the position of the Colonial Law Officers. The language of the passage quoted from the 1949 letter resembles in striking fashion that used two years later when explaining to the House of Commons at large the quasi-judicial character of the responsibilities imposed on the Law Officers of the Crown in making decisions concerning the enforcement or non-enforcement of the criminal law.

---

[46] Simon's reply to Shawcross, dated December 14, 1950—L.O.D. files. The same writer urged the Attorney General to take the opportunity of emphasising the true constitutional position.

[47] The following extracts from Mathew's letter to Shawcross have a special interest. "As I act under your superintendence and directions" the D.P.P. wrote "you are responsible for my decisions but you can and have, albeit politely, overruled decisions of mine. True, so far as the public is concerned, you have allowed me to reconsider my decision in the light of further representations, but you could give me a direction to act contrary to a decision that I had announced, which would not be open to you if it had been your original decision." And later "For the reasons which I outlined in . . . my lecture to the University of London on my office [see *ante*, pp. 39–41] in my view there is no qualification of your responsibility for my decision, and I suggest, therefore, that the words 'except where responsibility is delegated to him' might be misunderstood"—Mathew's letter bears the date January 15, 1951, L.O.D. files.

[48] Memorandum to the Cabinet on Illegal Strikes, June 28, 1950—L.O.D. files. Shawcross was particularly careful in limiting his approach to asking his colleagues "whether any circumstances are known to them which they think I ought to take into account in deciding whether or not to prosecute in the case of the present strike . . . ."

The spate of illegal industrial actions not having abated following the successful prosecution of the gas strikers there was a further discussion in Cabinet on December 11, 1950 in regard to the action that the Attorney General might take in relation to the latest body of striking workers. On December 13, in a formal memorandum to Cabinet, Shawcross communicated the final decisions that he had reached in these matters.[49] At the same time he outlined for the members of Cabinet the procedure that he proposed to adopt in any future cases which might arise. "Cabinet discussion of these matters," Shawcross wrote, "may be as embarrassing for my colleagues as indeed it is for me. For whilst my colleagues are scrupulously careful to remind me that they do not share any responsibility for the decision which is constitutionally placed upon me they do not fail to make clear what they consider my decision should be! In these circumstances, therefore, I think it would be more satisfactory if, in any future case in which I need advice, I should seek that advice on a less formal basis from the Prime Minister and any other Minister who may seem to be specially concerned."[50]

Distinct whiffs of political pressure being exerted, either individually or collectively, are evident in the above extract from Shawcross's memorandum to the Cabinet of which, it must be remembered, the Attorney General was not a member, but which could summon his attendance at any time the Prime Minister saw fit to call upon his services. The ability to resist such pressures will vary according to the experience, personality and determination of the Law Officer concerned. There is no reason to believe that the Cabinet in 1950 were successful in imposing their will upon the Attorney General by the sheer weight of the multiple expressions of identical opinions around the Cabinet table. On the other hand, by preferring to seek advice on a one-to-one basis the Attorney General enhanced the prospects of his being able to maintain a level of impartiality that should be inherent in the quasi-judicial function of the office.

Conservative administrations likewise provide useful insights into the attitude of modern Cabinets towards the question of the Attorney General's independence from government in deciding whether or not to institute criminal proceedings. Events in Kenya during the turmoil of the mid-1950s were the occasion for an unexpected discussion of this familiar subject by the Cabinet presided over by Winston Churchill, as Prime Minister. It would appear that the Attorney General, Sir Lionel Heald, was not present but Viscount Simmonds, the Lord Chancellor, intervened in the discussion in a way that, on reflection, led him to conclude that he

---

[49] The text of this memorandum, and that referred to in the preceding footnote, were kindly made available to the author by the Law Officers' Department.

[50] *Ibid.* In an unexpected, concluding paragraph Shawcross wrote: "Lest it should be thought that my concern for the integrity of my office and the due enforcement of the law is something peculiar and personal to myself I may perhaps add that the Solicitor General [Sir Frank Soskice] has for some time urged upon me the necessity for stricter enforcement of the law and that the matter is now the subject of comment in legal and other circles . . . "

may have misled his colleagues. In a Cabinet paper, prepared a few days later and headed "The Attorney General and Public Prosecutions."[51] the Lord Chancellor concluded that "it is only where a question of public policy arises that Ministers may express their views to the Attorney General and then on that question alone. The Attorney General must refuse to listen to any arguments based on political expediency . . . The line between politics and public policy is hard to draw; and there is always a danger that a Government which is known to have intervened by advice or direction to the Attorney General will be accused by its critics of using the plea of national interest as a cloak for political expediency. It is therefore, a matter of prudence for any Government to be extremely cautious in intervention."[52] Having reminded his fellow Conservative Ministers that both sides of the House of Commons had approved Sir Hartley Shawcross's statement in 1951 at a time "when it might be expected that the Attorney General in a Socialist Government would be under severe pressure from his own party,"[53] the Lord Chancellor added a postscript that, again on reflection, he might well think would have been better left unsaid. "I should perhaps add," he wrote, "that there is in my opinion no reason why the Cabinet should not discuss the propriety of a prosecution or of advice being offered to the Attorney General but to do so in his presence would generally be inadvisable."[54]

Since 1928 the policy has been consistently followed in Britain of excluding the Attorney General from membership in the Cabinet, a policy that has served to reinforce the tradition that the subject of criminal prosecutions is outside the purview of the Cabinet's decision-making

[51] Cabinet Paper c.(54)27 dated January 26, 1954—L.O.D. files.

[52] *Ibid.* Whether Simmonds consulted with Sir Lionel Heald, the Attorney General, before circulating his paper is not known. Certainly, the intervention of the Lord Chancellor, with respect to an office that he had never occupied, was extraordinary. What Heald's position would have been can only be conjectured—his interest in the subject is evident from correspondence which he had in July 1952 with the Downing Professor of the Laws of England at Cambridge University—L.O.D. files. In Wade and Phillips' *Constitutional Law* (4th ed., 1950) the statement appeared that "the institution of a prosecution for certain offences, *e.g.* sedition, may involve considerations of policy as well as law. In such cases the decision may be taken by the Home Secretary, or even the Cabinet, with the advice of the Attorney General, as chief law officer of the Crown" (*ibid* at p. 231). Writing to Sir Lionel Heald, the Attorney General, two years later, Professor E.C.S. Wade expressed his regrets if the compressed statement had led to the Law Officers being embarrassed. His letter continued: "The passage is intended to mean that the Home Secretary or, in a case of sufficient weight, the Cabinet may decide whether or not it is expedient to proceed with a prosecution. 'With the advice of the A.G.' means if the A.G. advises that there are in law grounds for initiating a prosecution . . . So far as my passage on p. 231 is concerned, I had in mind the *Campbell* case in particular but in the absence of a report on the case I did not insert a footnote. I have not, of course, ever seen the departmental papers on this case . . . ." No such limitations with respect to the parliamentary debates in 1924 concerning the Campbell affair can explain this unsupportable interpretation of the constitutional position, made, it is to be noted, in 1952. By that time also, Shawcross's exposition of the proper doctrine had been delivered in the House of Commons. The erroneous statement of principle was corrected in the 5th edition (1955) of the same work, *ibid.* p. 245.

[53] Cabinet Paper c.(54)27 dated January 26, 1954.

[54] *Ibid.*

functions.[55] Although stress is placed on responsibility for the actual decision making in prosecution matters, the consequence of adopting Viscount Simmonds's tolerance of Cabinet discussions as to the propriety of a prosecution, even in the absence of the Attorney General, would surely lead to a blurring of the line between considerations of public policy and arguments based on the government's political fortunes. The absence of the Attorney General and Solicitor General from the Cabinet deliberations is no guarantee of insulation against the pressures inherent in their subsequent reading of the Cabinet minutes, in which the strength or urgency of the opinions expressed around the Cabinet table are permanently recorded. This knowledge will reach the Attorney General in the normal course of conducting the government's business so that little reliance can be placed on Lord Simmonds's sanctioning of the Cabinet's right to formulate its collective opinion to be tendered to the Attorney General on the question whether or not he should prosecute, provided they do not do so directly lest he be embarrassed in the presence of his colleagues. Such a distinction carries little credibility.

In the early days of the 1945 Labour Administration Sir Hartley Shawcross, as Attorney General, informed himself of the views of his ministerial colleagues by bringing to the notice of the Cabinet any case of political significance in which he was contemplating authorising a prosecution.[56] This inevitably resulted in wide-ranging discussions in which, it is understood, some ministers exhibited an eagerness to express their views on the wisdom of instituting criminal proceedings. Dissatisfied with this state of affairs, as he might well be, Shawcross sought and obtained the Prime Minister's agreement to an arrangement whereby he would refer only the most important cases to the Cabinet.[57] In other cases, he would ascertain the views of the appropriate minister(s) informally, a practice that generally involved consulting the Minister of Labour on the political consequences of prosecuting the leaders of unofficial strikes in the gas industry and the docks.[58]

Later still even this modified procedure was abandoned by Shawcross with the support of Mr. Attlee, the Prime Minister, and the policy was followed of consulting individual ministers outside the framework of the Cabinet's deliberations.[59] Taking the initiative in supplying the Attorney General with information as to factors that could properly be taken into consideration when making the vital decisions to prosecute or not to prosecute, to halt proceedings or let them follow the normal course, may be at the behest of the minister(s) concerned or, preferably, by the Attorney General himself. What is not permissible and would be treated as constitutionally improper is the expression by the Prime Minister, another minister or the government of their individual or collective view on the

[55] Edwards, *op. cit.* Chapter 9, esp. pp. 172–176.
[56] Law Officers' Department files.
[57] *Ibid.*
[58] *Ibid.*
[59] *Ibid.*

question whether or not the Attorney General should prosecute. The same position must surely apply to the solicitation of such views by the Attorney General or anyone acting on his behalf.

However one attempts to delineate in unequivocal language the boundary line between what is proper and improper in these kinds of exchanges between ministers and the Attorney General it must be acknowledged that there will be occasions in which both the contents and manner of communicating factual information as to the likely effects of different courses of action is tantamount to expressing an opinion on the appropriate choice that should be made. It is a difficult line to sustain with the required degree of certainty that gives the appearance of stating a fundamental principle. Nevertheless, the essence of the principle is, I believe, capable of being demonstrated and understood and it is to that end that everyone concerned must be guided in their approach to the Attorney General's quasi-judicial responsibilities.

THE LEILA KHALID CASE

Glimpses of the innermost workings of government are unfortunately all too rare and, in the main, we must assess the conduct of ministers and their adherence to constitutional principles from the evidence publicly available. One such recent instance, the case involving the notorious *Leila Khalid* in 1970,[60] once more gave rise to much public speculation as to the part played by the government in the eventual release of the accused without trial. After an unsuccessful attempt to hijack an Israeli airliner, Miss Khalid was taken into custody at London Airport and held in a suburban police station. Urgent negotiations were entered into between the British, Swiss and German governments some of whose nationals were being held as hostages by Arab guerrillas belonging to the Palestine Liberation Organisation, of which Khalid was a prominent member. The price set for the release of the hostages was the freedom to be accorded the hijacker Khalid. This exchange of prisoners duly took place following a meeting at which Lord Hailsham, the Lord Chancellor, Sir Peter Rawlinson, the Attorney General, and other pertinent ministers met with Mr. Heath, the Prime Minister, to consider the various options open to them.[61] It would scarcely be believed if any of those present maintained that no consideration was given to the pros and cons of deporting Leila Khalid and wiping the slate clean so far as charging her with offences against British criminal law were concerned. Such was the eventual outcome of the case.

Subsequently, the Attorney General explained that throughout he had acted in accordance with the constitutional principles governing the

---

[60] The fullest account of this case and the problems associated with its handling by the D.P.P. is contained in Sir Norman Skelhorn's *Memoirs* (1982), pp. 122–126. See, too, Lord Hailsham's *Child Lecture 1978* (*ante* p. 218, fn. 38) in the course of which the Lord Chancellor confirmed the Att. Gen.'s explanation of what occurred during Rawlinson's consultations with his ministerial colleagues—*ibid.* pp. 7–8.

[61] *The Times*, September 28, 1970.

exercise of his discretionary powers. Before making his final decision and during the prolonged negotiations, Rawlinson told the Society of Conservative Lawyers, he had several times asked the Foreign Secretary what he thought would be the effect on the lives of the hostages if Leila Khalid were to be charged and made to stand trial for the hijacking. "On each occasion," Rawlinson disclosed, "I was advised that a charge would increase the danger to their lives. Accordingly, I informed the Government that I did not, in the circumstances then prevailing, intend to charge Leila Khalid. That was my decision and mine alone."[62] Faced with the awful dilemma of measuring the freedom, and possibly the lives, of political hostages against the non-enforcement of the criminal law in the circumstances presented by the *Khalid* case it cannot be said that the ultimate decision was misguided. It is clearly defensible. So, too, based on such limited information as the Attorney General was disposed to disclose after the event, was the decision by Sir Peter Rawlinson not to prosecute in the light of the judgment expressed to him by the Foreign Secretary as to the price that might have had to be paid if he had chosen to let the law take its normal course.

THE RHODESIA OIL SANCTIONS CASE

The political furor that surrounded the Attorney General's decision in December 1979 not to prosecute in what has become known as the *Rhodesia oil sanctions* case has now died down to the point where even the essential facts may be difficult to recall. We must wait many more years before a full and accurate account can be acquired of all the relevant considerations that ultimately dictated the negative decision announced in the House of Commons in 1979 by the Conservative Attorney General, Sir Michael Havers, after consultations with the Director of Public Prosecutions.[63] In the meantime, it would be unpardonable to by-pass this contentious decision and not venture an assessment as to the validity of the Opposition's claims that the decision was not reached impartially and that it was contrary to the public interest. What makes the case even more significant is that the events which, it was claimed, constituted blatant violations of the sanctions laws by the major oil companies, Shell and British Petroleum (B.P.), were alleged to have taken place with the knowledge and connivance of previous Administrations, both Labour (under Mr. Harold Wilson) and Conservative (under Mr. Edward Heath).

Immediately following the announcement of Ian Smith's unilateral declaration of independence (UDI) in 1965 the British Parliament, in fulfilment of its obligations under the United Nations resolution calling for economic sanctions against the illegally constituted regime, enacted the

---

[62] *The Times*, October 22, 1970. The Attorney General also emphasised the legal difficulties in establishing jurisdiction to try the case in the English courts, which would depend on whether the aircraft was in British airspace at the time of the alleged hijacking. For an elaboration of the jurisdictional issues, see Skelhorn *op. cit.* pp. 123–124.

[63] H.C. Deb., Vol. 976, cols. 627–639, December 19, 1979.

Southern Rhodesia (Petroleum) Order 1965.[64] It was later replaced by the Southern Rhodesia (United Nations Sanctions) Orders (Nos. 1 and 2) 1968, which extended the range of commodities and products which it sought to deny to the illegal regime in Rhodesia.[65] High among the list of these vital supplies were petroleum and its by-products but the efforts directed to this end were singularly ineffectual. Evasion of the prohibitions took several forms. The original route for leaking oil surreptitiously to Rhodesia was via Portuguese Mozambique. Later, a more circuitous strategy emerged whereby the French company Total, based in South Africa, accommodated all the oil needs of Rhodesia in the certain knowledge that its own stocks would be replenished by the South African subsidiaries of Shell and B.P., the British parent companies.[66] It is important to recognise at the outset that whereas the parent companies were in all respects subject to English law, their subsidiaries and their corporate officers were subject to the laws of South Africa, whose Government adhered firmly to the policy of non-interference in the choice of customers who sought to do business with its locally incorporated companies.[67]

The net effect, at least so far as the supply of oil was concerned, was to empty the legislative sanctions of any practical significance. Over the years rumours circulated suggesting that the United Kingdom Government connived at the state of affairs that effectively nullified its laws prohibiting the supply of oil to Rhodesia. Not until 1977, however, was any action taken to quell the rumours and to establish the extent of the oil companies' complicity in evading the law. In that year, Dr. David Owen, Secretary of State for Foreign and Commonwealth Affairs, appointed a Commission of Inquiry headed by Mr. T. H. Bingham Q.C. (now Mr. Justice Bingham) with the precise object of establishing the facts and obtaining evidence of the commission of any offences against the sanctions orders which might be disclosed.[68] A year later the inquiry submitted its report to the

---

[64] S.I. 1965 No. 2140.

[65] The first of these Orders (S.I. 1968 No. 885) obtained the necessary approval of the House of Commons but not of the House of Lords. A further Order was therefore introduced (S.I. 1968 No. 1020). This was duly approved by both Houses of Parliament. The terms of the 1965 and 1968 Sanctions Orders are conveniently set out in the Bingham Report (see fn. 69 below), pp. 24–25.

[66] The facts, as summarised in the above and following paragraphs, are derived from the Bingham Report, see especially pp. 212–223, 248–249, 251–253, 259–260, 268–270, 295.

[67] Ibid. pp. 256–259.

[68] The terms of reference of the investigation were: (a) to establish the facts concerning the operations whereby supplies of petroleum and petroleum products have reached Rhodesia since December 17, 1965; (b) to establish the extent, if any, to which persons and companies within the scope of the Sanctions Orders have played any part in the operations; (c) to obtain evidence and information for the purpose of securing compliance with or detecting evasion of the Southern Rhodesia (United Nations Sanctions) (No. 2) Order 1968 and (d) to obtain evidence of the commission of any offences against the Sanctions order which may be disclosed. Writing five years later on the need for an inquiry into the events surrounding the Falklands invasion by Argentina, Dr. Owen recalled his involvement in setting up the Bingham inquiry. He wrote: "The power of the Executive—which means both ministers and

Minister[69] who, in turn, referred the report to the Director of Public Prosecutions with a view to reaching a decision as to whether criminal proceedings should be instituted for breaches of the Southern Rhodesia (United Nations Sanctions) Orders 1968.[70]

Faced with the task of chronicling in detail the sequence of events that took place 12 years earlier, the Bingham Inquiry in its report made no effort to conceal the difficulties it had encountered. The most important obstacles were the amenability of most of the key witnesses, resident in Rhodesia and South Africa, to the domestic legislation of their own countries which made it an offence punishable by imprisonment to communicate information concerning oil stocks and supplies otherwise than in the course of ordinary commercial transactions.[71] The Bingham Inquiry concluded that there was no prospect of obtaining any useful information from those who might have been immediately involved in the transfer of oil supplies from South Africa to Rhodesia. Moreover, the Governments of Zambia, Mozambique and South Africa declined to cooperate by making available to the inquiry any information or documents in their possession.[72] The inquiry, accordingly, turned its attention to the activities of the parent companies, Shell and B.P., located in London and their negotiations with Ministers and senior officials of the British Government.[73]

As the Attorney General, Sir Michael Havers, readily acknowledged in his statement to the House of Commons in December 1979, highly confidential meetings had taken place in February 1968 and again in February 1969 between representatives of the Wilson Government and senior officers of Shell and B.P. The Bingham Inquiry report includes the minutes of these illuminating encounters,[74] from which it can be gleaned

---

civil servants—to dilute any findings is immense. As one who still bears the institutional battle scars of establishing, publishing and then attempting to implement the findings of the Bingham Inquiry into Rhodesian oil sanctions, I know only too well how hard it will be to discover the truth." *The Times*, June 18, 1982.

[69] *Report on the Supply of Petroleum and Petroleum Products to Rhodesia* by T.H. Bingham Q.C. and S.M. Gray F.C.A., published by H.M.S.O. for the Foreign and Commonwealth Office, 1978.

[70] See the statement of the Attorney General to the House of Commons, *supra*, fn. 63, col. 627. Included in the Bingham Report, but not immediately released with the rest of the report, was Annex III entitled "Evidence of Criminal Charges." It collects together references to evidence contained in the main report which would be relevant in considering whether offences against the sanctions orders had been committed. It also examined in detail the legal obligations and structure of the network of companies mentioned in the report.

[71] Bingham Report, p. iv.

[72] *Ibid.* p. v.

[73] The inquiry's approaches to other oil companies was unproductive, the report stating: "The parent companies of the major foreign Groups involved have been either unable or unwilling to give detailed assistance on the facts. Their subsidiaries in the United Kingdom, from which alone we have power to require information, have been fully cooperative but have had little valuable information to give"—*ibid.* p. iv.

[74] *Ibid.* Annex II, p. 256 *et seq.* (these are the minutes taken by officials of the Foreign and Commonwealth Office) and Annex II, pp. 259–260 (these are notes of the same discussion as recorded by officials of the Royal Dutch Shell Group and British Petroleum).

that the government's team, which included representatives from the Foreign Office and the Ministry of Power, was led by Mr. George (now Lord) Thomson, the Secretary of State for Commonwealth Affairs.[75] The overriding impression conveyed by the record of these frank discussions was the anxiety of the Wilson Government to refute allegations by African leaders that the British were directly involved in the circumvention of the United Nations sanctions.[76] To this end, for example, the minutes record: "In discussion, it was agreed that in any statements in the House of Commons or elsewhere, Ministers would be stating the position with complete accuracy if they used a formula along the lines: 'No British company is supplying P.O.L. to Rhodesia.' "[77] The same minutes leave no doubt of the full knowledge by the British Government's representatives as to the arrangements which were made through Shell and B.P. subsidiaries whereby British oil was leaked through Mozambique into Rhodesia, and later as to the exchange arrangements between Shell/B.P. (South Africa) and Total (South Africa) facilitating the diversion of substantial quantities of "French" oil into Rhodesia. The emphasis in the 1968 and 1969 discussions was on the ability of Ministers of the Crown to defend compliance with the strict letter of the sanctions orders notwithstanding the clearest evidence that the same laws were being subverted in spirit by the South African subsidiaries who could claim that, because they were registered companies outside British jurisdiction, they were obliged, by South African law, to supply oil to any customer who asked for it.[78] The entire plan reeks of hypocritical complicity that outwardly, at least, had all the appearances of being legally sound and therefore politically defensible. With justification, it seems to me, the Attorney General in 1979 could summarise the outcome of the London meetings with the Shell and B.P. executives in 1968 and 1969 as conveying to the oil companies tacit, if not express, approval to their operating, through their subsidiaries in South Africa, what had become known as the "exchange" scheme that ensured the continuous supply of oil and petroleum to Rhodesia during the years that U.D.I. was in place.[79]

What of the actions taken by the Director of Public Prosecutions? Faced with a mass of paper including the contents of 14,000 files amounting to 250,000 documents, which were considered relevant to the possibility of

---

[75] At the February 1969 meeting Mr. Thomson was Minister without Portfolio.

[76] *Ibid.* p. 256. Details of the mode of circumventing the sanctions orders are given by the senior representatives of the Shell and B.P. groups—*loc. cit.*

[77] *Ibid.* p. 257. The same minutes continue: "If asked whether P.O.L. consigned to the Transvaal by the British companies was being diverted to Rhodesia, Ministers could truthfully say something along the following lines. 'We have of course looked into this possibility. We are satisfied that this is not happening.' "

[78] *Ibid.* The Shell and B.P. representatives informed the Commonwealth Secretary, and the other United Kingdom Government representatives, of discussions which they had had on the same subject with the Prime Minister of South Africa and of the drastic repercussions to their assets that might follow if their South African companies failed to fulfill any orders placed with them by South African customers.—*ibid.* p. 259.

[79] H.C. Deb., Vol. 976, col. 627, December 19, 1979.

instituting criminal proceedings, the Director called upon the services of senior and junior counsel to advise him as to whether prosecutions should be brought and, if so, against whom.[80] Apart from the difficulties already adverted to wherein many of the principal officers in the South African subsidiaries were not amenable to the jurisdiction of the British courts, and could not be compelled to attend as witnesses, counsel were of the opinion that a jury might well be reluctant to convict if there appeared to be substance in the defence that those who might be charged acted in the belief that their conduct had the express or ostensible consent of the authorities.[81] A jury trial, it was estimated, would last for 12 months, and the complex investigation of identifying with exact precision, for the purposes of complying with the rules of evidence and enabling individual responsibility to be assessed, who had authorised which shipments, when and under what conditions, would occupy at least 4 years before everything was ready to proceed to trial.[82] In the light of all these considerations the Director of Public Prosecutions concluded that public expenditures in pursuing the massive further investigations called for would not be justified and that the whole matter should not proceed any further. This view was communicated to the Attorney General who concurred in the Director's decision.[83]

In responding to the Opposition's criticisms in the Commons the Attorney General, Sir Michael Havers, confirmed that there had been a series of relatively minor and successful prosecutions against companies and individuals for other violations of the sanctions orders, brought by the Director of Public Prosecutions and, separately, by the Customs and Excise authorities.[84] Challenged to deny that the decision not to prosecute the Shell and B.P. parent companies and their senior officials was a political decision made by the Government, the Attorney General totally rejected the accusation, stating " . . . this decision is remote and divorced from any decision of the Government. It is a decision by the Director of Public Prosecutions. Any comment to the contrary is a direct and totally unjustified attack upon the integrity of both counsel and the Director of

[80] *Ibid.* Initially, there was the obvious need—fully appreciated by the Bingham Inquiry—to undertake much more factual investigation and research in order to particularise offences, to identify the principal persons acting on behalf of the companies and to collect the admissible evidence. A team of senior police officers was assigned this laborious but essential task, if there was to be any prospect of launching successful prosecutions. The material disclosed by the Bingham Inquiry, on its own, was wholly insufficient for the purposes of a criminal trial. Just how extensive the police investigation actually developed was the subject of a critical article in *The Sunday Times*, January 28, 1980.

[81] *Ibid.* col. 629.

[82] *Ibid.* This estimate was based on the assumption that the defendants would be entitled to require full committal proceedings and strict proof of the essential ingredients required to establish criminal responsibility.

[83] *Ibid.* and see also cols. 637–638.

[84] *Ibid.* cols. 630, 639. Fuller details of these "minor" prosecutions, brought at the instance of the D.P.P., were released by the Director's office and published in *The Times*, January 10, 1980. Information on other prosecutions instituted by the Customs & Excise authorities appeared in *The Times*, January 9, 1980.

Public Prosecutions who is totally impartial in these matters."[85] Sir Michael Havers emphasised that whilst the initial decision not to prosecute had been determined by the Director he accepted equal responsibility as Attorney General for that decision.[86]

On the strictly legal arguments invoked by the Attorney General and the Director of Public Prosecutions to explain this conclusion it is hard to find persuasive grounds for seriously challenging the Director's decision. The Bingham Report, after all, was not a report based on evidence that could be produced in court. This, coupled with the jurisdictional problems and the prospect of a successful defence based on the express or implied consent of the government's own ministers to the alleged violations of the law, constituted the major explanation as to why the decision was made not to press forward with criminal proceedings years after the alleged violations had taken place. What was not answered in the Commons debate was the failure of previous administrations, both Labour and Conservative, to initiate serious investigations of possible criminal conduct and, instead, to draw a discreet veil over governmental involvement at ministerial level in circumventing the very laws the government itself had seen fit to enact.[87] That the essential facts were known to senior officials in both the Ministry of Power and in the Foreign and Commonwealth Affairs is beyond question. The same conclusion is irrefutable so far as the Secretary of State for Foreign and Commonwealth Affairs is concerned, since he presided over the meetings described earlier and the official minutes of which are available for public inspection.[88] Whether such

---

[85] *Ibid.* cols. 635–636.

[86] *Ibid.* col. 634.

[87] On February 1, 1979, the House of Commons, on a free vote, resolved by 146 votes to 67 to set up a parliamentary Special Commission on oil sanctions. The commission was "to consider, following the report of the Bingham Inquiry, the part played by those concerned in the development and application of the policy of oil sanctions against Rhodesia with a view to determining whether Parliament or Ministers were misled, intentionally or otherwise, and to report." The Commission was to have access to all material Cabinet papers and departmental files, sit in private, be chaired by a Lord of Appeal in Ordinary who would pre-vet confidential documents, and report without publication of the supporting evidence—see H.C. Deb., Vol. 961, cols. 1709–1814, February 1, 1979. A week later, the House of Lords, by 102 votes to 58, refused to support the Commons' resolution: H.L. Deb., Vol. 398, cols. 849–892, February 8, 1979. Nothing further was heard or done about setting up the special Parliamentary inquiry.

[88] Speaking of the period 1968–70, when the Labour Government was in power, Lord Thomson also wrote: "We could, it is true, have behaved differently towards the British oil companies in the winter of 1967–68. We could have tried to prosecute them for the breaches before 1968, of which their London managements claimed to have been kept in the dark by their subsidiaries. This was not a matter for the Commonwealth Office alone, and the suggestion that it was I who decided not to prosecute and even that I decided to take this course without consulting colleagues is ludicrous. What was accepted by the Government was that, up to 1968, the London boards of the oil companies had acted in good faith when they denied responsibility for what had happened. Even with the advantage of hindsight I personally cannot believe we would have been right to have acted differently. If there had been a prosecution at that time, whether successful or not, the revelation of the fact that British companies had been supplying oil would have given a great boost to the morale of the Rhodesians. We should also have provoked a crisis for British oil companies in South Africa, doing great damage to Britain's economic interests at a time of national weakness, and have alienated the South African authorities at a time we were seeking their political help again,

knowledge extended upwards to include other Cabinet Ministers and the Prime Minister cannot be established with the same degree of certitude.[89] Complicity among the higher levels of the government, however, can be inferred with some confidence, at least with respect to the Wilson Administration which was in office during the crucial years 1965–70. In a statement released by Lord Thomson of Montifieth shortly before the publication of the Bingham Report, the former Commonwealth Secretary stated: "I conveyed in writing to the Prime Minister and other Ministers most directly concerned a full account of all that passed at my meetings on behalf of the Government with the oil companies. The obvious ineffectiveness of the Rhodesian oil sanctions and the implications this constituted for the British oil companies were in fact discussed frequently by the ministers concerned before I joined the Cabinet, during my period as Commonwealth Secretary, and afterwards. The meetings I had with the oil companies in the winter of 1968–69 were the result of a collective decision of one of those ministerial committees."[90] It stretches credulity to be asked to believe that Mr. Heath's succession to power in 1970 was accompanied by a state of blissful ignorance of what had gone on before and what was continuing to be done without any serious expressions of disapproval as to the arrangements between the British oil companies, their subsidiaries, and the French Total company.[91]

without making any difference to the volume of oil reaching Rhodesia, or to the capacity for survival of the Smith regime. I cannot even now believe that on balance that would have been the better course" The message conveyed by this statement is loud and clear, that the government, in its attitude towards the oil companies, was acting in what it considered to be in the best interests of the British economy.

[89] Sir Harold Wilson, Prime Minister from before Rhodesia's unconstitutional declaration of independence in 1965 until 1970, and again between 1974 and 1976, was not asked to give evidence before the Bingham Inquiry. Prior to the release of Lord Thomson's statement, the former Prime Minister had publicly denied any knowledge that British oil companies were arranging for oil to be sold to Rhodesia in defiance of the sanctions regulations. See the correspondence between Mr. Wilson and Mr. R. W. Rowland, the head of Lonrho, the oil company that claimed to have suffered enormous losses, in compliance with the UN sanctions resolution, through the closure of its overland oil pipeline from Beira to Rhodesia—*The Times*, September 2, 1978. Set alongside Lord Thomson's claim, based on his review of the relevant Cabinet papers of the period when he was Commonwealth Secretary, to have conveyed in writing "to the Prime Minister and other ministers" a full account of what passed during the meetings between the oil companies and the Government's representatives, it is impossible to give unqualified credence to Mr. Wilson's denial of any knowledge or connivance on his part or that of his Government with respect to the circumvention of the sanctions orders.

[90] Thomson, *op. cit.* Before preparing his public statement, Lord Thomson indicated that he had exercised his rights as a former Cabinet minister to consult the appropriate papers.

[91] The major argument advanced in support of the Heath Government's ignorance of what had transpired before it assumed office in 1970 was the constitutional convention that denies a new administration the right to have access to the records of a previous Government of a different political party. See H.C. Deb., Vol. 957, cols. 991–992, November 8, 1978. The precise limits of this convention are authoritatively analysed by the former Secretary of the Cabinet (1973–79), now Lord Hunt of Tanworth, in [1982] *Public Law* 516. Excepted from the convention are the written opinions of the Law Officers of the Crown which are regarded as legal rather than political documents, and papers dealing with matters that are known to foreign governments (*e.g.* messages about inter-governmental negotiations). Former Ministers of the Crown may have access to, but not retain, any documents which they saw when in

Whatever levels of connivance may have been operating in those departments which had their own reasons for turning a blind eye to the oil companies' disobedience of the country's laws there is a total absence of any evidence that the Law Officers of the day were privy to such violations. Questioned in 1978 by the *Sunday Times*, Lord Elwyn Jones, who served as the Attorney General during the period 1964–70 but not as a member of the Cabinet, declared that "he had no recollection whatsoever that when he was Attorney General in 1968 he was asked to advise about a case to prosecute Shell for sanctions-busting. He would be surprised if his memory was at fault."[92] In response to my recent questioning on the same subject the former Attorney General instituted an exhaustive search of the official papers in both the Law Officers' Department and the Foreign and Commonwealth Office to ascertain whether there was any indication that either he, as the responsible Law Officer of the Crown, or the Law Officers' Department were ever informed or consulted about the part played by the British oil companies (Shell and B.P.), including their personnel and overseas subsidiaries, in evading the oil sanctions. This inquiry was directed specifically to the crucial years 1967 to 1969. No evidence of any kind was discovered in either of the two government divisions concerned, with respect to any correspondence or consultations with the Law Officers or their officials pertaining to possible breaches of the relevant Petroleum Order by the British companies concerned. Lord Elwyn Jones further confirmed that "to the best of my recollection I had no oral consultations with these matters. If these had taken place it is inconceivable that they could have taken place without some record of them or reference to their appearing in F.C.O. or L.O.D. papers."[93]

No indication was made as to the state of knowledge in the office of the Director of Public Prosecutions during the same period but it is reasonable to suppose that if the Director had been in a position to enlighten the Attorney General he would have felt it his duty to do so. Whatever rumours may have been circulating at the time it must be remembered that a very real dilemma would confront both the Law Officers and the Director of Public Prosecutions. Under the constitutional division of duties in relation to the criminal law, which we examined in Chapter 2, the responsibility for investigating crime basically rests with the police. In extraordinary circumstances, however, as illustrated by the Poulson corruption investigations in 1976,[94] a task force can be set up that includes

office. Furthermore, "officials have a duty to provide present Ministers with all relevant information about departmental policy or past events subject to not disclosing the personal views or comments of previous Ministers or the advice submitted directly to them"—*ibid*. p. 518.

[92] *Sunday Times* September 3, 1978.

[93] Personal communication to the author, January 21, 1983. "F.C.O." refers to the Foreign & Commonwealth Office and "L.O.D.", as seen in earlier footnotes, denotes the Law Officers' Dept. See, too, Lord Elwyn Jones' autobiography, *In My Time* (London, 1983) pp. 282–283. According to the same author neither of the Conservative Law Officers were consulted by the Eden Cabinet about the legality of the Suez action in 1956—*ibid*. p. 149.

[94] *Ante*, Chapter 4, pp. 81–85.

representatives of the police, the Director of Public Prosecutions and the Attorney General's office. This ensures that effective control is maintained both with respect to the investigative strategy and the provision of adequate resources. Exceptional circumstances both demand and usually receive the exceptional allocation of the manpower necessary to mount this kind of large scale investigation. But this is not normally possible and represents a serious limitation on the effectiveness of law enforcement authorities especially in the area of major frauds and other forms of "white collar crimes."

The results of the Bingham inquiry simply confirm the practical dimensions of this kind of problem. And where relevant information is withheld by ministers and officials who are in a position to know what is happening the difficulties confronting those charged with enforcing the criminal law are further compounded. The balance of justice may well have been properly served in Sir Michael Havers' decision in 1979 not to pursue the subject of possible criminal proceedings. The situation 10 years earlier, however, was significantly different in the sharpness of the issues involved, the immediacy of the events surrounding the breaches of the oil sanctions Orders, and the potential availability of important witnesses. Had the relevant evidence been brought to the attention of the then Attorney General, Sir Elwyn Jones, in 1968 and 1969 it is by no means inconceivable that different conclusions might appropriately have been drawn as to the necessity to set the criminal law in motion.

Reviewing the *Rhodesia oil sanctions* case in retrospect it is obvious that no simple set of criteria exists that can ensure an interpretation of "the public interest" which will command universal support by all political parties or by all segments of society. Inherent in the very concept of the public interest is the normal exercise of perceptions of what would be wise or foolhardy, beneficial or detrimental, proper or improper by the standards subscribed to by the person expressing his judgment of a particular event or course of conduct. We should not be surprised to discover that the government of the day, when representing different political parties, should reach diametrically opposite conclusions as to what is in the public interest and shape its policies accordingly. In doing so, the government may well be heavily influenced by what it considers to be conducive to favourable public support and hence to the advancement of its party's political fortunes. This is the stuff of everyday politics and must be recognised as central to the thinking of any government. There are times, however, when governments should be expected to act in accordance with the dictates of a higher conception of public standards of behaviour, notwithstanding the strong possibility that in doing so it will offend many or most of its political supporters. It is in these sorts of circumstances that the true character of governing is put to the test and on the basis of which the judgment of history will be declared. Many are the occasions in which governments fail to live up to these expectations. What really matters is that, whenever the Law Officers of the Crown become involved, society has the right to expect a consistent dedication to the more objective interpretation of the public interest when decisions have to be made that fall within the Attorney General's sphere of discretionary powers.

THE GOURIET CASE, THE CROSSMAN DIARIES CASE AND THE CLAY CROSS AFFAIR

During his tenure of the office of Attorney General for England and Wales from 1974 to 1979 Mr. Sam Silkin became a frequent target of public criticism, inside and outside Parliament, in which partisan motives were said to provide an explanation for some of the highly publicised decisions for which he was responsible. In a spirited defence of his record, delivered at the centenary meeting of the American Bar Association in 1978[95] Mr. Silkin ackowledged that "in politics you cannot win." Referring to those decisions which had been made with respect to the institution or non-institution of criminal proceedings against five of his parliamentary colleagues—three of whom were fellow members of Her Majesty's Privy Council—the former Attorney General declared that he had been subjected to deep embarrassment and misrepresentation, wilful or innocent, by his critics notwithstandng his disclosure in the House of Commons that the decision in each case had effectively been that of the Director of Public Prosecutions. Referring specifically to the *Thorpe* case in 1978, Mr. Silkin declared: "It is only a matter of weeks since ugly rumours were circulating of a cover-up . . . on the grounds that the Labour Government was anxious to promote harmony with the Liberals so as to damage the Conservatives at the forthcoming General Election. And since the men concerned have been charged there have been further ugly rumours that events were skilfully timed in order to destroy the Liberal Party at the forthcoming General Election. In fact, I have had no influence on either the decision or the timing."[96]

Fresh in the memory of Mr. Silkin's critics at that time was the Attorney General's refusal in 1977 to grant his consent to the application of Mr. Gouriet to bring relator proceedings for an injunction against the Union of Post Office Workers.[97] Speaking in the Commons, immediately following the decision of the Court of Appeal, but before that delivered by the House of Lords, Mr. Silkin defended his refusal to grant his fiat by explaining the considerations that had led him to reach that decision.[98]

[95] 100th annual meeting of the American Bar Association, New York, August 8, 1978. A brief summary of Mr. Silkin's address appeared in (1978) New L.J. 942, but I have been unable to trace any report in the United States legal literature.

[96] *Ibid.*

[97] See *ante*, pp. 129–137.

[98] H.C. Deb., Vol. 924, cols. 1699–1713, January, 27 1977. Much the same range of considerations governed the Attorney General's approach to the industrial dispute concerning *Grunwick Processing Laboratories Ltd.*—see H.C. Deb., Vol. 934, cols. 579–588, 591–592, 609–613, June 30, 1977. For the circumstances surrounding this dispute see the Report of the Court of Inquiry under Lord Justice Scarman (as he then was), Cmnd. 6922 of 1977.

When arguing before the Court of Appeal, it will be recalled, the Attorney General had steadfastly maintained that he was accountable to Parliament, not to the judiciary, for the decisions he made in the course of exercising his prerogative duties. True to this principle of ministerial responsibility, following the delivery of the Court of Appeal judgments in *Gouriet* v. *Union of Post Office Workers*, Mr. Silkin took immediate steps to explain and defend his actions on the floor of the House of Commons. The Attorney General maintained that he had adhered to well established principles applied by former Law Officers of all parties. In making his decision whether to grant a relator application, Mr. Silkin said, "the Attorney General is not confined to considering the chances of success. It is his duty also to consider broader issues of public interest and to base his conclusions on where the balance of public interest lies . . . On the face of the information available to me, and in my judgment, the taking of injunction proceedings in my name had the inherent risk, at that early stage, of inflaming the situation before the need for it was demonstrated and might well result in breaches of the law and inconvenience to the public over a much wider area than [the] two sections of Post Office employees affected by the circular. That possible reaction to court proceedings, based on a criminal offence, was all the more real in the light of the fact that the Conservative Government, in the Industrial Relations Act 1971, had, for very good reasons which were fully stated by the Solicitor General of the day, deliberately removed from the criminal law the principal existing provisions making industrial action a crime."[99] In an attempt to establish the common considerations that must have motivated his Conservative predecessors, Sir Peter Rawlinson and Sir Michael Havers, when serving as the Law Officers of the Crown in the Heath Government, Mr. Silkin reminded the House of Commons that no action had been taken in the virtually identical circumstances that prevailed in 1973 when the target of the Post Office workers' industrial action had been the proposed French nuclear tests.[1] In recognising that on that occasion, as well as in the *Leila Khalid* episode referred to earlier,[2] there had been no application for the Attorney General to intervene, Mr. Silkin was not prepared to accept that explanation as concluding the discharge of the Law Officers' responsibilities. "The Attorney General," he reminded the Lower House, "can bring proceedings *ex officio* without the intervention of a private citizen. I would need a great deal of convincing that the Law Officers of the Crown at that time had their heads so buried in the sand that they did not know what was going on around them."[3]

---

[99] *Ibid.* cols. 1701–1703, and see, too, cols. 1706 and 1710. As Solicitor General, Sir Geoffrey Howe had explained to the Commons that the purpose of clause 120 of the Industrial Relations Bill, 1971 was to reduce as far as possible the impact of the criminal law on industrial relations. Cl. 120 became section 133 in the Act.

[1] *Ibid.* col. 1703.

[2] *Ibid.* cols. 1704 and see *ante*, pp. 324–325.

[3] *Ibid.* col. 1706.

The Shadow Attorney General, Sir Michael Havers, offered no explanation of the 1973 precedent but claimed that nothing contained in Mr. Silkin's speech would allay suspicions about the political use of his prerogative discretion.[4] In reply, the Labour Attorney General reiterated repeatedly that the dominant consideration in his mind had been his judgment of what was in the public interest. The decision had been his alone, not that of the Cabinet,[5] though it can readily be deduced from Mr. Silkin's remarks that he had sought advice from some of his ministerial colleagues, most closely concerned with the effects of the industrial action, as to the possible repercussions of invoking the criminal law. "It is of great importance," Mr. Silkin concluded, "that the Attorney General should take a view of the public interest in cases of this kind on facts which may not be available to others which, indeed, in some cases he will not even be able to give to this House, although I hope that if challenged he will always be in that position—but certainly one cannot guarantee that would always be so. That being the case, until Parliament has worked out . . . the right way in which this public interest sieve can operate without the present antiquated methods of the Attorney General's fiat, it is right to follow the practice followed again and again by the Attorneys General of both parties."[6]

It might well have been anticipated that, even applying the same set of considerations as those outlined by Mr. Silkin in his House of Commons speech, including the overriding criterion of what is in the public interest, a Conservative Attorney General would have reached a different conclusion in the *Gouriet* situation. Indeed, it is no secret that had Sir Michael Havers been in the position then occupied by Mr. Silkin the Post Office workers would have had to face criminal charges, thus demonstrating what many observers would claim is a predictable divergence in the meaning accorded to "the public interest" by adherents of the major political parties in Britain. This largely depends on the way in which the actions of the Post Office workers and the response of the Attorney General is portrayed. On the one hand, the situation could be described as a direct challenge to the rule of law to which the State's response must be immediate and unequivocal, or, on the other hand, as calling for an appraisal of the dangerous consequences, by way of extending the dispute, that would be likely if precipitate action were taken in the form of bringing the strikers before the criminal courts.

Either of these decisions is capable of attracting criticism as having been dictated by a political ideology, and it is somewhat futile for the Attorney General of any political party to disclaim completely any political influences when making his decision on whether or not to enforce the laws of this country. The responsibility for making these decisions has

---

[4] *Ibid*. col. 1703.
[5] See Written Answers, col. 30, January 31, 1977.
[6] *Ibid*. cols. 1712–1713, January 27, 1977.

constitutionally been placed on the shoulders of the Law Officers of the Crown acting independently from the direction of the Prime Minister or the Cabinet. Judged by the public record of what transpired in each of the recent cases, reviewed above, there is no body of evidence to controvert the impression of a conscientious Attorney General endeavouring to balance the conflicting considerations in what he deemed to be in the best interests of society. Whichever decision is finally decided upon, public and parliamentary criticism must be expected. The ensuing public judgment will be influenced to a large degree by the previous decisions of the person occupying the office of Attorney General.

These decisions, moreover, are likely to cover a broad range of issues in which industrial disputes are but one of the high profile areas that call for the exercise by the Attorney General of his prerogative or statutory consent powers of discretion. These cases may entail consideration of such diverse laws as those regulating government secrecy, race relations, abortion, pornography, anti-nuclear demonstrations, picketing and the protection of property and employers' interests, or complaints against the police. The handling of situations that seem to involve the activities of powerful lobby groups—whether these represent the labour unions, big business or party interests—are very important criteria in judging an Attorney General's record of adherence to the standards of impartiality associated with the Law Officers of the Crown. The fact that the public's perceptions may be based on something less than a full appreciation of all the facts is a predicament that any Minister of the Crown must face. The Attorney General is accountable to Parliament for his decisions and that is the forum in which he can defend himself by demonstrating the grounds on which he acted in the particular circumstances.

The *Crossman Diaries* affair in 1975 and its handling by the Attorney General is another episode in Mr. Silkin's tenure of office that is likely to be recalled when assessments are made of individual Law Officers and their adherence to the basic concept of independence. Unfortunately, this kind of exercise sometimes becomes distorted by the critic's embellishment of the facts and the *Crossman* case is an apt illustration of how misapprehensions can colour the judgment of posterity. Richard Crossman's celebrated *Diaries of a Cabinet Minister*[7] derived from tape recordings of Cabinet deliberations in which he took part during the Wilson Government's rule in 1964–70. There was no secret amongst his Cabinet colleagues that he was doing so or of his intention to publish, at some politically opportune time, a "blow by blow" account of his ministerial experience including deliberations by the Cabinet and Cabinet committees. Crossman, it should be remembered, was a strong exponent of open government and, as appears in the introduction to volume one of

---

[7] Jonathan Cape, London, 1975. Volume 1 dealt with the period 1964–66, when Crossman was Minister of Housing; Vol. 2 is devoted to the years 1966–68, during which the author was Lord President of the Council and Leader of the House of Commons.

his *Diaries*,[8] disapproved of the practice requiring ministerial memoirs to be submitted for clearance by the Secretary of the Cabinet.

When, following the serialisation of extracts from the first volume in the *Sunday Times*, the Attorney General instituted proceedings to impose a permanent injunction against the publication of further extracts as well as the *Diaries* themselves, it was clearly within his prerogative powers to do so. The grounds on which the Attorney General, acting *ex officio*, sought the injunction was that the publication of the *Diaries* was contrary to the public interest. The application of this criterion, it was argued, required that the doctrine of collective responsibility be sustained and details of Cabinet deliberations not be disclosed until they became available for public scrutiny under the 30 year rule contained in the Public Records Act 1967. The public interest also required that there be no disclosure of confidential communications between Ministers and their senior civil servants. The judgment of Lord Widgery C.J. resolving the *Crossman Diaries* issue in *Att. Gen.* v. *Times Newspapers Ltd.*,[9] is yet another example of the necessity to balance conflicting public interests. On the one hand there is the call for readier public access to the inner workings of government, against which must be set the long established tradition of Cabinet secrecy.

According to the Chief Justice, the Attorney General had made out his claim that the expression of individual opinions by ministers in the course of Cabinet discussions were matters of confidence, the publication of which could be restrained by the court where this is clearly necessary in the public interest.[10] The degree of protection, however, to be accorded such material cannot be determined by a single rule of thumb. An arbitrary period of 30 years was held to be excessively restrictive.[11] Lord Widgery had wisely read the whole of volume one of the *Diaries* before delivering his judgment. His considered view, having regard to the interval of nearly 10 years that had lapsed since the events described in the first volume, was that there was nothing in the *Diaries* that "would inhibit free discussion in the Cabinet of today, even though the individuals involved are the same,

---

[8] *Ibid.* pp. 12–14. On the general issues of Cabinet confidentiality and their application to the Crossman diaries see Lord Chalfont's stimulating review article in [1977] *The Parliamentarian* 71.

[9] *Attorney General* v. *Jonathan Cape Ltd. & Others*; *Attorney General* v. *Times Newspapers Ltd.* [1975] 3 W.L.R. 606; [1975] 3 All E.R. 484. Publication by the *Sunday Times* on June 22, 1975 of an article "The jigsaw of truth" deliberately included unpublished Crossman material that had not previously been submitted to the Cabinet office. An application by the Attorney General for an interim injunction was granted by Ackner J. on June 26. This was vacated by the Court of Appeal in return for certain undertakings by the newspaper—see *The Times* Law Report, June 27 and 28, 1975, and see also Hugo Young (fn. 20 below) *op. cit.* p. 46.

[10] The Court accepted the view propounded by the Attorney General that, since the confidence is imposed to enable the efficient conduct of the Queen's business, the confidence is owed to the Queen and cannot be released to members of the Cabinet themselves. Thus, a resigning Minister who wishes to make a personal statement in the House, and to disclose matters which are confidential, under the doctrine obtains the consent of the Queen for this purpose—[1975] 3 W.L.R. 606 at p. 618.

[11] *Ibid.* p. 619.

and the national problems have a distressing similarity with those of a decade ago . . . The court should intervene only in the clearest of cases where the continuing confidentiality of the material can be demonstrated. In less clear cases—and this, in my view, is certainly one—reliance must be placed on the good sense and good taste of the Minister or ex-Minister concerned."[12] The injunction sought by the Attorney General was accordingly refused. The defendants, Times Newspapers Ltd., gave an undertaking to the court not to publish further extracts from the *Diaries* for a short period of time pending a decision by the Attorney whether or not to appeal the judgment of the Chief Justice. No such appeal was launched by the Law Officers of the Crown.

The decision was interpreted in many quarters as a resounding defeat for Mr. Silkin who was accused of trying to suppress the publication of the *Crossman Diaries* to avoid embarrassing his government colleagues. Some went further and implied that improper pressures by the Prime Minister and Cabinet were the real explanation behind the Attorney General's recourse to the court in pursuit of an injunction. More recently the view was once again aired that the Attorney General had acted on the prompting of the Secretary of the Cabinet, an implication strongly denied by Sir Robert Armstrong, the present occupant of that office.[13] Prior to the injunction hearing in July 1975, Mr. Silkin took the unusual step of issuing a public statement rejecting the suggestion made in *The Times* leading article that he had not acted of his own volition in the *Crossman Diaries* case.[14] According to the Attorney General's statement "the allegations that he was acting under the influence of the Prime Minister and the Secretary of the Cabinet are wholly unfounded. The decision to proceed with the applications for injunctions were the Attorney General's and his alone . . . The Attorney General wishes to emphasize that neither the Prime Minister nor any other Minister, nor the Secretary of the Cabinet, asked to be consulted by him in respect of either of the pending actions; nor did any of them seek to influence him in any way."[15] This explanation by the Attorney General was later confirmed to the House of Commons in a written reply to a question tabled by a Labour backbencher.[16]

The issues surrounding the publication of the first volume of the diaries, and the serialisation of extracts by *The Sunday Times*, had engaged the attention of the Attorney General, Treasury Counsel and the Attorney's legal and constitutional advisers long before the eventual decision was

[12] *Ibid.*
[13] See below, fn. 15.
[14] See *The Times* leader, June 28, 1975.
[15] The *Sunday Times*, June 29, 1975 and see also Mr. Silkin's letter to the Editor of *The Times*, June 30, 1975. So far as the Secretary of the Cabinet was concerned, corroboration of Mr. Silkin's statement was forthcoming some years later in a letter to the Editor of *The Times* (March 10, 1982) by the present incumbent in that office, Sir Robert Armstrong, who wrote to correct an error of fact in Bernard Donoughue's article on "open government" (*The Times*, February 25, 1982) "since it gives renewed currency to an old misapprehension."
[16] H.C. Deb., Vol. 940, Written Answers, col. 292, December 1, 1977.

made to proceed by way of injunctive proceedings. With a lack of legal precedent to guide the Attorney General there was uncertainty as to the basis for challenging the breach of Cabinet confidentiality. In the past, former Prime Ministers, Ministers, and other public figures (*e.g.* military leaders) had observed, with varying degrees of latitude, guidelines that were controlled by the Secretary of the Cabinet, acting as the delegate of the Prime Minister of the day. But these discretionary guidelines, operated in advance of publication, lacked the force of established law. Alongside this element of doubt as to the relevant legal principles was the pervasive issue of freedom of information and the cry for open government. Relations between the press and the Wilson Administration had been deteriorating for some time before the diaries issues surfaced publicly. A further confrontation was most assuredly calculated to exacerbate relations still further. There had been an inconclusive review of the question of Cabinet confidentiality in the closing stages of the 1964–70 Labour Government, instigated by Richard Crossman and Barbara Castle, the champions of open government. This philosophy had been actively resisted by those who favoured adherence to the traditional conventions governing the publication of ministerial memoirs.[17] No further action was taken until April 1975 when, following advice by the Attorney General, Mr. Silkin,[18] the Prime Minister announced the setting up of the Committee of Privy Councillors on Ministerial Memoirs under the chairmanship of Lord Radcliffe, with the expectation that it would submit its report and recommendations as speedily as possible.[19] In the event, the Radcliffe Committee tabled its report in January 1976,[20] nearly four months after Lord Widgery C.J. had delivered his judgment in *Att. Gen.* v. *Times Newspapers Ltd.* Had events moved more rapidly in terms of the Cabinet deciding what changes were necessary, for example, in limiting the length of time within which Cabinet papers should be kept secret, it is conceivable that the Attorney General's decision to seek an injunction in the Crossman diaries case might not have been seen to be necessary. That, however, was not the case in June 1975 when the writ was issued by the senior Law Officer of the Crown acting *ex officio*.

Somewhat paradoxically, in the light of the position which the Attorney General was forced to adopt in his *ex officio* capacity when arguing the case

---

[17] Personal communication to the author from Mr. Silkin, June 16, 1983.

[18] *Ibid.*

[19] H.C.Deb., Vol. 889, col. 483, April 11, 1975.

[20] Cmnd. 6386. The Committee's recommendations were accepted in full by the Wilson Government—see H.C.Deb. Vol. 903, Written Answers, cols. 521–523, January 22, 1976. According to one writer: "the net effect of the new 'rules', which it is emphasised do not have the force of law, is to construct a more formalised vetting system and to place on Ministers a more precise moral obligation to observe the code of behaviour than was previously evident. The existing conventions are not merely restated but amplified, hardened and given more suppressive force." See Hugo Young, *The Crossman Affair*, (London, 1977), p. 206. The official summary of the Radcliffe Committee's conclusions and recommendations are conveniently reprinted *ibid.*, Appendix 2.

for an injunction before the Queen's Bench Division, Mr. Silkin, a few weeks earlier, had appeared as a witness before the Radcliffe Committee to argue for a change in the legal position governing access to Cabinet confidential material.[21] In the course of his testimony Mr. Silkin suggested that there should be a substantial reduction in the 30 year period which governs the publication of material pertaining to Cabinet discussions. In Mr. Silkin's opinion, a ten year moratorium should suffice and he envisaged a statutory right of appeal against the initial ruling by the Cabinet Secretary.[22] In putting forward these ideas he stressed that he was expressing his personal opinion and not that of the Government. It is worth noting at this point that the Radcliffe Committee recommended a 15 year waiting period,[23] a position that the Wilson Administration quickly accepted and which now governs the discretionary authority exercisable by the Cabinet Secretary.

These changes, it should be stressed, were still in the realm of conjecture in June 1975 when the confrontation developed between the editor of the *Sunday Times* and the Cabinet office. According to the Attorney General he had to judge the situation as it stood, without the benefit of the opinion subsequently expressed by Lord Radcliffe and his colleagues to the effect that, in similar circumstances, legal action should be avoided except as a last resort.[24] It then becomes a question of judgment as to which side the balance tilts in terms of safeguarding the respective public interests at stake. Writing eight years later[25] Mr. Silkin remains convinced that in the circumstances facing him at the time he made the right decision. His only regret is that the policy review, which he had pressed for and which finally resulted in the adoption of the Radcliffe Committee's recommendations, had not taken place before the publication of the Crossman diaries had made its dramatic impact on everyone concerned. In the course of the same note to this writer the former Attorney General reconfirmed what he had previously stated publicly, first, in a letter to the editor of *The Times*[26] and, secondly, in the statement to which reference was made earlier,[27] *viz.*, that he had not acted on anybody's instructions or request. The decision to initiate injunction proceedings was his alone.

[21] *The Times*, July 15, 1975. The Attorney General made his suggestions in the form of three written memoranda and in oral evidence before the Committee.
[22] *Ibid.*
[23] *Op. cit.* pp. 30–31.
[24] *Op. cit.* pp. 22–26.
[25] *Ante*, fn. 17.
[26] Replying to *The Times* leader "The Secrecy of Government," of June 28, 1975, Mr. Silkin wrote: "The language which you employ plainly asserts that the Prime Minister and I are lying when we say that in decisions of that character, that is, in the enforcement of the present law as I understand it, I am totally independent and that no pressure is applied to me, whether by the Prime Minister or anyone else. You are utterly, hopelessly and dangerously wrong. When the Prime Minister invited me to accept my present office, he made that independence absolutely clear to me. He has done nothing since to modify or alter what he then said. You may fire if you wish, but are you firing at the wrong target."—Letters to the Editor, June 30, 1975.
[27] *Ante*, fn. 15.

In the absence of any further elaboration of the events surrounding the handling of the Crossman diaries, it would be proper to conclude that there had been a correct application of the constitutional conventions governing the Attorney General's exercise of his discretionary powers in matters affecting public rights and the protection of the public interest. Mr. Silkin's public statements at the time, in June 1975, do not suggest that there were no consultations. On the contrary, the implications to be drawn from the Attorney General's carefully phrased statement, rejecting the insinuation contained in *The Times* leader which dubbed as a "great absurdity and a great untruth" the pretence that the Attorney was acting purely of his own volition in the Crossman matter, are that Mr. Silkin did in fact seek the opinions of other members of the Wilson Government, as well as sounding out the reactions of the Secretary of the Cabinet.[28] In doing so, Mr. Silkin was acting entirely within the ambit of the principles set forth in the well known exposition by Sir Hartley Shawcross in 1951. There is also ample evidence that the decision was not reached in haste but after the widest possible consultations with his closest advisers within the Law Officers' Department.

This being the case, it is unfortunate that Mr. Silkin is on record as stating, in the course of a lengthy BBC radio interview and subsequently published in *The Listener*,[29] that it may well have been preferable that the commencement of the Crossman proceedings ought to have been a Cabinet decision. This attribution of doubt in the mind of the then Attorney General as to his constitutional duty and the role of the Cabinet is so startlingly at odds with both Mr. Silkin's contemporary statements at the time, as well as the exposition of his philosophy with respect to the office of Attorney General analysed earlier in this study, that caution is called for in according too much significance to this précis of Mr. Silkin's remarks. Placed in the wider context of the Cabinet's dilatoriness in formulating its position on Cabinet confidentiality, which was the setting within which the Attorney General had to make his decision, it is not unreasonable to conclude that it was to this question of Cabinet policy making, and not the actual decision to launch the court proceedings, that reference was being made on the course of the radio interview.

Another event that drew much public attention and parliamentary denunciation during Mr. Silkin's tenure of the Attorney Generalship was the *Clay Cross* controversy in 1975. It seems abundantly clear, in

---

[28] *Ibid.*

[29] July 3, 1980, p. 6. In the course of the same interview, the former Attorney General stated "I never gave way to pressure at all. It is one of the cardinal principles of government that Ministers do not press the Attorney General on matters that are within his own realm and they didn't do so. I never had any trade union pressure and I never had any security pressure. I formed my own judgments on the evidence that was presented to me. I made up my mind on a balance, which one has to, of public interest. And when it came to the 95 per cent. of matters behind the scenes which you never hear, I am quite confident that my colleagues accepted my judgment and believed that I was a person they could rely on, and I never hesitated to tell them when I thought that what they were doing was wrong."

retrospect, that his handling of the issues connected with that case coloured much of the suspicious feelings entertained by large sections of the public, including the Bar, towards his subsequent decisions. This was especially so in respect to the announcement, two years later, that the Attorney General had refused to grant his fiat in the *Gouriet* case. Perhaps the depths of the virulent comment provoked by Mr. Silkin's handling in the Clay Cross affair were reached in the columnist's atrocious observation that "No doubt they will find 'Clay Cross' inscribed on the heart of . . . Mr. Sam Silkin when he dies; indeed it is my pleasure . . . to make quite certain that they do, by carving the words there with a chisel."[30] Already, however, the details of that episode are beginning to fade in the public memory. A short summary of the pertinent facts is therefore advisable before we examine the role played by the Attorney General and form a judgment as to whether the widespread castigation of Mr. Silkin's conduct was justified in the circumstances.[31]

Clay Cross is a small community in the County of Derby. Its Urban District Council, with a Labour majority, decided to mount a direct challenge to the Housing Finance Act 1972. This measure was introduced by the Conservative Government as a means towards achieving economic rents and diminishing the level of government housing subsidies. To this end the Act imposed duties upon local authorities to make gradually progressive increases in the rents payable by tenants occupying council houses while at the same time providing for rebates to those tenants who could not afford to pay. These rebates were to be assessed by a means test, according to the tenant's needs and resources. Both before and after the Act came into law the members of the Clay Cross Urban District Council made publicly known their determination not to put into operation any of the provisions contained in the new legislation, claiming that to do so would be in violation of their pledges as to housing policy on which they were elected to the council. The clerk to the council and its chief financial officer warned the council members of the consequences that might flow from their actions. These warnings were repeated by the Secretary of State for the Environment, the responsible minister for housing, but to no avail.

In due course the Minister, having made a default order against the Clay Cross Council, directed that an extraordinary audit be conducted by the district auditor. He concluded that a loss of approximately £7,000 had been incurred by the councillors' negligence and misconduct. "This," the district auditor wrote "was no accidental omission to carry out their statutory duties, but a deliberate flouting of the law in furtherance of their political views."[32] Accordingly the councillors were surcharged, requiring that they personally make good the losses incurred by the housing revenue account

---

[30] Bernard Levin in *The Times*, March 13, 1975.
[31] The summary that follows is derived from the law report of *Asher & Others* v. *Lacey*, an appeal by the Clay Cross councillors to the Divisional Court against the district auditor's surcharge—see [1973] 1 W.L.R. 1412.
[32] [1974] 2 W.L.R. 466 at p. 473.

and they also became disqualified from being members of the local authority for a period of five years. In lieu of the now defunct Council, a housing commissioner was appointed by the Minister to carry out the functions of the Housing Finance Act. Resort by the Clay Cross councillors to the courts challenging, first, the district auditor's findings and, later, the Secretary of State's directives, received short shrift from, in turn, the Divisional Court[33] and the Court of Appeal.[34] The scene quickly shifted back to the political arena.

At the Labour Party conference in October 1973, a resolution was moved from the floor chastising the party's national executive committee for its failure to defend the Clay Cross councillors in their fight against the offensive legislation. The resolution concluded with these words: "Conference further agrees that upon the election of a Labour Government all penalties, financial or otherwise, should be removed retrospectively from councillors who have courageously refused to implement the Housing Finance Act 1972.[35] At least a year earlier a letter had been addressed to Mr. Silkin, as the Shadow Solicitor General, on behalf of the Labour Party's Home Policy Committee.[36] In the letter it was stated that the committee had been considering "the question of the next Labour Government repaying to Trade Unions, monies lost through the working of the Industrial Relations Act and to local councillors for any surcharging through the working of the Housing Finance Act." The same communication from Transport House recognised that the two items of legislation were very different in their legal implications but requested that Mr. Silkin give his considered opinion of "the possibilities and difficulties of a future Labour Government reimbursing either Trade Unions or Councillors or both." In a postscript the writer explained that in referring to "monies lost" the Home Policy Committee had in mind "fines and sequestered assets."

In thus emphasising the precise scope of the enquiry it must be presumed that the party leaders were not directing their minds to such other possibilities as imprisonment or disqualification from eligibility to act as a councillor. Whatever the precise thinking that lay behind the original letter it is apparent from Mr. Silkin's reply that he confined his statement of the constitutional position to the narrow issue of recompensing trade unions, councillors or both who might suffer financial loss as a result of their

---

[33] *Ante*, fn. 31.

[34] *Ante*, fn. 32. All the pertinent legislative provisions are set out in the Court of Appeal's judgment.

[35] See [1973] New L.J. 917. The resolution was accepted by Edward Short, Deputy Leader of the Labour Party, on behalf of the party's National Executive Committee, saying: " . . . you leave it to us when the time comes to see how this can be implemented. We believe it can. It will not be easy . . . " *ibid.*

[36] The extracts from the letters exchanged between the Research Officer (T. J. Pitt) at the Labour Party's Headquarters (Transport House) and Mr. Silkin are derived from copies of the correspondence kindly provided to the author by Mr. Silkin. The original enquiry bears the date "July 1972" and the reply "25th July 1972."

refusing to apply the legislation enacted by the Conservative Administration. Without hesitation the Shadow Solicitor General categorised legislation of the type contemplated by the committee as an Act of Indemnity. After explaining very briefly the kinds of circumstances in which such legislation had been resorted to in the past (*e.g.* after the cessation of martial law or to absolve ministers or others from legal liability incurred due to some excusable error in law) Mr. Silkin went on to state: "I know of no example of legislation by a Parliament to recompense persons or organisations for financial penalties incurred in consequence of refusing to obey the requirements of legislation passed by a preceding Parliament. An Act of Indemnity passed for this purpose would, in my opinion, contravene all constitutional practice and would set a dangerous precedent. . . . It is my opinion that no Law Officer of the Crown, of any political party, would be likely to advise the Government of which he was a member to initiate such legislation. . . . I will not comment on what is likely to be the political response to such action as is proposed. That is a matter on which others may have views to express."[37] It is understood that the contents of this reply were approved by the Shadow Attorney General (Sir Elwyn Jones) who, presumably, was unavailable at the time the original request was submitted for the opinion of the Shadow Law Officers.

Notwithstanding this clearly expressed opposition to indemnity legislation of the kind adverted to in the exchange of letters quoted above, it is a matter of public record that at its 1973 Conference the National Executive Committee of the Labour Party did not demur to accepting the resolution which had been supported by an overwhelming majority of the party membership. It should be noted also that the resolution specifically referred to the retrospective removal of "all penalties, financial or otherwise" from councillors who had refused to implement the terms of the Housing Finance Act, thus significantly extending the ambit of the proposed indemnity legislation. Such resolutions have never been accepted as having a binding effect upon the parliamentary wing of the party or the government when the party is in power. Nevertheless, with the advent of a solid majority in the country and in the House of Commons following the October 1974 general election, the expected indemnity measure, euphemistically described as the Housing Finance (Special Provisions) Bill, was duly introduced in March 1975 by Mr. Anthony Crosland, the new Secretary of State for the Environment.[38]

Its short title fully describes the Bill's underlying objectives, which were "to prevent surcharges under the Local Government Act 1933 arising out of the Housing Finance Act 1972; to substitute other means of making good losses or deficiencies in respect of which such surcharges would fall to

---

[37] *Ibid.*

[38] See Mr. Crosland's speech on the Bill's Second Reading, H.C. Deb., Vol. 889, cols. 35–51, March 24, 1975. The Bill, with the omission of the controversial clause lifting the automatic disqualification, was finally passed into law as the Housing Finance (Special Provision) Act 1975, c.67.

be made; (and) to terminate any disqualification for election to a local authority arising from a surcharge made in consequence of failure to implement the said Act of 1972." It was estimated that, apart altogether from the Labour council at Clay Cross, twenty other local authorities had failed to raise their rents as required by the Act of 1972, leaving some 400 councillors liable to be individually surcharged on an average of £10,000 each.[39] The contents of the Indemnity Bill purported to draw certain distinctions in terms of legal and financial responsibility. Thus, with respect to those local authorities whose accounts had not yet been subject to scrutiny by the district auditor, (this only excluded Clay Cross where, as noted earlier, an extraordinary audit had already taken place), the audit was to go ahead but the power to surcharge was to be retrospectively prohibited thus effectively precluding the prospect of disqualification.[40] Instead, the auditor was empowered to certify the sum of money lost by reason of a council's failure to implement the Housing Finance Act leaving the local electors to exact such retribution as they saw fit against the errant councillors. The level of this form of retaliation would be dependent on the degree of hostile reaction engendered by an increase in the general rates, whereby the financial liabilities incurred by the defiant councillors were to be discharged. The council tenants, on the other hand, who had enjoyed a honeymoon period of protection from rent increases, were to be saddled with the treatment originally provided for by the 1972 legislation, albeit in arrears.[41]

Reading the debates in the House of Commons there appears to have been a considerable amount of common ground among all the parties that the proposed relief from the financial surcharge could be accepted as a matter of clemency. It was the interference with the automatic disqualification penalty that brought forth a chorus of denunciation.[42] Valiant attempts were made by Government supporters to demonstrate how earlier Conservative Administrations had not balked at the prospect of legalising retrospectively unlawful expenditures by local authorities and absolving individual councillors of the surcharges levied against them by the district auditor. Among the precedents cited was the action of Mr. Neville Chamberlain in 1927 with respect to the Poplar, Bethnal Green and Woolwich councillors who faced the possibility of imprisonment because of

[39] *Ibid.* col. 38.

[40] c. 67, s. 1.

[41] *Ibid.* ss. 2 and 3. Unlike all the other councils involved, the Clay Cross councillors had already been surcharged to the tune of £7,000. No indemnification for this highly publicised surcharge was proposed by the Bill—"The surcharge was a decision upheld by the courts, and we have no intention of retrospectively upsetting such a decision of the courts" (*per* Crosland, and H.C. Deb., Vol. 889, col. 42). The proposed termination of the disqualification, as provided for in the Local Government Act 1933 s.59(1)(*d*), was based on two arguments—first, the inequity of continuing the disqualification of the Clay Cross councillors for failure to implement the Housing Finance Act when other local authorities would be released by the Bill from the threat of such disqualification, and, secondly, "to get the bitterness and rancour out of this whole business"—*ibid.* cols. 42–43.

[42] See, *e.g.* Mr. Emlyn Hooson, *ibid.* cols. 84–89.

their intransigence in persisting to make illegal payments to council employees[43]; also the decision of the Secretary of State for Wales in 1971 in retrospectively sanctioning the illegal expenditures on school milk by the Merthyr Tydfil borough council[44]; and that of the Secretary of State for Scotland in 1973 in overriding the district auditor's decision to impose surcharges against members of the Glasgow City Council for expenditures incurred in distributing publicity material opposing the Scottish equivalent of the Housing Finance Act 1972, the Conservative legislation that gave rise to the Clay Cross debate.[45]

These earlier episodes did much to blunt the Opposition's outright condemnation of the Bill as a whole but the Attorney General, Mr. Silkin, was singled out for some trenchant criticism. The sharpest of these attacks was launched by the Conservative Shadow Attorney General, Sir Michael Havers, who concluded his speech on the second reading of the Bill by stating that, if the Bill was passed into law, future Law Officers would remember the episode with cringing shame.[46] As Havers saw the situation, nothing short of the Attorney General's voting against the measure and resigning could sustain the independence and detachment necessary for the proper discharge of the Law Officers' responsibilities. Attempting to put aside the political aspects of the measure, Sir Michael Havers asked Mr. Silkin how he could justify his support of the Bill of indemnity to his colleagues in the Temple, when he is the leader of the Bar, and to the country "which is entitled to believe that the Law Officers of the Crown are fair and impartial and fiercely proud of their independence."[47] More contentiously, Havers asserted that the quality of detachment associated with the office of the Attorney General required that there be no blurring of the lines separating policy decisions from legal advice.[48] As we have noted earlier, this interpretation of the role of the Law Officers is in marked contrast to the philosophy subscribed to by Mr. Silkin who has argued that no hard and fast line can be drawn between the two concepts and that it is both theoretically sound and practical for the Attorney General to keep distinct in his mind, and in his contributions to the decision process, the inter-relationship between legal advice and policy direction.[49]

Mr. Silkin was repeatedly reminded of his unequivocal statement of constitutional principle in 1972 when he had warned his Labour colleagues in opposition that " . . . no Law Officer of the Crown, of any political party, would be likely to advise the Government of which he was a member

---

[43] *Ibid.* col. 44. The indemnity clause was incorporated in the Audit (Local Authorities) Act 1927. See, H.C. Deb., Vol. 892, cols. 492–498. May 14, 1975.
[44] H.C. Deb., Vol. 889, col. 46.
[45] *Ibid.* col. 158.
[46] *Ibid.* cols. 143–153, at col. 153.
[47] *Ibid.* col. 153.
[48] *Ibid.* col. 151.
[49] See *ante*, pp. 70–71.

to initiate such legislation," adding that to do so would "contravene all constitutional practice and set a dangerous precedent."[50] Exactly how far Mr. Silkin injected his own views into the policy discussions preceding the introduction of the Housing Finance (Special Provisions) Bill in 1975 is not known, but the public record makes it clear that the Attorney General subscribed to the measure introduced by Mr. Anthony Crosland, the Secretary of State for the Environment. Mr. Silkin's apparent *volte face* from the position he took when acting as the Shadow Solicitor General in 1972 prompted Sir Michael Havers to ponder upon the likelihood that a different response might have been forthcoming on Mr. Silkin's part if the Labour Government had been dealing with councillors of a different political colour.[51] This thinly veiled accusation of political partisanship on the part of the Attorney General contained seeds of all the criticisms levelled against Mr. Silkin's decisions in subsequent situations with political overtones of which the *Gouriet* case stands out as the most dramatic instance.

Replying in his own defence, Mr.Silkin dismissed as misconceived and unworthy the Opposition's portrayal of the debate as a battle between those who would uphold the rule of law and those who would suppress it. Claiming that he yielded to no one in his conviction that the rule of law was the lifeblood of democracy, Mr. Silkin reminded the Commons and his ex-Law Officer critics that, like all his predecessors, he had had to take decisions that were unpopular with his political colleagues because of his insistence in maintaining a position of independence when making up his mind.[52] In the present circumstances, he maintained, the issue was how to apply the rule of law with fairness and compassion towards those who acted unlawfully but in the deep and sincere belief that they were called upon to administer a bad and unfair law.[53] In the case of the Clay Cross councillors, the Attorney General readily acknowledged that the degree of defiance of the law had been of a different order from the general situation in other

[50] See *ante*, p. 345. "The advice which he gave as Shadow Law Officer" Havers declared "was the only advice which a reputable and responsible lawyer could give"—H.C. Deb., Vol. 889, col. 150.

[51] *Ibid*. col. 146. *Cf.* the opinion expressed by Mr. Hooson, the Liberal Party's spokesman on legal affairs: "This is a really shabby Bill. There is no way in which the Attorney-General can mitigate the matter. I shall not deal with the personal vendetta against the Attorney-General which the newspapers suggest should be conducted. I am sure that the Attorney-General has suffered torment over this matter. I have been a Member of Parliament for long enough to have seen honourable and decent men of all parties under party pressure to do something of which they did not entirely approve. But I think that the Attorney-General has gone too far with this Bill. He will find it difficult to recover from his part in it. He should reconsider the measure with the Government"—*ibid*. col. 89.

[52] See *ibid*. cols. 153–162, especially at cols. 153–154.

[53] *Ibid*. col. 154. As explained later in the text, Mr. Silkin's speech in his own defence was abruptly terminated by the House dividing to vote on the second reading. To enable me to get a grasp of the former Attorney General's thinking behind his support of the indemnity Bill I have had recourse to the manuscript of Mr. Silkin's speech on second reading and will be making reference to both those portions which were delivered in the Commons and those parts which remained unspoken. Appropriate identification of the several parts is made in the accompanying footnotes.

parts of the country. "We believe" he argued "that the surcharges on the Clay Cross councillors and their disqualification until the Bill becomes law will be sufficient deterrent; no more is required."[54] Here is the nub of the confrontation that set the Commons alight and which carried over to the Lords where the controversial clause 4 relating to disqualification was defeated and deleted from the Bill. Wisely, the Government accepted defeat on this contentious issue and took no steps to reinstate the provision when the Bill returned to the House of Commons.[55]

Continuing with his reply to the debate, Mr. Silkin next adverted to the accusations levelled against him that he had exhibited double standards, first, in his original letter to the Labour Party's Home Policy Committee declaring as unconstitutional the kind of compensatory legislation which the party's political leaders had in mind in 1972 and, secondly, in lending his support to the contents of the Bill of indemnity presented for the approval of Parliament. Before the Attorney General was able to conclude his speech, the House dividing to register its vote on the second reading, it become apparent that Mr. Silkin perceived no fundamental inconsistency between his stance in respect to each of these situations. Quite correctly, he reminded the Commons that his original opinion in the 1972 letter to Transport House had been specifically directed towards the question whether a future Labour Government could introduce legislation to reimburse trade unions or councillors for any sums of money that they might have paid by way of damages, fines or surcharges for not obeying the law as contained in the Housing Finance Act and the Industrial Relations Act.[56] According to Mr. Silkin the underlying purposes of the Bill of indemnity were essentially different, there being no intention of repaying any financial losses incurred. Instead, he maintained that the measure before the House was intended to prevent surcharges arising, to terminate disqualifications and to substitute other means of making good the losses attributable to the transgressors of the earlier legislation. In doing so, Parliament was being asked to balance respect for the law with the need to avoid imposing financial ruin upon large numbers of otherwise responsible citizens. "This Bill" according to Mr. Silkin "did not contravene all constitutional practice. It is a sensible measure to deal with a difficult situation—just as was the [Poplar and Bethnal Green] Act of 1927 before it."[57]

It must be recognised at once that Mr. Silkin's argument, under the best of circumstances where religious beliefs or conscientious objections are the motivating force behind disobedience of the law, has received scant sympathy in the development of the principles of criminal liability. Rather

---

[54] *Ibid.* In actual fact, the Clay Cross councillors remained disqualified, having been surcharged to the tune of £50,000 in respect of other matters wholly unconnected with the Housing Finance Act. See H.C. Deb., Vol. 897, col. 155, August 4, 1975.
[55] *Ibid.*
[56] H.C. Deb., Vol. 899, cols. 161–162, March 24, 1975.
[57] *Ante*, fn. 53.

more tolerance has been exhibited towards such sentiments when a trial judge has to decide upon the appropriate penalty to administer. In the Clay Cross situation, however, the evidence was overwhelming that the objections to applying the law, as contained in the Housing Finance Act 1972, were of the most politically partisan nature. The sincerity and honesty of those objecting to participating in enforcing the new law was not in question. On the contrary, it was the undisguised political character of the councillors' actions that drew forth the accusations in the House of Commons that to support the indemnity Bill in its fullest extent made a mockery of the rule of law. Another major influence on the tenor of the debate was the invidious position, to put it most charitably, of a Labour Government seeking to indemnify its own political supporters for their opposition to legislation enacted by the previous Conservative Administration. In this context the laudable objectives of compassion and wiping the slate clear, to which the Attorney General alluded in justification of his support of the Bill, were not surprisingly viewed with deep suspicion.

Looked at in the cool dispassionate atmosphere of weighing the arguments for and against Mr. Silkin's defence of his conduct, and bearing in mind his well known interpretation of the office of Attorney General as requiring active participation in government policy making, it is understandable that he should have approached the difficulties presented by the Labour Party's 1973 resolution as calling specifically for his intervention to modify any indemnity legislation in the direction of moderation. That would be in keeping with his conception of the ministerial role assigned to the Law Officers of the Crown in our modern constitutional form of government. Believing as he did in the imperative need to act as legal counsellor to his government colleagues throughout their policy discussions it is not difficult to understand Mr. Silkin's motives in assuming the uncomfortable mantle of defending the Bill before a bitterly hostile House of Commons. Were it not for the unequivocal nature of his earlier denunciation of the kind of indemnity legislation comtemplated by the Labour Party in 1972, it is doubtful if the Clay Cross affair would have aroused such strong political passions with the unfortunate Mr. Silkin as its principal target. The legal refinements, however, which he sought to draw between the questions raised in 1972 and those arising out of the Bill of indemnity were lost sight of in the face of what the Opposition saw as an act of politically motivated dispensation from the law in force. Set in that context it was an uphill task all the way to persuade Parliament and other public critics that relief by way of removing the element of disqualification was distinguishable from relief by way of financial compensation, or that denying the imposition of prospective surcharges was different from affording relief with respect to surcharges that had already been imposed. No matter how substantial these distinctions may have been in the mind of the Government, and of Mr. Silkin in particular as the basis for explaining the alleged double standards, the Attorney General's critics were not assuaged.

Within a few years, Mr. Silkin was to find himself in the position to subject his erstwhile accusers to a taste of their own medicine, but it is to his credit that instead he elected to remain true to the need to show compassion even to his political opponents. In introducing the National Health Service (Invalid Direction) Bill in March 1980[58] the Conservative Secretary of State for Social Services offered his full and unqualified apologies for having to introduce the measure for parliamentary approval and for which he accepted full ministerial responsibility.[59] Its purpose was to regularise, by means of retrospective indemnity provisions, the minister's invalid exercise of a statutory direction under section 86 of the National Health Service Act 1977,[60] seeking to bring to heel the recalcitrant members of the Lambeth, Southwark and Lewisham health authority who had repeatedly refused to accept the consequences of a reduced budgetary allocation by the central government. The minister's directive was challenged successfully in the High Court, Woolf J. holding that the Secretary of State's action appointing commissioners to take charge of the affairs of the area authority acting under their direction, if not regularised by law, was open to attack from any number of directions.[61] Briefly, the minister's mistake was that he invoked the wrong statutory provision as the legal authority under which he sought to accomplish his objectives.[62] All the evidence, moreover, pointed to his having been given bad advice from the legal advisers in his own department, advice that was criticised in the judgment of the court. Notwithstanding the potential political fall-out associated with such a drastic policy decision it seems clear that the Law Officers of the Crown were not consulted beforehand, either by the minister himself or his departmental legal advisers.[63] This regrettable omission was subsequently

[58] Enacted in due course as the National Health Service (Invalid Direction) Act 1980, c.15.

[59] See H.C. Deb., Vol., 980, col. 1158 *et seq.* March 11, 1980.

[60] c. 49.

[61] *R. v. S. of S. for Social Services ex p. Lewisham, Lambeth and Southwark London Borough Councils, The Times* Law Report, February 25, 1980.

[62] See H.C. Deb., Vol. 980, cols. 1164–1167, 1203–1206, March 11, 1980.

[63] *Ibid.* cols. 1160–1161, 1174, and 1206. The Minister concerned made valiant efforts to shelter his departmental officers by invoking the constitutional practice that the Government of the day, or individual Ministers, do not disclose to the House of Commons on whose advice a decision has been taken. As to the limits of this so-called "convention" see Edwards, *op. cit.* pp. 256–261. If there was any doubt as to the substance of the claims made by back benchers that "it is common knowledge in the legal profession that neither the A.G. nor the S.G. was consulted,· and that they were not responsible for the advice that was criticised in the judgment of the Court" (*ibid.* col. 1160) these doubts were dispelled when the Shadow Attorney General spoke in the debate. Addressing the Secretary of State for Social Services, Mr. Silkin inquired: "If he did seek legal advice why, on a matter of such consequence, were not the Law Officers asked to advise? It was a serious constitutional action. It was plainly a matter on which the Law Officers should have been asked to advise. I have no doubt that they were not so asked. The Secretary of State must take responsibility for his failure to seek the advice of the Law Officers"—*ibid.* cols. 1239–1240. Earlier in his speech the former Attorney General had stated: "The House is entitled to know who advised him so badly. I have no doubt whatsoever that the Law Officers could not possibly have advised him on this Bill of indemnity—it is backed by the Attorney-General—but I have no doubt that they advised the Secretary of State after the litigation was concluded that he had no hope whatever of success if he went to the Court of Appeal."

rectified and the Attorney General's name appeared as one of the backers of the Bill to regularise the invalid direction of the Secretary of State.

Belatedly, the Law Officers were called to the rescue and advised the minister to forego any appeal through the courts. The only alternative left was to resort to indemnity legislation, a course of action that the Government must have swallowed with acute embarrassment. For however innocuous its title might be there is no denying that the National Health Service (Invalid Direction) Bill was tantamount to a Bill of indemnity, against which Sir Michael Havers had pontificated so eloquently in the Clay Cross debate. If there had been no indemnifying statute it was entirely conceivable that both the Secretary of State and others could have been held personally liable for the expenditures that were not authorised by law. Speaking from the Opposition benches in support of the Bill, the former Attorney General, Mr. Silkin recalled the campaign of vilification to which he had been subjected in 1975.[64] Evoking memories of the public furor surrounding the Clay Cross affair Mr. Silkin declared: "Perhaps it is too much to hope that some of the distasteful words that were uttered in 1975 will be eaten by the Law Officers in 1980. I recall in particular the doubts that were expressed as to whether I would have supported—as I do today—a Bill had it been one to indemnify my political opponents."[65] He went on to state that he approached the present measure with the same concern for balancing the competing values of mercy and adherence to the rule of law. There was no denying, Mr. Silkin acknowledged, the minister's strong political interest in wanting to see the government's tight budget policies adhered to, but such a political motive was infinitely less significant than the fact that he had received bad legal advice from within his own department.

Any such attempt to draw comparisons between the application of competing values in different sets of circumstances is unlikely to produce universal agreement. Such is bound to be the case when examining the background to the two recent Bills of indemnity. Each was introduced by a different political party, confirming that expediency and a lack of dedication to principle are not the prerogative of any political group. It may be a matter for regret that circumstances ever arise where a government is forced to face up to the choice of evils that present

[64] *Ibid.* col. 1241. Mr. Silkin recalled the words used by Mr. Levin (see *supra*, fn. 30) and which were adopted by the Shadow Solicitor General, speaking from the Opposition benches during the Clay Cross debate in 1975. On that occasion Mr. Ian Percival had stated: "If we pass this Bill [the Housing Finance (Special Provision) Bill] it will be, to borrow the words of Mr. Levin, 'to proclaim that those who spit upon the law may do so with impunity provided that they do so in a sectional or political interest' "—see H.C. Deb., Vol. 892, col. 610, May 14, 1975. Mr. Silkin continued, "Mr. Levin has remained strangely silent about this Bill. Let me assure the Secretary of State that I do not accuse him of spitting on the law for a political interest. Certainly he had a strong political interest, and certainly his action was high handed in the extreme. But spitting on the law is a vulgarism which I decline to repeat"—*ibid.* col. 1239. Apart from one small intervention, the Attorney General did not take part in the Second Reading debates on the Bill.

[65] *Ibid.* col. 1240.

themselves for decision. The future will surely produce further examples of the kind of controversial decisions we have examined in this chapter. The basic approach of any government is likely to be more a matter of degree than of any clear cut demarcation between permissible acts of clemency and the subversion of that basic core of integrity that sustains the rule of law. Political sympathies may incline the government's critics and supporters to draw the line at slightly different points in the scale that separates legality from outright expediency.

The role of the Attorney General in these situations needs to be clearly understood. It must first be distinguished from those situations for which he and he alone is constitutionally responsible. Thus, in the sphere of prosecution policy, including those circumstances in which immunity from prosecution is contemplated, the Attorney General's ministerial colleagues do not share collective responsibility for his decisions. This is not the case where the government elects to introduce indemnity legislation. The Law Officers have every right to be heard before any policy decision is taken by the Cabinet to go ahead and face Parliament on such an issue. Even if the Law Officers oppose the introduction of such an extraordinary measure it is clear that, as members of the administration, they share collective responsibility for the final decision to proceed. The option of resignation is always open to an Attorney General or Solicitor General who, on grounds of principle or in the actual circumstances of a particular situation, feels sufficiently strong that he must take a public stand in opposition to the rest of his political colleagues. Recent experience would suggest that such a prospect must be weighed carefully by each incumbent if respect and public confidence in the truly independent character of these offices is to be maintained and strengthened.

12

Politics and the Independence of the Attorney General—Some Commonwealth Experiences

The history of colonial government in those countries that are now regarded as the older independent members of the Commonwealth reveals a common theme wherein the Attorney General has always been regarded as an indispensable member of the Executive Council. From the days of direct colonial rule by London, through the evolving stages of representative and responsible legislatures, the Attorney General has laid indisputable claim to one of the senior portfolios in what we now term the Cabinet, the supreme policy making body of government. Of all the characteristics that generally distinguish the office of Attorney General outside of the United Kingdom this membership of the supreme governing body is the most visible hallmark. Not all member states of the Commonwealth have seen fit to perpetuate this significant departure from the British constitutional practice that has been in place since 1928.[1] For example, there are a number of Commonwealth countries including Kenya, Singapore, Pakistan, Sri Lanka, Malta, Cyprus and the Bahamas which have opted for the public servant model in which the Attorney General combines with his office the functions of the Director of Public Prosecutions who is not subject to the directions or control of any other person or authority.[2] It is not my intention in this chapter to review the ever increasing number of constitutional provisions that, with the achieving of independent sovereignty, regulate the offices of Minister of Justice, Attorney General

---

[1] The variety of models that exist throughout the Commonwealth were reviewed in a paper that I prepared for the 1977 Meeting of Commonwealth Law Ministers, see *Minutes of Meeting and Memoranda*, Commonwealth Secretariat, pp. 195–204.

[2] For details of the respective constitutions see Blaustein & Flanz, *Constitutions of the Countries of the World*, (New York, Oceana Publications, 1983 ed.); the pertinent provisions are as follows—Kenya, Constitution Act 1979, s.109; Singapore, Constitution of 1980, s.35; Pakistan, Islamic Constitution 1973, s.100; Sri Lanka, Constitution of 1978, s.54; Malta, Constitution of 1978, s.92; Cyprus, Constitution, Arts. 112–114; Bahamas, Constitution of 1973, s.78.

and Director of Public Prosecutions in the constituent members of the Commonwealth.

It must suffice to note that different solutions have been resorted to by different countries in assigning responsibility for the inter-related areas that are usually identified under the general heading of the administration of justice. These principal areas include: (1) police and law enforcement, (2) the initiation and conduct of prosecutions, (3) the courts, including judicial appointments and the legal profession, (4) representation of the government and the State before the courts and tribunals, (5) the penal system, (6) legal advice to the government and governmental agencies, and (7) the drafting of legislation and law reform. The question that naturally arises is whether, in practical terms or as a matter of principle, it is desirable that these variegated responsibilities should come under one portfolio or be shared among separate ministries. Various solutions to this question have been adopted ranging from the English system, in which the responsibilities are divided amongst three ministers, the Lord Chancellor, the Attorney General and the Home Secretary, to the system prevailing, for example, at the federal level in Canada prior to 1966, in which most of these responsibilities resided ultimately in the Minister of Justice and Attorney General of Canada.[3] Partly as a result of a public inquiry which examined the incumbent minister's failure to separate his functions in the initiation of federal prosecutions from his responsibilities as the minister in charge of the Royal Canadian Mounted Police, the Department of the Solicitor General was established in 1966 to encompass the Royal Canadian Mounted Police, the penitentiaries and national parole service, areas previously dealt with by the Justice Minister.[4] In other Commonwealth countries, e.g. federal Nigeria[5] and, until very recently, New Zealand,[6] all the responsibilities listed earlier, except those of police and law enforcement, are concentrated in the one minister who holds the separate portfolios of Minister of Justice and Attorney General concurrently. In such situations, responsibility for the police and law enforcement is usually assigned to a Minister of Police, Minister of Internal Affairs or to the Prime Minister. The pattern of vesting control of the police and security forces in the Prime Minister, and sharing the remainder of the administration of justice duties between a Minister of Justice and the Attorney General, is exemplified by many countries including Malta and Sri Lanka.[7] And there are many precedents for assigning responsibility for the police and its investigative and crime prevention roles to the Attorney

[3] See Edwards, *Ministerial Responsibility for National Security, as it relates to the Offices of Prime Minister, Attorney General and Solicitor General of Canada* (Ottawa, 1980), Chapter 2.
[4] *Ibid*. Chapters 5 and 6, and see also the *Second* [Final] *Report of the* [McDonald] *Commission of Inquiry Concerning Certain Activities of the Royal Canadian Mounted Police*, (1981), Vol. 1, pp. 80–81, Vol. 2, pp. 856–863.
[5] Constitution of the Federal Republic of Nigeria 1979, s.138. *Cf.* s.176 which defines as a public, non ministerial office the post of Attorney General in the respective States.
[6] See *post*, p. 390, fn. 47.
[7] See constitutional provisions cited in fn. 2 *ante*.

General, *e.g.* Cyprus, Zambia, Kenya, the Commonwealth of Australia[8] with respect to the Australian Capital Territory, and those provinces of Canada which have not yet split the Attorney General's portfolio and created a separate ministry, customarily designated as the Solicitor General, to oversee the police aspects of the criminal justice system.[9]

Whatever constitutional alternative is adopted there has never been any suggestion that overriding control over the machinery of criminal prosecutions should reside in any other minister than the Attorney General. It may be useful therefore to take stock of experience outside the United Kingdom in terms of the public perception of how far political pressures and political influences determine the exercise of the Attorney General's discretionary powers and what store is placed on the independent exercise of prosecutorial decision making by the Attorney General and his agents.

I. Canada[10]

Unlike most modern constitutions within the Commonwealth the British North America Act 1867,[10a] is somewhat less than explicit in stating the legal foundations on which the powers and functions of the Canadian offices of the Attorney General and Solicitor General are said to rest. Executive power is declared "to continue and be vested in the Queen" (s.9). The Executive Council, to aid and advise in the Government of Canada, is to consist of "persons who . . . shall be from time to time chosen and summoned by the Governor General and sworn in as Privy Councillors" (s.11). No specific reference is made in the Act to the portfolios that would initially comprise the Executive Council of the Dominion Government, but there can be no doubt that, following the pattern established since the advent of British rule in Canada, it was envisaged that the office of Attorney General would be included. Neither would it have occasioned surprise at the time, in 1867, that the first Canadian Prime Minister, Sir John A. Macdonald, elected to join the duties of the Attorney General with his responsibilities as First Minister.

---

[8] *Ante*, fn. 2; for Zambia, see Constitution Act 1974, s.57.

[9] In Canada, only the provinces of Ontario (in 1972) and Alberta (in 1973) have seen fit to create separate Departments of the Solicitor General with responsibility for the administration of the Police Act. *Cf.* the Attorney General's Dept. in British Columbia which has been described by its Deputy Attorney General as one of the few "unified ministries of justice" in Canada, a phrase that would be equally applicable to the provinces of New Brunswick, Newfoundland, Quebec and Saskatchewan. For the background to these moves see Edwards, *Ministerial Responsibility op. cit.* pp. 18–19, 32, and for the separate history of the office of Solicitor General in Quebec see *ibid.* pp. 32–34. On the theoretical aspects of the need to separate policing and prosecutorial functions in terms of ministerial responsibility, see *ibid.* pp. 30–31.

[10] Much of the material contained in this section derives from the background study which I prepared for the [McDonald] Commission of Inquiry—see *ante*, fns. 3 and 4.

[10a] 30 & 31 Vict. c.3 (U.K.). By virtue of the Canada Act 1982, c.11 (U.K.), Sched.1, the earlier enactment is to be cited henceforth as the Constitution Act 1867.

The British North America Act is more precise when dealing with executive power in the provincial constitutions. The Attorney General, according to section 63, heads the list of executive officers named as initially constituting the executive council in the provinces of Ontario and Quebec.[11] This provision confirmed the long established tradition which had prevailed from the earliest days of colonial rule in the Province of Quebec. Commencing with the period preceding the British conquest of New France, when Paris, not London, was the seat of the prevailing colonial power, the Attorney General was an *ex-officio* member of the Sovereign Council.[12] With the subsequent institution of British colonial rule, a succession of English lawyers were appointed to the office of Attorney General in the distant colony and participated actively, alongside the Governor, in determining and executing policies within the mandate laid down by Whitehall.[13] With the division, following the Quebec Act 1774,[14] of the former province into Upper and Lower Canada, the practice of including the Attorney General within the small body of persons selected by the colonial Governor to advise him in administering the government was continued. The early minutes of the executive council of Upper Canada show how actively the legal members, the Attorney General and the Chief Justice, participated in the deliberations of that

[11] Special reference is made in the same provision to the inclusion of the Solicitor General within the Executive Council of Quebec. It is noteworthy that the office of Solicitor General nowhere appears in the establishment of government offices prepared at the time of the Quebec Act 1774, nor in the list of appointments which were sent to Governor Haldimand in April 1775 by the Secretary of State for the Colonies. In appointing Jenkin Williams, a Welshman and former clerk of the Executive Council, as Quebec's first Solicitor General, Haldimand seems to have been prompted more by a determination to ensure a more dependable and less politically active government lawyer, with an added desire to divert away from Attorney General James Monk some of the lucrative sources of income associated with the office. See A.L.Burt in *The Old Province of Quebec*, 1933, Vol. II, pp. 40, 215 and Hilda Neatby, *The Administration of Justice Under the Quebec Act* (1937), pp. 339–340. Originally patterned on the model associated with the office of Solicitor General for England, all the available evidence points to the Solicitor General in both Upper and Lower Canada being regarded as the *secondarius attornatus*, the lieutenant who was expected to assist the Attorney General in the discharge of his duties as the senior Law Officer of the Crown. For an account of the antecedents of the office of Solicitor General of Canada prior to the reorganisation in 1966 see Edwards, *Ministerial Responsibility op. cit.* Chapter 4.

[12] See W.J. Eccles, *The Government of New France*, (1968), pp. 10–12, and Mason Wade, *The French Canadians* (1760–1967), Vol. 1, (1968), pp. 17–18. For an authoritative account of the Government of New France between 1627 and 1760 see Governor Carleton's Report upon the Laws and Courts of Judicature in the Province of Quebec (1769) which is published in full in W.P.M. Kennedy and G. Lanctot, *Reports on the Laws of Quebec*, 1767–1770—see especially pp. 55–56.

[13] As examples of the earliest functioning of the office of Attorney General in distant parts of the British Empire see the literature referred to, for New Zealand, at *post*, p. 388, fn. 34 and, for Barbados, in the unpublished thesis by S.L. Richards, "The Role of the Attorney General in the Administration of Justice in Barbados," 1982, esp. Chapter 2.

[14] 14 Geo. 3, c. 88. For a synopsis of the principal landmarks in the importing of British governmental institutions and legal systems into Canada during the 17th, 18th and 19th centuries, see J.D. Whyte and W.R. Lederman: *Canadian Constitutional Law*, (2nd ed. 1977), Chapter 1.

body.[15] By the time the British North America Act 1867, was enacted the imperative needs to separate the judiciary from the executive and legislative branches of government had been fully recognised. The position of the Attorney General, however, as a key figure in the executive councils of the expanding confederation remained unchanged and it is of notable significance that the office to this day is regarded as one of the more senior Cabinet posts in both the federal and provincial governments.

Furthermore, the precedent set by the first Prime Minister of Canada in combining from 1867 to 1873 his duties as First Minister with those associated with the joint appointment of Minister of Justice and Attorney General of Canada[16] was in no way regarded as extraordinary.[17] Many instances are on record, well into the present century, where the Premier of a provincial government has simultaneously fulfilled the duties of Attorney General.[18] The most credible explanation for this practice was the paucity of suitable qualified lawyers to discharge the special functions associated with the office of Attorney General, coupled with the pre-eminent standing of the legally trained appointee who was chosen to occupy the position of First Minister. Such an eventuality was, and is forever likely to remain, unheard of in Britain. On the question of the Attorney General's inclusion within the ranks of Cabinet members it is a matter of note that no other country in the Commonwealth, which subscribes to the principle of politically appointed Law Officers, has seen fit to embrace the British constitutional theory that it is more appropriate that the independence of the Attorney General and Solicitor General should not be blurred by their inclusion in the Cabinet, the body that may have to take decisions on policy after receiving legal advice from the Law Officers.[19]

---

[15] See State Books of Upper Canada, Records of the Executive Council, Vols. B, C, E and F, *passim*. Volume K, for example, contains a minute directing the Attorney General to forbear from prosecuting certain persons unless they were leaders of the 1838 revolt—see pp. 77–78, April 10, 1838.

[16] The principal components of the first statute, the Department of Justice Act 1868 (31 Vict. c. 39), enumerating the duties of the Minister of Justice and the Attorney General of Canada, respectively, remain as operative today as when the enactment was originally promulgated. The Minister of Justice is *ex officio* Her Majesty's Attorney General of Canada. For a review of the division of responsibilities and the consequences that can flow from a blurring, or ignoring, of the boundary lines that separate the two offices, see Edwards, *Ministerial Responsibility, op. cit.* Chapter 2.

[17] *Ibid.* p. 8. In addition to his duties as Prime Minister and Minister of Justice Sir John A. Macdonald personally assumed responsibility for overseeing the reorganisation of the North West Mounted Police—*loc. cit.*

[18] *Ibid.* p. 132, fn. 115. Exemplifying a situation that can exceptionally be encountered in modern times in some parts of the Commonwealth, Alberta's Attorney General in the 1930s was not a lawyer and had never received any training in the law. In addition to being the province's Law Officer, William Aberhart was also the Premier and Minister of Education—see (1939) 17 Can. Bar Rev. 416.

[19] See *The Law Officers of the Crown*, Chapter 9. For the Canadian experience, from the period of its colonial status up to the present, see Edwards, *Ministerial Responsibility, op. cit.* Chapter 7.

CABINET INVOLVEMENT IN THE DISPOSITION OF SENSITIVE CRIMINAL CASES

The question may well be asked, therefore, what effect has Canadian adherence to the contrary practice, of including the Attorney General within the Cabinet, had upon the conception of that office as the guardian of the public interest and in its adherence to the classic statement of Sir Hartley Shawcross as to the principles of independence that should govern decisions in the area of criminal prosecutions. In a statement made by the Attorney General of Canada, Mr. Ron Basford, to the House of Commons in 1978,[20] explaining the reasons for his decisions whether or not to authorise prosecutions under the Official Secrets Act against Mr. Tom Cossitt M.P.,[21] and the *Toronto Sun*,[22] the Minister went to unusual lengths to expound on the parliamentary, constitutional and legal principles that guided him in the discharge of his discretionary powers[23]

[20] H.C. Deb., Vol. 121, pp. 3881–3883, March 17, 1978.

[21] In the event, the Attorney General's fiat, required under s.12 of the Official Secrets Act, was granted with respect to the prosecution of the Toronto Sun Publishing Ltd., together with its publisher and editor, but declined in the case of Mr. Cossitt, a member of the Opposition. No explanatory reasons by the Attorney General of Canada were forthcoming in the only other recent prosecution under the Official Secrets Act, *R.* v. *Treu* (1978). The accused in that case was charged with "unlawfully retaining" (s.4(1)(*a*)) and "failing to take reasonable care of" (s.4(1)(*d*)) NATO documents relating to secret air communication systems that he had obtained as an employee of the Northern Electric Company which was party to a defence contract with NATO. Treu's conviction was reversed on appeal to the Quebec Court of Appeal—see *Globe & Mail*, February 21, 1979. More recently, the handling of the *Hambleton* case in 1982 gave rise to intense questioning in the Canadian House of Commons of both the Attorney General of Canada and the Solicitor General as the Minister responsible for the Security Service—see H.C. Deb., Vol. 14, pp. 2111–2112 (November 30, 1982), pp. 21342–21348, (December 7, 1982) and 21392–21397 (December 8, 1982). Uncertainty still prevails as to the exact circumstances in which Hambleton was led to believe that, in return for his collaboration with the Royal Canadian Mounted Police Security Service, he would not be prosecuted under the Canadian Official Secrets Act. During a later visit to England in June 1982, and despite apparent warnings by the responsible authorities in both Canada and Britain as to the likely consequences of his entering British jurisdiction, Hambleton was arrested and charged with offences against the English Official Secrets Act, in having supplied the Russians with NATO secrets. At the trial in the Old Bailey before Croom Johnson J., at which the Attorney General, Sir Michael Havers, led for the prosecution, the accused entered a plea of guilty at a later stage in the proceedings and was sentenced to 10 years imprisonment. See *The Sunday Times*, December 12, 1982.

[22] The Toronto newspaper, together with its publisher and editor, were charged under the Official Secrets Act, s.4(1)(*a*) and s.4(3), after printing an article based on a Royal Canadian Mounted Police report entitled "Canadian related activities of the Russian Intelligence Services." Parts of the same documents had previously been made public, independently of the *Sun* article, in a CTV television broadcast and during exchanges in the House of Commons. On April 23, 1979 the preliminary hearing concluded with the discharge of the accused, there being insufficient evidence to place the accused on trial. The previous publicity accorded to the report, classified "Top Secret—For Canadian eyes only," in the view of the court, had brought the "shopworn" document into the public domain and thus outside the purview of the Official Secrets Act. It would not be surprising if the unsuccessful outcome of the *Sun* and *Treu* (*supra*) prosecutions had exerted a powerful influence on the decision of the Attorney General of Canada not to authorise criminal proceedings under the Official Secrets Act against *Hambleton*.

[23] In an interesting insight into the influences that guided the Canadian Attorney General in clarifying the appropriate governing principles Mr. Basford informed the House of Commons: "In arriving at these I have been guided by recognized authorities such as Lord Shawcross, Edwards, Erskine, May and Bourinot, and more recently and very helpfully, my

and the nature of his accountability to Parliament. Remarkable as it may seem, no comparable statement of the relevant principles will be found in the annals of the Canadian House of Commons stretching back to its inception in 1867. "The first principle," the Attorney General declared, "is that there must be excluded any consideration based upon narrow, partisan views, or based upon the political consequences to me or to others. In arriving at a decision on such a sensitive issue as this, the Attorney General is entitled to seek information and advice from others but in no way is he directed by his colleagues in the government or by Parliament itself."[24] In this passage is contained the nub of the problem. An Attorney General who seeks to sustain his privileged constitutional status as the guardian of the public interest, in the widest sense of that term, may seek, and frequently would be seriously at fault in failing to do so, advice from whatever quarter, ministerial or otherwise, that may help to illuminate the decision confronting him. What is absolutely forbidden is the subjection by the Attorney General of his discretionary authority to the edict of the Prime Minister or the Cabinet or Parliament itself. Parliament has the right to question and criticise the Law Officers. It does not have the right to direct them in the discharge of their constitutional duties.[25]

Applying these considerations to the cases before him in the *Cossitt* affair, the Attorney General of Canada further emphasised that, in exercising his discretion as to whether or not he should consent to a prosecution under the Official Secrets Act, it was incumbent upon him to ensure that the widest possible public interests of Canada were taken into account. In this task he had to balance the rights, privileges, traditions and immunities so necessary for the proper functioning of Parliament, and the doubts that exist as to the application of parliamentary privilege to statements made by Members of Parliament outside the House of Commons.[26] It was Mr. Basford's view that he should not grant his consent to a prosecution unless the case was free from substantial doubt. Accordingly, he announced his decision not to proceed against the individual Member of Parliament whose disclosures had prompted the Attorney General into action. Conversely, the first Law Officer of the Crown said that, in the case of the *Toronto Sun*, he had due regard to the principle of freedom of the press which did not embody absolute rights. Rather it must be exercised pursuant to the rule of law. Parliament not

---

valuable discussions with Commonwealth Attorneys General in Winnipeg last summer on the office of Attorney General, and more particularly my personal conversations at that time with the Attorney General of England and Wales and the Lord Chancellor." *ante* fn. 20, *ibid.* p. 3881.

[24] H.C. Deb., Vol. 121, pp. 3881–3883.

[25] For an unusual instance of a legislative body being invited by the Government of the day to determine whether criminal proceedings should be instituted, see the Dutch Parliament's handling of the Prince Bernhard affair in 1976—see *The Times*, August 27, 28 and 31, 1976.

[26] No doubt Mr. Basford had in mind the findings of the Select Committee of the British House of Commons regarding the *Duncan Sandys* case in 1939, see H.C. Paper 101.

having seen fit to extend to any other person or body the rights, privileges or immunities that are accorded by law to Parliament and its members, the Attorney General concluded that, after balancing the various competing interests, he should issue his fiat for the launching of criminal proceedings against the Toronto newspaper and its editor and publisher.[27]

The accountability of the Attorney General to Parliament was readily acknowledged in the extensive review submitted to the Commons of the considerations that lay behind the Attorney General's decisions. The unique qualities of independence that are attached to the office were said to be"clearly embedded in our parliamentary practice."[28] Furthermore, Mr. Basford declared, "based on these authorities and my own experience as a member of the Government for ten years, which has included my three immediate predecessors, this special position has been diligently protected in theory and in practice."[29] The underlying philosophy contained in the above extracts from the Attorney General's statement is clearly in conformity with the British constitutional theory and practice, and this despite the major difference between the two countries in terms of the Attorney General's membership in the Cabinet. Sadly, however, and contrary to what Mr. Basford said, the evidence of previous administrations, irrespective of party affiliation, suggests that earlier Prime Ministers and Attorneys General subscribed to a totally different philosophy in which decisions in highly political cases were made by the Cabinet and carried out by the Attorney General.

A few instances may suffice to illustrate the misconceptions that have prevailed within Government and Parliament, without serious challenge prior to the carefully prepared statement by the Minister of Justice and Attorney General of Canada in 1978. Thus, in the course of a debate in the House of Commons in 1965 as to the handling of a case involving two members of the Soviet Embassy who were alleged to have induced a Canadian civil servant and a naturalised Canadian citizen to take part in espionage activities, the Prime Minister, Mr. Lester Pearson, was asked who had the final authority to determine whether criminal proceedings were to be taken against the two Canadians. Would it be the Royal Canadian Mounted Police, the Minister of Justice or one of his officials, or the Government as a whole, the inquirer asked. Mr. Pearson's reply was that "In this situation, it will be the responsibility of the Government on the advice of the Minister of Justice,"[30] a statement that he reiterated a short while later in response to a further question by the leader of the New Democratic Party.[31] No minister, none of the leaders of the Opposition

[27] H.C. Deb., Vol. 121, pp. 3881–3883, March 17, 1978.

[28] *Ibid.*   [29] *Ibid.*

[30] H.C. Deb., Vol. II, p. 1147, May 11, 1965.

[31] *Ibid.* p. 1148. Earlier, in his prepared statement to the House of Commons on the involvement of Canadians in Russian espionage acts, the Prime Minister had stated "certainly there can be no question of prosecution for wrongdoing in this case; quite the contrary"— *ibid.* p. 1139. The Attorney General, Mr. Favreau, contributed nothing to the debate.

parties and no member of the House of Commons saw fit to controvert this interpretation of the constitutional principles involved. Statements by Mr. Diefenbaker, then Leader of the Opposition, concerning his Government's role in handling the *Hal Banks* affair in 1957 and in 1963 concerning the blocking of the St. Lawrence Seaway by the Seafarers Union, of which Banks was the president, leave no doubt either as to the Conservative leader's perception that the decision whether or not to prosecute the labour official was one that would have been taken by the Cabinet and not left to the independent judgment of the Attorney General.[32] More recently, during the course of a general election, the Conservative Leader of the Opposition, Mr. Joe Clark, speaking in the course of a television interview, stated that, if he became Prime Minister, he would prosecute any Liberal Cabinet Minister found responsible for alleged illegalities by the Royal Canadian Mounted Police. "If legal action was called for," Mr. Clark said, "I would certainly not grant an exception to anyone for the consequences of breaking the law."[33] Allowance must be made for the fact that this statement was made in the context of an election campaign. Nevertheless, it is in keeping with similar views expressed by earlier leaders of the major political parties in Parliament and which, apart from the Basford statement quoted earlier, have never been disavowed.

If any conclusion is to be derived from the above statements of Canada's political leaders it is the uncritical assumption that some prosecution decisions will naturally assume a high political profile because of the position which the accused enjoys in society, the circumstances that give rise to possible criminal charges or the political consequences that will flow from the outcome of the trial. There is good reason to suppose that prior to the Basford statement in 1978 most Ministers of the Crown would have viewed their involvement in the disposition of such prosecutorial questions in Cabinet as a natural application of the principle of collective responsibility for unpalatable political decisions. In making these decisions it should not be assumed that the Cabinet would necessarily be governed by politically partisan motives. At the same time, it would be unrealistic not to envisage situations in which, in the absence of any clearly understood constitutional prohibition against the referral by the Attorney

---

[32] The Commons' exchanges are recounted in Edwards, *Ministerial Responsibility, op. cit.* p. 66. The pertinent *Hansard* references are as follows: H.C. Deb., Vol. III, pp. 2997–98, June 29, 1965; H.C. Deb., Vol. VII, pp. 7684–7691, September 4, 1964. The same theme is discernible in the remarks of Mr. Guy Favreau when, speaking as Minister of Justice and Attorney General of Canada on the same subject of bringing Hal Banks before the criminal courts, he stated: " . . . in 1963, as soon as the Norris report was published, as soon as the government could do something, legal action was taken and complaints were lodged after the government had retained the best Toronto and Montreal lawyers. So, this government is the first to do something about Mr. Banks; this government is the first to assume its responsibilities and prosecute Mr. Banks with the results we know . . . I must inform the House that, if necessary, this government will continue to act in the same way concerning Banks or anyone else who must be prosecuted." H.C. Deb., Vol. VI, pp. 6083, 6085, July 28, 1964.
[33] As reported in the *Toronto Star* and the *Ottawa Journal*, May 5, 1979.

General of prosecution matters for decision by the Cabinet or any group of ministers or by the Prime Minister, partisan influences would rise to the surface and prevail in whatever decision ultimately emerged.

Confirmation of the federal Cabinet's active involvement in prosecution decisions, as well as providing evidence of the then Attorney General's readiness to bring politically sensitive cases before that body, was forthcoming in the recent release for public examination of the Cabinet minutes for 1952. At its meeting on May 15, 1952 the Prime Minister (Mr. St. Laurent) and the Minister for External Affairs (Mr. Lester Pearson) expressed their views forcibly on the political fallout that would attach to the launching of criminal proceedings for treason against *James Endicott*, a Canadian clergyman.[34] Endicott's father had been Moderator of the United Church of Canada and he himself had served as a missionary in China for 21 years. Endicott became convinced that the United Nations forces had engaged in bacteriological warfare during the Korean War and persisted in making these allegations publicly in the course of his travels through Russia, China and Europe.[35] For example, in a broadcast that he made over Radio Prague, Mr. Endicott accused "American germ war criminals" of dropping anthrax, typhoid and cholera germs on the Chinese mainland.[36] These statements were given wide publicity in Canada and this was followed by repeated calls in Parliament that Endicott be prosecuted for treason.[37]

Opening the Cabinet discussion of the *Endicott* case the Minister of Justice and Attorney General (Mr. Garson) explained that, of all the alternative charges that might be relied upon, treason was the only serious possibility since, unlike other relevant counts,[38] it would not be necessary to establish that the germ warfare assertions were false. The major difficulty, according to the Attorney General, was that the only punishment for treason at that time was the death penalty. After the Minister for External Affairs had reviewed the prosecution practices in the United Kingdom, France and the United States in similar cases, emphasis was placed on the amount of unwelcome international attention that the prosecution of Mr. Endicott would generate. After further discussion, the concluding paragraph of the minutes noted, the Cabinet agreed that the matter be considered again at a later date following a further report by the Minister of Justice. This appears never to have taken place, since the Cabinet minutes throughout the remainder of 1952 contain no further reference to the *Endicott* case. In drawing conclusions from the handling of

[34] Public Archives of Canada, R.C. 2, Series 16, Vol. 29.
[35] For a sympathetic account of Rev. Endicott's exploits see *James G. Endicott: Rebel out of China*, written by his son Stephen Endicott, (Univ. of Toronto Press, 1982), esp. Chapter 26.
[36] *Globe & Mail*, January 5, 1983.
[37] H.C. Deb., Vol. 2, pp. 2100–2104, May 12, 1952.
[38] These included sedition, spreading false news and the common law offence of public mischief.

this high profile event it is apparent that the Cabinet in 1952 assumed that the decision which had to be made was a collective responsibility and not that of simply communicating the views of individual ministers which the Attorney General would take into account in reaching his decision whether or not to prosecute.

PROSECUTION BY GOVERNMENT OR AT THE IMPARTIAL DETERMINATION OF THE ATTORNEY GENERAL

What is applicable to Cabinet decision-making is equally associated with the deliberations of Parliament and the Legislative Assemblies of the Provinces.[39] Perhaps because of the strongly embedded Canadian tradition of regarding the parliamentary system as essentially an exercise in partisan politics, it may be thought to be impractical to attempt to imbue these assemblies with a concept of impartiality that is so foreign to their interpretation of their customary functions. The issue, however, should not be looked upon in terms of customary practice alone or even in seeking accord with the practicalities of existing governmental and parliamentary practice. The issue must be lifted on to a higher plane and the question posed—in what form is the broadest public interest likely to be served when the quality of our system of criminal justice is at stake? Are all questions that savour of political ramifications to be treated alike and made subject to the will of the government in power and to the collective responsibility of the Cabinet? Or are there certain areas of ministerial responsibility, especially those involving the exercise of the Attorney General's prerogative and statutory discretion with respect of criminal prosecutions, which require that the Prime Minister and other ministers in the government refrain from becoming directly involved in the final decision that is made? If any true meaning is to be given to the discharge of this kind of discretion the collegial system of Cabinet involvement must be confined to a consultative role. Such consultation, however, must never be allowed to become dictation.

It is satisfying to note that the recent McDonald Commission of Inquiry, in its Third (and final) Report dealing with the question of governmental knowledge of alleged illegal activities by members of the Royal Canadian Mounted Police,[40] saw fit to address this subject in a manner calculated to reinforce the special position that has been constitutionally accorded to the office of Attorney General in Canada. The volume in question reviews in extensive detail the evidence adduced during the course of the Commission's investigations and hearings, from which it became possible to

---

[39] See, *e.g.* the statement made by the Attorney General, R. McMurtry in announcing the decision not to prosecute Mr. Francis Fox, a member of the federal Cabinet—Ontario Legislature Debates, December 23, 1978.
[40] The report was released in August 1981. See, too, the other volumes containing the findings and recommendations of the McDonald Commission—*First Report, Security and Information* (October 1979); *Second Report*, Vols. 1 and 2, *Freedom and Security under the Law* (August 1981), (Government Publishing Centre, Ottawa).

determine the degree of knowledge acquired by senior members of the Royal Canadian Mounted Police, senior governmental officials and ministers as to certain investigative practices by members of the security service that were not authorised or provided for by law. These illegal practices included theft, arson, surreptitious entries, electronic surveillance, mail check operations, access to and the use of confidential information held by various departments of the federal government. The McDonald Commission acknowledged that it was not within its jurisdiction to advise the Attorney General of Canada or the pertinent provincial Attorneys General whether, in any particular situation, criminal proceedings should be instituted. These decisions were a matter solely for the discretion of the Attorneys General. Nevertheless, the Commission deemed it necessary to expound on the principles that should govern the exercise of executive power in regard to prosecutions.[41]

Emphasis was placed on the need to satisfy both of the relevant criteria, *viz.*, the sufficiency of the evidence and the public interest, before making an affirmative decision to launch a criminal prosecution. Special difficulties, it was pointed out, arise where doubts are entertained as to whether the illegal practices in question were a matter of choice for the individual officer or could be characterised as official investigative procedures that enjoyed the express or tacit approval of the senior management of the Royal Canadian Mounted Police. Similarly, assuming that the conduct of the members of the security service had become institutionalised in the manner just described, when assessing whether a prosecution should lie against the senior officers who authorised the illegal practice it becomes a matter of the greatest moment to ascertain whether the practice had either expressly or by implication received the approval of the government. This might mean the approval of the responsible minister or possibly the Cabinet as a whole.

Some guidance was found in a 1977 report prepared by the United States Department of Justice in somewhat analogous circumstances. The issue faced in that instance was the institution of criminal proceedings against members of the Central Intelligence Agency who had regularly engaged in mail opening activities contrary to the federal law. According to the Justice Department, "whatever its cause, the failure of officials at the highest levels, who were generally aware of these activities, to clarify the law and establish institutional controls, and their apparent contentment to leave the individuals operating in this field to proceed according to their best estimates of legal constraints in a vague and yet vitally important area—all this would render a prosecution by the government hypocritical."[42] The McDonald Commission, however, was emphatic in dissociating itself from the principle that it was the same government ministers who, having turned a blind eye to the bending or outright violations of the criminal law by any

---

[41] *Ibid.* Part VII, pp. 503–515.
[42] Quoted in the McDonald Commission of Inquiry, *Third Report*, (1981), pp. 509–510.

of its agencies, should also be accorded the responsibility of deciding whether or not criminal prosecutions should be instituted. Such decisions, it must be remembered, might involve allegations of possible complicity by members of the executive branch itself, whether these persons were senior departmental officials or ministers of the Crown.

Speaking of Canada and its constitutional system the McDonald Commission of Inquiry stated " . . . it is quite erroneous to speak of 'prosecution by the government': when an Attorney General decides whether or not to prosecute the decision is his, not that of the government, even though he is also a minister in that government. Thus, for example, if the person against whom criminal proceedings are contemplated happens to be a minister of the Crown or a deputy minister, or, for that matter, anyone in the executive branch of government, it is the duty of the Attorney General to reach his decision without regard to any embarrassment or prejudice that his decision to institute proceedings may cause either the individual concerned or the government of which he happens to be a member. Consequently, that part of the passage just quoted which speaks of government 'hypocrisy' should be regarded as inapplicable to Canada."[43]

In his public response to the McDonald Commission the present Attorney General of Canada, Mr. Mark MacGuigan, has reiterated the ultimate responsibility of his office, and not that of the government, for prosecutorial decisions within the federal jurisdiction.[44] With respect to Criminal Code violations it was noted that only Quebec had decided to institute proceedings. Mr MacGuigan's predecessor had earlier decided that there would be no prosecutions for such federal offences as tampering with the mail or the unlawful use of confidential information.[44a] In reaching the decision not to institute proceedings the most important factors identified were "the institutional nature of the practices engaged in, the expiry of limitation periods with respect to a vast majority of the incidents, . . . the question of motive on the part of the members of the R.C.M.P. who participated in these activities, the uncertain direction received in connection with certain practices such as mail opening, and fundamental disagreement [between the McDonald Commission and the legal officers in the Department of Justice] as to the legal status of activities such as entries in connection with the installation of electro-magnetic surveillance devices pursuant to a lawful authorization."[45] Whatever

---

[43] *Ibid.* p. 509.

[44] See "The Position of the Attorney General of Canada on Certain Recommendations of the McDonald Commission," Department of Justice, Canada, August 1983, esp. pp. 8 and 9.

[44a] In a letter dated July 20, 1982, addressed to Mr. Robert Kaplan, the Solicitor General of Canada, and tabled before the House of Commons Standing Committee on Justice and Legal Affairs on November 11, 1982—see Minutes of Proceedings and Evidence, Vol. 110, pp. 10–11 and Appendix "Just 43."

[45] *Ante* fn. 44, *op. cit.* p. 19, The Alberta C.A. (three to two decision) has ruled in favour of the McDonald Commission's interpretation of the law. The question is now to be taken to the Supreme Court of Canada: *Globe & Mail*, December 16, 1983.

reactions this ministerial statement may have stimulated among the general public it is a depressing fact to record that, apart from one brief encounter in the Standing Committee on Justice and Legal Affairs in November 1982,[45a] neither the government nor the opposition has seen fit to ensure an adequate opportunity in which to subject the Attorney General of Canada to an intensive accountability for these prosecutorial decisions.

II. Australia

The early colonial histories of New South Wales, Victoria, South Australia, Queensland, Tasmania and Western Australia, the founding states of what in 1900 became the Commonwealth of Australia, contain many similarities to those features of government by Whitehall, alluded to in the previous section, as they applied to the Provinces of Lower and Upper Canada.[46] Direct rule from London, through the instrumentality of a British appointed Governor was facilitated by the appointment of a Chief Justice and Attorney General recruited from the ranks of the English Bar. Both lawyers were made *ex officio* members of the colony's Executive and Legislative Councils and took an active part in every aspect of local government. The realisation that judicial independence necessitated a withdrawal from both the executive and legislative branches of government came slowly but surely, leaving the Attorney General as the longest surviving office to be closely associated with the functioning of the executive council, and its modern successor the Cabinet, at both the State and Commonwealth levels of government. Thus, for example, by virtue of section 64 of the Commonwealth of Australia Constitution Act 1900,[47] the Attorney General is one of the officers appointed to administer a Department of State of the Commonwealth established by the Governor General, namely the Department of the Attorney General. As such, the Attorney General is a member of the Federal Executive Council and one of the Queen's Ministers of State for the Commonwealth. Along with other ministers, the person appointed as the senior Law Officer of the Crown may not hold office for more than three months unless he is or becomes a Senator or a member of the House of Representatives.[48]

Even in this context, however, the passage of time has brought with it constitutional adjustments in keeping with the political inclinations of individual governments. Thus the practice has long been recognised that the holder of the office of Attorney General does not, *ex officio*, occupy a seat within the Cabinet or inner council of ministers of the Commonwealth

---

[45a] *Supra*, fn. 44a, *loc. cit.*
[46] See, generally, Todd, *Parliamentary Government in the British Colonies*, (2nd ed., 1894), *passim*, and Edwards, *The Law Officers of the Crown*, pp. 165–169.
[47] 63 & 64 Vict., c. 12.
[48] *Ibid.*

Government sitting in Canberra.[49] Neither is there any constitutional convention, paralleling that adhered to in the United Kingdom since 1928, that the Attorney General be excluded from the ranks of Cabinet ministers. Rather, in Australia, membership in the Commonwealth Cabinet is determined in accordance with the political standing and seniority of the individuals invited by the Prime Minister to hold the various portfolios of the government. Looking at the list of Attorneys General during the past few decades it comes as no surprise to learn that Sir Robert Menzies and Sir Garfield Barwick were ranked as senior members of the Cabinet. Menzies went on to become the Prime Minister of Australia but prior to that appointment he had combined the duties of Attorney General with those of Acting Prime Minister, an association of responsibilities that he described as "frightening."[50] Earlier still, Menzies had held office as Attorney General of the State of Victoria simultaneously with occupying the portfolios of Minister of Railways and State Treasurer, a combination of functions that is by no means unique in Australian experience.[51] Prior to leaving the political arena and becoming Chief Justice of Australia, Sir Garfield Barwick at one time was required to discharge the seemingly unconnected responsibilities as Attorney General and Minister of External Affairs. In doing so, he was following in the footsteps of Sir John Latham[52] and Dr. H. R. Evatt.[53] There are also

[49] It is of some interest to note that, paralleling the situation that arose in Scotland with the first Labour Administration (see *ante*, pp. 281–283), H.B. Higgins, though not a member of the Labour Party, held the Attorney General's portfolio in the first Commonwealth Labour Party Government (1903–04), see G. Sawer, *Australian Federal Politics and Law, 1901–29*, Melbourne 1956, p. 38. See also the editorial note in (1978) 52 Aust.L.J. pp.4–5, canvassing recent experience with respect to the Cabinet status of the office of Federal Attorney General.

[50] Personal communication to the author in Melbourne, April 2, 1968. An earlier notable precedent, wherein the two offices of Prime Minister and Attorney General were occupied by the same person was set by the redoubtable W.M. Hughes from 1915 to 1921—Sawer, *op. cit.* p. 189.

[51] In the course of my talk with Sir Robert Menzies, (see *ante*, fn. 50), he drew a sharp contrast between his own and Dr. Evatt's approach, when Attorney General, to tabling before the House of Representatives the advice that they each had received from the Solicitor General of the day, a non-political office. According to Menzies he had consistently refused to accede to Opposition demands of this kind, maintaining that he expressed his own views for which he was answerable to the House if he was wrong. Evatt, in Menzies' opinion, felt no compunction in disclosing the Solicitor General's opinion "particularly when these were favourable to the Labour Party's position as the Government in power." Speaking of Sir John Latham (*infra*) as Attorney General and his relationship to Prime Minister Bruce, Menzies described the Attorney as "an able lawyer but with a rigid mind" and criticised some of Latham's decisions as Law Officer as "stupid political moves".

[52] Latham first became Attorney General of the Commonwealth from 1925 to late 1929. He resumed the duties of Attorney General in 1931 in conjunction with the responsibilities of Deputy Prime Minister, Minister for External Affairs and Minister for Industry. From 1935 until his retirement in 1952, Latham was Chief Justice of the High Court of Australia. During his first tenure of the Attorney General's office a series of motions were introduced in the House of Representatives seeking to censure the Attorney for his handling of several notorious criminal cases. In the *Abrahams* case (1928), before a prosecution could be launched for fraud and evasion of income tax two of the defendants fled the country secretly without obtaining passports. The subsequent settlement of the Government's claims for income tax and penalties, and the suspicion that this had been premised on the understanding

numerous instances in which the joint offices of Attorney General and Minister of Justice have been occupied by a non-lawyer without any evident loss of public confidence in the carrying out of the duties associated with these positions.[54] Unlike the Commonwealth situation, however, the convention of including the Attorney General within the Cabinet of each State Government has, to the best of my researches, never once been broken.[55]

In marked contrast the office of Solicitor General has taken several distinct turns in the course of its Australian evolution. Prior to the advent of the federal constitution in 1900, appointments to the Solicitor Generalship followed the British tradition, insomuch as the holding of a seat in the legislature was deemed a necessary qualification for appointment. In those colonies that possessed a portfolio designated as the

that there would be no prosecution for criminal conspiracy, sparked the Opposition's unsuccessful censure motion. Strong words of criticism had previously been expressed by Starke J., as to the Government's handling of the fraudulent avoidance of income tax by the defendants—(1928) Aust.L.J. 388. What the court was not told, but which was disclosed in the House of Representatives, was the advice given to the Attorney General by five senior counsel, including Owen Dixon Q.C. (as he then was) not to proceed by way of criminal prosecution but rather by way of a civil action to recover the tax penalties for the Revenue Department—see Parl. Deb., H.R. Vol. 118, pp. 4051–5078, March 22, 1928. Another controversial decision, in which Latham was closely involved, was the withdrawal of criminal proceedings against the coal mining firm, *John Brown & Co.*, in 1929. The company had originally been charged, under the Conciliation and Arbitration Act and the Industrial Peace Act, with conducting a lock-out. According to his version of the events, Latham had launched criminal proceedings against the company with the express agreement of the Cabinet. This action at once exacerbated the tense industrial situation, so that Prime Minister Bruce became actively involved in seeking a resolution to the problem. After consultation with the Attorney General, the withdrawal of the prosecution was announced by the Prime Minister who proceeded to give instructions to the Solicitor General to take the necessary executive and court action to bring the proceedings to a halt—see Parl. Deb., H.R. Vol. 121, pp. 7–20, 34–57, August 5, 1929, especially the P.M.'s statements at pp. 17–18 and Latham's defence of the Government's handling of the case at pp. 50–57. No criticism of the Government's actions have been voiced by post hoc academic writers in Australia—see, *e.g.* G. Sawer, *op. cit.* pp. 313–315 and Zelman Cowen, *Sir John Latham & Other Papers*, (1965), pp. 14–15, 31–32. R. Plehwe, "The Attorney General and Cabinet: Some Australian Precedents" (1980) Fed.L.R. 1–18, presents a careful assessment of the significance of the *John Brown Co.* and *Mercantile Bank* cases to the recognition of a convention regarding the Attorney General's exclusive control over criminal proceedings.

[53] Dr. Evatt, prior to serving as the federal Attorney General and Minister for External Affairs in the period 1941–49, and deputy Prime Minister from 1946 to 1949, had served as a Justice of the High Court of Australia for 10 years from 1930 to 1940. He became leader of the federal parliamentary Labour Party in 1951 and sat on the Opposition benches until his retirement from politics in 1961.

[54] Thus, as recently as 1968, the Queensland Attorney General and Minister of Justice was a pharmacologist by training. What must be remembered in such exceptional situations, is that there generally will be found a Solicitor General, an experienced lawyer, who occupies a non-political appointment on the public service side of government.

[55] In Victoria and South Australia the State's Constitution Act expressly provides that the Ministers of the Crown are to be *ex officio* Executive Councillors. This approach "merely makes explicit what has always by constitutional convention been the understood practice in the other states. The Executive Council, in other words, consists of the Governor and his Ministers"—see S.R. Davis, *The Government of the Australian States*, p. 10. The Department of the Attorney General and Minister of Justice, in each of the founding divisions of Australia, was one of the basic departments of state government—*ibid.* p. 144.

Solicitor General, the appointee was always drawn from the ranks of politicians.[56] If the Solicitor General was legally trained so much the better. This pattern, outside of the Commonwealth Government in Canberra, was not abandoned until the 1950s, of which more will be said later. Moreover, the initial break with tradition was not occasioned by any theoretical arguments but as an act of outright political expediency designed to make the life of the Prime Minister more bearable.

Sir Robert Garran was the first incumbent, the position of Solicitor General of the Commonwealth as a non-political office being specially created[57] by statute in 1916[58] when W.M. Hughes was doubling the parts of Prime Minister and Attorney General. The enactment conferred the widest powers of delegation, thus enabling Hughes to relieve himself of practically all his duties as the Attorney General.[59] Garran had been for many years the permanent Secretary of the Attorney General's Department, a position that he continued to hold in conjunction with his new duties as Solicitor General. In 1964 the two appointments were again separated, as they had in fact become in practice before the Law Officers of that year gave better definition to the functions of the respective offices. The machinery within the Attorney General's Department remained the same but it was now enshrined in statutory form.[60]

---

[56] See *post*, fn. 65.

[57] See R.R. Garran, *Prosper the Commonwealth*, (Melbourne, 1958), p. 152. Garran describes the beginning of the Attorney General's Department in 1900 as "a one man show of which the head and the tail was myself. Its principal work at the outset was to give legal advice, especially on constitutional matters, to all other departments, to draft bills and statutory regulations, and to conduct litigation in which the Commonwealth might be involved. I was anxious to keep it as far as possible a professional department with as little as possible of administrative work"—*ibid*. p. 151. During his 32 years as permanent head of the Department Garran served under 11 Attorneys General. Five of the 11 had left the Attorney's portfolio before the Commonwealth of Australia was six years old and did not occupy the office again—*ibid*. p. 155. Of Sir Isaac Isaacs Garran had this to say, "By day his capacity for work was amazing. By day he carried the biggest practice of the Victorian Bar; by night he did full justice to the duties of Attorney-General. He sometimes slept, I must believe, though I could never discover when. I once left him at the office at midnight, and on my way home took to the printer a draft Bill that was to be ready in the morning. Coming to the office early, I found on my table an envelope from the Government Printer, containing an entirely different draft, which, in some wonderment, I took in to the Attorney. He confessed that in the small hours he had had a new inspiration, had recovered the draft from the printer, and had reshaped it, lock, stock and barrel." *ibid*. p. 157.

[58] Commonwealth Acts, No. 28 of 1916.

[59] The circumstances that dictated the introduction of the measure were frankly explained to the House of Representatives by the Prime Minister but at the time no copies of the Bill were available. All stages of the Bill were completed in two days—Parl. Debates, H.R. & Senate, September 27 & 28, 1916. For an appreciation of Garran's indispensable role as the first Solicitor General of the Commonwealth and permanent head of the Attorney General's Department in its earliest years, see J.A. La Nanze's biography of *Alfred Deakin*, (Melbourne U.P., 1972), pp. 263–264, 270; and L.F. Fitzhardinge: *W.M. Hughes—A Political Biography*, Vol. 1, (1964), pp. 252–275. In 1913, Garran was seriously considered for one of the vacancies on the High Court of Australia—*ibid*. p. 275.

[60] Commonwealth Acts, No. 91 of 1964. For the Government's explanation of the Bill's underlying philosophy, see Parl. Debates, Senate, October 19 and 30, 1964. The last holder of the joint appointments was Sir Kenneth Bailey who, on his retirement as Solicitor General, was made the Australian High Commissioner to Canada.

The Solicitor General, who henceforth was to be appointed from among counsel practising at the Bar,[61] was formally designated as the second Law Officer of the Commonwealth[62] with primary responsibility to appear as chief counsel for the Crown and on behalf of the Commonwealth in litigation, as well as furnishing opinions on questions of law referred to him by the Attorney General.[63] These matters generally include constitutional questions, the existence of rights against the Commonwealth Government, issues having a political flavour but which are essentially legal concerns, and areas in which the Cabinet might be considering proposals for legislation affecting the federal constitution. When responding, the Solicitor General does not act as the exclusive source from which the Attorney General derives legal advice, it being the normal practice to find the Secretary of the Department and his legal officers being brought into the discussions. In cases of special importance or difficulty, however, where an independent judgment is called for, the opinion of the Solicitor General would generally be sought.[64] There exist obvious similarities with the office of Solicitor General of the United States and his functions within the federal Department of Justice but the parallel should not be pressed too far.

In the Australian States there is a broad consistency, rather than uniformity, in the ministerial arrangements for supervising the administration of justice. At the apex carrying ultimate responsibility to the Legislature is the Attorney General who may or may not be designated as the Minister of Justice. No inflexible score is placed on appointing a lawyer to the portfolio, or, where the profession is bifurcated, restricting the appointment to a member of the Legislature who is also a member of the Bar. In terms of legal expertise and judgment the burden rests on the shoulders of the Solicitor General, a non-political office.[65] Interestingly, in

---

[61] *Ibid.* s.6.

[62] *Ibid.* s.5. Appointments to the non-political office were to be for a fixed term, not exceeding 7 years, but with eligibility for re-appointment—*ibid.* s.6.

[63] *Ibid.* s.12. The original powers of delegation by the Attorney conferred by the 1916 statute were preserved and extended by the new measure to include the Secretary to the Department as well as the Solicitor General—see s.17.

[64] This account of the internal workings of the Attorney General's Department derives from discussions with the Solicitor General, A.F. Mason Q.C. (now Mr. Justice Mason of the High Court of Australia) and the then Secretary of the Department, Mr. E.J. Hook, on March 25, 1968. At the request of the present Prime Minister (R. J. Hawke), formal opinions were submitted by the Attorney General (Senator Gareth Evans) and the Solicitor General (Sir Maurice Byers) recommending against the prosecution of *Mr. Mick Young*, Special Minister of State for disclosing to a lobbyist information obtained when Young was a member of the National Intelligence Security Committee of the Cabinet—see *The Australian*, August 31, 1983.

[65] This was not always so, as indicated by the Prime Minister of Australia in 1916 when introducing his Bill to create the office of Commonwealth Solicitor General. At that time, Mr. W.M. Hughes stated: "In New South Wales, until recently and in Tasmania, Western Australia, and New Zealand, the Solicitor General is an official, and not a member of Parliament." Parl. Debates, H.R. September 27, 1916, p. 8996. In Victoria, Queensland, South Australia, the Solicitor General was a political Minister and a member of the State Cabinet.

Victoria the move was instituted in 1958,[66] and in New South Wales in 1969,[67] to confine eligibility to the Solicitor General's position to those holding the rank of Queen's Counsel, itself an appointment subject to the recommendation of the State's Chief Justice. Moreover, the legislation expressly provides that the office of Solicitor General shall not be held by a minister of the Crown.[68] The motive behind such a move is clear, emphasising as it does the independent status of the office and the need to encourage leading counsel to assume the duties of being the State's chief legal adviser. A further reflection of these essential attributes is the general understanding that the advice of the Solicitor General is available in appropriate circumstances not only to the government and its ministers but also to the Governor of the State and members of the Opposition.[69] The same understanding prevails at the federal level, as evidenced during the constitutional crisis in 1975 when Governor General Kerr saw fit to dismiss Mr. Gough Whitlam, Leader of the Labour Party, from office as Prime Minister. An examination of the roles played in that affair by the Attorney General and the Solicitor General of the Commonwealth[70] must be deferred to another occasion.

[66] Statutes of Victoria, No. 6374 of 1958, s.3(1). The precedent set by this legislation was obviously influential in the Commonwealth Government's decision in 1964 to follow the same principles.

[67] Statutes of N.S.W., No. 80 of 1969, s.2(1); and see, too, the Crown Advocate Act 1979, (N.S.W.), Act No. 59 of 1979, an office designed to provide assistance to the Solicitor General, the Attorney General, crown prosecutors and the police. Under the N.S.W. Constitution Act 1902, the Governor may authorise any member of the Executive Council to exercise the powers appertaining to any other executive councillor but it is expressly provided by that section that no such authority shall be granted in respect of the powers, duties and obligations by law annexed to and incident to the office of the Attorney General. In his absence or incapacity, or where the office is vacant, the duties at common law devolve upon the Solicitor General.—see S.G. v. Wylde (1945) 62 W.N. (N.S.W.) 246 and the Solicitor General Act (N.S.W.), 1969, ss.3 and 4.

[68] Statutes of Victoria, No.6374 of 1958, s.3(2); Statutes of N.S.W., No. 80 of 1969, s.2(6). More recent developments in Australia, designed to insulate the prosecution decision-making process from political influences, include the federal Special Prosecutors Bill 1982 (see (1983) 9 C.L.B. 15–17) and the appointment of a Director of Public Prosecutions for the State of Victoria in January 1983 (see A.L.R.C.'s Reform, no. 30 (April 1983) pp. 78–79). Under the federal bill the Attorney General is restricted to giving directions as guidelines of a general nature and not with reference to any particular case. The new Victoria D.P.P. will enjoy the status of a Supreme Court judge and assume sole responsibility for the prosecution of all indictable offences, Crown appeals and presentments. Both of the new officials will report on their activities directly to the legislative bodies concerned.

[69] This understanding is based on my helpful discussions with the then Solicitor General of Victoria, Mr. B.L. Murray (now Mr. Justice Murray of the Supreme Court of Victoria) on March 29, 1968, and with Sir Henry Winneke, Chief Justice of Victoria, on April 2, 1968. Prior to his appointment as Chief Justice, Winneke served as the first non-political Solicitor General from 1958 to 1964.

[70] Some of the preliminary sources to which reference must be made include Sir John Kerr's book Matters for Judgment, 1978 and, by way of reply, Mr. Whitlam's account of the same events, The Truth of the Matter, 1979. A critical evaluation of the constitutional propriety of the action taken by the Governor General, and by Sir Garfield Barwick, Chief Justice of Australia, who was consulted by Sir John Kerr against the advice of the Prime Minister and without the knowledge of the other High Court Justices, is contained in Professor Geoffrey Sawer's Federation Under Strain, (Melb.U.P. 1977), esp. Chapter 8, pp.

ISAAC ISAACS AND THE MERCANTILE BANK CASE IN 1893

If there is certainty today as to the proper constitutional relationship that should prevail between the two Law Officers, one the political minister and the other a non-political civil servant subordinate to the minister's final authority, this was far from being true in the remarkable events surrounding the handling of the *Mercantile Bank Case* in the State of Victoria in 1893.[71] With the collapse of the bank, one of the many prosperous institutions that had sprung up during the land boom in the 1880s, the financial dealings of the bank's chairman and his senior associates became the subject of widespread comment in the newspapers and in the legislature. Summonses charging conspiracy to defraud and the publishing of false and fraudulent balance sheets were issued on the instructions of the Attorney General, William Shiels, against Sir Mathew Davies, the chairman and former Speaker of the Legislative Assembly, as well as against Millidge, the manager of the bank, and sundry other directors and auditors.[72] Before the committal proceedings began there was a change of government and Sir Bryan O'Loghlen was named as the new Attorney General. After some dramatic confrontations at the close of the long preliminary hearing among the presiding Justices of the Peace, Davies and Millidge were committed for trial. This event took place amid a fresh crop of failures among the banking and financial houses in Melbourne. Public feelings were running high when Sir Bryan O'Loghlen, Attorney General and a former Premier of Victoria, announced that there would be no prosecution.[73] Almost immediately the Solicitor General, Isaac Isaacs, later to achieve fame as Chief Justice of Australia and that country's first native born Governor General, announced that he proposed

141–172. The same source describes the weight accorded during the crisis to the opinions prepared by the former Commonwealth Solicitor General (Mr. R.J. Ellicott) and his successor in that office (Mr. M. Byers). For the published documents in the Prime Minister's dismissal see Sawer, *op. cit.* Appendix 2, pp. 203–211. See also A. Reid, *The Whitlam Venture*, (1976), pp. 411–414.

[71] For an eminently readable account of this case and the surrounding events, see Michael Cannon, *The Land Boomers*, (Melbourne, 1966), pp. 157–177. See, too, Zelman Cowen's biography of *Isaac Isaacs*, pp. 30–36, which concentrates more on the legal aspects of Isaacs' involvement in the case.

[72] As the Attorney General in 1892, Shiels had resisted persistent attempts by the Opposition to force him into authorising criminal proceedings against the Melbourne directors of the Bank stating, with respect to a motion debated on December 15, 1892: " . . . it would, if carried, amount to a command from the House that the Government should, without any sufficient case having been laid before the Attorney General or his advisers, punish certain individuals . . . So strongly had he felt that this was not a matter which should be brought into the political arena, he had always refused to discuss these questions in Cabinet. From first to last he had exercised this power apart altogether from his colleagues, and they had not been taken into his confidence; they had simply seen the result of his action in the newspapers. And it was absolutely necessary, if the House wanted to keep the fount of justice pure, that they should religiously say that in the administration of justice in cases of a criminal character, all political motives and all political considerations must be refused admission." See Leg. Assembly Debates, December 15, 1892, pp. 3517–3532.

[73] Cowen, *op. cit.* pp. 30–31.

to consider the question of instituting criminal proceedings against the directors of the Mercantile Bank, notwithstanding the contrary decision communicated to the court by the senior Law Officer of the Crown, the State's Attorney General.[74]

Isaacs based his claim to having an independent authority vested in him as the Solicitor General on the terms of the Crimes Act 1890,[75] section 338 of which reads: "Subject to the provisions hereinbefore contained, it shall be lawful for Her Majesty's Attorney-General or Solicitor-General for Victoria or for any prosecutor for the Queen in the name of a law officer to make presentment at the Supreme Court of General Sessions of the Peace of any person for any indictable offence cognisable by such courts respectively, and every such presentment . . . shall be as good and of the same force, strength, and effect in law as if the same had been presented and found by the oaths of twelve good men and true." According to Isaacs this provision conferred a separate and concurrent authority on the Solicitor General to proceed with a criminal prosecution notwithstanding the contrary view being held in the same matter by the Attorney General. This dubious interpretation of the concurrent powers exercisable by the senior and junior Law Officers was categorically rejected by O'Loghlen in a letter addressed to Isaacs. In it the Attorney General wrote[76]: " . . . once I have decided and taken action as Attorney General acting as a grand jury, no one has any right to interfere with, or review officially, that decision or nullify action taken by me on behalf of the Crown. You must consider the constitutional position and what differences of judgment may lead to. The Queen cannot speak with two varying voices through two responsible ministers on one and the same occasion, the one perhaps saying 'no prosecution' and the other saying 'I must make a presentment'. You must remember too, in interpreting the section you refer to . . . that that section has to be read with the knowledge of Parliament of the constitutional position of Her Majesty's Attorney General from the conception of that office. The Attorney General is the chief law officer of the Queen, and the Solicitor comes after him. Only in the absence of or at the request of the Attorney General does the Solicitor General act as a grand jury in this colony. No Solicitor General has ever acted independently as a court of review in any case decided by his senior Law Officer, the Attorney General. It would be manifestly most unconstitutional for him to do so, as well as against all precedent . . . For all these reasons, I, as Attorney General, cannot sanction your proposed action, nor can I submit to it, nor can I ignore it. I must therefore officially request of you with the

---

[74] Cowen, *op. cit.* p. 31.

[75] 54 Vict. no. 1079 (Vict.).

[76] The increasingly acerbic correspondence between the Attorney General and the Solicitor General was later published in the columns of *The Argus*, May 26, 1893. O'Loghlen's letter to Isaacs is quoted in full in Cowen, *op. cit.* pp. 31–32.

utmost urgency to abstain from carrying out your intentions as announced in the papers."

Isaacs was not to be moved from his intransigent claim[77] that, as a matter of interpretation of the plain words of the statute, an independent discretion was reposed in the Solicitor General as well as that accorded to the Attorney General. "My power to set justice on its way," Isaacs replied, "is, if I read the law aright, absolutely independent of your sanction and beyond your prohibition, and its exercise is wholly within my own discretion so long as I occupy my present position. The Attorney General and the Solicitor General are by the act *personae designatae* and of equal authority in this respect."[78] Unassailable as the Attorney's legal position might be, there were patent weaknesses in the grounds on which the Attorney General purported to stop the prosecution, it having been publicly stated by the Crown Prosecutors in the Crown Law Department that, in their view, it was justifiable to initiate criminal proceedings against the accused directors.[79] Despite being deprived, by order of the Attorney General, of the services of the Crown Solicitor in preparing the papers for his proposed presentment against Davies and Millidge, Isaacs pressed forward with his initiative to the embarrassment of the Government and his political colleagues.[80] By now the *Mercantile Bank* case and the dispute between the Victoria law officers had become a *cause célèbre* throughout Australia, each incident and each statement being given great prominence in the daily newspapers.

Never one to entertain doubts as to the correctness of any position that he took in public life Isaacs called upon his colleagues in the Cabinet to resolve his dispute with the Attorney General by affirming his claims to independent discretionary powers as the State's Solicitor General. It will be remembered that, at that period in 1892, the Solicitor General's office was a political appointment, the appointee enjoying equal status as a member of the Cabinet with the Attorney General. Isaacs' advocacy of his cause fell on deaf ears and he received instead what amounted to a letter of dismissal from the Premier, James Patterson.[81] Having regard to subsequent developments in the case the contents of this message are deserving of notice. "After the consideration which the Cabinet gave to the question of your claim to make the prosecution in the case of the *Mercantile Bank* a

[77] "No amount of custom" Isaacs declaimed "red tape, officialdom, of personal consideration, or of etiquette, or relative status of law officers of the Crown, can in any way lessen my individual responsibility for the due, honest and fearless performance of the functions entrusted to me"—*The Argus*, May 26, 1893.

[78] *Ibid.*

[79] Cowen, *op. cit.* p. 32.

[80] The Solicitor General ensured that a full statement of his position appeared in the Melbourne newspapers, see, *e.g. The Argus*, May 25, 1893.

[81] The full text of the Premier's peremptory letter, calling on Isaacs to forward immediately his resignation of the office of Solicitor General, appeared the following morning in *The Argus*, May 25, 1893. Cowen, *op. cit.* p. 33 concludes that the Premier's letter was communicated to the press before it reached its recipient.

Cabinet matter,"[82] the Premier wrote, "I am quite confirmed in the view which I have always held, and which the Cabinet has affirmed, that the proprieties of the administration of justice demand that the function of filing or not filing a presentment should be discharged by the Attorney General, and in his absence by the Solicitor General, and entirely apart from the political Cabinet, and together distinct from any personal view any member of the Cabinet may entertain. You are, of course, aware that out of consideration to you the following resolution was adopted at the meeting of the Cabinet on Monday last: 'That, in the opinion of this Cabinet, it is unconstitutional for it, or any member of it, to interfere with the Attorney General in the discharge of his functions as a grand jury either directly or indirectly.'[83] In that resolution you concurred, and it was unanimously adopted by the Cabinet. The Cabinet affirming this view as its deliberate and well considered opinion, I was greatly pained to observe by the press this morning that you have expressed a determination to improperly involve the Cabinet in your action. Whatever may be the motives impelling you in your proposed course its effect is plainly to expose the Government to ridicule."

In the light of Isaacs' rejection of the Cabinet's position that the Attorney General's decision was supreme, coupled with the imminence of Isaacs' move to lay presentments before the Supreme Court charging the directors of the Mercantile Bank with conspiracy and the issuing of false balance sheets, the Premier was left with no option but to peremptorily demand that the Solicitor General resign. Isaacs complied at once and followed this up by resigning his seat in the Legislative Assembly so that he could contest the ensuing election.[84] He was returned unopposed with wide acclaim for the stand he had taken with respect to the *Mercantile*

---

[82] Isaacs strongly disavowed that this was his intention. In his reply to the Premier written immediately on receipt of the dismissal notice, the Solicitor General wrote: "Any person ignorant of all that has taken place between us might from the terms of your letter imagine that I have been desirous that the Cabinet should exercise the functions of a grand jury and determine on the evidence whether the prosecution should continue. If such an idea could arise let me dissipate it at once by referring to the following passage in my letter to you of the 21st inst.:—'First of all it never was part of my intention to ask the Cabinet to deal with the case. All I wish is that the Cabinet should say whether on the view of the possible conflict between my opinion and that of Sir Bryan may be allowed to exercise the functions assigned to me by law and co-equal with those of the Attorney General in this respect—or whether the Cabinet insist that the decision of one law officer shall be final, thus practically repealing the legislative enactment.' What I distinctly wished above all things to avoid was that the Cabinet should either interfere or permit any interference with either of the law officers in the discharge of their respective functions. That position I have reiterated so many times in correspondence and verbally in the Cabinet that even to your own mind your statement that I claimed 'to make the prosecution in the case of the Mercantile Bank a Cabinet matter' must present a wretchedly weak appearance."

[83] Isaacs' letter further contested that the insertion of the words "directly or indirectly" was never part of the resolution adopted by the Cabinet with his approbation. Without the additional condition, Isaacs wrote that he would be prepared to go further and declared that "such conduct as is deprecated by that resolution is not only unconstitutional but quite illegal"—*The Argus*, May 25, 1893.

[84] *The Argus*, May 26, 1893.

Bank prosecutions, an acclaim that sprang from the disillusionment of a susceptible public with what were regarded as corrupt financiers and a belief, however ill-founded, that the Government was disposed to lend protection to those who were responsible for the bursting of the economic boom and the resultant ruin to innocent investors.[85] The constitutional proprieties involved in the dispute between the two Law Officers, and that which estranged Isaacs from his fellow members in the Victoria Cabinet, were lost on the general public but featured prominently in the heated debate that took place in the Legislative Assembly some months later.[86]

By that time the final chapter of this precedent setting episode had been played out, but not before it had become quite apparent that the same Cabinet had quickly forgotten the important resolution it had passed unanimously in the face of the rebellious Solicitor General. Moreover, in this instance the Attorney General is seen capitulating under the pressures of his Cabinet colleagues. After Isaacs' forced resignation, the Supreme Court of Victoria, without Crown opposition and at the instigation of a private citizen, granted an application for a grand jury to investigate the *Mercantile Bank* issues.[87] In the midst of this new manoeuvre to bring the original accused to trial, the principal defendants suddenly disappeared from Melbourne. Notified of the latest developments, the Cabinet, sensitive to the public clamour that had earlier propelled Isaacs back into political prominence, moved with scant regard for the constitutional principles it had so recently endorsed. Over the opposition of the Attorney General who maintained that, in the event of a true bill being returned by the grand jury, it was within his prerogative to enter a *nolle prosequi*, the Cabinet decided to take immediate action to apprehend the accused and bring them to trial.[88] Failing the assistance of the Attorney General, this task was delegated to the Postmaster General, a lawyer by training, who hastily repaired to the Crown Law Office and instructed the Crown

[85] *e.g.* the lead editorial of the same issue of Melbourne's foremost newspaper wrote: "Although Mr. Isaacs has been repulsed we may hope that he will continue with unabated zeal in the good work which he has commenced by removing the right of entering a *nolle prosequi* or of filing a presentment from the Attorney General of this day . . . The administration of justice should be removed from an atmosphere of strife and suspicion. And the fact that there is strife and that there is suspicion in Victoria today is conclusive proof that 'a new order' is wanted."

[86] See Leg. Assembly Debates, June 29, 1893, pp. 29–47, July 4, 1893, 82–99, and again on August 17, 1893, pp. 1040–1049. Constitutional writers in Australia would do well to study the notable speeches made on that occasion with regard to the independence of the office of Attorney General. Plehwe (*ante*, fn. 52) *op. cito* pp. 4–6 has done so with careful discrimination.

[87] *R. v. Davies and Millidge* (No. 2) (1893) 19 Vict. L.R. 246 and 251.

[88] *The Argus*, June 1, 1893. According to the newspaper report "the view upon which [the Cabinet] now took action was that the decision of the Full Court to grant a grand jury had taken the matter entirely out of the Attorney General's hands and that the moment had now come for the Cabinet to intervene. To this otherwise unanimous decision there was one dissentient and it is hardly surprising to find that this was the Attorney General . . . he could find no supporters, and the upshot will probably be his early retirement from the Ministry." In fact, O'Loghlen did not resign and took an active part later in the Legislative Assembly in defending the Administration's handling of the entire episode.

Solicitor to prepare warrants for the arrest of Sir Mathew Davies and Mr. Millidge. The Crown Solicitor at first demurred but on the production of definite instructions from the Cabinet raised no further opposition. The Attorney General was summarily by-passed. The accused were apprehended in Colombo and returned for trial in the criminal court. After a 13 day hearing verdicts were returned acquitting each of the accused.[89] It remains to record the judgment expressed by Isaac Isaacs' biographer, Professor Sir Zelman Cowen, that the Attorney's stated reasons for declining to proceed with the *Mercantile Bank* prosecutions were "poor and inept."[90] Cowen goes on: " . . . more careful reflection suggests the unwisdom and one may even say the impropriety of Isaacs' action. Surely the appropriate course for him to have pursued in face of the Attorney's action and the government's support of that action was to resign his portfolio, and then to attack the government as a private member."[91] A more trenchant critic, the late Sir John Barry, of the Supreme Court of Victoria, has written[92]: "Isaacs was right in his opinion that the prosecution should go on; his manoeuvering was politically astute and effective, but his biographer's comment that the course taken by Isaacs was unwise and even improper is unquestionably correct . . . only a man impervious to any view but his own could have behaved as he did . . . An obnoxious element in his complex character was his absolute and invincible conviction of the rightness of his opinions and the stupidity, or worse, of those who disagreed with him. Unhappily, it was a fault that worsened with the years."

Resort in the case of the Attorney General or Solicitor General to the ultimate weapon of his dismissal from office by the First Minister is an extremely rare occurrence. The same infrequency attaches to the alternate procedure available to any minister or public official who feels so strongly opposed to a course of action, directly involving the position he holds, that resigning the office, after due warning of his intentions, is the last remaining sanction exercisable in keeping with the individual's conscience. Nevertheless, it must be recognised that such risks are inevitable in those circumstances where the Attorney General insists on prosecuting a case in opposition to the strongly held views of his Prime Minister and other

---

[89] Cowen, *op. cit.* p. 35.

[90] *Ibid.*

[91] *Ibid.* Zelman Cowen prefers O'Loghlen's argument, at the time, that the section of the Crimes Act under which Isaacs claimed to act must be read in the light of cabinet responsibility—*ibid.* p. 36.

[92] "From Yackandandah to Yarralumla: the Enigma of Isaac Isaacs," *Meanjin Quarterly*, December 1967, 443 at p. 446. Of Cowen's account of the *Mercantile Bank* case, Barry's judgment is that it was "thorough and judicious," *loc. cit.* Speaking of the customary tributes to Isaacs' memory paid by the High Court of Australia on his death, Barry wrote, "deserved though they were, there was a hollowness about some of the utterances . . . The speech of the Chief Justice, Sir John Latham, consisting of three paragraphs, was brief to the point of perfunctoriness. Isaac Isaacs' life was long and in the main honourable. As a tale of success and brilliant achievement, it was without parallel in the nation to which he was devoted. It was his tragedy that death did not come to him a decade sooner."*Ibid.* at p. 451.

ministerial colleagues. Any Law Officer who, rightly or wrongly, persists in maintaining his prerogative right to institute or continue proceedings in the face of clearly expressed condemnation of his proposed course of action must not be surprised if he is asked to surrender the seals of his office. At the same time it must be emphasised that to recognise the inevitability of dismissal or resignation in these circumstances in no sense represents a weakening of the Attorney General's constitutional position. What it entails is the removal of the issue from the confidential environment of Cabinet deliberations and its exposure to the full glare of public attention. The political judgments that ensue as to the respective merits of the stance adopted by the parties concerned will have short term and long term variations. Anticipating what these external judgments are likely to be will undoubtedly command the attention of the Attorney General or Solicitor General concerned before he resolves the conflict in favour of adhering to what he conceives to be his public responsibilities.

THE RESIGNATION OF ATTORNEY GENERAL ROBERT ELLICOTT IN 1975

As we have seen, the judgment of Australian publicists, writing in the calm atmosphere of retrospection, has been as severely critical of Isaac Isaacs' conduct in the *Mercantile Bank* case as his constituents were enthusiastic in ensuring his unopposed return to the Legislative Assembly. In more recent times, Australia has again been the setting for a highly controversial dispute that resulted in the resignation of Mr. Robert Ellicott, the Commonwealth Attorney General, following what he conceived to be the Cabinet's interference with the exercise of his independent discretion in criminal proceedings. These proceedings began with the laying of an information by a private citizen, a New South Wales lawyer, against Mr. Gough Whitlam, Prime Minister of Australia from 1972 to 1975, Senator Lionel Murphy, the former Attorney General of the Commonwealth (presently a Justice of the High Court of Australia), and other sundry ministers of the Crown[93] in the Whitlam Administration.[94]

---

[93] Of the other defendants Mr. Connor had been Minister for Minerals and Energy, and Dr. Cairns had been Treasurer, in the Whitlam Administration.

[94] At the outset of the committal hearing before the Court of Petty Sessions at Queanbeyan objections to the validity of the proceedings were registered by the former ministers of the Crown. The presiding stipendiary magistrate having ruled against the objections, the defendants sought to terminate the private prosecution by applying for orders of certiorari, prohibition and mandamus and a declaration before the New South Wales Court of Appeal. For a variety of reasons the court declined to interfere with the continuance of the proceedings—*Connor* v. *Sankey et al*; *Whitlam* v. *Sankey et al* [1977] 2 N.S.W.L.R. 570. When the committal proceedings were resumed the Commonwealth objected to the production of certain documents sought to be introduced by the prosecutor and Mr. Whitlam. After much manoeuvering and adjustments in the court below, the question of state privilege was removed, on application by the Attorney General of the Commonwealth, for resolution in the High Court of Australia. By consent, an order was made that Mr. Justice Murphy, as a member of the court and one of the defendants in the private prosecution, cease to be a party to the cause so removed. The judgments of the High Court, to be discussed later, are reported as *Sankey* v. *Whitlam et al*, (1979) 21 Aust. L.J. 505; [1980] C.L.R. 1.

The information charged the defendants with conspiring to effect an unlawful purpose, contrary to section 86 of the Commonwealth Crimes Act, the alleged unlawful purpose being that of deceiving the Hon. J.R. Kerr, the Governor General, into approving a loan of $4,000 million "for temporary purposes," when in fact the borrowing was for 20 years and was designed to meet the long term energy needs of the Government. If these assumptions were correct, the loan would be in violation of the relevant constitutional instruments, *viz.* the Financial Agreement 1927, the Constitutional Alteration (State Debts) Act 1928 and the Financial Agreement Act 1944.[94a]

In two separate applications, first on behalf of the informant and later at the behest of three of the defendants, the Attorney General's consent was sought to his taking over the proceedings.[95] In response to these applications, and earlier on his own initiative, Mr. Ellicott had taken steps to obtain statements from relevant witnesses as to the subject matter of the private prosecution. Statements were supplied by the Solicitor General, the Secretary of the Attorney General's Department and also certain officers of the Executive Council.[96] Ellicott's approach to the Secretary of the Treasury, however, was met with an outright rejection, the public official taking the position that the evidence sought from him related to events that took place during the period of the previous administration, when the Labour Party was in power, and consequently should not be produced even to the senior Law Officer of the Commonwealth.[97] In due course, the difficulties experienced by Mr. Ellicott in gaining access to all the documents that pertained to the overseas loan negotiations, which he deemed an essential precondition to deciding whether or not to take over the private prosecution, came before the Cabinet for resolution. It discussed the Attorney's request on several occasions, eventually deciding

---

[94a] For a detailed analysis of the legal and constitutional implications of the Petro-Dollar Loan affair see Geoffrey Sawer's *Federation Under Strain, Australia 1972–75*, (Melbourne U.P. 1977), pp. 65–90.

[95] Mr. Ellicott, the Commonwealth Attorney General, had taken up his appointment more than one month after the inception of the committal proceedings.

[96] The summary of the facts concerning the Attorney General's involvement derives from the lengthy statement made by Mr. Ellicott to the House of Representatives when announcing his resignation. No questions were raised as to the accuracy of Mr. Ellicott's recollection of the surrounding events. See Parl. Deb. H.R., September 6, 1977, pp. 721–727.

[97] *Ibid.* p. 722. A parallel problem, illustrated by Canadian experience, is the extent to which a Government is constitutionally entitled to call upon a police force to produce for its inspection details of political intervention in police investigations by the members of a previous administration. Mr. Pearson, when he was Prime Minister in 1964, and arising out of the events that led to the Dorion Inquiry (see Edwards, *Ministerial Responsibility, op. cit.* Chapter 6), instructed the Commissioner of the Royal Canadian Mounted Police to conduct such an examination of its files over the preceding 10 years. The Opposition, led by Mr. Diefenbaker, refused to cooperate and maintained that the Prime Minister's motives were themselves highly suspect. The essentials of this story and its constitutional implications are to be found in H.C. Deb., 1964, Vol. 1, pp. 4627–4631; Mike, *The Memoirs of Lester B. Pearson*, Vol. 3, pp. 187–194; and Diefenbaker's *Memoirs, The Tumultuous Years*, pp. 266–273.

that it should invoke Crown privilege with respect to the key papers that Mr. Ellicott wished to examine.[98]

In taking this stand in opposition to the Attorney General the Cabinet rejected the philosophy adumbrated by Mr. Ellicott that "there is no place where the criminal law does not run, even in the Executive Council, nor can any convention that a government should not look into the affairs of a previous government prevent inquiry for the purposes of enforcing the criminal law."[99] The confrontation in Canberra, it will be readily recognised, bears a striking resemblance to that which took place in Washington a few years earlier at the height of the Watergate affair when President Nixon sought to resist, also under the cloak of executive privilege, the no less determined efforts of the special prosecutor, Archibald Cox, to gain access to relevant evidence in the form of tapes of Richard Nixon's discussions with ministers and senior officials.[1] Even at this distance in time it is possible to feel the sense of frustration that each side in the Australian dispute must have experienced at the turn of events, to which was added the no less dogged determination to prevail, if not by the force of logic then by resort to what each conceived to be the source of final constitutional authority.

Before proceeding to outline the events that ensued from the basic disagreement between Mr. Ellicott and his Cabinet colleagues it is worth noting that, subsequent to his resignation, the Attorney General's philosophy was resoundingly supported by the High Court of Australia in an unanimous ruling given in the case of *Sankey* v. *Whitlam et al.*[2] The High Court was faced with an application by the private prosecutor to have much the same list of documents, pertaining to the controversial Middle East loan proposal, produced as evidence before the pending preliminary hearing. In ordering that, with one exception, all the documents sought to be introduced should be placed at the disposal of the private prosecutor the Justices of the High Court swept away the last vestiges of the special privilege hitherto accorded that class of documents generally described as Cabinet papers, minutes, memoranda and other communications concerned with policy decisions at a high governmental level. The traditional view of English law had been that the disclosure of the contents of documents falling within this special class, no matter what they might individually contain, would inhibit the proper functioning of executive

[98] Parl. Debates, H.R., September 6, 1977, *loc. cit.*
[99] *Ibid.*
[1] In *U.S.* v. *Nixon* (1974) 418 U.S. 683, 712 the Supreme Court of the United States, in an unanimous decision, ruled that "when the ground for asserting privilege as to . . . materials sought for use in a criminal trial is based only on the generalised interest in confidentiality it cannot prevail over the fundamental demands of due process of law in the fair administration of justice. The generalised assertion of privilege must yield to demonstrated specific need for evidence in a pending criminal trial." For a comprehensive account of the special prosecutor's tribulations and eventual successes see the *Final Report of the Watergate Special Prosecution Force*, (Washington, 1975), *passim*, and the *Report of the American Bar Association's Special Committee to Study Federal Law Enforcement Agencies*, (1976), *passim*.
[2] *Ante*, fn. 94.

government and accordingly their non-disclosure was necessary for the proper operation of the public service. Gradual inroads into this expansive umbrella of protection were given a powerful stimulus by the voluntary restrictions announced in 1956 and 1962 by the Lord Chancellor, speaking on behalf of the executive branch of government.[3] Later, substantial modifications of the original doctrine stemmed from the leading decision of the House of Lords in *Conway* v. *Rimmer*[4] authorising the trial judge to make up his own mind on the question whether production of the evidence, contained in the Cabinet documents, would or would not be harmful to the public interest despite official views to the contrary.[5]

In the judgment of the Australian High Court the fundamental principle should be that documents, including State papers at the highest level, may be withheld from disclosure only if, and to the extent that, the public interest renders it necessary. The real difficulty arises in determining on which side the balance of conflicting public interests should fall. The fact that members of the executive council are required to take a binding oath of secrecy, it was stated by the High Court, does not assist the argument that the production of State papers cannot be compelled.[6] As Gibbs C.J. aptly described the dilemma in the case before the court: "If the defendants did engage in criminal conduct, and the documents are excluded, a rule of evidence designed to serve the public interest will instead become a shield to protect wrongdoing by ministers in the execution of their office."[7] Stephen J., spoke in similar terms when he

---

[3] See Cross on *Evidence* (5th ed.) pp. 311–312. The English cases formerly relied upon in support of this principle included *Duncan* v. *Cammell Laird & Co. Ltd.* [1942] A.C. 624 and *Ellis* v. *Home Office* [1953] 2 Q.B. 135.

[4] [1968] A.C. 910; see also *Burmah Oil Co.* v. *Governor and Company of the Bank of England* [1979] 3 All E.R. 700, and *Air Canada et al.* v. *Secretary of State for Trade* [1983] 2 W.L.R. 494.

[5] In Canada, doubts as to the justification for the absolute protection claimed for certain classes of documents had been expressed as early as 1954—see *R.* v. *Snider* [1954] S.C.R. 479 and Schiff, *Evidence in the Litigation Process*, (1978), Vol. 2, pp. 1048–1070. For the likely future direction of Canadian law see the *Report of the Federal-Provincial Task Force on the Uniform Rules of Evidence*, (1982), Chapter 32 and the amendments to the Canada Evidence Act (R.S.C. 1970, c.E–10, ss.36.1–36.3) enacted by 1980–81–82, c.111, s.4, Sched. III and proclaimed in November 1982. Under these provisions absolute privilege in the public interest area is maintained only with respect to "a confidence of the Queen's Privy Council for Canada" which encompasses the Cabinet and committees of the Cabinet. The breadth of this exclusionary exception is potentially very wide, including as it does information contained in Cabinet memoranda and discussion papers, Cabinet records of communications or discussions between Ministers of the Crown and draft legislation (see s.36.3(2)). New South Wales has taken a similar initiative in its determination to spike the High Court of Australia's landmark decision in *Sankey* v. *Whitlam*—see the Evidence (Amendment) Act, No. 40 of 1979. The New Zealand Court of Appeal, however, in *Environmental Defence Society* v. *South Pacific Aluminium Ltd.* [1981] N.Z.L.R. 146, has ranged itself alongside the High Court of Australia and the House of Lords in asserting an unconditional right to exercise judicial scrutiny of Cabinet papers prior to determining the issue of admissibility. Also in line with the more recent decisions of the House of Lords (*ante*, fn. 4) the New Zealand Court of Appeal has emphasised that such a procedure is not to be regarded as routine.

[6] (1978) 142 C.L.R. at p. 42. *Cf.* the view expressed on the same question by Lord Widgery C.J. in *Attorney General* v. *Jonathan Cape Ltd.* [1976] Q.B. 752 at p. 767.

[7] *Ibid.* p. 47.

stated "to accord privilege to such documents as a matter of course is to come close to conferring immunity from conviction upon those who may occupy or may have occupied high offices of State if proceeded against in relation to their conduct in those offices. Those in whom resides the power ultimately to decide whether or not to claim privilege will in fact be exercising a far more potent power: by a decision to claim privilege dismissal of the charge will be well nigh ensured."[8] The further important point was made, by Stephen and Mason JJ., that the High Court's ruling in favour of disclosure stemmed from a combination of factors, *viz.* that the course of justice should not be impeded and also the unusual character of the criminal proceedings, involving charges against a former Prime Minister and senior members of his ministry related to their conduct in office.[9] The same combination of circumstances resulted in the unanimous rejection of President Nixon's arguments in *U.S.* v. *Nixon*, a decision that was cited with obvious approval by the Australian High Court in the case before it.[10]

These views by the High Court of Australia were not known a year earlier when Mr. Ellicott was waging a solitary campaign against the Prime Minister, Mr. Malcolm Fraser, and the other members of the Cabinet. In repeatedly refusing to agree that the Attorney General should have unrestricted access to documents in the possession of the government's servants the Cabinet made its position even more plain by urging the Attorney General to take over the proceedings and terminate the prosecution.[11] Mr. Ellicott's reaction to this advice, conveyed in the course of a meeting of the Cabinet on July 26, 1977, set the course for his ultimate decision to resign. This decision, moreover, was preceded by earlier intimations to the Prime Minister by Mr. Ellicott that he was prepared to resign because of the "collision course" which he regarded as inevitable so long as he was thwarted in the execution of his responsibilities.[12]

In the event, after taking counsel's advice, the Attorney General decided against taking over the committal proceedings.[13] The record strongly suggests that one of the principal reasons for this decision was a letter received from Mr. Justice Murphy, the former Attorney General and one of the co-defendants, who indicated that he would strongly object to the prosecution being taken over by the present Attorney General if this was to be done with the purpose of continuing the proceedings.[14] Mr.

[8] *Ibid.* p. 56.

[9] *Ibid. per* Mason J., at p. 100: "My impression, as that of Stephen J., is that to insist on non-disclosure in a case such as this would be to confer immunity on Ministers from prosecution. And with him I agree that it is not to the point that the prosecution is a private prosecution."

[10] *Ibid. per* Mason J., at pp. 98–99.

[11] Parl. Debates, H.R. September 6, 1977, p. 724.

[12] *Ibid.* p. 725.

[13] *Ibid.*

[14] The text of Murphy J.'s letter was read to the House of Representatives by the resigning Attorney General—*ibid.*

Justice Murphy's objection was based on certain statements made by Mr. Ellicott when sitting as a member of the Opposition and which could be interpreted as colouring his approach to the case against the defendants.[15] It should, at this stage, be noted that during the initial years of the Whitlam Ministry Robert Ellicott was the serving Solicitor General in the Department of the Attorney General, a non-political appointment. In 1975 he resigned as the junior Law Officer in order to contest a by-election as a member of the opposition Liberal party. On being successfully returned to sit in the House of Representatives, his opponents claimed that the new member actively participated in the partisan debates surrounding the proposed foreign loan in the course of which Mr. Ellicott was on record as condemning "the deceitful, illegal and unconstitutional nature of the government's actions."[16] It is scarce wonder, therefore, that the defendants in the conspiracy charges should entertain, rightly or wrongly, serious reservations as to the Attorney General's ability to demonstrate the essential qualities of impartiality and detachment when making his decision in their case.

Fortunately, for historical purposes, no dispute exists as to the accuracy of the account given to the House of Representatives by the resigning Attorney General. Most of the significant steps preceding the resignation have already been outlined above. The crux of Mr. Ellicott's complaint against his Cabinet colleagues is contained in his letter to Prime Minister Fraser which explained that he was resigning "because decisions and actions which you and the Cabinet have recently made and taken have impeded and in my opinion have constituted an attempt to direct or control the exercise by me as Attorney General of my discretion in relation to the criminal proceedings in *Sankey* v. *Whitlam and others*. In the circumstances I feel that I have no other course but to resign my office. I regard it as vital to our system of government that the Attorney General's discretion in criminal matters remains completely independent."[17] It will be noted that Mr. Ellicott, no doubt choosing his words carefully, accused the Cabinet of "an attempt to direct or control" the exercise of his prosecutorial discretion. Whatever opinions may have been exchanged around the Cabinet table and however expressed, it is obvious that the Attorney General interpreted those views, and particularly the decision to refuse him access to the overseas loan papers, as impeding the exercise of his discretion. Add to this the repeated intimation, conveyed by the Prime

---

[15] Mr. Ellicott's speech, when in Opposition, on the Whitlam Government's handling of the Loan Affair is presumably what Mr. Justice Murphy was alluding to—see Parl. Debates H.R., July 9, 1975, pp. 3642–3646.

[16] These remarks were directed specifically against the legal advice tendered orally to the Governor General by the former Attorney General, Senator Murphy, that the proposed borrowings could probably be regarded as a borrowing for temporary purposes within the meaning of the constitutional law pertaining to financial agreements entered to by the government. *Ibid.* pp. 3645–3646.

[17] Parl. Debates, H.R., September 6, 1977 at p. 721.

Minister as expressing the considered opinion of the entire Cabinet, that the Attorney General should take over the private prosecution and discontinue the proceedings,[18] and it is understandable, from Mr. Ellicott's point of view, that he should interpret this "advice" as tantamount to an "attempt to direct or control" his ultimate decision.

According to the Prime Minister, Mr. Malcolm Fraser, there was, throughout the Cabinet discussions, a clear understanding that "It is the traditional role of the Attorney General, as First Law Officer, to institute and, where appropriate, to take over prosecutions for offences. The Government recognises that this is his role. It is not questioned that the Attorney General has a full discretion in relation to these matters. It is, nevertheless, proper for the Attorney General in such matters to consult with and to have regard to the views of his colleagues, even though the responsibility for the eventual decision to prosecute or not rests with the Attorney General, and with the Attorney General alone. This practice of consultation is a long-standing practice."[19] It is, of course, a truism that individual perceptions of the same event or of the same discussions are capable of being translated into totally different descriptions of what actually transpired. In this instance, interpretations were compounded by the respective parties' judgment of what was in the public interest. By denying the Attorney General access to the papers in the Government's possession and at the same time counselling the termination of the embarrassing criminal proceedings it can scarcely be wondered that the first Law Officer perceived the Cabinet's actions as an indirect interference with his independent discretion.

For a few weeks the matter lay dormant while Mr. Ellicott attended the meeting of the Commonwealth Law Ministers in Winnipeg, Canada. Quite fortuitously the agenda for that meeting included an item described as "Emerging problems in defining the modern role of the Attorney General."[20] The Australian Attorney General did not take part in the wide-ranging discussions[21] but, in his resignation speech to the House of Representatives, he chose to draw particular attention to the pertinent paragraph in the Winnipeg communiqué, summing up the views of all the 31 Law Ministers present irrespective of their country's constitutional arrangements.[22] "In recent years," the communiqué reads, "both outside and within the Commonwealth, public attention has frequently focussed on the function of law enforcement. Ministers endorsed the principles already

[18] *Ibid.* pp. 723 and 725.

[19] *Ibid.* p. 727. The Prime Minister distinguished a decision as to whether a prosecution should be instituted or taken over from decisions that concerned claims of Crown privilege or whether the costs of the defendants should be met out of public funds. Each of these questions had arisen in the course of the *Sankey* v. *Whitlam* case. Decisions as to the latter matters, Mr. Fraser maintained, were properly matters for the government and did not fall within the exclusive province of the Attorney General—*loc. cit.*

[20] See, *ante*, pp. 62, 354.

[21] Parl. Debates, H.R., September 6, 1977, p. 725.

[22] 1977 Meeting of Commonwealth Law Ministers, *Minutes of Meeting and Memoranda*, (*1978*, Commonwealth Secretariat), p. 138, paras. 22–25.

observed in their jurisdictions that the discretion in these matters should always be exercised in accordance with wide considerations of the public interest, and without regard to considerations of a party political nature, and that it should be free from any direction or control whatsoever. They considered, however, that the maintenance of these principles depended ultimately upon the unimpeachable integrity of the holder of the office whatever the precise constitutional arrangements in the State concerned."[23] It is also noteworthy that Mr. Ellicott, in explaining his actions, took the well known Shawcross exposition as the principal text embodying the principles that must guide Attorneys General in Australia, no less than in the United Kingdom, in deciding whether or not to authorise a prosecution.[24]

At the theoretical level the Prime Minister and the Attorney General were of one mind in defining the nature of the Attorney General's role. The serious rift that emerged in the *Whitlam* case arose in the application of the theoretical principles and in determining the significance that should attach to the advice tendered by the Cabinet to the decision-maker. There is good reason to believe that the Prime Minister's innocuous reference to "the practice of consultation being a long-standing practice in the Commonwealth Government"[25] describes the regular, if infrequent, practice of Cabinet discussion of pending criminal cases that have political overtones. It may fall well short of the notorious Cabinet minute concerning the *Campbell* case in Britain in 1924, but an Attorney General might be forgiven in failing to discern any relevant difference between a formal directive from his Cabinet colleagues and the communication of the Government's unanimous opposition to his proposed course of action. In either alternative the Attorney is placed in an invidious position that challenges his otherwise independent discretion. The situation that faced Mr. Ellicott may or may not have been experienced by any of his predecessors. Certainly, no record exists of any previous Attorney General of the Commonwealth resigning office on a matter of high principle. In doing so with reference to such well publicised circumstances it cannot be doubted that Robert Ellicott succeeded in alerting his fellow Australians, and his colleagues among the ranks of Law Ministers in other Commonwealth countries, to the issues at stake and to the constant need to reinforce the independence of the Law Officers by exemplifying the integrity of the holder of these offices.

Editorial opinion on the conflict of principle that led to the Ellicott resignation was divided among the leading Australian newspapers.[26] The

---

[23] Quoted by Ellicott, *op. cit.* pp. 725–726.
[24] *Ibid.* pp. 721–722.
[25] *Ibid.* p. 727.
[26] *e.g. The Australian*, September 7, 1977 supported the stand taken by the Attorney General; *The Age*, on the same date, considered that Mr. Ellicott had "concentrated on legalistic detail to the exclusion of parliamentary convention which may be seen as fundamental to the smooth government of the country, certainly to the smooth transfer of power from one Government to another."

New South Wales Bar Association passed a resolution extolling the stand taken by the Attorney General as in keeping with the highest traditions of the office which he had left.[27] A similar commendation was forthcoming from the back-bench members of the administration's own Law and Government Committee in the House of Representatives.[28] These conclusions were not adopted in the assessment of the constitutional dispute contained in the influential *Australian Law Journal*.[29] Careful as its editorial was in presenting both sides of the denouèment between Mr. Ellicott and the Prime Minister the final message was unmistakeable. Since the nature of the criminal proceedings was inseparably connected with politics, the *Journal* concluded that the Cabinet, not the Attorney General, was the better judge of the relevant public interest. Had the prosecution been taken over and continued in the name of the Attorney General, even through independent counsel, the appearance of one government prosecuting its predecessor, it was claimed, would constitute an undesirable constitutional precedent.[30] In the same philosophic strain the *Australian Law Journal* doubted whether the Shawcross and Winnipeg principles were ever designed to extend to criminal proceedings of the kind portrayed in *Sankey* v. *Whitlam et al.*[31]

Part of the answer to this line of argument was contained in the unanimous judgment of the High Court of Australia, already referred to, which represents a resounding vindication of the stand taken by Mr. Ellicott on the question of access to documents emanating from a previous ministry and which were considered relevant to the enforcement of the criminal law. The citizen's historic right to launch a private prosecution may frequently be viewed as an irritation but no outright challenge to its continued existence was to be heard in Australia during the Whitlam affair.[32] There remains the essential characteristic of Australian constitu-

[27] *The Sydney Morning Herald*, September 17, 1977.
[28] *The Canberra Times*, September 10, 1977.
[29] (1977) 51 Aust. L.J. 675.
[30] *Ibid*. p. 678.
[31] *Ibid*. p. 679. Examples of the Australian federal Cabinet discussing and making decisions concerning the institution of criminal proceedings are contained in Plehwe (*supra*, fn. 52) *op. cit*. p. 11. These illustrations are derived from a search of Cabinet records before 1949. For confirmation of the continuation of this practice post–1949 see Edwards, "The Integrity of Criminal Prosecutions—Watergate Echoes beyond the Shores of the United States" in *Reshaping the Criminal Law* (1978, Ed. Glazebrook) p. 377, fns. 53 and 54.
[32] On the contrary, in the High Court judgments in *Sankey* v. *Whitlam et al.* it was stated: "The fact that the informant is a private citizen and that the committal proceedings are not the result of any initiative on the part of government or police force can, I think, have no effect upon the question of Crown privilege. The nature of proceedings may affect the relative weight to be given to the respective public interest considerations but should not otherwise be of significance"—*per* Stephen J., (1948) 142 C.L.R. 67, and later: "that the informant was entitled to institute the committal proceedings is unquestioned, s.13(*a*) of the Crimes Act 1914 (Cth.) confers that right and to the extent that it does so it reflects the position at common law. It has always been the position, subject only to occasional statutory exceptions, that it is 'the right of any member of the public to lay an information and to prosecute an offence,' *per* Diplock J. in *Lund* v. *Thompson* [1959] 1 Q.B. 283 at p. 285, and see *Duchesne* v. *Finch* (1912) 28 T.L.R. 440 at p. 441." As Lord Wilberforce observed in *Gouriet* v. *Union*

tional practice, as in Canada, of looking upon its Attorney General as the leading legal minister at both levels of government. As such, the first Law Officer of the Crown is generally, though not universally, accorded a seat in the Cabinet. The consequences of this membership cannot be ignored and the lessons of the Ellicott affair are likely to prove enduring. If the Attorney General is to remain within the Cabinet circle, privy to, and participating in, all its deliberations, it behoves his ministerial colleagues to gain a better grasp of the unique nature of the functions associated with the Law Officers and to respect, in reality as well as in theory, the reasons behind the independent judgment required of the Attorney General as *the* ultimate guardian of the public interest in the enforcement and administration of the criminal law.

III. NEW ZEALAND

This most distant of the former British colonies has long enjoyed an enviable reputation for its pioneering measures in the areas of law reform and social justice. New Zealand's history relating to the office of Attorney General is marked by the same willingness to embark on new experimental measures even if they subsequently become discarded as unworkable. Thus, the contentious question of Cabinet membership by the Attorney General was being actively debated in the New Zealand Legislative Assembly in the mid-nineteenth century long before the same subject became the object of lively discussion in Britain.[33] At first, in conformity with the practice of other Crown colonies, the Attorney General was one of the three permanent officials (the others were the Colonial Secretary and the Colonial Treasurer), who, under the Governor, comprised the Executive Council.[34] The same set of British appointed officials also sat as members of the nominated Legislative Council.[35] This system of preroga-

---

of Post Office Workers [1977] 3 All E.R. 70 at p. 84: "All citizens have sufficient interest in the enforcement of the law to entitle them to take this step," that is, to institute a prosecution—and see *per* Viscount Dilhorne at p. 90 and Lord Fraser of Tullybelton at p. 116."

[33] See Edwards, *Law Officers of the Crown*, pp. 167–169.

[34] For the early history of the office of Attorney General in New Zealand see P.A. Cornford, "The Administration of Justice in New Zealand, 1841–46" (1970) 4 N.Z.U.L.R. 18 and pp. 120–138; and the official booklet *Crown Law Practice in New Zealand*, 1961. The latter publication was based, to considerable measure, on an article by E.J. Haughey, a Crown Solicitor, on "The Legal Work of the Crown" (1957) 38 N.Z.L.J. 203–207, and an anonymous contribution on "The Attorney Generalship" (1929) 4 N.Z.L.J. 268 and (1934) 10 N.Z.L.J. 81. See, too, P.A. Cornford's note on the early history of the Crown Law Office in [1964] N.Z.L.J. 423.

[35] The government of the colony in its earliest days was the responsibility of the Governor of New South Wales. On January 14, 1840 Sir George Gipps, the Governor, published a proclamation declaring such parts of New Zealand as were or might be acquired in sovereignty by the Queen. This proclamation coincided with the arrival in Sydney of Captain Robson R.N., who was declared Lieutenant Governor of the new territory. A Royal Charter of November 16, 1840 constituted New Zealand as a separate colony. At first there was no Law Officer in the new colony but Robson contrived to appoint Francis Fisher as provisional Attorney General on May 3, 1841, thus gaining, together with the Colonial Secretary and the Colonial Treasurer, three *ex officio* members on the Legislative Council. Fisher had served as

tive appointment by the Crown continued into the first years of representative government that was proclaimed under the Constitution Act of 1852. Following the advent of responsible government in 1856 the Attorney General's office was transformed into a political appointment with the portfolio being occupied by a member of one or other House of the General Assembly.[36]

Within a decade New Zealand embarked on a series of experimental measures born out of the doubts that swirled around the proper role expected of the Law Officers of the Crown and the appropriate constitutional arrangements that should exist to ensure the fulfilment of their independent functions. Under the first of these enactments, the Attorney General's Act (N.Z.) 1866,[37] the office was changed from its erstwhile political character into a non-political, permanent appointment. Adopting the principle incorporated in the Act of Settlement 1701 with respect to the English judiciary, the New Zealand statute provided that the commission of the Attorney was to be continued "during good behaviour," removal from office being dependent upon an address of both Houses of the General Assembly.[38] To further underline the new conception of the Attorney Generalship, the same enactment expressly declared that during his continuance in office the Attorney General was to be ineligible for membership in the Executive Council of the colony or of either House of the General Assembly. For reasons that have never been clearly demonstrated the 1866 experiment was not a resounding success and it was discontinued in 1876. By that time the sole occupant of the non-political version of the Attorney Generalship, James Prendergast, had been

Crown Solicitor for New South Wales from 1834 to 1839 at the handsome salary of £800 per annum. Fisher, who is thus regarded as New Zealand's first Attorney General, served in that capacity for only three months. He was succeeded by William Swainson who retained the position for the remainder of the Crown Colony period of government. When he sailed for New Zealand, Swainson was accompanied by William Martin, the colony's first Chief Justice. In each case the new incumbent had been in conveyancing practice for only a few years—see Cornford *op. cit.* pp. 20–24, 32. Of these key appointees the same author writes: "It is generally accepted that upon the voyage from England to New Zealand Martin and Swainson drafted the first Supreme Court Ordinance and rules of procedure for the court"—*ibid.* p. 33.

[36] See N.Z. Parl. Debates, Leg. Assembly, Vol. 23, pp. 20–22, October 4, 1876 and *Crown Law Practice in New Zealand*, p. 12. The list of persons who occupied the office of Attorney General during this period indicates that changeovers were rapid. Thus, Henry Sewell is shown as holding the appointment three times between 1851 and 1855. These comings and goings, it has been surmised, were considered undignified for in March 1867 James Prendergast was appointed to the office "for life" under the Attorney General's Act, 1866 (see *supra*) a tenure that ceased with his subsequent elevation to the office of Chief Justice—see N.R.A. Netherclift "Colonial Justice" [1973] N.Z.L.J. 164.

[37] 30 Vict. (N.Z.), cap. 63.

[38] *Ibid.* s.3. The minimal labours of the office, as anticipated at the time, were exemplified in the further provision that: "It should be lawful for the A.G. to hold any other office under the Crown the duties of which are not incompatible with the office of A.G. and it shall be lawful for him to practise as a Barrister of the Supreme Court but only in such place as shall for the time being be the Seat of Government or at the Court of Appeal when held elsewhere, except with the sanction of the Governor—*ibid.* s.6. The customary limitations were also imposed so far as acting as counsel for accused persons or those suing against the Crown were concerned.

elevated to become Chief Justice of the Crown Colony.[39] The new formula, embodied in the Attorney General's Act (N.Z.) 1876,[40] demonstrated again the uncertainties that prevailed at the time concerning the role and functions of the same office. Under the new legislation the office of Attorney General could be a political or non-political appointment, tenure of the office being changed from "good behaviour" to occupancy "during [the] pleasure" of the Governor in Council.[41] The holder could be, but was not required to be, a member of the Executive Council and the same flexibility prevailed with respect to elected membership in the Legislative Assembly.[42] Perhaps some clue to this ambivalence is to be found in the simultaneous revival in 1875 of the office of Solicitor General as a permanent government official,[43] the first appointee occupying the junior office for the next 25 years.[44]

In changing so rapidly its approach to the nature of the office of Attorney General New Zealand was following the precedent set by the colony of South Australia in 1873.[45] Similar uncertainty can be seen in the actions of the New South Wales Legislative Assembly which, in the same year, agreed to resolutions rendering both the offices of Attorney General and Solicitor General non-political government appointments, only to reverse their decision in 1878 so far as the office of Attorney General was concerned.[46] Back in New Zealand, despite the alternative models provided for in the Act of 1876, the office of Attorney General has ever since been always held by a member of the New Zealand Parliament who enjoys Cabinet rank, usually in association with the portfolio of Minister of Justice.[47] It only remains to add that the office in 1920 reverted to its

---

[39] See *ante*, fn. 36.   [41] *Ibid*. s.3.
[40] 40 Vict. (N.Z.), cap. 71.   [42] *Ibid*.

[43] For the informative debates in the Legislative Council, anticipating by half a century the disputes in England concerning the Attorney General's membership in the Cabinet, see N.Z. Parl. Debates, Leg. Council, Vol. 23, pp. 249–254, October 12, 1876, and in the House of Assembly, *ibid*. pp. 20–22, October 4, 1876. Specific reference was made in the Legislative Council to the fact that "the appointment of a political A.G. would not deprive the country or the House of Assembly of the assistance of the permanent Law Officer of the colony. There would still be a Solicitor General and a permanent officer to whom the House of Assembly could have recourse in the future as they did in the past." *Ibid*. p. 254.

[44] *Crown Law Office in New Zealand*, p. 21.

[45] See the *South Australian House of Representatives' Votes*, (1871), p. 202.

[46] See Todd, *Parliamentary Government in the British Colonies*, (2nd ed. 1894), p. 57, citing *Votes and Proceedings of the Legislative Assembly of New South Wales*, Dec. 3, 1873.

[47] From time to time the Attorney General of New Zealand has not held any other office, *e.g.* 1879–82, 1887–91 and 1915–18. Between 1884 and 1887 the Attorney General, Robert Stout, combined that appointment with the offices of Prime Minister and Minister of Education. This conjunction of portfolios was surpassed by George Forbes in 1933–35 who was Prime Minister, Attorney General, Minister for External Affairs, Minister of Railways and Native Minister (see fn. 48). No discernible or predictable pattern emerges from a review of the other offices simultaneously held by the Attorney General during the present century, though, until 1976, it seemed safe to say that since the occupancy of the senior Law Officership by H.G.R. Mason, 1935–49, there was a consistent expectation that the two offices of Minister of Justice and Attorney General would be held jointly by the Cabinet member concerned. This "tradition" was departed from in 1976 with the appointment of Mr. D.S. Thomson as Minister of Justice and Mr. P.I. Wilkinson as Attorney General.

original prerogative character with no statutory provisions to hamper the choice of appointees.[48]

SPECIAL POSITION ACCORDED TO THE OFFICE OF SOLICITOR GENERAL

The office of Solicitor General of New Zealand has also undergone a number of changes during its history, the initial political character of the appointment in 1867 being short lived.[49] On the elevation of Prendergast, the Attorney General, to become Chief Justice of the colony in 1875[50] the Solicitor Generalship, as noted above, became a permanent non-political post that has been its distinctive characteristic ever since. The absence of any specific statutory authority for the office of Solicitor General prompted action in the Supreme Court in 1875 in *Solicitor General ex rel. Cargill* v. *Dunedin City Corporation*.[51] The ruling of Williams J., in that case remains the authoritative statement of the status and powers of the Solicitor General of New Zealand, it being declared that "unless taken away by legislation, the Crown has the power of appointing an Attorney and Solicitor General; and I apprehend that the duties of the persons appointed would be similar to those of persons filling corresponding offices at Home; and that there would be no necessity to specify, by statute or otherwise, the nature and extent of duties already sufficiently defined by long usage."[52] The prerogative nature of the office of Solicitor General of New Zealand remains the same to this day, though occasion was taken in the Acts Interpretation Act (N.Z.) 1924, s.4, to declare that "any power, duty, authority or function enforced upon or vested in the Attorney General by virtue of that office includes the Solicitor General and that any such power, duty, authority or function may be performed and exercised either by the Attorney General himself or the Solicitor General."[53]

To appreciate the special relationship that exists in New Zealand between the Solicitor General and his ministerial superior, the Attorney General, it is essential to recognise at once that, in practical terms, it is the Solicitor General, the junior Law Officer, who is the chief legal adviser to the government. As such, he presides over the Crown Law Office which is

---

[48] Attorney General G.W. Forbes was not a lawyer. As might be expected, criticism of his appointment was voiced by the legal profession, including the passing of a resolution by the New Zealand Law Society condemning the break with constitutional history—see (1934) 10 N.Z.L.J. 90 and see, too, pp. 81–83. The precedent is unlikely to be repeated.

[49] *Crown Law Practice in New Zealand*, p. 21.

[50] *Ibid.* p. 12.

[51] (1875) 1 N.Z. Jur. (N.S.) 1. The issue before the court was the validity of an information sworn by the Solicitor General at the relation of three ratepayers against the Corporation of the City of Dunedin.

[52] *Ibid.* pp. 14–15.

[53] A similar provision had first been enacted as part of the Attorney General's Act (N.Z.) 1876—see s.5; and *cf.* the N.Z. Interpretation Act 1868, which declared that the words "Attorney General" in any Act shall include "Solicitor General" during any vacancy in the office of Attorney General, and during the absence of the Attorney General from New Zealand.

an independent department of the public service separate from the Department of Justice.[54] The legal work of government, including the provision of opinions and advice on the widest range of governmental activities, is done by the legal staff of the Crown Law Office.[55] Litigation, including prosecutions, in the lower courts is conducted by the Crown Solicitor for the district concerned but other cases brought before the Supreme Court and Court of Appeal, and appearances before commissions of inquiry or other tribunals, are generally handled by counsel from the Crown Law Office led, if the subject matter is of considerable importance, by the Solicitor General himself.[56] Only very rarely will the Attorney General appear as the chief advocate for the Crown or the government.

[54] The existence of this office is recognised in the annual Appropriation Act but otherwise there is no statutory provision governing its functions.

[55] For an early account of the Crown Law Office see (1878) 3 N.Z. Jur. (N.S.) 36 and cf. with the more recent description of its responsibilities contained in the booklet Crown Law Practice in New Zealand, (1961), pp. 21–27. Among the many notable occupants who have presided over the office as Solicitor General reference should be made to Mr. J.W. (better known as Sir John) Salmond. First appointed in 1907 to the new post of Counsel to the Law Drafting Office, Salmond became Solicitor General in 1910 and reorganised the Crown Law Office and the functions it is expected to perform. He served as the junior Law Officer until 1920, and was then appointed to the Supreme Court Bench. A major review of the Crown Law Office work was undertaken in 1962 as part of the terms of reference of a Royal Commission of Inquiry into the State Services in New Zealand headed by McCarthy J., who subsequently became a member of the Court of Appeal. Among the proposals it considered was that put forward by the Solicitor General to centralise the legal business of the Crown in the Crown Law Office with a few exceptions. One of these was the legal section in the External Affairs Department whose specialised legal services were accepted as necessarily forming part of the departmental organisation. The arguments advanced in support of the proposal for centralised legal services paralleled those which were adopted in Canada by the Glassco Commission and subsequently implemented—see ante, pp. 183–184. In New Zealand, the Solicitor General's arguments were opposed by the Law Draftsman, whose organisation would have been absorbed within the Crown Law Office, and the Civil Service Legal Society, whose members were averse to losing the prospects of promotion to senior administrative posts within the regular government departments. The McCarthy Commission declined to pass judgment on the Solicitor General's submissions, preferring instead to call upon the State Services Commission to examine the problem—see the Report of the Royal Commission, pp. 161–163. The same Commission gave short shrift to a suggestion that had been put forward before it, not by the Attorney General nor the Solicitor General, to amalgamate the Crown Law Office with the Department of Justice. "The Solicitor General" it was stated "is required to make recommendations, and give advice, to all Ministers. This advice must be objective and independent. His independence would be eroded if he were incorporated into the Department of Justice which services the Courts and administers prisons, and in respect of whose actions or proposals the Solicitor General may be required to advise. We believe that his independence must be maintained and oppose any amalgamation which would prejudice it"—ibid. p. 173.

[56] Under the Crimes Amendment Act 1966 (No. 98), s.9(2), power is conferred upon the Solicitor General, with the leave of the Court of Appeal, to appeal against a sentence passed on conviction of any person on indictment, unless the sentence is one fixed by law. Consideration was given, but rejected, by the then Minister of Justice (Mr. Hanan) to making the Attorney General the authorising Law Officer in appeals against sentence. This is the situation in Canada, New South Wales, Queensland and Tasmania. In preferring to confer this right upon the Solicitor General, the Minister recognised that it eliminated "direct ministerial responsibility" but argued that it emphasised the need to avoid any suggestion of political overtones in matters of sentencing.—see N.Z. Parl. Debates, H.R. June 15, 1966, pp. 490–504. The same enactment, it is noted, abolished the former right of a Law Officer to the "last word" when appearing as prosecution counsel at a trial—ibid. s.6(3), and see also Edwards, op. cit. pp. 271–276.

In view of the largely independent role accorded in practice to the Solicitor General in conducting the legal business of government, there has been a consistent reluctance to express in formal terms the ultimate deference owed by the Solicitor General to the opinion of the Attorney General if and when the senior Law Officer elects to become involved in any aspect of the administration of justice. Normally it is the Solicitor General who is seen as the final arbiter in legal matters, with constant recourse to his opinions being made by the Attorney General, the Prime Minister and the Cabinet of the day.[57] This reflection of the normal practice cannot, however, distort the constitutional relationship between the Law Officers of the Crown in New Zealand wherein the Attorney General occupies the senior position of authority. This question, moreover, has become increasingly significant in recent years as more and more criminal cases arise with political overtones. In the official publication describing *Crown Law Practice in New Zealand* in 1961 the statement is made that "the only recorded instances in which the Attorney General has expressed an opinion at variance with that of the Solicitor General are a couple of occasions when Sir Francis Bell[58] (Attorney General 1918–26) differed from [Sir John] Salmond.[59] In those cases it was the opinion of the Attorney General that was adopted because he is, of course, the senior Law Officer."

If this statement was intended to underline the unquestioned authority, in terms of general practice, of the Solicitor General in legal questions of concern to the government it fails to recognise the increasing difficulty, experienced in every country, of delineating the boundary line that separates law from political considerations, a difficulty that exerts pressure on the Attorney General to become involved in exercising his ministerial discretion as to the course to be followed by the Crown Law Office. Other considerations that bear on the sensitive nature of this relationship, in which the junior partner, as it were, generally exercises *de facto* authority, must include the relative years of experience in office that each of the Law Officers can draw upon, the individual personalities and the strength of

[57] See the carefully phrased statement in the official publication *Crown Law Practice in New Zealand*, (1961), at p. 23 which reads: "In practice the Solicitor General is the chief legal adviser to the Government (subject to any views that the Prime Minister or Cabinet may seek from, or that may be expressed by, the Attorney General), and he is its chief advocate in the Courts."

[58] Attorney General, 1919–25.

[59] Solicitor General, 1910–20. The divergence of views, reflected in the memoranda that passed between Bell and Salmond between August 1918 and January 1919, was concerned with (i) the entry of a stay of proceedings in criminal cases after one or more trials in which the jury have disagreed, and (ii) the extent to which the views of the trial judge should govern the decision by the Attorney General or the Solicitor General as to whether a *nolle prosequi* should be entered. The outcome of the internal dispute was the issuance on June 9, 1919, of a circular to all Crown Prosecutors, replacing an earlier one dated October 17, 1917, and containing the Attorney General's directions in the several circumstances that might arise. The 1919 circular was revised and re-issued on January 29, 1945. It is of interest to note that Salmond, writing on August 22, 1918, said of majority verdicts "I do not think that any more important improvement could be made to the system of criminal trials."

commitment that each is prepared to invest in their respective constitutional roles. As often as not the focus for any possible divergence of
approach between the Attorney General and the Solicitor General will
concern the degree of influence that political considerations should exert
on the decision to institute or to terminate criminal proceedings. In
interpreting where the balance of public interests should fall it should not
occasion too much surprise if the Law Officers, with their different
perspectives, should sometimes disagree.

In the course of the discussion that flowed from the paper which I
prepared for the Commonwealth Law Ministers meeting in Winnipeg in
1977 the then Minister of Justice of New Zealand, Mr. D. S. Thomson,
intervened to correct what he considered to be an error in my statement
that "discussion by the Cabinet of the initiation and extent of criminal
prosecutions . . . is a common occurrence in New Zealand."[60] The
Minister of Justice quoted from a memorandum prepared by the Solicitor
General of New Zealand,[61] prior to the Winnipeg meeting, which stated
that "the firm view and consistent advice of this office has been that it is not
proper for Cabinet or a Minister, in the absence of specific authority, and
no such case comes immediately to mind, to decide that any person or
persons should be prosecuted or not prosecuted for the reason that this
decision should not be made, or even appear to be made, politically. We
understand that to be accepted by ministers."[62] According to the Minister
of Justice, whose experience, he explained, dated back to 1966, that
philosophy was followed by ministers and by the New Zealand Cabinet.[63]

If the Solicitor General's memorandum is correct it is a matter for
considerable satisfaction, conveying as it does the declaration that New
Zealand has adopted the constitutional doctrine followed in the United
Kingdom since the *Campbell* case in 1924. The information on which my
statement was based derived from long conversations in 1968[64] with the
then Minister of Justice and Attorney General, the late Mr. J.R. Hanan,
who held both offices from 1960 until his death in 1969. The unmistakeable
conclusion conveyed to me was that the New Zealand Cabinet, at least
during Mr. Hanan's period in office, regularly discussed both general
situations that might develop with reference to criminal prosecutions and
also individual cases. Among the latter, identified by the Attorney General
as having been the subject of Cabinet deliberations, were the *SS. Tiri* case
in 1966 and the private prosecution, under the Indecent Publications Act
1963, which required the consent of the Attorney General, instituted by a
local school committee with respect to the publication of the masochistic
details associated with the "Profumo affair" in England.[65]

---

[60] *Minutes of Meeting and Memoranda, op cit*. 195 at p. 202.
[61] Prior to becoming Solicitor General, Mr. Savage had served as Senior Crown Counsel in
the Crown Law Office.
[62] *Ibid*. p. 40.   [63] *Ibid*.   [64] On March 12, 1968 in the Minister's office.
[65] *Ibid*. The SS. Tiri was a radio ship operating outside territorial waters in violation of
New Zealand laws. On the advice of the then Solicitor General criminal proceedings were

In addition to these relatively minor cases the Attorney General referred to the Exchange Control Act prosecutions in 1967, as illustrating the manner in which the decisions whether to institute criminal proceedings, and against whom, became a major preoccupation of the Cabinet and the Cabinet's Finance Committee. The New Zealand overseas balance and currency were being seriously affected through private arrangements entered into between residents and New Zealand citizens overseas, whereby the exchange control regulations were being infringed daily. Investigation by the police of the activities of large companies, stock-brokers and the like, with respect to the more extensive amounts involved in violating the exchange control laws, eventually led to a recommendation by the Solicitor General that criminal proceedings should be brought. When this became known to the Government, political pressures began to be exerted, with the Reserve Bank, an active party in the whole matter, advising the Minister of Finance, and the Solicitor General performing his normal duty as the Attorney General's principal adviser. Both ministers were members of the Cabinet Finance Committee. Had the Finance Ministry prevailed in eliminating the possibility of prosecution it is understood that the Solicitor General, Mr. (later Mr. Justice) J. C. White, would have submitted his resignation. The Attorney General was well aware of this fact. In discussing the matter with me after the event, Mr. Hanan disclosed that he had been prepared to reach an accommodation with other views within the Cabinet as to the exact boundaries of the proposed criminal proceedings. The matter was ultimately resolved pragmatically and, according to the Minister of Justice, recorded in the minutes of the New Zealand Cabinet.[66] The criminal process having been set in motion pleas of guilty were quickly forthcoming. This particular case, especially the Cabinet's involvement in settling the range of defendants against whom criminal proceedings were to be instituted, may help to explain the reference to New Zealand Cabinet practice that I inserted in my paper for the 1977 meeting of the Commonwealth Law Ministers. If there has indeed been a dramatic reversal of Cabinet practice in that country it is a matter of much importance to reinforce the principles described in the Solicitor General's memorandum addressed to the Minister of Justice prior to the same meeting.

instituted but the charges were dismissed by the stipendiary magistrate. The Solicitor General wanted to enforce the law with respect to subsequent breaches but the Attorney General refused to give his consent to the fresh prosecutions. There was a major difficulty in obtaining first hand evidence of the radio ship having entered New Zealand territorial waters, but the implications of criminal prosecution were discussed by Mr. Hanan with the Minister of Marine, the Minister of Posts and Telegraph, and all the other members of Cabinet. The SS. Tiri case flared up on the eve of the 1966 general election in the course of which the Opposition Labour Party made the issue of illegal radio broadcasting a part of their electoral platform.

[66] Ibid.

For, whatever level of commitment may have been accorded in 1977 to the principle that political intervention is not acceptable in the enforcement of the criminal law, it is very evident that public perceptions of government involvement in specific cases continued to be surrounded by serious doubts as to the depth of any such commitment. So much so that in October 1978 the Solicitor General of the time, Mr. Richard C. Savage (now Mr. Justice Savage of the Supreme Court of New Zealand), took the unusual step of addressing an open letter to the country's leading morning newspaper[67] with the specific aim of furthering public understanding of the total unacceptability of political considerations in making decisions pertaining to the application of the criminal law. The choice of such a public organ and its nation-wide circulation was a calculated one. Moreover, the prominence accorded to the Solicitor General's clarification of the law probably achieved more in dispelling misunderstandings as to the nature of the independent functions of the Attorney General and Solicitor General[68] than a host of parliamentary statements or pronouncements to gatherings of the legal profession. The junior Law Officer's foray into the public arena, it should be noted again, was prompted by public accusations of alleged government involvement in the staying of a cluster of criminal prosecutions each exhibiting distinct political ramifications.

THE SUPERANNUATION ACT CASE IN 1976

The best known of these interventions by the Attorney General involved a private prosecution that arose out of the set of circumstances that have come to be known as the *Superannuation Act* case in 1976. In separate civil proceedings, the Chief Justice of New Zealand, Sir Richard Wild, robustly delivered a judgment declaring New Zealand's Prime Minister, Mr Richard Muldoon, to be in breach of section 1 of the Bill of Rights Act 1688.[69] Within a matter of days after being sworn in following his party's

---

[67] *The Dominion*, October 2, 1978. The letter was given great prominence in the news columns of the newspaper. Commenting on the remarks made by the New Zealand Minister of Justice at the 1977 Meeting of Commonwealth Law Ministers (*ante*, fn. 60) Mr. Savage asserted his belief that at least since 1970, when he assumed the duties of Solicitor General, the principles set forth in his letter to the editor had been generally accepted and applied by ministers in New Zealand. The purpose of his public letter, he concluded "is to make clear that political intervention is not, and has not been, acceptable in the enforcement of the criminal law. It does not follow that I am asserting that there have never been attempts to influence the criminal process for political or other reasons; but I believe that the concept of the unacceptability of political considerations in the prosecution process is steadily growing in Parliament, the Government generally and the community."

[68] If justification were thought necessary for the Solicitor General's extraordinary intervention in the public debate, Mr. Savage reminded all and sundry that as "the junior Law Officer with the same powers, duties and responsibilities as the Attorney General in the role of a [New Zealand] Law Officer, I am much concerned to ensure the position may not be misunderstood by the public." *Loc. cit.*

[69] *Fitzgerald* v. *Muldoon et al.* [1976] 2 N.Z.L.R. 615. The background facts are fully set out in Wild C.J.'s judgment. Referring to the invoking of the Bill of Rights and its prohibition against "the pretended power of suspending of laws or the execution of laws by regall authority without consent of Parliament" the Chief Justice declared: "It is a graphic illustration of the depth of our legal heritage and the strength of our constitutional laws that a

victory in the November 1975 general election, the Prime Minister issued a press statement purporting to suspend certain mandatory sections of the Superannuation Act 1974.[70] Government departments and private industry alike immediately stopped deducting employee contributions and making the corresponding employer payments to the superannuation fund. In the light of the Prime Minister's further declaration, that when new legislation was introduced it would ensure that all persons who had relied on his press statement and acted in accordance with it would be excused from any penal provisions of the Act,[71] the Superannuation Board decided not to take any action to enforce payment of deductions and contributions.[72] The 1974 Act, it should be noted, created a number of offences for violations of its provisions with penalties of up to 12 months imprisonment, fines of $2,000 or both.

It was left to a clerk in the public service to successfully challenge, in *Fitzgerald* v. *Muldoon*, the constitutionality of the Prime Minister's action, a case destined to find an honoured place in New Zealand textbooks on constitutional law and history.[73] Another public spirited citizen had

statute passed by the English Parliament nearly three centuries ago to extirpate the abuses of the Stuart Kings should be available on the other side of the earth to a citizen of this country which was then virtually unknown in Europe and on which no Englishman was to set foot for almost another hundred years." *Ibid.* at p. 623. The Chief Justice concluded that Mr. Muldoon's public announcement of December 15, must be regarded as made "by regall authority" within the meaning of section 1 of the Bill of Rights.

[70] The general election took place on November 29, 1975. The former Opposition party became the Government of New Zealand on December 12, 1975 when its leader, Mr. Muldoon, was sworn in as Prime Minister. He also became Minister of Finance. The first press statement on the Government's intentions and actions with respect to the compulsory element in the country's superannuation scheme was released on December 15.

[71] *Loc. cit.*

[72] See the evidence in *Fitzgerald* v. *Muldoon* (*ante*) of Sir Arnold Nordmoyer, Chairman of the New Zealand Superannuation Board, which disclosed that the Prime Minister had sent him a letter on December 12, enclosing a draft of the proposed press statement and inviting the Board's comments. No changes of any substance were suggested by the Board members. According to the Chairman there had been no prior communications between the Prime Minister and himself. The Board had acceded to the Prime Minister's request because it believed that the new Government's majority in Parliament was adequate to enable it to carry out the policy it proposed.

[73] An important footnote to the decision, that may easily be overlooked, concerned the independence of counsel who was instructed to act on behalf of the plaintiff. After the judgment had been delivered in *Fitzgerald* v. *Muldoon* the Prime Minister was asked by a journalist if the State would consider paying the plaintiffs' costs, to which Mr. Muldoon replied: "I think that [the plaintiff] probably got a very good deal from his counsel, who I rather suspect had a good deal to do with the original decision to take the case." Later in the House of Representatives, the Prime Minister confirmed that he stood by his statement as reported in the press, an allegation that was tantamount to a charge of having perpetrated the tort of maintenance. The highly respected and experienced counsel concerned, Mr. George P. Barton, Q.C. chose to make a public statement at the subsequent hearing of the Supreme Court to determine the issue of costs. In his prepared remarks counsel rejected the Prime Minister's allegation absolutely, giving chapter and verse of events that led to his accepting the brief to act on behalf of the plaintiff, and of his normal consultations on the subject of fees with the instructing solicitors. "I wish to make it clear beyond any doubt whatsoever" Mr. Barton informed the court "that no matter what imputation may be made and however high in the land he may be who makes them, I shall not be deterred from discharging my duty as counsel for my client." Had counsel seen fit, instead, to launch proceedings for defamation against the Prime Minister it could have occasioned no surprise in the circumstances.

previously launched a series of private prosecutions against the Ford Motor
Company for failing to perform its statutory obligations, but on each
occasion the Attorney General intervened to halt the proceedings. These
stays, it is proper to recognise, were entered nearly four months after the
Prime Minister had issued his press release on December 15, 1975
effectively terminating the compulsory aspects of the superannuation
scheme. In a public statement explaining his action the senior Law Officer
of the Crown, Mr. P. I. Wilkinson, disclosed that he had deliberately
refrained from submitting the question of entering his stay of proceedings
to the Cabinet.[74] He had advised Mr. Muldoon of what was happening but
the Prime Minister was not a party to the Attorney General's decision.[75]
The Solicitor General's letter to the editor of *The Dominion*, referred to
earlier, gives every indication that the Crown Law Office had concurred in
the Attorney General's proposed stay of the private prosecutions. It was
stated, for example, that neither the national nor district law societies had
condemned the Attorney General's action or his reasons for so doing.[76]
Other public bodies and newspaper editorials were more critical, and
induced a second press statement by the Attorney General defending his
decision in the *Superannuation Act* prosecutions.[77] Emphasis was placed
on the fact that the Prime Minister's statement in December 1975,
purporting to suspend the operation of the Superannuation Act, was an
acknowledged fact and had been acted upon by virtually everyone in the
community affected by it. To permit the private prosecutions to proceed
could cause chaotic results in the administration of justice. "The danger in
a controversy of this nature," the Attorney General's statement concluded, "is that the factor of common sense can get overlooked—
particularly when the arguments become too theoretical or hypothetical.
We cannot run a Government by theory and hypothesis."[78]

This line of thinking in which common sense becomes the mother to
expediency might have persuaded a different court to dismiss the argument
that the Prime Minister's actions infringed section 1 of the Bill of Rights, it
being as certain as could be that the Government had the power to
implement its policies when Parliament reassembled.[79] And yet constitutional theory is clear that Parliament having made the law, the law can only
be amended or repealed by Parliament or with its authority. There is no
suggestion here that the Attorney General was acting beyond his statutory
power of staying summary proceedings under section 77A of the Summary

[74] Press statement dated April 1, 1976.
[75] *Ibid.*
[76] *Ante*, fn. 67.   [77] Press statement dated April 7, 1976.   [78] *Ibid.*
[79] Due regard to the realities of the situation, which included the knowledge that
Parliament was due to assemble in 10 days time, was recognised in the decision of the Chief
Justice not to grant injunctive relief to the plaintiff. Wild C.J. stated "In my opinion the law
and authority of Parliament will be vindicated by the making of the declaration [that the
Prime Minister was in violation of the Bill of Rights Act, 1688] and the appropriate course is
to adjourn all other matters in issue for six months from this date." [1976] 2 N.Z.L.R. 615 at
620.

Proceedings Act (N.Z.) 1957.[80] The Law Officer's actions, nevertheless, are open to criticism suggesting as they do the readiness of the Attorney General to adapt the policy of criminal law enforcement to the politics of the situation and to use his power of stay in anticipation of the government's intention to repeal the pertinent legislation that was said to have been breached. It is inviting to conjecture what position the Attorney General would have taken if the private prosecution had been expanded to include the Prime Minister as a defendant for having counselled the commission of the offence and thus rendered himself liable under section 66 of the Crimes Act 1961 as a party to the substantive crime.[81]

CONTROVERSY SURROUNDING THE STAY OF SOME RECENT PROSECUTIONS BY THE ATTORNEY GENERAL

The further entry of a stay by the same Attorney General in the series of *Bastion Point* cases in 1978[82] regenerated the controversy that swirled around the disposition of the superannuation proceedings. Of the large body of protesters who crusaded against what they perceived to be exploitation of the Maoris, and who received summonses alleging wilful trespass,[83] the majority were diverted out of the criminal justice system by virtue of stays entered by the Attorney General, but not before some 50 of their number had already occupied the attention of the magistrates' court. The Attorney General's action came immediately after the police had consulted the Solicitor General and it became apparent that the magistrates, though convicting, were not imposing any penalty and not ordering the defendants to pay costs or witnesses' expenses. The Solicitor General having formed the opinion that no useful purpose was to be served in solemnly parading the outstanding 120 defendants through the court to receive the same treatment,[84] the actual decision to stay the remaining

[80] s.77A was added to the 1957 statute by virtue of the Summary Proceedings Amendment Act 1967, s.2. For the background to the latter piece of legislation see *ante*, p. 72, fn.56. One writer, however, goes so far as to suggest that the Attorney General's stay in the Superannuation Act cases was not merely of doubtful propriety but was by reason of its purpose actually unlawful, arguing "an Attorney General cannot lawfully use s.77A [of the Summary Proceedings Act, 1957] as a means of anticipating changes in the criminal law that Parliament has still to enact"—see F.M. Brookfield (1978) 22 N.Z.L.J. 467 at p. 469. The Attorney General's response to this criticism, expressed after he had left the Law Officership, was that "the stays were entered because the prosecutions, if allowed to continue, would have inflicted needless harm to the administration of justice; they were not entered because the legislation was shortly to be changed"—(1979) 23 N.Z.L.J. 116, and see, too, N.Z. Parl. Deb., Vol. 417, pp. 306–309, May 25, 1978.

[81] This hypothetical possibility was raised in a comment on *Fitzgerald* v. *Muldoon* by W.A. McKean in [1982] *Public Law* 7 at p. 14.

[82] For a balanced and critical examination of the issues raised by this case, see Brookfield, "The Attorney General and the Staying of Proceedings" (1978) 22 N.Z.L.J. 467.

[83] No denial was heard to the claim that the Crown's decision to invoke the Trespass Act to clear the protesters from its land was taken as a matter of government policy and represented a Cabinet decision for which, under the New Zealand system of government, the Attorney General shared in the collective responsibility—*ibid.* p. 470.

[84] See the Solicitor General's letter to *The Dominion*, October 2, 1978.

prosecutions was taken by the Attorney General.[85] Writing in the *New Zealand Law Journal*, after he stepped down from office, Mr. Wilkinson confirmed that the Government had not taken part in the decisions which had been made by him alone.[86] One of the main considerations involved in the Bastion Point decision, he wrote, was the need to consider the future protection of the court system from organised attempts to undermine it by provoking mass arrest situations leading to mass prosecutions, which in turn could seriously clog and overtax its resources. No strong arguments were ever advanced that the Bastion Point stays were dictated primarily by reasons that originated in the political advantage to the government,[87] and there were responsible voices to be heard saying that the Attorney's decision was thoroughly sensible.[88]

The experience of New Zealand in recent years demonstrates beyond question that its Law Officers have become deeply committed to the policy of explaining prosecutorial decisions that engender public controversy or which touch off those indefinable features that capture the public's attention. These discretionary judgments may involve the authorisation of proceedings, a refusal to intervene or the intervention and staying of a private prosecution. Once the circumstances are judged to have the potential for widespread public interest there appears to be a growing

[85] Press statement issued from the office of the Attorney General, August 1, 1978. Two broad factors were said to lie behind the Attorney's decision to discontinue further proceedings. First, the interests of justice had been served by the judgment of the Supreme Court making the legal position clear, *viz.* that the land at Bastion Point was Crown land and the defendants had no right to be upon it. Secondly, the public interest would not be served by continuing with the outstanding multiple prosecutions that could only be processed at the rate of three or four cases a day. With no penalties having been imposed on the earlier defendants the sensible course to follow was to stop now. The substance of the Attorney General's statement is quoted by Brookfield, *ante*, fn. 82 at p. 469.

[86] [1979] N.Z.L.J. 116 at p. 118. The former Attorney General also disclosed that he had decided to act within 24 hours of an approach from the Commissioner of Police seeking his intervention—*loc. cit.* The Commissioner had initially made his approach through the Solicitor General, as the non-political head of the Crown Law Office—see *The Dominion*, October 2, 1978.

[87] *Cf.* the sceptical view expressed by Brookfield: " . . . the fact is that, as with his exercise of the same power in staying the Superannuation Act prosecutions, the public interest was found to coincide with what is arguably the political advantage of the government" *ante*, "The Attorney General and the Staying of Proceedings" (1978) 22 N.Z.L.J. 467 at p. 470.

[88] *e.g.* the editorial in (1978) 22 N.Z.L.J. 321, and *cf.* the interpretation of the inter-relationship between the respective Law Officers of the Crown in relation to the granting of stays of prosecution, contained in Mr. Wilkinson's press statement concerning the *Ravensdown* and *Mangere Airport* cases—see next fn. Having regard to the legislative provisions discussed earlier *ante*, pp. 391–393, it is beyond question that the Solicitor General in New Zealand has concurrent authority, with the Attorney General, to enter a stay of criminal proceedings. Judicial confirmation of this position was forthcoming in *Daemar* v. *Solicitor General of N.Z.* A.868/77, *per* McMullin J., (judgment delivered on November 4, 1977). And in *R.* v. *Mcdonald* [1980] N.Z.L.R. 102 at p. 105, the Court of Appeal affirmed that the giving of an undertaking to grant immunity from prosecution by the entry of a stay of proceedings was within the proper scope of the office of the Solicitor General. Furthermore, the court stated that "without finally determining the point, . . . it seems highly unlikely that this exercise of discretion in the course of his office by the Solicitor General is capable of review by the Courts even in appropriate proceedings" *ibid.* p. 106, *per* Richmond P. delivering the judgment of the court.

inclination for the Attorney General to become involved in the decision making. This rather recent tendency must be taken into account when considering the earlier description of the Crown Law Office, headed by the Solicitor General of New Zealand, as the location where the bulk of day to day decisions are made in the realm of criminal law.[89]

Political undercurrents are invariably associated with the resolution of industrial disputes. It is understandable therefore that in the latest New Zealand situations, the *Ravensdown* and *Mangere Airport* cases in 1981 that inspired another public exposition of the role of the Attorney General, it was the senior Law Officer, acting on the advice of the Solicitor General, who once again made the decision not to intervene in the labour disputes.[90] Other sources of advice to which the Attorney General disclosed that he had had recourse included the Federation of Labour and the Employers Federation. And, as in the previous cases reviewed in the preceding pages, the Attorney General went out of his way to emphasise in his public statement that the final decision on the matter had been his alone. "As is required in such cases" the Minister's statement read, "my Cabinet colleagues have left it entirely to me to make the decision and have not interfered in any way; particularly bearing in mind the political overtones of this issue I am very grateful for that fact."[91] In the *Ravensdown* case 33 people were charged, under section 33 of the Police Offences Act, with using unlawful intimidation to prevent engineers from entering a factory to attend to dangerous sulphuric acid equipment. The company, acting in accordance with the terms of its settlement with the union which resolved the dispute, requested the Attorney General to stay the criminal proceedings. The request was rejected. Picketers were also involved in the *Mangere Airport* case, criminal proceedings being brought under the Civil Aviation Regulations for trespassing beyond the areas set aside for public use. In this instance it was the Federation of Labour that sought the Attorney General's intervention. Whilst the union did not disagree with the rules to preserve airport safety and security, it did not want the law to apply to the picketers. In the negotiations towards settling both these industrial disputes some public statements suggested that industrial action would only be terminated if the Attorney General authorised a stay of pending prosecutions.

[89] The Attorney General's press statement explaining his reasons for not intervening is quoted verbatim in (1981) *Commonwealth Law Bulletin* 1446. An earlier situation, involving the refusal of the Law Officers to step in and stop the prosecutions was the *Ocean Beach Freezing Works* cases—see the press statement issued by the Attorney General's office, July 20, 1978, which traversed the customary ground in explaining the legal and constitutional principles that govern the Law Officers in the exercise of their statutory powers. The Ocean Beach statement of the Attorney General is, moreover, of special significance. In his letter to *The Dominion*, October 2, 1978, the Solicitor General at the time, Mr. R.C. Savage, drew particular attention to the Attorney General's public acknowledgment that "It was a well settled principle, and one which both he and the Solicitor General had invariably followed, that the decision to exercise the power [of entering a stay] was made by them alone and was not considered by Cabinet or by any other Minister".
[90] (1981) 7 C.L.B. 1447.
[91] *Ibid.* p. 1448.

The Attorney General's response was unequivocal and to the point. "I do not intend," his public statement declared, "to allow the office of, or the powers given to, the Attorney General to be used whether by employers or employees or anyone else as a convenient means of avoiding the proper legal consequences of their own actions. These are criminal proceedings. There must be no place to which the criminal law and its consequences cannot reach—whether it be to Parliament, the streets, the houses of New Zealanders, the boardroom or the picket line. To seek to have the law changed is one thing: to break it with impunity, for whatever reason, is another." These resounding sentiments emulate the philosophy which guided Mr. Robert Ellicott, the former Attorney General of Australia, and eventually compelled his resignation in 1977. Whether consciously or by accident perhaps, a rather unlikely supposition, it will be observed that the doctrine as expounded by New Zealand's Attorney General omitted "the government" and "the Prime Minister's office" from the illustrative categories to which the scope of the criminal law was said to apply. Having regard to the measure of inconsistency that can be drawn between the theory as enunciated in relation to the *Ravensdown* and *Mangere Airport* cases in 1981 and the public's perception of its selective application in the circumstances revealed in the *Superannuation Act* cases in 1977, New Zealanders are unlikely to carve the Attorney General's latest declaration in tablets of stone.

It is well to remember that it is the precedents established by the handling of earlier individual cases which are the more likely basis on which future Attorneys General and Solicitors General in New Zealand will hopefully stand when discharging the lofty ideals associated with their offices. The most recent occupants of these singular appointments have served their country's laws and constitution well in the many instances wherein they have sought to explain in detail the nature of the Law Officers' responsibilities and how individual decisions were reached. Past transgressions too, and departures from the doctrine of independence associated with the role of the Law Officers, represent equally significant chapters in the development of the constitutional principles examined in this chapter. Between the ability to recall the lessons of past mistakes and the expectation that the non-political Solicitor General will always be alert to condemn any encroachment of partisan political considerations into the decision making process, New Zealand should look confidently to the future integrity of its system of administering the criminal law.

13

Discretionary Factors in the Decision to Prosecute

The factors that control the outcome of discretionary authority in the area of law enforcement and criminal prosecutions have been aptly described as exhibiting the quality of low visibility.[1] Calls for the public disclosure of the reasons behind individual decisions is symptomatic of a growing unwillingness to accept unquestioningly the exercise of authority whether by government, statutory bodies or other public institutions. The model frequently invoked as epitomising openness and public accountability is the long established tradition of the judiciary in giving reasons in open court for their decisions. The nature of the adversary system supports judicial commitment to this ideal with its concern for identifying the legal issues before the trial commences and for confining the admissibility of evidence to what is relevant in accordance with well established rules. Far less certainty prevails in those other areas of the administration of justice that are concerned with the preliminary steps leading up to the actual trial of a criminal case.[2]

---

[1] J. Goldstein, "Police Discretion Not to Invoke the Criminal Process: Low Visibility Decisions in the Administration of Justice" (1960) 69 Yale L.J. 543 and see, too, W.R. La Fave, *Arrest: The Decision to Take a Subject into Custody*, (1965), pp. 67–143, and J. Vorenberg, "Narrowing the Discretion of Criminal Justice Officials" (1976) 4 Duke L.J. 651.

[2] For general discussions of the exercise of discretionary authority and the governing criteria pertaining thereto, see Glanville Williams, "Discretion in Prosecuting" [1956] Crim. L.R. 222–231 (one of the earliest examinations in the English literature of this growing topic); A.F. Wilcox, *The Decision to Prosecute*, (London, 1972), *passim.*, (written from the perspective of a former chief constable of a county police force); D.G.T. Williams, "Prosecution Discretion and Accountability of the Police" in *Crime, Criminology and Public Policy* (Ed. Hood), (1966), pp. 161–195; B.A. Grosman, *The Prosecutor*, Toronto 1969 (a Canadian perspective of the problem); K.C. Davis, *Discretionary Justice: A Preliminary Inquiry*, and a collection of essays edited by the same author, *Discretionary Justice in Europe and America*, (1976), particularly Chapter 2 which describes the highly formalised system of controlled discretion that prevails in West Germany, pp. 16–74. See, too, L.H. Leigh and J.E. Hall Williams, *The Management of the Prosecution Process in Denmark, Sweden, and the Netherlands*, (1982). For the most comprehensive examination of various aspects of prosecutorial discretion in the Australian context, see Enid Campbell and Harry Whitmore, *Freedom in Australia* (2nd ed.) (Sydney, 1973), pp. 96–124.

These manifold steps include decisions by the police whether or not to charge a citizen, whether to issue a summons or to arrest a suspect to ensure his appearance before the court, whether to support or oppose a bail application, and most importantly, whether and when to lay an information before a justice of the peace that sets the formal process of the criminal courts in motion. There may be some inexperienced police officers who believe that no discretion exists in the face of evidence that discloses the commission of a criminal offence. It is certainly not unknown to hear senior officers publicly claim that no discretion is exercisable by the police when confronted with otherwise unexplained circumstances pointing to an offence having taken place.[3] In truth, however, neither the law nor the practice of police forces recognises an inflexible rule that requires a prosecution to be launched irrespective of the particular circumstances surrounding the crime, the victim and the perpetrator. Whether the question arises at the initial contact of the police with the crime or at the level of intervention by the Director of Public Prosecutions or a Law Officer of the Crown, the basic principle that applies is enshrined in the passage from Sir Hartley Shawcross's speech in the House of Commons in 1951 when he declared[4]: "It has never been the rule in this country—I hope it never will be—that suspected criminal offences must automatically be the subject to prosecution. Indeed the very first Regulations under which the Director of Public Prosecutions worked provided that he should . . . prosecute . . . wherever it appears that the offence or the circumstances of its commission is or are of such a character that a prosecution in respect thereof is required in the public interest. That is still the dominant consideration." In deciding whether or not to authorise a prosecution, Shawcross added, the Director's office must have regard to "the effect which the prosecution, successful or unsuccessful as the case may be, would have upon public morale and order, and with any other considerations of public policy."[5] These views continue to represent the proper theory of criminal prosecution.

Whilst the general principle is correctly expressed in Shawcross's dictum it would be unrealistic to equate in any exact sense the evaluation of the relevant factors at every level of the criminal process. Thus, the exercise of judgment by uniformed police officers on the street or by detectives in the interrogation room is likely to be somewhat circumscribed by the knowledge that their initial response will be reviewed by senior officers in the force.[6] In difficult, important or highly sensitive cases this review will

---

[3] See Edwards, "Discretionary Powers by the Police and Crown Attorneys in the Criminal Law" (1970) 59 *Canadian Police Chief* 36.

[4] H.C. Deb., Vol. 483, col. 681, January 29, 1951 and see *ante*, pp. 318–324.

[5] *Ibid.*

[6] Among the important empirical studies of police work, to which reference should be made, are J. Skolnick, *Justice Without Trial*, (New York, 1966); P. Greenwood et al., *The Criminal Investigation Process*, Vol. III, 1975; and R.V. Ericson, *Making Crime: A Study of Detective Work*, (Toronto, 1981).

likely extend upwards to include the chief constable. We have discussed at length in an earlier chapter the relationship that exists in English constitutional law between the chief constable and the local prosecuting solicitor.[7] It was noted then that the solicitor-client characterisation of their respective roles means that the final decision whether or not to prosecute is firmly in the hands of the chief constable, or such subordinate officer to whom the delegated power is given to make decisions of this kind. If the recommendations of the recent Royal Commission on Criminal Procedure are adopted and translated into legislation the authority of the prosecuting solicitor will change dramatically but that struggle for supremacy is essentially concerned with the location of the final decision-making power.[8] Our present concern is with identifying the considerations that guide those who have to make the decisions to prosecute or not to prosecute.

DISCRETION AND THE BALANCING OF COMPETING VALUES

Only in very recent years has there been any serious public airing of the discretionary factors that are taken into account by prosecutors. We have now had revealed for public examination some inkling of the balancing of competing values that is the hallmark of discretionary power. The major initiative in opening the windows of disclosure is attributable to the present holder of the office of Director of Public Prosecutions. Since assuming office in 1977 Sir Thomas Hetherington, unlike his predecessors,[9] has gone out of his way to explain in considerable detail how decisions are made in his department. National and regional newspapers,[10] the radio and television media,[11] and occasionally professional bodies and universities,[12] have afforded the Director opportunities to convey a better understanding of the role of the public prosecutor and his relationship to the police forces and to the Attorney General. The precedents set by Hetherington in England have been paralleled in other countries of which the United

---

[7] *Ante*, pp. 87–89.

[8] *Ante*, pp. 98–104.

[9] Comparison should be made with the contents of the public lectures given by Sir Theobald Mathew—see *The Office and Duties of the Director of Public Prosecutions*, (1950, University of London, Athlone Press) and *The Department of the Director of Public Prosecutions*, (1952, The Law Society). See, too, Sir Norman Skelhorn's interview "Between the Devil and the D.P.P.", *Punch*, November 24, 1976 and his chapter on "The Machinery of Prosecution" in *English Criminal Law: The Way a Briton Would Explain it to an American*, pp. 32–36.

[10] See, *e.g.* the extended interviews reported in the *Daily Mirror*, November 1, 1979; *The Times*, May 11, 1980; the *Sheffield Morning Telegraph*, May 19, 1980 and the *Sunday Times*, January 13, 1980.

[11] BBC Radio 4, *The World This Weekend*, April 19, 1981, and BBC Radio 4, *Inside Parliament*, February 16, 1980.

[12] Examples of Hetherington's public lectures include the Upjohn Memorial Lecture at King's College, University of London (November 2, 1979—see *post*, fn. 30); to Gray's Inn Moots (April 24, 1980) and to the Media Society (May 22, 1980).

States,[13] Canada,[14] Australia,[15] and New Zealand[16] can be cited for individual examples of releasing prosecution guidelines or *ex post facto* explanations for public scrutiny. Former Directors in charge of the Department of Public Prosecutions revealed as little as possible as to the actual operations of the institution and this approach was accepted as invevitable if the integrity of the system was to be maintained. The change of policy, instituted by the present Director, has now been in operation for sufficient years to demonstrate that the integrity of the Public Prosecutions' office can remain unimpaired notwithstanding the Director's determination to take the public into his confidence by frankly admitting his mistakes, when called for, or otherwise explaining repeatedly how complex and subjective is the process of reaching an impartial decision as to the enforcement of the criminal law.

In the main, the Director's remarks have been associated with the exercise of his "consent" powers or those conferred upon the Attorney General but with respect to which the Director of Public Prosecutions would normally be involved in advising the Attorney. The focus of these "revelations" has usually depended on the current *cause célèbre*, so that the involvement of a public figure or the contentious nature of prosecutions involving riots, obscenity, race relations, deaths in police custody, or corruption have all tended to figure prominently in the public discussion of the Director's activities. The opportunity for a more dispassionate analysis of the Director of Public Prosecutions' discretion arose in connection with the appearance of Sir Thomas Hetherington before the Royal Commission on Criminal Procedure. Prior to doing so, Hetherington had submitted a

[13] See (1978) 24 *The Criminal Law Reporter* 3001 which contains, in their entirety, United States Justice Department documents issued under the authority of a memorandum by Attorney General Edward H. Levi (January 18, 1977) on the exercise of prosecutorial discretion in such areas as decisions to prosecute, selection of charges, plea agreements and agreements to forego prosecution in return for cooperation. See, also, John T. Elliff, *The Reform of F.B.I. Intelligence Operations* (1979, Princeton), Appendices I, II, III and IV.

[14] *e.g.* in the province of Ontario 21 directives to the Crown Attorneys have been issued by, or in the name of, the Attorney General during the period from 1972 up to the present time. These cover a wide range of subjects including: plea discussions, disclosures to the defence, strict enforcement of new Criminal Code provisions relating to firearms, drinking and driving offences, child abuse prosecutions, prosecution of police officers who lie under oath, pornography and obscenity prosecutions, high speed police pursuits, child abduction, hockey violence, vandalism, sentences in sexual cases and preferring indictments for offences founded on evidence taken at a preliminary inquiry. Most of the directives are issued under the signature of the provincial Attorney General, with the others emanating from the Director of Crown Attorneys or the Assistant Deputy Attorney General.

[15] In early 1982 the Commonwealth Attorney General, Senator Peter Durack Q.C., announced that he would be tabling in the Australian Senate during the current session a statement setting out "the Australian Government's (*sic*) prosecution policy." Australia had decided to make public the principles which would guide it in such matters—see (1982) 8 *Commonwealth Law Bulletin* 826. The statement, *Prosecution Policy of the Commonwealth*, was tabled in the Australian Senate on December 16, 1982—see *post*, p. 432, fn. 25.

[16] See the numerous instances in recent years, referred to in the previous chapter, wherein both the Attorney General and the Solicitor General of New Zealand have provided elaborate *ex post facto* explanations of prosecution decisions that became the subject of public debate.

volume of written evidence which includes the most authoritative exposition of the factors underlying the decision to prosecute, as practised within the Department of Public Prosecutions.[17] It would be a signal omission, however, when dealing with this subject, not to recognise the even earlier exposure of the inner workings of the office of Director of Public Prosecutions prepared by Mr. Peter Barnes, then an Assistant Director, and delivered to a conference on the prosecution process held at the University of Birmingham in 1975.[18] Perhaps it was the cosy setting that prompted the latter to open his remarks by describing the view of the department probably entertained by the police as being rather like "a sort of voracious Whitehall monster which demands to be fed an unending flow of files and, what is more, sometimes repays all their hard work and kindness by flatly refusing the fare it is offered."[19]

As we have already noted, the police are obligated to submit to the Director of Public Prosecutions full reports, including witness statements and material documents, in all consent cases that require the statutory approval of the Director, the Solicitor General or the Attorney General before criminal proceedings can be commenced.[20] And, in accordance with the Prosecution of Offences Regulations, chief officers of police are also required to provide the Director's office with the same kind of information concerning those categories of offences that are specifically listed in the regulations or which the Director may direct to be the subject of reports to his office because of their individual importance or difficulty.[21] In all, these statutory directives generate some 14,000 cases annually that flow into the Department of Public Prosecutions to be assessed by the relatively small establishment of 53 barristers and 17 solicitors who comprise its full time professional officers.[22]

---

[17] *Written Evidence of the Director of Public Prosecutions*, December 1978.

[18] *The Prosecution Process*, an edited transcript of the proceedings of a conference held under the auspices of the Institute of Judicial Administration, University of Birmingham, in April 1975. Mr. Barnes' address on "The Office of the Director of Public Prosecutions" and the ensuing discussion is at pp. 22–36 of the *Proceedings*.

[19] *Ibid.* p. 22.

[20] See *ante*, p. 13.

[21] *Ante*, pp. 14–16. An interesting insight into the changing character of the Director's advisory and prosecuting roles was provided in Sir Thomas Hetherington's *Written Evidence* where it was pointed out that, whilst the total number of cases referred to the D.P.P. has increased steadily over the years (see *post*, fn. 22) the actual proportion of cases in which the Director has undertaken the prosecution, either directly or through a local agent, has declined. In 1977, the percentage of cases in which the Director assumed the conduct of the prosecution was 13·55 per cent., or 2130 cases out of the total of 15,724 cases referred to the D.P.P. The current feature emphasised by the D.P.P. was the increasing number of court days required to complete the more complex cases that are earlier processed through the department. "During the last three years at the Central Criminal Court" Hetherington wrote "I have prosecuted 37 cases lasting between 5 and 10 weeks; 17 cases which took 11 to 20 weeks and 3 cases which lasted far more than 20 weeks—one of the latter occupied 135 court days or 27 weeks in all." A not dissimilar trend was evident in the provinces—*op. cit.* pp. 69–70.

[22] A chart showing the professional staff structure as of October 1978 is included as Appendix 8 of the D.P.P.'s *Written Evidence* to the Royal Commission on Criminal Procedure (*ante*, fn. 17). Appendix 13 gives an overall summary of the volume of work

DECISION MAKING IN THE DEPARTMENT OF PUBLIC PROSECUTIONS

At the apex of this organisation, of course, is the Director, with a Deputy Director immediately beneath him.[23] The Department is divided into nine divisions, the responsibility for which is shared between two Principal Assistant Directors. Metropolitan London police cases occupy the attention of two of these divisions, the work of the central office being separated from that of the Metropolitan divisions. Three other divisions take care of police cases that emanate from the rest of England and Wales, which is divided into three parts, east, west and south, for purposes of administrative orderliness and an even distribution of case loads.[24] The remaining divisions are designed to deal with specialised work that has expanded in recent years. One of these, the research division, handles requests for advice from police forces, coroners and magistrates' clerks as well as preparing submissions, for example, to the Law Commission, the Criminal Law Revision Committee, or to the Parliamentary Counsel on points that arise in draft Bills and which impinge upon the Director's functions.[25] Another division, the fraud and bankruptcy division, concerns itself with major company frauds and the Director's responsibilities in connection with the making of criminal bankruptcy orders by the Crown Courts under the provisions of sections 39 to 41 of the Powers of the Criminal Courts Act 1973.[26]

Finally, there are two divisions of the Department of Public Prosecutions entirely devoted to the handling of public complaints of alleged offences committed by police officers. Under section 49(3) of the Police Act 1964[27] complaints made by a member of the public have to be reported to the Director of Public Prosecutions unless the chief officer of police is satisfied that no criminal offence has been committed. The number of such reports has risen steadily since 1964 and shows no sign of diminishing.[28] To gain a true appreciation of the significance of this development, in 1977 (the latest year for which statistics are available) the Director's office received 9068

processed through the department for the years 1950, 1955, 1960, 1965, 1970 and each of the succeeding years to 1977. For a comparison with the number of applications received and prosecuted by the Office of Public Prosecutions between 1895 and 1907, and 1949 and 1961, see Edwards, *Law Officers of the Crown*, p. 387, fn. 77.

[23] The description that follows draws heavily on both Hetherington's *Written Evidence* (*ante*) and Barnes' paper to the University of Birmingham Conference (*ante*, fn. 18).

[24] See Appendix 9 of the Director's *Written Evidence* which shows geographically the distribution of police forces in England and Wales among the respective divisions of the D.P.P.'s office.

[25] The D.P.P.'s role in handling extradition applications, which falls within the assigned responsibilities of the research division, rarely merits attention. Occasionally the foreign government will instruct its own solicitor but that practice is changing and the Director may find himself increasingly representing the foreign state involved or acting as *amicus curiae* in the Divisional Court in habeas corpus applications by the fugitive. *Written Evidence, op. cit.*, pp. 63–64.

[26] c. 62.

[27] c. 48.

[28] The relevant statistics for each of the years 1970–77 are usefully collected in Appendix 14 of the D.P.P.'s *Written Evidence, op. cit.*

such complaints, which accounted for just over half the department's total intake in terms of numbers of files received from every outside source. Not all of these complaints involved allegations of assaults, corruption of other serious crimes. On the contrary, the bulk of the complaints were concerned with relatively trivial matters such as careless driving and other minor infringements of the traffic laws. This burden on the Director's office is accepted as inevitable[29] and involves a very special category of discretionary power in the area of criminal prosecutions, to which we shall return in due course.

Whatever the assigned responsibilities of each division may be it is headed by an Assistant Director. The remainder of the professional officers, who may be solicitors or barristers, are distributed among the respective divisions according to the volume of work. The important thing to remember is that, by virtue of section 1(5) of the Prosecutions of Offences Act 1908, "an Assistant Director of Public Prosecutions may do any act or thing which the Director of Public Prosecutions is required or authorized to do by or in pursuance of any Act of Parliament or otherwise." Consequently, in any discussion of the decision to prosecute it is necessary to bear in mind that the Director's direct involvement in the assessment of the varying factors involved will be truly exceptional and not the normal course of procedure. Speaking in the course of delivering the Upjohn Memorial Lecture in 1979,[30] the present holder of the office of Director revealed that in the two and a half years during which he had been

[29] According to the present Director, the nature of most of the offences contained in complaints against the police are relatively trivial and are inconsistent with his policy of dealing only with major crime. Nevertheless, he added: " . . . in view of the anxiety of both the police and the public that all cases involving police officers should be considered by an independent body, I can see no viable alternative at the moment to the present practice continuing"—*Written Evidence*, p. 55. Changes, however, appear inevitable following the recommendations contained in the *Fourth Report of the Select Committee on Home Affairs* (H.C. 98–1 (1981–82)). In its considered reply to this report the Government has proposed a new set of police complaints procedures, the net effect of which, if adopted, will be a severe curtailment on the present burdensome involvement of the D.P.P.—see Cmnd. 8681 of 1982 and the comment in [1982] *Public Law* pp. 509–511. Moreover, an increasing body of opinion is being heard to the effect that the responsibilities of the Police Complaints Board are independent of, and not subject to the final disposition of a case by, the Director of Public Prosecutions—see *R.* v. *Police Complaints Board, ex p. Madden*, [1983] 1 W.L.R. 447 *per* McNeill J., who held that the board had wrongly concluded that the Police Act 1976, precluded the institution of criminal proceedings where the D.P.P. has determined not to bring criminal proceedings on the same or similar evidence. After receiving McNeill J.'s ruling, the Board issued a public statement expressing its view that the effect of the judgment in *Madden* is that the conduct of police officers may be subjected to disciplinary proceedings and notwithstanding the Director's view the Board may recommend or direct the preferment of a disciplinary charge on their own evaluation of the evidence—see *The Times*, February 11, 1983. See, too, the well informed discussion paper on "Complaints against the Police" by Professor Sir Roy Marshall (a member of the Complaints Board) prepared for the 1983 Meeting of Commonwealth Law Ministers, especially paras. 52–63.
[30] The Ninth Upjohn Lecture given at King's College, University of London, on November 2, 1979, and subsequently published in (1981) 14 *The Law Teacher* paras. 92. In it, Hetherington essays a biographical portrait and assessment of his predecessors, Sir Archibald Bodkin and Sir Theobald Mathew, and their handling of some of the prominent obscenity cases that occurred during their respective regimes.

in office he had never been required to take any decision on whether to prosecute in a murder case.[31] He added: " . . . in all I have taken the decision to prosecute, or been concerned in consultations with the police and with counsel, in not more than 10 or 12 cases a year—usually when they are exceptionally sensitive because of the subject matter or because of the persons involved."[32] The majority of cases brought to the attention of the Department of Public Prosecutions, either by way of mandatory edict, to obtain the formal consent of the Director or one of the Law Officers, or to be subject to the guiding discretion of the Director, will not proceed beyond the Assistant Director in charge of the appropriate division or the Principal Assistant Director responsible for co-ordinating the cluster of divisions assigned as his mandate within the department.

The fullest description of the actual functioning of the decision-making process in the Department of Public Prosecutions is contained in the address given to the conference on "The Prosecution Process" by Mr. Peter Barnes, presently the Deputy Director of Public Prosecutions.[33] In it, Barnes emphasised the high level at which decisions to prosecute are taken in the office, decisions which, in his words, "should only be taken after a very careful consideration of all the available evidence, quite calmly and in the light of day because a wrong decision either way can have pretty disastrous consequences."[34] He may well have had in mind the handling of the *Confait* case in 1972 and the strong criticisms subsequently levelled against the professional staff in the Department of Public Prosecutions by Sir Henry Fisher, the former High Court judge, who was appointed by the Home Secretary to conduct a public inquiry into the affair.[35] Three youths, aged 18, 15 and 14 years respectively, were convicted in 1972 of the killing of Maxwell Confait, a homosexual prostitute. They were freed three years later after a successful public campaign to prove their innocence. The entire case depended on confessions by the accused in which they admitted having gone to Confait's home for the purpose of stealing. The victim had been strangled and the three accused were said to have sprinkled paraffin about the home in order to destroy any fingerprints they may have left. At the conclusion of the trial, verdicts of murder, manslaughter by reason of diminished responsibility, and arson were returned by the jury. Leave to appeal against conviction was refused by the Court of Appeal but the case

[31] *Ibid.* p. 101.
[32] *Ibid.*
[33] See *ante*, fn. 18.
[34] *Ibid.* p. 26.
[35] *Report of the Inquiry into the circumstances leading to the trial of three persons on charges arising out of the death of Maxwell Confait and the fire at 27 Doggett Road, London S.E.6*—H.C. Paper 90 of 1977. The original trial took place in November 1972. Applications for leave to appeal were refused by the Court of Appeal in July 1973. Following fresh police enquiries instigated by the Home Office the Secretary of State in June 1975 referred the case back to the Court of Appeal under the terms of s.17(1)(*a*) of the Criminal Appeal Act 1968. As a result, the original convictions were quashed and a warrant issued setting up the Fisher Inquiry in November 1975.

was referred back to the court three years later following the emergence of
fresh pathological evidence. It informed the court that a substantial
amount of time had elapsed between the setting fire to the house and the
death of the victim. In direct contradiction to the confessions obtained by
the police there was incontestable evidence that the three youths were
elsewhere at the time of the fire. The prime suspect for the murder, a
transvestite who lived in the same house as Confait, hanged himself in
1974. He gave evidence at the original trial about the time the fire had
started.

Evidence adduced before the Fisher inquiry as to the handling of the
papers in the *Confait* case indicated that the professional officer concerned
in the Department of Public Prosecutions had treated the case as
straightforward because of the independent nature of the respective
confessions and their having been repeated in the presence of the youths'
parents.[36] He was not aware that there had been another suspect. Sir
Norman Skelhorn, the then Director of Public Prosecutions, expressed
doubts as to whether the discrepancies, revealed later, should have been
spotted and regarded as important by the professional officer who first
reviewed the file and whose recommendations were adopted by his
superiors.[37] This view was rejected in forthright terms by Sir Henry Fisher,
the chairman of the departmental inquiry, who concluded: "It seems to me
clear that it was [the professional officer's] duty to look for weaknesses or
contradictions in the prosecution's case, and to see whether there were
matters which should be further enquired into . . . If (as he said) he did not
notice anything which required further investigation or specific reference
to counsel, then in my view he was at fault, though in extenuation it can be
said that he was under great pressure of work. If (as the police say) his
attention was drawn to them and he did nothing, then his fault was
greater."[38] Before leaving the subject of his inquiry, Sir Henry Fisher
turned his attention to the administrative practices then in force in the
office of Director of Public Prosecutions. Noting that the Director had not
seen fit to criticise his subordinate's handling of the *Confait* case, the
chairman of the inquiry concluded that "the experienced and conscientious
officer did as much as under prevailing practice was expected of him."[39]
Based on this assumption the procedures then in place were condemned as
unsatisfactory.[40] The lessons of that case are unlikely to be readily
forgotten within the Department of Public Prosecutions.

Describing the present mode of administering the Department, it has
been authoritatively explained that under no circumstances can a decision
to prosecute be made by anyone below the rank of Assistant Director who,
before obtaining that rank, will generally have served in the department

[36] *Op. cit.* p. 213.
[37] *Ibid.* paras. 26.6 and 26.8, p. 216.
[38] *Ibid.* para. 26.7, p. 216.
[39] *Ibid.* para. 26.8, p. 216.
[40] *Ibid.*

for something like 17 years on average.[41] All cases, in the first instance, are sent to the Assistant Director in charge of the particular geographical area where the crime occurred. Short, straightforward cases can be dealt with expeditiously by the Assistant Director reaching a decision himself and communicating at once with the chief constable giving any necessary advice regarding charges and evidence. In all other cases the files will be allocated between the senior legal assistants who constitute the backbone of the division concerned. The individual officer who takes charge of the police file will read the case in greater detail, eventually returning the file to the Assistant Director with a minute summarising the salient facts, identifying any legal or evidential problems and registering his opinion as to the proper disposition of the case. Depending on the seriousness, sensitiveness or difficulties of the case the resolution of the decision to prosecute will be made from among the senior echelons of the office, often after informal discussions that ensure the exercise of all the accumulated experience that is at the disposal of the Director. In addition, if the case is of a highly complex character, either as to its facts or the legal issues involved, the Director may invoke the assistance of counsel. In London, this is likely to be one of the eight senior and ten junior Treasury Counsel who conduct all Crown prosecutions at the Central Criminal Court and the Inner London Crown Courts, or one of the supplementary counsel whose name is on the Attorney General's list drawn from the various circuits.[42] Normally, counsel are not instructed by the Director of Public Prosecutions until after committal for trial but this practice will be departed from if the circumstances warrant it and then the same counsel will likely take charge of the committal proceedings. Resort to the opinion of counsel, in the circumstances described above, means exactly that and no more. It does not entail the transfer of responsibility for making the prosecutorial decision from the Director to Treasury Counsel. As Sir Thomas Hetherington explained to the Royal Commission on Criminal Procedure, in the initial stages of a prosecution brought or taken over by the Director of Public Prosecutions he has complete control. It is entirely for the Director to decide against whom proceedings should be brought and on what charges.[43] Once the case has been committed to the Crown Court, however, as Hetherington went on to elaborate, "the position is not so straightforward, since the view is taken that the final responsibility for the

---

[41] In recommending a revision of the Prosecution of Offences Regulations 1946, Sir Henry Fisher noted that "the demands made of the Director's professional staff are excessive . . . If the present system is to continue, there can be no assurance that cases like the *Confait* case will not recur if the Director's staff is not increased"—*op. cit.* pp. 30, 207–208. Sir Henry Fisher's disposition to see a greater measure of involvement of the D.P.P.'s staff in supervising the police investigation of those cases which the Director is under a statutory duty to "institute, undertake or carry on" was opposed by Sir Norman Skelhorn, *ibid.* pp. 24–27, 30–31. With reference to the handling of the *Confait* case itself by the professional officer in the D.P.P., see esp. the conclusion reached at p. 216.

[42] Hetherington, *Written Evidence, op. cit.* paras. 165–167.

[43] *Ibid.* para. 170, p. 60.

conduct of the trial rests with counsel instructed by me to appear for the Crown. The convention, though, is that where questions of substance arise, for example, the acceptance of a plea to a lesser offence than that charged in the indictment, counsel consults me before arriving at a final decision. It is rare that there is any fundamental disagreement between us, but should such a situation arise, the arrangement is that the matter would be referred to the Attorney General."[44]

SUFFICIENCY OF THE EVIDENCE: THE FIFTY-ONE PER CENT RULE

At whatever level of authority the decision is ultimately taken to prosecute or not to prosecute, the evaluation process involves three separate but inter-related stages. It is possible to compress these exercises into two stages but the position will probably be made clearer if we adhere to the tripartite division of the assessment procedure. How separate the various stages are actually observed in practice may well be open to question, given the years of experience that most of the professional staff can draw upon in reaching their conclusions on the succession of files assigned for their attention.[45] It may be stretching credulity to be asked to believe that each and every such review is conducted with an inflexible adherence to the cycle of analysis that is about to be described. However compressed may be the evaluation of the run of the mill cases that occupy most of the professional officer's time on a regular basis, the following analysis is necessary in order to identify the separate issues that must be resolved in reaching the eventual decision to prosecute or not to prosecute.

The first objective is to ensure that there are no insuperable legal or jurisdictional obstacles that could constitute a fatal flaw to the prosecution of a case. Was the offence, for example, committed outside the jurisdiction of the English courts? Have any pertinent time limits for prosecution already passed? Are there any definitional problems that require compliance and which are deficient in the evidence accumulated by the police? It is possible that some of these deficiencies can be rectified by further police investigation, and advice to this effect will be conveyed by letter or in person to the police force concerned. In the absence of such a possibility it stands to reason that it is pointless to pursue the merits of the case if the essential legal underpinnings are not in place.

The second stage must next be addressed. It is concerned with the issue whether the evidence in the case is sufficient to justify instituting criminal proceedings. The present Director of Public Prosecutions has repeatedly sought to explain to all and sundry the criterion that applies throughout his department, at whatever level of authority the operational decision is made. Different wording has been used on occasion to explain the

---

[44] *Ibid.*

[45] For a realistic analysis of the relationship between theory and practice in adhering to the successive stages leading up to decision making in individual cases, see Barnes, *op. cit.* pp. 26–32.

governing test, some less felicitous than others, and we can begin by referring to the Director's written submission in 1978 to the Royal Commission on Criminal Procedure in which Hetherington stated: "The test normally used in the Department . . . is whether or not there is a reasonable prospect of a conviction; whether, in other words, it seems rather more likely that there will be a conviction than an acquittal. We set an even higher standard if an acquittal would or might produce unfortunate consequences. For example, if a man who has been convicted of some offence is subsequently acquitted of having given perjured evidence at his trial, that acquittal may cast doubt on the original conviction. Likewise, an unsuccessful prosecution of an allegedly obscene book will, if the trial has attracted publicity, lead to a considerable increase in sales. In such cases we are hesitant to prosecute unless we think the prospects of a conviction are high. We also tend to adopt a somewhat higher standard if the trial is likely to be abnormally long and expensive and the offence is not especially grave."[46]

On another occasion, this time in a memorandum prepared in 1980 for the House of Commons Select Committee on Deaths in Police Custody, the Director of Public Prosecutions confirmed that the standards applied in police complaint cases are the same as those invoked in all other cases reported to the department. The first consideration, the memorandum stated, is "whether the totality of the available evidence is of such quality that a reasonable jury (or magistrate, in respect of summary offences) is more likely than not to be satisfied beyond reasonable doubt that the accused is guilty of the offence charged. If so, the evidence is sufficient to justify proceedings. If it fails that test, we would not consider it proper to prosecute."[47]

In thus delineating the standard of sufficiency the Director of Public Prosecutions was very conscious of the contrary school of thought that maintains it is incumbent upon the Crown to prosecute whenever there is a "bare prima facie case" and that to raise the minimum standard any higher is to "usurp the proper function of the courts."[48] According to this view, in the absence of unassailable evidence that the prospective Crown witnesses are lying, it is not the function of the prosecutor to decide whether he believes a witness or not. Where the question is whether the prosecution's evidence is likely to be believed, it is argued, this is strictly a matter for the jury (or the magistrate in summary cases) and not the Director to decide.

---

[46] *Written Evidence, op. cit.* p. 33, paras. 92–94. The criterion "whether or not there is a reasonable *prospect* of conviction," repeatedly referred to by Hetherington in his public utterances should be compared with the formula "a reasonable *certainty* of conviction" used by his predecessor as the D.P.P., Sir Norman Skelhorn (*ante*, fn. 9) at p. 35. In his memoirs, *Public Prosecutor* (1982), Skelhorn describes the acid test, used during his period as D.P.P., to be "whether on the evidence before us, if that evidence stood up in court and was not eroded, there was in our considered opinion a likelihood that a conviction would result," *ibid.* p. 70 but *cf.* his formulation on p. 71.

[47] H.C. Paper 401—iii, February 14, 1980, see p. 27.

[48] *Written Evidence, op. cit.* p. 34, para. 95.

Hetherington's response to this argument is an outright rejection of its underlying thesis. The resolution of the sufficiency of evidence test, in the opinion of the present Director of Public Prosecutions, requires that proper attention be paid to the credibility of the witnesses since "the universal adoption of a prima facie case standard would not only clog up our already overburdened courts but inevitably result in an undue proportion of innocent men facing criminal charges."[49]

The elucidation of the key passages in the above extracts from the Director's written submissions, *viz.* "the reasonable prospect of a conviction" and it is "more likely that there will be a conviction than an acquittal" resemble the difficulties in giving realistic meaning to the task imposed upon examining justices in deciding whether there is "sufficient evidence" to warrant committing the accused for trial,[50] and upon a trial judge when explaining to a jury the standard of "proof beyond a reasonable doubt" in a criminal case,[51] or in deciding whether the evidence is sufficient to justify him in withdrawing the case from the jury and which is determined according to "whether or not there is any evidence upon which a reasonable jury properly instructed could return a verdict of guilty."[52] It is not my intention to venture into a comparative analysis of the respective meanings accorded by the appellate courts to the various criteria mentioned above. These comparable situations are introduced in order to draw attention to the difficulties experienced in applying such nebulous standards, and the additional problem encountered by the Director in explaining to the general public how he and his staff approach the task of defining "sufficiency of evidence." In a no doubt sincere attempt to elucidate this piece of legalise, Hetherington has acquired for himself the immortal title of "Mr. Fifty-one per cent.," a reference to his resort to mathematical percentages as a vehicle for simplifying the

---

[49] *Ibid.* and see the exchange of views on this question with the Director defending his position before the Select Committee on Home Affairs, (*ante*, fn.4), p. 35.

[50] The Magistrates' Courts Act 1952 (15 & 16 Geo. 6 & 1 Eliz. 2, c.56) s.7(1), and *Archbold*, (41st ed.), para. 4–193, afford little assistance in interpreting the "sufficiency of evidence" test, stating only that the function of the committal proceedings is "to ensure that no one shall stand trial unless a prima facie case has been made out." And see *R.* v. *Epping & Harlow Justices, ex p. Massaro* [1973] Crim. L.R. 109. In interpreting a similar provision in the Criminal Code, s.475, the Supreme Court of Canada (in *U.S.A.* v. *Sheppard* [1977] S.C.R. 1077) has declared (by a majority) that "sufficiency of evidence" to warrant committal for trial bears the same meaning as that accorded the same formula when deciding whether to withdraw the case from the jury, *viz.*, "whether or not there is any evidence upon which a reasonable jury properly instructed could return a verdict of guilty."

[51] The leading authorities are reviewed in *Cross on Evidence*, (5th ed. 1979) pp. 110–115, according to which the *locus classicus* remains the judgment of Denning J., in *Miller* v. *Minister of Pensions* [1947] 2 All E.R. 372 at pp. 373–374. See, too *Archbold, Criminal Pleading, Practice and Procedure*, (41st ed., 1979), para. 4–426.

[52] The decision to uphold or reject a submission of no case to answer does not depend on whether the adjudicating tribunal (if compelled to do so) would at that stage convict or acquit—Practice Note issued by the Divisional Court, [1962] 1 All E.R. 448; and see *R.* v. *Mansfield* [1977] 1 W.L.R. 1102.

governing criterion.[53] Formulated in these terms the question to be asked in contemplating a prosecution is this—is there a better than 50 per cent. chance that a jury will find the accused guilty on the evidence that the prosecution are in a position to present? Hetherington's words of caution, uttered in another public lecture, that it is not possible to evaluate to a percentage degree of accuracy have been lost sight of in the public's preference for simple, uncomplicated metaphors.[54] Talk of cases falling within the marginal 49 to 51 per cent. category are equally unhelpful because of the false conception implicit in such language that the prosecutor's decision-making bears the stamp of scientific objectivity. Nothing could be more misleading insomuch as it obscures the reality of the situation. An experienced Assistant Director disclaimed any ability on his part to offer a neat yardstick as to how to assess the prospects of a conviction or an acquittal. "All I can say" he frankly admitted "is that we do our best to call upon the experience that we have accumulated over the years, and that in itself is a strong reason for the high level at which our decisions are taken."[55] The truth of the matter lies closer to recognising the subjective nature of the prosecutorial decision in individual cases, it being at least likely that something less than identical answers would be forthcoming if the same set of files were to be given to a sample of, say, 20 or 50 professional officers all working in the same Department of Public Prosecutions.[56] With the restriction of the actual decision-making to the small coterie of senior staff of Assistant Directors and above, vagaries of subjectivity are probably kept to a minimum.

A special consideration that we should look at is the weight attached to an earlier police decision to charge, before the papers in the case have been submitted to the Director's office. This election by the police to go ahead may be necessary, for example, where there are substantial grounds for believing that the accused will leave the country, interfere with witnesses or commit further crimes. In these circumstances it is understandable that the police should wish not only to charge the suspected person but to strongly oppose bail. Other situations, however, arise when the Director's consent is refused on policy grounds notwithstanding the existence of ample evidence to support a prosecution, and it is obviously preferable if the issue of consent is first determined before a formal charge is laid by the police. Pre-emptive action of this kind by the police, it has been readily acknowledged, exerts pressure upon the Director of Public Prosecutions and his staff in sustaining the objective of a dispassionate decision.[57] It is

[53] See, e.g. the headline in the Sunday Times, January 27, 1980, which compounds the difficulties by dubbing the present Director as "Mr. Fifty per cent." Hetherington himself refers to "the 50 per cent rule" in his address to the Media Society, ante, fn. 12.

[54] Op. cit. Media Society address, at pp. 7–8.

[55] Barnes, op. cit. p. 27.

[56] The likelihood of such an outcome was readily acknowledged by the Deputy D.P.P. in the course of my discussion with him in his office on July 7, 1980.

[57] Barnes, op. cit. pp. 25–26.

also understandable that a team of detectives who have worked laboriously and conscientiously for an extended period in solving a case should feel an acute sense of having been let down by the Director if approval to the bringing of criminal proceedings is not forthcoming. The police may be firmly convinced of the guilt of the suspect, but if the evidence is insufficient in terms of the probability of a conviction the policy of the Department of Public Prosecutions, as stated by its Director, is to oppose the initiation of a prosecution.[58] Any substantiated indications that the Director of Public Prosecutions and the staff of the Department are prone to succumb to police pressures in making their decisions instead of adhering to the principle of fearless impartiality would surely contribute to the erosion of public confidence. It may be assumed that nowhere is this fact better appreciated than in the office of the Director of Public Prosecutions itself.

AN EVALUATION OF SOME RECENT CONTROVERSIAL DECISIONS

Criticisms of particular decisions made by the Director have usually centred around cases that have already attracted public attention, in which cultural or political prejudices are readily given rein. In the early years of the office of Public Prosecutions the practice of the Director was to defer a public response to criticisms of his decisions until he prepared his annual report for Parliament.[59] This avenue for defending the Department's actions has long since disappeared[60] and it is doubtful whether, in present day conditions of accelerated communication, public opinion would be satisfied to await a yearly accounting of the Director's work. What is evident is the readiness of Sir Thomas Hetherington to defend his record after the event by whatever media resources are placed at his disposal.

Some of the more notorious cases in recent times have centred on the narrow question of the sufficiency of evidence. In the *Blair Peach* case in 1979, for example, one of several situations where a suspect has died in police custody in suspicious circumstances, Hetherington has admitted that the reason why there was no prosecution against any particular officer is that it was impossible to tell which of any policemen committed the crime. In an interview with *The Times*,[61] and referring expressly to the *Blair Peach* case, the Director stated: "I am not absolutely certain that he was hit on the head by a police officer, but I think it is probable that he was. There was no evidence as to which one, literally no evidence, and no evidence really as to what the weapon was, except that it was a blunt

---

[58] One qualification to this policy is the reluctance of the D.P.P.'s office to turn around a police decision to charge, unless the evidence is totally without substance. If there is some evidence to support the original police charge, the tendency is to let the lower court make the decision not to commit for trial by "soft pedalling" the evidence in support of the prosecution's case. *Per* the Deputy D.P.P. in discussion with the author, July 7, 1980.

[59] Edwards, *Law Officers of the Crown*, pp. 377–387.

[60] *Ibid.* p. 386.

[61] *The Times*, May 11, 1981.

instrument. We don't have the evidence. What they did in fact was to remain silent, which they are entitled to do."[62] This unusually frank disclosure of the thinking that contributed to the decision not to prosecute in that case should not be extended by inference to the 26 other cases involving complaints against a police officer or police officers that resulted from deaths in suspicious circumstances over a period of 10 years between 1970 and 1979.[63] According to figures published by the Home Office in February 1980, a total of 274 people had died while in the custody of the police during the same period.[64] 48 deaths, the highest total in any single year, occurred in 1978 during which the number of persons taken into custody was 1·25 million. The disparity in the respective totals mystified many people at the time, including the members of the House of Commons Select Committee. The explanation for the lower figure is that these cases represent those where a public complaint was registered and where the particular chief constable felt it incumbent upon him to submit the papers to the Director of Public Prosecutions under the test laid down in section 49 of the Police Act 1964.[65] The remainder would be cases in which either no complaint was received or the chief officer of the police was satisfied that no criminal offence could have been committed. Furthermore, the suspicious circumstances surrounding the deaths were not necessarily confined to deaths that took place while the victim was "in police custody," a phrase that can encompass a variety of situations ranging from an arrest in the home or on the street to the actual detention of the person concerned in a police station or in a hospital.

Prominent among the cases generally referred to as having given rise to widespread public concern, in addition to *Blair Peach*, are those of *James Kelly* (1979) and *Liddle Towers* (1976), who died after release from custody. The continuous attention devoted to these cases in the press[66] and in Parliament was reinforced by the remarkable fact that, arising out of the 26 situations in which the deceased allegedly died at the hands of the

---

[62] *Ibid.*

[63] This is the figure adhered to by the D.P.P. in the course of his evidence before the Home Affairs Committee—see *Report*, February 14, 1980, H.C. 401–iii. A breakdown of the 26 cases where the deceased allegedly died at the hands of the police or as a result of action taken by the police formed part of the Director's written memorandum to the Committee. Annex 1 (p. 29) analyses the statistics according to the attributed cause of death (7 being due to natural causes, 4 to misadventure, 4 to suicide, 2 to accidental death, 2 to lawful killing—the remainder are classified as no inquest, inquest adjourned or no known cause). Annex II (p. 30) indicates that 11 of the deaths took place in hospital, 5 while the deceased was in police custody, 7 as having taken place "elsewhere," and 3 "not known."

[64] *Justice of the Peace*, February 23, 1980, pp. 111–112. At first, the Home Office refused to disclose the names of the deceased "because of the disproportionate cost involved" (*The Times*, January 7, 1980), but later provided the relevant information (*The Times*, January 14, 1980).

[65] *Minutes of Evidence* of the Home Affairs Committee, H.C. Paper 401–iii, at p. 31. For a further elaboration of the responsibilities defined in section 49 see *post*, p. 419.

[66] See, *e.g. The Times* editorial, January 14, 1980; the *Sunday Times*, January 6, 1980 (reporting the call by Sir Harold Wilson for a public inquiry into the death of James Kelly in a police cell).

police, in different parts of the country, not one prosecution had been instituted by the Director of Public Prosecutions. Questioned on this subject by the members of the House of Commons Select Committee, the Director stated that in each of the 26 cases the decision not to prosecute was based on the failure to surmount the first hurdle of meeting the sufficiency of evidence test.[67] Sir Thomas Hetherington disclosed that he had personally considered 3 of the 26 deaths, presumably the most controversial cases, and that he had been fully satisfied in each case that there was no further witness that needed to be interrogated and that no further inquiries needed to be undertaken.[68] In some of the cases the papers had been referred to outside counsel whose conclusions were the same as those eventually reached by the Director.[69] Experience and statistics alike, however, confirm the fact that it is only in the very strongest of cases that a jury will convict a police officer of assault. The same pattern of a very high rate of police acquittals exists with respect to all types of indictable offences. Thus the overall acquittal rate in cases brought against police officers is 59 per cent. compared with a national rate in trials on indictment against other citizens of about 17 per cent.[70] Like it or not, juries appear to view with a high degree of scepticism the testimony of prosecution witnesses who have a criminal record or whose background casts a shadow on their degree of credibility. Another statistic which requires some explanation is the remarkably low figure of cases, involving complaints of assault by the police, in which the Director has initiated prosecution of the police officer(s) concerned. In 1979, for example, which is the last full year for which results are available, the percentage of assault cases prosecuted was slightly in excess of 2 per cent.[71] A partial explanation for this state of affairs is the demonstrated tendency on the part of chief constables, anxious to avoid public criticism that they have sought to protect their own, to send forward for the Director's consideration cases that do not have the semblance of sufficient evidence to support a prosecution.[72] Many of the circumstances involve nothing more than

---

[67] *Ante*, fn. 65, p. 31, Q. 152. To the chairman's supplementary question "So in these [26] cases of death in custody which you were considering, you do not think that the public interest criterion came into it all?" the D.P.P. answered "No, we never got to that stage" (*ibid.* p. 32).

[68] *Ibid.* p. 33, Q. 164.

[69] *Ibid.*

[70] Barnes, *op. cit.* p. 27.

[71] *Per* the D.P.P. in the course of an interview with the *Daily Telegraph*, February 15, 1982. This represents an average of 47 prosecutions out of an annual total of 2,600 assault complaints.

[72] See *Written Evidence, op. cit.* p. 54. Referring to the Police Act 1964, s.49(3) of which requires that complaints made by a member of the public have to be reported to the D.P.P. unless the chief officer is "satisfied that no criminal offence has been committed," Hetherington commented: "In practice almost every chief officer is extremely anxious to divest himself of responsibility for deciding whether one of his officers should be prosecuted, however trivial the allegation, so that there can be no suspicion of improper bias. Hence they normally report all cases involving an officer even if the evidence is virtually non-existent and regardless of whether the complaint has been made by a member of the public"—*loc. cit.*

technical assaults. Even so the perception of different standards being applied is not such that it can be dismissed and there will be a constant need to explain the Director's policies in this regard.

Adherence to the same strict standards as to the quantum of evidence necessary to justify prosecution is confirmed by the attitude of the Director of Public Prosecutions in the *Cowley Shop Stewards* case in 1966, several years before the formulation of Hetherington's "51 per cent. rule." Questions were asked in the House of Commons as to why criminal proceedings had not been brought against the stewards who had admittedly conducted a "kangaroo court" and expelled several workers for not taking part in an official strike.[73] Quintin Hogg (as he then was) had earlier accused the Attorney General of failing to prosecute for improper motives[74] and Randolph Churchill had trotted out the ghosts of the Campbell affair in 1924 as a warning of the fate that might befall the Government because of the Attorney General's decision not to prosecute.[75] Sir Elwyn Jones, the then Attorney, explained that he had been consulted by the Director but that there was insufficient evidence to justify proceeding against any identified individual.[76] Confirmation of this wholly non-political explanation for the decision became available years later when Mr. Peter Barnes in his Birmingham address, referring to circumstances that seem to match the Cowley case in 1966, stated: "We eventually managed to satisfy him that that the evidence really was insufficient but I was left with no doubt whatsoever that the Attorney General was anxious that there should be a prosecution if possible, although I had equally no doubt that such a prosecution would have been embarrassing to his Government from the political point of view."[77]

The failure to institute major prosecutions arising out of the revelations contained in the Bingham report to the alleged violations of the Rhodesia Oil Sanctions orders has already been addressed in an earlier chapter.[78] In the present context it is only necessary to remind ourselves of the explanation proferred by the Director of Public Prosecutions in defence of the decision not to launch criminal proceedings against the international companies involved in circumventing the statutory prohibitions. According to Sir Thomas Hetherington the true explanation lay in the inability of the Crown to satisfy the 51 per cent. standard.[79] The Director had sought the advice of outside counsel, Mr. Michael Sherrard Q.C., who concluded that, whatever the Bingham report may have revealed about political and economic realities, the evidence it contained would not alone justify a

---

[73] H.C. Deb., Vol. 727, Oral Answers, April 27 and May 18, 1966.
[74] *Sunday Express*, March 13, 1966.
[75] *Evening Standard*, March 16, 1966.
[76] *Ante*, fn. 73.
[77] Barnes, *op. cit.* p. 32.
[78] *Ante*, pp. 325–333.
[79] The *Sunday Times*, January 13, 1980. As illustrative of the evidentiary obstacles to a successful prosecution the Director disclosed: "We do not even have the documents to prove that oil was carried from Mozambique to Rhodesia."

prosecution.[80] An investigation in search of the necessary evidence would have taken several years, involving uncooperative witnesses who were outside the purview of the British courts' jurisdiction. Even then, in Hetherington's judgment, there was insufficient likelihood of obtaining convictions. As with other high profile cases, it is often difficult to separate convincingly the evidentiary reasons for a negative decision as to prosecution and those other public interest considerations that tend to loom large in the decision-making process.

There are, of course, numerous instances in which the go-ahead signal is given by the Director of Public Prosecutions and the outcome is a spectacular failure, when judged in the narrowest terms of a conviction against an acquittal. The *Jeremy Thorpe* case will often come to mind in this kind of comparison,[81] demonstrating as it does the unpredictability of juries or, if it is preferred, the fallibility of the judgments reached in the calm atmosphere of the Department of Public Prosecutions. Asked about the outcome of the Thorpe prosecution, Hetherington rejected any feeling of embarrassment and instead gave the verdict a sense of perspective by declaring that it would be stored away as evidence to guide his instinct when similar facts present themselves again for assessment.[82] Asked whether given another chance he might have prosecuted on different charges, Hetherington insisted that the charges of conspiracy to murder were absolutely right on the evidence before him.[83] More recently, speaking publicly on the legal dilemma concerning well-meaning doctors who deliberately accelerate the death of a patient, Sir Thomas Hetherington described as "his most difficult prosecutorial decision" the institution of a murder charge in 1981 against *Dr. Leonard Arthur*, a consultant paediatrician of unimpeachable reputation, who admitted to taking steps to hasten the death of a baby suffering from Down's syndrome.[84] The child died after only 69 hours of life. It had been rejected by its natural parents and the prosecution maintained that the accused had thought it more humane and more in keeping with informed medical opinion to let the mongoloid baby die. In consequence of the parents' rejection Dr. Arthur ordered nursing care only and prescribed the drug dihydrocodeine to relieve distress. Other effects of the drug are a suppressed appetite and impaired breathing. Evidence from other leading paediatricians confirmed that Dr. Arthur had acted within accepted medical limits. Following the

---

[80] See *ante*, pp.328–329.

[81] See also *ante*, pp. 52–57 for the respective roles played by the D.P.P. and the Attorney General in reaching the decision to proceed with the prosecution in the *Thorpe* case.

[82] The *Sunday Times*, January 13, 1980.

[83] *Daily Mirror*, November 1, 1979. In the course of the same interview Hetherington stated: "I thought there would be a conviction but I was wrong. Having decided that I thought there would be a conviction, I then had to consider whether it was in the public interest to go ahead. I had no doubt at all that it would be in the public interest. It would have been quite wrong to have covered it up. I still think I was right about that."

[84] *Daily Telegraph*, February 15, 1982. For the related contempt proceedings against the *Daily Mail*, arising out of the *Arthur* case, see *Att. Gen.* v. *English* [1982] 2 W.L.R. 959.

cross examination of the Home Office consultant pathologist, who had performed the post mortem on the child and whose findings were subsequently reversed by the same witness, the murder charge was withdrawn from the jury's consideration. The jury later acquitted the accused of the remaining charge of attempted murder. Speaking to the press several months later after the high emotions of the highly publicised trial had died down, the Director of Public Prosecutions stated that if the prosecution had known in advance of the expert medical evidence to be produced by the defence "it might have changed the whole course of the trial. We might not have charged murder in the first place." The uncertainties of the criminal law, Hetherington maintained, had left no scope in which to bring another charge other than murder.[85]

The *Bristol Riot* case, on the other hand, in retrospect appears to have been a genuine error of judgment on the part of the Director and he candidly admitted as much after the original trial which produced eight acquittals and four jury disagreements.[86] In a charge of riotous assembly, the legal requirement of establishing a common purpose among the various defendants illustrates the importance of the very first stage in the process leading a decision to prosecute. As it transpired, the fatal defect in the prosecution's case was not recognised in the initial evaluation of the evidence. The jury's verdict at the original trial demonstrated the danger of re-indicting those accused with respect to whom there had been jury disagreements. So it came as no great surprise to learn that, after consultations between the Attorney General, the Director of Public Prosecutions, Crown counsel and the chief constable of Avon and Somerset it was agreed that it was not in the public interest to proceed with a second trial of the four defendants in respect of whom the jury had failed to agree upon a verdict.[87]

---

[85] *Loc. cit.* Hetherington also issued a warning to the medical profession that, unless and until a legal solution is found to the problem of a doctor who eases the pain and suffering of a terminal patient, "if there is clear evidence that a doctor has deliberately ended the life of a baby, then because of the position of the law as it stands, we shall certainly have to consider whether the public interest requires a prosecution"—*loc. cit.* It seems likely that the D.P.P. had in mind the public statement attributed to the secretary of the British Medical Association, immediately following the acquittal in the *Arthur* case, who had stated: "I hope that the D.P.P. will now realise that it is not appropriate to bring criminal proceedings against eminent and distinguished paediatricians." There can be no doubt, however, as to the correctness of the D.P.P.'s position under the existing law, the classic statement being that of Devlin J.'s direction to the jury in the *Bodkin Adams* case: *The Times*, April 9, 1957; [1957] Crim. L.R. 365. See, too, the D.P.P.'s recent decision to authorise a charge of attempted murder of an aborted baby against the senior consultant gynaecologist of a hospital—*The Times*, July 1, 1983.

[86] Speaking on the BBC Radio 4 programme *The World This Weekend*, April 19, 1981 and reported in *The Times*, April 20, 1981. Hetherington re-affirmed the same sentiments in his extended interview with the present editor of *The Times*, May 11, 1981, emphasising the significance of the judgment expressed by the local chief constable as to the likely repercussions of a further trial being instituted.

[87] *The Times*, April 7, 1981 and see H.C. Deb., Oral Answers, April 16, 1981, p. 262.

THE BOUNDARIES OF RELEVANT PUBLIC POLICY FACTORS

We turn next to the final stage in the process leading up to the ultimate determination whether to prosecute or not. That decision, it should be emphasised, is not sufficiently explained in terms of answering "Yes" or "No" to the question of prosecution. The decision may involve a choice between the following alternative dispositions: (a) to prosecute if no charge has yet been preferred by the police or other governmental authority; (b) to proceed with any charge(s) already laid; (c) to reduce (or increase) the offence already charged; (d) to charge any other person with the offence; (e) to ask the police to make further inquiries; (f) to discontinue further police investigations in favour of the decision not to prosecute for any offence. Having decided that the evidence is sufficient to justify criminal proceedings, the Director and his senior colleagues must then go on to consider whether the provable facts and the whole of the surrounding circumstances are such that it is incumbent upon them, in the public interest, to institute a prosecution and with respect to what offence(s). This final decision is, without doubt, the most difficult of all since it involves a subjective attempt to determine what course of action will best reflect the interests of the community as a whole. No ready made yardsticks are available to solve the myriad circumstances recorded in the files submitted to the Director for his decisions. What is apt to be misleading is the impression conveyed in Sir Thomas Hetherington's written submission to the Phillips Commission and repeated in his public statements explaining how the department functions. The description of the process as an orderly sequence of cumulative judgments, each separated from the other but each requiring an affirmative resolution in order to achieve the final judgment, ignores the impact that public interest considerations are bound to make in borderline cases. Rigid adherence to the separation of the evidentiary and public interest questions is a standard incapable of fulfilment and it is unhelpful to exaggerate the exclusive nature of the separate exercises.

The boundaries of public policy factors that can properly be taken into account when making prosecutorial decisions are slowly becoming identified. This is a positive contribution towards public understanding and support for the substantial element of discretion that is involved in every such decision.[88] Several of these factors are relatively non-contentious and can be described as exculpatory or mitigating in their possible impact. Staleness of the crime will likely influence the Director's eventual decision, it being stated that there is much hesitation to prosecute if three or more

---

[88] One of the recommendations of the Royal Commission on Criminal Procedure (see *Report, op. cit.* pp. 173–175, 188) urged the preparation of a statement setting forth the appropriate criteria that should govern the decision whether or not to prosecute. Action to this end has produced a document entitled "Criteria for Prosecution" which, bearing the seal of authority of the Attorney General, has been distributed to prosecuting solicitors and police forces for their guidance—see *ante,* p. 112, fn. 27.

years have lapsed between the date of the offence and the probable date of trial.[89] The gravity of the offence will naturally diminish the significance of the element of staleness and the same applies if the complexity of the case explains the prolonged police enquiries. A similar response will likely occur if the accused has contributed to the staleness by disappearing or covering his tracks. Lack of diligence on the part of the police, on the other hand, will tend to enhance the relevance of the time interval.[90]

The youthfulness or advanced age of the accused will have to be taken into consideration in appropriate cases. In sexual cases, for example, high regard for the respective ages of the persons involved is generally regarded as a proper balancing of the values at stake. The consenting nature of the victim's participation and the issue of corruption will also bear heavily on the way in which discretion is exercised.[91] In other cases, the younger the offender the greater must be the inclination to examine alternative possibilities such as a caution if the accused has no previous blemishes and, in addition, has a good home background and employment record. Against these positive qualities must be set the seriousness of the crime and the extent to which it has aroused public concern. With respect to a defendant who is of advanced age there must always be concern as to whether he is likely to be fit enough to stand trial. Apart from such a practical matter, there is general reluctance to prosecute anyone who has passed his seventieth birthday and is infirm, unless there is a real possibility that the offence will be repeated or, of course, that the offence is of such a grave character that a prosecution cannot be avoided.[92]

Caution is called for when the mental condition of the accused is brought into the discussions preceding the decision to prosecute.[93] Its relevance during court proceedings is unquestioned and the court has broad powers to authorise psychiatric examinations if called for in the particular case. No one can doubt either the importance of evidence of mental illness to the issue of criminal responsibility. What we are presently concerned with is the possible impact that evidence of mental instability should have in avoiding the subjection of the accused to a criminal trial. The initiative in this regard will usually come from the defendant's solicitor who may point to the dangers of a permanent worsening of his client's condition if the prosecution goes ahead. The possible spurious nature of any such claim can be met in part by ensuring an independent examination of the defendant's mental condition. The healthy scepticism that prevails in the Director's office in such matters is perhaps best captured in the view expressed by Mr. Peter Barnes that: "On the one hand it is somewhat distasteful to

---

[89] See the D.P.P.'s *Written Evidence, op. cit.* p. 38 and Barnes, *op. cit.* p. 29.

[90] *Ibid.* The same reaction is to be expected if there has been dilatoriness "on the part of those who have some sort of moral responsibility for reporting the matter to the police in the first place."

[91] *Written Evidence, op. cit.* pp. 38, 40–41, and Barnes *op. cit.* pp. 29–30.

[92] *Written Evidence, op. cit.* p. 39 and Barnes, *op. cit.* p. 29.

[93] *Written Evidence, op. cit.* pp. 39–40.

prosecute someone who is mentally subnormal but on the other hand that very subnormality or abnormality may itself increase the risk of an offence being repeated and so it may be necessary for us to prosecute in the hope that this may result in some form of effective treatment."[94]

Perjury is an offence that the public might be forgiven for believing that it has become as much of a dead letter crime as, say, bigamy. In his evidence to the Royal Commission on Criminal Procedure, the Director of Public Prosecutions acknowledged that experience has shown that the modern tendency is for the judges to impose no more than a nominal penalty in cases of bigamy unless there are exceptional or aggravated circumstances. Faced with this reality very few prosecutions for bigamy are nowadays approved, the normal advice being to issue a caution against any repetition of the offence.[95] With perjury, on the other hand, a far more serious view is taken of the crime and it is pertinent to note the principles that guide the Director in his approach to such cases.[96] A clear distinction is drawn between alleged perjury by a witness and that sought to be laid at the door of the accused. In the case of the former, assuming there is sufficient corroboration as required by the Perjury Act 1911 and a reasonable prospect of a conviction, the Director's office will sanction a prosecution if the perjured evidence goes to the heart of the issue before the original trial. On the contrary, should the evidence, whilst technically in breach of the Act, relate to a peripheral issue and the intent of the witness is more to protect his own skin than to prevent the course of justice, then it is most likely that a prosecution will be approved.

The position of a defendant who commits perjury is seen in a different light, especially if his effort is unsuccessful and a conviction has been registered in the case. In these circumstances, the Director's submission to the Commission stated: " . . . it is necessary to have regard to the punishment inflicted by the court and to assess whether a subsequent prosecution for perjury would be likely to result in any substantial increase of the sentence. It is also essential that the evidence should be so exceptionally strong that a conviction is virtually certain, because of the doubts which an acquittal would cast upon the verdict of guilty in the original case. Usually, although not necessarily, it is the emergence of some additional and compelling evidence, after the original trial, which removes the last trace of doubt. Even, however, where there is abundant evidence against a defendant who has unsuccessfully lied without involving others, I would not normally think it right to prosecute unless there are aggravating factors."[97] The imperative obligation to balance subordinate considerations one against the other is well illustrated in the further observation that the Director's office "will consider whether the lies

[94] Barnes, *op. cit.* p. 30.
[95] *Written Evidence, op. cit.* p. 43.
[96] *Ibid.* pp. 41–42.
[97] *Ibid.* p. 42, paras. 121–122.

necessary involved an attack on the truthfulness (as opposed to recollection or ability to identify) of one or more prosecution witnesses; whether the lie was clearly planned before the hearing or arose on the spur of the moment during cross-examination; and the degree of persistence in maintaining the lie."[98]

This kind of analysis of the conflicting considerations that must be taken into account when contemplating possible proceedings for perjury highlights the impracticality of ever laying down hard and fast rules that will confer a high degree of predictability as to the result of their application. The very nature of discretionary authority requires resistance to any attempt to develop rigid rules that cannot encompass every possible contingency. Take another factor, that of public expense in maintaining a long drawn out trial. Any suggestion of imposing upon the police or the Director of Public Prosecutions a predetermined ceiling as to the costs that can be incurred in connection with different categories of prosecutions would be abhorrent to the principles of justice and law enforcement. At the same time, lack of any restraint in the face of predictable major expenditures in bringing accused persons to trial would likewise be regarded as irresponsible. Hence the careful balancing of costs against the purposes to be achieved through prosecution that must occupy the minds of the decision-makers in the office of Public Prosecutions when the magnitude of the bill to be paid out of the public purse cannot be ignored.[99]

As one illustration of this unusual factor reference can be made to the crop of potential defendants enmeshed in the *Poulson* affair.[1] By mid-1974 the list of candidates for investigation and possible prosecution for corruption numbered around 300, most of whom were individuals in subordinate positions whose involvement was relatively trivial. In the event only the leading figures in the conspiracy were brought to trial. Commenting on the decision to single out the principal conspirators in this fashion, Sir Thomas Hetherington has stated; "It is not necessarily in the public interest to prosecute every minnow connected with an offence, provided the whales are tried . . . In the Poulson case . . . after the prosecution of John Poulson, Dan Smith, George Cunningham and other public servants there were still a number of leads which had not been investigated fully . . . They were retired, old, and a lot more money would have to be spent. Was it really in the public interest to go ahead?"[2] The Director of Public Prosecutions has frequently found himself the target of public criticism as a result of his authorising prosecutions that have involved enormous public costs and resulted in the acquittal of the accused. The implication, whether intended by the critics or not, is that it is

[98] *Ibid.* p. 42, para. 123.
[99] Barnes, *op. cit.* p. 30. The D.P.P. made no reference to the public expense factor in his written submission to the Royal Commission.
[1] See *ante*, pp. 81–85.
[2] *The Times*, May 11, 1981.

acceptable to proceed if convictions are obtained, otherwise the ends do not justify the costs incurred. This is asking the impossible of the Director of Public Prosecutions and it is doubtful if there has been any serious criticism of the Director's judgment by those whose responsibility it is in government to guard against the extravagant use of public money.

Another amorphous factor that is difficult to pin down relates to the attitude of those who, directly or indirectly, can be said to have a special stake in the outcome of a prosecution. Mention has already been made of the indefinable relationship that occurs between the professional officers who have been in charge of the case up to the point where the papers are transmitted to the Director for decision. The imperceptible pressures engendered by this relationship cannot be dismissed, a senior member of the Director's office going so far as to acknowledge the Department is reluctant to turn around a police decision to charge, unless the evidence is totally without substance.[3] If there is some evidence to support the original police charge the tendency is to let the court make the decision not to commit for trial by soft-pedalling the evidence in support of the charge. The attitude of victims and complainants may not exert as powerful an influence, there always being the possibility that the accusation was made in the heat of the moment or as the last straw in a relationship that has been simmering in intensity for some time. A change of heart on the part of the complainant, be it a person (in a case of assault) or a company (in a case of fraud) will be assessed in the light of the seriousness of the offence and the harm inflicted, as well as exploring any suspicion that the withdrawal was actuated by fear.[4] Then there is the current mood of the local community, which may have given expression to its concerns as to the prevalence of the offence in its area, or as in the *Bristol Riot* case where the views expressed by the chief constable of Avon and Somerset as to the detrimental effects which a new trial would have on racial harmony in the city appears to have been a powerful factor in persuading the Attorney General and the Director not to pursue charges against the remaining four defendants.[5]

There remains the sensitive aspect of the position occupied in society by the defendant, and his or her previous character. At times, it may be difficult to separate these variables and it may even be more of a challenge to demonstrate that equality before the law has been adhered to in the decision to prosecute or not to prosecute, as the case may be. The circumstances surrounding the handling of the prosecution of *Jeremy Thorpe*, and in particular the transfer by the Attorney General to the Director of Public Prosecutions of responsibility for making the decision in that case, have already been examined in detail in this work.[6] Apropos our

---

[3] *Per* the Deputy Director of Public Prosecutions in the course of my talk with him in his office on July 7, 1980; and see, too, Barnes, *op. cit.* pp. 25–26, expressing much the same views in relation to circumstances where the Director's consent is a pre-requisite to launching a prosecution.

[4] *Written Evidence, op. cit.* p. 43.

[5] *Ante*, p. 422.

[6] *Ante*, pp. 52–57.

present concern, it can readily be imagined that Sir Thomas Hetherington was acutely conscious of the public position occupied by the suspect, and at the same time sensitive to the enormity of the charge of conspiracy to murder and the penalty for such a crime. Questioned by *The Times* representatives in the course of a wide ranging interview on the Director's handling of prominent cases during his tenure of office, Hetherington was asked what his response would have been if Mr. Silkin had instructed him not to prosecute Jeremy Thorpe. The Attorney's instruction, the Director replied, would have been "most unconstitutional."[7] In the event of his proving unsuccessful in persuading the Attorney to change such a hypothetical ruling, Hetherington declared that he would probably have resigned. "It was so basic," he said, "that I wouldn't have been able to carry out my duties thereafter."[8]

The position of the Director becomes more vulnerable where he decides against prosecuting and the proposed charge involves a prominent public figure. Allegations of bias and of protecting "the Establishment" will surface quickly in this kind of situation, presenting the Director and the Attorney General with the choice of riding the storm in silence or responding quickly in a way that is calculated to dispel uninformed criticism. A case in point was that involving *Sir Peter Hayman*, formerly this country's High Commissioner in Canada.[9] In 1978 a packet containing obscene literature and other written material was found in a London bus. The subsequent police investigation revealed the existence of correspondence of an obscene nature, involving young children, between Hayman and a number of other persons. Altogether a total of seven men and two women were named in the report submitted by the Metropolitan London Police to the Director of Public Prosecutions, as possible defendants to charges under section 11 of the Post Office Act 1953. A further report revealed that one of the nine men, not Sir Peter Hayman, was also carrying on correspondence with another person which indicated that the two shared an obsession about the systematic killing by sexual torture of young people and children. In view of the extreme nature of this latter material the Director decided to prosecute them for conspiring to contravene the 1953 Act.

There was no evidence that Hayman had ever sent or received material of this kind through the post. Simultaneously with these inquiries, the police investigation into the activities of the "Paedophilic Information Exchange" resulted in a separate trial for conspiracy to corrupt public morals, the defendants being involved in the management or organisation of the body concerned. Hayman did not fall within this group. With respect to the original group of nine persons, which did include Sir Peter Hayman,

[7] *The Times*, May 11, 1981.
[8] *Ibid.*
[9] The facts set out in the text above are based on the Attorney General's statement, H.C. Deb., Vol. 1(6s.) Written Answers, cols. 139–140, March 19, 1981.

the Director advised against the bringing of criminal proceedings,[10] the principal factors being stated to be, first, that the correspondence had been contained in sealed envelopes passing between adult individuals in a non-commercial context and, secondly, none of the material was unsolicited. The Attorney General defended the Director's decision in a full statement to the Commons, saying that he was in agreement with the decision.[11] Previously, before Hayman's name was disclosed to the Commons by a Labour back-bencher, the Attorney General had appealed to the Member of Parliament concerned to spare Sir Peter and his family public humiliation in naming him when the decision had been taken not to prosecute Hayman or any of the potential defendants.[12] Subsequently, the Director explained that the public position occupied by Hayman had had nothing to do with his decision. It had been dictated by the fact that the spirit of the Post Office Act offence had not been infringed, given that it is no offence to possess indecent material and the recipients had not been unwilling victims of the obscene literature in the sense of being shocked and disgusted by the contents.[13]

DECISIONS NOT TO INSTITUTE PROCEEDINGS—THE NEED FOR RESTRAINT IN PUBLIC EXPLANATIONS

This kind of explanation, in such detail, has come to be expected from the present Director. It should be noted, however, that there is a general reluctance to elaborate on the particular considerations that led to a decision *not* to institute proceedings in specific cases. Such reluctance is explained on two grounds. First, whilst it is reasonably safe to expound in abstract terms on the kind of discretionary factors, reviewed in this chapter, which enter into the decision-making process, there is a marked

[10] For conflicting views on the merits of the D.P.P.'s decision see *The Times*, March 26, 1981 and Sir David Napley's statement to the press, *ibid.* March 20, 1981 and his letter to the editor, *ibid.* March 27, 1981. Napley was the defending solicitor in the case.

[11] *Ante*, fn. 9.

[12] *The Times*, March 18, 1981.

[13] *The Times*, May 11, 1981. Elaborating on the reasoning that lay behind his decision not to prosecute Hayman, the D.P.P. stated: "It would be quite wrong of me to say that Parliament should have repealed the Act and it hasn't, and therefore I am never going to prosecute anyone for sending obscene literature through the post. It is for Parliament to decide whether an offence should be on the statute book, but it is part of the constitution law that I have a discretion to prosecute. Parliament is really saying: 'This is the offence. We haven't abolished it but we leave it to you, director, or to the police, to decide whether, in the individual circumstances, it requires prosecution'. Sending indecent material through the post, bearing in mind that it is no offence to possess indecent material, is not the sort of offence that affects members of the public. The only people who can be affected by it are the postmen, if it is written on the outside of the packet, which it wasn't, or the unwilling recipient, who is shocked and disgusted, which wasn't the case. And therefore the spirit of the statute was not infringed and that is why we didn't prosecute." It is impossible to estimate whether Hetherington's explanation, fortified by the Attorney General's view that the right decision was reached, has succeeded in dissipating public suspicions of the kind exemplified in a feature article "Pain, Anguish and the DPP" in the *Sunday Times*, March 22, 1981. For an analysis of the current law, the enforcement policies of the Post Office and recent proposals for reform, see Colin Manchester, "Obscenity in the Mail" [1983] Crim.L.R. 64.

resistance to disclosing publicly the specific in-house policies that have been developed to guide the professional staff in their approach to certain kinds of offences. The explanation for this resistance, departed from so visibly in the Peter Hayman situation, is that "it would not be in the public interest to risk it becoming known that certain offences of medium or minor importance can in fact be committed with relative impunity."[14] This remark, on the part of the present Deputy Director, contains more than a hint of exaggeration in its basic assumption that the incidence of criminal activity is directly related to the level of prosecutorial activity. The fundamental questions implicit in this assumption have been addressed in the parallel context of law enforcement activity with little evidence to support the proposition that a strong statistical nexus exists between levels of police action and the levels of criminal activity.[15] This conclusion, it is acknowledged, does not control the public's perception of how the criminal justice system functions and it is these perceptions that principally influence individual behaviour.

As for the other ground on which the Director and his colleagues studiously maintain a veil of silence in relation to specific cases, the explanation is principally dictated by the ethics of the Director's relationship to the police, the undisclosed witnesses and the defendant himself. Pressed by the Select Committee on Deaths in Police Custody to go beyond the Department's customary resort to explaining its decision in terms of the insufficiency of the evidence, Sir Thomas Hetherington drew no distinction between police complaint cases and other cases.[16] To make public the grounds on which the evidence was judged to be insufficient to secure the likelihood of a conviction would, in the first place, breach the confidentiality of police reports and statements taken by the police from potential witnesses. Disclosure of the reasons for not believing prospective witnesses might require revealing the criminal record of those witnesses. The same reasons would apply to making public details about the defendant with the result that there would be a public "trial" of the potential defendant without his or her having all the safeguards that are an integral part of a criminal trial in open court. Much as a very substantial body of public opinion might savour the opportunity to engage vicariously in this kind of trial by the media, the Director's adherence to the contrary principles favouring non-disclosure is to be preferred. This choice is not as easy to make as might sometimes be supposed, and the present Director has confessed to the frustration that he has experienced in the more emotive cases, such as *Blair Peach* and *James Kelly*, in not being able, because of the principle of confidentiality, to answer publicly the bombardment of criticism to which he and his Department have been subjected.[17]

[14] Barnes, *op. cit.* p. 30.
[15] See *post*, p. 446, fn. 15.
[16] *Ante*, fn. 47, at pp. 34–35.
[17] The *Sunday Times*, January 13, 1980.

In its Report the Select Committee recommended that the Director of Public Prosecutions should make it his normal practice to supply a complainant with at least a summary of the considerations which led him to decide against prosecution.[18] It also proposed that the police investigation report be made available to the legal representatives of the deceased when appearing at the ensuing coroner's inquest.[19] Both recommendations were rejected by the Director, a decision supported by the Attorney General, for the same grounds as those explained to the Select Committee as governing established practice.[20] That indefinable concept, the public interest, might in exceptional circumstances deem it sufficiently imperative to enforce full public disclosure but it would have to be done after the most careful balancing of the conflicting principles at stake, and with the necessity of requiring the Attorney General to defend before the House of Commons a decision that runs counter to the general practice faithfully observed by the Director of Public Prosecutions.

PUBLIC DISCLOSURE OF PROSECUTION GUIDELINES

Most of what has been written in this chapter will have equal application whatever the jurisdiction in which the decision to prosecute or not to prosecute has to be made. There are growing signs too of a disposition to follow the example set by Edward H. Levi, an outstanding Attorney General of the United States who, during his term of office in 1977, embarked on a programme of formulating the principles upon which prosecution decisions should be made. In his prefatory note to the document setting forth such principles[21] Attorney General Levi stressed that the materials being circulated were not to be construed as Department of Justice "guidelines" and that they imposed no obligations on United States Attorneys, their Assistants, or other attorneys acting on behalf of the United States Government.[22] Ascribing the most modest of objectives to this pioneering initiative Mr. Levi said that it was intended solely for use by government attorneys to the extent that the principles were found to be appropriate in discharging their responsibilities as federal prosecutors.[23] The Attorney General's "materials" covered such topics as the decision to prosecute, the election of charges, plea negotiations and, a procedural feature that is peculiar to United States law, opposition to *nolo contendere* pleas.[24] Not surprisingly, there is much common ground between the

[18] H.C. Paper 631 of 1980, pp. 30–40.
[19] *Ibid.* p. xiv.
[20] H.C. Deb., Written Answers, Vol. 993, cols. 150–153, November 11, 1980.
[21] "U.S. Department of Justice Materials Relating to Prosecutorial Discretion" (1978) 22 *The Criminal Law Reporter*—see Text Section, pp. 3001–3008.
[22] *Ibid.* p. 3001.
[23] *Ibid.*
[24] *Ibid.* pp. 3005–3006. See also *Federal Rules of Criminal Procedure*, Rule 11(a) and (b) and *American Bar Association Standards Relating to the Administration of Criminal Justice*, Vol. 18, 1974, "Pleas of Guilty", pp. 299–308.

relevant factors that are said to guide the Director of Public Prosecutions in England and Wales, and those expressed in the Levi documents as the advisable guideposts within the federal criminal justice system of the United States. In Australia, the impact of the Levi statement of principles has been immediate, the Attorney General of the Commonwealth of Australia breaking new ground in bringing together in a public document the guidelines that will govern the actions of all counsel and Crown solicitors whose authority derives from the senior Law Officer of the Crown and who are engaged in the prosecution of Commonwealth offences. The policy paper containing the guidelines and considerations upon which prosecutorial decisions are to be made within the federal sphere of jurisdiction was tabled in the Australian Senate in December 1982.[25] Included within this precedent-setting statement is a reaffirmation of the "Shawcross doctrine" as a fundamental tenet that must govern the Attorney General's personal involvement in prosecution decision making.[26] Added to which the document contains the necessary reminder that this philosophy was accepted by the Government in the speech made by Prime Minister Fraser on the occasion of the Endicott resignation debate in September 1977.[27] None of these prosecution blueprints is in the nature of hard and fast rules. Within any such sets of guidelines, including those issued by the Attorney General of England and Wales on the effects of jury vetting and disclosure, and now the criteria for prosecution,[28] there is a considerable measure of discretion as to how the relevant standards are to be applied in the particular circumstances.[29]

[25] *Prosecution Policy of the Commonwealth*, tabled in the Australian Senate on December 16, 1982 on behalf of the Commonwealth Attorney General, Senator Peter Durack Q.C. Among the subjects covered are (i) who may institute and conduct Commonwealth prosecutions, (ii) the decision to prosecute and police involvement, (iii) private prosecutions and stays of proceedings, (iv) no bill applications, (v) granting of indemnities or pardons to witnesses, (vi) plea negotiations, (vii) special prosecutors. So far as I am aware, no comparable statement exists in any of the States of Australia, each of which has its own body of criminal law and procedure. Adherence to the principles set forth in the Commonwealth policy statement is explicitly acknowledged by the Attorney General (Senator Gareth Evans) in the detailed opinion prepared for the Prime Minister with respect to the *Mick Young* case—see *ante*, p. 371, fn. 64.

[26] *Ibid.* p. 9.

[27] *Ibid.* and see *ante*, pp. 384–385.

[28] On the subject of prosecution guidelines see *ante*, p. 423, fn. 88 and on the issues of jury vetting and disclosure to the defence see *post*, Chapter 14, pp. 476–490.

[29] Despite the disclaimer by former Attorney General Levi that his expansive treatment of the various items included in the Justice Department's memorandum was nothing more than "suggestions," it is noticeable that each principle is accompanied by detailed comments as to the meaning that is intended to be attached to the several propositions. Moreover, the language used in the comments have the distinct ring of departmental expectations that the policies enunciated in the document will be either followed strictly or an explanation provided for any departure from the existing departmental policies. The same level of expectation runs through the growing number of policy directives issued by the Attorney General of Ontario, referred to *ante*, p. 406, fn. 14. For the arguments in favour of seeking Parliamentary approval of prosecution guidelines, see the note by Francis Bennion in (1981) 125 S.J. 534.

This discretion, moreover, attaches to each of the documents that have
been referred to, irrespective of whether they are described as "guidelines" or "appropriate considerations that are not to be regarded as
departmental requirements," and whether they emanate from the office of
the Attorney General in London, Canberra, Toronto or Washington. They
do not, it is true, carry the force of a "practice direction" similar to those
issued from time to time by the Lord Chief Justice after consultation with
the Judges of the Queen's Bench and Family Divisions. These latter
statements of practice have the same binding force as all other rules of
procedure that derive their statutory authority from the Supreme Court of
Judicature Acts.[30] Nevertheless, since the Prosecution of Offences Act
1879, section 2 ordains that the Attorney General is the Minister
responsible for the actions of the Director of Public Prosecutions and can
issue directives to his subordinate official with respect to any of his
functions, it cannot be doubted that there exists a secure statutory basis for
the Attorney General's emerging forays into the setting of guidelines
concerned with subjects that lie within the Law Officers' prerogative
authority. In this respect, the approach favoured by the Attorney General
of the United States in expressly disclaiming any mandatory component for
the guidance afforded to the United States Attorneys would be a highly
inappropriate parallel to use in describing the modest incursions of the
English Attorney General into the same field. At the same time it is
interesting to note that, as the federal Minister of Justice in charge of the
United States Department of Justice, Attorney General Levi attached no
qualifications to the series of formal guidelines that he imposed upon the
Federal Bureau of Investigation when executing his policy of bringing that
agency back into the fold of ministerial control and accountability.[31] This
fascinating exercise must regrettably be left to others to recount,[32] as we

[30] See Supreme Court of Judicature (Consolidation) Act 1925, (c.49), s.99.
[31] For authoritative descriptions of the legacy of F.B.I. abuses left by its founder J. Edgar
Hoover at his death in 1972 see United States House of Representatives, Committee on the
Judiciary, Subcommittee on Civil and Constitutional Rights, *Hearings: FBI Oversight*, Serial
No. 2, Parts 1–3, 94th Congress, 1st and 2nd session, 1975–76; and United States Senate,
Select Committee to Study Governmental Operations with respect to Intelligence Activities,
Hearings, Vols. 2–6, 94th Congress, 1st sess. 1975, and *Final Report*, Books I–IV, 94th Cong,
2nd sess. 1976.
[32] The best informed and succinct account of this exercise is contained in John T. Elliff's
The Reform of the F.B.I. Intelligence Operations, (Princeton, 1979), see especially pp. 37–76.
Among the guidelines promulgated by Attorney General Levi during his tenure of office were
those relating to (1) F.B.I. Domestic Security Investigations (released March 10, 1976), (2)
Reporting on Civil Disorders and Demonstrations involving a Federal Interest (released
March 10, 1976) and (3) White House Personnel Security and Background Investigations
(ditto) and (4) Informants in Domestic Security, Organised Crime and Other Criminal
Investigations (released December 15, 1976). These guidelines are conveniently reprinted in
Elliff, *op. cit.* Appendices 1 to 4. The machinery for preparing the guidelines, in which the
F.B.I. under its new Director, Clarence M. Kelly, took a fully cooperative part, is described
by the same author, *op. cit.* pp. 58–61. Levi had made a commitment to prepare new
guidelines for the F.B.I. during his confirmation hearings before the Senate but had not
completed the task by the time he left office following a change in the office of United States
President—*ibid.* pp. 55 and 60.

move on to describe the substantial restriction on the powers of the Attorney General for England and Wales, and by derivation those of the Director of Public Prosecutions, in the matter of preferring an indictment without prior resort to a preliminary hearing. This powerful discretionary jurisdiction, frequently exercised in such Commonwealth countries as Canada, New Zealand, and Australia is not available to the English Attorney General. At least, not in relation to his functions in England and Wales. On assuming the duties of Attorney General for Northern Ireland, however, the same Law Officer inherited the power of presenting a direct Bill of indictment in the Northern Ireland courts, a power created by the Stormont Parliament when it abolished the grand jury.[32a]

PREFERRING BILLS OF INDICTMENT—BRITISH AND COMMONWEALTH DIFFERENCES

Prior to 1933 the Attorney General or the Solicitor General exercised concurrent jurisdiction with a judge of the High Court in sanctioning the presentation of a voluntary bill of indictment by a private citizen. These restrictions on private accusations were introduced by the Vexatious Indictments Act 1859[33] to counter the abuse and hardship incurred by those accused of crimes who had no right to appear before or to be heard by the grand jury before it decided whether or not to return a true bill. Proceedings to determine whether leave should be granted,[34] by one of the Law Officers[35] or by a High Court judge, was always *ex parte*[36] and the grand jury's subsequent involvement of returning a true bill became a mere formality. Under the provisions of the Administration of Justice (Miscellaneous Provisions) Act 1933[37] the grand jury was recognised as a useless anachronism and abolished.[38] At the same time the discretionary power of the Attorney General and the Solicitor General to authorise the presentation of a bill of indictment, that would effectively by-pass the

---

[32a] See Grand Jury (Abolition) Act (N.I.) 1969, c.15, s.2. I am indebted to Mr. David Haggan of the Law Officers' Department for drawing my attention to this unique feature of Northern Ireland statute law pertaining to the powers of the Att. Gen. for Northern Ireland.

[33] 22 & 23 Vict. c.17, s.1. The restrictions extended to the following offences only: perjury, subornation of perjury, conspiracy, false pretences, keeping a gaming or disorderly house, indecent assault.

[34] An indictment could also be preferred "by the direction" of the same authority.

[35] Both of the Law Officers were named in the legislation thus conferring equal authority to act in their own right. No instance is on record, however, paralleling the extraordinary events in Australia in the *Mercantile Bank* case in 1893—see *ante*, pp. 372–379.

[36] The earlier background to the *ex parte* procedure resorted to in such cases was examined in considerable detail by the Court of Appeal in *R.* v. *Raymond* [1981] 3 W.L.R. 660 at pp. 665–667. Despite subsequent legislation, repealing the 1859 statute, and the introduction of new rules of procedure the court unanimously held that the defendant was not entitled to be heard in person before leave is granted to prefer a bill of indictment. For the transformation in the practice of hearing the parties concerned, prior to the Attorney General's issuance of a *nolle prosequi*, see Edwards, *op. cit.* pp. 229, 236.

[37] 23 & 24 Geo. 5, c. 36.

[38] *Ibid.* s.1.

procedure of a preliminary inquiry before examining justices, was likewise terminated.[39]

The avenues remaining to a prosecutor in England and Wales who seeks to bring an accused person to trial by indictment are two-fold. The first, and most regularly followed, is by way of committal to the Crown Court following either the taking of depositions as part of the preliminary hearing or by resort to the accelerated procedure which, since the coming into force of the Criminal Justice Act 1967, s.1,[40] allows a committal, in given circumstances, without consideration of the evidence. Briefly, the circumstances require that all the evidence be in the form of written statements or exhibits and that no objection is voiced by the defendant or his lawyer that there is insufficient evidence to put the defendant to trial by jury for the offence(s) charged.[41] What have come to be known as "section 1 committals" cannot be resorted to if the defendant is not legally represented.[42] The second avenue open to a prosecutor is to circumvent the committal procedure altogether by way of seeking the leave of a High Court judge *ex parte* in accordance with the provisions contained in section 2(2) of the Administration of Justice (Miscellaneous Provisions) Act 1933 which states: " . . . no bill of indictment charging any person with an indictable offence shall be preferred unless either—(a) the person charged has been committed for trial for the offence; or (b) the bill is preferred . . . by the direction or with the consent of a judge of the High Court or pursuant to an order made under section 9 of the Perjury Act 1911."[43] These powers merely replicate the jurisdiction originally conferred on the High Court under the terms of the Vexatious Indictments Act 1859.[44] It is this procedure which the Director of Public Prosecutions, like any other private prosecutor, has to invoke when faced with unexpected obstacles that arise in the course of seeking a normal committal by the examining justices.

A prolonged preliminary hearing, for example, with little prospect of an expedited committal, may prompt drastic action by the Director as occurred in the *Terence May* case in 1981 when 15 black youths were charged with a variety of offences including murder, affray, and riotous assembly following the death of a motor cyclist in South London.[45] The

[39] *Ibid.* s.2(7).
[40] c.80. Such statistical evidence as is available points to the virtual supplanting of the conventional preliminary hearing (under the Magistrates Courts Act 1952, s.7) by the expedited committal procedures (under section 1 of the 1967 Act)—see the Report of the Royal Commission on Criminal Procedure, p. 70. For the further recommendations of the Commission see *ibid.* pp. 181–183.
[41] *Ibid.* s.1(1)(*b*).
[42] *Ibid.* s.1(1)(*a*).
[43] 24 & 24 Geo. 5, c.36.
[44] See *ante*, p. 434. There is no longer any restriction on the list of indictable offences with respect to which the procedure of preferring a bill of indictment applies.
[45] *The Times*, October 23 & 24, 1981 and November 7, 1981. The D.P.P.'s action was prompted by a request from the chairman of the Croydon magistrates' court that committal be sought by way of a voluntary bill of indictment. This move was explained by the magistrates' "profound concern at the lack of progress." Leave to prefer a bill of indictment was granted

conduct of several counsel representing the defendants at the committal hearing was the subject of a formal complaint made by the Attorney General to the Professional Conduct Committee of the Bar Council, a step that was later repeated at the conclusion of the actual trial.[46] In another recent situation, involving the unexplained death of *Barry Prosser*, an inmate of Winson Green Prison, Birmingham, and a second refusal of the examining magistrate to commit the three accused prison officers to trial because of the insufficiency of the evidence presented by the Crown, the Director of Public Prosecutions changed his mind after first stating that the case was closed.[47] After consultations with the Attorney General, *ex parte* proceedings were begun that resulted in the Director obtaining leave from Stephen Brown J., for the presentation of a direct indictment against the prison officers concerned.[48] At the subsequent trial in Leicester Crown Court all three accused were acquitted of murder.[49] In yet another case, *R. v. Raymond*,[50] that eventually found its way before the Criminal Division of the Court of Appeal, it was said that the defendant "gave such unmistakable indications of an intention seriously to disrupt the committal proceedings as to make a mockery of them"[51] that counsel for the Crown decided to abandon them and sought leave to prefer a bill of indictment from a High Court judge. The principal ground of the appeal against conviction of the accused for theft of more than £2 million worth of currency from the storerooms of Heathrow Airport was the failure of the judge, hearing the *ex parte* application, to afford the appellant an opportunity to be heard if he wished to do so. After carefully reviewing the entire history of preferring bills of indictment, Watkins L.J., speaking for the court, rejected the argument that the 1933 Act had conferred any such

---

by Michael Davies J., on the basis that "there was no prospect of committal proceedings, if they continued, being completed within a reasonable or tolerable time. Any trial by jury would thus be delayed for an excessive and unacceptable period." Sitting as the presiding judge at the Central Criminal Court, Lawson J., refused to disturb the decision to grant the bill, stating that he was only empowered to quash the bill if there had been an excess of jurisdiction in making the original decision. No such grounds had been established before him. Verdicts of guilty were subsequently returned against the 10 accused charged with various offences ranging from riot to manslaughter that arose from the stabbing to death of Terence May, a crippled teenager—*The Times*, April 16, 1982.

[46] *The Times*, October 23, 1981 and see also *The Times*, April 15 and 16, 1982. Following a three-day hearing by a disciplinary tribunal of the Bar Council, presided over by Staughton J., Mr. Narayan, the Secretary of the Society of Black Lawyers, was found not guilty of professional misconduct when he issued a press statement accusing the Attorney General and D.P.P. of being "corrupt, incompetent and an unholy alliance with the National Front." The defendant claimed that he had issued the statement not as a barrister but in his capacity as chairman of an organisation called "Black Rights U.K." *The Times*, April 9, 1983. The tribunal issued a formal reprimand with respect to charges of abusing the D.P.P.'s staff during a murder trial at the Old Bailey and ordered that Mr. Narayan be suspended for 6 weeks on the other charges of professional misconduct. *The Times*, June 25, 1983.

[47] *The Times*, October 2, 1981.

[48] *The Times*, October 24, 1981.

[49] *The Times*, March 1, 17 and 20, 1982.

[50] [1981] 3 W.L.R. 660.

[51] *Ibid.* at p. 664.

rights[52] or that the elimination of the roles formerly associated with the Attorney General and Solicitor General was an indication that the executive element was dispensed with leaving only procedures in which the High Court was required to conform to the *audi alteram partem* rule.[53] In his concluding remarks Watkins L.J. said: "There can be no doubt that the defendant is becoming, if he has not already become, a practised disturber of court proceedings. In agreeing to receive and consider the written representations made by his solicitor on the defendant's behalf, Michael Davies J., probably paid him much more regard than he ever deserved."[54]

By English standards, the legislation of many Commonwealth countries confers extraordinary authority upon the Attorney General and his agents who are empowered to prefer an indictment irrespective of whether a preliminary inquiry has or has not been held or that such an inquiry has resulted in the accused being discharged.[55] There is, for example under the Canadian Criminal Code, the parallel procedure whereby a private individual can seek leave to prefer a direct indictment by order of a judge of a provincial Supreme Court, or in certain limited circumstances a county or district court judge sitting as a court of criminal jurisdiction, or from the Attorney General.[56] In some circumstances the Attorney General may elect to proceed by way of seeking leave from the court,[57] notwithstanding

---

[52] *Ibid.* at p. 665. Speaking of the 1933 legislation, the court (*coram* Watkins L.J., Boreham & Hodgson JJ.) stated: "The Act merely did away with a virtually useless anachronism, the grand jury, and with the powers of the Attorney-General and Solicitor-General. It perpetuated the other existing procedures along with the existing powers of a High Court judge and justices. We reject the submission that the Act of 1933 did not have this effect, and disagree with the proposition that a precise effect of it was to substitute the High Court judge for the grand jury. The powers of a High Court judge, be it noted, find identical expression in the Acts of 1859 and 1933." Parliament, it was inferred, must have been aware that prior to the Act of 1933 High Court judges had been using their powers under the Act of 1859 by a procedure which was exclusively *ex parte*. According to the Court of Appeal the Indictments (Procedure) Rules 1971 (S.I. 1971 No. 2084/L.51), enacted under the Lord Chancellor's rule-making power (1933 Act, s.2(6)), must be taken as a determination to perpetuate the *ex parte* procedure which had been in effect since 1859. The Rules contained no reference to the defendant and expressly conferred judicial power to act without requiring the attendance before the High Court judge of the applicant, counsel or any witnesses (*ibid.* rule 10).

[53] *Ibid.* at p. 667.

[54] *Ibid.* at p. 672.

[55] Criminal Code R.S.C. 1970, c.C–34, ss.505(4) and 507(3). For the historical background to these provisions see esp. *R.* v. *Harrison* (1975) 33 C.R.N.S. 62 *per* Henry J. The original provisions in the Criminal Code of 1892, s.641(2) and (3) were derived from the English Draft Code of 1879, s.505, as to which Stephen wrote (*H.C.L.* i. 293–294): "The Criminal Code Commissioners of 1878–9 recommended that this Act [the Vexatious Indictments Act, 1859] should be applied to all indictments whatever, and that the power of secret accusation . . . should be taken altogether away." Under a proposed amendment to the Canadian Code, made known in a recent information paper released by the federal Minister of Justice in July 1983, only the appropriate Attorney General or Deputy Attorney General could consent to the preferring of a direct indictment by Crown prosecutors, *op. cit.* p. 5. No alterations are proposed in the procedure involving private prosecutors, *ibid.*

[56] *Ibid.* ss.505(1)(*b*) and 507 (1) and (2).

[57] *Ibid.* ss.505(1)(*b*) and 507(2).

his having jurisdiction in his own right to prefer an indictment.[58] Electing to proceed by the former route might be explained, in some situations, by the desire of an Attorney General not to risk further criticism in unilaterally re-activating a prosecution that failed to secure a committal by the examining justice.[59] There is a similar sensitivity evident in the accepted judicial view that "If the Attorney General has definitely refused to prefer, or to consent to the preferring of a charge, the court should hesitate to order or consent to the laying of the charge as to which his refusal has been made, and should refuse its order of consent when it is made to appear that the administration of justice is being prejudiced or jeopardised by the proper action of that officer who by custom, tradition and constitutional usage, as well as by law, is charged with the administration of justice in the province."[60] It is by virtue of the co-equal jurisdiction conferred upon the court in preferring indictments, under the provisions of sections 505 and 507 of the same Code, that in this instance a departure is justified from the fundamental proposition that the Attorney General's prosecutorial discretion is not examinable by any court but is subject to review by the legislature, to whom the Attorney General is answerable.[61]

[58] *Loc. cit.* For the Crown's right to indict under s.307(2) for offences disclosed by the evidence taken on a preliminary inquiry but for which the accused was not specifically charged, see *R.* v. *Chabot* [1980] 2 S.C.R. 985 and (1981) 23 Crim. L.Q. 454, and *R.* v. *McKibbon* (1982) 35 O.R. 124.

[59] *Cf., e.g.* the judicial positions taken in *R.* v. *Brooks* (1971) 6 C.C.C. (2d) 87 and *R.* v. *Murphy and Saik* (1972) 19 C.R.N.S. 236 with that expressed in *R.* v. *Nellis et al.* (1981) 64 C.C.C. (2d) 470. Even more calculated to arouse public criticism would be the situation canvassed in *Nellis* (*supra*) that: "There is nothing in the Criminal Code to prohibit the Attorney General from bringing a direct indictment *after* the Court has adjudicated on an application for consent. I do not see this possibility as being one intended by Parliament yet it could hardly be avoided in those circumstances where there is no indication the Attorney General is refusing to indict or is at least equivocal"—*ibid.* p. 476.

[60] *Re Johnson and Inglis et al.* (1980) 17 C.R. (3d) 250 at p. 261 *per* Evans C.J., High Court of Ontario (adopting the view previously expressed in *Maloney* v. *Fildes* (1933) 60 C.C.C. 7 at p. 13). *Cf.* the statement by Haultain C.J.S. in *R.* v. *Weiss* (1915) 23 C.C.C. 460, 463 " . . . there is nothing in the Criminal Code to prevent me from consenting to a charge being preferred by any person but I think that very strong reasons should be shown to justify me in taking such a step, in face of the deliberate action of the Crown authorities. If the evidence taken on the preliminary inquiry disclosed such a strong prima facie case against the accused as to suggest an abuse of his judicial discretion by the A.G., or an attempt to stifle a proper prosecution, I should have no hesitation about consenting to a charge being preferred."

[61] For a strong and unequivocal acceptance of the basic constitutional position see *Re Johnson and Inglis et al., supra* (at pp. 267–268), in the course of which the Chief Justice added: "This power to prosecute . . . must be distinguished from the s.507 power to grant a consent to the preferring of an indictment. This latter statutory power is given to both the Attorney-General and the court and is one which places them in positions of equality. While the court cannot interfere with the Attorney-General's exercise of his discretion, so too the Attorney General cannot interfere when a court sees fit to grant a consent. A court may, in exercising its discretion, choose to consider the position taken by the Attorney-General in any given case. This does not mean, however, that it must do so, or that if it does it is compelled to adopt his position. Our jurisdictions are and must remain separate but equal." 17 C.R. (3d) 268. This analysis, as Evans C.J., himself recognised (*loc. cit.*), is incomplete since there remains the residual power of the Attorney General to enter a stay to an indictment preferred with the approval of the court. The possibility of such a clash might be extremely remote but its implications cannot be ignored.

This principle of judicial deference to the Attorney General in matters pertaining to the institution of criminal prosecutions makes it totally unrealistic to contemplate the adoption in Canada and other Commonwealth countries of the law that now prevails in England and Wales in which, as we have seen, the leave of a High Court judge is the only route open to the Attorney General, the Director of Public Prosecutions or any private person who seeks to present a bill of indictment as the most expeditious procedure for commencing a trial on indictment. Until the Criminal Law Act 1967, there was always the possibility that the Attorney General could invoke his prerogative authority to file an *ex officio* information, the origins of which are traceable as far back as the reign of Edward I. A full account of this procedure's chequered history is set forth in my previous study.[62] The Divisional Court's condemnation in *R. v. Labouchere*[63] of the laxity with which, in the early part of the nineteenth century, the normal process of presentment and indictment was by-passed, exerted a powerful restraint upon holders of the office of Attorney General in resorting to their prerogative discretion of filing an *ex officio* information. The last recorded instance in which a criminal trial was launched in this manner was *R. v. Mylius* in 1910 when Sir Rufus Isaacs, as Attorney General, without resort to a preliminary inquiry, filed an *ex officio* information charging the accused with criminal libel against King George V.[64] This special privilege of the Attorney General survived the legislative scythe that, in the Administration of Justice (Miscellaneous Provisions) Act 1938, abolished outlawry proceedings, the exhibiting of articles of peace in the High Court, and criminal informations "other than informations filed *ex officio* by His Majesty's Attorney General."[65] The Criminal Law Revision Committee in its Seventh Report, observing that the procedure had not been used since 1911, described the Attorney General's prerogative right as "plainly unnecessary" and recommended that it should be abolished.[66] The final demise of the Attorney's *ex officio* information was effectuated in the Criminal Law Act 1967,[67] section 6(6) of which declared that "Any power to bring proceedings for an offence by criminal information in the High Court is hereby abolished." No voices in opposition to this move were raised during the passage of the Bill through Parliament. We must presume, therefore, that the Law Officers, as well as

---

[62] Edwards, *op. cit.* pp. 262–267.

[63] (1884) 12 Q.B.D. 320.

[64] *The Times*, February 2, 1911 and see Edwards, *op. cit.* p. 186 fn. 31 and also p. 266.

[65] 1 & 2 Geo. 6, c. 63, s.12.

[66] Cmnd. 2659, para. 63, the full extent of the Committee's treatment of the subject being contained in a single paragraph that reads as follows: "For misdemeanour, though not for felony, a person may be tried on a criminal information *ex officio* filed by a Law Officer instead of an indictment. This procedure has not been used since 1911, and it is plainly unnecessary and should be abolished."

[67] 1967, c. 58. Action to the same end in Canada had been taken in the revised Criminal Code 1955, s.488(2), and in New Zealand, by implication, under the provisions of the Crimes Act 1961, s.345—see Adams, *Criminal Law and Practice in New Zealand*, (2nd ed.), pp. 705–706.

past holders of those offices, were reconciled to the need to obtain the leave of a High Court judge as the most expeditious procedure for bringing accused persons speedily to trial.

One interesting postscript, from Australia, is the confirmation by its High Court in *Barton* v. *R.* in 1981[68] that *ex officio* informations (or *ex officio* indictments as they are there described) are alive and well in New South Wales in accordance with the powers conferred by the Westminster Parliament in the Australian Courts Act 1828.[69] This law was intended to confer upon the colonial counterparts the same prerogatives as those practised by the Attorney General of England.[70] Due note was taken in *Barton* of the abolition in 1967 of the English Attorney General's former

---

[68] *Sub nom. Gruzman* v. *A.G. for N.S.W. & Others* (1980) 32 A.L.R. 449.

[69] 9 Geo. 4 (U.K.), c. 83, s.5 of which provided "that until further provision be made as hereinafter directed for proceedings by juries, all crimes, misdemeanours, and offences, . . . shall be prosecuted by Information, in the name of His Majesty's Attorney General, or other officer duly appointed for such purpose by the Governor of New South Wales and Van Diemen's Land respectively." For a recent illustration, arising out of the Street Commission's findings dismissing allegations of interference with the course of justice against the Premier of N.S.W. (Mr. Wran) but leading to the laying of ex-officio indictments by the Attorney General (Mr. Landa) against the Commissioner of the N.S.W. Rugby League and a former chief stipendiary magistrate, see *The Australian*, October 19, 1983.

[70] Each of the Australian States has conferred upon its Attorney General a statutory power to file an indictment whether the accused person has been committed for trial or not. The language chosen to accomplish this purpose, however, displays the confusion that can arise in failing to keep distinct (1) the original common law power of the Attorney General of England to file an *ex officio* information in the Queen's Bench Division without a previous indictment and (2) the statutory power first created under the Vexatious Indictments Act 1859, that effectively controlled the right of any person to prefer an indictment before a grand jury by requiring, if no committal proceedings had taken place, "the direction or consent of a Judge or the Attorney General." For examples of this confusion see the Queensland Cr. Code, s.561: "Ex officio informations. A Crown Law Officer may present an indictment . . . for an indictable offence. . . . "—interpreted and commented upon in *R.* v. *Webb* [1960] Qd. R. 443 and *R.* v. *Johnson & Edwards* (1979) 2 A. Crim. R. 414; the Tasmanian Cr. Code, s.42: "A Crown Law Officer may, without leave, file an indictment (herein called an ex officio indictment) for any crime." The proper distinction is maintained in the Victoria Crimes Act between the power of the Attorney General, or Solicitor General or any prosecutor for the Queen in the name of a Law Officer, to make presentation for any indictable offence (s.353(1)) and the later provision that "Nothing herein contained shall in any manner alter or affect the power which the A.G. possesses at common law to file by virtue of his office an information in the Supreme Court etc.," (s.355), a clear reference to the transposition to Victorian law of the English *ex officio* information. The New Zealand Crimes Act, s.345 empowers "the A.G., or any one with the written consent of a judge of the Supreme Court or of the Att. Gen., to present an indictment for any offence." Adams, *Criminal Law & Practice in New Zealand*, (1971), unhesitatingly points to the historical connection between the above section in New Zealand's Criminal Code and the British Vexatious Indictments Act 1859, the principles of which were re-enacted for N.Z. in that country's Vexatious Indictments Act 1870, and subsequently incorporated into New Zealand's Criminal Code Act 1893. The present section 345 is essentially on a par with the Canadian provisions (Code ss.505 and 507) examined earlier, but Adams, *op. cit.* para 2755 is seriously wrong in claiming that "substantially the same result has been arrived at in England by section 2 of the Administration of Justice (Miscellaneous Provisions) Act, 1933." As we have seen (*ante*, pp. 434–435) the 1933 legislation in England effectively eliminated the former jurisdiction of the Attorney General and Solicitor General to direct or to grant leave for the preferment of an indictment, the exclusive control over this form of expedited procedure now resting in the hands of the judiciary.

privilege of filing an *ex officio* information in the Queen's Bench Division of the High Court, but there was no disposition to urge that similar action be instituted in the Australian legislative bodies. The remarkable feature of the High Court's decision was the lengths to which a majority of the justices were prepared to go in according the accused a fundamental right to have the prosecution present its case through a preliminary inquiry. No suggestion was made that the Attorney General's decision to commence a prosecution was examinable by the courts.[71] Rather, the approach was more indirect in its adoption of the position that "a trial held without antecedent committal proceedings, unless justified on strong and powerful grounds, must necessarily be considered unfair."[72] According to the majority of the justices of the High Court: "It is for the courts, not the Attorney General, to decide in the last resort whether the justice of the case required that a trial should proceed in the absence of committal proceedings. It is not for the courts to abdicate that function to the Attorney General, let alone to Crown Prosecutors whom he may appoint . . . If the courts were to abdicate the function there is the distinct possibility that the *ex officio* indictment, so recently awakened from its long slumber, would become an active instrument, even in cases in which it has not been employed in the past, notwithstanding the criticism which has been directed to it and the assertions of commentators that it was appropriate for use of in a very limited category of cases."[73] Reconciliation of the two principles adumbrated by the High Court of Australia is to be found in the unanimous assertion that, notwithstanding the non-reviewability of the Attorney General's decision to launch the prosecution, the courts may postpone or stay the ensuing trial on indictment in circumstances where such action is necessary to prevent an abuse of process and ensure a fair trial for the accused person.[74]

Stephen and Wilson JJ., refused to subscribe to the theory that a prima facie case of abuse of process would arise whenever the accused was denied the essential prerequisite of committal proceedings.[75] The detriments associated with a preliminary hearing, they maintained, could be overcome by resort to speedier and less cumbersome forms of pre-trial discovery.[76]

---

[71] (1981) 32 A.L.R. 449 at pp. 455–459. The High Court rejected the contrary view advanced by Fox J. in *R. v. Kent, ex p. McIntosh* (1970) 17 F.L.R. 65, and overruled that decision.

[72] *Ibid.* at p. 463, *per* Gibbs and Mason JJ.

[73] *Ibid.*

[74] *Ibid.* at p. 459 (*per* Gibbs and Mason JJ.) and at p. 465 (*per* Stephen J.).

[75] *Ibid.* at pp. 466 and 470.

[76] Murphy J., in lending his support to the views of Stephen and Wilson J., cited with approval J. Seymour, *Committal for Trial, An Analysis of Australian Law Together with an Outline of British and American Procedures*, (Australian Institute of Criminology, 1978), a study to which the present writer is also indebted. In Canada, likewise, there are distinct signs that the preliminary hearing, with the taking of depositions, is destined to be replaced by procedures analogous to those of "section 1 committals" under the English Criminal Justice Act 1967. The abolition of committal proceedings, described as "a cumbersome and expensive vehicle for obtaining discovery," was recommended by the Law Reform Commission of Canada in 1974, *Working Paper No. 4 on Discovery*. A somewhat more

In each jurisdiction, except New South Wales, it is possible for the committal to rest on written statements. And in four of the Australian states, Victoria, Queensland, Tasmania and Western Australia, what is tantamount to the English procedure of "section 1 committals" (under the Criminal Justice Act 1967) is already in place.[77]

This attention to the Australian High Court's ruling in the *Barton* case is less important for the actual decision, that pertains to the unique character of New South Wales law, than the deeper issues it explores in connection with the court's role in examining the prosecutorial discretion exercised by the Attorney General. We have seen that the Australian justices adhered closely to the constitutional separation of powers doctrine that impels the English courts likewise to reject any jurisdiction by way of reviewing the Attorney General's decision to institute criminal proceedings,[78] to enter a *nolle prosequi,* to seek an injunction to prevent the commission or repetition of a serious offence, or the Director's intervention to take over a private prosecution and to end the proceedings by offering no evidence. The same general principles govern the approach of the Canadian courts in declining to become too closely involved, except when required to do so by express statutory provision, in questions that will decide whether a prosecution should be commenced.[79] When the ultimate function of the court is to determine the accused's guilt or innocence it is rightly concluded that the judges should not be seen to be associated with the initial step of allowing the prosecution to take place. The broad consistency of the judicial approach to this problem is departed from in dramatic fashion under present English law when the issue of approving the presentment of a bill of indictment, without resort to a committal hearing, is conferred exclusively upon a judge of the High Court.

This extraordinary jurisdiction is of moderate antiquity dating back to the Vexatious Indictment Act 1859, and it is doubtful whether its exercise has ever been so frequently resorted to as in the turbulent years of recent memory. The elimination in 1933 of the former concurrent jurisdiction of the Attorney General and the Solicitor General to grant leave in this regard may well have been dictated by the desire to provide safeguards against the abuses associated with the filing of *ex officio* informations in the eighteenth and nineteenth centuries. In remedying one possible ground of public dissatisfaction with the criminal process, Parliament may unwittingly have laid the foundations for a future conflict of purpose between the judiciary and the Law Officers of the Crown.

---

cautious approach, recommending a period of voluntary experimentation with a pre-trial disclosure system prior to the enactment of reform legislation, is reflected in the report of the influential Ontario committee on preliminary hearings 1982, chaired by Mr. Justice G. Arthur Martin, Ontario Court of Appeal.

[77] *Ante*, fn. 76.
[78] *Ante*, fn. 71.
[79] *Ante* fnn. 60 and 61.

14

Immunity and Other Interventions in the Criminal Process

Public disclosure of intervention by the Attorney General or the Director of Public Prosecutions in terminating a prosecution after it has commenced, or notification that a grant of immunity from prosecution has been authorised, can give rise to heated debates as to the appropriateness of the action taken in the name of the Crown. Among recent events that may readily be recalled is the belated disclosure of the grant of immunity to Anthony Blunt,[1] the promise of immunity extended to the leading witness for the Crown in the trial of Jeremy Thorpe for conspiracy and incitement to murder,[2] and the protection from prosecution for treason accorded to Bishop Muzorewa and Mr. Ian Smith prior to their setting foot on British soil for constitutional talks on the future of Rhodesia-Zimbabwe.[3] At the height of public interest in these and other similar cases questions are rarely directed towards the nature and source of the legal authority under which the decisions of the Attorney General and the Director of Public Prosecutions are made. As will readily become evident, the exercise of veto powers to prevent the institution of criminal proceedings, or to suppress a prosecution in mid-stream, epitomise the magnitude of the discretionary authority vested in the Attorney General for England and Wales. This residual discretion, with its universal application throughout the criminal law process, derives from the prerogative authority of the Crown supplemented by specific statutory provisions contained in the Prosecution of Offences Acts and Regulations.

More recently, we have seen the present Attorney General and his predecessor take the initiative in issuing formal policy statements that are intended to provide guidance to the Director of Public Prosecutions, prosecuting solicitors, counsel, and the police, relating to jury vetting,[4] the

---

[1] See *post*, pp. 466–471.
[2] See *post*, pp. 462–463.
[3] See *post*, pp. 475–476.
[4] See *post*, pp. 476–490.

disclosure of information to the defence before trial on indictment,[4a] identification evidence[5] and the exercise of prosecutorial discretion.[5a] Considerable hostility was generated towards the original set of guidelines governing jury checks by the police, a procedure that was condemned in some quarters as undermining the essential quality of randomness that should permeate the process of jury selection. Although significant changes were introduced in the later version of these guidelines many important questions remain to be considered as we proceed in this chapter to examine the range of sensitive powers at the discretionary disposal of the Attorney General in influencing the outcome of the criminal process.

NOLLE PROSEQUI

Pre-eminent amongst the prerogative powers exercisable by the Attorney General, as the chief legal representative of the Crown in the area of criminal prosecutions, is the entry of a *nolle prosequi* whereby the proceedings are effectively brought to a halt.[6] The exact origin of the plea is unclear though its underlying basis would seem to be fairly evident in that it was natural for the Crown, in whose name indictments embodying criminal charges were brought, to reserve the right to terminate the criminal proceedings at will. The first recorded instance of resort to this arbitrary procedure dates back to 1555,[7] and for a considerable period thereafter there was judicial uncertainty as to the precise consequences of a *nolle prosequi* being entered. On the basis of the decisions of the Court of King's Bench in *Goddard* v. *Smith* (1704),[8] *R.* v. *Ridpath* (1712)[9] and *R.* v. *Allen* (1862)[10] it can now be stated incontrovertibly that the effect of a *nolle prosequi* is neither a bar to a fresh indictment nor a discharge of the original offence. What it does is to postpone *sine die* the prosecution. Should the Attorney General decide at a later date to reopen the original charges he can, theoretically speaking, reactivate the earlier indictment that was placed in suspension when the *nolle prosequi* was filed in the court's records. Alternatively, fresh proceedings leading to a new indictment can be commenced to which the accused will be precluded from raising a plea of *autrefois acquit* on the basis of the *nolle prosequi*.

Considerations of fairness and oppressiveness can be expected to occupy a prominent place in any determination by the Attorney General to set aside his own original *nolle prosequi*, or that entered by one of his predecessors, and thus recommence a prosecution that may legitimately

---

[4a] See *post*, pp. 478–479.

[5] See *Archbold*, (41st ed.) para. 14.–1. The guidelines were first disclosed to the House of Commons, on May 29, 1976—H.C.Deb. Vol. 912, Written Answers, cols. 287–289.

[5a] See previous Chapter, pp. 431–434 and also *ante*, p. 112, fn. 27.

[6] See, generally, Edwards, *op. cit.* pp. 227–237.

[7] *Op. cit.* p. 228.

[8] 6 Mod. 261; 11 Mod. 56.

[9] 10 Mod. 152.

[10] 1 B. & S. 850, *per* Cockburn C.J. at p. 854 and *per* Crompton J. at p. 855.

have been understood by the accused to have been finished with months or years earlier. The spectre created by allegations of harassment and persecution is a powerful deterrent to the renewal of a criminal prosecution against the same accused at the instigation of the Crown. On the other hand, as we shall see later, there is in theory no obstacle to a fresh prosecution being launched at the behest of a private individual, in which event additional considerations arise as to the justification for intervening, possibly by way of entering a fresh *nolle prosequi*, to deprive the ordinary citizen of his constitutional right to maintain a private prosecution under his own authority and expense.

Until quite recently there was a body of authoritative opinion that maintained that, in practical terms, the entry of a *nolle prosequi* was confined to two categories of cases, first, to dispose of technically imperfect proceedings instituted by the Crown, and, secondly, to put a stop to oppressive but technically impeccable proceedings instituted by private prosecutors.[11] Both of these categories find support in the reported case law[12] but the emphasis seems to be shifting towards an even more restrictive interpretation of the grounds upon which the Attorney General might properly use his common law powers of *nolle prosequi*. Recent practice on the part of Attorneys General suggests adherence to a policy of confining the exercise of the power to cases where, after the indictment has been signed, it is found that the accused, for reasons of ill-health or other medical reasons, is unlikely ever to be fit to stand his trial and there is no other way of disposing of the indictment.[13] Such situations would arise, for example, if the accused was known to be suffering from a terminal disease or where the prospect of undergoing the trial might well be regarded as

---

[11] Edwards, *op. cit.* p. 234. These conclusions were based on a critical review of the earlier case law in an authoritative article on the subject of *nolle prosequi* in [1958] Crim. L.R. 573, at p. 577. Published anonymously, it can now be disclosed that its author was Mr. G.E. Dudman, Legal Secretary (at that time) of the Law Officers' Department.

[12] [1958] Crim.L.R. 573 at pp. 575–577.

[13] Speaking with the authority of first hand familiarity with the policies followed by the principal Law Officer of the Crown, the same writer stated: " . . . the current practice is to confine the exercise of the [*nolle prosequi*] power almost entirely to cases where, after the indictment has been signed, it is found that the accused is unlikely ever to be fit to stand his trial (so that it is not possible to place him in charge of the jury with the object of bringing the proceedings to an end with a formal verdict of not guilty). In short, a power which was previously exercised largely (but not, of course, exclusively) in order to enable the Crown to present a fresh indictment is now exercised largely for the purpose of disposing of an indictment which would otherwise remain on the file." *Ibid.* p. 578. For an analysis of three cases in the 1950s which represent a departure from the policy enunciated above see *ibid.* pp. 579–580 and Edwards, *op. cit.* pp. 235–236. More recently, in a Home Office memorandum on "The prosecution process" submitted to the Royal Commission on Criminal Procedure it was stated: "The *nolle prosequi* is chiefly used to dispose of proceedings where it would be oppressive to pursue the prosecution, *e.g.* where the accused is suffering from some serious permanent complaint such as heart disease" (*Memorandum* no. VII, p. 8). The above policy statement bore the full authority of the Attorney General, considerable care having been exercised to ensure that the submission to the Royal Commission accurately reflected the current policies adhered to by the Law Officers' Department and the office of Director of Public Prosecutions.

oppressive. Accordingly, the Attorney General in such cases has authorised the entry of his *nolle prosequi* without occasioning a ripple of comment.[14]

No longer is it thought justifiable, at least in English law, to dispose of technically imperfect proceedings instituted by the Crown by resort to the *nolle prosequi* procedure. The advantages that formerly accrued to the prosecution in this fashion were theoretically unlimited, permitting the Crown to meet procedural objections with the utmost equanimity. A sense of injustice was inevitably associated with the use of the Crown's prerogative powers to these ends and thus the policies of the Crown's prosecutors have shifted towards either seeking the leave of the court to the withdrawal of the charges or in offering no evidence and thereby ensuring a directed verdict of acquittal.[15] From the point of view of the defendant the latter procedure is to be preferred, since his discharge in these circumstances is a reality not a fiction and the erasure of the indictment from the court's active file is proof that the proceedings in question have been permanently and irrevocably terminated. A withdrawal, albeit with the consent of the presiding judge, is of a very different nature since it permits the prosecution to re-order its case at a later time when the difficulties that led to the request to withdraw the original charge(s) have been ironed out and the prosecution is ready to proceed afresh.

[14] *e.g.* in a Written Answer, H.C. Deb., Vol. 945, col. 15–16, February 27, 1978, the Attorney General disclosed that he had exercised his *nolle prosequi* power four times in 1976 and six times in 1977. No supplementary questions followed by way of either eliciting further information or questioning the grounds on which the decision in any case was based. See too [1958] Crim. L.R. 582. Infinitely more interest was exhibited with respect to the entry of a *nolle prosequi* by the Attorney General, Sir Michael Havers, in *R.* v. *Bogdanov* (1982), better recognised as the *Romans in Britain* case which centred on a homosexual rape scene in the controversial play at the National Theatre. Having been refused the Attorney General's consent to launching criminal proceedings under the Theatres Act 1968, Mrs. Mary Whitehouse instituted a private prosecution against the director of the play charging gross indecency under the Sexual Offences Act 1956—see *The Times*, October 29 and November 27, 1980. Notwithstanding the trial judge's ruling that there was evidence for the jury to consider, counsel for the prosecution decided to terminate the case. This course of action was criticised by Staughton, J., the trial judge, who had not been consulted before the accused was informed and who stated: "Although I do not doubt that it was done with a good motive I am bound to say that any notion that the trial could then and there be brought to a conclusion was misconceived and improper"—*The Times*, March 20 1982. The Attorney General's entry of a *nolle prosequi* followed. This action was explained to the House of Commons in a written answer that stated: "There was no way that the wish of the prosecution, which he had been told had the express agreement of the defendant, could be effected without my intervention and since it could have been oppressive to the defendant to put him again in jeopardy after he had been told that the case was to be stopped at that stage, I thought it right to enter a *nolle prosequi*"—H.C. Deb., Vol. 20, ser. 6, col. 237–238, March 22, 1982. This resort to the *nolle prosequi* procedure was quite exceptional, dictated as it was by the prosecution's inability to opt for offering no evidence (that stage having passed by the time the decision to terminate was reached) or a withdrawal (in view of the trial judge's refusal to accede to this alternative). See, too, the views expressed by the C.A. in *R.* v *D. The Times*, November 1, 1983

[15] See, *e.g.* S. McCabe & F. Sutcliffe, *Defining Crime: A Study of Police Decisions*, (Oxford, Blackwell, 1978); R. Sparks, D. Dodd and H. Glenn, *Surveying Victims*, (London, Wiley, 1977); and Wesley Skogan (Ed.) *Sample Surveys of Victims of Crimes* (esp. Chapter 6 on "Crime and Crime Rate") (Cambridge, Mass. Bellinger, 1976).

Control, however, in these circumstances is exercised by the court[16] in contradistinction to the entry of a *nolle prosequi* which is within the absolute discretion of the Attorney General.[17] Moreover, the Attorney's discretionary power is one that in English law cannot be delegated.[18] Prosecuting counsel, acting on their own authority, cannot invoke the common law power of terminating criminal proceedings by resort to a *nolle prosequi*.[19] And, as the Court of King's Bench declared in the leading case of *R. v. Allen*[20] in 1862, should any question arise of an abuse of power or of an injustice occasioned by the entry of a *nolle prosequi* the Attorney General may be held accountable to the High Court of Parliament. Opportunities for the House of Commons to challenge the exercise of the Attorney General's prerogative authority are nowadays few and far between because of the relatively small number of instances in which a *nolle prosequi* is entered. This, in turn, is dictated by the emphasis which English law places on the personal responsibility of the senior Law Officer in making such decisions. This accentuates, rather than diminishes, the sense of accountability to Parliament. This is not emptied of its significance

---

[16] Edwards, *op. cit.* pp. 235–236.

[17] *Ibid.* p. 236.

[18] *Ibid.* p. 231. This exclusive authority of the Attorney General, enunciated in 1843 in *R. v. Dunn* 1 C. & K. 730, 731 and never once challenged since that time, is peculiar to England and Wales and has not been copied in other Commonwealth countries. A correction is called for in the statement which appears in *Archbold, Criminal Pleading, Evidence & Practice* (41st ed.) para. 1–121. The need to act in any of the predicated emergencies suggests the desirability of amending the 1944 statute to encompass such an eventuality. To do so would in no way diminish the importance attached to requiring, in normal circumstances, the personal decision of the senior Law Officer of the Crown.

[19] *Cf.* the position in Canadian law which extends the power of entering a stay (the equivalent of a *nolle prosequi*) to both proceedings on indictment (Criminal Code, s.508) and on summary conviction (*ibid.* s.731.1). In an amendment to the interpretation section made in 1968–69 (c. 38, s.2) any reference to the "Attorney General" includes "the lawful deputy" of that official. The latter category, moreover, is not restricted to the "Deputy Attorney General" (a title denoting the most senior public official in the ministry) but comprehends "all persons appointed to act on behalf of the Attorney General when acting within the scope of their authority," *perc*kson J., speaking for the Supreme Court of Canada, in *R. v. Harrison* (1977) 28 C.C.C. (2d) 279 at p. 285. In an information paper released in July 1983 by the Minister of Justice the federal government disclosed a series of proposed amendments to the Criminal Code, including changes whereby (i) the reactivating of a prosecution stayed by a Crown prosecutor would require the written personal consent of the pertinent Attorney General or Deputy Attorney General, and (ii) proceedings not recommenced within three months of the original stay would be dismissed for want of prosecution—*op. cit.* pp. 4–5. In New Zealand, the power of the Attorney General to enter a *nolle prosequi* (Crimes Act 1961, s.378) is normally exercisable by the Solicitor General in accordance with the general interpretation of the term "Attorney General" as including the junior Law Officer—Acts Interpretation Act 1924, s.24. Furthermore, "a Crown Solicitor or other counsel appearing for the Crown in criminal prosecutions has no authority to enter a stay of proceedings. Only the Law Officers themselves can exercise this power"—*Crown Law Practice in New Zealand* (1961), pp. 17–18. Australia adheres more closely to the Canadian approach, many of the States declaring the power to enter a *nolle prosequi* to be exercisable by Crown prosecutors as well as the Attorney General—see Qd. Cr. Code 1899, s.563; Tasm. Cr. Code 1924, s.350; and West. Aust. Cr. Code 1913, s.581.

[20] (1862) 1 B. & S. 850 at p. 855 and see also Edwards, *op. cit.* pp. 231–232, and *ante*, fn. 14.

by the absence of situations in which the Attorney's decision has been questioned by the Commons. The important fact to note is that the power to do so is there and represents the normal channel of accountability of a Law Officer of the Crown to Parliament for every action that he takes.

VEXATIOUS AND OPPRESSIVE PROSECUTIONS—WHOSE RESPONSIBILITY IS IT TO INTERVENE?

The question of how best to handle vexatious or oppressive prosecutions, to which we turn next, provides a potential source of disagreement between the Attorney General and the Director of Public Prosecutions as to whose responsibility it is to make the determination whether to intervene and by what procedure. On the one hand, there is a long and substantial body of case law which illustrates how resort to the Attorney General's common law power of directing the entry of a *nolle prosequi* has effectively maintained control over the troublesome features that may be associated with the citizen's right to institute a private prosecution. Not that it should be assumed that oppressive prosecutions are confined to the activities of private citizens. Harassing other members of society, by resort to the criminal law process, is just as capable of emanating from the police, local authorities or any of the other groups associated with what we describe as private prosecutions.[21] To intervene in any such private prosecution with a view to stifling the proceedings is not a decision that is taken lightly. Not to do so, however, in glaring circumstances may just as readily be criticised as an abdication of responsibility.

Exactly whose function it is to make these invidious decisions has been the subject of much discussion in recent years between the two offices having supervisory roles to play in the field of criminal prosecutions. The reluctance of the Attorney General to resort to his prerogative powers has already been noted. In support of this conservative approach by the principal Law Officer of the Crown, the case is advanced for utilising, in appropriate cases, the statutory power conferred upon the Director of Public Prosecutions under the Prosecution of Offences Act 1908, s.2(3) of which declares that "Nothing in the Prosecution of Offences Acts 1879 and 1884 or in this Act shall preclude any person from instituting or carrying on any criminal proceedings but the Director of Public Prosecutions may undertake at any stage the conduct of those proceedings if he thinks fit." This subsection, as already noted, preserves the rights of the private prosecutor while giving the Director the authority to intervene in any prosecution at any stage. In the case of a vexatious or oppressive prosecution, ·it is argued, the Director can effectively stop such a prosecution in its tracks by taking over the conduct of the case and offering no evidence, thereby disposing of the proceedings and erasing the charges

---

[21] To guard against malicious, vexatious and "utterly unreasonable prosecutions" see the approach propounded by the Royal Commission on Criminal Procedure, *Report* (Cmnd. 8092) at pp. 160–162, and its *Law and Procedure* volume (Cmnd. 8092–1) at pp. 59–63.

against the accused. One major practical advantage that is seen as inherent in the Director's statutory power of intervention is its availability for use in both proceedings on indictment in the Crown Court and in summary prosecutions.[22] This is in sharp contrast to the scope of a *nolle prosequi* which, as illustrated by the case of *Nina Ponamavera*,[23] cannot be resorted to in cases brought before a magistrates' court for summary disposal or at the preliminary hearing stage of an indictable offence. In both of the latter situations the leave of the court is necessary to achieve a withdrawal of the prosecution's case. According to English law, the filing of the Attorney General's *nolle prosequi* is strictly confined to trials before a judge and jury on the presentation of a bill of indictment and then only after the indictment has been signed.[24]

A recent example of this important practical distinction involved charges of corruption and conspiracy to pervert the course of justice, which were brought in the name of the Director of Public Prosecutions against a 20 year veteran of the Metropolitan London Police.[25] At a late stage in the preliminary inquiry psychiatric evidence was tendered indicating a belief that the accused would take his life if the case went ahead. Normally, if the case had proceeded to trial and the indictment had been filed this would have resulted in the Attorney General filing a *nolle prosequi* but the technical limitations of this procedure prevented its being utilised. Accordingly, application to withdraw the charges was reluctantly agreed to by the stipendiary magistrate, counsel having informed the court that the Attorney General had considered the case and had instructed the Director of Public Prosecutions not to proceed.

So far as is known no concerted effort has been mounted within the Law Officers' Department or the Department of the Director of Public Prosecutions to rid the law of this anomaly. Reforms towards this end, executed in New Zealand and Canadian law, are referred to below.[26] It

---

[22] Edwards, *op. cit.* pp. 230, 236–237.

[23] [1956] Crim. L.R. 725–730. See, too, the opinion expressed by Lord Dilhorne (*arguendo*) in *D.P.P.* v. *Brown et al* (unrep.) (*post*, p. 465, fn. 89) referring to "the difficulty about the possibility of entering a *nolle prosequi* in the magistrates' court. It is very doubtful if that can be done. The main view is that it cannot" (Transcript, p. 17).

[24] Edwards, *op. cit.* pp. 236–237. This position should be contrasted with that of New Zealand which, by virtue of section 378 of the Crimes Act 1961 and section 173 of the Summary Proceedings Act 1957, empowers the Attorney General to stay proceedings by indictment at any time from the laying of the information until judgment is given in the Supreme Court. And, as already noted (*ante*, pp. 72, fn. 56 and 398, fn. 80), under an amendment to section 77A of the same Summary Proceedings Act, the Attorney General of New Zealand can enter a stay in any summary proceedings at any time before the defendant has been convicted or otherwise dealt with. Canada followed New Zealand's example in 1972, see c. 13, s.62, and now embodied in the Criminal Code, s.732.1.

[25] *R.* v. *Mathews, The Times*, November 12, 1980.

[26] *Ante*, fn. 24. It remains unclear under Canadian law whether the Attorney General's power to enter a stay in regard to an indictable offence (Code s.508) extends to a preliminary hearing. To ensure that such a power was legally exercisable, an amendment to the Code was recommended by the criminal law section of the Uniformity Commissioners of Canada, 1977 *Proceedings* 44, and was incorporated as clause 92 of the Criminal Law Amendment Bill 1982 (Bill C-21). Due to a change of government the Bill made no progress. Had the amendment

must be assumed that the statutory powers of intervention by the Director to take over any criminal case and bring the proceedings to a halt is viewed as providing ample authority for circumventing the limitation attached to the Attorney General's *nolle prosequi* powers. At the same time, doubts may be entertained whether Parliament, in 1908, in conferring upon the Director a discretion to undertake *the conduct* of a private prosecution if he thinks fit,[27] visualised the use of this authority as supplanting the Attorney General's prerogative power of intervention by way of entering his *nolle prosequi*. What is known is that serious misgivings have long been entertained in the Department of the Director of Public Prosecutions with respect to the broader interpretation of the Director's powers to stay proceedings. So much has this feeling been subscribed to that a tradition has grown up which maintains that it would be an improper exercise of the Director's power of intervention to take over the proceedings with the primary objective of smothering the prosecution by offering no evidence,[28] since this was not the purpose for which the statutory power was originally granted. The comparison is usefully drawn with "D.P.P.'s consent" provisions which are scattered throughout the statute book and which, it is asserted, are a clear indication of Parliament's express intention to confer unqualified control upon the Director with regard to the institution or non-institution of criminal proceedings. In the absence of any similar express authority the position adopted by successive Directors is to disclaim any power to intervene where the object is to bring a private prosecution to a premature halt. Instead, support is extended to the principle that the protection of the public from vexatious or oppressive[29]

reached the statute book it would have brought Canadian law into line with New Zealand—see section 173 of the Summary Proceedings Act (No. 87) (N.Z.) of 1957. A significant aspect of the same problem surfaced in Australia in 1979 in connection with the private prosecution, *Sankey* v. *Whitlam* (see *ante*, pp. 381–383), the question being raised as to whether the Commonwealth Attorney General could take over the prosecution of committal proceedings instituted by a private informant. In the booklet *Prosecution Policy of the Commonwealth*, tabled recently in the Australian Senate, that country's Attorney General referred to the statutory powers in English law whereby the D.P.P. may, at any stage, intervene in a private prosecution and, by offering no evidence, terminate the prosecution. There being no equivalent Commonwealth statutory provisions the Attorney General concluded: " . . . in my view it is highly doubtful that the A.G. has this power of intervention"—*op. cit.* p. 6.

[27] See Edwards, *op. cit.* pp. 397–398 and the references to the D.P.P.'s intervention in the *Arundel* murder case in 1950 and his declared intention to intervene in the *Linda Smith* case in 1961.

[28] D.P.P.'s *Written Evidence* to the Royal Commission on Criminal Procedure, p. 76, para. 214.

[29] See Costs in Criminal Cases Act 1973, ss.3, 4, 12(1), 12(4), and the latest Practice Directions on the subject (1982) 74 Cr. App. R. 48 (Crown Court) and [1982] 3 All E.R. (magistrates in the summary trial of indictable offences or as examining justices). Both courts are empowered to order payment out of central funds of the costs of the defence, it being stated that an order should normally be made for the payment of the costs of an acquitted defendant out of central funds under section 3 of the 1973 Act unless there are positive reasons for making a different order. Examples of such reasons are: (a) where the prosecution has acted spitefully or has instituted or continued proceedings without reasonable cause the defendant's costs should be paid by the prosecutor under section 4 of the 1973 Act; (b) where

private prosecutors lies with the courts, especially through the medium of awarding costs.[30] This approach, however, can turn out to be a double edged weapon, insomuch as it tacitly recognises the court's jurisdiction to embrace both the Crown and other prosecutors within its inherent powers of controlling abuse of process situations. If, as most recent precedents suggest, a more flexible and pragmatic approach to this difficult problem appears to be gaining acceptance, this points yet again to the importance of recognising the breadth of the Attorney General's discretionary powers and his ultimate authority in the development of policies within the office of the Director of Public Prosecutions.

"Withdrawals" and "Offering No Evidence": is Ultimate Control in the Court or the Prosecutor?

Remarkable as it may seem at this stage in the development of criminal procedure, uncertainty still prevails as to the precise distinction between the "withdrawal" of a charge and the prosecution's "offering no evidence" against the accused. This uncertainty, moreover, contains the potential for some far-reaching implications. There appears to be universal agreement on one aspect of the differentiation, namely, the consequences that flow from resort to the respective procedures. As stated already, the effect of offering no evidence in support of a charge, irrespective of the court before whom the accused appears, is to end the prosecution by what, to all intents and purposes, amounts to a verdict of acquittal. The same prosecution cannot be reopened at some future date without the accused having available to him a complete answer in the form of a plea of *autrefois acquit*. The result of a withdrawal, on the other hand, assuming the court's approval to such a course is forthcoming, is the same as that which attaches to the entry of a *nolle prosequi*. There is no verdict of acquittal. The prosecution is simply postponed *sine die* and may be reactivated at a later date. Only the Attorney General is authorised to enter a *nolle prosequi* but any prosecutor or prosecuting counsel can seek the leave of the court to withdraw a charge that is pending.

---

the defendant's own conduct has brought suspicion on himself and has misled the prosecution into thinking that the case against him is stronger than it is the defendant can be left to pay his own costs; (c) where there is ample evidence to support a conviction but the defendant is acquitted on a technicality which has no merit. Here again the defendant can be left to pay his own costs. The power to award costs to an acquitted defendant is limited to cases in which the accused is acquitted on *all* counts in the indictment. There is no power in summary cases to award costs out of public funds.

[30] In discussing the subject of costs with the author (July 7, 1980) the present Deputy D.P.P. opined that "With the rate of *directed* acquittals of prosecutions launched by the police (with the agreement of the prosecuting solicitors) running between 7 and 9 per cent. of total prosecutions, it is likely that the decisions not to award costs against central funds will transfer the responsibility for paying the costs to the local authority. Any significant increase in this burden will likely see pressure being brought to bear upon the county prosecuting solicitors to take greater care in exercising their prosecutorial discretionary power and not to go along with police decisions to prosecute in cases that should not have been launched at all or not committed for trial."

The uncertainties surrounding these different steps in the criminal process mainly arise in connection with the court's authority to control the actions of prosecuting counsel. In this context, moreover, there appears to be no legal basis for differentiating between the position of counsel representing the Director of Public Prosecutions, a local prosecuting authority, or a private prosecutor. From at least as early as 1848, in *Tunicliffe* v. *Tedd*,[31] the position seems to have been generally accepted that provided no plea had been taken the prosecution could be withdrawn. It is also clear from the well known passage by the Court of Appeal in *R.* v. *Comptroller General of Patents, ex p. Tomlinson*[32] that the consent of the court to a withdrawal is necessary. Comparing the situation with the pre-eminence of the Attorney General in his power to enter a *nolle prosequi*, A.L. Smith L.J. declared: "I do not say that when a case is before a judge a prosecutor may not ask the judge to allow the case to be withdrawn, and the judge may do so if he is satisfied that there is no case, but the Attorney General does have the power to enter a *nolle prosequi*, and that power is not subject to any control."[33] Lord Parker C.J. in *R.* v. *Phipps ex p. Alton* was no less explicit in stating that " . . . it is always a matter for the discretion of the court, and the court alone, whether it allows the process to be withdrawn."[34]

The implications of a withdrawal in a summary trial, as illustrated by *R.* v. *Phipps*, may preclude the magistrates' court from making an order for costs in favour of the defendant because the outcome of the proceedings has not resulted in an acquittal, as required by the Costs in Criminal Cases Act 1973.[35] To achieve a dismissal of the charges against the defendant the procedure of offering no evidence must be adopted by the prosecution. It, therefore, becomes a matter of importance to determine whether ultimate control over this procedure rests with the presiding judge or the prosecutor. According to Lord Goddard C.J., delivering the judgment of the Divisional Court in *R.* v. *Chairman, County of London Quarter Sessions, ex p. Downes*[36]: "It is, of course, well known to every practitioner that, if the prosecution is satisfied that there is a good defence to the charge or that for some reason it is inadmissible to proceed, it is permissible, with the leave of the court after issue joined, to offer no evidence, when a verdict of acquittal will be directed. Again, if there were

---

[31] (1848) 12 J.P. 249; 5 C.B. 553.
[32] [1899] 1 Q.B. 909.
[33] *Ibid.* at p. 914.
[34] (1964) 128 J.P. 323 at p. 326. Among the questions to be considered in the case of a summary trial would be: "Is the nature of the offence such that the defendant should be acquitted, which will prevent further proceedings being brought, whereas a discretion to allow process to be withdrawn will not amount to an acquittal? There is also the consideration . . . that the accused may have incurred costs and desire to recover those costs or have an opportunity of recovering those costs which he will not have if the summons is withdrawn" (*loc. cit.*).
[35] 1973, c. 14, ss.1 & 2.
[36] [1954] 1 Q.B. 1 at p. 6.

more than one of them, to direct that the others are to remain on the file and not to be prosecuted without leave." Reference to the terms of the Criminal Justice Act 1967,[37] which is included in the authorities cited by *Archbold*[38] on this subject, is not particularly helpful insomuch as the provision is less than crystal clear as to the exact scope of the trial judge's discretion. The relevant section reads as follows: "Where a defendant arraigned on an indictment or inquisition pleads not guilty and the prosecutor proposes to offer no evidence against him, the court before which the defendant is arraigned may, if it thinks fit, order that a verdict of not guilty shall be recorded without the defendant being given in charge to a jury, and the verdict shall have the same effect as if the defendant had been tried and acquitted on the verdict of a jury." The discretionary element here would seem to be associated with the placing of the accused in the jury's charge and not to be concerned with the question whether the trial judge has a discretion to refuse to permit the prosecution to offer no evidence. If Lord Goddard's statement of the law is correct, however, there is no distinction between the authority of the court to control either situation, *i.e.* an application for withdrawal or a proposal to offer no evidence.

Support for Lord Goddard's interpretation of the trial court's discretionary powers is to be found in the recent decision of the Court of Appeal (Criminal Division) in *R. v. Broad*.[39] The facts which gave rise to the appeal were fairly straightforward. A number of valuable mares having been stolen from a stud in Cheshire, three persons were later apprehended in the South of England to which the mares had been transported in the dead of night. At the close of the arraignments in the Crown Court, the appellant entered a plea of not guilty to handling stolen goods and prosecuting counsel intimated his intention of offering no evidence in support of the charge. The trial judge, Mars-Jones J., demurred to the prosecutor's proposal indicating that, in his view, the whole surrounding circumstances were such that Broad ought to stand trial on the charge of assisting in the disposal of stolen property. Counsel representing the prosecuting solicitor for Chester accepted that the decision whether or not to continue was subject to the presiding judge's consent.[40] Such consent not being forthcoming, the trial proceeded and resulted in the conviction of all three accused. Broad subsequently sought leave to appeal against his conviction on the specific ground that the trial judge was wrong in law in not approving the proposal of counsel for the prosecution to offer no evidence against the accused. The response was unequivocal. Delivering the unanimous judgment of the Court, Roskill L.J. stated[41]: "We can see

[37] c. 80, s.17.
[38] *Archbold, Criminal Pleading, Practice and Procedure* (41st ed.), paras 4–76, and 4–176.
[39] (1978) 68 Cr. App. R. 281.
[40] *Ibid.* p. 283.
[41] *Ibid.* p. 284.

no logic in that submission. There is no authority for it. It seems to us to be against all principle. When counsel for the Crown invites the judge to give approval to some course which he wishes to take, the seeking of that approval is no idle formality. The judge in the circumstances is not a rubber stamp to approve a decision by counsel without further consideration, a decision which may or may not be right and which, in the present case, in view of each member of this Court, with respect to the experienced counsel concerned, was not one with which this Court agrees." In the particular circumstances of that case it may well have been "quite unrealistic" for prosecuting counsel to have concluded that there was no evidence to go to the jury. But such an interpretation avoids the central question of whether the trial judge has the authority in the first place to impose his direction upon the prosecutor.

In view of the singular lack of previous authority specifically dealing with the main ground of appeal in *Broad*[42] it might have been expected that the relevant passage in *Archbold's Criminal Pleading, Evidence and Practice* would have been cited to the court in the course of argument. In the then current edition it was stated: "It is customary for prosecuting counsel to seek the approval of the judge before offering no evidence. Views differ as to whether the judge can refuse to allow the Crown to offer no evidence if they insist on doing so. It is submitted that strictly the judge has no such power, though clearly he is entitled to express his view strongly upon the matter."[43] What may well have become a customary practice, as an act of courtesy to the presiding judge, is quickly transformed into a question of principle where the judge deems it to be within his prerogative to deny prosecuting counsel the right to conclude the proceedings by offering no evidence against the accused.

Some further doubts as to the authority to be accorded to the Court of Appeal's decision in *R. v. Broad* derive from the reference, later in the court's judgment, to the trial judge's refusal to sanction the "withdrawal" of the charge.[44] Such imprecision in the language used by the Court of Appeal suggests the advisability of adopting a cautious approach to the ruling enunciated in *R. v. Broad*. Additional grounds for caution derive from the court's postscript[45] which disclosed that, since giving judgment, their Lordships' attention had been drawn to the dictum of A.L. Smith L.J.

---

[42] *R. v. Soanes* (1948) 32 Cr. App. R. 136, referred to *arguendo* and approved in *Broad*, was concerned with the distinguishable issue of a trial judge's discretion not to permit a more serious charge to be reduced to a lesser charge. *Cf.* the provision in the Canadian Criminal Code, s.534(4) which states " . . . where an accused pleads not guilty of the offence charged but guilty of an included or other offence, the court may in its discretion with the consent of the prosecution accept such plea of guilty and, if such plea is accepted, shall find the accused not guilty of the offence charged."

[43] 40th ed., 1970, para. 399. The passage quoted in the text above has been eliminated in the latest edition (41st ed. 1982) which adopts the view expressed by the Criminal Division of the Court of Appeal in *R. v. Broad*. The principle in *Broad* does not apply to committal proceedings: *R. v. Canterbury and St. Augustine JJ., ex p. Klisak* [1982] Q.B. 398.

[44] 68 Cr. App. R. 281 at p. 285.

[45] *Ibid.* p. 286.

in *ex p. Tomlinson*,[46] cited above, which the Court of Appeal found to be entirely consistent with its own judgment in *Broad*. A reference back to the well known passage from *ex p. Tomlinson* indicates that the Court of Appeal in 1899 was speaking of the trial judge's power to deny an application for a withdrawal, and this begs anew the question whether a similar power extends to controlling the prosecution's discretion to terminate the charge by offering no evidence.

SOME MODERN PRECEDENTS AND NEW DIRECTIONS

How far then do modern precedents lend support to the approaches outlined above in terms of adherence to principle? Because it represents a notable departure from the customary practice on *nolle prosequi*, consistently followed by the more recent holders of the office of Attorney General, we should first examine the unusual circumstances portrayed in *Gleaves* v. *Deakin and others* in 1979.[47] This case involved a prosecution for criminal libel, under section 5 of the Libel Act 1843.[48] Proceedings were instituted by a private citizen against the authors and publishers of a book called "Johnny Go Home" which contained allegations, *inter alia*, that the prosecutor had been guilty of gross sexual offences with minors, that he belonged to a Fascist movement and that he was a "monster" of a kind similar to other notorious criminals. No prior consent is necessary under the existing law for the institution of proceedings for an alleged criminal libel in a book, whereas section 8 of the Law of Libel Amendment Act 1888,[49] requires the leave of a judge in chambers before a criminal prosecution for criminal libel can be brought against a newspaper proprietor, publisher or editor. Interestingly, in an earlier private prosecution, *Goldsmith* v. *Pressdram Ltd.*,[50] a successful application was launched before Wien J. for leave to proceed under the 1888 statute charging criminal libel against the satirical magazine *Private Eye*, its editor and distributors. In that case the private prosecutor was a public figure associated with the Bank of England, who claimed that his integrity had been infringed by an allegation that he was the ringleader of a conspiracy to obstruct the course of justice in what became known as the "Lord

---

[46] *Ante*, fn. 32.

[47] [1979] 2 All E.R. 497, H.L. affirming the decision of the Div. Ct. in *R.* v. *Wells Street Stipendiary Magistrate, ex p. Deakin* [1978] 3 All E.R. 252.

[48] 6 & 7 Vict. c. 96.

[49] 51 & 52 Vict. c. 64.

[50] [1977] 2 All E.R. 557. The exceptional nature of these proceedings, by way of a private prosecution against a newspaper for criminal libel, was adverted to by the Master of the Rolls in a related civil action, one of a large number of similar suits brought by the plaintiff against one of the major distributors of the satirical magazine. Lord Denning stated that he could not recall any such private criminal prosecution in his professional life—*Goldsmith* v. *Sperrings Ltd.* [1977] 2 All E.R. 566, at p. 571. See, too, *Desmond* v. *Thorne et al.* [1983] 1 W.L.R. 163 in which Taylor J., in refusing to grant leave under section 8 of the 1888 Act, assimilated the judge's role to that normally discharged by the D.P.P. when deciding whether to institute criminal proceedings—*ibid*. p. 169.

Lucan" affair.[51] The defendants were later committed for trial but when the proceedings reached the Central Criminal Court the prosecution was, by leave of the court, withdrawn.[52]

Prior to 1888, under the terms of the Newspaper Libel and Registration Act 1881,[53] s.3, the fiat of the Attorney General or the consent of the Director of Public Prosecutions was a necessary prerequisite to the commencement of libel proceedings against a newspaper or those connected with its publication. But this provision, as we have just seen, had no application where the alleged libel appeared in a book and not a newspaper. It was the unanimous recommendation of the Lords of Appeal in *Gleaves* v. *Deakin*[54] that, with respect to all criminal prosecutions for libel, the consent of the Attorney General should be made necessary. Such a projected change in the law lies in the future and, if enacted, will transform the involvement of the Attorney General from the present situation, in which he has to consider the advisability of intervening to stop the proceedings after they have been launched, to a consideration of whether it is in the public interest that he issue his fiat in the first place authorising the libel prosecution to go forward. The precise issue on which *Gleaves* v. *Deakin* reached the House of Lords was the examining magistrate's ruling that evidence of the general bad reputation of the prosecutor was inadmissible at the preliminary hearing. The magistrate had, in fact, allowed the private prosecutor to be cross-examined as to his long record of prior convictions for buggery and attempted buggery, indecent assault, and assault occasioning bodily harm but the appeal was not concerned with this part of the examining justice's rulings on evidence. The Divisional Court, in rejecting applications for certiorari and mandamus, upheld the magistrate's decision and so, in turn, did the House of Lords. Lord Scarman, alone of their Lordships, ventured the opinion that because of the seriousness of the libels complained of, he would expect

---

[51] A sampling of the allegations in *Private Eye* pertaining to this case and other notorious affairs in the public domain is contained in Lord Denning's judgment, *ante*, fn. 50.

[52] *The Times*, May 10, 1977.

[53] 44 & 45 Vict. c. 60. This section was superseded and repealed by the Law of Libel Amendment Act 1888, s.8, referred to above. Under the 1881 provision, the words "criminal prosecution" were held not to apply to a criminal information whether instituted *ex officio* by a Law Officer or filed by leave of the court—*Yates* v. *R.* (1885) 11 Q.B.D. 750; 14 Q.B.D. 646. And see *R.* v. *Labouchere* (1884) 12 Q.B.D. 320.

[54] [1979] 2 All E.R. 497. Viscount Dilhorne expressed the consensus of opinion among the Appellate Committee in stating: "It would, I think, be an improvement in our law if no prosecution for criminal libel could be instituted without leave. There are many precedents for the leave of the Attorney-General or the Director of Public Prosecutions being required for the institution of prosecutions. In considering whether or not to give his consent, the Attorney-General and the Director of Public Prosecutions must have regard to the public interest. The leave of a judge must be obtained for the institution of a prosecution for criminal libel against a newspaper (Law of Libel Amendment Act 1888, s.8), and where such leave is sought the judge must consider whether a prosecution is required in the public interest. As I do not myself regard it as very desirable that judges should have any responsibility for the institution of prosecutions, I would like to see it made the law that no prosecution for criminal libel could be brought without the leave of the Attorney-General or of the Director of Public Prosecutions" (*ibid.* at p. 502); see, too, *per* Lord Edmund Davies, at p. 507.

a prosecuting authority to authorise prosecution because the complainant, however bad his reputation, should be allowed the verdict of a jury on the libellous allegations.[55]

The ensuing trial resulted in the acquittal of the defendants and the payment out of public funds, on the direction of the trial judge, of costs in the region of £50,000, it being said that the private prosecutor was virtually unemployable and without any means.[56] Undeterred by the outcome of the trial the incorrigible complainant set about invoking the criminal law in another batch of informations against the same journalists and Yorkshire Television which had made a television documentary based on the book. This time the charges alleged conspiracy to commit fraud over the copyright of two photographs. Not surprisingly, editorial comment questioned the propriety of allowing the fresh prosecutions to proceed to trial with the prospect of further demands on the public purse to meet the legal costs.[57] Both private prosecutions generated the dilemma discussed earlier as to whether, when and how such intervention is considered necessary. Had the Attorney General, Sir Michael Havers, adhered to the modern practice of restricting the entry of a *nolle prosequi* to cases where, because of medical reasons, it was improper to proceed to trial, the impecunious Mr. Greaves would have been free to pursue his vendettas at the public expense. The Attorney General had refrained from intervening in the proceedings for criminal libel though, no doubt, he would have taken note of the criticisms levelled against the existing law by the House of Lords and by Comyns J. who presided over the trial at the Old Bailey. Shortly before the second trial for conspiracy to defraud was due to begin the Attorney announced his intention to enter a *nolle prosequi* in the case,[58] thus departing markedly from the established practice of recent times and, at the same time, manifesting the absolute nature of the Attorney General's *nolle prosequi* discretion in determining what the public interest requires.[59] Sir Michael Havers' decision is also significant for his reported rejection of the representations made by the defendants' lawyers that the Director of Public Prosecutions be asked to take over the outstanding prosecutions and bring the process to an end by offering no evidence against the accused.[60] It was for the House of Commons to denounce the decision if it saw fit to do so. In this case all the evidence points to overwhelming expressions of public support for the Attorney General's intervention.

---

[55] Lord Scarman, in lending his support for the suggested reform of the law advocated by Viscount Dilhorne, condemned the existing law under which the examining justices were indirectly responsible for the decision whether to allow a prosecution to proceed under the Libel Act 1843. (*Ibid.* at p. 509).

[56] *The Times*, February 29, 1980.

[57] See, *e.g. The Times*, February 28, 1980.

[58] *The Guardian*, March 1, 1980; New L.J., March 6, 1980.

[59] Edwards, *op. cit.* pp. 234–235.

[60] *Daily Telegraph*, February 29, 1980.

In another recent controversial case there was much criticism and misconception surrounding the handling of the prosecution in *R.* v. *Lemon; R.* v. *Gay News Ltd.*, in 1977.[61] The charge of blasphemous libel was brought at the instance of another well-known and controversial figure, Mrs. Mary Whitehouse. It arose out of publication in *Gay News*, a newspaper catering for homosexuals, of a poem entitled "The love that dares to speak its name." It purported to describe in explicit detail acts of sodomy and fellatio performed upon the body of Christ immediately after the moment of his death, as well as ascribing to Christ promiscuous homosexual practices with the Apostles and other men. An application for leave to prefer a voluntary bill of indictment for blasphemous libel against the newspaper's publisher and editor was brought before Bristow J., by Mrs. Whitehouse as a private prosecutor.[62] Leave to proceed was granted and at the subsequent trial before Judge King Hamilton and a jury at the Central Criminal Court both defendants were convicted by majority verdicts. Appeals against the convictions were rejected by the Court of Appeal and later by the House of Lords, in the course of which attention was mainly focussed on the relevant principles governing the requirement of *mens rea* in cases of blasphemy.[63]

Public interest, meanwhile, was fastening on to the question of the costs of the prosecution, which were perceived as a public charge following the taking over of the prosecution by the Director of Public Prosecutions, coupled with the dubious wisdom of lending the Crown's name to what some regarded as a moral crusade. *The Times*, in its leader,[64] set the tone that was to be followed by other newspapers and journals. It foresaw a danger that the success of the prosecution against "Gay News" would encourage other individuals and organisations to start similar, perhaps less reasonably founded, private prosecutions. To counteract any such tendency the editorial rejected a solution that would require the consent of the Attorney General or the Director of Public Prosecutions as a condition precedent to the bringing of a private prosecution, preferring to place its faith in the sanction of costs as the best means of deterring all but the most genuine prosecutions. The problem of the impecunious but determined private prosecutor, illustrated by the case of *Gleaves* v. *Deakin*, was to make its presence felt further down the road. According to *The Times* leader "The Crown should not normally take over such prosecutions . . . as it did in the *Gay News* case."[65]

[61] [1979] A.C. 617; affirming decision of the Court of Appeal [1979] Q.B. 10.

[62] *Ibid*. p. 620. This procedure was in accordance with the Law of Libel Amendment Act 1888, s.8. (*ante*, fn. 49.)

[63] By a majority of 3 to 2 (Lord Diplock and Lord Edmund-Davies dissenting), the Appellate Committee ruled that the offence of blasphemous libel did not depend on the accused having an intent to blaspheme, it being sufficient for the prosecution to prove that the publication had been intentional and that the matter published was in fact blasphemous. *Cf.* the approach followed by the Law Commission is its Working Paper No. 79 (1981) on *Offences against Religion and Public Worship*, reviewed in [1981] Crim. L.R. 811.

[64] *The Times*, July 13, 1977.

[65] *Ibid*.

Showing an understandable sensitivity to this misrepresentation of the true facts surrounding the prosecution, the Legal Secretary of the Law Officers' Department promptly despatched a letter to the editor pointing out that the proceedings had been commenced and continued as a private prosecution and that the Crown, in actual fact, had not taken over the case.[66] In a charitable afterthought, the opinion was ventured that confusion on this point had arisen because all prosecutions on indictment, whether privately instituted or not, are brought in the name of a written accusation made at the suit of the Crown.[67] This does not mean that the Crown takes over responsibility, financial or otherwise, for the proceedings in a private prosecution. This remains the sole responsibility of the private prosecutor. Even this prompt correction of the true facts behind the *Gay News* prosecution failed to persuade some critics. In its lead editorial on the case the *New Law Journal* persisted in condemning the "take over" of the prosecution by the Crown.[68] "Why," it inquired, "if the Crown did not consider it desirable that it should be the instigator of a prosecution of *Gay News* did it not have the courage of its convictions and leave Mrs. Whitehouse to carry the burden which she had, of her own free choice, assumed?"[69] For a publication with the standing enjoyed by this periodical to persist in its misrepresentation, despite a further communication from the Law Officers' Department categorically denying the factual basis of the journal's denunciation,[70] is a revealing commentary on its editorial standards.

IMMUNITY FROM PROSECUTION: UNDERTAKINGS BY THE DIRECTOR OF PUBLIC PROSECUTIONS

Earlier in this chapter I referred to the simmering problem of upon whose shoulders, the Attorney General or the Director of Public Prosecutions, rests the normal responsibility for intervening to stop a criminal prosecution that is in process, assuming it is considered to be in the public interest to do so. Given the prevailing attitude as to the limited circumstances that warrant resort to the Attorney General's *nolle prosequi* powers, the alternative procedure is to look to the Director of Public Prosecutions to invoke his statutory powers of intervention and to bring the proceedings to an end by offering no evidence. But as already explained, a notable lack of enthusiasm for this role has been evident on the part of recent holders of the office of Director of Public Prosecutions, each of whom has made it known that, in his opinion, it would be an improper exercise of the Director's statutory authority to use his powers of intervention in order to terminate a private prosecution by offering no

[66] *The Times*, Letters to the Editor, July 14, 1977.
[67] *Ibid.*, see, too, H.C. Deb., Vol. 935, Written Answers, col. 259, July 14, 1977.
[68] Vol. 127, pp. 701–702, July 21, 1977.
[69] *Ibid.*
[70] Letter dated July 28, 1977 from the Legal Secretary of the Department. The letter, without comment, appeared in the issue of the journal dated August 4, 1977—see *ibid.* p. 771.

evidence.[71] This high minded approach towards the citizen's right to pursue a private prosecution in his own behalf, however, has its own built-in limits.

A well established exception to these reservations against intervention arises in those situations where an accomplice decides to give evidence against his criminal confederates. The Director's motives for doing so, and the considerations that might encourage the accomplice turning Queen's evidence, are irrelevant in the present context. If the erstwhile accomplice, in the course of giving evidence, objects to answering an incriminating line of questions, the representative of the Director of Public Prosecutions will have to give an assurance to the court that the witness is not in peril, insofar as it is the Director's intention not to prosecute him for his participation in the crime in question or possibly other criminal activities. In effect, the Director's action amounts to a grant of immunity from prosecution. Until very recently, such immunity could legitimately be regarded as an impregnable sanctuary behind which an accomplice could retreat with a sense of absolute safety. Only theorists were disposed to conjecture what might happen if a private prosecutor sought to circumvent the Director's assurance of immunity by proceeding against the accomplice and charging him with the very offence that he admitted committing during the course of his evidence at the earlier trial.

Prior to the extraordinary case of *Turner* v. *D.P.P.*[72] in 1978 this eventuality had never been known to happen, let alone the prospect of a convicted person seeking to wreak revenge on his previous partner in crime by himself launching a private prosecution. Turner's attempt to turn the tables on his former accomplice was thwarted but his case provides useful illumination as to the extent of the Director's statutory powers of intervention and, no less importantly, that of the court to review and control the exercise of those powers. In the *Turner* case a formal undertaking by the Director of Public Prosecutions not to prosecute the accomplice Saggs was not given until close to the date of the actual trial. Turner was convicted of robbery and sentenced to seven years' imprisonment. Prior to the trial Saggs had made several statements under caution in the course of which he disclosed details of the robbery. Throughout this period of investigation Saggs and his family were under constant police protection. In prison, Turner petitioned the Home Office for permission to bring a private prosecution against Saggs. Before a decision on this unprecedented request was reached by the Home Office, counsel representing Turner successfully applied to a magistrates' court for the issue of a summons against his former confederate, charging him with the robbery to which he had confessed to the police. The next day a letter, signed by a Principal Assistant Director, was despatched to Turner's

---

[71] *Ante*, pp. 450–451.
[72] (1978) 68 Cr. App. R. 70, the essential chronology of events described in the text above are set out in the judgment of Mars-Jones J.

solicitors conveying the information that "the Director [of Public Prosecutions] is of the view, in these circumstances, that it is not in the interests of either justice or the public for the prosecution of Saggs commenced by your client to continue, and accordingly I have decided to assume responsibility for the proceedings with a view to offering no evidence when Saggs appears before the court."[73]

Clearly, by virtue of section 1(5) of the Prosecution of Offences Act 1908, the Principal Assistant Director was empowered to act with the same authority as the Director of Public Prosecutions. And section 2(3) of the same Act, as we have noted before, confers upon the Director and his Assistant Directors a wide, unfettered discretion to undertake at any stage the conduct of any private prosecution "if he thinks fit." Undeterred by the Assistant Director's initiative, Turner responded by bringing an action against the Director of Public Prosecutions contending that his intervention was unlawful and *ultra vires*, a claim that the Director asked should be struck out as being vexatious and an abuse of the process of the court.[74] And so the case of *Turner* v. *D.P.P.* came before Mars-Jones J. for decision, it being perhaps worth noting that it was the same judge whose view, in *R.* v. *Broad*, that the court could refuse consent to a prosecutor desirous of offering no evidence had been upheld by the Court of Appeal.[75]

The trial judge was under no illusions as to the important questions of public policy which arose out of the case before him. If the proceedings were to be prosecuted to a successful conclusion they would have the result of punishing the accomplice Saggs for giving evidence as a witness for the Crown in the original trial against Turner. "Such a result or even the threat of it," said Mars-Jones J., "would obviously have very grave consequences so far as the administration of justice is concerned. I do not need to spell out in detail the effect on future criminal investigations or proceedings if a witness giving evidence for the prosecution in these circumstances could not rely upon the undertaking of the Director of Public Prosecutions and his cooperation in ensuring that such a witness would be protected against a private prosecution of this kind."[76] In ordering that the plaintiff's claim be struck out, Mars-Jones J., declared that it was impossible to argue, having regard to the wide powers conferred upon the Director of Public Prosecutions, that it was unlawful and *ultra vires* for the Director to intervene in the private prosecution only for the purpose of offering no evidence. Such a procedure, the judge continued, paralleled that of the Attorney General entering a *nolle prosequi* as to which "the courts have never sought to interfere with the exercise of that power. It was natural for the Crown in whose name the criminal proceedings were instituted to reserve the right of Attorney General to stay proceedings at will. Likewise,

---

[73] *Ibid.* at p. 73.
[74] R.S.C., Ords. 18, 19.
[75] *Ante*, pp. 453–454.
[76] (1978) 68 Cr. App. R. 70 at p. 73.

in the case of proceedings before courts of summary jurisdiction, the Director of Public Prosecutions has the same power and has exercised it time and time again . . . Although this was a private prosecution it was, and in the nature of things had to be, brought in the name of the Crown."[77] There being no suggestion that the Director or his staff had acted in bad faith and had clearly acted in the public interest to prevent a witness from being prosecuted after being given an undertaking by the Director of Public Prosecutions that this would not happen, the court concluded that there was no case for the trial of a preliminary issue as to whether the Director's statutory discretion had been exercised properly.

An earlier challenge to the immunity extended to the leading prosecution witness in the trial of *Jeremy Thorpe* was similarly rejected on the grounds of lack of jurisdiction by the Divisional Court, consisting of Lord Widgery C.J., Griffiths and Gibson JJ.[78] The challenge to the Director's grant of immunity was launched before the preliminary hearing had taken place. It will be recalled that Mr. Thorpe, formerly Leader of the Parliamentary Liberal Party, was charged, along with three other accused, with conspiracy to murder and incitement to murder. The terms of the Director of Public Prosecutions' letter extending immunity to Mr. Bessell, a principal witness but not an accomplice, were conditional on the witness giving evidence for the Crown at the magistrates' court and, if the case went to trial, at the Crown Court. The letter continued: "No criminal proceedings will be instituted by the police or any other prosecuting authority against Mr. Bessell in respect of matters forming part of the subject matter of the proceedings against John Jeremy Thorpe and others; or in respect of matters which may be referred to in court in such proceedings; and in the event of the private prosecution of Mr. Bessell in respect of any such matter, the Director will assume responsibility for the conduct of those proceedings and offer no evidence against Mr. Bessell."[79] It will be noted at once that the Director's letter indicates a readiness to intervene and stop the proceedings even if the later prosecution were to be instituted by a private citizen. This kind of undertaking considerably dilutes any weight that might otherwise attach to protestations by the Director of Public Prosecutions that it would be an improper exercise of his statutory powers to stifle a private prosecution which has otherwise been properly set in motion.

---

[77] *Ibid*. p. 76.

[78] *R.* v. *D.P.P. ex p. Thorpe* file no. SCN/12291/77, transcript of Div. Ct. hearing, November 16, 1978. The case was reported in *The Times*, November 17, 1978.

[79] *Ibid*. pp. 2–3. Counsel explained that, so far as the Director was aware, there was no evidence to suggest that Bessell could properly be prosecuted for any offence, whether arising out of the *Thorpe* case or any others; "so that in this case the immunity which is being extended is not by way of an indulgence or shield; it is simply by way of reassurance to a witness outside the jurisdiction that, as far as the D.P.P. is concerned, he will not be prosecuted for any matters 'arising, during or out of the actual trial' "—*ibid*. p. 8. See too the uncommunicative statement by the Attorney General in the House of Commons on the same subject, H.C. Deb., Vol. 959, cols. 28–29, November 27, 1978.

Everyone concerned in the hearing before the Divisional Court recognised the unique character of the application to quash or vary the immunity authorised by the Director of Public Prosecutions. No other case could be cited where the witness, upon whom immunity from prosecution was conferred, was not a self-confessed accomplice.[80] Counsel for Mr. Thorpe argued vigorously that the unedifying bargain struck between the Director and the witness was contrary to public policy and hideously unfair in that it gave a blanket immunity, not in terms of the subject matter of the actual proceedings but against perjury or the revelation of any other crime. For his part the Director of Public Prosecutions viewed the application for certiorari or prohibition as an invitation to the court to restrict his unfettered jurisdiction in deciding who and who not to prosecute and how the prosecution should be conducted.

Counsel representing the Director argued that the actual interpretation of the immunity was not a matter for the court, whilst acknowledging at the same time that the trial judge may take the view, as he can about any witness, that the interests of justice would not be served by allowing evidence to be heard on the part of the witness to whom immunity had been extended. It is in this sense only, it was argued, that the Director's decision is subject to review by the trial judge. In refusing the application challenging the immunity, Lord Widgery C.J. stressed that the Divisional Court's decision was not to be taken as limiting in any way "the power and duty of the presiding judge at the trial to deal with the evidence and any matters of inducement then before him in accordance with the law."[81] This reconciliation of the respective discretionary powers, those of the Director and the trial judge, does not invalidate the protection afforded the Crown witness, but it is capable of creating a major obstacle to the fulfilment of the purposes that gave rise to the conferring of immunity. To that extent only can it be said that the Director's statutory power is constrained by the possibility of judicial review, for example, as to the scope of the immunity or the existence of a continuing inducement by holding in abeyance other criminal proceedings to which the witness was subject.

Exactly how far judicial intervention of this kind may extend will depend largely on the view taken of the discretionary powers conferred by Parliament upon the Director of Public Prosecutions. Two distinct lines of thought can be discerned from judicial dicta in recent cases involving accomplices who turn Queen's evidence following a promise of immunity. These undertakings by the Director were judged to be an acceptable price to pay in order to secure the presentation of crucial evidence at the trial, and without which convictions against the leading members of organised groups resorting to crimes of serious violence would never have been possible. The elaborate contents of the immunity granted in the case of R. v. Turner et al.,[82] provide some indication of the importance attached to

[80] Ibid. p. 14.
[81] Loc. cit.
[82] (1975) 61 Cr. App. R. 67.

the accomplice's statement incriminating his partners in crimes. These activities, involving a series of major robberies, netted proceeds well in excess of £1 million. The Court of Appeal had few kind words to say regarding the contents of the letter from the Department of Public Prosecutions to the accomplice's solicitors, setting forth conditions under which immunity would be obtainable. Speaking for the entire court, Lawton L.J. stated: "Above all else the spectacle of the Director recording in writing, at the behest of a criminal like Smalls, his undertaking to give immunity from further prosecutions, is one which we find distasteful. Nothing of a similar kind must ever happen again. Undertakings of immunity from prosecution may have to be given in the public interest. They should never be given by the police. The Director should give them most sparingly; and in cases involving grave crimes it would be prudent of him to consult the Law Officers before making any promises. In saying what we have, we should not be taken as doubting well-established practice of calling accomplices on behalf of the Crown who have been charged in the same indictment as the accused and who have pleaded guilty."[83]

No doubt the feelings of the Court were dictated by their assessment of Smalls as "one of the most dangerous and craven villains who had ever given evidence for the Crown."[84] Nevertheless, as Lawton L.J. reminded his colleagues, it is in the interests of the public that criminals should be brought to justice. Employing Queen's evidence to accomplish this end is distasteful, he continued, and has been distasteful for at least 300 years to judges, lawyers and members of the public. Hale C.J., writing about 1650, used strong language in condemning the plea of approvement which was the precursor of the modern practice of granting immunity from prosecution, or further prosecution, to accomplices willing to give evidence for the Crown. "The truth is," Hale wrote, "that more mischief hath come to good men, by these kinds of approvements by false accusations of desperate villains, than benefit to the public by the discovery and convicting of real offenders."[85] In the judgment of the Court of Appeal, Hale's comment should be constantly in the minds of the Director of Public Prosecutions and his staff, an observation that, as Lawton L.J. readily recognised, neither added to the weight of ethical condemnation nor dissipated it.[86]

---

[83] *Ibid.* at p. 80. Lawton L.J.'s exhortations may have exerted some influence in the Crown's refusal to disclose to the court the terms of the immunity conferred by the D.P.P. for Northern Ireland upon a "supergrass," a self-confessed commander in the outlawed Ulster Volunteer Force. On the basis of his evidence, 14 other principal members of the same organisation were convicted of terrorist offences including bombing attacks and murder. The immunity conferred extended to the killing of a post-mistress, in which the informer had participated. The Crown's refusal to give evidence about the terms of the immunity was criticised by the trial judge, Murray J.—*The Times*, April 12, 1983.

[84] *Ibid.* at p. 79.

[85] *Pleas of the Crown*, Vol. 2, p. 226, and *cf.* the views expressed by Radzinowicz, *History of the English Criminal Law*, Vol. 2, pp. 52–56.

[86] *Ibid.*

Opinions will differ as to the ethical justification for resorting to immunity guarantees in pursuit of the larger goal of bringing a large number of notorious criminals to the bar of justice. What defines "the public interest" in these circumstances will naturally depend on the person who sets the governing criteria. The close association of the police and the Director of Public Prosecutions has been the subject of fuller treatment earlier in this work, and the case of *R. v. Turner et al.* provides a vivid insight into the degree of collaboration that prevails in the investigation of serious crime. Promises of immunity extended by the police are not worth a candle in the strict sense, there being neither statutory nor common law power in any police officer to grant immunity from prosecution. References by the Court of Appeal to the need for the Director to exercise his immunity powers most sparingly would not have occasioned any strong reaction, as there is no empirical evidence to suggest that such authorisations are made with regularity or what might be regarded as disturbing frequency. On the need for consultation with the Law Officers in cases involving grave crimes no possible objection can be taken to the court's intimation that political prudence suggests the advisability of involving the responsible Minister of the Crown who must defend the Director's decision if it is challenged on the floor of the House of Commons.

The most debatable statement by Lawton L.J. is that in which he declared: "Nothing of a similar kind must ever happen again."[87] This would appear to go beyond the bounds of legitimate criticism by the judiciary of actions taken by the Director of Public Prosecutions. It is entirely proper, if the circumstances call for public censure, for such criticism to be expressed forcefully and independently by the Bench. With respect, however, to the Court of Appeal's denunciation of the Director's undertaking in *R. v. Turner et al.* it comes very close to the issuing of a direction that implies a judicial power to exercise control over this aspect of the Director's discretionary authority. It was so interpreted by the editor of *Archbold's Criminal Pleading, Evidence, and Practice* according to which the observations made by Lawton L.J., during the course of delivering the judgment of the Court of Appeal, were "apparently intended (at least to some extent) to regulate the conduct of the Director of Public Prosecutions should circumstances of a similar nature arise again."[88]

If this interpretation correctly reflects the attitude of the Lord Justice of Appeal in *R. v. Turner et al.* the implications of the principle being espoused are far-reaching and unlikely to pass unchallenged. At the first opportunity which presented itself in *D.P.P. v. Brown and others*, the unreported application by the defendants in *R. v. Turner et al.* for leave to appeal against conviction,[89] both Lord Salmon and Lord Dilhorne strongly

[87] *Ante*, fn. 83.
[88] 41st ed., para. 4–128.
[89] Transcript of the hearing before the Appellate Committee, June 23, 1975.

disapproved of the passage quoted above. "What I think is a little disturbing," said Lord Salmon, "is that if that comment of Lord Justice Lawton was not justified, that it should be left standing, because it might put considerable inhibition on the Director in future, if exactly similar circumstances arose."[90] As a former Attorney General, Lord Dilhorne was quick to grasp the potential significance of the position adopted in *R.* v. *Turner* by the Court of Appeal. "I am wondering," he said, "to what extent it is right for any court to give directions to the Director as to how he should conduct his business. The Director of Public Prosecutions works under the Attorney General; he does not work under any judges at all and any directions he receives as to the way in which he does his work surely must come from the Attorney General. I would have thought it quite wrong for it to come from any judicial authority at all. He may be condemned for what he has done but he must not be told what he has got to do in the future."[91]

Constitutionally speaking, there can be no serious challenge to the analysis contained in Lord Dilhorne's statement in *D.P.P.* v. *Brown.* It conforms to the doctrine admirably summarised in a very short passage in *Gouriet* v. *Union of Post Office Workers* in the course of which Lord Dilhorne enlarged on its application to the relationship of the Attorney General to the courts. "He may stop any prosecution on indictment by entering a *nolle prosequi.* He merely has to sign a piece of paper saying that he does not wish the prosecution to continue. He need not give any reason. He can direct the institution of a prosecution and direct the Director of Public Prosecutions to take over the conduct of any criminal proceedings and he may tell him to offer no evidence. In the exercise of these powers he is not subject to direction by his ministerial colleagues or to control and supervision by the courts."[92] The contrary doctrine, expounded by the Court of Appeal in *R.* v. *Broad* and *R.* v. *Turner,* is dangerous and should not be followed. The obvious dangers derive from its implications for both inhibiting intervention by, and restricting the ability of, the Director of Public Prosecutions to follow through on an undertaking, given bona fide and in the public interest, to an accomplice or other witness not to prosecute him if he measures up to his part of the agreement. Criticism should never be stifled but there is a very wide gulf that separates judicial comment, however forcefully expressed, and judicial claims to control certain decisions made by the Director of Public Prosecutions or any other prosecutor acting in the name of the Crown. It is for the Attorney General, not the courts, to exercise control over his subordinate the Director of Public Prosecutions and for Parliament to hold the Law Officers accountable for actions that are said to have been taken in the public interest.

[90] *Ibid.* p. 20.
[91] *Ibid.*
[92] [1978] A.C. 435 at p. 487.

IMMUNITY FROM PROSECUTION: UNDERTAKINGS BY THE ATTORNEY GENERAL

Immunity from prosecution can also be conferred directly at the hands of the Attorney General though this form of immunity is much less frequently resorted to. Its exercise in recent times with respect to the politically sensitive areas of treason and espionage has aroused Parliament to unusual bursts of activity in seeking full explanations from the Attorney General as to the reasons for his predecessors' actions. The circumstances surrounding the handling of the *Blunt* affair were to be thoroughly aired in the House of Commons[93] 15 years after the Attorney General of the day, Sir John Hobson, had authorised the grant of immunity to Anthony Blunt, art historian and surveyor of the Queen's pictures. Blunt had joined the security service during the early days of the Second World War and served in that capacity until 1945. He first came under suspicion of passing information to the Russians in the course of the inquiries that followed the defection in 1951 of Burgess and Maclean, the high-ranking Foreign Office diplomats. Between then and 1963, when Philby's espionage activities on behalf of the Russians were exposed, Blunt was interviewed on 11 separate occasions. Throughout these interrogations Blunt persisted in his denial of spying and no evidence against him was forthcoming. In 1964 new information was received from a United States citizen, Mr. Michael Whitney Straight, that directly implicated Blunt in espionage activities of long standing.[94] This new evidence, however, did not provide a sufficient basis on which to bring charges of treason against Blunt. As a result of further interrogation by members of M.I.5. and the special branch of the Metropolitan London Police it became apparent that, provided he first received immunity from prosecution, Blunt was prepared to make a confession and to co-operate fully with the security authorities.

According to the various pieces of evidence that can be gleaned from the Government's statements in the House of Commons on the *Blunt* case the actual decision to grant immunity was taken following a meeting convened by the Attorney General, Sir John Hobson, and attended by the Acting Director of Public Prosecutions, Mr. Maurice Crump, the head of M.I.5, Sir Roger Hollis, and Commander Leonard Burt, head of the special branch.[95] No special importance seems to have been attached to the

[93] The first carefully prepared statement was made by the Prime Minister in the form of a Written Answer to a private notice question—see H.C. Deb., Vol. 973, cols. 679–681, November 15, 1979.

[94] Mr. Straight's account of his involvement with Blunt, Burgess and the other self confessed Soviet agents is contained in his unimpressive apologia, *After Long Silence*, (Collins, 1983).

[95] *Ante*, fn. 93, *loc. cit.* Speaking in November 1979, many years after his retirement from the position of Deputy Director of Public Prosecutions, Mr. Crump did not dispute the account given by Mr. F.D. Barry of how the Blunt file had been handled in the D.P.P.'s office. Mr. Barry was an Assistant Director at the time. According to his recollection the file was extremely thin and did not contain Blunt's confession. "At that stage Blunt had simply made the offer to confess and to reveal what he knew but would only have made his full statement after immunity was agreed." Crump's recollection was that "a meeting of that kind [with the Attorney General] would not have been unusual. In fact, dealing with a file like Blunt's would have been all in a day's work." *Sunday Telegraph*, November 18, 1979.

Attorney General's decision at the time. The grant of immunity was regarded as the only means whereby the security authorities could get a firm handle on the full extent of Blunt's espionage activities, his association with Burgess, Maclean and Philby, and generally the dimensions of Soviet penetration of this country's security and intelligence services. Because of the inducement associated with the making of the confession, however, its contents could not be introduced in evidence against Blunt, should the Crown have brought him to trial. And without Blunt's confession there appears to have been insufficient evidence to support a prosecution for treason.

That was the position in 1964. According to the Commons statements made in 1979 by Prime Minister Thatcher and the present Attorney General, Sir Michael Havers, the *Blunt* case had been reviewed during the intervening years by successive Attorneys General on assuming office—in 1973 by Sir Peter Rawlinson, in 1974 by Mr. Sam Silkin and in 1979 by Sir Michael Havers. The decision in each instance was to abide by the immunity authorised by Sir John Hobson in 1964.[96] Implicit in this approach is the conditional nature of the Attorney General's grant of immunity, it being co-terminous with the first Law Officer's tenure of office. Each subsequent Attorney General is free to re-examine the file and make a fresh determination. It is doubtful whether such an understanding has been widely recognised and its correctness may well be questioned. It has never been suggested, for example, that a pardon could be revoked by the Sovereign acting on the advice of a new Home Secretary who took a different view of the merits of the case from that of his predecessor. Furthermore, as pointed out by the Appellate Committee of the House of Lords in *D.P.P.* v. *Brown*, no case could be recalled in the past hundred years in which fresh proceedings have been brought at the instance of the Crown following the entry of a *nolle prosequi* by the Attorney General of the day.[97] By analogy it could be argued that something akin to a moral estoppel should ensure that there was no reneging on a solemn undertaking

---

[96] The first intimation of this series of reviews of the original decision to grant immunity was contained in the Prime Minister's written reply—*ante*, fn. 93. It was repeated in Mrs. Thatcher's fuller statement during the Commons debates on the Blunt affair on November 21, 1979—*ibid.* Vol. 974, cols. 402–410. Speaking in the same debate, the former Attorney General, Mr. Sam Silkin, confirmed that on taking his new duties in 1974 the Cabinet Office had wished to be satisfied that the incoming Attorney General took the same view as his predecessors and, if not, what advice he had to give. After reviewing the case and learning that no new evidence, which would be admissible in a trial, had been disclosed to him that had not been available to his predecessors, Mr. Silkin advised that a prosecution was out of the question. Later, in 1978, when Andrew Boyle's book *Climate of Treason* was in contemplation, the question of instituting a prosecution was again brought before the Attorney General with a much fuller account of Blunt's pre-war activities. Mr. Silkin remained of the same opinion that "there was no prospect of embarking on a successful prosecution and that, even if there were, the grant of immunity would have formed an unshakeable obstacle to such a possibility." Mr. Silkin's later opinion was communicated to the Prime Minister, Mr. Callaghan, in person. H.C. Deb., Vol. 974, cols. 422–427, November 21, 1979.

[97] *Ante*, fn. 89 at p. 17 *per* Lord Salmon.

by a Law Officer of the Crown to grant immunity. On the other hand, circumstances can be envisaged in which the national interest might require that a person be placed on trial, notwithstanding an earlier grant of immunity. Such action would be constitutionally proper.

Support for this view, it is suggested, appears in the Attorney General's revised policy concerning the granting of immunity in criminal cases which was disclosed to the House of Commons during the debate on the handling of the *Leo Long* case in 1981.[98] "True immunities" Sir Michael Havers declared "are uncommon because it is now the practice not to go further than [give] an undertaking that any confession obtained as a result will not be used against the maker." If other evidence to justify the prosecution becomes available then proceedings may be brought.[99] It is not known whether the introduction of this new policy governing grants of immunity was dictated by the public reactions to the *Blunt* affair or whether it derives from a reconsideration of the basic philosophy underlying the question of immunity in general, including those cases in which the Director of Public Prosecutions has acted without reference to the Attorney General. Whatever may have been the moving force behind the change it would be wrong to ignore the ethical considerations that inevitably come into play in situations of this sort.

The holding out of a promise of immunity from prosecution as the price that must be paid by the Crown in return for a confession effectively reaffirms the well-established privilege against self incrimination. For the Crown, in those circumstances, to proceed to sustain the prosecution's case against the accused by relying on other evidence generated as a result of the confession, creates an impression of sharp practice that ought not to be countenanced, unless it can be shown that there are other substantial grounds justifying the practice. Such allegations of bad faith, it is suggested, might be confidently met if it can be demonstrated that in holding out the promise of immunity its precise limitations were revealed

---

[98] H.C. Deb., Vol. 12, ser. 6, cols. 12–13, Written Answers, November 9, 1981. The criteria used by the Attorney General or the D.P.P. in deciding whether or not to grant immunity from prosecution were stated by Sir Michael Havers to include: (i) whether in the interests of justice it is of more value to have a suspected person as a witness for the Crown than a possible defendant; (ii) whether in the interest of public safety and security the obtaining of information about the extent and nature of criminal activities is of greater importance than the possible conviction of an individual; (iii) whether it is very unlikely that any information could be obtained without an offer of immunity and whether it is also very unlikely that any prosecution could be launched against the person to whom the immunity is offered." *Loc. cit.*

[99] As a direct result of the handling of the *Long* case, the procedures followed by the security service have also been changed. Henceforth, a person suspected of an espionage offence will not be interviewed on the basis that he need not fear prosecution unless the case has first been referred to the Attorney General and permission has been given for the interview to be conducted on that basis—H.C. Deb., Vol. 12, ser. 6, col. 13, and Oral Answers, col. 306, November 9, 1981. An earlier indication of this new policy had been given by the Attorney General during the major debate on the Blunt affair, H.C. Deb., Vol. 974, col. 512, November 21, 1979. On that occasion the Attorney General had prefaced his statement with the qualifying words "this is more usually the case nowadays."

and not obscured in any way. This would require the court to be satisfied that the accused person had been adequately informed, at the time of the immunity negotiations, that he might still be the object of a prosecution if independent evidence, unrelated to his confession, made the institution of criminal proceedings possible and necessary.[1] If, however, the immunity conferred is expressed in unconditional language there should be no question of circumventing its existence on the grounds that the accused's resulting confession is not necessary to maintain the prosecution's case. Some critics might even find intolerable the distinctions drawn in the above analysis but I would maintain that the emphasis is properly placed on making explicit the exact terms on which the inducement is held out to the prospective accused. The issuance of formal guidelines confirming the Attorney General's revised policy in this regard would be a progressive step towards full disclosure of the principles governing the exercise of the discretionary power vested in the Law Officers of the Crown.

During the height of the controversy in November 1979 surrounding the handling of the *Blunt* case in 1964, much of the criticism was directed against the apparent failure to notify and, presumably, to seek the prior approval of, in turn, the Home Secretary, Lord Brooke, and the Prime Minister of the time, Sir Alec Douglas Home. The facts, as disclosed to the House of Commons,[2] indicate that the Attorney General acted in strict accordance with the constitutional principle that the decision was his, and his alone, to take. Sir John Hobson was aware that the Home Secretary had been apprised of the possible granting of immunity to Blunt[3] but chose not to consult with his ministerial colleague or, so far as is known, any other member of the Government. There was no contact whatsoever with the Prime Minister.[4] The political sensitivity of the case appears not to have registered with either the Acting Director of Public Prosecutions[5] or the Attorney General, suggesting, at best, that the decision was taken on strictly national security grounds. On reflection, it appears inevitable that the decision to grant Blunt immunity from prosecution contained all the necessary ingredients for generating political waves, as evidenced by the lively Commons exchanges in 1979 and again in 1981. All the indications

---

[1] *Ibid.*

[2] *Ante*, fn. 93. In her statement to the House on November 15, 1979 the Prime Minister disclosed that the Director General of the Security Service, acting in accordance with the Maxwell Fyfe directive of 1952 (see *ante* fn. 6), had met with the Home Secretary on March 2, 1964 to tell him of the new information implicating Blunt and indicated his intention to consult with the D.P.P. on how to conduct the interview with Blunt, bearing in mind the security service's need to obtain as much intelligence as possible about Soviet penetration. There is no record of the Home Secretary informing or discussing the Blunt situation with the Prime Minister of the day, (now Lord Douglas Home)—Vol. 974, cols. 405–406, November 21, 1979.

[3] *Ibid.* col. 407.

[4] *Ibid.*

[5] In the opinion of the Assistant Director, Mr. F.D. Barry, who handled the *Blunt* file and who was informed by his colleague of the outcome of the meeting at which the decision was taken to grant immunity: "From my experience I consider it to be most unlikely that any politicians would have been informed at the time"—fn. 95, *op. cit.*

point to what would have been an even more turbulent reaction had the news of the Attorney General's action become publicly known at the time his decision was made.

So far as the future is concerned, new procedures were announced by the Prime Minister that maintain inviolate the well-established relationship of the Attorney General to the government and his ministerial colleagues in matters pertaining to the machinery of criminal prosecutions. Primary responsibility for the security service, it was again emphasised, lies with the Home Secretary to whom the Director General of M.I.5 normally reports.[6] In exceptional circumstances, as for example where the security risk involves a minister or senior public servant, the head of the security service could report directly to the Prime Minister who has overall responsibility for the nation's security. The normal channels of reporting would be for the Home Secretary to advise the Prime Minister of situations that require the head of government being brought into the picture.[7] As to the responsibilities of the Attorney General, the Prime Minister informed the House of Commons: "If the Attorney General is asked to authorise a grant of immunity from prosecution in a case involving national security, he should satisfy himself that the Home Secretary is aware that the request has been made. In cases of especial doubt or difficulty, the Attorney General or the Home Secretary, or both, may wish to see that the Prime Minister is also aware that the request had been made. The Attorney General and the Home Secretary should always be informed of the outcome of the offer of immunity. It is the Home Secretary's responsibility to ensure that the Prime Minister is informed."[8] It can be confidently surmised that this statement by Mrs. Thatcher had received the prior approval of the Attorney General, Sir Michael Havers,[9] and it will be seen that it in no way qualifies the independence of the Law Officers of the Crown in reaching the final decision whether to grant immunity or authorise the institution of criminal proceedings.

There is nothing unconstitutional in charging the Attorney General with responsibility for ensuring that the Prime Minister and the Home Secretary

[6] A convenient account of the administrative controls and ministerial responsibility for the operation of the security service, that were in place at the time of the decision to grant immunity in the *Blunt* case, is contained in *Lord Denning's Report* into the handling of the Profumo affair, see Cmnd. 2152, para. 238. Foremost among the official documents defining the constitutional position in authoritative terms is the directive issued in 1952 to the Director General of the British Security Service by the then Home Secretary, Sir David Maxwell Fyfe (*loc. cit.*). For a discussion of the comparative constitutional positions on this subject, in the United Kingdom and Canada, see Edwards, *Ministerial Responsibility for National Security*, pp. 58–64.

[7] H.C. Deb., Vol. 974, col. 407, November 21, 1979.

[8] *Ibid.* cols. 407–408. As noted earlier (*ante*, fn. 96), Mr. Silkin informed Prime Minister Callaghan of his decision, following his re-examination of the Blunt file in 1978. The Attorney General, likewise, informed Mr. Wilson, when he was Prime Minister, at the conclusion of his earlier review of the *Blunt* case in 1974. According to Mr. Silkin: "Both [P.M.s] entirely properly accepted my decision without question but, again quite properly and naturally, wanted to know why a self-confessed traitor was able to remain a free man."—personal communication to the author, June 12, 1983.

[9] *Ibid.* cols. 511–514 and esp. col. 520.

are aware of the circumstances that require the Attorney to make up his mind on the issue of immunity. Each minister has a separate function to perform in the field of national security but there is no suggestion, and neither should there be, that the Attorney General is obliged to take directions from either the Home Secretary or the Prime Minister. The country's interests can be expected to be uppermost in the minds of the respective participants and the final decision to be made by the Attorney General will be all the more defensible if he takes into consideration any views that his ministerial colleagues, in charge of the nation's security and intelligence services, may see fit to make to him.

There was another flurry of excitement in 1981 when the country learnt that yet another Soviet intelligence agent, *Leo Long*, had transmitted secret information to the Russians while he was on the staff of M.I.14, the War Office branch of military intelligence that dealt with the deployment of German forces.[10] Long's name had been disclosed by Blunt as being among those whom he had recruited in Cambridge in the 1930s and whose espionage activities on behalf of the Soviet Union he had controlled during the war years. It is understood that Long, like his mentor, requested immunity from prosecution but, unlike Blunt, his request was turned down for reasons that have never been publicly disclosed. A reasonable conjecture would conclude that Long was not as strategically placed in negotiating with the security service as Blunt, whose confession preceded the disclosures made by Long in his statement. What is known is that Long, prior to confessing in 1964, had been told that he was not likely to be prosecuted if he co-operated with the security service's interrogators.[11] Since neither the Attorney General nor the Director of Public Prosecutions was consulted before the interrogation[12] we can only conclude that the security service representatives were flying a kite that was not within their power to control. The ploy may have been effective in its result but it rendered impossible the use of Long's confession in any criminal proceedings that might have been contemplated against him. From answers given in the House of Commons by the present Attorney General[13] it is possible to conclude that there were a few other cases connected with the Burgess-Maclean-Philby affair in which inducements were offered by the security authorities to persons suspected of espionage, resulting in the same insurmountable obstacle as to the inadmissibility of such statements in a criminal trial.[14]

---

[10] H.C. Deb., Vol. 12, ser. 6, cols. 305–306, November 9, 1981.

[11] *Ibid.*

[12] *Ibid.* col. 306. The Attorney General also had previously so informed the House of Commons in a written answer the significance of which had escaped most people's attention—see H.C. Deb., Vol. 974, col. 99, November 20, 1979.

[13] In his statement to the House of Commons on November 9, 1981 the Attorney General confirmed that Mr. Long was one of the persons to whom he had been referring in his 1979 statement on the same subject.

[14] Sir Michael Havers stressed repeatedly that in matters of national security true immunity from prosecution, at the behest of the Attorney General or the D.P.P., had been granted in only the one case—Anthony Blunt—since the end of World War II.

It is a matter of concern that no obligation exists upon the Attorney General to disclose to Parliament any grant of immunity that he may have authorised. As the circumstances revealed in the *Blunt* and *Long* cases demonstrate, there may well have been good reasons for not making public the Attorney General's decision to grant immunity in the one case and withhold it in the other. Those reasons would likely be described as in the interests of national security, a compendious phrase the exact definition of which is generally avoided.[15] Presumably, the same reasoning dictated the response of the Home Office to the Private Secretary to the Queen in 1964 recommending that no action be taken to strip Blunt of his official title as curator of the Queen's pictures,[16] a step that, almost certainly, would have become public knowledge and with it the communication to the Soviet intelligence authorities that Blunt's espionage activities on their behalf had been discovered. To acknowledge the logic of this approach does not diminish the contrary expectation that a self-confessed traitor be made to stand trial and not treated differently than other, less prominent, Soviet agents.

The balancing of these conflicting considerations is always difficult, added to which may be the complication of inadmissible statements. My present purpose is not to criticise the particular decisions that were reached in the *Blunt* and *Long* cases. It is to question the absence of any constitutional obligation upon the Attorney General to inform Parliament of his decision. At a minimum, this should involve imparting to the Shadow Attorney General and the leaders of the major parliamentary parties, in appropriate conditions of confidentiality, sufficient details that will ensure that the immunity decision is subject to independent scrutiny. The new procedure, set in place following the recent parliamentary debates into the Blunt and Long affairs, is designed to ensure that the Prime Minister and the Home Secretary, the key members of the executive responsible for the nation's security service, are fully briefed as to the Attorney General's intentions. In my judgment, this does not go far enough and fails to give the proper emphasis to the principle of ministerial accountability. The kind of circumstances we are concerned with in espionage cases, involving possible grants of protection from the criminal process, may not lend themselves to public debate at the time the decisions are taken. It is, however, a serious omission to neglect considering ways and means of establishing some kind of parliamentary sounding board that combines the need to protect the country's security interests with the fundamental

---

[15] For an admirable exposition of the elements contained within the compendious phrase "national security," defining the interests requiring protection and the threats posed to those interests, see the *Second Report of the [McDonald] Commission of Inquiry* Vol. 1., pp. 39–47.

[16] This recommendation was conveyed by the Home Secretary at a meeting in the Home Office on June 17, 1964, attended by the Queen's Private Secretary, the Permanent Under Secretary and the Director General of the Security Service. This meeting took place after the Attorney General had decided to grant immunity and Blunt had made his statement admitting to spying for the Russians during the war when serving in the security service—*per* Prime Minister Thatcher in H.C. Deb., Vol. 974, cols. 405–406, November 21, 1979.

principle of accountability that justifies the degree of independence accorded to the Attorney General in exercising his prerogative powers.[17]

IMMUNITY BY THE GRANT OF A PARDON BY THE SOVEREIGN

The prerogative of mercy, vested in the Sovereign, includes the power to confer a pardon upon a person who claims that he has been the victim of a miscarriage of justice in, for example, having been wrongfully convicted. According to constitutional practice followed in Britain over the past 150 years, this action is taken on the exclusive advice and recommendation of the Secretary of State for Home Affairs. During the nineteenth century it was common practice to grant a pardon to an accomplice who was prepared to turn Queen's evidence, but this resort to the machinery of pardons, prior to the registering of a conviction, has long since become obsolete.[18] Where the reluctance of a witness to testify on behalf of the Crown did not stem from his being an accomplice but arose on the ground that he would incriminate himself, it was also known for the Crown to prepare a free pardon in advance, ready to be produced by prosecuting counsel. The last occasion when a free pardon was granted to a witness in these circumstances was in 1891.[19] There is now a general understanding among British constitutional law authorities[20] that the practice of

[17] An expression of the same concerns was voiced by the former Prime Minister, Mr. James Callaghan, during the Blunt debate, H.C. Deb., Vol. 974, cols. 510–511, November 21, 1979. For the Canadian proposals, recommended by the McDonald Commission of Inquiry but as yet not implemented or approved by the Government and Parliament, see *op. cit. Second Report*, Vol. 2, pp. 881–905. See also Bill C-157 and the *Report of the* [Pitfield] *Senate Committee on the Canadian Security Intelligence Service* November 1983. *Cf.* the recommendation contained in the [British] House of Commons Liaison Committee's *First Report (session 1982–83) on the Select Committee System*, para. 25 calling for the exercise of parliamentary accountability with respect to the security services through the medium of the Select Committees on Home and Foreign Affairs.

[18] See L. Radzinowicz, *A History of English Criminal Law*, Vol. 2, pp. 40–56. Whether the pardon incentive was used "as an absolute right under statutes, as an equitable claim to the mercy of the Crown, under proclamation or in response to individual applications the various methods employed during the 18th and 19th centuries were on such a scale that 'pardon ultimately became a major instrument for bringing criminals to justice' "—*op. cit.* p. 52.

[19] Home Office historical note on "Pardons before conviction," kindly provided to the author. The same document states: "When in 1947 counsel prosecuting in a criminal case inquired as to the possibility of using the prerogative in that way he was informed, after consultation with the Director of Public Prosecutions, that it was no longer the practice to grant free pardons for this purpose."

[20] See, *e.g.* Wade and Phillips, *Constitutional and Administrative Law* (9th ed. by A.W. Bradley) p. 338, and S.A. de Smith, *Constitutional and Administrative Law* (1971), p. 128, who wrote, "It would seem that a pardon may be granted before conviction; but this power is never exercised. The line between pardon before conviction and the unlawful exercise of dispensing power is thin." R.F.V. Heuston, on the other hand, in his *Essays in Constitutional Law* (2nd ed.), makes no reference to modern English practice and states without qualification. " . . . the monarch may pardon any offence against the criminal law whether before or after conviction" (p. 69). A review of the "independence" constitutions within the Commonwealth, negotiated with the United Kingdom Government prior to the transfer of sovereignty, provides substantial support for a pre-conviction limitation on the pardoning power. Examples are to be found in the constitutions of Kenya (1963), Guyana (1966), Barbados (1966), the Bahamas (1973), Zambia (1973) and St. Lucia (1978). In comparison,

conferring a pardon upon a principal offender before conviction has fallen into disuse,[21] the most important objection being that such practice is out of harmony with modern views as to the propriety of granting dispensation before the normal process of the criminal law has run its course.

There is all the more reason, therefore, to take note of the unusual precedent established in recent years with little fanfare, when the British Government took action to ensure immunity from prosecution for Bishop Muzorewa, then the Rhodesia Prime Minister. Muzorewa was on the point of visiting Britain for talks with Prime Minister Thatcher and her Cabinet colleagues when it became known that members of the Anti-Apartheid Movement, led by a Labour Member of Parliament, were proposing to have Bishop Muzorewa arrested and charged with treason and murder. The same problem arose when Mr. Ian Smith, the former Prime Minister of Rhodesia who was responsible for that country's unilateral declaration of independence in 1965, set foot on British soil as a member of the Zimbabwe-Rhodesia delegation to the constitutional conference in 1979.

To meet these contingencies the Government invoked its statutory powers under the Southern Rhodesia Act 1965, which empowers Her Majesty by Order-in-Council to make such provision in respect to persons connected with that country "as appears to Her to be necessary or expedient in consequence of any unconstitutional action taken therein."[22] The action taken to ensure immunity from prosecution for Muzorewa, Smith and other residents of that country, who might otherwise have faced charges of treason, was the enactment of the Southern Rhodesia (Immunity for Persons attending Meetings and Consultations) Order 1979.[23] Under its provisions a person to whom the Order-in-Council applies "shall, while within the United Kingdom, be entitled to the like immunity from suit and legal process and the like personal inviolability as is accorded, under the law in that behalf, to a diplomatic agent accredited to Her Majesty." The Order-in-Council was approved, laid before Parliament and brought into operation all on the same day, July 13, 1979. This extraordinary timetable scarcely permitted an opportunity for intelligent debate by the House of Commons with respect to its contents.

---

reference may be had to Trinidad and Tobago which, at the time of acquiring its independence in 1962, followed the pattern described above. Subsequently, in 1976, the power of its President was enlarged to permit the granting of a pardon before or after conviction. The Nigeria Constitution (1963) and that of Malawi (1966) contain earlier precedents of the more extensive availability of the presidential pardoning power.

[21] It is noteworthy that in a circular addressed by the Colonial Secretary to all the colonial governors on November 1, 1871 it was stated that in England a pardon is not granted before the trial of an offender. At the same time it was recognised that a proclamation of amnesty for past offences against the Crown is within the Royal Prerogative, examples of which include those issued by Lord Durham, Governor General of Canada in 1838; Sir George Grey, Governor of New Zealand in 1865; and by Lord Dufferin, Governor General of Canada in 1875—see Todd, *op. cit.* pp. 267–268.

[22] Cap 76, s.2.

[23] S.I. 1979 No. 820, O.2.

In this regard the procedure of conferring prosecutorial immunity by Order-in-Council resembles the difficulties that formerly confronted the Opposition when seeking to question the Home Secretary as to the exercise of the prerogative of mercy. So long as the death penalty remained on the statute book there existed a well-recognised limitation on the right of a Member of Parliament to question the Home Secretary whilst the execution was pending. Moreover, the uncommunicativeness of successive holders of that office in providing explanations, after the event, was rarely challenged successfully. This attitude and the support given to it by successive Speakers of the House of Commons has been trenchantly criticised.[24] It will be interesting to see what stance future Home Secretaries will adopt now that the emotional atmosphere of an impending execution has been removed from the forum in which the doctrine of ministerial accountability is invoked. Attorneys General, in recent times, have been relatively more forthcoming in providing an account of their reasons for instituting or discontinuing prosecutions, though the invariable practice has been to defer answers to members' questions until after the criminal proceedings have been concluded.[25]

There can be no doubt as to the legality of the recent Order-in-Council, conferring what amounts to a free pardon with respect to possible crimes committed in the course of "unconstitutional action in Southern Rhodesia." After all, Parliament in 1965 saw fit to confer upon the government statutory power of a remarkably wide nature, within which the recent Order-in-Council is comfortably ensconced. It would be an altogether different situation if the prerogative rather than an Act of Parliament were to be invoked as the constitutional authority for extending a similar immunity from criminal prosecution. In subjecting the Attorney General, and the Prime Minister, to intensive questioning with respect to the immunity conferred on *Blunt* it is to be hoped that Members of Parliament were at least prompted in part by the recollection that such action evokes memories of the Stuarts' dispensing power which was roundly condemned by the Bill of Rights in 1688.[26]

JURY VETTING AND DISCLOSURE TO THE DEFENCE

Suggestions of tampering with the jury process surfaced in many quarters following the disclosure in 1978 that the Attorney General had issued a set of guidelines several years earlier designed to provide prosecuting counsel with selective information about potential jurors'

[24] See Geoffrey Marshall's essay on "Parliament and the Prerogative of Mercy" [1961] *Public Law*, and *cf.* the position taken by O.R. Marshall in [1948] 1 *Current Legal Problems* 104 at pp. 106, 113, 117.

[25] The precedents and arguments concerning this question are analysed in Edwards, *op. cit.* pp. 224–225 and pp. 253 *et seq.*

[26] See Wade & Phillips (9th ed.), p. 11. For the relevance of the Bill of Rights in a contemporary setting see the New Zealand case *Fitzgerald* v. *Muldoon*, discussed, *ante*, pp. 396–399, and the Manitoba C.A. decision in *R. v Catagas* (1978) 2 C.R. (3d) 328.

convictions and other kinds of activities that engage the attention of police special branches.[27] The underlying purpose of these inquiries is to enable prosecuting counsel, if there is good reason to believe that any jurors are biased towards either the prosecution or the defence, or are susceptible to improper pressures, to pronounce that such persons "stand by for the Crown," thus effectively withdrawing them from being on the jury. Lord Denning M.R. in *R. v. Crown Court at Sheffield, ex p. Brownlow*[28] denounced the practice as "unconstitutional," only to be followed by a differently constituted Court of Appeal in *R. v. Mason*[29] declaring the jury vetting procedures to be perfectly lawful. Nevertheless, certain changes were instituted in 1980 following the views expressed in *R. v. Mason*, and we must now take stock of this unusual aspect of the Attorney General's intervention in the criminal process.

Unfamiliar as the practice may be in England and Wales of issuing such guidelines, there is no need to look further than Ireland during the nineteenth century to find ample precedents where the Attorney General issued specific instructions to the Crown Solicitors in each circuit of Ireland on the subject of empanelling a jury and the grounds on which the Crown's representatives should exercise the right to set jurors aside.[30] The practice appears to have begun around 1835 at a time when political and religious affiliations were often the underlying motives behind the commission of crimes. The jury system came under intense pressures as a consequence of the political turmoil of the times and this resulted in the occasional temporary suspension of jury trials. It was against this background that successive Irish Attorneys General saw fit to issue directions stating, for example, that "no person should be set aside by the Crown on account of his religious or political opinions" and that "the Crown Solicitor should be able in every case in which the privilege is exercised to state the grounds on which he thought proper to exercise it."[31] Special provision was made in the instructions to cover the case of members of secret societies, one

[27] See, *e.g.* New L.J. May 17, 1979, *The Guardian* editorial, September 21, 1979; *The Guardian*, letter to the Editor, October 15, 1979; *The Times*, November 19, 1979; *The Law Society's Gazette*, November 28, 1979; and *The Times*, August 1, 1980.

[28] [1980] 2 All E.R. 444 at p. 453.

[29] [1980] 3 All E.R. 777.

[30] I am indebted to J.F. McEldowney's article on "Stand by for the Crown: an Historical Analysis" [1979] Crim. L.R. 272, for the Irish references that follow. Mr. McEldowney appears to have drawn heavily on the memoranda and evidence tendered to the series of Parliamentary Select Committees that examined the subject of jury trial in Ireland in the late nineteenth century.

[31] *Ibid.* p. 277, instructions issued in April 1841 and quoted in (1843) Parl. Papers, Vol. xx, 334. *Cf.* the instruction given in 1894 by the Attorney General for Ireland, " . . . the Crown Solicitor shall not inquire into the religious or political opinions or calling of any juror, and no person shall be directed to stand by on account of his religious or political opinions or of his calling—cited in McEldowney *loc. cit.* Echoes of this policy are to be found in the Practice Direction issued by the Queen's Bench Division in January 1973 which stated, *inter alia*: "It is contrary to established practice for jurors to be excused on more general grounds such as race, religion, political beliefs or occupation"—[1973] 1 All E.R. 240. On this subject see G. Marshall "The Judgment of One's Peers: Some Aims and Ideals of Jury Trial," Cropwood Round-Table Conference on the British Jury System, *Proceedings*, (1974), pp. 1–9. Shortly

Attorney General stating: "I consider that members of secret and exclusive or political societies to whatsoever sect or party they may belong or whatever be the object of such societies, are objectionable as jurors, more especially in cases where it it known or supposed that the individual on trial is himself a member of such society."[32] Notwithstanding these principles of guidance allegations of "jury packing" by the Crown's agents in Irish criminal trials were rampant. Invariably the target was the suggested policy of the Crown in excluding Roman Catholic jurors from serving in jury trials.[33] Whatever truth there was to these allegations of jury manipulation it will be noted that the Attorney General of Ireland was fulfilling his normal functions of providing direction for his agents, the Crown Solicitors.[34] The same framework explains the long established practice, dating back to 1765, of the Lord Advocate issuing directives through the Crown Office to his agents, the procurators fiscal, with a view to ensuring uniformity of practice throughout Scotland's system of public prosecutions.[35] Precisely the same relationship exists between the Attorney General for England and Wales and the Director of Public Prosecutions, to whom the jury vetting guidelines of recent years were principally addressed. Insofar as the Director saw fit to ensure that the Attorney's statement was incorporated in his advice to the chief officers of police, as provided for in the Prosecution of Offences Regulations,[36] there appears to be little ground for questioning the legal foundation on which rests the application of the guidelines.

A further illustration of the same authority of the Attorney General to issue "guidelines" or "directives" to prosecuting counsel and solicitors is contained in the later set of guidelines, issued in December 1981, which relate to the disclosure of information to the defence in cases to be tried on indictment.[37] This comprehensive statement is dictated by a philosophy that favours disclosure to the defence solicitor of witness statements and documents if they have some bearing on the offences charged and the surrounding circumstances of the case. At the same time a cautionary note is evident throughout these guidelines, as a series of exceptions are developed making it clear that a discretion exists to withhold certain kinds of information. This is not the place to examine these categories in detail

---

before his retirement from the Bench, in his book *What Next in the Law* (London, Butterworths, 1982), Lord Denning suggested that juries should no longer be selected at random from the electoral register, the argument for reform resting on the premise that the same standards of conduct no longer were shared by all the races that together made up British society. The strong criticism generated by the views expressed by the Master of the Rolls, including an allegation of jury packing by the accused at the *Bristol riots* trial, led to the withdrawal of the book and the issuance of a public apology by the author to the black community, *The Times*, May 20, 22, 29, 1982.

[32] *Ibid.* p. 278.
[33] *Ibid.* pp. 279–280.
[34] *Ante*, pp. 262–264.
[35] See *ante*, p. 297.
[36] S.I. 1978 No. 1357 (L. 33), reg. 4.
[37] [1982] 1 All E.R. 734.

but it is noteworthy that amongst the exceptions to the normal rule of disclosure are many of the situations also encompassed in the jury vetting guidelines, and which refer to those circumstances in which the identity of an informer or a member of the security service or some matter of national security is involved.[38] In these kinds of cases it is envisaged that reference will be made to the Director of Public Prosecutions for his advice, with the distinct possibility of having to resolve the dilemma by offering no, or no further, evidence.[39]

The background leading up to the first set of jury-vetting guidelines was the disturbing evidence of "hung juries" in some major terrorist cases, and other prosecutions involving gangs of professional criminals, that pointed to the possible existence of bias or corruption on the part of some members of the jury panels. The practice of exploring the background of jurors in these kinds of trials had been followed since at least 1948, and probably much longer, in the Central Criminal Court where the problem just described was experienced in its most acute forms.[40] Police and prosecutors collaborated in what was regarded as a well intentioned attempt to secure an unbiased jury, not unlikely to be subject to outside pressures. The extent of the practice came to light following a highly publicised I.R.A. trial in 1974.[41] Discussions followed between the Attorney General, Mr. Sam Silkin, the Home Secretary, Mr. Roy Jenkins, and the Director of Public Prosecutions, to determine whether the practice should be allowed to continue and if so under what safeguards.[42] As a result, a series of what were described as "guidelines" for vetting jurors' lists in certain cases were issued in August 1975 under the signature of the Attorney General and subsequently distributed to all police forces in the form of a Home Office circular.[43] No further public disclosure was made at

[38] *Ibid*. para. 6.
[39] *Ibid*. paras. 10 and 15.
[40] H.C. Deb., Vol. 958, cols. 28–30, November 13, 1978 *per* Attorney General Silkin. Speaking in the course of a radio interview in 1966, with respect to the problem of communists serving on juries in spy cases or Official Seerets Act cases, Viscount Dilhorne stated: "I was very worried when I conducted those cases, that one might get a communist on the jury, because one juror disagreeing in any of those cases, even though the cases were very clear, would have meant a new trial, possibly followed again by disagreement, and abandonment of the prosecution. I did take steps in one of those cases to find out whether there were any well-known communists on the jury panel, and in fact I had to ask for one juror to stand down for the very reason that he was an active member of the Communist Party and therefore I thought unsuitable to be a member of the jury in that case." *The Listener*, August 11, 1966. Lord Shawcross, speaking on the same occasion, recalled similar experiences when he was the Attorney General but added: "I don't think I would inquire into the political antecedents of juries but I would inquire into their criminal convictions." It is believed that Viscount Dilhorne was alluding to the trial of George Blake, the Soviet spy who in 1961 was sentenced to 42 years imprisonment—*The Financial Times*, September 24, 1979.
[41] *R. v. Pettigrew, O'Sullivan, Allen*, June 1972, and referred to by Mr. Silkin in his article on jury-vetting, the *Observer*, November 11, 1979.
[42] The full text of the Attorney General's statement, including the original set of 1975 guidelines as amended, appears as an annexure to the report of *R. v. Crown Court at Sheffield, ex p. Brownlow*, (1980) 71 Cr. App. R. 19 at pp. 30–33.
[43] Home Office circular 165/1975 dated October 10, 1975.

the time of either the existence or the contents of the Attorney General's directions.[44]

As already stated, the guidelines derive their legal authority in part from the statutory powers conferred upon the Director of Public Prosecutions to give advice to chief officers of police in any situations that appear to the Director to require his attention. As such the guidelines are truly advisory in character and do not constitute directions that have the force of law.[45] Two general principles were enunciated at the outset as representing the fundamental approach to the selection of any jury. The first was that members should be selected at random from the jury panel, and, secondly, that no matters other than those prescribed by Parliament in the Juries Act 1974[46] should be regarded as legally disqualifying a person from serving on a jury in a criminal trial. These disqualifications are restricted to persons (a) who have at any time been sentenced to life imprisonment or for a term of five years or more, (b) who have been sentenced to be detained during Her Majesty's pleasure, or (c) who, during the previous 10 years, have served a sentence of three months or more in prison, detention or in a borstal institution. Failure to disclose any such disqualification when called upon to serve on a jury is subject on a summary conviction to a fine of not more than £400.[47] This sanction, and the provision for majority verdicts,[48] are the sum total of the safeguards provided for by Parliament to meet the

[44] Some inkling of what was afoot, but lacking in concrete information, was the statement to the Commons in 1975 by Mr. Silkin, as Attorney General: "It is not the practice of the Crown to object to jurors on the grounds of their political beliefs as such. Political beliefs are relevant only to the extent that, depending on the nature of the charges, political views held to an extreme may impair the impartiality of jurors or give rise to the possibility of improper pressure . . . The Home Secretary and I are reviewing the position to ensure that the balance between the prosecution and defence is held as fairly as possible." H.C. Deb., Vol. 892, Written Answers, cols. 216–217, May 19, 1975. This statement was in reply to a private notice question tabled by Mr. Brian Sedgmore, a Labour backbencher. The same M.P. had previously raised the issue of checks on potential jurors on March 25, 1974, in a question answered by Mr. Alex Lyon, then Minister of State, Home Office—see H.C. Deb., Vol. 871, Written Answers, cols. 10–11. Strangely, in the light of later public reaction, neither the statement by Mr. Silkin, *supra*, nor the letter to Sedgmore by the Home Secretary, Mr. Roy Jenkins, of May 30, 1975, evoked any comment at the time. In the latter instance, moreover, the Home Secretary stated explicitly that checks were necessary in certain exceptional cases and set out the safeguards that should be observed to ensure that abuses did not happen.
[45] The *advisory* nature of such guidelines is to be distinguished from the *mandatory instructions* (or circulars) which the D.P.P. is authorised to issue to chief officers of police in respect of those offences that must be reported to the Director and the form which such reporting should take—regs. 6 and 7 of the Prosecution of Offences Regulations 1978.
[46] c. 23, s. 1 and Sched. 1, Part II. For the position before 1974 see the *Report of the Departmental Committee on Jury Service*, Cmnd. 2627 (1965), pp. 41–45. Moves to amend the grounds of disqualification have been launched, as yet with no success, by both the government and by a private members Bill. In each instance the proposal would impose a 10 year disqualification from jury service for anyone convicted of an offence punishable with imprisonment (of whatever duration)—*Daily Telegraph*, June 2 and 30, 1982 and *The Times* February 17, 1983. Also, the House of Lords has given a second reading to the Juries (Amendment) Bill introduced by Lord Wigoder, under which a person would not be eligible to serve as a juror if within the last 10 years he was twice convicted of an indictable offence—H.L. Deb., Vol. 436, col. 597, November 17, 1982.
[47] *Ibid.* s.20(5).
[48] *Ibid.* s.17.

problems addressed by the Attorney General's guidelines for jury checks. The comment might be permitted that, if the dangers contemplated by the guidelines are so enormous in terms of their consequence to the integrity of the administration of justice, a re-evaluation is called for of the existing criminal penalties for serving when disqualified. The penalty provided for under the Juries Act 1974, can only be described as grossly inadequate to meet the kind of exceptional cases of public importance that are seen as justifying a departure from the basic principles governing jury selection. In the only two prosecutions brought since 1974 for serving on a jury while disqualified, an acquittal was returned in one case and in the other a fine of £10 was imposed. An ad hoc review of the jury panel at Northampton Crown Court, instituted at the direction of the Court of Appeal hearing the case of *R. v. Mason*,[49] led to the inescapable inference that many persons who are disqualified are sitting on juries and not disclosing the reasons why they should be excluded. Speaking for the Court of Appeal, Lawton L.J. described this state of affairs as "disturbing"[50] and as exposing the unreliability and over-optimism of the earlier opinion expressed by Lord Denning M.R. who tended to dismiss the problem as insignificant in its proportions.[51]

From the inception of the first set of guidelines the greatest difficulty was experienced in defining the classes of criminal cases which would justify exceptional inquiries being authorised with respect to the jury panel's activities. The 1975 criteria were described in the broadest terms as encompassing "serious offences where strong political motives were involved such as I.R.A. and other terrorist cases and cases under the Official Secrets Act" and "serious offences committed by a member or members of a gang of professional criminals."[52] Assuming that the particular circumstances fell within one or other of the above categories,

---

[49] [1980] 3 All E.R. 777 at p. 779.

[50] *Ibid*. Out of a hundred prospective jurors, summoned for jury service at Northampton Crown Court, the police, on searching the local criminal records, found that ten appeared to have previous convictions but the similarity of names in some instances precluded any positive identification for the purposes of disqualification. The disturbing feature of this small scale pilot inquiry, in the minds of the Court of Appeal, was the likelihood of a much higher proportion of disqualified jurors when a panel is summoned from an urban area with a high level of crime. It might have been useful to quote from the evidence of the Commissioner of Police of Metropolitan London before the [Morris] Departmental Committee on Jury Service in 1965 when it was stated that "on a recent occasion, when the names of 38 jurors summoned to the Central Criminal Court were checked, it was found that four definitely had convictions registered in the Central Records Office, and nine others appeared to have records." In the opinion of Theobald Mathew, then the D.P.P., "there was nothing irresponsible in the verdicts reached by the juries chosen from this panel" and "although convicted persons did undoubtedly serve on juries there was no reason to suppose that this was resulting in perverse verdicts." Cmnd. 2627, para. 132.

[51] In *R. v. Crown Court at Sheffield ex p. Brownlow*, the Master of the Rolls had stated: " . . . as a matter of practical politics, even if jury vetting were allowed, the chances are a thousand to one against any juror being found unsuitable (*sic*); and; if he should be, the chance of his being on any particular jury of 12, so as to influence the result, are minimal, especially in these days of majority verdicts"—[1980] 2 All E.R. 444 at p. 453.

[52] 1975 Guidelines, para. 4.

three alternative justifications were put forward in the Attorney General's statement of October 1975. First is the possibility of potential jurors being susceptible to improper pressures. The second situation enlarges on this possibility, it being necessary to safeguard against improper use being made, "either voluntarily or under pressure," of *in camera* evidence heard in Official Secrets Act cases. The final justification for the introduction of the vetting guidelines was said to be the bias towards the prosecution or the defence which a juror's extreme political beliefs may engender. Recognition of the dangers that any such criteria pose to the democratic process is evident in the Attorney's statement but these reassurances could hardly expect to allay public suspicion that the pertinent tests might be pushed too far in the wrong direction. A juror's political connections or philosophy, the Attorney General emphasised, is wholly irrelevant to the discharge of his responsibilities in a criminal trial "unless they are of so extreme a character as to make it reasonably likely that they will prevent the jurors from trying the case fairly or that he may exert improper pressure on his fellow jurors."[53] Making this kind of distinction involves the exercise of an essentially subjective judgment and it is not surprising, therefore, to note that certain safeguards are introduced in terms of who can authorise the investigation of a jury panel. At first, this power of authorisation was assigned to the Director of Public Prosecutions or his deputy, with the intention that it should be the personal decision of either of the two most senior officers in the department. In addition, when the authorisation was issued the Attorney General had to be notified.[54] Under the revised guidelines, however, issued in 1980[55] after a general review of the public criticisms that the original document had evoked, the Attorney General in person has displaced the Director of Public Prosecutions as the signing authority for searches that involve the examination of records kept by police special branches, thus ensuring the most clear assumption of ministerial responsibility for any mistakes or excesses perpetuated in administering the guidelines. Recommendations to conduct such sensitive inquiries will continue to emanate from the Director of Public Prosecutions, to whom the results of an authorised check will be sent. The Director will then decide having regard to the purport of the guidelines, what information ought to be brought to the attention of prosecuting counsel.

Special branch inquiries are carefully distinguished in the latest set of

---

[53] *Ibid.* para. 5.

[54] *Ibid.* para. 7.

[55] The revised guidelines incorporate changes agreed upon following consultations between the Attorney General, the Home Secretary, the Lord Chancellor and the D.P.P. Particularly significant in this review were the opinions expressed by the Court of Appeal in *R. v. Mason, infra.* The amended set of guidelines, with an accompanying explanatory statement by the Attorney General, is inserted as a note to the report of *R. v. Mason* [1980] 3 All E.R. 777 at pp. 785–788. And see H.C. Deb., Written Answers, col. 18, July 6, 1981, in which the Attorney General disclosed that since the revised guidelines were promulgated he had received only 2 applications for his authorisation of special branch checks. Both related to terrorist offences and both requests were granted.

provisions from the examination of ordinary criminal records which may be necessary in order to ascertain whether any juror is disqualified under the terms of the Juries Act 1974, as already described. This latter objective falls squarely within the normal preventive functions of the police.[56] The earlier guidelines, in marked contrast, envisaged investigations that would comprise one or more of the following sources available to the police: a criminal record check, an exploration of special branch records, and a check with local C.I.D. officers to ascertain if a potential juror is known to be an associate of an accused or of those known to be sympathetic or antagonistic to his cause. The breadth of this original conception of the boundaries of necessary jury vetting might have inclined some jaundiced critics to view with circumspection the claim made in the 1975 guidelines that "there is no question of telephone intercepts or the instigation of inquiries, by way of surveillance, or otherwise, into occupations, family, backgrounds, associates, political views and activities . . . No inquiries are made other than with or by the civilian police."[57] Furthermore, only the most naive observers could profess to have been taken by surprise when it was confirmed to the House of Commons by the Attorney General in February 1980, that, despite the clear instruction contained in the Home Office circular of October 1975 to chiefs of police, saying that all cases in which it was intended that a check be made should first be referred to the Director of Public Prosecutions, the Northamptonshire police were checking all jury panels against criminal record office information.[58] Moreover, this practice had been continuing into 1980 despite assurances conveyed to the Home Office in June 1979 by the Association of Chief Police Officers that the Attorney General's guidelines were being adhered to by all police forces in the country.[59] Between October 1975, when the first guidelines were introduced, and October 1978, when the first public disclosure of the guidelines' existence was made, 25 cases were recorded in which a jury check had been authorised by the Director of Public Prosecutions: 12 of these were in connection with I.R.A. related trials, 2 were Official Secrets Act prosecutions, and the remainder concerned the offences of murder, armed robbery and international fraud.[60]

[56] The recommendations of the Association of Chief Police Officers with respect to "disqualification" checks of prospective jurors are published as an Annex to the Attorney General's 1980 guidelines—(1981) 72 Cr. App. R. at pp. 16–17.

[57] (1980) 71 Cr. App. R. at p. 32.

[58] H.C. Deb., Vol. 979, ser. 5, Oral Answers, cols. 948–950, February 25, 1980.

[59] *Ibid.* The Attorney General made no bones in expressing his complete disapproval of what had happened in Northamptonshire. Only a year earlier, his predecessor, on being informed of the failure of the Northamptonshire police to follow the vetting guidelines, had also made known his concerns at that force's practice of checking all jury panels against C.R.O. records. By the time the final grounds of appeal in *R.* v. *Mason* had been filed with the registrar, word of the police violations of the Attorney General's guidelines had been communicated by a journalist to the applicant's legal representatives. Before the Court of Appeal, however, it was accepted by counsel on both sides that what happened before the trial could not be relied upon as a material irregularity "in the course of the trial," as required by the Criminal Appeal Act 1968 (c. 19), s.2(1)—[1980] 3 All E.R. 777 at pp. 779, 780.

[60] See (1980) 71 Cr. App. R. 30 at p. 32 and *ante*, fn. 55.

What is significant is the much tighter rein introduced in the revised set of guidelines released in July 1980. No longer is the broad category of "serious offences committed by a member or members of a gang of professional criminals"[61] a conditional licence to set in motion a review of special branch records as might pertain to members of the jury panel. Instead, the emphasis is confined to "(a) terrorist cases and (b) cases in which national security is involved and part of the evidence is likely to be heard in camera. In the latter situation, the danger envisaged is the prospect of a juror, voluntarily or under pressure, making improper use of evidence which, because of its sensitivity, has been given in camera."[62] There is also the further argument that "in both security and terrorist cases the danger (exists) that a juror's beliefs are so biased as to go beyond normally reflecting the broad spectrum of views and interests in the community to reflect the extreme views of sectarian interest or pressure group to a degree which might interfere with his fair assessment of the facts of the case or lead him to exert improper pressure on his fellow jurors."[63] There is no doubt that the public debate that swirled around the original guidelines issued by Mr. Silkin, as Attorney General, contributed significantly to the tightening up that is revealed in a comparison between the 1975 and 1980 versions. For example, there is an implicit awareness in the current provisions of the dangers inherent in allowing jury checks to explore the political beliefs of prospective jurors, especially in such pejorative terms as those which purport to be able to distinguish beliefs that exceed those which "normally reflect the broad spectrum of views and interests in the community." This concern is confirmed by restricting authorised special branch investigations of jury panels to "terrorist cases." In other criminal prosecutions, even those involving "so called strong political motives," authorised checks by the Attorney General will not be resorted to. Moreover, the new guidelines envisage both the trial judge and defence counsel being informed when an authorised check of special branch records has been undertaken under the personal signature of the Attorney General.[64] These changes are no less than were absolutely necessary if the discretionary system of jury checks is to maintain some semblance of public confidence.

That element of confidence was seriously challenged by the decision of the Court of Appeal in *R.* v. *Crown Court at Sheffield, ex parte Brownlow*,[65] which declared as "unconstitutional" any order or direction of a court designed to facilitate the selection of a jury by methods not directly provided for in the Juries Act 1974, or recognised by the common law. Jury vetting by the police, albeit under the 1975 guidelines prepared

---

[61] *Ante*, fn. 52.
[62] 1980 Guidelines, (1981) 72 Cr. App. R. at p. 15.
[63] *Ibid.*
[64] Explanatory statement by the Attorney General, issued in conjunction with the revised guidelines—*ibid.* p. 18.
[65] [1980] 2 All E.R. 444.

by Mr. Silkin, the then Attorney General, suffered a temporary set-back by this decision, but its impact turned out to be short lived. The trial in the Sheffield Crown Court involved two police officers charged with assault occasioning bodily harm. The defendant's counsel requested that the prosecuting solicitor arrange to have the jury panel vetted for previous convictions. The request was refused. Application was then made to the Crown Court judge for an order directing the police to investigate the jury panel. This application was granted, prompting the chief constable to seek an order of certiorari to quash the judge's order. The Divisional Court declined to interfere on the grounds that it was a matter "relating to a trial on indictment" and thus outside their jurisdiction,[66]—in accordance with section 10(5) of the Courts Act 1971.[67] The Civil Division of the Court of Appeal, with Lord Denning dissenting, took the same view on this aspect of jurisdiction but the court was prepared to entertain the appeal since the trial judge's order was not a "criminal cause or matter" within section 31(1)(a) of the Supreme Court of Judicature (Consolidation) Act 1925,[68] and therefore the Court of Appeal had jurisdiction.[69]

Having thus seized itself of the opportunity to review the much debated question of jury vetting, the members of the Court of Appeal in *ex p. Brownlow* gave expression to their individual views on the practice embodied in the Attorney General's guidelines. Lord Denning M.R. was opposed to the police authorities engaging in jury vetting on the grounds that the practice was "unconstitutional." "So long as a person is eligible for jury service, and is not disqualified" he said, "I cannot think it right that, behind his back, the police should go through his record so as to enable him to be asked to 'stand by for the Crown' or to be challenged by the defence. If this sort of thing is to be allowed, what comes of a man's right of privacy?"[70] The Master of the Rolls was not disposed to challenge the legitimacy of the Attorney General's guidelines but pointed out that the order made in the instant case, involving a charge of assault occasioning bodily harm, was far outside the guidelines. Shaw L.J., who also used the strong language of unconstitutionality to describe the judge's order,[71] was prepared to conceive of very special cases where the protection of the interests of the public at large demands that the special knowledge derived from police checks of jurors' backgrounds should be sought and used. Even then, he maintained, the process should be subject "to the prior sanction of the Attorney General who is ultimately responsible for the conduct of prosecutions by way of indictment . . . Such procedure should

[66] [1980] 2 All E.R. 444 at pp. 447–449.
[67] c. 23.
[68] 15 & 16 Geo 5 c. 49.
[69] Brandon L.J. declined to express a concluded opinion on the jurisdictional point concerning the 1925 legislation, but declared that he had serious doubts whether there should be any jury vetting, either by the prosecution or the defence—[1980] 2 All E.R. 444 at p. 450.
[70] *Ibid.* at p. 453.
[71] *Ibid.* at p. 455.

not be adopted merely because it might reinforce a prosecution by excluding from a jury persons who might be anti-authority or pro an accused. The Juries Act 1974 makes statutory provision as to information which should appear on the jury panel. The courts should not in my view lend their aid to the extraction of further information by making orders in that regard . . . Apart from the exceptional cases I have indicated, jurors must not be exposed to prodding or probing if they are to discharge their function fearlessly and impartially."[72]

A short while later, in *R.* v. *Mason*,[73] the Criminal Division of the Court of Appeal, consisting of Lawton L.J., together with Michael Davies and Balcombe JJ., refused to follow the path set by their colleagues in the Civil Division in *R.* v. *Crown Court at Sheffield, ex parte Brownlow*. In neither case were the circumstances so exceptional as to fall within the wider ambit of the Attorney General's guidelines. In *R.* v. *Mason* the indictment consisted of counts of burglary and handling stolen goods. Only after the conviction of the accused did it become known to his counsel that the trial jury may have been empanelled in breach of the guidelines. The grounds for this assertion was the use made of criminal convictions, not for the purpose of establishing disqualification under the Juries Act 1974, but to activate the common law right of prosecuting counsel to require that any member of the jury panel "stand by for the Crown" and thus be excluded from serving on the actual jury. Adopting the line of approach favoured by the Court of Appeal in the earlier case of *ex p. Brownlow*, the argument was advanced that, on its true construction, the 1974 enactment envisages that all persons who are qualified to serve as jurors in the Crown Court should be allowed to do so unless they are ineligible or disqualified or excused by virtue of the terms of the consolidating statute. This interpretation of the Juries Act, favoured by the Master of the Rolls and his brother judges in the Civil Division, was totally rejected by the Criminal Division of the Court of Appeal.

Far from altering the old law, the court in *R.* v. *Mason* referred to section 21(5) of the 1974 Act as making it abundantly clear that all the rules of law relating to juries and jurors prior to 1974 continue in force, leaving it to the judges and the parties in criminal cases to decide which members of a jury panel were suitable to try a particular case. The court reminded everyone that the so-called principle of random selection of jurors has always been subject to qualification by way of the defence's right to a certain number of peremptory challenges and unrestricted right to challenging for cause.[74] To this must be added the ancient right of prosecuting counsel to request that a member of the jury panel "stand by for the Crown" and that this right can be exercised without there being a

---

[72] *Ibid.* p. 456.
[73] [1980] 3 All E.R. 777.
[74] *Ibid.* at p. 781.

provable valid objection.[75] As to what had transpired in the trial below the Criminal Division of the Court of Appeal was of one mind in stating that the practice of supplying prosecuting counsel with information about potential jurors' convictions "is not unlawful and has not until recently been thought to be unsatisfactory."[76] Speaking for the entire court, Lawton L.J. went on to say[77]: "We have not been concerned in any way with, and make no comment on, the giving to prosecution counsel of information other than that relating to convictions, or with the desirability of making other inquiries about members of a jury panel. In so far as the *obiter dicta* of this court in *R. v. Crown Court at Sheffield. ex parte Brownlow* differ from what we have decided in this case we justify our presumption by the knowledge that we have been able to examine the issues raised in greater depth than our brethren were able to do. Further, it is no part of our function to criticise either the contents of Home Office circular 165/1975 or the Attorney-General's statement entitled 'Checks on Potential Jurors,' which he issued in October 1978. Both the circular and the statement contain advice: they were not directions having the force of law, as counsel as *amicus curiae* accepted. Whether the advice should be changed in the light of this judgment is for the Home Secretary and the Attorney General to consider." This broad hint was acted upon at once. In the revised set of guidelines issued by the Attorney General following the decision in *R. v. Mason* the point was once again emphasised that, although the selection of those who are summoned for jury service from among those qualified must be random, both parties to criminal proceedings have the right to object to a juror called to serve, the exercise of which inevitably limits the truly random nature of the jury which eventually tries the case. Neither in practice nor in strict legal terms can it be said that the principle of random selection is inviolable. After all, the categories of persons excluded by the Juries Act from serving on a jury embrace not only serving police officers, prison and probation officers, parole board workers and clerks to the justices, to name but a few classes, but also the same categories for a period of 10 years after the conclusion of their active service.[78] In effect, the Attorney General was resting the vetting system on the solid theoretical foundation of the Crown's right to make inquiries about a jury panel with a view to exercising its centuries-old right to "stand by" a potential juror.

One further important principle has been incorporated into the current set of guidelines, no doubt prompted by the desire to reflect a greater sense of equality in the protection available to the defence as well as the Crown. Thus, in addition to the defence's unqualified right to inspect the panel and to institute its own lawful investigations, the Attorney General has set in

---

[75] See *Mansell* v. *R.* (1857) 8 E. & B. 54 *per* Lord Campbell C.J., *R. v. Chandler* [1964] 2 Q.B. 322 at pp. 328–330 (argument of the Solicitor General).
[76] [1980] 3 All E.R. 777 at p. 784.
[77] *Ibid.*
[78] See c. 23, s.1 and Sched. 1, Group B.

place a procedure whereby the defence can also apply to the Director of Public Prosecutions for assistance in gaining access to information that derives from a police check of any criminal records that pertain to potential jurors.[79] Because of the inherently sensitive nature of the security information that might surface in the course of the additional investigations of special branch files, which it will be recalled must be authorised only by the Attorney General, limitations are placed on the prosecution's use of this information. Thus, it cannot be used to justify the right to "stand by" a juror unless the information is such as to afford strong reason for believing that a particular juror might be a security risk, be susceptible to improper approaches or be influenced in arriving at a verdict for corrupt or biased reasons.[80] Where the circumstances warrant the Crown's intervention to stand by a juror, the guidelines state there is no duty to disclose to the defence the information on which it was founded, but counsel is given a discretion to disclose it if its nature and source permit.[81] Additionally, if the information revealed by the special branch check is not of a kind that prompts counsel for the Crown to ask a juror to "stand by" but it discloses grounds for believing that he might be biased against the accused then the defence should be alerted to this fact with such detail as is consistent with the security aspects of the information.[82]

If the revised guidelines convey the impression that a sincere effort has been made to eliminate the more questionable features associated with the original document few would dissent from the improvements that are now in place. Some critics, it is true, would gladly assign the whole procedure to the scrap heap of legal antiquities, as reflected in the Jury Vetting (Abolition) Bill, introduced by several prominent Labour backbenchers in 1979.[83] It proposed a blanket prohibition against any investigation of jurors of the kind described in the Attorney General's guidelines, coupled with the abolition of the Crown's right to "stand by" members of the jury panel. Under the Bill any challenge of a juror by the prosecution would have to be for reasons disclosed to the court, leaving it to the trial judge to decide whether the objection should be upheld.[84] Other critics have resurrected the dubious argument that the "stand by" rights of the prosecution lack legal foundation. This line of attack derives from the language of the Ordinance for Inquests in 1305[85] which abolished peremptory challenge by the Crown stating: " . . . if they that sue for the King will challenge any of the jurors they shall assign for their challenge a cause certain, and the truth of the same challenge shall be inquired of

---

[79] (1981) 72 Cr. App. R. 17 at p. 18.
[80] 1980 Guidelines, para. 9.
[81] *Op. cit.* para. 10.
[82] *Op. cit.* para. 11.
[83] Bill 81; noted in [1980] C.L.B, p. 396.
[84] *Ibid.* cl. 3.
[85] 33 Edw. 1, stat. 4.

according to the custom of the court . . . " Prior to 1305, at common law, the Crown had the right to challenge peremptorily an unlimited number of jurors. This right led to abuse in that, by exhausting the panel with peremptory challenges, the Crown was able to ensure that the defendant was kept without trial and in custody until the next sessions. However self evident might be the intention of the 1305 statute that the Crown should only be able to challenge for cause, subsequent judicial interpretations saw fit to place a gloss on the language cited above and to hold that the Crown was not bound to state the grounds of its challenge until the whole panel had been gone through without a complete jury being sworn. In practical terms, given the number of names appearing on the panel, this meant that the Crown could exercise an almost unrestricted right of peremptorily excluding particular individuals from jury service. Although challenged in several of the state trials during the seventeenth century, the practice of permitting the Crown, without showing cause, to ask a juror to "stand by for the Crown" until the panel was exhausted has never been successfully assailed.[86] The re-enactment of the language of the 1305 statute in section 29 of the Jury Act 1828[87] brought about no change in the established practice which has long since crystallised into a right in law. Confirmation of this position was accorded by the Court of Criminal Appeal in *R. v. Chandler* (No. 2).[88]

If change is to be effected in the mode of selecting a jury it must be by the legislative route. There is an obvious inequality in the rights accorded to the Crown and the defendant, the latter being confined to what has become a progressively fewer number of peremptory challenges. At one time these extended to 35 such challenges for treason and 20 for murder and other felonies.[89] This entitlement was further reduced to seven by the Criminal Justice Act 1948,[90] s.35 and, finally, to three in the provisions of the Criminal Law Act 1977.[91] Once he has exhausted his quota of peremptory challenges the defendant must show cause for any further objections he may have to individual jurors acting in his case. It has been fairly pointed out that the resources, both financial and manpower, available to the respective sides in the matter of investigating jurors' backgrounds are also grossly disproportionate. Little wonder, therefore, that a chorus of concern was exhibited in the wake of the first public intimation that the Crown's investigative resources were being invoked in

[86] For the history of this subject see Forsyth, *History of Trial by Jury*, (1851), *passim*; J.B. Thayer, *Preliminary Treatise on Evidence at the Common Law*, (1898) Chapters 2–5; W.S. Holdsworth, *History of English Law*, Vol. 1, p. 312 *et seq.*; W.R. Cornish, *The Jury*, (1970), pp. 44–48 and J.F. McEldowney, *op. cit.* pp. 272–283.

[87] 6 Geo. 4, c. 59.

[88] [1964] 2 Q.B. 322.

[89] 7 & 8 Will. 3, c. 3, s.2, and 6 Geo. 4, c. 50, s.29.

[90] 11 & 12 Geo. 6, c. 58, s.35(1). For a while, between 1940 and 1948, the defendant had been deprived of all peremptory challenges by virtue of the Defence (Administration of Justice) Regulations 1940 (S.R. & O. 1940, No. 1028), reg. 13(1).

[91] c. 45, s.43 and see too Juries Act 1974 (c. 23), s.12.

support of its already privileged position in the matter of requiring potential jurors to "stand by for the Crown." Some of the sting in these criticisms may well have been removed by the latest set of guidelines, but the remaining grounds for maintaining the favoured position of the Crown in choosing the jury are untenable and must be changed to accord more closely with the public's expectations of fairness and equality.[92]

[92] The Republic of Ireland acted in 1976 to remove the advantages previously enjoyed by the Attorney General in the matter of challenging the jury panel. Under the provisions of its Juries Act 1976, the power to "stand by" has been abolished, the prosecution and the defence each now being entitled to challenge up to seven jurors without cause shown—*ibid*. s.20. For the background to this legislation see J.P. Casey, *The Office of the Attorney General in Ireland*, pp. 134–135. In New South Wales, likewise, the Jury Act 1977, s. 42, has equalised the rights of the prosecutor and the defendant in this regard. The same legislation prohibits the Crown from ordering a juror to stand by until all the jurors on the panel have been called, thus effectively nullifying the advantages previously enjoyed by the Crown—*ibid*. s.42(2). There are also growing signs of dissatisfaction with the Canadian law, under which the Crown is entitled to four peremptory challenges and up to 48 stand-bys. On special leave being granted, the latter figure can be increased in the court's discretion. If the offence is punishable with more than five years imprisonment, the accused is given up to 12 peremptory challenges. These inequitable provisions (Crim. Code, ss.562, 563) have been assailed, so far unsuccessfully, on the ground that they infringe the newly enacted provisions of the Charter of Rights and Freedoms relating to a fair trial—see *R. v. Piraino* (1982) 67 C.C.C. (2d) 28.

BIBLIOGRAPHY

BOOKS

Adams: *Criminal Law and Practice in New Zealand* (1971) 440
Alison on *Criminal Law of Scotland* (1832), Vol. ii...295, 303
American Bar Association: *American Bar Association Standards Relating to the Administration of Criminal Justice*, Vol. 18 (1974) 431
Amissah, A.N.E. *Criminal Procedure in Ghana* (1982) 66, 67
Archbold: *Criminal Pleading, Evidence and Practice*
    (40th ed.) 444
    (41st ed.)...23, 415, 444, 447, 453, 465
Bell, Griffin: *Taking Care of the Law* (1982) 60
Bingham, T.H. and Gray, S.M.: *Report on the Supply of Petroleum and Petroleum Products to Rhodesia* (1978) 327
Blanstein and Flanz: *Constitutions of the Countries of the World* (1983) 354
Blom Cooper and Drewry: *Final Appeal* (1972) 154
Boyle, Andrew: *Climate of Treason* (1979) 468
Bradley, A.W. (Ed.): *Wade and Phillips, Constitutional and Administrative Law* (1977, 9th ed.)..30, 147, 218, 227, 228, 474, 476
Burt, A.L.: *The Old Province of Quebec* (1933, Vol. 11) 357
Butler and Halsey (Eds.): *Policy and Politics* (1978) 38
Campbell E. and Whitmore, H.: *Freedom in Australia* (1973, 2nd ed.) 403
Cannon, Michael: *Land Boomers* (1966) 373
Casey, J.P.: *The Office of the Attorney General in Ireland* (1980)........................202, 244,
    262–266, 490
Cobden Institute: *Justice in Northern Ireland – A Study in Social Confidence* (1973)..253–255
Cockburn, Lord: *Memorials of his Time* (1856) 211
Cohen, S.A.: *Due Process of Law* (1977) 17
Cornish, W.R.: *The Jury* (1970) 489
Cowen, Zelman: *Isaac Isaacs* (1967)..373, 375, 377, 378
——: *Sir John Latham and Other Papers* (1965) 369
Critchely, T.A.: *A History of Police in England and Wales* (revised ed., 1978)...39, 81, 115
Cross: *Evidence* (1979, 5th ed.)...382, 415
Crossman, Richard: *The Diaries of a Cabinet Minister* (1975, 2 vols) 203
Cummings, H. and Macfarland, C.: *Federal Justice* (1937) 59
Dale, W: *The Modern Commonwealth* (1983) 65, 66, 71
Davies, Anne: *Reformed Select Committees: The First Year* (1980) 228
Davis, K.C.: *Discretionary Justice in Europe and America* (1976) 403
——: *Discretionary Justice, A Preliminary Inquiry* (1969) 403
Davis, S.R.: *The Government of the Australian States* (1960) 369
de Smith, S.A.: *Constitutional and Administrative Law*
    (1971, 1st ed.) 474
    (1973, 2nd ed.) 218, 227
——: *Judicial Review of Administrative Action*
    (1959, 1st ed.) 139
    (1973, 3rd ed.) 130
    (1980, 4th ed.) 130
——: *The New Commonwealth and its Constitutions* (1964) 65
Denning, Lord: *What Next in the Law* (1982) 477
Diefenbaker: *Memoirs: The Tumultuous Years* (1977) 380
Easby-Smith, J.S.: *The Department of Justice: Its History and Functions* (1904) 59

491

Eccles, W.J.: *The Government of New France* (1968) 357
Edwards, J.Ll.J.: *The Law Officers of the Crown* (1964)................................1–3, 5, 8, 9,
                    18, 21, 23, 26, 28, 50, 51, 63, 73, 77, 80, 105–107, 111, 118, 119, 130, 132,
                    139, 140, 144, 180–182, 195, 196, 199, 200, 207–210, 225, 226, 230, 238,
                    244, 257, 261, 269, 271, 272, 281, 289, 291, 300, 305, 310, 312, 313, 317,
                    318, 322, 358, 367, 388, 392, 408, 417, 438, 444–450, 457, 476
——: *Ministerial Responsibility for National Security as it relates to the offices of Prime
    Minister, Attorney-General and Solicitor of Canada* (1980) 39,
                    44, 74, 191, 355–358, 380, 471
Elliff, John T.: *The Reform of the F.B.I. Intelligence Operations* (1979)......................59,
                    406, 433
Elwyn-Jones, Lord: *In My Time – An Autobiography* (1983)............ 179, 193, 201, 214, 332
Endicott, Stephen: *James G. Endicott, Rebel out of China* (1982) 363
Ericson, R.V.: *Making Crime: A Study of Detective Work* (1981) 97, 404
Feeley, M. and Sarat, A.D.: *The Policy Dilemma: Crime Policy and the LEAA
    1968–1978* (1980) 192
Fitzhardinge, L.F.: *W. M. Hughes – A Political Biography*, Vol. 1 (1964) 370
Forsyth: *History of Trial by Jury* (1851) 489
Fountainhall: *Decisions of the Lords of Council and Session 1678–1712*, Vol. i (1759–61,
    2 Vols.)..272, 277
Garran, R.R.: *Prosper the Commonwealth* (1958) 370
Glassco, J.G.: *Report of the Royal Commission on Government Organization* (Canada)
    (1962, 4 vols.) 183
Glazebrook, P. (ed.): *Reshaping the Criminal Law: Essays in Honour of Glanville
    Williams* (1978)..58, 66, 67, 120, 154, 387
Gordon, G.H.: *Criminal Law* (2nd ed.) 299
Greenwood, P. *et al*: *The Criminal Investigation Process*, Vol. III (1975) 404
Grosman, B.A.: *The Prosecutor* (1969) 403
Hale: *Pleas of the Crown*, Vol. 2 (1650) 464
Halsbury: *Laws of England*, Vol. 13 (1955, 4th ed.) 154
Heuston, R.F.V.: *Essays in Constitutional Law* (1964, 2nd ed.) 474
Holdsworth, W.S.: *History of English Law*, Vol. 1 (1903) 489
Hood R. (Ed.): *Crime, Criminology and Public Policy* (1966) 403
Hume: *Commentaries on the Law of Scotland*, Vol. ii (1844) 274, 275,
                    294, 297, 300–302
——: *Crimes*, Vol. ii.. 35, 303
Jackson, R.M.: *The Machinery of Justice in England* (1972, 6th ed.) 193
Jennings, Ivor: *Parliament* (1957, 2nd ed.) 218
Justice: *The Prosecution Process in England and Wales* (1970) 3, 270
Kelly, J.M.: *The Irish Constitution* (1980) 267
Kennedy, W.P.M. and Lanctot, G.: *Reports on the Laws of Quebec* (1767–1770) 357
Kerr, Sir John: *Matters for Judgment* (1978) 372
La Fave, W.R.: *Arrest: The Decision to Take a Subject into Custody* (1965) 403
La Nanze, J.A.: *Alfred Deakin* (1972) 370
Langeluttig, A.: *The Department of Justice of the United States* (1927) 59
Lasok, D. and Bridge, J.W.: *European Communities* (1982, 3rd ed.) 177, 178
Leigh, L.H. and Hall Williams, J.E.: *The Management of the Prosecution Process in
    Denmark, Sweden and the Netherlands* (1982) 403
Lidstone, K.W. Hogg, R. and Sutcliffe, F.: *Prosecutions by Private Individuals and
    Non-Police Agencies* (1980)... 12, 144
McCabe, S. and Sutcliffe, F.: *Defining Crime: A Study of Police Decisions* (1978) 446
Mackinnon, Justice: *On Circuit (1924–1937)* (1941) 276
McLarty, M.R. and Campbell, Paton G.: *A Source Book and History of Administrative
    Law in Scotland* (1956) 294
Macmillan, Lord: *A Man of Law's Tale* (1933) 269, 276, 281, 282, 301–303, 317
Marshall, Geoffrey: *Police and Government* (1965) 39
Masson, D. (Ed.): *The Register of the Privy Council of Scotland*
    Vol. iii (1880) 273
    Vol. x (1545–1689) 274
Mathew, Sir Theobald: *The Office and Duties of the Director of Public Prosecutions*
    (1950).. 39, 405

——: *The Department of the Director of Public Prosecution* (1952) 41, 405
May, Erskine: *Parliamentary Practice*
    (18th ed.) 166, 218
    (19th ed.) 224
Meador, D.J.: *The President, the Attorney General and the Department of Justice* (1980) 58, 60, 61, 69, 191
Middlemas, Keith (Ed.): *Thomas Jones, Whitehall Diary*, Vol. 1 (1969) 313
Miller, C.J.: *Contempt of Court*
    (1959) 163
    (1976)... 162, 166
Milne, Sir David: *The Scottish Office, and Other Scottish Government Departments* (1957)...278, 288, 293
Morris, A. (Ed.): *The Growth of Parliamentary Scrutiny by Committee* (1970) 228
National Association of Attorneys General: *The Office of Attorney General* (1971) 59
Neatby, Hilda: *The Administration of Justice Under the Quebec Act* (1937) 357
Omond, G.W.T.: *The Lord Advocates of Scotland* (1883).................................... 269, 271–274, 276, 287, 289, 295
Pearson, L.B.: *Mike: The Memoirs of Lester B. Pearson* (Vol.3) 380
Pinkerton, J.M. (Ed.): *The Minute Book of the Faculty of Advocates 1661–1712*, Vol. 1 (1976) 281
Radzinowicz, L.A.: *A History of the English Criminal Law*, Vol. 2 (1956) 464, 474
Reid, A.: *The Whitlam Venture* (1976) 373
Renton and Brown: *Criminal Procedure According to the Law of Scotland* (1971, 4th ed.) 298
Sawer, G.: *Australian Federal Politics and Law 1901–29* (1956)...................... 367, 368, 369
——: *Federation Under Strain, Australia 1972–75* (1977)............................... 372, 380
Scarman, Lord: *English Law – the New Dimension* (1974) 177
Schiff: *Evidence in the Litigation Process* (1978) 382
Seymour, J.: *Committal for Trial, an Analysis of Australian Law Together with an Outline of British and American Procedures* (1978) 123, 441
Shetreet, Shimon: *Judges on Trial* (1976) 193
Skelhorn, Sir Norman: *Public Prosecutor: Memoirs of Sir Norman Skelhorn D.P.P. 1964–1977* (1982) 42, 324, 325
Skogan, Wesley (Ed.): *Sample Surveys of Victims of Crimes* (1976) 446
Skolnick, J.: *Justice without Trial* (1966) 404
Smith, Professor T.B.: *British Justice: The Scottish Contribution* (Hamlyn Lectures) (1961) 270, 300
——: *A Short Commentary of the Law of Scotland* (1962) 270
Sparks, R. Dodd, D. and Glenn, H.: *Surveying Victims* (1977) 446
Stair Society: *An Introduction to Scottish Legal History* (1958) 272
Stenning, P.C.: *The Legal Status of the Police in Canada* (Canada) (1981) 39
Straight, W.: *After Long Silence* (1983) 467
Thayer, J.B.: *Treatise on Evidence at the Common Law* (1898) 489
Thio, S.M.: *Locus Standi and Judicial Review* (1971) 143
Todd: *Parliamentary Government in the British Colonies* (1894, 2nd ed.) 367, 390, 475
Twiss: *The Public and Private Life of Lord Chancellor Eldon*, Vol. 1 (1846, 3rd ed.) 318
Wade, Mason: *The French Canadians (1760–1967)*, Vol. 1 (1968) 357
Wade and Phillips: *Constitutional and Administrative Law* (1977, 9th ed.).................. 30, 147, 194, 218, 227, 228, 474, 476
Whitlam G.: *The Truth of the Matter* (1979) 372
Whyte, J.D. and Lederman, W.R.: *Canadian Constitutional Law* (1977, 2nd ed.) 357
Wilcox, A.F.: *The Decision to Prosecute* (1972) 403
Wyatt, D. and Dashwood, A.: *The Substantive Law of the EEC* (1980) 177
Young, Hugo: *The Crossman Affair* (1977) 340

PERIODICAL ARTICLES AND PAMPHLETS

Anon: "A Procurator Fiscal – What he was, What he is, and What he will be" (1877) 21 Jo. of Jurisprudence 24 296

——: "The Attorney Generalship" (1929) 4 N.Z.L.R. 268 388
Archer, P.: "The Role of the Law Officers" (1978) 339 *Fabian Research Series* 23 78,
  177, 182
Arora, R.S.: "Parliamentary Scrutiny: The Select Committee Device" [1967] Public Law
  30 227
Atkins, S. and Rutherford, A.: "The Police and the Public: In Search of New Styles of
  Accountability" [1983] Public Law 241 39
Bailey, S.H.: "The Contempt of Court Act 1981" (1982) 45 M.L.R. 301 172
Barnes, P: "The Office of the Director of Public Prosecutions" [1975] *The Prosecution
  Process* 22 ....407, 408, 416, 419, 420, 423, 425, 426, 427, 430
Bennion, Francis: "Who should Lay Down Prosecution Guidelines?" (1981) 125 S.J.
  534 432
Blom Cooper, Louis: "The New Face of Judicial Review: Administrative Changes in
  Order 53" [1982] Public Law 250 153
Bowley, A.S.: "Prosecution – A Matter for the Police" [1975] Crim. L.R.
  442 88
Brookfield, F.M.: "The Attorney General and the Staying of Proceedings" (1978) 22
  N.Z.L.J. 467 ....398, 399
Cockburn, Henry [?]: "The Powers and Importance of the Lord Advocate of Scotland"
  (1824) 39 *Edinburgh Review* 363 300
Cohen, Stanley A.: "Observations on the Re-Emergence of the Doctrine of Abuse of
  Process" (1981) 19 C.R. (3d.) 310 120
Cornford, P.A.: "The Administration of Justice in New Zealand 1841–46" (1970) 4
  N.Z.U.L.R. 18 388
Crown Law Practice in New Zealand, 1961 ....388, 392, 393, 447
Danks, P.K.L.: "The Public Prosecutor" *The Magistrate*, October 1970, 148 88
Devlin, J.D.: "Police Prosecutors" (1970) *Police Review* 1245 88
Dias, R.W.M.: "Götterdämmerung: gods of the law in decline" (1981) 1 *Legal Studies*
  3 129
Dickens, B.M.: "Discretion in Local Authority Prosecutions" [1970] Crim.L.R. 618 117
Dickey, A.: "Prosecutions under the Race Relations Act 1965, s.6 (Incitement to Racial
  Hatred" [1968] Crim. L.R. 489 21
Drewry, G.: "Parliament and the Sub-Judice Convention" (1972) 122 New.L.J.
  1158 ....166, 184
——: "Lawyers in the U.K. Civil Service" (1981) 59 *Public Administration*
  15 ....182, 183
Durack, Sen.P.: *Prosecution Policy of the Commonwealth* (Aust.) (1983) 450
Edwards, J.Ll.J.: "Special Powers in Northern Ireland" [1956] Crim.
  L.R. 7 237
——: "The Administration of Criminal Justice in N. Ireland" [1956] Crim. L.R. 466 244
——: "Discretionary Powers by the Police and Crown Attorneys in the Criminal Law"
  (1970) 59 *Canadian Police Chief* 36 404
——: "Emerging Problems in Defining the Modern Role of the Office of Attorney-
  General in Commonwealth Countries" (1977) *Proceedings of the Meeting of
  Commonwealth Law Ministers* 195 ....62, 199, 385
Feldman, D.: "Standing in the Lords: A Matter of Interest" (1982) 45 M.L.R. 92 148
Goldstein, J.: "Police Discretion Not to Invoke the Criminal Process: Low Visibility
  Decisions in the Administration of Justice" (1960) 69 Yale L.J. 543 403
Gordon, Gerald H.: "Institution of Criminal Proceedings in Scotland" (1968) 19
  N.I.L.Q. 249 ....243, 270, 292–294, 298, 300
Griffith, J.A.G.: "The Unaccountable Prosecutor" *The New Statesmen*, October 19,
  1979 ....44, 48
——: "Mickey Mouse and Standing in Administrative Law" [1982] C.L.J. 6 148
Hammonds, O.W.: "The Attorney General in the American Colonies" (1939) 2 *Anglo
  American Legal History Series* 59
Hanham, H.J.: "The Creation of the Scottish Office 1881–1887" (1965) *Juridical Review*
  205 ....276, 278, 279
Harris, D.J.:"Decisions on the European Convention on Human Rights during 1979 – a
  commentary on *The Sunday Times* case" (1979) 50 B.Y.I.L. 257 172
Harrison, Ruth: "The Attorney General's Reference" (1980) 32 *King's Counsel* 20 159
Haughey, E.J.: "The Legal Work of the Crown" (1957) 38 N.Z.L.J. 203 388

Sutherland, P.F.: "The Use of the Letter of Request (or Letter Rogatory) for the
    Purpose of Obtaining Evidence for Proceedings in England and abroad" (1983) 31
    I.C.L.Q. 784 156
Vorenberg, J.: "Narrowing the Discretion of Criminal Justice Officials" (1976) Duke
    L.J. 651 403
Wade, H.W.R.: "The Attorney General and the Trade Unions" (1978) 94 L.Q.R.
    4.. 129, 143
Weatheritt, M. and Kaye, D.R.: *The Prosecution System – Organisational Implications of
    Change* Research Studies, Nos. 11 and 12, H.M.S.O. 1980 87
Williams, D.G.T.: "The Prerogative and Parliamentary Control" [1971] C.L.J. 178 30
——: "The Prerogative and Preventative Justice" (1977) 36 C.L.J. 201 .... 129, 144
——: "Preventative Justice and the Courts" [1977] Crim. L.R. 703...................... 129, 144
Williams, Glanville: "Discretion in Prosecuting" [1956] Crim. L.R. 222 403

PARLIAMENTARY PAPERS

1845 Criminal Law Commissioners, Eighth Report (Parl. Papers, Vol. xiv (No. 656))   2
1847–48 Report of the Select Committee on Public Business (Parl. Papers, Vol. xvi (No.
    644)) 227
1854–1855 Report of the Select Committee on the Public Prosecutors Bill (Parl. Papers,
    Vol. xii (No. 481)).. 17, 263
1856 Report of the Select Committee on Public Prosecutors (Parl. Papers, Vol. vii
    (No. 206)) 2, 17
1870 Report of the Commissioners appointed to inquire into certain Civil Departments in
    Scotland [C. 64] (H.C. Paper xviii) 279, 291
1877 Departmental Committee on the System upon which the Legal Business of the
    Government is Conducted, First, Second, and Third Reports (H.C. Papers 199,
    Parl. Papers, Vol. xxvii) 182, 184
1894 Law Officers of the Crown in Scotland (Remuneration) (H.C. Paper 327) 290
1915 Report of the Royal Commission on the Civil Service (Cd. 7832) 292, 293, 295, 296
1915 Royal Commission on the Civil Service, Minutes of Evidence (Cd. 8130) 292
1918 Report of the Haldane Committee on the Machinery of Government (Cd. 9230) 193
1920 Report of the Select Committee on the Remuneration of Ministers (H.C. Paper
    241) 291
1929 Report of the Royal Commission on Police Powers and Procedure (Cmd. 3297)   80
1930–33 Report of the Select Committee on Capital Punishment (Parl. Papers, Vol. 6
    (No. 15)) 227
1936 Report of the Budget Disclosure Tribunal of Inquiry (Cmd. 5184) 199
1939 Report of the Select Committee on the Official Secrets Act (H.C. Paper 173) 360
1939–40 Report of the Select Committee on the Conduct of a Member of Parliament
    (H.C. Paper 177) 231
1940–41 Report of the Select Committee on the Conduct of a Member of Parliament
    (H.C. Paper 5) 231
1949 Report of the Tribunal Appointed to Inquire into Allegations Reflecting on the
    Official Conduct of Ministers of the Crown and other Public Servants (Cmd.
    7616) 199
1950 Report of the Select Committee on the Election of a Member (Clergyman of the
    Church of Ireland) (H.C. Paper 68) 231
1952–53 Report of the Select Committee on Nationalised Industries (H.C. Paper 235) 227
1952–53 Convention for the Protection of Human Rights and Fundamental Freedoms—
    Rôme, November 4, 1950; U.K. ratification, March 8, 1951; Treaty Series 71/1953
    (Cmd. 8969) 177
1958 Report of the Bank Rate Leak Tribunal of Inquiry (Cmnd. 350) 200
1958 Report of the Select Committee on Obscene Publications (H.C. Paper 123–1) .. 26, 230
1962 Royal Commission on the Police, Final Report (Cmnd. 1728)......................... 80, 87
1963 Lord Denning's Report (Cmnd. 2152) 471
1964 Report of the Committee on the Remuneration of Ministers and Members of
    Parliament (Cmnd. 2516) 195
1964–65 Report of the Select Committee on Procedure (H.C. Paper 303) 228

1981–82 Report of the Select Committee on Home Affairs, Deaths in Police Custody
(H.C. Paper 631) 234, 270, 298, 431
1982 Report of the Federal-Provincial Task Force on the Uniform Rules of Evidence
(Dept. of Justice, Canada) 382
1982 Report of Inquiry into action taken by the Police, the Crown Office and the Scottish
Home and Health Department relating to the murder of Mrs. Rachel Ross in 1969
both before and after the trial of Mr. Patrick Meehan (H.C. Paper 444) 4 Vols. ... 294
1983 White Paper on an Independent Prosecution Service for England and Wales
(Cmnd. 9074) 104

INDEX

This is a consolidated index of both the present volume and the earlier work, *The Law Officers of the Crown*, by the same author.

References to the latter volume are prefixed by the abbreviation [LOC] and are shown in italics.